Understanding Adolescence

SECOND EDITION

Understanding Adolescence
Current Developments in Adolescent Psychology

edited by

James F. Adams
Temple University

Allyn and Bacon, Inc.   Boston

Library of Congress Catalog Card Number: 72–92890

Second printing . . . August, 1973

To Our Adolescents
Past—Present—Future

Robert B. Adams
Dorothy L. Adams
James E. Adams
Bill Amos
Randy Amos
Laura Amos
Lisa Amos
Terri L. Bachman
Steven J. Bachman
Jon A. Bachman
Paul S. Beller
Daniel R. Beller
Susan D. Block
Jody L. Block
David L. Block
Carol A. Block
Carolyn J. Borow
Nancy J. Borow
Charles R. Cross
Catherine F. Cross
Timothy J. Davis
Bradford L. Davis
Gregory H. Davis

David F. Gallagher
Karl C. Garrison, Jr.
Mary Haan Shiroff
Peter A. Haan
John S. Hackman
Patricia Hackman
    Kendall
Helen Havighurst
    Berk
Ruth Havighurst
    Neff
Dorothy Havighurst
    Kucera
James P. Havighurst
Walter M.
    Havighurst
Debbie E.
    Hamachek
Dan E. Hamachek
Greg Lynas
Arthur W. Jalkanen,
    Jr.
Leif E. Jalkanen

Timothy J. Jalkanen
Karen L. Jalkanen
Douglas L. Johnston
John Detre
Peter Detre
Ann McGovern
    Mead
Susan McGovern
    Rowen
Teresa McGovern
Steven McGovern
Mary McGovern
David K. Nichols
James E. Nichols
Richard A. Loomis
Joshua H. Smith
T. Daniel Smith
Rebecca M. Smith
J. Torquil Smith
Timothy Wellford
Katherine Wellford
Isabel Garcia
    Gutierrez

Contents

Preface

Organizing a book on the topic of "adolescence" is a fascinating as well as a thought-provoking task. Since the first edition of this book, an increasing awareness of national and international problems has spread throughout the youth culture of the United States (and the world). The priorities of our country are being examined closely as the youth of today realize that never before has mankind faced the possibility of extinction through the exhaustion of the world's physical resources (minerals, water, etc.). Concern with population and pollution has increased tremendously within a short space of five years. We have become aware that the issues of peace and poverty are also ecological problems. Adolescents are facing the almost impossible task of reordering national and world priorities if they wish to salvage an earth which is dying—largely unnoticed by past generations. The tone of this book, then, is to focus on the issues which this generation of adolescents must resolve if there are to be other generations to follow.

Understanding Adolescence was planned for those who are interested in understanding the problems of youth today. It contains chapters which are traditional in nature, as well as chapters which are focused on the immediate present. It is probable that this book could be read, with profit, by any interested and concerned adult, but it has been written, in particular, for the individual who is preparing for his future role of parent, teacher, psychologist, social worker, and most importantly, responsible citizen.

I am indebted to many individuals who, over the years, have stimulated my interest in adolescence, not the least of whom are my own children. Most young people of this age group, including the three adolescents in my own family, do not like the term *adolescent*. Since there seems to be no other word which describes this age group as adequately (I suggested "elderly children"), they have accepted the title of the book and agree that *understanding* would help. I am particularly indebted to my youngest son, Robert B. Adams, who has read many of the chapters in this book and who has been most helpful with his constructive criticism. He has encouraged me to believe that much of the book is relevant to the youth of today.

Most of all, I am indebted to the authors who have contributed the chapters to this book. Many areas in psychology have become just too involved for a single person to cover with comprehensiveness and integrity. Whatever merit the book may have will be found in their contributions.

Finally, during the year in which I have put this manuscript into its final form, I have been Visiting Professor of Psychology at Catholic University in Ponce, Puerto Rico. Without the friendliness and the time to write and edit which the university provided, this book would not have been revised. I am grateful for the cooperation which they extended so freely.

James F. Adams

Understanding Adolescence

1

Adolescents in an Age of Crisis
James F. Adams*

There was a time when the world was moving along at a reasonably slow pace. The task of growing from childhood into becoming an adult could be accomplished with temporal leisure. Children had time to be children, and adolescents had their years of development with but few of the pressures which they encounter today. We are now faced with a fact of life: Science has moved us forward far faster than our capabilities of adaptation. While the rate at which knowledge increases is difficult to estimate, its acceleration and the accompanying tempo of life have reached frightening speeds.

It has been estimated, for the child who is born today, that by the time he graduates from college, the fund of the world's knowledge will have increased fourfold. When this same child reaches fifty years of age, the world's knowledge will have increased thirty-two times, and 97 percent of everything known in the world will have been learned since he was born (Toffler, 1970).

The writer's own field of psychology is an excellent example of what is occurring in science as a whole. For the year of 1960, the *Psychological Abstracts* listed 8,532 contributions to the psychological literature. By

* James F. Adams is Professor of Psychology and Educational Psychology at Temple University. In addition to the first and second editions of this book, he has edited or written *Problems in Counseling: A Case Study Approach, Counseling and Guidance: A Summary View, Human Behavior in a Changing Society,* and numerous journal articles on such topics as counseling, adolescent psychology, psychological testing, and the history of psychology.

1970, the total had increased to 21,722. It would be no exaggeration to say that if I have some inkling of 20 percent of what is occurring in my profession, and an in-depth understanding of 5 percent, I should consider myself fortunate. It is just impossible for a scientist today to be broadly conversant within his own chosen field of specialization. And what is true for the scientist has also become true for the industrialist, the business-man, the laborer, and the average citizen.

Our attempts to keep pace with the commercial changes of our society and of our world have made many of us myopic in our concern for human values and our fellowman. We have become blinded to, and blinded by, the by-products of our exploding economies, our exploding populations, and the ecological disasters which may soon present unre-solvable crises. It is within this age of crisis that our adolescent of today develops.

In this first chapter of a book devoted to the task of furthering the understanding of the adolescent period, I shall attempt to set the stage. The point will be made that never before have adolescents been raised in a period fraught with more difficulties, more potential for disaster, and more frustration. I shall also touch upon a number of topics which will be developed in greater magnitude by the authors of this book.

Adolescence Defined

Adolescence has been considered from a variety of viewpoints. In the main these viewpoints have approached the subject from a consideration of physiological and hormonal development, social influences, economic determination, or emotional development. Often it is considered from a combination of approaches, usually including physiological and hor-monal maturation. We know, for example, that the age of puberty, the time when the young person is capable of reproducing his kind, usually occurs sometime between the tenth and fifteenth year of the individual's life. For some this has been considered the onset of adolescence, as it is most certainly a part of adolescent development.

Historically, one could make the case that adolescence, if it existed at all, has frequently been very short in duration. In past centuries primi-tive, agrarian, and urban cultures needed the contributions of their youth at a very early age. In these cultures children went from childhood to the responsibilities of adulthood with scarcely a pause for what we now call adolescence. The short life spans of adults, as well as economic and social pressures, often forced the age of adult responsibility downward.

It is only within the last one hundred years or so that adolescence, as a focus of interest and study, has blossomed forth into the literature in great quantities. G. Stanley Hall, at the turn of the twentieth century, launched the increasing flood of research which has continued unabated to the present time. Why, we might ask, has this happened? Perhaps the simplest explanation would be to note that as a function of increased life spans, technological and industrial developments, and exploding populations, we have much less need for our youth. Their contributions to society are no longer of economic importance. We do not need their sexual reproductive capacities, for the world is already overpopulated. We do not need their economic contributions to the world of work, since mechanization, automation, and population have left us with vast reservoirs of unemployed workers. We do not need their minds and intellects, to any degree, because we have become satisfied with the tradition of adult leadership. We have very effectively communicated to our youth that their major contribution is to hang around, grow up, become educated, and stand in line until it is their turn to take over the reins from their elders. We have, in short, *created* a prolonged period of adolescence which has stimulated interest and research.

Adolescence then, can be defined as a holding period in which education, maturation, and waiting are the major tasks to be faced. For this reason it seems scarcely profitable to define the adolescent period as being tied in with age, although there would be no objection to doing so if it had any meaning or utility. Adolescence, as a meaningful concept, is best considered within a broad framework of the total development of the individual. At the time when the child begins to feel less need for the security of familial supervision and protection; at the time when his physiological and hormonal development begins to approximate adult maturity; and lastly, at the time when his psychological maturity moves him in the direction of becoming responsible in society, adolescence has begun. It should be readily apparent that in using these criteria, vast individual age differences for the onset of adolescence may be expected. It should be equally apparent that the termination of adolescence, for some, may never occur. Maturity, defined as being a contributing, relatively self-sufficient member of society, is a goal for which we all strive. Some are more successful than others in reaching this goal. These variable years of developing are considered the adolescent years. The thrust of this book is to consider the nature of the forces, issues, and problems with which the young person must cope on his road to responsible adulthood.

The World of Today's Adolescents

Our generation of adolescents, who have not yet faced the necessity of specialization, of being overwhelmed by the vast frontiers of expanding knowledge, or of earning a living, may well be far more conversant with the major problems facing humanity than are we—their elders! Their concerns, by exclusion from other areas of life, are focused on a human level which is a disappearing focus within a highly industrialized society.

While it is true that every generation of adolescents has had certain problems which were unknown to previous generations, it is equally true that the problems facing *this generation* may be problems which will end what we call civilization. Ecology, as yet an infant science, is already being called upon to salvage a world environment which has been raped beyond comprehension by a mankind which has been largely unconcerned. But even now, the call for salvation comes only from youth and a small minority of concerned adults. Many, not all, of our young people are aware that, within a short span of fifty years, the world's resources for human habitation may be destroyed or exhausted by a mankind which has not appreciated Mother Earth. Is it surprising that some of our youth have withdrawn into "doing their own thing," while others have rioted and protested over the priorities of their country? A whole new youth consciousness has sprung into being (Reich, 1970), while many of us have passively encouraged and tolerated the status quo.

It seems to me that a major share of the adult's confusion concerning the difficulties of growing up comes from his own confused thinking. This is not to say that the adolescent does not have his share of confusion. He does. However, it would be safe to estimate that the overlap between these private domains is minor (although a causal relationship can be frequently seen).

The adult world derives its confusion from a recognition that the increasing chaos in the world is becoming even more chaotic. We do not understand why. Take the typical father. In his need to provide financial support for his family, to advance in his business or profession, and to provide some stability for his family, he has not had time (or taken the time) to consider what is happening on the broader scene. His parents had similar problems to his; why should the world of his children be that much different? His observations of his nation and its civil unrest usually result in his appealing for a return to law and order—to the good old days. He does not realize that the good old days are gone forever. The cycle of generational similarity has stopped. There will never be another generation which will grow up in similar times or similar places. He has but vaguely realized that we have moved into an era of what has been called *future shock* (Toffler, 1970). He will never be able to return to the past; indeed, society is changing so rapidly that we cannot adjust even to the present.

An even sadder fact of life is the need to recognize that our children may not live long enough to die of old age. They are a generation which is facing the inevitable approach of the world's destruction through over-population and pollution. This process of self-destruction is already an accomplished fact in some areas of the world (Adams, 1972). But youth are aware! They are reading Ardrey (1968), Morris (1969), De Bell (1970), and Ehrlich and Ehrlich (1970). They are talking and listening. They are concerned with what is happening. It is not surprising that they are intolerant of our national priorities, for they will not survive unless they can change these priorities.

The establishment, as viewed by many adolescents, is unknowing and unconcerned; and they have ample materials with which to demonstrate their case. With but few exceptions such as Ralph Nader, who fights for consumer and environmental rights; Senator George McGovern, who has waged an unremitting warfare on the immorality of Vietnam and other issues; and Martin Luther King, who had a "dream," it is difficult for concerned youth to look to their civic and political leaders with pride. They are told that life is a matter of compromise, which indeed it is. But they find that compromise is not reasoned or just. Oil companies, with impunity almost, can pollute the environment. Financial resources define whether one is right or wrong; whether one is prosecuted or not prose-cuted. The wealthy pay no taxes; the poor have no income. Justice would seem to be a legal word which has increasingly little meaning. They view President Richard M. Nixon and they observe his actions. They con-clude, not unreasonably, that expediency is the hallmark of leadership—not morals, concern, or principles. The eighteen year old is given the vote only to find that, if he is in a college away from his home, it is unlikely that he will be able to exercise his rights of citizenship.

To make the adolescent period even more difficult, the phase is viewed by many adults as a period of maladjustment to home and society. Psychologists and psychiatrists contribute to this view as they call atten-tion to the disturbed young people who pass through their offices. Sur-prisingly enough to many, most adolescents make remarkably good adjustments to a maladjusted society. Be this as it may, the impression is conveyed to the public that all adolescents are maladjusted. The news media make greater financial gains by focusing on the adolescent who deviates in his behavior from what adults would expect. Television, movies, and the press create the image that most adolescents are hooked on drugs, that protest movements contain the criminal or politically unfavorable elements in our society, and that the adjusted young person is the one who spends his time studying, working for good grades, and preparing to make an adequate income as his contribution to his country. Perhaps it is this latter adolescent who should be of concern. Many of us were cast in the same mold; and it is our very acquiescence and unin-volvement that has brought our nation and world to a state from which there may be no time to recover. We have polluted and destroyed our natural and human resources to an unbelievable degree. In our self-centeredness and in our noncaring attitudes, we stand condemned.

Adults and Adolescents

Let us turn our discussion into a more personal vein of thought. Up to this point we have been considering the awareness of the adolescent of the difficulties he faces as he moves into an adult world in which he will find insurmountable problems never before faced by previous generations. But now, as a present or future parent, assume that you have an adolescent within your own home.

I wonder if you have ever stopped to consider that there is no such thing as a professional parent. We are all amateurs in our roles of rearing children. By the time we have learned a little, our children are grown and we have already made our mistakes (and had our triumphs, hopefully). Reading about the raising of children can prove to be helpful, and certainly Spock (1946) has influenced a generation of parents. However, we should remember that while this literature may have been written by experts (educators, physicians, psychiatrists, psychologists, and sociologists), when it comes to being parents, we too are amateurs. Rearing one, two or three children is just as personal with us as it is with you. We share, in spite of our professional training, the same fears, misgivings, joys, and hopes for our children. What we can contribute from our various disciplines is an objectivity about other people's children—not our own. Many of the writers of this book have spent their lives studying and trying to understand children and adolescents. All of us would quickly admit that having our own children has had a humbling effect on our expertise. However, by controlled study and observation, much has been learned which is true with respect to young people in general and even specifically (on occasion). This knowledge should make you a more intelligent parent, teacher, or adult when it comes to working with or understanding the adolescent. In addition, the same information should provide the adolescent with greater self-understanding. One of the basic needs in growing toward maturity is to discover that many of the concerns you have are shared by others; that many of the difficulties you are encountering, have been encountered and solved by others.

Adult-Adolescent Confusion

Let us return to that relative in your home. As a parent you are suddenly aware that you no longer have a child. The child has become a more or less independent young adult—the adolescent. Day by day you wonder if you have prepared him adequately for the new world that he is facing. You find yourself concentrating on many of the minutiae of growing up. You may become suddenly concerned with his table manners (which you too have been neglecting), and he, just as suddenly, becomes totally unconcerned. You find that there are times when he is affectionate and that there are times when he goes his own way without seeming to need that closeness that you once had together. As a parent you try to comfort yourself with some old cliché, such as "The love of a parent for a child is the one love that should grow toward separation." It does not help much.

In short, you are a little confused with respect to this new state of affairs. Then you suddenly become acutely aware of teenage problems and they take on a new meaning. You hear of gang wars, drinking, and pot parties. Your adolescents are covering their rooms with posters that have implications of thinking which you do not entirely understand. A young girl down the street is killed in an automobile accident, and a friend of your son's commits suicide. School grades become of increasing concern as the possibility of going to college approaches. You find out that your daughter has been smoking when she is with her friends. A neighbor's sixteen year old becomes pregnant. You read that suicide rates have gone up on college campuses and that boys and girls are living together in the same residence halls. Have you raised your son or daughter to cope with these pressures? You hope that you have, but there is a strong element of doubt in your mind. Do you now understand what I mean when I say that you have joined, or absorbed, the adult world's adolescent-confusion?

Adolescent Idealism

There is another side to the coin. The adolescent stands on the threshold of adult responsibility. He is beginning to think for himself and to question the wisdom of his parents. He finds that there are major issues in the destiny of the world with which his parents are relatively unconcerned. He attends a sit-in on the pollution problems facing the world and leaves the sit-in more polluted than he found it (Norman, 1971). There is an inconsistency to his behavior which adults do not understand. Sometimes he finds that his parents are not very receptive to discussing the issues which concern him; and these issues range all the way from environmental destruction to what time he should be home at night. He looks at his school and his teachers critically. He finds that no one in the adult world is perfect, including his parents. Yet, his high idealism makes it difficult for him (Horrocks, 1969) to accept imperfection.

The adolescent finds that there is a discrepancy between what he has been taught is right and how people conduct themselves. This young person lives in a world of high hopes and aspirations (which he has difficulty in meeting himself), but he finds that others, the adults, do not share either his enthusiasm or his ideals. He observes that, as a congressman, it is permissible to steal if you are relatively quiet about the matter. The crime is in being caught. As a citizen, it is more laudatory to steal "big" than to steal "small." Americans admire private enterprise.

He reads such writers as Hesse (1929, 1951), Teilhard de Chardin (1959), and Camus (1961) in an attempt to reach some conclusion about the nature of man (and himself). Or he may withdraw from any attempt at a reasoned approach to the nature of man and seek his identity with his peers. In either case, he has not found the answer to his question within his everyday environment.

The Adolescent and Educational Institutions

The adolescent may turn to educational institutions to find the answers. It doesn't take too much of an investigation to find that education might better be called *hedgeucation*. He hears that learning for learning's sake is to be greatly admired. Then he observes that what adults are really interested in are those grades. He finds that education is great at *hedging* when he asks questions.

Democracy, supposedly, should give people freedom to choose their own governments. Why then, he asks, does this country try to enforce its style of living on other countries? Why is the going to the moon more important than eliminating, or at least trying to eliminate, poverty in the United States? Why does his school organize its teaching around the College Boards when it tells him they are preparing him for enlightened citizenship? What is so important about teaching calculus in the ninth grade? Just what is education anyway?

All his friends are going to college; well, at least most of them. He hears his father say: "Where else can they do less harm for four years?" He reads that keeping young people in school is important because it keeps them off the labor market. His counselor tells him that it is important to go to college because he is likely to earn a quarter of a million dollars more in his lifetime. Is this what education is for—to make money? Why can't or won't adults give him a straight, honest, meaningful answer? Is it that they have no answer?

I wonder why we are so surprised when the adolescent decides to ignore the adult world and build his own peer-group culture. Fortunately for us, many adolescents do not withdraw but work for positive change. Universities throughout the country have felt the impact of concerned youth who have insisted on meaningful and relevant education. I think that it would be safe to estimate that 90 percent of the innovations occurring in higher education in the last ten years were a direct result of the pressures which students exerted upon their institutions. This is not to say that all their efforts have been positive. They, too, have made mistakes. When viewed in retrospect, however, the changes which occurred—frequently with great misgivings on the part of educators—opened up a new era of willingness to change. We now realize that education is a process of change, and that youth have given us the stimulus to move us out of our conservative positions on topics as varied as grading, government, and curricula.

Personal Concerns of Adolescents

On top of all the foregoing considerations, the adolescent also has his own personal concerns. Socially he may be very ill at ease, but he is learning to converse as an equal in both an adult and a heterosexual peer world. He wishes to be accepted by the girls and boys of his peer group. There is much verbal fencing and the trying on of roles for size. Well over one-fourth of adolescents' major problems focus on interpersonal relationships, emotions, growing maturity, and their families. Girls have more problems in these areas than do boys. About the same number of proportionate problems exist for the adolescent in his school environment, except that there the boys have a greater concentration of difficulties (Adams, 1964). As we consider the personal problems of adolescents, let us bear in mind that we are not emphasizing the *problem* aspect as being the private property of the adolescent. Children and adults also have personal problems. The spotlight is really on those matters which are of *concern* to this age group.

A Focus on Parents

Our adolescent finds that the adults (his parents being the representatives of this group) are strangely reticent to recognize his newly assumed maturity. When he acts mature, they convey to him that he is still a child. Adults use a double-barreled shotgun on their adolescent. They point one barrel at him when his behavior is considered childish; they use the other barrel when he is asking for recognition of his developing maturity.

I think, that as adults, the burden of understanding reasonably should rest on our shoulders. As we learn more about the world of the adolescent, we should be better able to aid him in his transition into our complex adult world. As a function of understanding, we should become more secure and efficient in our desire to help youth whether we are parents, educators, politicians, or concerned adults. In short, at least some of the fog of confusion should be rolled away through our mature understanding.

This is not to say or imply that *understanding* will ever completely insure our feelings of security as adults or parents. Living, itself, is not a secure proposition at best (and becoming less so all the time), and there are no final proven answers to most of the important issues of life.

The Meanings of Words and Concepts

One of my sons introduced me to a book with which I was totally unfamiliar. It is entitled *The Devil's Dictionary* (begun in 1881), by Ambrose Bierce.* In our relationships with adolescents (and people in general), his definitions are priceless. Consider the following examples:

> *Absurdity:* A statement or belief manifestly inconsistent with one's own opinion.
>
> *Accuse:* To affirm another's guilt or unworth; most commonly as a justification of ourselves for having wronged him.
>
> *Acknowledge:* To confess. Acknowledgment of one another's faults is the highest duty imposed by our love of the truth.
>
> *Admonition:* Gentle reproof as with a meat-axe. Friendly warning.
>
> *Age:* That period of life in which we compound for the vices that we still cherish by reviling those that we have no longer the enterprise to commit.
>
> *Alone:* In bad company.
>
> *Battle:* A method of untying with the teeth a political knot that would not yield to the tongue.
>
> *Brain:* An apparatus with which we think we think.
>
> *Christian:* One who believes that the New Testament is a divinely inspired book admirably suited to the spiritual needs of his neighbor.
>
> *Comfort:* A state of mind produced by contemplation of a neighbor's uneasiness.
>
> *Conversation:* A fair for the display of the minor mental commodities, each exhibitor being too intent upon the arrangement of his own wares to observe those of his neighbor.
>
> *Friendship:* A ship big enough to carry two in fair weather, but only one in foul.

* New York: Hill and Wang, Inc., 1957. Used by permission.

Impartial: Unable to perceive any promise of a personal advantage from espousing either side of controversy or adopting either of two conflicting opinions.

Ultimatum: In diplomacy, a last demand before resorting to concessions.

As growth into adulthood occurs, the adolescent finds that there is a difference in the way Webster defines words and the way in which they are often used. The adolescent must, sooner or later, learn that the world is a most imperfect place. This task is more difficult for some adolescents than for others. It is particularly difficult when we adults raise our children as if society practiced the principles which we teach them. Undoubtedly society would be far worse if we did not raise our children in this manner, but it can be a difficult and embittering process which they go through when they discover that life is not based upon love and respect for one's fellowman. I am not suggesting that we should teach our children differently, but, rather, that we should encourage them to live up to their fullest potential at the same time that we inform them of the frailty of human nature and of their responsibility to leave the world a little better than they found it.

Internationalization of Standards

Many of the familial problems, which are of great importance for the adolescent, are a result of conflicts over behavioral standards. Every adult, at one time or another, has had an adolescent object to recommended behavioral principles by saying, "So-in-so's parents don't make him (or, let him) " or, "It isn't fair," or, "Give me a good reason." What they are reflecting is an attempt to cope with one of the most difficult tasks of life, viz., internalizing a set of personal standards which stand at least relatively independent of the influences of society. Consider the words of fifteen-year-old Debbie Deliere* (killed in an automobile accident) : "I must reach for a goal reached only by a few, but this makes me an individual . . . I must make my own decision. I can either continue striving for the goals I place in front of myself, or I can go along with 'The Crowd.' Do what they want and go where they want. But then I am a fake."

We become quite adept in using the psychological mechanism of rationalization to justify our own unacceptable behaviors. Much of our middle-class society is a society of tranquilizers and sleeping pills, yet we object to our youth compounding our errors with additional drug experi-

* *The San Juan Star,* March 30, 1972, p. 41.

mentation—and quite correctly so. Attempting to escape from the realities of life does not make those realities any the less real or more palatable, and because there are many evils in the world does not mean that we should add to the collection from our own experiences.

Peer Approval. The adolescent has an additional problem: the need for peer approval. As he moves into adulthood, he gains much of his security from his companions within his own age group. Their standards and behavior are most important to him. If he loses their approval and sanction, he stands by himself. This is difficult to do during a period in which he is moving away from the security of his home and in the direction of complete independence. It is quite likely that the adolescent will agree that he should have his own standards to live by; that he should stand on his own two feet without parental admonition for support. The uncomfortable fact is that he may yet lack the internal strength to follow his own ideals. It is much easier for a girl to say, "My parents told me to be home by eleven," than it is to say, "I think I should be home by eleven." Adults need to exercise tolerance and understanding during this phase. If there has been an overall pattern of mutual trust between family members (Peck, 1958), it is likely that the adolescent will be moved in a positive direction by his parents' suggestions. This would assume, of course, that familial standards are both reasonable and consistent with the general goals and behaviors which are acceptable within the broad ethical principles of mankind.

The Need for Self-Expression

One of the interesting phenomena of our times, is the increasing number of adolescents, both male and female, who are turning to prose and poetry as a means of expressing their inner feelings. Writers such as Kahlil Gibran (*The Prophet; Tears and Laughter*) have captured the emotions of our youth with the beauty which can be expressed through the written word. Poetry is a medium through which many of the innermost thoughts of our youth are revealed. The work of McKuen is an excellent example of this type of poetry (1954, 1967). Adolescents' thoughts portray the way in which they would like the world to be; through their poetry, they ask for understanding. They share their poetry with each other and with interested adults.

Music, frequently at a decibel level that produces adult howls of discomfort, is another mode of expression and sometimes a type of escape from painful reality. The words of the songs of today focus on protest, or a plea for the positive things in life, such as peace and human understanding. The protests are against a deviant society, war, the establishment, and the rules that prohibit individuals from doing "their own thing." The musical sounds take youth away from their immediate problems and bathe them in an aura of their emotional reactions. Their musical "trips" may become a means of tolerating what they may consider an intolerable world.

It is probable that never in the history of the world has more music been produced by so many individuals with so little talent. Talent is not a prerequisite; the ability to express one's self is. Almost every youth firmly believes that he has the "talent" to become a successful musician. He creates his own inner music as he listens to others. He attempts self-expression through music in the same manner as he does through poetry. Individualized music has never been a major part of our culture (as, for example, in Latin countries), but it is rapidly becoming so.

Why this youth movement into poetry and music? I think that there is a sadly simple explanation. We have, by and large, walled youth out from participation within their own society. They are more conscious than are their elders of the evils of the world, but they are effectively prevented from their attempts to remedy those ills.

In the agricultural societies of the past, youth were considered adults when they were old enough to till the soil and to marry; that is, when they were economically independent. They participated much more fully within their communities. Today many of our youth are not economically self-sufficient until they reach their twenties, if then. But their minds have been educated, and they grasp the issues which inundate the world. These problems have become so great in magnitude that they are creating desperation within the young (as they should within the old).

There is nothing more frustrating for an adult than to know what is wrong in a situation and yet to be effectively stymied from initiating the solution. If this is true for the adult, think of how much greater magnification the problem assumes in the eyes of youth, for whom patience is a still-to-be-developed virtue! Greater involvement of youth is a mandate which I shall discuss in greater detail later.

Developing Sexuality

There are a number of very normal biological needs which are a part of every human being. Most of these needs are satisfied in an unprohibited manner, e.g., no one objects to our breathing, drinking water, eating, or relieving ourselves from our waste products. However when we reach the area of sex, the meeting of needs is not so simple. It is the only biological need for which society claims a restrictive right.

To be fulfilled completely, our sexual needs involve two individuals, both of whom are extremely vulnerable in their interpretations as to the meanings of the sexual act. Procreation, which has always been considered a major function of intercourse, is relatively minor when compared to the significance of the emotional communication which should occur in the sexual union. Marriages are seldom satisfactory when there is poor sexual-psychological adjustment. Couples who may not converse meaningfully in their daily contacts become increasingly distant if their sexual contacts become merely an expression of physiological pleasure. Sexual relationships can provide the closest and most meaningful approach to unity in a human experience that two people will ever experience.

The adolescent's sexual needs cannot be ignored. Sex, as many other human experiences, is a learning experience. We have hastened the learning process in our society with the emphasis we have placed on heterosexual contacts at an early age. If we insist that our children learn to dance together in the elementary school, we should not be surprised when they sleep together during their high school years. If we were preparing our youth for meaningful and lasting sexual relationships upon graduation from high school, the learning experiences which we provide would be admirable. As it is, most of our youth must put off marriage, and the responsibilities which should accompany sexual relationships, for a prolonged period of time.

Even more unfortunate is the fact that many of our youth are unable to tolerate the waiting period. They desperately need the human closeness which the sexual experience can provide. The speed with which our industrialized society has developed has removed many of the possibilities for human involvement and companionship which were available to many of us as we were growing to maturity (Toffler, 1970). The average family in the United States remains in one locality about the same length of time that a student spends in college or in a four-year high school.

In addition to the lack of geographical stability of the average family, the pressures and the frightening realities facing our aware youth as they move toward adult status make a close relationship with at least one other human being almost a necessity. It is scarcely surprising that adolescents turn to their peers of the opposite sex for their emotional and physiological needs. In many respects it may not be desirable, but in every respect it should be understandable. If we expect premarital sex to decrease, we must first look toward changing the society that produces the situations which cause the need for the sexual involvement. In addition, we should give our youth both an intellectual and an emotional understanding of the implications of the sexual relationship.

National and International Concerns of Adolescents

A number of years ago (Adams, 1963), I canvassed some four thousand adolescents on their feelings concerning the problems of their country.

Approximately two-thirds of their responses focused on the international scene. Our adolescents did not restrict their horizons to the internal problems of the United States, although they were cognizant of these problems. At the time I conducted these studies, I cannot recall one adolescent who mentioned pollution as a problem of major magnitude, and only 1 percent mentioned the population explosion as a concern. Think of the change in awareness which has occurred in less than ten years! Today the concerned adolescent is focusing on the four Ps: *Peace, Poverty* (with racial and educational implications), *Population,* and *Pollution.* All other areas have become secondary priorities. One cannot talk with our university students without being impressed with their sincerity of purpose, and the same sincerity is extending itself down to the high and junior high school levels.

It is our youth who must straighten out the ecological mistakes of their elders. It is tragic that so few adults have awakened to the emergency and that the legacy which we are leaving them is imminent disaster. Most certainly, if our national priorities give us some indication of what we think is important, we are communicating unconcern to our youth. Without our help and support, there is no future for the children and adolescents of tomorrow.

Today's Adolescents—Tomorrow's Adults

Let us turn back to the adolescent of today. What type of an adult will he become tomorrow? Will he fall into the pattern of previous generations, or will there be a new breed of concerned adult? Whatever I say, of course, will be conjecture. However, from my experiences and observations of our youth, I should like to categorize the adjustments to adult life which I believe our adolescents will follow.

Poverty Youth Reactions

When one is hungry for bread and education, it is a luxury to worry about such problems as overpopulation and ecology. Minority-group youth, and other poverty peoples, have enough difficulty in surviving on a day-to-day basis without being concerned with more than their immediate future.

For a number of years I have been working with Puerto Rico's youth and educational institutions. If there is one area in the world which should be concerned with ecological and populational disaster, it is Puerto Rico (Adams, 1972). Yet the typical university student there is completely unaware and unconcerned. The future of Puerto Rico is not bright, and I predict that nature will solve the island's problems through a Darwinian process in which only a select "fit" will survive. Many small Latin American countries will suffer a similar fate unless there is massive assistance by a world body or a world power.

Within our own country, our minority youth will not be in a position to assist their country unless the inequalities of employment, education, and social status are resolved. As this is not likely to occur in the foreseeable future, one can predict an increasing militancy and disillusionment with the so-called democratic process. Crime rates will increase, and drug usage will skyrocket (a reaction of despair). There will be some assistance from enlightened leaders in this sector; but on a proportionate basis, not much can be expected. Their hands will be full with their own, immediate, pressing needs.

Middle-Class Youth Reactions

It is really here that we should expect to find most of our leadership. Middle-class youth can afford the luxury of thinking and of being politically active. As a group, they are not faced with the day-to-day problems of having enough to eat, adequate housing, adequate education, or adequate income. The question is, will they provide the leadership we need? I think that their concern, or lack of concern, will divide them into several different camps.

Activists. This movement which has involved a relatively large group within the last ten years, has contained many dedicated young people. It has also contained large numbers who went along because it was the popular thing to do. The movement has been concentrated within our universities; and, as we sum up their efforts on the national level, it is difficult to see that they have made much of an impact. Undoubtedly, this will cause many activists to reassess their efforts and to wonder if they should continue. In addition, many of the issues which rallied the protestors have begun to disappear. For example, our involvement in Southeast Asia has been decreased. It is difficult to demonstrate for peace when it *appears* that we are moving in that direction.

On the local level, this group has been much more successful. There have been a number of instances where active involvement in politics has been successful (e.g., Berkeley, California), and almost every university in the country has felt the impact of their demands for educational reform. Students are now involved in contributing to the government of the nation's universities in a meaningful way. They are represented on many committees and governing boards for the first time in our educational history.

They have also become involved in assisting disadvantaged minority groups. Business school students have worked with small businesses in an attempt to help the owners understand modern accounting and marketing methods. Day-care centers and nurseries have been staffed by youth who have cared, and tutoring programs have sprung up across the country. Efforts such as these are likely to continue.

However, to sum up the future of the activist groups, I believe that they will become much less popular. They will lose many of their fringe adherents who have contributed little except impressive numbers. The youth who are now moving into this age group seem to be much less impressed with the causes of the activists. Most of the causes began before they were old enough to become concerned or involved. The new youth will be aware of the issues, but he has also observed the effectiveness of the activists in many areas, and is likely to be cynical about the amount of effort involved and the returns gained.

The Counterculture. This group of youth and adults has received more attention and less understanding than all the other groups combined. They have been typed as freaks and addicts, and indeed some of them do fit the labels. Still there has been a solid nucleus who have been honestly looking for a new approach to life: a return to basic values. There is an element within this group whom we might type as having an existential neurosis but who have had the same basic goal; viz., finding a reason for man's existence.

In their search for meaning, many of the counterculture have separated themselves into communes or communities which have been apart from society at large. They have thought that in a return to nature—one which they would not pollute—they would find a new meaning to life. A number have been successful, and some have returned to society with new and wholesome values.

On the other hand, many of the communes have failed, and others are doubtful successes. Perhaps the basic error of many of the counterculturists has been an error which man has committed since the beginning of time (Alexander and Selesnick, 1966). The ancients looked to the stars to find their destinies. Failing in this, the next movement was to look to nature for the answer to the essence of man's being. This, too, was unsuccessful. Science was then the orientation of the quest, and the result was, again, failure.

The answer to the nature of man must be found, for each of us, within ourselves, and we are singularly reticent to look within. The degree to which the counterculture has provided the opportunity for its adherents to look inwardly, with sincerity, is the degree to which it has been successful for each individual. It is probable that the popularity of

the movement will phase itself out. Certainly, the counterculture movement has provided few, if any, leaders for the needs of our country.

The Youth of Tomorrow. If we tally our discussion up to this point, it
should be noted that the youth movements of the sixties are not viewed
with much promise for the needs of the seventies and the eighties. If this
is true, where will we find the impetus of enlightened leadership which
we so desperately need?

As I talk with our youth today, I notice a new development and a
new trend in their thinking. The first characteristic of this new youth is
that he is aware. As a group they are aware of ecological and political
issues. They are aware of the youth movements of the past, their successes, and their failures; and they are not identifying themselves with
any of the currently operating movements. This is not to say that they
will not march again; they may. Youth will always react to a challenge. It
is rather to say that they have become somewhat cynical! They are much
more likely to operate *individually* but in a *collective* fashion. Their
goals and priorities are similar, so they will provide a collective impact.

They are seeking what a productive life will bring, for each of them,
in terms of financial security and the good things of life. This means that
their orientation is in the direction of improving the nation's economy.
At the same time, they have a collective sense of the directions in which
our political priorities should go. They will provide leadership and
support those leaders who place the emphasis on resolving the issues of
Peace, Poverty, Population, and *Pollution.* They see their own security
irrevocably determined by these issues. Their altruism is a practical
altruism which says that to better themselves, they must change the directions of the nation and the world; that to improve their own lot they
must improve the lot of the others. They are increasingly realizing that
the individual cannot live by himself—that "no man is an island."

I am optimistic as to the potential of this group. However, to enable
youth to attain their full potential, we must involve them within our
society at a much earlier age than we have done in the past. Let us consider how this might be accomplished.

Greater Involvement of Youth

In the history of our country, the sector of youth involvement has been
pitifully small. Our nation has built educational systems that have
insured better-educated and more aware young people than can be found
in any other nation of the world. Yet, we have effectively locked youth
out from active participation in the development of those agencies of

society with which they are intimately involved. (Less than 4 percent of President Nixon's appointments have gone to individuals under thirty years of age.) With the major exception of universities, where youth have forced the issue, it would be safe to say that young people have been ignored as a resource which could contribute much in the development of their society.

To a marked degree, the lack of effective leadership at the national level can be traced to our ignoring the possibilities of participation by our youth in their developing years. As a nation, we have been the loser in two senses: we have not had the benefits of their contributions in their younger years, and we have thereby discouraged their participation in their adult years. Most of us were raised in an era when "children should be seen but not heard." Consider how few of us are involved in our communities, states, and national issues. Yet, all of us complain about the quality of our leaders and the directions in which they are moving society.

We just cannot fall back on the cliché that age and wisdom are synonymous. There is too much evidence to the contrary. In fact, age tends to produce a desire for stability and a fear of change, regardless of the evils that are perpetuated. Youth are willing to risk, and dare, and change, and change again if necessary. Their very impatience is a desirable quality in many instances. I have been continually impressed by the contributions of the young people with whom I have served. While we, their elders, would sit around and discuss the difficulties of needed changes, they would say: "Let's implement the change and worry about the difficulties later. We can always try something else if this doesn't work." Of course, not all their ideas were good ideas, but has our record been so much better?

What I am suggesting is that we involve our adolescents in all the meaningful sectors of life, as full-fledged participants wherever possible. They should be represented on school boards, on city councils, and on advisory committees to governors and presidents. They should be represented intimately on most university committees and should be represented on boards of trustees in their colleges. They should be challenged to participate to the fullest possible extent in all the phases of society which touch them personally.

Is there an alternative? Most certainly there is. We can continue to go in the directions we are currently pursuing. We can continue to watch our society and civilization destroy itself. We can continue to watch selfish interest groups in our country destroy our air and water and land. It seems to me that a better alternative is to involve our youth in helping us to change our priorities and to salvage a nation which still has great untapped resources—its youth.

Summary

In this chapter I have attempted to outline some of the developmental problems faced by the adolescent as he moves in the direction of maturity. He is developing in a period of world crisis in which the alternatives to solving the challenges are the destruction and the end of civilization. Our adolescents are aware of the issues; at the same time they are looking for meaning in life. The period between childhood and adulthood is not an easy period, and it has never been more difficult than it is at the present time. The aware adolescent of today is developing in an age where he sees little concern for the environmental emergencies which surround him. He lives within a world that does not practice the ideals which have been taught him by his parents. Man, he finds, is essentially self-centered or selfish. The adolescent needs encouragement to live up to his potential and to contribute of himself, for the welfare of others.

The age in which our adolescent is living is an age which is moving along at an amazing rate of speed. Science is developing knowledge at a pace which makes adjustment impossible. There is no return to the past, and the present changes more rapidly each day. Science has contributed to accumulating a vast storehouse of knowledge, but has provided little which has helped man to better understand himself. As has always been true, each of us must look within ourselves to find our identities, to find a meaning in our existence. The adolescent seeks for the answers in different ways: Some give up the quest; some withdraw from society; and some continue to seek for life's meaning in service to their communities, nation, and world.

I have suggested that we should involve the aware and service-oriented adolescent in all phases of our society. We can ill afford to lose his contribution during his youth, or the training which his involvement will provide for future leadership. In the process we will add meaning to his search for his identity. The contributing potentials of our young have never been tapped as a national resource, and we need their assistance. Giving the eighteen year old the right to vote is not enough; we need the involvement of those youth who wish to be involved, to encourage all youth to become involved.

In the remainder of this book, the reader will find topics relevant for understanding today's adolescent. Such current topics as activism, involvement in politics, the counterculture, disadvantaged youth, and drugs are discussed. In addition, the more traditional areas, such as theories of adolescent development, physiological development, heredity and environment, creativity, cognition, and the role of educational institutions in adolescent development, are discussed. I have begun to develop these topics in this first chapter. The thoughtful reader will find the merit of this book in the expanded discussions which follow.

REFERENCES

Adams, J. F. Adolescent opinions on national problems. *Personnel and Guidance Journal,* 1963, *42,* 397–400.

———. Adolescent personal problems as a function of age and sex. *Journal of Genetic Psychology,* 1964, *104,* 207–214.

———. Overpopulation: A Puerto Rican catastrophe. *San Juan Star,* March 10, 1972.

Alexander, F. G., and Selesnick, S. T. *The history of psychiatry.* New York: Harper and Row, 1966.

Ardrey, R. *The territorial imperative.* New York: Delta–Dell, 1968.

Bierce, A. *The devil's dictionary.* New York: Hill and Wang, 1957.

Camus, A. *Resistance, rebellion and death.* New York: Alfred A. Knopf, 1961.

De Bell, G. *The environmental handbook.* New York: Ballantine Books, 1970.

Ehrlich, P. R., and Ehrlich, A. H. *Population, resources, environment: Issues in human ecology.* San Francisco: E. H. Freeman and Co., 1970.

Hesse, H. *Steppenwolf.* New York: Holt, Rinehart and Winston, 1929.

———. *Siddhartha.* New York: New Directions, 1951.

Horrocks, J. E. *The psychology of adolescence.* Boston: Houghton Mifflin, 1969.

McKuen, R. *Stanyan street and other sorrows.* New York: Random House, 1954.

———. *Listen to the warm.* New York: Random House, 1967.

Morris, D. *The naked ape.* New York: Dell Publishing Co., 1969.

Norman, G. Project survival. In Editors of *Playboy, Project survival.* Chicago: HMH Publishing Co., 1971.

Peck, R. F. Family patterns correlated with adolescent personality structure. *Journal of Abnormal and Social Psychology,* 1958, *57,* 347–350.

Reich, C. A. *The greening of America.* New York: Pocket Books, 1970.

Spock, B. *The commonsense book of baby and child care.* New York: Duell, Sloan and Pearce, 1946.

Teilhard de Chardin, P. *The phenomenon of man.* New York: Harper and Row, 1959.

Toffler, A. *Future shock.* New York: Random House, 1970.

2

Development and Dynamics of the Adolescent Self

*Don E. Hamachek**

Adolescence is a remarkable phenomenon. It is not only a time when girls stop climbing trees, but also a time when boys stop thinking that girls who do are neat. It is a period when boys and girls emerge slowly but surely from the cocoon of childhood to become young men and women ready and anxious to sample the fruits and privileges of their new developmental status. It is a time for adjusting to an incredible welter of biochemical and psychosocial changes which make separate and sometimes collective withdrawals on the growing adolescent's energy bank. Most of all, it is a time for raising such questions as Who am I, How am I coming across to others, and How did I ever get to be this way in the first place?

Before we move into a discussion of the dynamics of adolescence, we first of all need to address ourselves to a more basic question.

What Do We Mean by *Adolescence?*

To begin with, adolescence is neither a universal happening nor does it have lengthy historical credentials. For example, the Greeks and Romans

* Don E. Hamachek is Professor of Educational Psychology and Child Development at Michigan State University. He has edited or written such books as *The Self in Growth, Human Dynamics in Psychology and Education,* 2d ed., and *Encounters with the Self.* He has also contributed a sizeable number of journal articles to his field.

did not view it as a separate growth stage, except for the relatively short one- to two-year period it took to change from sexual immaturity to sexual maturity. Although the Roman Emperor Claudius was regarded by his relatives in the Claudian and Julian families to be somewhat dull and slow in developing, he nonetheless married at twelve and was a high priest at thirteen. The leap from childhood straight into adulthood with no adolescent apprenticeship was typical not only of classical cultures but of the Middle Ages and Renaissance as well. One writer (Ariès, 1962), for example, notes that in the 1300s and 1400s young elementary-age boys frequently went to school armed with sabers, no less! Thus, age has not always been a criterion for deciding what a growing youngster could do or what he should be taught. Referring to Ariès again (1962), he observes that, in 1677, pupils in some of the French primary grades ranged in age from nine to seventeen, and those in the highest grade were anywhere between twelve and twenty. Cultures were not age-graded. For both those who went to school and those who did not, seven years of age was considered to be the age of adulthood in most of the early Western culture. Even today adolescence as a separate growth stage is often absent in entire cultures. For example, within certain hunting cultures childhood terminates by age eight, and within certain agrarian cultures it ceases anywhere between ten and twelve (Landis, 1945). Only within our contemporary Western culture is this period we call adolescence viewed as an extension of childhood dependency. Havighurst focuses on cultural differences, in a separate chapter, so I shall not discuss this topic in greater detail.

In a purely physical sense, adolescence is a universal phenomenon. What varies are the meanings and expectations which different cultures and various subcultures within the same culture place upon a growing youngster as he moves through this growth stage. In terms of physical development, adolescence commences with the prepubertal growth spurt and ends with the attainment of full physical maturity. Although physical maturity is difficult to define with precision, it usually refers to the idea that one has reached the upper limits of his genetic potentials for endocrinal development, skeletal growth, and total height.

In a purely psychological sense, adolescence refers more to a state of mind, an attitude, a style of existence that begins with puberty and ends when one is relatively independent of parental control. As you may know from your own observations, the cessation of adolescence varies from individual to individual. For one person, psychological adolescence is terminated when he is about eighteen, while for another person his psychological adolescence persists into his twenties or thirties or, sadly enough, even later.

All in all, we can reasonably conclude that adolescence begins with signs of sexual maturity in both physical and social development, and ends when the individual becomes self-supporting, responsible, and is accepted in most ways by the reference group peers toward whom he looks for some measure of approval, recognition, and advice. I want to emphasize the importance of shifting one's needs for approval, recognition, and advice to the peer group because one of the major symptoms of a persisting *psychological* adolescence, particularly when physical adolescence has been completed, is continued dependence on parents as a major source of approval, recognition, and guidance. This does not mean that one must completely outgrow or give up needing anything from his parents, whether it be their counsel or love, in order to leave psychological adolescence successfully. It is more a matter of the *degree* to which an individual remains dependent on his parents and "needs" them for emotional and social support when physical adolescence is concluded. A twenty-five-year-old woman who persists in calling mother every time that she has a rift with her husband or a twenty-four-year-old male who gives up his vocational plans because his parents disapprove could very well be psychological adolescents in their dependency ties and inability to think for themselves.

Suffice it to say, a major task of adolescence—one that usually signals its conclusion—is the capacity and willingness of a growing youngster to fall out of love with his parents, which is the necessary first step to falling in love with another person, beginning a new family, or making one's way as an independent person.

Major Developmental Tasks of Adolescence

Emergence of the adolescent self does not happen simply because a developing youngster grows older and taller, but occurs, rather, because of certain interpersonal experiences and educational outcomes or accomplishments. Havighurst (1953) refers to these accomplishments as developmental tasks. The idea here is that there are certain rather specific "tasks" which a developing youngster must accomplish at his various stages of growth in order to reach the next level of development. A developmental task, then, is an event which occurs at a certain point in the life of an individual, successful achievement of which spurs him to further growth and probable success with later tasks, while failures inhibit growth, lead to disapproval by society and difficulty with later tasks.

The major developmental tasks confronting the adolescent boy and girl include the following:

> Achieving new and more mature relations with age-mates of both sexes.

Achieving a masculine or feminine social role.

Accepting one's physique and using the body effectively.

Achieving emotional independence of parents and other adults.

Achieving assurance of economic independency.

Selecting and preparing for an occupation.

Preparing for marriage and family life.

Developing intellectual skills and concepts necessary for civic competence.

Desiring and achieving socially responsible behavior.

Acquiring a set of values and an ethnic system as a guide to behavior.

In a sense, these ten developmental tasks are the prerequisite learnings and accomplishments necessary for successful adult living. Each task, in its own way, contributes to one's expanding sense of self, of who he is, of what he wants to be, and how he can best achieve his goals. Unless, for example, the adolescent boy or girl achieves greater maturity and confidence in his or her relations with the opposite sex during adolescence, the difficulty of acquiring these qualities increases with the move into adulthood. The adolescent girl, let's say, who remains emotionally attached to her parents, who dates hardly at all, who fails to test her feminine self in different social roles, and who persists in attaching too much importance to what other people think is a poor risk to leave the psychological safety of perpetual adolescence.

Just as there are some individuals who remain psychological adolescents most of their lives, there are others who, unfortunately enough, scramble headlong into adulthood without completely working through the tasks of adolescence. An example is the boy who drops out of school before he is either emotionally or educationally ready for economic independence. Another example is the teenage boy and girl who marry before they understand themselves well enough to know that the marriage partner is really the one they can live with in an intimate relationship. One twenty-three-year-old girl, unhappily married after six years, expressed it this way during a counseling session:

> When Bill and I got married right after high school it was great. We dated each other all through high school and never really considered dating others. Marriage just seemed a natural outgrowth of our relationship. But now, I don't know, it's sorta like we've missed out on something—at least I feel that way and I think he does, too. Isn't it stupid? Here I've been married six years and I feel I'm into something I wasn't ready for in the first place.

This young lady is saying what many young adults feel as they look back over their adolescent years; namely, the wish to have done things differently or at least to have had more heterosexual experiences while the opportunity was available.

The developmental tasks of adolescence are not simply hurdles which must be jumped in some mechanical way, but they are, in a deeper sense, highly personalized experiences, each of which helps the adolescent to define himself to himself as a person and to develop a recognizable and reasonably predictable "self." Which brings us to a logical question:

What Is the Self?

Acquiring a sense of *self* involves a slow process of differentiation as a person's identity gradually emerges into focus out of his total world of awareness. Jersild (1952, p. 9) is probably as clear as anyone about what the self is when he says:

> A person's self is the sum total of all that he can call his. The self includes, among other things, a system of ideas, attitudes, values, and commitments. The self is a person's total subjective environment; it is the distinctive center of experience and significance. The self constitutes a person's inner world as distinguished from the outer world consisting of all other people and things.

It is through the door of the self that one's personality is expressed. In fact, we could say that the self is that portion of our personality of which we are aware. How the self is reflected is a complex phenomenon expressed in different ways by different people. It is one person's assertiveness and another person's shyness; it is one individual's openness and another individual's guardedness; it is one man's independent manner and another man's dependent clinging. Each of us has images of himself constructed from our conception of the "sort of person I am." All of us have beliefs about our relative value and our ultimate worth.

Indeed, how any person feels about himself depends on many things, not the least of which are his perceptions of where he sees himself standing in relation to persons whose skills, abilities, talents, and aptitudes are similar to his own. For example, if Sally perceives herself to be an excellent student but gets a report card with three C's and a B, or if John perceives himself to be an excellent athlete but can make only third-string halfback, then each will have either to rationalize their subpar performances, to lower their expectations for themselves, or to go on to something else in which greater success is possible.

Thus, the self can be best understood as a social phenomenon growing in the context of comparative interpersonal relationships. That is, one's sense of self is nurtured not only by what one would ideally like to be, but also by how one views himself as actually performing in relation to other people. We live in a social world, and it is no surprise that the self is very much a social product. In this regard, the self has two aspects—concept and feeling. That is, we know ourselves to have certain qualities and we have certain feelings about these qualities.

Acquiring a sense of self, then, is a major undertaking of the adolescent. At times it seems like a terribly bewildering experience, an idea one adolescent girl (Williams, 1968, p. 674) expressed by asking:

> How do you tell anyone:
> This is me.
> I am this and that
> and—then again—
> I am not?
> Can you put down
> in black and white
> why you are as you are
> if sometimes it is not clear to you
> that you are at all?

However confusing it may at times seem, most adolescents do make the transition into young adulthood with at least some tentative ideas about their assets and liabilities, about their goals, and about the course they will chart to reach them. Many different people and experiences feed into the development of the emerging adolescent self. Let's turn our attention now to some of the people who play important parts during this stage of growth.

Impact of Parents on the Adolescent's Growing Self

Inasmuch as a major developmental task of adolescence is that of progress toward greater self-sufficiency and self-direction, it is not surprising that an air of tension exists between the adolescent and his parents as he struggles to find himself in his expanded social world. Parents, of course, are anxious to have their children grow up. Indeed, as you may have noticed yourself, when parents criticize an adolescent it is likely to include the observation that he is acting childishly. Although the young person is continually prodded toward adulthood, parents sometimes behave as if his reaching it is in some remote and far-off future. One frustrated sixteen-year-old boy expressed it this way during a group discussion: "You know, I think my parents want me to be independent and think for myself, but apparently not while I'm still living at home." This is true, I suspect, for many homes where adolescent age youth reside. Perhaps the observation that adulthood comes about two years later than the adolescent claims, and about two years earlier than his parents will admit, is more accurate than we realize.

The fact is, most parents do not easily let go of their emerging adolescents, a reality which has both good and bad points. The positive side is that the adolescent boy and girl must work harder and withstand stiffer challenges to prove to their parents and *themselves* that they really can make it on their own and that their self-concepts are sturdy enough to withstand both the responsibilities and setbacks accompanying independent adult living. The negative side is that parents who hang on too tightly can cause a young person struggling to be free to either feel guilty (My parents need me so—how can I leave them?) or inadequate (They don't trust me on my own—maybe I'm not able enough). As Douvan and Adelson (1966) point out in the results of their study of a large number of adolescents, there is a curvilinear relation between parental involvement with a young person and the young person's developing sense of personal autonomy. What this means is that either too much or too little involvement can inhibit the adolescent's achievement of independence. If parents are too little involved, the security necessary for self-direction is underdeveloped. On the other hand, too much involvement may generate dependency needs which interfere with the growth autonomy.

The general trend in many homes seems to be that the adolescent grows away from his family, both in spirit and presence, until it appears that "home" is transformed into something of a rooming house where, for convenience' sake, he eats (sometimes), sleeps, deposits his clothes to be washed and ironed, watches television, and is party to an endless stream of incoming and outgoing phone calls. Mealtimes, at least in those families which eat together, are frequently the only time in a day when there can be communication among all members of the family. Although the dinner table may serve as a pleasant forum, it can also be an arena for conflicts and dissension. Whatever the case, a substantial portion of the time an adolescent spends with his family is likely to be colored by feelings—on both sides—of frustration, humiliation, some sullenness, a little resentment, and even a bit of melodramatic despair from time to time.

Sex of Parent and Child as a Variable

Research shows that the specific impact that parents have on an adolescent's emerging self depends not only on whether the youngster is a boy or girl, but also on the sex of the parent. For example, there is evidence to indicate that a boy's adjustment during adolescence depends to some extent on the level of affection existing in his relationship to his father. An interesting cross-cultural study of a group of adolescent boys (Mussen, Young et al., 1963) found that boys who experience "insufficient paternal affection" were less secure, less self-confident, and less well adjusted socially than boys whose fathers showed sufficient affection.

An investigation by Bronfenbrenner (1961) examined parental behaviors and the development of responsibility and leadership qualities in a large group of fifteen- and sixteen-year-old youth. It was found that three parental behavior variables were related to the development of responsibility in young people, these being rejection, neglect, and affiliative companionship. The adolescent who was judged to be the least responsible was most likely to describe his parents as inclined to complain about and ridicule him, compare him unfavorably with other children, and spend little time with him. An interesting sex difference was observed, however. For example, responsibility in boys was associated with nurturance, affection, and companionship, especially from the mother, and with relatively high amounts of discipline and authority from the father. At the same time, these same variables were negatively related to responsibility in girls, for whom heavy paternal discipline, in particular, was deleterious to a high rating on responsibility.

The antecedents of a self-attitude which encourages leadership qualities in the adolescent were not too different from those related to responsibility. It was noted, however, that parental overprotectiveness seemed to undermine an adolescent's leadership attempts. Again, a marked sex difference was apparent. Specifically, it was noted that "affiliative companionship, nurturance, principled discipline, affection, and affective reward appear to foster the emergence of leadership in sons but discourage it in daughters" (p. 256).

This sex difference in antecedents of the self-attitudes leading to a high level of responsibility and leadership apparently means something different for the adolescent girl than for the adolescent boy in terms of personality needs. At least one explanation is that in our culture both of these characteristics are important and rewarded aspects of the male sex role but less so for the female sex role. Thus, the explicit expression of these characteristics in a girl is not as likely to win her the plaudits of a proud father or a pleased mother as might more likely be the case for a boy.

The fact is, boys and girls within and outside the family unit are treated differently by adult men and women, and this contributes significantly to how the adolescent views him- or herself. For example, there is increasing evidence to suggest that expressions of affection and punishment, as two major factors in parent-child interactions, are used in somewhat different ways, for somewhat different purposes, and with somewhat different effects when applied to boys and girls. An illustration of this is in the evidence showing that girls are more likely than boys to be subjected to love-oriented child-rearing techniques and that such techniques are effective in encouraging healthy social adjustment (Miller and Swanson, 1958; Sears, Maccoby, and Levin, 1967). In contrast, a rather different child-rearing style is used for boys. That is, parents are more likely to use physical punishment, to be permissive of and even encourage aggressiveness, to minimize the emphasis on conformity, and to stress the value of independence and achievement. With boys, parent-child interactions seem to be focused more specifically on *directing him toward the environment,* when with girls the emphasis is more on *protecting her from the environment.* (Although it is too early to tell, this is a distinction which the women's liberation movement, if powerful enough, may homogenize to some extent. We can probably better assess this as the adolescents of the late sixties and seventies become, of all things, parents themselves.) The reader is encouraged to consider Beller's discussion of psychoanalytic theory in conjunction with these sex differences in family orientations.

These contrasting means and ends help explain why it is that girls are usually found to be more obedient, cooperative, and, in general, better socially adjusted than boys of comparable ages (Terman and Tyler, 1954). At the same time, research also indicates that girls also tend to be more anxious, dependent, and sensitive to rejection. Apparently characteristics such as independence, self-confidence, initiative, and self-sufficiency, which are included among the top criteria of an adolescent boy's successful socialization in our culture, require for their development a different balance of authority and affection than is found in the more "love-orientated" strategies employed with girls. Although parental affection is important for a boy's overall socialization and self-concept development, it must be accompanied by, and be compatible with, a strong blend of parental discipline. Otherwise, the adolescent boy is likely to find himself in the same situation as the girl, who, having been the object of greater affection, is also more sensitive to its withdrawal. In other words, since the girl is likely to *receive* more affection than the boy, she is also likely to be *more responsive* to its loss, which is, in fact, why her self-attitude is marked by predispositions to greater anxiety, dependency, and sensitivity to rejection. Along this same vein, Hoffman et al. (1958, p. 5) have noted: "It seems likely that assertiveness in girls is less valued by others," and that girls are more likely to "respond to the emotional rejection that coercion (being aggressive, getting others to do what she wants, etc.) implies." This is not the sort of behavior normally encouraged in an adolescent boy, and, as you might suspect, the more dependent behaving boys at any age have a more difficult time developing a healthy self-concept than those boys who are more independent and aggressive. Returning to Bronfenbrenner again (1961, p. 260), he makes the point that "for boys, who tolerate and require higher levels of discipline on an affectional base, problems derive most commonly from the failure on the part of parents to provide adequate emotional support and—especially—firm authority."

In general, research is showing that the emergence of a healthy adolescent self-image is a function of an optimal balance of affection and control, which is different for boys and girls and involves different risks in the process of child-rearing. A healthy self-concept, at least as it is expressed in getting along with others, being accepted as a leader and assuming responsibility, is most likely to be encouraged when sons and daughters experience the parent of the same sex taking an active part in the child-rearing process.

There are definite indications that appropriate sex-role identification results in better adjustment to the day-to-day demands of living. For example, Heilbrun (1965a, 1965b) found that male college students who identified with their fathers were better adjusted and had a stronger sexual identity (more certain about their "maleness") than males who were not so identified with their fathers. In a similar vein, Helper (1955) found that the degree of "likeness" or "identification with" the father was related to the popularity of high school boys. That is, popular, likeable boys were more identified with their fathers. Just as the father plays an increasingly important role in the boy's life as he grows older, there is also evidence (Schaefer and Bayley, 1963) to show that the mother assumes a more prominent role in the girl's life as she grows older. In sum, boys thrive in a patriarchal context and girls in a matriarchal one.

Although both adolescent boys and girls share the goal of emotional independence as a major developmental task, the data reported by Douvan and Adelson (1966) suggest interesting sex differences in the expression and achievement of autonomy.

Surprisingly, adolescent girls seem to be more advanced in behavioral autonomy despite the fact that they are somewhat more restricted and protected by parents. For example, by the time they are eighteen more girls than boys report holding jobs, dating earlier, and taking a greater share of household responsibilities. Even though girls mature earlier than boys, socially as well as physically, they remain closer emotionally to the family. Contrary to what popular and fictional literature may lead us to believe, few adolescents of either sex go through a dramatic struggle for independence, and such an occurrence is even less prevalent among girls. Although an early- or middle-adolescent girl may have disagreements with her parents about such things as clothes, makeup, dating, how late she stays out and so on, most of these issues are pretty well resolved by the time the girl is seventeen or eighteen. Conflicts which occur after that point are more likely to center around differences in attitude and values related to the more general and ambiguous area of philosophy of living or life style.

This route toward emotional independence is not so smooth for boys. They are more inclined to rebel against their parents actively and to look to their peers as a primary reference group. In fact, you may recognize this behavior as being quite consistent with the earlier observation of boys' greater aggressiveness and the extent to which dependency is approved of in girls and disapproved of in boys. All in all, mild expressions of antisocial activity, especially if engaged in with a gang of friends, seem to be a pretty normal way for the adolescent boy to test his emotional biceps and burgeoning masculinity.

On the whole, the main trend during the adolescent years as far as influence of parents is concerned is toward a more thorough internalization of parental values, even though there may be considerable hassling about particular points. This generalization is especially true for girls, who are more apt to be identified with the parental point of view.

In fact, the influence of parents on an adolescent's developing self extends well into adult life. It is not uncommon that the very boy who battles his parents' beliefs and values so ferociously in his teens comes to adopt those same beliefs and values as his own as he enters his twenties (Bath and Lewis, 1962). Others retain undercurrents of bitterness toward their parents, and still others acquire a deeper feeling of respect. Some, when they have children of their own, recognize and appreciate for the first time what their parents meant to them. Suffice it to say, parents play a critical part in influencing the shape and direction of an adolescent's growing self. So do peers, an idea to which we turn next.

Impact of Peer Relationships on the Adolescent's Growing Self

It is no secret that a young person's relations with his own age-mates become increasingly more important as he moves into his adolescent years. Peer group influence hits a peak around middle adolescence and begins to decline after that, when young people go their separate ways, marry, and begin setting up standards for their own nuclear families. However, during the junior high and high school years, adolescents have a society or "youth culture" of their own, overlapping with, and yet separate from, the larger society in which they live.

There is little question but that the peer group has an enormous impact on an adolescent's developing sense of self. Why is the adolescent peer culture successful in shaping the behavior and self-attitudes of young people? Medinnus and Johnson (1969, p. 709) look at it this way:

> It succeeds because it is dangerous and exciting and it requires real skills . . . ; because it is *not* based on such things as class distinctions, which are contrary to our expressed adult values system but not to our actual behavior; because it *is* based on the idea that the individual should be judged in terms of personal attributes and accomplishments; because it is in many ways more humane and accepting of individual differences than adult cultural values; because it is concerned with expanding self-awareness at a time when people have few means of discovering themselves; because it is against sham; and because it fulfills the needs of young people better than does the adult culture.

Major Functions of the Peer Group

Ausubel (1954) has listed seven basic functions that the peer group serves during adolescence. In somewhat modified form, in view of research which has appeared since Ausubel wrote, these functions are as follows:

Family Replacement. To some extent, the peer group takes the place of the family, which is to say that a youngster can feel a certain status, or lack of it, quite independent of what or who his family is. As you might suspect, this is invaluable preparation for adulthood because it gives one a chance for more objective feedback than parents can usually provide.

Stabilizing Influence. Peer-group membership is a useful stabilizer during a period of rapid transition. In light of the incredible endocrinal, developmental, and social changes which occur during the brief period of adolescence, it is comforting to know that others are going through the same thing. As one sixteen-year-old boy put it, "I hate these dumb pimples, but I'd hate them more if I was the only one who had them."

Self-Esteem. The peer group can be an important source of self-esteem, in the sense of being important to someone outside the primary family unit. Of course it can work the other way, too, particularly for the adolescent who is isolated or scapegoated.

Standards. Ausubel takes more or less for granted an issue over which there is some disagreement, namely, that adolescents allow their peer group the authority to set standards. The reasoning is that adolescents thereby affirm their own right to self-determination, since the peer group basically represents what they value in the first place.

This may be, but it is not certain that the impact of the peer group is any more intense than the influence of the family. Although the adolescent moves initially in the direction of the more liberal peer group, there is evidence (McDill and Coleman, 1965; Douvan and Adelson, 1966; Reiss, 1968; Levitt and Edwards, 1970) to suggest that, for basic life decisions, the standards of the family carry more weight than the peer group when the two are in conflict.

There are exceptions to this. For example, if parental warmth and a sense of "equal rights" within the home are at a minimum, as is sometimes the case, the peer group may provide both the security and the models that youngsters need. We can say with some certainty that the greater the wall between the adolescent and his family, the more elaborate the peer culture becomes and the more he will turn to it for support and identity. Not infrequently those teenage youth who are most involved and identified with their peer culture are those who have strained and difficult relationships with their parents.

Protection. The peer group insulates and protects adolescents to some extent from the coercion that adults are likely to impose on young people. When the adolescent says something on the order of "Well, everyone else is going (or doing it, or wearing it, or whatever), why can't I?" he is raising what has become an almost universal wail of defensive protest designed to implore restricting adults to change their minds. As you can imagine (or remember from your own adolescent years), there is a certain safety in lodging this protest while holding membership within the security of one's peer group. Being able to say, for example, that "everyone" is doing it is a much more persuasive statement than "he" or "she" is doing it. There is both safety and strength in numbers, and membership in the peer culture provides both.

Practice by Doing. Another thing the peer group provides is an opportunity to practice by doing. Dating, participation in extracurricular activities, bull sessions about life, sex, future goals, and the world generally are all important rehearsal experiences for eventual adulthood. As one practices by doing, the peer group is a source of instant feedback; it is an audience of self-proclaimed critics watching for flaws in the performances of their own kind and in themselves. Feedback from peers is important because it is objective (sometimes unmercifully so), and it provides cues and information which can be used to modify and refine the adolescent's emerging concept of who he is as a person.

Modeling. Particularly for disadvantaged youngsters, the peer group offers a psychosocial moratorium that many parents simply cannot provide. For example, Hoffman and Saltzstein's (1967) research relating parent discipline to a child's moral development found that there was substantial moral and conscience development modeling of their parents among middle-class youngsters, but almost none among lower socioeconomic status subjects. It may very well be that lower socioeconomic youth are more psychologically dependent on their peers and thus use them for models "to be like" more extensively.

Peer Acceptance and Social Adjustment

Being liked and accepted is important at any age, but it seems particularly crucial during the adolescent years. Sometimes the dependence on group approval is so severe that it seems something on the order of "popularity neurosis." Being noticed and feeling reasonably accepted are important prerequisites to getting feedback and to taking the necessary risks to try out different personalities or relationship "styles" from time to time. Boys show themselves off in what they consider to be their masculine best and girls in their most feminine, extravagantly vivacious, and alluring. No matter how interested in their own group various clusters of boys and girls seem to be, at a deeper level they are really proclaiming and advertising *they are*. Individuals within any given peer group may be busy politicking and making time, but so is everyone else. In a sense, they are all campaigning for office, for the esteem and acclaim and recognition that will tell them where they finished in the voting. Actually, the adolescent's concern about getting along with people or having a "good personality" is sometimes less a search for inner strength and more a search for the tricks that will gain him approval and acceptance, whether it be in making the varsity team, playing a musical instrument, getting high grades, developing into the class clown, being active in extracurricular activities, and so on. But so what, so long as his search for approval leads him to be more involved and competent than he was before?

Ironically, the occasional adolescent who is mature enough to be more independent of the whims, wishes, and fads of his contemporaries and goes his own way may find that his peers flock around him as if he were a tower of strength. It is almost as if they want to find what his secret is so as to be more that way themselves. When you think about it, there are very few people (young or old) who enjoy the ingratiating submissiveness demanded of them when they are dependent on another person or group of people as their source of self-esteem and self-worth. Perhaps this is one of the reasons that most of us admire and even feel a bit envious of the strong person able to hold his own in the face of strong adversity or group pressure.

The intense need to be liked and accepted during adolescence is neither a negative characteristic nor in any sense abnormal. In fact, the youngster who reflects the qualities which make him more or less acceptable to his peers has many advantages. In a study by Feinberg (1953) of over two thousand adolescents, it was found that young persons who were accepted by others had, on the whole, a more favorable view of themselves than the rejected ones. In addition, they had better relationships with their parents and teachers.

There is also evidence to show that peer acceptance is related to success in high school, at least as far as its completion is concerned. For example, Gronlund and Holmlund (1958) examined the high school careers of children who had high or low sociometric status as determined by tests administered when they were in the sixth grade and compared these with the records of these same individuals seven years later. What they found was that 82 percent of the high-status pupils, as compared to low-status pupils, graduated from high school. In other words, about three times as many students in the low-status group as in the high-status group dropped out of high school. We might also note that the difference in intelligence between the two groups (high-status average IQ was about 109; low-status IQ about 101) was not large enough to account for this difference in the number of dropouts. Although we cannot conclude from this that low social acceptance causes poor high school performance or that high social acceptance leads to superior high school performance, we can conclude that low peer-group acceptance may be an important factor contributing to a particular adolescent's subpar academic achievement record. Not surprisingly, perhaps, it was also noted that a considerably larger number of those who had been most accepted by their sixth-grade peers joined clubs and organizations, participated in varsity sports, and held various leadership positions in high school.

Although it is true that acceptance by one's peers very often leads to social success, we cannot take for granted that social success, as indicated by high popularity ratings, automatically leads to healthy personal adjustment. Nor, for that matter, can we assume that a low degree of acceptance by peers is indicative of current or future social maladjustment. Why?

In the first place, to judge the meaning of high or low peer acceptance it is necessary to consider the criteria of standards and values being applied. In some high schools, as you know, athletics are prized above all else and in fact the morale of an entire school may fluctuate with the won-loss column of the current varsity sport. In still other high schools, honor rolls and a college orientation are so highly esteemed that even the team's best fullback has to show academic promise to be fully accepted. Johnston and Bachman's chapter contains the results of some interesting research in this area.

In the second place, to understand the meaning of high peer acceptance it is also necessary to consider the price a person may pay to get it. For example, the adolescent who gives up his own natural bent and inclinations so he can "go along with the crowd" may be the very one who so lacks confidence in himself that he will do anything to almost anything to be liked, no matter what the price. Sometimes the most popular members of a crowd include those whose sense of personal adequacy and mental health is so tenuous that they can feel worthwhile only by being a friend to all and an enemy to none. There is research evidence, for example, to show that among those who attain a high level of social acceptance on a sociometric test, there are some who are "seriously disturbed" (Northway and Wigdor, 1947). So, in order to assess all the implications of peer acceptance or lack of it, we have to put it in perspective by first of all determining its criteria and its price. We probably all know persons with whom we went to high school who never really "made" it with their peers during that stage of growth, but who went on to be quite successful—educationally, socially, and economically—as they moved into young adulthood when being popular, in terms of getting along with people, was less important than being competent, in terms of accomplishment and getting things done.

All in all, the peer group and the youth culture provide the medium within which one secures an identity, however tentative it may be. Because the adolescent must separate himself from his parents, he must initially at least, reject their dictates and, occasionally, their values. Why should this be? As any one of us can probably testify to, "achieving" an identity is an active process, not one of passively purchasing the achievements of others. The typical adolescent is driven by a strong need to become who *he* is, not who his parents are. In order to do this, the adolescent becomes less like his parents and more like his peers. Unfortunately some parents overreact to this shift in affiliation by behaving as if their youngsters had sworn a blood allegiance to a group of youthful desperadoes bent on overthrowing the entire concept of parenthood. Nothing could be further from the truth. It is simply a necessary phase which all adolescents go through (just as each of us did) in finding himself. If a growing boy or girl is psychologically healthy, each must fill the need of being his or her own man or woman before he can be anyone else's.

Another reason behind the peer group's being an important medium for the adolescent's total socialization and self-definition is that adults have been negligent in providing clear landmarks and in institutionaliz-

ing systematic steps to autonomy. Not surprisingly, the adolescent constitutes his own society. Why? Paul Goodman, a most articulate spokesman
for youth, suggests that society has ceased to make sense to young people.

> It's hard to grow up when there isn't enough man's work. There is
> "nearly full employment," but there get to be fewer jobs that are neces-
> sary or unquestionably useful; that require energy and draw on some of
> one's best capabilities; and that can be done keeping one's honor and
> dignity. In explaining the widespread troubles of adolescents and young
> men, this simple objective factor is not much mentioned (Goodman, 1956,
> p. 17).

The result has been a youth culture which provides a series of
eccentric, substitute vehicles toward the achievement of independence
and maturity which, though characteristically nonadult, nonetheless
encourages many of the same behaviors found in the adult world such as
conformity and stereotype. What is important is that the adolescent peer
culture develops its own criteria of good and bad, right and wrong,
successful and nonsuccessful, and thereby offers its own series of demarca-
tions of identity. Thus, through an elaborate system of rewards and
punishments, the vast social system of the peer culture is defined and
constituted.

Adolescence is the time, and the youth culture is the place in normal
growth when a developing youngster begins to question all those things—
parents, religion, education, self, you name it—he had heretofore simply
accepted on faith. Among those things which an adolescent assesses and
which contribute to his overall socialization and feelings of adequacy and
worthwhileness is his physical growth and development, an idea to which
we now turn.

The Adolescent Self as Related to Physical Growth and Development

As we have said, a major developmental task of adolescence is that of
shaping an identity, of arriving at a sense of self in relation to the world
at large. A significant aspect of an adolescent's self-awareness is in large
part expressed in self-consciousness, a concern for how well he measures
up. Although he worries about how he stands on a number of measures—
intelligence, wit, popularity, daringness, and so on—his primary concern
is with his progress toward physical maturity. The fact is, whether maturing takes place too fast or too slowly, it can be a source of agonized self-

consciousness. An adolescent's height, weight, birth, eye color, hair color and texture, complexion, and general body proportions are very much related to his feelings of personal adequacy. The pace of a boy's total growth in relation to other boys in his class, or the extent of a girl's overall development in comparison to other girls her age play an important part in how they feel about themselves.

Like all other aspects of the self-concept, the image a person has of his body is subjective. A person may have a generally positive body image—he likes the way he looks; or he may have a negative body image—how he looks falls short of his expectations for himself. Garrison's chapter provides additional information which the reader should integrate into our discussion in this section.

The Body and Self-Esteem

The most material and visible part of the self is our physical body. Like any other object in our physical environment, our bodies are perceived through the various senses. Occupying as it does a substantial portion of our visual and auditory field, we see and hear a lot of ourselves.

This being the case, it is not surprising to find a considerable amount of evidence to suggest that one's *appearance* is an important determiner of self-esteem, both among men and women. For example, in a series of studies (Secord and Jourard, 1953; Jourard and Secord, 1955), it was found that the feelings an individual had about his body were commensurate with the feelings that he had about himself as a person. That is, the person who had negative feelings about his body was also likely to feel negatively about himself as a total person and vice versa.

Body image, appearance, and self-esteem do seem to be related. Indeed, research has shown that how one feels about himself is related not only to total appearance but also to the rate and pace of growth as one moves through his developmental years.

Individual differences in physical growth have been found to affect personal and social adjustment not only during adolescence, but beyond that time as well. Since the effects of early or late growth are different for boys than for girls, perhaps we can more clearly see these differences if we separate the two and examine them one by one. Let's take the boys first.

Effect of Early versus Late Physical Maturity on Boys

Highly significant and classical growth studies have emerged from the Institute of Human Development at the University of California. One of these studies, conducted by Jones and Bayley (1950), focused on a group of boys who were the sixteen most accelerated growers and the sixteen who were the most consistently slow growers for a four-and-a-half-year period between the ages of twelve and seventeen.

Many significant differences between the two groups were found. For example, when rated by adults, the slower-growing boys were judged as lower in physical attractiveness, less masculine, less well groomed, more animated, more affected, and more tense. They did not, however, differ from the more advanced boys in ratings of popularity, leadership, prestige, or social affect on the group. They were considered, though, to be less mature in heterosexual social relations.

When rated by their peers, the slower growers were judged to be more restless, talkative, and bossy. In addition, peer ratings showed them to be less popular, less likely to be leaders, more attention-seeking, and less confident in class situations. Significantly, perhaps, they were also judged by their peers as being shorter on a sense of humor about themselves.

In contrast, boys who were physically accelerated were usually more accepted and treated by adults and peers as more mature. They were more matter-of-fact about themselves, and had less need to strive for status and recognition, although from their ranks came the outstanding student body leaders in high school. The investigators concluded by stating: "The findings give clear evidence of the effect of physical maturing on behavior. Perhaps of greater importance, however, is the repeated demonstration of the multiplicity of factors, psychological and cultural as well as physical, which contribute to the formation of basic personality patterns" (p. 146).

In a study designed to see if there were any differences between the self-conceptions, motivations, and interpersonal attitudes of late- and early-maturing boys (Mussen and Jones, 1957), it was found that boys who mature late in adolescence are more likely to be insecure and dependent than their faster-growing peers. In addition, they more frequently behave in childish, affected, attention-getting ways.

These findings are consistent with those in another study reported by Mussen and Jones (1958), in which they investigate the motivations of late- and early-maturing boys. In general, they discovered that high drives for social acceptance and for aggression are more characteristic of the slower-growing than the faster-growing boys. This may suggest that a later maturer's needs for social visibility may stem from feelings of insecurity and dependence, which conceivably serve as the basic motivators for recognition in order to compensate for underlying feelings of inadequacy and rejection. It is as if these boys were saying in many different ways, "Hey lookit me!"

In line with the evidence thus far, Weatherly (1964, p. 1209), in a study related to physical maturation and personality in late adolescence concluded:

> . . . the late-maturing boy of college age is less likely than his earlier-maturing peers to have satisfactorily resolved the conflicts normally attending the transition from childhood to adulthood. He is more inclined to seek attention and affection from others and less inclined to assume a position of dominance and leadership over others. Yet he is not ready to accept the dictates of authority gracefully; he is inclined, rather, to defy authority and assert unconventional behavior in a rebellious vein. In view of the evidence of these potentially competing forces within him [it is not] surprising that he tends to see himself different from his peers and parents.

Taken together, these findings make it clear that the rate of physical maturing may affect self-concept development specifically and personality development generally in crucial important ways. We can reasonably infer that adult and peer attitudes toward the adolescent, as well as their treatment and acceptance of him, are related to some extent to his perceived physical status. This suggests that the sociopsychological environment in which a late-maturer grows may be significantly different and less positive from that of their early-maturing peers. As a consequence, according to the studies we have examined above, they acquired different patterns of overt social behavior.

On the basis of both observations and research, we can reasonably conclude that during adolescence late-maturing is a handicap for many boys and rarely offers special advantages. Early maturing, on the other hand, is a two-sided coin. On the positive side it frequently lends itself to certain competitive advantages, but on the negative side it sometimes means that the adolescent has to respond to expectations which are determined more by size and appearance than to other aspects of maturing. All in all, however, the early-maturing boy is likely to have a better time of it both in terms of certain physical advantages and more positive self-concept outcomes as he moves through his adolescent years.

Effect of Early versus Late Physical Maturity on Girls

What is perhaps most noteworthy in the research dealing with the relationships between developmental maturity and personality variables in girls is the fact that they are so much less dramatic than those for boys. For girls, early maturing provides no obvious prestige-gaining advantages. Indeed, at the peak of their growth, early-maturing girls are not only taller than their girl classmates, but also are actually taller than most of the boys in their class. In addition, thère is evidence to suggest that many early-maturing girls consider their accelerated growth status to be a physical stigma which interferes with their opportunity for wider social experiences (Stolz and Stolz, 1944). Such girls have also been judged to have little influence on their peers and seldom attain a high degree of popularity, prestige, or leadership (Jones, 1958).

As you may sense, the evidence favoring positive self feelings is hardly on the side of the early-maturing girl, particularly during her early adolescent years. If anything, the evidence seems to suggest that girls who mature at a slower rate enjoy more social advantages mostly because they are inclined to be less stocky and less apt to tower over so many of their age-mates. On the other hand, we have to bear in mind that when we are talking about early-maturing girls, we are considering girls who are experiencing their peak growth years somewhere between eleven and fourteen years of age, which is during their junior high and early high school years. You may recall from your own junior high and early high school days the vast individual differences among both boys *and* girls when it came to height, weight, and assorted measurements. Considering that junior high is, for the most part, full of little boys and young women, it is not surprising that the buxom seventh-grade girl feels a degree of social isolation and receives feedback to reinforce a somewhat "out of it" feeling. It is not uncommon for early-maturing girls to date boys and seek social outlets with other older adolescents, which probably does a great deal to counteract feeling *too* out of it.

In an effort to determine whether the psychological impact on girls of early or large growth persisted into later adolescence, Jones and Mussen (1958) studied the self-conceptions, motivations, and interpersonal attitudes of thirty-four seventeen-year-old girls. Sixteen of these girls had been consistently fast growers, and eighteen had been consistently slow growers. They assumed that, since the early-maturing girl had a harder time of it during her peak growing years, she might be expected to reveal negative self-feelings and poor interpersonal attitudes as a late teenager. However, when the *Thematic Apperception Test* scores of early- and late-maturing girls were compared it was found that early-maturing girls had significantly lower scores on the category *negative characteristics*, indicating more favorable self-concepts. From the picture we have to this point, we would have expected early-maturing girls to have lower self-concepts. Although this was not true, the fact that early-maturing girls did have a higher self-concept in later adolescent years is consistent with the conclusion of Faust (1960) who found that, for girls, precocious physical development tends to become a decided asset as the girl moves from junior high and into the high school years. On the other hand, Weatherly's (1964) efforts to find whether late physical maturation was a liability or asset to the personality development of girls did not result in a definite answer to the question. He did, however, observe that late physical maturation had adverse affects on personal adjustment in *both* sexes in late adolescence. This is quite consistent with the conclusion reached by Jones and Mussen (1958, p. 498) :

> When the differences between early- and late-maturing girls are compared with the differences between early- and late-maturing boys, they are found to be in the same direction more often than in the opposite. These findings are interpreted to indicate that late-maturing adolescents of both sexes are characterized by less adequate self-concepts, slightly poorer parent-child relationships, and some tendency for stronger dependency needs.

As you can see, the relationship between physical maturation and personality variables is much less definite for girls than for boys. A logical conclusion is that rate of physical maturation is a less influential variable influencing personality development in girls than for boys. This is not surprising. Elsewhere (Hamachck, 1971) the point has been made that the cultural sex-role prescription for males in our society is relatively clear and is one which places a high value upon attributes associated with physical strength, coordination, and athletic deftness, especially in the adolescent and young adulthood years. For girls, however, the feminine sex-role prescription is less definite and stereotyped and is, therefore, not as likely to be connected to any specific pattern of physical attributes. In addition, whereas people seem to respond more to a boy's or a man's total physical makeup, the response to a girl's physical makeup is apt to be more specific. That is, the physical qualities of a girl capable of eliciting a favorable response include her face, bosom, hips, legs, and total proportions (although not necessarily in that order). For example, one girl might have a pretty face and very little else, but this could be sufficient to win her signs of approval. Another girl may have an extremely attractive figure and only very plain facial features, but her nice legs or substantial bosom may be quite enough to win her some feeling of social approval. In other words, it may be more possible for a girl than for a boy to elicit different responses to different parts of her body so that even though she may fall short in one area, she can make it up in another. Girls are expected to do little else with their bodies except adorn them and make them as attractive as possible. Boys, on the other hand, are expected to *do* something with their bodies and are judged more on that basis. Another way of stating it, I suppose, would be to suggest that when it comes to the physical side of the self, at least, girls tend to be judged more in terms of how they look and boys more in terms of how they perform. If this is true, then a tentative speculation about why it is that the rate of physical maturation has less dramatic effect on girls than boys is that girls have greater flexibility for altering or changing their looks than boys do for altering or changing their performances. Even a somewhat unattractive girl can look attractive with the aid of proper dress, padding, and cosmetics.

Summary

The adolescent self is a tenuous, fragile thing which not uncommonly is marked by continual shifts in emphasis, direction, and expression. When we talk about the adolescent "self," what we have reference to is a kind of experimental personality "style" which may change, chameleonlike, on a moment's notice, depending on the strength of current social fads. Probably the most important considerations to keep in mind regarding the adolescent self are that it is incompletely formed and that many of its expressions are simply temporary mimicries of the youth culture in which it is nurtured. Persons who either work with or are the parents of adolescent youth would do well to keep in mind that a teenager must necessarily experience a great deal of changing and growing during the adolescent years. Sometimes we forget this and act as if the normal signals and stresses of growing up were symptoms of personality malfunction and disorder.

Adolescence is both a psychological and physical growth stage. The personality style or "self" we see expressed during adolescence is not unrelated to the adult self which will emerge from it. Generally speaking, the adolescent self will continue to develop in the direction it starts and will be influenced both by parental and peer values.

REFERENCES

Ariès. P. *Centuries of childhood.* Translated by R. Baldick. New York: Alfred A. Knopf, 1962.

Ausubel, D. P. *Theory and problems of adolescent development.* New York: Grune and Stratton, 1954.

Bath, J. A. and Lewis, E. C. Attitudes of young female adults toward some areas of parent-adolescent conflict. *Journal of Genetic Psychology,* 1962, *100,* 241–253.

Bronfenbrenner, U. Some familiar antecedents of responsibility and leadership in adolescents. In L. Petrullo and B. Bass (eds.), *Leadership and interpersonal behavior.* New York: Holt, Rinehart and Winston, 1961.

Douvan, E., and Adelson, J. *The adolescent experience.* New York: Wiley, 1966.

Faust, S. Developmental maturity as a determiner in prestige of adolescent girls. *Child Development,* 1960, *31,* 173–184.

Feinberg, M. R. Relation of background experience to social acceptance. *Journal of Abnormal and Social Psychology,* 1953, *48,* 206–214.

Goethals, G. W., and Lkos D. S. *Experiencing youth.* Boston: Little, Brown and Co., 1970.

Goodman, P. *Growing up absurd.* New York: Alfred A. Knopf, 1956.

Gronlund, N. E., and Holmlund, W. S. The value of elementary school sociometric status scores for predicting pupils' adjustment in high school. *Educational Administration and Supervision,* 1958, *44,* 255–260.

Hamachek, D. E. *Encounters with the self.* New York: Holt, Rinehart and Winston, 1971.

Havighurst, R. J. *Human Development and Education.* London: Longmans, Green and Co., 1953.

Heilbrun, A. B. The measurement of identification. *Child Development,* 1965, *36,* 111–127. (a)

———. The measurement of identification. *Child Development,* 1965, *36,* 789–799. (b)

Helper, M. M. Learning theory and self-concept. *Journal of Abnormal and Social Psychology,* 1955, *51,* 184–194.

Hoffman, L., Rosen, R., and Lippin, R. Parental coerciveness, child autonomy, and peer group role at school. Paper presented at 66th Annual American Psychological Association Convention, Washington, D.C., September, 1958.

Hoffman, M. L., and Saltzstein, H. D. Parent discipline and the child's moral development. *Journal of Personality and Social Psychology,* 1967, *5,* 45–57.

Jersild, A. T. *In search of self.* New York: Teachers College Press, Columbia University, 1952.

Jones, M. C. A study of socialization at the high school level. *Journal of Genetic Psychology,* 1958, *93,* 87–111.

———, and Bayley, N. Physical maturing among boys as related to behavior. *Journal of Educational Psychology,* 1950, *41,* 129–148.

———, and Mussen, P. H. Self-conceptions, motivations, and interpersonal attitudes of early and late maturing girls. *Child Development,* 1958, *29,* 491–501.

Jourard, S. M., and Secord, P. F. Body-cathexis and personality. *British Journal of Psychology,* 1955, *46,* 130–138.

Landis, P. H. *Adolescence and youth.* New York: McGraw-Hill, 1945.

Levitt, E. E., and Edwards, J. A. A multivariate study of correlative factors in youthful cigarette smoking. *Developmental Psychology,* 1970, *2,* 5–11.

McDill, E. L., and Coleman, J. Family and peer influence in college plans of high school students. *Sociology of Education,* 1965, *38,* 112–126.

Medinnus, G. R., and Johnson, R. C. *Child and adolescent psychology.* New York: Wiley, 1969.

Miller, D. R., and Swanson, G. E. *The changing American parent.* New York: Wiley, 1958.

Mussen, P., Young, H., Gaddini, R., and Morante, L. The influence of father-son relationships on adolescent personality and attitudes. *Journal of Child Psychology and Psychiatry,* 1963, *4,* 3–16.

———, and Jones, M. C. Self-conceptions, motivation and interpersonal attitudes of later- and early-maturing boys. *Child Development,* 1957, *28,* 243–256.

———, and Jones, M. C. The behavior-inferred motivations of late- and early-maturing boys. *Child Development,* 1958, *29,* 61–67.

Northway, M. L., and Wigdor, B. T. Rorschach patterns related to the socioeconomic status of children. *Sociometry,* 1947, *10,* 186–199.

Reiss, A. L. America's sex standards: How and why they're changing. *Trans-action,* 1968, *5* (March), 26–32.

Sears, R. R., Maccoby, E. E., and Levin, H. *Patterns of childrearing.* Evanston, Ill.: Row, Peterson, 1957.

Secord, P. F., and Jourard, S. M. The appraisal of body-cathexis: Body-cathexis and the self. *Journal of Consulting Psychology,* 1953, *17,* 343–347.

Stolz, H. R., and Stolz, L. M. Adolescent problems related to somatic variations. *Yearbook of the National Society for the Study of Education,* 1944, *43,* Part I, 80–99.

Terman, L. M., and Tyler, L. E. Psychological sex differences. In L. Carmichael (ed.), *Manual of child psychology.* New York: Wiley, 1954.

Weatherly, D. Self-perceived rate of physical motivation and personality in late adolescence. *Child Development,* 1964, *35,* 1197–1210.

Williams, J. Chronology of a self. In D. E. Hamachek (ed.), *Human dynamics in psychology and education.* Boston: Allyn and Bacon, 1968.

3

A Cross-cultural View
of Adolescence

*Robert J. Havighurst**

For the purposes of this chapter we shall define adolescence as the age period from twelve to eighteen, though occasionally extending the upper limit to age twenty. We shall take a long cross-cultural look at adolescent youth.

A *culture* is a set of common and standard behaviors and beliefs shared by a group of people and taught by them to their children. Different nations have different cultures. Also, within a complex society there are always a number of subcultures. A subculture is a culture shared by a subgroup in a complex society and different from the subcultures of other subgroups in that society. For example, the American society has a number of subcultures, including those of Italian-Americans, Mexican-Americans, Japanese-Americans, American Indians, Puerto Ricans, Appalachian whites, New Englanders, Middle Westerners, Southerners, Texans, Negroes, Catholics, Jews, Protestants. From this list it should be clear that a given American takes part in a number of subcultures, as well as in the common culture shared by all or nearly all citizens of the United States. Thus, a subculture does not include all the learned behaviors and beliefs of its members.

* Robert J. Havighurst is Professor of Education and Human Development, Emeritus, at the University of Chicago. In his distinguished career he has written such books as *Adolescent Character and Personality*, *Growing Up in River City*, *Human Development and Education*, and *Society and Education*. In addition he has published over two hundred scholarly articles on a diversity of topics.

Another form of subculture is that of a *social class*. This is important for the understanding of American adolescents, and will be discussed in some detail later in this chapter.

Cultures change with time, in most societies. Therefore, the culture of today is different from that of a century ago, or even of a generation ago. We will limit ourselves to the twentieth century in our cross-cultural comparisons, but will note frequently that the American culture and subcultures of the 1970s are different from those of 1910 or 1940, even though they carry the same names.

Universal Aspects of Adolescence

A cross-cultural view of adolescence requires us to answer the question: What is there about adolescence that does not depend upon culture? What is universal about adolescence—common to adolescents everywhere?

The answer to this question depends on empirical study—study and comparison of adolescent boys and girls all over the world and in all the subcultures of the complex societies. There was a time, not long ago, when people generally thought that the experience of adolescence was very much the same all over the world. They looked at adolescence in their own society and thought it must be very similar in other societies.

This was an error and, when the error was discovered, it taught us an important lesson. For example, only fifty years ago there was a widespread belief, on the part of American teachers and opinion leaders, that adolescence is inevitably a period of "storm and stress" for all boys and girls everywhere. They were bound to have a difficult time, full of uncertainty and feelings of self-doubt. At the same time they were bound to be in conflict with their elders. This is the way adolescence was described in the nineteenth-century literature of Europe and North America. Then an American anthropologist, Margaret Mead, went to live on the South Pacific island of Samoa, to observe the lives of the adolescents there. She found little or no stress during adolescence. This period of life was one of easy growth toward adulthood. Reasons for this became evident as she studied the Samoan culture. Her book *Coming of Age in Samoa* made a great change in our understanding of adolescence. It became clear that we should compare adolescence in several widely different cultures before we could state with assurance that a given characteristic of adolescence is universal.

Still, there are many universal aspects of adolescence, and they will be listed and discussed briefly.

Biological Development

The adolescent growth cycle appears to be universal, with girls preceding boys by about two years. Briefly, this cycle consists of the following:

A very brief slowdown of growth in height, coming at the age of ten for girls and twelve for boys, followed by a spurt in height, which lasts for about three years, and then a rapid decline in growth rate, until adult height is reached for the average girl at about age sixteen and for the average boy at about eighteen. There is a wide variation in the age of beginning and ending the adolescent growth cycle.

Appearance of pubic hair and hair in the armpits for both sexes. Growth of facial hair for boys; growth of breasts for girls. Widening of the shoulders in boys; widening of the hips in girls. Growth and development of the external genital organs in boys and girls, and of the internal genital organs in girls. Closure of the epiphyses of the long bones, which means that the bones cannot grow longer, and growth in height has stopped.

Physiological changes, triggered by changes in the pituitary and the adrenal glands, and the gonads. The beginning of menstruation and the establishment of the menstrual cycle in girls. The parallel but not directly observable sexual maturation of boys.

Development of interest in the opposite sex, and feelings of sexual desires.

These events are universal, as far as we know. Only the age at which they occur seems to depend partly on individual inheritance and partly on external factors, such as diet. The age of menarche (beginning of menstruation) appears to have been lowered about two years between 1800 and 1950 in Europe. This is probably due to improved nutrition in the preadolescent years, and probably the age when boys reach sexual maturity has been lowered to the same degree. There is some uncertainty as to whether climate affects the age of sexual maturing. Garrison, in the following chapter, discusses physiological development in some detail.

Sex-Role Differentiation

During adolescence, boys acquire a masculine sex role, with "appropriate" attitudes about the male's behavior toward females, about the male's responsibility for a family, about career, etc. Girls acquire a feminine sex role. To a limited extent these roles have a biological base. But they also have a cultural base—a nearly universal cultural base. The sex-role differences are very nearly the same in most societies. However, Margaret Mead found a society in the South Pacific where the roles were almost reversed. Men behaved like Western women, and women behaved like the men in Western societies. Furthermore, the role of women has changed a great deal during the present century in Europe and North America. The contemporary Women's Liberation Movement in North America is an attempt to change the sex role of women in the direction of making their roles more like those of men. Thus the nature of sex-role differentiation is not free from cultural variations.

Assuming Adult Roles under Societal Guidance

In all societies that we know about, adolescent youth take on the adult roles of worker and husband or wife, under the general stimulation and regulation by the society. They vary in the age at which they take on these roles, especially that of husband or wife. The average age of marriage varies greatly among modern societies, and is set by a number of factors which vary from one society to another. Many societies, including the United States, do not generally expect marriage by the end of adolescence, but rather during the early adult period. But it is a universal fact that young people take on adult roles, and are influenced and ruled by the society concerning their manner of taking on these roles.

Becoming Emotionally Independent of Parents and Other Adults

The major decision for a child's life are made for him by his family or by adults who are responsible for his rearing. But during adolescence a boy or girl begins to "take charge" of himself. His life becomes his own, and he has a private life which he does not share with his parents. He begins to make such major decisions as whom shall he have as friends, whom he will marry, what clothing he will wear, what occupation he will learn. (Within this book, Borow discusses the occupational area for adolescents within our culture.)

The universality of this aspect of life is rather severely limited by culture in two ways. There are some cultures in which the family makes nearly all of these decisions for a girl, and almost as many for a boy. The family will choose a husband or wife for their adolescent child, and will determine his occupation. This is less true of the modern complex societies than it is of simpler and agriculture-based societies. The second limitation of universality is in the age when major decisions are made by or for a person growing to adulthood. In some cultures there is considerable emotional independence from his family for an adult, but he gains this very slowly over a period of years, extending far beyond his biological adolescence. Generally speaking, males achieve emotional independence considerably earlier than females do, in most societies.

Acquiring an Ideology

Erik Erikson (1959) has defined ideology as "a coherent body of shared images, ideals, and ideas which—whether based on formulated dogma, an implicit *Weltanschauung,* or highly structured world image, a political creed, or a way of life—provides for the participants a coherent if systematically simplified overall orientation in space and time, in means and ends."

It is the fact of acquiring an ideology that is universal, not the actual ideology itself. This latter varies from one culture to another. It may be acquired by "absorption" from the family and the local community, and never be put into words. It may be made explicit by some initiation ceremony at adolescence, such as confirmation in a church, or becoming a full member of a clan in a simple society. Or it may be the result of much individual study and introspection. For example, George Bernard Shaw, in an autobiographical sketch, reports that he went to London from his native Ireland to work in a business concern, and that he struggled to work out an ideology over a period of some years. At last he adopted Fabian Socialism, and then was able to organize his life effectively. It was the "clear comprehension of life in the light of an intelligible theory" which set his life into "triumphant operation" (Erikson, 1959).

In such a case, ideology is not completed by the end of biological adolescence. It may be barely started. The universal aspect is that the growing boy or girl does at least get started on an ideology during adolescence.

Achieving Identity

In his illuminating description of the major tasks of growing up and developing throughout the life cycle, Erikson (1950) defines a central, crucial developmental task for each of eight age periods of life (see Beller's chapter). The task for adolescents is the achievement of *identity.* In its simplest form, this task amounts to the discovery and the defining by a growing adolescent of *who he is* and *what he is.* Up to the beginning of adolescence a boy or a girl is seen as part of a family, and his identity comes from the family. He is "the Jones boy" or "the Smith girl." Then, during adolescence, the child becomes individualized as a person in his own right as Tom Jones or Sally Smith. This process takes some effort by the individual. The amount and nature of this effort depends partly on the culture or subculture. The process includes several related elements. One is the formation of an ideology. Another is the formation of an ego-ideal or the kind of person one wants to be. Another is the choice of an occupation or some other central determinant of a way of life. In modern democratic societies the choice of an occupation and the preparation for an occupation have become the major steps in identity achievement for males and for many females.

The urban-industrial democratic societies tend to give the adolescent a good deal of personal freedom and responsibility in his task of choosing an occupation. On the other hand, the simpler societies generally provide less individual freedom of choice. The boy is expected to follow in the footsteps of his father; the girl learns from her mother by an informal apprenticeship. The religious beliefs are taken from the family and the local church. Political attitudes are absorbed in the family. Thus there is less variation in identity from one generation to the next.

The achievement of identity is a universal aspect of growth through adolescence, but the amount of individual effort and responsibility varies from one culture to another.

The Adolescent Peer Culture

It is well known that a given age group has its own somewhat truncated culture. While the members of this age group participate in the culture of the larger society, they also have common and standardized ways of behaving and believing that are pretty much limited to their own age group. For instance, the eight-year-old boys of a community are likely to have their own game culture—a set of games with rules handed from one age cohort of eight-year-old boys to the next: Rules for games of marbles, hide-and-seek, cops and robbers, etc. To this extent, the eight-year-old boys have a peer culture; that is, a culture of a group who are approximately equal in age. There is a culture of twelve year olds, one of fourteen year olds, sixteen year olds, eighteen year olds, and one such culture for boys with a different one for girls.

There may also be a more generalized peer culture for teenagers, into which the thirteen year olds enter slowly and unsurely, while the eighteen year olds are dropping their participation in their *adolescent peer culture* in favor of the culture of young adults. The adolescent peer culture is the set of ways of behaving and believing of the age-group from thirteen to eighteen, which they pass on to their successors. This is the kind of definition to be found in a modern democratic society, where teenagers are allowed to be "adolescents" with a minimum of control by the adult society.

In a few societies, the adolescent peer culture actually opposes the adult culture at points, and there is a long drawn-out contest between adults and adolescents. The adolescent peer culture may have certain values and interests that conflict with the values and interests of the adults. In this case the adult society may seek to put down the adolescent peer culture. This was clearly the case in the United States in the late 1960s, when the adolescent peer culture encouraged boys to let their hair grow long, and girls to shorten their skirts. There were a number of battles between the adolescent peer group and the adult generation, which was usually represented by teachers and school principals.

More generally, the adolescent peer culture has its own existence more or less outside the ken of adults, although they know it exists, and they make sure it does not interfere with the general adult culture.

In the United States there has been something of a controversy over the question of whether an adolescent peer culture actually opposes some of the educational values of the high schools, encouraging athletics and social activities at the expense of academic study. In an influential book entitled *Adolescent Society,* Professor James S. Coleman (1961) reported his study of students in several midwestern high schools. This study appeared to show that adolescent boys and girls in high school were more influenced by their peers than by their parents and teachers.

A critical analysis of Coleman's study and other studies was made by Gottlieb and Reeves (1963). They concluded that there is a vaguely defined adolescent peer culture, made of varying peer cultures from various groups of adolescents, and that this peer culture has a common basis of disagreement with the adult culture at some points. However, there is no solid monolithic adolescent peer culture that is common to all adolescents in a modern society.

A study similar to that of Coleman was made by a Swede, B-E. Andersson (1969), of adolescents aged fourteen–sixteen in the city of Goteborg in 1963–65. He found evidence of an adolescent peer culture which was somewhat independent of the adult culture, but it was clear that school and family were also exerting a great deal of influence on those Swedish youth.

It appears that nearly every society has an adolescent peer culture, generally different for boys and for girls, and that the adolescent culture is not related in any simple way to the adult culture. This topic is discussed in greater detail by Hamachek in a separate chapter within this book, with a focus on the American culture.

Summary on the Problem of Universal Adolescent Characteristics

From this attempt to find truly universal characteristics of adolescence, we see that the development of the body and physiological changes in the

body are about the only universal aspects of adolescents, and even these
are affected in their timing by diet, which is a cultural factor. The other
six aspects are only universal in the most general sense. Something under
those titles can be found in every culture, but there is a wide cross-
cultural variation in their details.

Cultural Variations of Adolescence

Accepting the fact that most of adolescent experience is affected by
culture and shows cross-cultural differences, one may ask what are the
cultural forces that impinge upon young people. These appear to be the
forces of nationality, race, social class, age-group, sex, and religion. The
best-known cultural variations are those of sex, age-group, and social
class. These have been studied in a number of countries. They can be
studied inexpensively, since groups of different sex, age, and social class
can be located and studied in almost every community, and the studies
can be compared in a search for cultural differences.

Studies of Cultural Factors in Adolescent Behavior, Keeping Nationality Constant

Since 1940 there have been a number of studies of secondary school
students made in relatively small cities or areas in the United States.
Generally these studies compare the sexes and the social classes. Sometimes they also compare age-groups. By relatively simple statistical procedures, it is possible to study the effect of one cultural factor at a time.
Hollingshead (1949) reported in his study of the youth of Elmtown, a
pseudonym for a midwestern county seat of six thousand residents, where
he lived for a year while making his study. He found very large social
class differences in educational, social, occupational, and sexual behavior
and attitudes. Peck and Havighurst (1960) reported on their intensive
study of moral character development in thirty-four adolescent boys and
girls in a small city (that they called Prairie City). This group was
studied from the age of ten to eighteen, against the background of data
collected on the whole age-group in the town. The social class factor
proved to be more important than sex in differentiating the character
development of these young people.

Sewell and his coworkers at the University of Wisconsin (1965, 1968,
1970) made an extensive set of studies of high school students in the state
of Wisconsin, paying special attention to their educational achievement
and aspirations. He found that the social class factor was related to their
educational characteristics, as also was the factor of urban versus rural
residence. There was some indication of a rural subculture that was

causing rural youth to differ from those who grew up in small and larger cities.

Levine, Mitchell, and Havighurst (1970) reported on a study of the seniors in over fifty schools in the Kansas City metropolitan area (from the years of 1968 to 1970). They were interested in the possible effects of different peer group cultures on the desire of young people to attend college. They divided the schools into three categories on the basis of social class composition and two other categories (Catholic and small schools), and then studied the college-going expectations and performance of the students in relation to their social class, school achievement, and skin color. They found evidence for the "reference group" hypothesis—that students would show expectations of going to college, and actual college entrance, related not only to their own social class and school achievement but also to the predominant social class composition of their school.

Havighurst and his colleagues (1962) studied all the children in the public schools of a midwestern city of forty thousand, from the time they were in the fourth grade until they had reached the age of twenty-three. They found that social class was closely related to the educational and occupational achievement and the marital experience of this group.

Cross-National Studies of Adolescents

When there is interest in studying the influence of national culture on adolescents, it is necessary to compare persons of different nationality. But, since there are other subcultural factors which we have noted, it is important to make sure that these other factors of age, sex, social class, religion, etc., are the same in the two or more national samples that are being studied. However, sometimes religion is a part of the national culture, as in the case of Sweden, which is nominally Protestant; and Italy, which is nominally Catholic. Comparisons of adolescents in Sweden and Italy would include the religious subculture as a part of the national culture.

One form of cross-cultural research involves a study of two or more national groups which involve differences in age, sex, and social class, at the same time. The task is to find out how much of the differences between the groups being studied is due to each of the several possible subcultural factors. For example, Havighurst et al. (1965) made a systematic comparison of Buenos Aires and Chicago adolescents aged thirteen and sixteen, male and female, upper-middle and upper-lower class. One outcome of this research was to compare the size of the differences between social classes, age levels, sex groups, and nationality groups. It turned out that the differences between nationalities were greater than the differences between the other subcultural groups. But there were differences of substantial size between age groups, sex groups, and social classes.

A cross-national research study in which the emphasis was on differences between nationalities was made (without deliberate planning) by James S. Coleman (1961) for the United States and Bengt-Erik Andersson (1969) for Sweden. Coleman's study of adolescent social and personal values was published in 1961, and Andersson used some of Coleman's methods to study Swedish adolescents in 1965. Both researchers agreed in finding the socioeconomic status of their adolescent subjects and their sex to be the causes of most of the variability. But they also found that American-Swedish differences did exist. One such difference lay in the importance of excellence in sports and athletics as a source of popularity of boys. The Swedish youth, especially girls, did not think that success or interest in athletics was important for popularity of boys. Yet Coleman's study in the United States placed success in athletics as the most important attribute of a popular boy (also see Johnston and Bachman's chapter). The two nationality groups were very similar, however, in giving low importance to high marks for scholarship as a criterion for popularity.

A major cross-national study of fourteen-year-old boys and girls from eight countries is now under way (Peck, 1971). In this case the subjects are all fourteen years of age, but they come from two different socioeconomic status groups—upper-middle and upper-lower class, and they are both sexes. Preliminary findings indicate that substantial nationality differences exist in occupational values, and in ways of coping with a variety of problem situations.

Another cross-national comparison shows that national differences between Brazilian and United States adolescents are very great in the area of employment. Havighurst and Gouveia (1969) studied a sample of Brazilian students at the end of the first cycle of middle school (about the equivalent of ninth grade in the United States) and at the end of the second cycle of middle school (the equivalent of twelfth grade). They found that approximately 30 percent of the Brazilian first-cycle youth were employed thirty hours or more a week, while 50 percent of the second-cycle youth were so employed. It was clear that employment experience is far more widespread among Brazilian than among American adolescents.

The Nature of Cross-cultural Differences

Some kinds of cultural differences can be traced fairly easily to certain subcultures. For example, the masculine and feminine subcultures differ in predictable ways. Other differences cannot so easily be attributed to sex or social class or national cultures. The student who is interested should read several of the studies mentioned here, but I shall summarize some of the cross-cultural differences that appear to be well established.

National Differences. The experiences of adolescents with employment and with schooling related to employment are quite different in different countries, and the associated values and attitudes are also quite different. Countries which need the work of adolescents encourage positive attitudes toward employment, and they adapt the school system by maintaining night schools, requiring work experience as a part of education, and giving preference for entrance to higher schools to students with employment experience. The Brazilian example has been pointed out. The socialist countries—Russia, China, Cuba, etc.—have needed the work of adolescents as an aid to their economic development and have encouraged positive attitudes toward employment. Most European countries have a relatively large number of jobs as formal or informal apprentices for adolescents in shops and offices, as well as in the manual trades. But the United States has very few jobs for adolescents, and consequently both the work experience and the attitudes toward work are very different in the United States from what they are in these other countries.

Another nationality difference is found in attitudes toward the opposite sex, and in social-sex behavior. For example, Havighurst et al. (1965) found the Chicago thirteen year olds were more interested in the opposite sex than were youth of the same age and social class in Buenos Aires. This was true in 1961–62, when the study was conducted, but it may be less true now, since there has been a widespread development of sexual interest and behavior in practically all modern countries.

There are also nationality differences in the dominant social values of adolescents. For example, comparisons have been made with the *Uses Test,* a list of common objects for which the respondent is asked to indicate their use. The responses are then grouped into common categories, such as instrumental, esthetic, hedonistic, benevolent, malevolent. Havighurst et al. (1965) found that Chicago adolescents gave more *instrumental* responses, while Buenos Aires adolescents gave more *hedonistic, benevolent,* and *malevolent* responses.

Social Class Differences. The major social class differences are pretty much what one would expect. Educational aspirations and expectations vary with social class, as do occupational interests and values.

Sex Differences. The masculine and feminine subcultures produce the expected differences with respect to occupational interests and values. Here it is likely that the sex differences are decreasing. This is a useful

area for research on present-day adolescents, the results to be compared
with similar studies of 1960 or earlier.

Social Mobility and Adolescence in a Modern Society

Perhaps the most widespread ambition of adolescents and their families
in modern societies during the past century has been the desire to move
up the socioeconomic ladder—to rise in social status, to get a higher
income, to get more prestige. And it was evident that the widest road of
upward mobility lay through achievement in adolescence and early
adulthood. This achievement might take the form of educational progress that opened the way to higher status occupations, or of hard work
and cleverness in a series of ever-improving jobs, or of marriage (for
girls) to a man of higher status.

To be upwardly mobile, to move from one social class or socioeconomic level to a higher level, means a change from one subculture to
another, or a change of life style.

The Social Class Subcultures of a Modern Society

Research by social anthropologists and sociologists has discovered that
social classes exist as crudely defined subcultures in a number of modern
societies. While most of this research has been done in the United States,
there is confirmation of the social class phenomenon from research of the
last twenty years in Sweden, Canada, Australia, New Zealand, Brazil, and
England.

A social class is defined as a group of people who share certain values
and attitudes and feel themselves to be similar to each other. It may also
be seen as a group of people who share a particular life style. There is
much intermarriage within a social class and much informal social relationship. When a social scientist studies a particular community, he
observes the various social groupings and economic groupings, and he
asks people in the community about the "social structure" of the community. Invariably, if the community is as big as several thousand, and if
it contains a population with a range of income and occupation, the
residents of the community report that there is a hierarchy of social
groups, or social classes, with the highest group having the highest
prestige and power in the community. The metaphor of vertical distance
is used by the residents, who speak of "our upper class, our middle class
or classes, and our lower class or classes."

The number of visibly different social classes depends on the size and
complexity of the community. It may be as many as seven, or as few as
three. The American community studies tend to settle on a five-class

structure, named as follows: upper, upper-middle, lower-middle, upper-lower, and lower-lower. These five classes can be found in any cross-sectional community of five thousand or more. The placing of an individual in the class system depends on his social relationships, his occupation, income, educational level, the type of house and area of the community in which he lives, and the clubs or churches to which he belongs. All these social characteristics are judged by people in the community in terms of social prestige.

A democratic society has an "open" class system, with people moving into and out of a given social class on the basis of their performance in various sectors of socioeconomic life. Hence there are always some people at the margin between two classes, and therefore some people cannot be placed as exactly as others in the class structure.

Social mobility is defined as movement within a lifetime by an individual from one class to another. Generally the move is up or down one step on a five-class scale, but sometimes a person moves two or more steps. The degree of social mobility in a society is usually measured by comparing the social class of adult sons and daughters with their fathers. Often the measurement is limited to sons and fathers, since the occupations of males can be easily determined, and occupational level is a very good indicator of social class position, all over the world in complex societies.

The proportions of people in the various social classes are substantially as follows in the United States: upper, 3 percent; upper-middle, 10 percent; lower-middle, 27 percent; upper-lower, 45 percent; lower-lower, 15 percent. In effect, the white-collar occupations are middle class, and the blue-collar occupations are lower class or working class, with significant exceptions. Some highly skilled handworkers, such as electronic technicians and interior decorators, would be placed by their incomes and their associations in the lower-middle class. Also, owners of substantial farms who work their own farms would be placed in one of the middle classes.

Social Mobility

The degree of social mobility in a society depends on several factors. One is the nature of the technology. Societies which have moved into mass production and labor-saving technology have increased their proportion of white-collar jobs and have decreased their proportion of unskilled, lower-class jobs. This has been characteristic of the United States during the past fifty years and has resulted in a high degree of upward mobility. Societies which were formerly underdeveloped industrially and had very large proportions of unskilled agricultural workers experience a great deal of upward mobility when they enter a phase of industrial development. Thus Brazil, which had about 90 percent of its labor force in unskilled and semiskilled labor jobs in 1940, now has 75 percent of the labor force in such jobs, and has had a very high degree of upward social mobility in the past thirty years.

Great Britain, on the other hand, was already highly industrialized by 1900 and did not change its social class structure quantitatively until after 1950. Therefore, Great Britain showed almost no net upward mobility between fathers and sons in the study made by Glass (1954) about 1950. Yet there was a great deal of individual social mobility in Great Britain, with many boys rising above their fathers' status, while almost as many boys fell below their fathers' status. Glass found that 27 percent of young men had been upwardly mobile at least one step on a five-step scale, while 33 percent had been downwardly mobile. Contrasting with this, Coleman and Neugarten (1971), studying a sample of men in the Kansas City metropolitan area, found 33 percent upward mobility and 12 percent downward mobility, with 55 percent of men maintaining the same social class position as that of their fathers.

The Soviet Union and other socialist societies experienced a relatively high degree of social mobility at the time the society became officially socialist. Educational and economic policies were adopted to give special educational opportunities to the children of working-class parents. In some cases the property and therefore the power of some of the upper-class families was expropriated, and their children had to compete on more nearly equal terms with the working-class children for adult social status.

In general, a society with high net upward mobility has high morale among its young people, because such a large proportion of them are "improving themselves." In this connection the United States has been fortunate.

Amount and Nature of Social Mobility of Adolescents

Upward mobility has been studied critically in the United States by a number of sociologists. Boys who are upwardly mobile, and some girls, achieve this by securing jobs and forging careers at a higher status level than that of their fathers. This may be done by hard work combined with intelligence, ambition, and luck. The adolescent starts at the bottom of the occupational ladder and works up. This process was more common at the beginning of the century than it is now, since so many high-status occupations require education at the college level. Therefore, the usual route to higher status in the United States is to graduate from high school, go to college and possibly to a professional school for medicine, law, engineering, business administration, or education, and then to enter a high-status occupation.

However, most girls who have been upwardly mobile in the past have achieved this through marriage. By common consent, a woman takes the social status of her husband, though she sometimes helps him or hinders him by her own individual achievement or personality. Since more than half of American girls are married by the age of twenty, they could hardly have established their own adult social class position by that time. A study of all the girls of a given age cohort in a middle-sized midwestern city showed that by the age of twenty-three, 33 percent of the girls were upwardly mobile one or more steps on a four-step scale, and 18 percent were downwardly mobile. There was a subgroup of girls who had not married and were establishing their own adult social status outside of marriage, just as boys do. In this subgroup, 5 percent of the total group of girls were upwardly mobile and 2 percent were downwardly mobile (Havighurst and Moorefield, 1964).

Within this same age cohort of boys, 31 percent were upwardly mobile, 24 percent were downwardly mobile, and 45 percent were stable, in terms of "initial adult status" (Havighurst et al. 1962). The tentative adult status of young men and women aged twenty-three was based on consideration of the educational level they had reached; the nature and prospects of their jobs, if they were employed; and the initial adult status of their husbands, if they were married females. These figures must be regarded as tentative, since the group were too young to have established themselves reliably in the adult social class structure.

Social Mobility Involves Learning a New Subculture. A social class has a subculture or life style of its own. Consequently, an adolescent who is in the process of moving up or down the social scale is also in process of learning a new subculture. This consists of ways of dressing, language forms, behavior with the opposite sex, eating and drinking habits, choice of room and home decorations, attitudes toward saving and spending money, etc. While a certain occupation or educational level tends to identify one's social class to strangers, the life style is the permanent proof. Therefore, mobile adolescents are learning the new life styles from various sources. They learn most fully from age-mates who are in the social class to which they are going. Thus it is useful for upward social mobility of working-class youth if they can attend a comprehensive high school where they will find models of middle-class behavior.

Ethnic and Racial Subgroups of Adolescents in the United States

With the very large emigration from Europe and Asia and the Middle East to various parts of the world in the nineteenth and early twentieth centuries, and with the export of Africans as slaves in the sixteenth to eighteenth centuries, there is no large modern country where residents are all over even 90 percent of one racial group or nationality group. The ethnic subgroups within a society have subcultures of their own, and their adolescent members show evidence of these subcultures.

The nationality and racial subcultures interact with the social class subcultures to produce somewhat different adolescent behavior for each subgroup. Thus each of the following groups of adolescents has certain subcultural features that make them different from other American youth.

American Indians. There are about 100,000 American Indian and Alaskan adolescents, scattered in fifty or more tribal groups and living in considerable numbers in about twenty states and in most of the big cities. The various tribal subcultures are all different, but, as Indians, these young people have a common subculture that makes them somewhat similar to each other and different from non-Indians. If teachers study the Indian subcultures and adapt their teaching to it, they do a better job than is ordinarily done by the school system for Indian youth (Fuchs and Havighurst, 1972).

Chinese-Americans. Chinese-American adolescents are found in practically every big city. Though their grasp of the English language is generally good, most of them were raised in Chinese-speaking families, and in a subculture in which family influence and family loyalty are very strong. They do very well in school, on the average, and they make great use of educational opportunities. For instance, the Titus Lowe High School in San Francisco is open to students from all over the city who have especially good scholarship. Though located several miles from Chinatown, it has more than 40 percent Chinese and Japanese students (Havighurst, Smith, and Wilder, 1971). Japanese-Americans, of course, have a subculture of their own, and are much "acculturated" to the ways of Americans, and they, too, do very well in school. The U.S. Census calls Japanese and Chinese-Americans "Orientals," and notes that Oriental males have a higher average number of years of schooling and a higher proportion of white-collar jobs than do the white native Americans.

Appalachian Whites. The native-American whites of that hill country that ranges from West Virginia through Kentucky, Tennessee, and Southern Missouri and Northern Arkansas are in some ways the oldest and most native Americans, with the exception of the Indians. Since the land did not make them rich as farmers, and the coal did not make them rich as miners, these people have had to scramble for a living ever since the Revolutionary War. Many of them have migrated to the industrial cities of the Middle West, and they make up a substantial portion of the white working class in most of the cities from Pittsburgh on the east to Chicago and Kansas City on the west. The adolescents of this group appear to divide themselves into two subgroups. One group does well in school and moves upward in the social structure into a variety of white-collar and skilled blue-collar jobs. The other seems to keep closer to the Appalachian subculture, to do less well in school, and to stay in the lower working class. Since the Appalachian white group is not distinguishable by skin color or by name from the majority white group, they have not been studied very much or understood very well by school teachers and directors. It would be useful for someone to make studies of the Appalachian white subculture in several of the industrial centers, and to relate their findings to studies made of the same group in the hill country.

Blacks, or Negroes. The largest easily visible minority group are the blacks, who comprise about 11 percent of the population of the United States. Whether this group, under 1970 conditions, has a significant subculture, is a question which will probably be debated by the sociologists for some time to come. The blacks do not have a separate language, or even a separate English dialect, although there is a southern black lower-class dialect that is not spoken by the majority. The blacks are distributed through the social class structure, in all five classes, though they have a larger proportion of poor people and therefore, of lower-class people, than does the majority white group. There is no cultural characteristic that is common to all or nearly all blacks and absent in whites, unless it is the experience of being black, and elements of ideology that flow from that experience.

In spite of some prejudice against blacks in certain occupations, the proportion of black men and women in middle-class occupations has been increasing since 1940. There is a higher percentage of black men and women who are teachers than there is of white men and women.

Black adolescents are especially conscious of themselves as a separate interest group, if not a subculture. It appears that the high schools and colleges will pay special attention to this group for another decade, at least. After that, there may be little or no separate black subculture, and little or no economic discrimination practiced against black people. The American big city high schools are especially involved in the issues of black-white relations, because there is a concentration of black families in the larger central cities, and many high schools are practically all black. The study of big city high schools, made for the National Association of Secondary School Principals (Havighurst, Smith, and Wilder, 1971) revealed that 20 percent of the public high schools in cities of 300,000 or more population were 80 percent or more black, while 10 percent were between 20 and 80 percent black in 1968–69. Among these 30 percent of high schools, 5 percent were mainly middle class in composition, and 25 percent were mainly working class. The school principals reported on such matters as the nature of foreign language courses, the relations of the school to the local community, student protest activities, demands for more freedom of dress, etc. The schools in the various categories of racial composition and social class differed in ways which indicated that there was a black subculture operating as well as the various social class subcultures. Amos and Wellford, in their chapter on the disadvantaged, concentrate primarily on this group.

Spanish-surname Student. Four groups with Spanish surnames are now in American high schools. They are Puerto Ricans, Cubans, Mexican-Americans (Chicanos), and Spanish-Americans of the Southwest whose families have lived there for three centuries. These are four different subcultures, which interact with social class subcultures to produce different kinds of high school populations.

Other European-American Groups. It is not very useful, from the point of view of understanding American adolescents, to try to differentiate the various European national groups or subcultures. Fifty years ago there were definite Italian-American, Irish-American, Polish-American, Hungarian-American, and Greek-American subcultures that influenced their adolescent members. Now these groups seem to have merged into a general American culture, with social class differences the principal ones. However, the Jewish-American group seems to have continued as a subculture with considerable influence on its adolescents.

Emerging Subcultural Differences in a Modern Affluent Society

When a society is changing rapidly and pervasively, as the contemporary American society is changing, the lives of adolescents are likely to react to these changes in a highly visible way. To put it simply, the modern affluent society does not *need* adolescents, except as the raw human material out of which the next adult generation is formed. Before this time in history, all societies have needed and required the work of adolescent boys and girls, while at the same time these societies taught adolescents to become adult members of the society largely through the experience of adolescent work. A small proportion of adolescents were spared from employment so that they could study to become knowledgeable and skilled adults for the kinds of work that required intensive formal education.

Then the technological development of the modern highly productive society made the work of adolescents unnecessary, and denied all but 15 percent of sixteen to eighteen year olds the opportunity to work. At the same time the technology created more positions that required formal educational training through high school or even beyond high school. But there were not enough such positions in the labor force to need more than about 40 percent of adolescent males aged eighteen–twenty and even fewer females. Thus there were four broad groups of American youth aged sixteen–twenty by the year 1970:

Some 40 percent of males and 20 percent of females who finished high school and then went to college.

Some 50 percent of females who married before the age of twenty, and thus took on an adult role generally outside of the labor force. Many of these also went to college.

Some 45 percent of males and 15 percent of females who entered the labor force with some saleable skills between the ages of sixteen and twenty and gradually worked into stable employment by the age of twenty.

Some 15 percent of males and of females who dropped out of school around the age of sixteen and did not obtain any stable adult role, either as worker or housewife. Amos and Wellford speak of this group as the "young retired."

These four groups were not subcultures. They were categories based on their participation in the labor force and in the educational system. However, they were affected by the pervasive value changes of contemporary society, and by the subculture known as the *counterculture* which developed during the 1960s.

The Counterculture, or Consciousness III

To understand what was happening to adolescents in the 1960s, it is necessary to look behind the facts of their participation in the labor force and the school system to the changing ethics of the United States as it moved into the "postindustrial" era. The highly productive industry and commerce of the period since 1950 had reduced the moral value of work. The work of the contemporary society is done with less hours of human effort than ever before, and there is actually an oversupply of workers unless the work week and the span of the work life are reduced. When work becomes less necessary to a society, its moral value is likely to decrease, and this is what has been happening in the United States since

1950. The *ethics of work,* on which Western Europe and North America
have based their value systems since about 1600, is losing force; and a new
basis for ethics is emerging, with its characteristics still unclear. In the
past, the American society of the nineteenth and early twentieth centuries gave priority and precedence to *instrumental activities*—such
actions as plowing virgin prairie to make a farm, mining coal and iron
ore and creating a steel industry, building a railroad system and then an
airline system to facilitate transport and travel. Instrumental action is
action to change the present situation for one which will satisfy human
needs better. It is a method to achieve something that is beyond the
method. For example, studying algebra in high school may be instrumental to getting into an engineering school, and that may be instrumental to becoming an engineer with a good job for life.

The instrumental activities that dominated North American society
and were regarded as most valuable are giving way to *expressive activities.* Expressive action is action for the sake of the action itself. The
reward is in the act, not something that follows from the act, as in the
case of instrumental action. For instance, a boy may study algebra in
high school because he likes algebra, with no thought for its usefulness in
his subsequent career. The emerging society favors expressive activity
such as enjoying the present moment without worry about the future,
spending time on activities which broaden and deepen experience—
"doing one's thing."

This move away from the *instrumental* toward the *expressive* will
eventually reach a new equilibrium, since people will demand the
material goods and service of a high material standard of living and will
have to engage in enough instrumental action to maintain this. Thus we
are now working uncertainly toward the new equilibrium, and young
people are working out their way of life as part of this process.

A popular exposition of this process is given by Charles Reich
(1970) in his best-selling book *The Greening of America.* The state of
society toward which Reich thinks we are moving is characterized by an
ideology and a set of values which he calls Consciousness III. This book
has aroused controversy. My own view of it is that it oversimplifies the
situation, and that we are in the process of achieving a useful and desirable combination of Reich's Consciousness III and Consciousness II
(the value system of 1910 to 1960), in which useful work and service of
an instrumental character will be balanced by more expressive activity
than we have enjoyed in the past.

The culture of Consciousness III has been called the *counterculture*
by some writers, because it runs counter to the instrumental culture
which dominated American action and ethics before 1950. This counterculture is not the new dominant culture of the United States—it is a

movement within the American culture, which has its greatest effect on the emerging generation of adults, though it does not really control the lives of more than a small minority.

The counterculture has two rather different elements which are not altogether in harmony with each other. One is a kind of self-indulgent quest for pleasant expressive experience. The other is a strong desire for a better society, in which peace, freedom, and beauty are the main elements. Thus the counterculture includes the desire to bring the American wars in Southeast Asia to an end, the desire to eliminate poverty, and the desire to raise the status of nonwhites. This may require instrumental activity that is not fully harmonious with the expressive activities of individual freedom to seek satisfaction wherever and however it may be found.

There are a number of aspects of the counterculture which are disturbing to the older adult generation whose values and life style were formed in the first half of the current century. Not the least of these is the personal grooming which the counterculture seems to favor.

The Adolescent Grooming Phenomenon of 1965–73. We have noted that the adolescent peer culture is especially influential in the dress and grooming of young people. Adolescents in high school and postadolescents in college are especially apt to follow clothing and grooming fashions in the manner of sheep.

When the counterculture appeared on the scene about 1965, one of its first signs was the growth of long hair, then of sideburns, then of beards by young men, and the wearing of "rough and ready" clothing—blue jeans, levis, open shirts, sandals, dark glasses, etc. To people who grew up in the 1920s, '30s, '40s, and '50s, these fashions seemed "sloppy," to say the least, and even disruptive of students' morale in school and college. Hence there was a period of several years in which school and college administrators attempted to set levels on hair length and style for boys and young men. But a few court cases, backed by parents who believed in being permissive, favored the school directives to be more permissive with respect to grooming.

What happened in the case of males was tame compared to the happenings among females. In the perception of men and women who grew up in preceding decades, adolescent and postadolescent girls seemed to be deliberately trying to look repulsive. They waddled down the streets in torn blue jeans. They colored their eyelids green. They wore lipstick that looked like lard. Their fingernails were dirty. In so-called "hot-pants" those with large buttocks exposed their nether "cheeks" to the gaze of all. Those with visible breasts made them more visible by omitting brassieres. Only a minimum was left to the imagination.

To their mothers and older sisters these girls seemed bent on repelling the opposite sex, yet they more than compensated by taking the initiative in public love-making. Instead of playing "hard to get," the girls initiated kissing in public. They became the pursuers, and their boyfriends the pursued. Since so many of the boys looked like girls, the publicly observable difference in sexual appearance and sexual behavior became reversed.

From the point of view of cultural differences, it is important to note that the standard-bearers of the counterculture were generally upper-middle class young men and women, with college education. The upper-middle class subculture seems to have produced this kind of behavior in a number of different nations at about the same time. It was a subculture of the upper-middle class culture, since only a minority of upper-middle class youth followed these fashions. It came to public notice at about the same time in London, Amsterdam, San Francisco, Los Angeles, Copenhagen, Stockholm, Munich, New York, Buenos Aires, Sydney, and Cambridge (Massachusetts, U.S.A.). The summer of 1971 saw a peak of this kind of behavior in Copenhagen, on the Stroget, where all the modern nations and races were represented, and in Munich, in the Schwabing area. Meanwhile, it was receding at Haight-Ashbury in San Francisco, where it seems to have started.

Perhaps before this book goes out of use, this phenomenon will have disappeared, and the new generation of college students will find this account to be grossly exaggerated. Yet this is a mild statement of what adults of 1970 thought they perceived.

Influence of the Counterculture on the Several Groups of Adolescents

The counterculture is something broader than a subculture of adolescents. It is a projected culture that could affect all age groups, though adolescents and young adults appear to be its principal exponents at the present time. Its effects on adolescents depend very much on which of the four work-school experience groups they belong to.

Group A. High School Graduates and College Entrants. This group, consisting mainly of middle-class youth, is most influenced by the counterculture, but only a minority of this group have really adopted Consciousness III as their ideology. The vast majority of this group would be called "squares" by the exponents of the counterculture.

Yet the life style and value patterns developed by Group A for their adult lives during the remainder of this century and into the next will be very much influenced by the contemporary reevaluation of the ethics of work, and by an emerging ethics of beauty, service, and international peace and justice. For a closer look at this group, read the chapter by Block et al.

Group B. Girls Who Marry before Age Twenty and Do Not Enter the Labor Force as Young Women. This group of young girls will be influenced by the counterculture to a lesser degree than will the girls of Group A. Nevertheless, as wives of Groups A and C, and as mothers of the children growing up during the next two decades, they will be more expressive and less instrumental in their roles of wife and mother, and they will be a most significant segment of the coming adult culture.

Group C. High School Graduates and Nongraduates in Working-Class Occupations. This group is least affected by the counterculture. They come mainly from working-class homes and are carrying on the tradition of stable work and family life. They will be conservative, politically and in life style. However, as they secure more free time and more real income due to increasing productivity of the society, they will probably go in for leisure-time activities of an expressive sort.

Group D. High School Dropouts Who Are Marginal to the Labor Force. This group represents two forms of social pathology which will cause trouble for the society until it substantially eliminates them. The largest subgroup are those who come from working-class homes which have not helped them to become competent in school or work. They will be unemployed and on welfare rolls much of their adult lives. The other pathological group of boys and girls, often from middle-class homes, who have "copped out" of the task of growing up, establishing an identity, and making an adult life style for themselves. They are "hippies" but not the only ones, since a subgroup of Group A are also "hippies."

Relation of the Counterculture to the Adolescent Peer Culture. These four groups are engaged in working out life styles for themselves, through the interaction of their social class, their adolescent peer culture, the counterculture, and their own personality makeup. They can be found in all the modern societies, though in varying proportions. For example, Andersson (1969) in his study of Swedish adolescents, found rather similar subgroups. The adolescent peer culture, by giving young people some protection from the pressures of the adult subcultures, helps to experiment with life styles that will enter into the composition of the major life styles of adults during the coming decades. For a further discussion of the counterculture, the reader will find the chapter by Cross and Pruyn of great interest.

Cross-cultural Differences in Schooling

The amount and kind of schooling which an adolescent receives is partly determined by the subculture in which he lives. If a society is conscious of its social structure and wishes to preserve this structure unchanged, it will develop a separate educational program for each separate subculture in the social structure. On the other hand, if a society wants to encourage movement of individuals from one place to another in the social structure, it will design an educational system to teach young people to be mobile.

Until very recently, there was no widespread formal educational program for all adolescents in any country. The secondary schools and middle schools were highly selective on the basis of family social status and of probable occupational goal. In the United States, which carries adolescents the farthest up the age scale in public schools, only 50 percent of young people aged fourteen–seventeen were in school in 1930, compared with 95 percent in 1970. Most countries made education in elementary schools free and compulsory up to age fourteen, and made secondary or middle schooling selective on socioeconomic criterias. A major exception to this rule was the Soviet Union, which encouraged the entrance of children of working-class parents into the middle school and gave special advantages to them. This was part of an effort to increase the amount of educational opportunity for the children of workers and peasants.

Since 1950, there has been a general movement toward making the secondary school or the middle school into a "comprehensive" school which receives students from all social classes and tries to teach them all together. The aim is to increase the amount of upward social mobility for children of low-status families, and also to encourage the development of democratic social attitudes by bringing youth of all social classes together in a single educational institution.

This was already the pattern in the United States, where there was only a single type of public high school in most communities. Only a few large cities had separate vocational-technical high schools. Of course there were private schools, most of them operated by the Catholic Church, but some maintained by other churches. There were a few independent, rather expensive schools to which only well-to-do parents could afford to send their children.

The British Secondary School. Great Britain had a very selective social class-oriented system following the primary school at about age twelve. There were the high-status *private schools* (known peculiarly as "public schools"). There were the state-maintained *grammar schools* which required the passing of an admission examination. And there were the "modern" secondary schools that were really extensions of primary schools to the age of fourteen or fifteen, for pupils who could not pass the admission examinations for the grammar school. After World War II, there was a strong movement to democratize the state school system by introducing a "comprehensive" secondary school starting at age twelve, for all pupils, though with ability grouping and special vocational courses that tended to retain some of the social class separation of the prewar system.

Sweden. This country has done something very similar since about 1960. Before that time, there were several types of postprimary schools, which were closely related to the occupational levels of the parents. In 1960 only 34 percent of the age group sixteen through eighteen were in school at all. This proportion increased to 62 percent in 1970, and the several postprimary schools were combined in 1971 into a single comprehensive *gymnasieskolan,* which includes university entrance and vocational classes. Furthermore, secondary school pupils receive a cash payment from the state of 100 Swedish crowns ($20) a month, and this amount may be increased up to 275 Swedish crowns for students whose parents have relatively low incomes.

Brazil. This is an example of an educational system which is moving in the same direction at a much slower rate. The Brazilian system of middle schools is divided into two levels or cycles. The first cycle of four years is for students from about twelve to fifteen years of age (though many are older), and the second cycle of three years carries on the level of university entrance. Most middle schools have charged tuition, even if they were operated by the state, and they also have required entrance examinations. Furthermore, they have been divided into a number of vocational schools (commercial, industrial, normal, agricultural, as well as academic), and there have been many night schools. The proportion of an age group entering a middle school is relatively small (about 25 percent) but increasing, and the proportion completing the second cycle of the middle school is only about 7 percent.

Nevertheless, the Brazilian government is attempting to extend educational opportunity through operating more middle schools in small cities, through eliminating the entrance examination for the first cycle in some cases, and through a system of tuition scholarship grants. Also, the first two years of the first cycle have recently been given practically the same curriculum (stressing general academic education) so as to encourage working-class children to keep themselves in the path of entrance to the second cycle as long as possible before a definite choice of a vocational curriculum is made. A study by Havighurst and Gouveia (1969) found that 30 percent of the pupils in the fourth year of the first cycle were from manual working-class homes in 1962, and this proportion varied from 20 percent in the poorer northern states to 33 percent in the wealthier and more progressive southern states.

Secondary Education in the United States. Although the American pattern has been that of a single comprehensive secondary school to serve students of all social classes in a single institution, and 95 percent of the age-group fourteen–seventeen inclusive are in school, there is in fact a considerable degree of social class segregation in cities of 100,000 or more, where there are generally three or more public high schools. A study of public high schools in the forty-five largest cities (300,000 or larger) in 1968–69 (Havighurst, Smith, and Wilder, 1971) showed that most of these schools were rather clearly marked in social class composition, with 21 percent of the schools mainly upper-middle class, 40 percent more nearly comprehensive drawing from a wide range of social class, and 40 percent being primarily working-class schools. This economic segregation is a consequence of the residential segregation of large American cities. Furthermore, the big city schools were substantially segregated by color or by Spanish surname. Only 16 percent were integrated in the sense that they had no more than 60 and no less than 20 percent students who were in one of the following subgroups: either white or black, or Spanish surname. On the other hand, 62 percent had more than 80 percent of students who were of one skin color.

Thus the United States, which has explicitly attempted to maintain a system of economically integrated secondary schools and which during the 1960s attempted to move toward racial integration, still is far from being a system of secondary schools which bring adolescents of all economic and racial groups together in a single school building. Within this volume, Johnston and Bachman consider the role of educational institutions in the future development of our adolescents.

Summary

The American adolescent grows up in the general American culture and also in a number of subcultures. A culture or a subculture is a set of common and standard behaviors and beliefs shared by a group of people and taught by them to their successors. In the United States there are social class subcultures, ethnic, religious, and regional subcultures. In the world there are a variety of national cultures, and a number of subcultures in the more complex nations.

Before looking at the difference of adolescent experience and behavior in various cultures, it is useful to ask what is universal about adolescence—common to adolescents everywhere? The universal or quasi-universal aspects of adolescence are biological development, sex-role differentiation, assumption of adult roles under societal guidance, establishing emotional independence of parents and other adults, acquisition of an ideology, achievement of identity, and participation in an adolescent peer culture. But the last six of these seven show a good deal of variation of behavior among cultures.

A number of studies have been made of subcultural variations in a complex society, limited to one nationality. Generally these studies have reported on sex and social class subcultures. The truly cross-national studies of adolescents should be read with care, to make sure that only the nationality differences are identified, keeping subcultural factors such as social class, age, and sex constant. Studies are reported from Sweden, Brazil, Argentina, Italy, Yugoslavia, Japan, England, Mexico, and West Germany.

Within a complex society, the adolescent is often a candidate for social mobility, out of the social class into which he was born and into a different social class where his own efforts and experience can carry him. Comparative studies of social mobility have shown different patterns and degrees of social class mobility in England, Brazil, and the United States. The patterns of social mobility are rather different for girls than for boys. Marriage is an important means of mobility for girls.

The following American ethnic subcultures show different patterns of adolescent behavior: American Indians, Chinese-Americans, Appalachian whites, blacks, and Puerto Ricans and Mexican-Americans. The youth culture takes different forms for the following subgroups: college entrants, girls who marry before the age of twenty, youth in working-class jobs, high school dropouts who are marginal to the labor force. There is an emerging youth subculture, sometimes called the "counterculture" or "Consciousness III."

A major cross-national difference in the experience of adolescents is the nature and the amount of formal schooling which differ among modern societies, such as Britain, Brazil, Sweden, and the United States.

REFERENCES

Andersson, B-E. *Studies in adolescent behavior.* Stockholm: Almqvist and Wiksell, 1969.

Coleman, J. S. *The adolescent society.* New York: Free Press, 1961.

Coleman, R. P., and Neugarten, L. *Social status in the city.* San Francisco: Jossey-Bass, 1971.

Erikson, E. H. *Childhood and society.* New York: W. W. Norton, 1950.

———. *Identity and the life cycle. Psychological Issues.* Vol. 1, No. 1. New York: International Universities Press, 1959.

Fuchs, E., and Havighurst, R. J. *American Indians and their education.* Garden City, N.Y.: Doubleday, 1972.

Glass, D. *Social mobility in Britain.* London: Routledge and Kegan Paul, 1954.

Gottlieb, D., and Reeves, J. *Adolescent behavior in urban areas.* New York: Free Press, 1963.

Havighurst, R. J., et al. *Growing up in river city.* New York: Wiley, 1962.

———, and Moorefield, T. Marriage and social mobility among girls. *Journal of the National Association of Women Deans and Counselors,* 1964, *27,* 160–171.

———, et al. *A cross-national study of Buenos Aires and Chicago adolescents.* New York: Karger, 1965.

———, and Gouveia, A. *Brazilian secondary education and socioeconomic development.* New York: Praeger, 1969.

———, Smith, F., and Wilder, D. Profile of the big city high school. *Bulletin of the National Association of Secondary School Principals,* 1971, *55,* 3–160.

Hollingshead, A. B. *Elmtown's youth.* New York: Wiley, 1949.

Levine, D. U., Mitchell, E. S., and Havighurst, R. J. *Opportunities for higher education in a metropolitan area. A study of high school seniors in Kansas City, 1967.* Kansas City, Mo.: Center for the Study of Metropolitan Problems in Education. University of Missouri–Kansas City, 1971.

Mead, M. *Coming of age in Samoa.* New York: Mentor Book, 1949.

Peck, F. *An international study of coping behavior of children and adolescents.* Description of the Study. Austin, Texas: University of Texas, Personality Research Center, 1971.

———, and Havighurst, R. J. *The psychology of character development.* New York: Wiley, 1960.

Reich, C. *The greening of America.* New York: Random House, 1970.

Sewell, W. H., and Haller, A. Educational and occupational perspectives of farm and rural youth. In L. Burchinal (ed.), *Rural youth in crisis: Facts, myths and social change.* Washington, D.C.: U.S. Government Printing Office, 1965.

————, and Shah, V. Social class, parental encouragement and educational aspirations. *American Journal of Sociology,* 1968, *73,* 559–572.

————, Haller, A. O., and Ohlendorf, G. W. The educational and early occupational status attainment process: Replication and revision. *American Sociology Review,* 1970, *35,* 1014–1027.

4

Physiological Development
Karl C. Garrison*

Physiological and biological development in the individual is a continuing process from birth to old age and death. In this chapter we shall consider the multiplicity of factors which contribute to and maintain the human organism. To understand adolescent development, we must place the adolescent within the context of the total picture of development which begins at conception and continues throughout the life span of the individual. Life is an interaction between man's organic being and the environment within which he lives. The psychology of man cannot be meaningfully separated from physiological considerations.

Man, like other organisms, has a biological nature. His bodily system consists of fluids, bones, skin, connective muscular and neural tissue. The functioning of these, separately or in various combinations, is the *physiology* of the organism. A generation or more ago, special attention was focused on the close parallel between secretions from the endocrines and certain manifestations of behavior or personality structures. This was followed by an increased interest in the electrical rhythms of the brain (brain waves) as possible substrata of differences in personality structure. Certainly, if we are to keep abreast of personality theory we must remain

* Karl C. Garrison is Emeritus Professor of Education at the University of Georgia. He has had a most distinguished career and has authored and coauthored a number of books which have included: *Psychology of Adolescence*, 6th ed., *Psychology of Exceptional Children*, 4th ed., *Educational Psychology*, *Child Psychology*, and *Psychology of Human Development*. His many articles have focused on growth and development, problems related to learning, and problems of adolescents.

alert to progress in anatomy, neurology, and physiology in general. Brown (1959) pointed out over a decade ago that biological clocks appear in virtually all species, including man, bees, and flowering peas. Furthermore, environmental programing of cycles seems to be produced by such regularities as feeding and elimination schedules, provided these are not too distant from the natural schedule of the infant.

Neurological and physiochemical processes manifest themselves in a wide range of both complex and simple ways such as electrical impulses, chemical reactions, respiratory rate, heart rate, and perspiration. There has been a pronounced increase in psychophysiological research in the past two decades, which has furnished new ideas about the role of physiology in behavior adjustment and has opened up the field to research on many problems. Because of this research the prospect of resolving the mind versus body issue that has plagued scholars for many centuries may be attained. This chapter provides materials which attempt to provide for the reader the beginning of an increased understanding of the relation between physiology and psychology in the developing maturity of the individual.

Physiological Bases of Behavioral Patterns

There is a physiological basis underlying each pattern of behavior. Every behavior pattern depends upon connections between the receiving mechanisms and responding mechanisms. The maturation of structures upon which specific behavioral patterns depend takes place with age. As the child develops, his receptors (sense organs) become more mature and more sensitive to stimuli. His entire nervous system increases in complexity, significant changes take place in the ductless glandular system, and the muscles become stronger and more able to respond.

The Endocrine System

A group of structures that exercises a great deal of influence over the behavior of an individual is the system of ductless glands, usually referred to as the *endocrine glands*. These glands are well supplied with blood vessels but have no ducts through which to channel the substances which they produce; these are passed directly into the bloodstream. The chemical substances secreted are called *hormones* and are very important to bodily development and functioning.

An outstanding challenge of this generation of endocrinologists has been to understand the biochemical mechanisms of action of the various hormones discovered by previous generations of endocrinologists. The early studies of endocrinology involved bearded women, dwarfs, rooster-fied hens, and femininelike roosters, together with the effects of minute quantities of glandular extracts on behavior. With the maturity of biochemistry, a shift has been made in the nature and problems of research; although there are still investigations related to the control of the endocrine systems and the role of hormones in homeostasis, or its counterpart homeokinesis.

While the scholars in the field of endocrinology are not in complete agreement as to the exact nature of endocrine glands, they have supplied us with a rather complete description of the following: the pituitary, the thyroids, the parathyroids, the adrenal, the islets of Langerhans, the pineal, the thymus, and the gonads. A brief description of each of these should be useful to an understanding of the physiological bases of behavior.

The Pituitary. The pituitary body is attached to the underside of the brain and lies in the center of the head. This gland secretes a number of different hormones, two of which are very important to human adjustment and development: the *growth hormone* and the *middle man hormone*. Proper production of the growth hormone (somatotrophin) is essential to normal bodily development.

The "middle man" hormones act directly upon other ductless glands to stimulate their functioning. It is thus regulatory in nature and has been referred to as the "master gland." The hormones from this gland affect the functioning of the adrenals, sex glands, as well as other glands. Laboratory studies indicate that without the normal function of this gland, the otherwise normal peripheral glands such as ovaries and testicles remain quiescent and unstimulated. The importance of properly timed action of the growth and gonad-stimulating hormones for normal development is well known.

The importance of the pituitary hormones may also be observed in *Simmonds disease,* which, due to damage to the gland, produces a lack of the pituitary secretion. Individuals afflicted with this condition show rapid aging, loss of weight, wrinkling of the skin (as a result of dryness) , and weakened muscles. There is also evidence that hormones from this gland affect one's temperament and emotional behavior.

The Thyroids. The thyroid glands are located on either side of the "Adam's apple" in the neck. Hormones from these glands affect physical and sexual development, body metabolism, and emotional behavior. Thyroid secretions also affect the structure and function of the nervous system. An extreme deficiency of hormones from these glands during early childhood results in a condition known as *cretinism*. This is a condition characterized by an inhibition of normal development, particularly of the nervous system, accompanied by low-grade intelligence. Insufficient thyroid secretion occuring later in life usually results in a depressed mood, inability to concentrate, and sometimes actual mental deterioration. An excessive secretion from the thyroid gland usually leads to irritability, restlessness, excessive perspiration, and failure to sleep soundly.

The Parathyroids. The parathyroid glands consist of two or more pairs of small bodies located near or imbedded in the thyroids. Their removal produces convulsions, agonizing muscular cramps, and death. Overactive parathyroids produce a condition of sluggishness, loss of weight, and finally death if not treated. The parathyroid hormones are concerned mainly with regulating the amount of calcium in the blood.

The Adrenal Glands. The two adrenal glands are located near the kidneys and consist of two parts: an inner core, *the adrenal medulla;* and an outer layer, *the adrenal cortex.* The adrenal medulla regulates bodily changes during an emotional period. During this period there is a secretion from the medulla called *adrenin,* which has a stimulating affect. There is, then, an increase in blood pressure, pulse rate, and stomach activity.

The adrenal cortex acts as a separate gland from the adrenal medulla; it regulates body activity and the development of masculine traits. An overactive adrenal cortex produces both heightened body activity and an accentuation of certain masculine features, such as the "bearded lady." Underactivity of the adrenal cortex results in a condition known as *Addison's disease*—low blood pressure, loss of self-control, tired feelings, and loss of sex interest.

The Islets of Langerhans. The tiny endocrine structures known as the islets of Langerhans are located in the pancreas. They are not connected with the pancreatic duct system but deliver their hormones directly into the bloodstream. The hormones from these tiny bodies are known as *insulin,* and control the sugar level in the blood. They also assist the assimilation of carbohydrates by the body tissue. A deficiency of hormones from these bodies results in a condition known as diabetes, which is characterized by a general wasting away and, if not properly treated, by rapid death.

An oversupply of insulin may produce severe changes in behavior, such as a mental stupor and strange sinking sensations in the stomach.

The Pineal. Near the center of the head, the pineal gland is attached to the underside of the brain. Its central position influenced Descartes, a seventeenth-century philosopher, to identify this gland as the seat of the soul. Although its functions are still largely unknown, its activity is related to sexual development. During infancy and childhood it apparently serves to hold back sexual maturation; it seems to lose its function as adult sexual characteristics begin to appear during the adolescent years. Damage to the pineal gland during early childhood may result in early sexual maturing.

The Thymus. The thymus gland is located in the chest. Little is known about its functions. It is relatively large in infancy and childhood and tends to atrophy or disappear after puberty. Hormones from this gland are believed to be associated with growth and retardation of sexual development. There is also some evidence from clinical studies that the thymus is related to normal muscular development.

The Gonads. The gonads, or sex glands, have a dual purpose: the first is the production of gametes (sperms or eggs), and the second is the secretion of sex hormones. The development and function of sex hormones are discussed later in this chapter. Research has furnished us with much information about the operation of the endocrine system and the effects of the different hormones on behavior and development. Additional research should enable us to chart with more exactitude the many possible interactions among the ductless glands and the role of the different hormones on the development of personality.

The Nervous System

The nervous system consists of billions of tiny nerve cells, or *neurons,* which connect with receptors (sense organs), effectors, or other neurons to form the complex neural patterns that underlie all behavior. The development of behavioral patterns depends upon the development of the nervous system and learning. With maturation there is an increase in the size of the brain and an increase in the complexity of the neural patterns which connect the receiving mechanisms with the responding mechanisms.

There is much research going on at the present time which involves a study of brain surgery, brain waves, brain stimulation, psychosurgery, and the location and study of the sensory and motor areas of the brain. An attempt will be made here to provide you with a better understanding of the operation of the brain as a part of the physiology of adjustments.

The Brain. The brain's major components, which have developed to their present state over a period of millions of years, furnish us with a good record of man's development. It is only within relatively recent years that man has probed into the interior workings of the brain as intensively as he had earlier explored the heart, stomach, and liver. Yet, the pinkish-gray jelly that makes up the brain remains a wonder to all researchers.

The major motor and sensory areas of the brain, as well as its constituent parts were charted decades ago. These are described as follows ("Probing the Brain," *Newsweek*, 1971, p. 61):

> At the top of the spinal cord lies the brain stem which is critically involved in respiration, blood pressure and other involuntary functions essential to life. The top part of the brain stem and the deeper part of the cerebral cortex (paleocortex or "old bark") composes the so-called "limbic system" which plays a key part in controlling the emotions and basic drives of fear, hunger, pleasure and sex. At the rear of the brain lies the cerebellum (little brain) that regulates fine coordination. The top of the cerebral cortex accounts for man's supremacy over the world he inhabits. This is the neocortex (new bark) that governs not only movement and the senses, but which also permits man to acquire new skills and gives him rational control over his baser drives.

Recently acquired knowledge about the location of the pleasure center, and the demons of anger and rage, has led to an era of psychosurgery. Dr. Thomas Ballantine of Massachusetts found that eight of ten patients with severe manic-depressive psychosis showed an improvement in their mental state with no adverse side effects following psychosurgery ("Probing the Brain," *Newsweek*, 1971, p. 62). Electrical stimulation of the brain and other forms of neurosurgery have been employed to treat individuals subject to violent outbursts of rage that are associated with temporal lobe epilepsy. Electrical stimulation of the brain (ESB) has been applied by remote control to control rage and aggression in entire colonies of monkeys. The potentialities for the future use of this and other methods for dealing with brain injuries, psychotic conditions, and other behavioral problems are impossible to estimate at the present time, although they appear to be enormous.

Specialized Roles in the Brain. It was formerly believed by researchers that all neurons were more or less alike and had adapted to specialized roles because of environment and experience of the organism. Recent studies have shown that at least some neurons are genetically made for remarkably specific tasks. Dr. Roger Sperry of California Tech cut the optic nerves of frogs and newts and rotated their eyes 180 degrees. After the nerves had regenerated, as they do in amphibians, the animals saw upside down—if food was hung from the ceiling, the animals moved down to reach it. Sperry concluded, "The nerve cells of the eyes were programmed to reconnect with only one specific point in the brain" ("Probing the Brain," *Newsweek,* 1971, p. 61).

Specialized roles may also be observed in connection with hormones from the endocrines. Although the mechanism by which the pituitary-adrenal hormones regulate or influence behavior is largely unknown, they must do so by acting on the brain. It is known that hormones in general are targets to specific sites, and the body tissues have a remarkable selectivity for them (Levine, 1971).

The uterus, for instance, picks up and responds selectively to estrogen and progesterone among all the hormones circulating in the blood; also the seminal vesicles and prostate gland of the male select testosterone. There is now much evidence that organs of the brain may be similarly selective. ". . . studies indicate that the lateral portion of the hypothalamus may be a receptor site for gonadal hormones. We have the inviting prospect, therefore, that exploration of the brain to locate the receptor sites for the hormones of the pituitary-adrenal system, and studies of the hormones' action on the cells of these sites, may yield important information on how the system regulates behavior" (Levine, 1971, p. 31).

Autonomic Nervous System

Early in the nineteenth century a French physiologist, Bichat, suggested that the activities of the nervous system could be divided into two parts: "voluntary" and "involuntary." The involuntary system has been further divided into the *sympathetic* and *parasympathetic* nervous systems. Most visceral organs are supplied by both systems, each having an opposite effect from the other. This is referred to as a reciprocal relation and helps to keep the activities of the different organs in balance. For example, while nerves from the sympathetic nervous system stimulate the heart, others from the parasympathetic slow it down.

The role of the autonomic nervous system in psychosomatic and homeostatic functions is well established. Miller (1969) has conducted experiments involving the autonomic nervous system which he believes have important implications for learning homeostatic responses. The results of such studies may help us to understand better why some people react to stress in a more rational or learned manner than others.

Although the sympathetic and parasympathetic systems are triggered by the preganglionic neurons that come from the spinal cord, these ganglionic neurons receive impulses from the cerebrospinal system by way of the hypothalamus. Thus, it appears that if there is a *seat of emotions,* it lies within the hypothalamus; and that it is the principal center in which the components of emotional reactions are organized into definite patterns. This is true even though the various components, as such, are separately activated at the lower points of the brain stem (Eysenck, 1967).

Biological Drives: Homeostasis, Hunger, and Sex

Few topics in psychology have been treated in so many different ways as motivation. Some terms that have been or are presently used with reference to motivation are *instincts, drives, activation, needs, conscious* and *unconscious motives,* and *wishes* or *desires.* Motivation as an activating force or condition affects every area of human behavior. It is not the purpose here to present theories of motivation; neither will an attempt be made to differentiate between drives that are essentially biological and those that are largely learned.

Biologic drives have their origin in the biological requirements or needs of the organism, and are sometimes referred to as tissue needs. The focus of the behavior of the organism is in behavior leading to the satisfaction of these needs.

Homeostasis

One important aspect of the body's function is referred to as *homeostasis.* According to the homeostatic theory of drives, the organism acts in such a way as to maintain internal stability or normal physiological balance. Some of these behavior patterns involve the regulation of body temperature, the heart, and certain other bodily functions, the maintenance of appropriate calcium, and the control of the acid-base balance of the blood. One example of the change in homeostasis in the aged is the regulation of the acid-base balance of the blood.

Actually, drives operate as homeostatic mechanisms when we realize that they originate in essential tissue needs. In order to maintain homeostasis the organism must be able to obtain the needed substances in its environment; to maintain itself within a limited range of external temperature; and to protect itself from attacks and adverse conditions in its environment.

In 1932 Walter Cannon wrote *The Wisdom of the Body,* which had an important influence in providing us with a better understanding of the operation of the physiological system. Cannon described the manner in which the physiological system functions in order to maintain internal equilibrium. It has been observed that children suffering from certain nutritional deficiencies, and given freedom to select their food, tend to choose those foods that will aid in overcoming such deficiencies. Animals with certain deficiencies are known to profit from the same process. It has been frequently observed that there are changes in rate of heartbeat as a result of temperature changes, physical activity, or emotional stress. People living in frigid or torrid zones tend to maintain a constant body temperature.

There is a great variety of body needs, and there are many ways in which essential homeostasis can be disrupted. Sooner or later, the automatic homeostatic mechanisms can no longer maintain the necessary "steady states" in the body. It is at this critical time that the organism as a whole must be aroused to take voluntary action to correct the body condition. At this time needs as bodily deficits become conscious (Krech et al., 1969).

The Hunger Drive

An understanding of the mechanism of hunger has been advanced by the combined efforts of psychologists and physiologists, who have manipulated the hunger stimulus under varying conditions.

Some Effects of the Hunger Drive. Although hunger is usually described in terms of stomach contractions, there is evidence that the hunger drive can operate in the absence of stomach contractions. It seems likely that stomach contractions are a by-product of some basic condition in the physiological state of the hungry organism and have no essential role in the hunger drive, although serving as a useful sign of hunger.

The hunger drive is still far from being understood; even though studies of the behavior of adults on a starvation diet have furnished us with interesting information about the effects of near-starvation upon human behavior. Historical records of peoples suffering from famine reveal something of the degenerative nature of man when faced with starvation. The behavior was that of self-concern and survival. This tended to pit brother against brother, parents against their children, and neighbors against neighbors. In more recent times, famine that has at times plagued certain areas of war-ravaged Europe and Asia has produced the same violence, lack of charity, and concerns only for the self that was noted in earlier records.

The behavioral effects of severe malnutrition upon war prisoners furnishes us with the same description of that for the famine victims. All thoughts of the prisoners were affected by their insatiable hunger; food became an obsession. Their behavior was further marked by extreme lethargy, a marked decrease in sexual desire, and a deterioration of moral standards. In some instances, their unrelenting hunger has led to a form of cannibalism with those remaining alive feeding upon the bodies of the dead (Markowski, 1945; Niremberski, 1946).

Integration of Cognitive and Physiological Determinants

The integration of cognitive and physiological determinants was studied by Schachter (1964) with obese subjects. His experiments involved manipulating bodily states by injections of Adrenalin or placebo and simultaneously manipulating cognitive and situational variables that were presumed to affect a subject's interpretation of his bodily feelings. The results of these studies have shown that cognitive factors play an important role in determining how a subject interprets his bodily feelings.

The 1964 study by Schachter manipulated bodily states by the exogenous administration of Adrenalin or some other agent, while Stunkard's studies have suggested that the same conclusion might be valid for endogenous physiological states. Stunkard and Koch (1964) had their subjects forego breakfast and come to the laboratory at 9:00 A.M. They swallowed a gastric balloon, and for the next four hours stomach contractions were continuously recorded. Every fifteen minutes the subjects were asked, "Do you feel hungry?" Comparisons were made between the subjects' hunger responses and the recordings of the stomach contractions. For normally sized subjects there was a general agreement; for the obese there was little correspondence. That is to say, when their stomachs contracted, the normal subjects reported hunger; but there was little or no relation between the contractions of the stomach and reports of feelings of hunger on the part of the obese subjects. Based on these and later studies (Schachter et al., 1968; Schachter, 1969), Schachter (1971, p. 130) concludes:

> Eating by the obese seems unrelated to any internal, visceral state, but is determined by external food-relevant cues such as the sight, smell, and taste of food. Now, obviously, for normals these external factors clearly interact with the internal state.

Further evidence of the interaction of cognitive and physiological determinants on hunger has been obtained from studies of the eating behavior of lesioned hyperphagic rats (Teitelbaum and Campbell, 1958). It was found that lesioned, obese rats eat more of good-tasting food than do their normal controls. They also eat fewer meals per day, eat more per meal, and eat more rapidly than do normal animals. Each of these results has a parallel for humans.

The Sexual Drive

During the past two decades there has been considerable research on the sexual drive. Following the studies by Freud, we have come to realize the importance of this drive as it relates to personality development. Studies of both animals and humans show that the strength of the drive is profoundly influenced by the hormones from the sex glands.

Sexual Drive in the Male. The sexual drive of the male is controlled by the *androgens,* which are hormones secreted by the testes, and certain "middle man" hormones, which are secreted from the pituitary body. The supply of the androgen hormones seems to be relatively constant; it does not show the monthly periodic cycle characteristic of the female.

The "middle man" hormones affect the sex drive both by acting directly on the testes, and thus on the supply of androgens, and by stimulating the adrenal cortex, which then secretes a hormone that speeds up sexual maturation. Here we note the close interrelation of the glands making up the endocrine system.

Sexual Drive in the Female. The sexual drive of the female is more complex than that of the male. The ovaries are responsible for the secretion of the principal sex hormones—the *estrogens,* which control the sexual drive, and the *progestins,* or progestational hormones, which are associated with ovulation in pregnancy.

Estrogens are secreted into the bloodstream each month at the time of ovulation. The female sexual drive is definitely influenced by these hormones. This relationship is most clearly observable in the lower mammals. At ovulation, when the bloodstream is enriched with estrogens, the female dog or other mammal not previously interested in the male becomes very receptive or aggressively suggestive in her sexual behavior.

Money (1961) has brought together considerable evidence to support the hypothesis that androgen is the hormone which is related to sexual arousability in women as well as in men. However, androgens in women seem to originate in the adrenals.

Physiological Basis of Sexual Behavior. It should not be concluded that sex behaviors emanate from the sex hormones. These behaviors are most complex and involve highly coordinated reactions to stimuli by complicated sequences of motor activity. Nash (1970, p. 166) concludes from a study of the role of the hormones:

> . . . it would appear, that, especially in higher animals, hormones are less specific than was once believed, and that their influence on sex behavior is less direct; moreover, sexual activity may continue in their absence. In humans at least, it might seem possible to conclude that the hormones do not provide either a necessary or a sufficient basis for sexual behavior, but this would be too hasty a conclusion.

A distinction should be made between sexual drive, sexual arousal, and sexual arousability. The sexual drive has been closely related to sexual hormones—androgens and estrogens. Sexual arousal, on the other hand, refers to the current level of sexual excitement. Sexual arousability, according to Whalen (1966, p. 152) is "an individual's characteristic rate of approach to orgasm as a result of sexual stimulation." Although sexual arousal can be measured by behavioral and verbal reports, physiological measures offer the advantage of objectivity. Such measures make use of blood volume changes, hyperventilation, temperature changes, muscle tension, and tachycardia (Zuckerman, 1971).

Sexual arousal in man appears to be mediated through the central and autonomic nervous systems and may involve the pituitary gonadotrophic and gonadal systems. Money (1961, p. 1396) states:

> . . . among the coordinates of sexual functions there are three: local genital surfaces, the brain, the hormones, any of which can fail in its contributions without total destruction of sexual function. . . . Nonetheless, it is evident that loss of any of the three constituents is an immense handicap to effective sexual functioning.

Sexual Maturation and Behavioral Changes. There is both scientific and empirical evidence that with the onset of puberty there is an increase in sex hormones that brings about an increased sexual tension. The increased interest and changed attitude toward members of the opposite sex has been observed and studied by students of developmental psychology. This was emphasized in an early study by Jones and Bayley (1950). Comparisons were made between two groups of boys approximately equal in chronological age but two years apart in skeletal development. As expected, the early-maturing boys displayed a greater interest in personal grooming and a different attitude toward girls than the late-maturing boys.

There is a close relationship between the morphological development of the body and social-sex behavior during adolescence. Late sexual maturing adolescents tend to display less dating and similar behaviors than their earlier maturing age-mates, and, conversely, those advanced in sexual maturation show more. It has also been noted that males low in androgen tend to show passive behavior patterns and rank low in dominance hierarchies.

There are also pronounced changes in attitudes and interests among girls with the onset of pubescence. Girls select books of romance; in their social activities they prefer those activities involving both sexes; they tend to shun activities that interfere with their playing a feminine role. In order to determine the effect of the menarche, or beginning of menstruation, Stone and Barker (1939) studied the interests and attitudes of a thousand girls from two large junior high schools of Berkeley, California. The girls were matched with respect to chronological age and social status, but were significantly different in physiological development—one group being postmenarcheal, the other premenarcheal. Significantly more postmenarcheal girls displayed an interest in boys than premenarcheal did. They were also more given to daydreaming and were more interested in personal adornment. These comparisons indicate a growing interest in adult activities, an increased independence, and an increased interest in the opposite sex, as a result of forces and conditions associated with the menarche.

Some of the behavioral activities so frequently cited as characteristics of the adolescent period may well have a physiological background. It is well known that the internal environment of individuals is in a state of flux during the early adolescent years. Thus, the unpredictable behavior and variations in mood during this period may often have a physiological basis. Such behavior may range from restlessness, resulting in part from an increased production of sex hormones within the individual, to the opposite state of apathy and listlessness, especially likely during periods of lowered metabolism. It is at this time that the individual is expected to reconcile his own internal environment with social and cultural demands.

Homosexuality was once thought to be controlled by endocrine factors (Krafft-Ebing, 1892). At a later stage, following research on androgen and estrogen hormones, it was thought to be associated with an estrogen-androgen imbalance (Swyer, 1954). Most psychiatrists have long maintained that the etiology of homosexuality is entirely psychological and environmental—that under the scrutiny of biochemical analysis homosexuals are not different from heterosexuals (Kinsey, 1941).

Investigators have continuously noted that small amounts of female sex hormones (estrogens) are found in males, while androgens circulate in all females. Thus, many investigators have attempted to link male homosexuality with an excess of female hormones and female masculinity, or homosexuality, with an excess of male hormones. These efforts, however, have not been successful.

Margolese (1970), a Los Angeles endocrinologist, attacked the problem of homosexuality in a different manner by concentrating solely on the male hormone. The subjects of his study consisted of ten heterosexuals in "good health," ten active homosexuals in "good health," and four heterosexuals not in "good health." Urines collected over a twenty-four-hour period were analyzed for 17-ketosteroids, androsterone, and etiocholanolone. A statistical analysis on the androsterone and etiocholanolone values obtained from the ten heterosexual and ten homosexual males showed a clear discrimination between the two groups. The results for an additional group of six healthy subjects, whose classification was withheld prior to the urine analysis, furnished a discrimination score which accurately predicted the four homosexuals and the two heterosexual males.

The androsterone etiocholanolone ratios and the discriminant scores of the four heterosexual males who did not fulfill the criteria of good health were in ranges similar to those of the homosexuals. One of these subjects had diabetes mellitus; the other three had severe depression. Thus, the change in ratio and discriminant score may occur in cases of individuals other than homosexuals. This suggests that the reversed ratio does not in itself furnish a safe basis for predicting homosexuality. Margolese concludes further:

> The present data could lead to the hypothesis that the metabolic condition which results in a relatively high androsterone value is the cause of sexual preference for females by either sex, whereas a relatively low androsterone value is associated with sexual preference for males by either sex (p. 154).

I have concentrated on the hormonal development of adolescent sexual characteristics, but the reader should also direct his attention to the chapters on sex education by Juhasz and Staton.

Neurology and Biology of Emotion

In recent years there has been considerable attention given by psychologists and others to "activation" or arousal theory in emotion and motivation. Much of this dates back to Cannon's theory of the emotions, in which he suggests that such emotions as anger, fear, and rage serve emergency functions in that they prepare the organism for action by mobilizing its resources to meet an apparently dangerous situation. Activation theory, according to Cofer and Appley (1964, pp. 392–393), has arisen in relation to two main bodies of fact:

> . . . first, that behavioral efficiency varies as a function of energy mobilization and muscular involvement; and, second, that recent neurophysiological discoveries have suggested that cortical function is related to activity in an arousal system of the brain stem.

Arousal Theories

Studies performed in physiological laboratories, using front-limbic brain lesions have been successful in separating at least two components of arousal. One component is an indicator of searching and sampling; the other component is manifest when a novelty is registered (Pribram, 1967). It is only after such registration that habituation occurs. The experimental results cited by Pribram raise the question as to when arousal leads to disruption. The classical answer to this question has been that the *amount* of arousal determines the outcome (Hebb, 1955). However, on the basis of experimental studies of the orientation reaction, amount seems to depend on experiential organization, and on the configuration of the expectations by the novel output.

While habituation reflects redundancy, novelty implies information and uncertainty. Amount of arousal or activation, should not be thought of as some quantitative change in intensity; rather it is a change in the uncertainty and information of the system. The arousal theories may then be thought of as uncertainty theories. These theories suggest that disruption of control is involved.

Hormonal Factors

The function of hormones in connection with homeostasis was discussed earlier. Cannon's (1929) early viewpoints about the secretion of the adrenal medulla in emotional behavior are well known. He regarded this hormone as being responsible for the sustaining state of emotional arousal first triggered off by the autonomic nervous system. His notion that the liberation of adrenalin into the bloodstream increases the vigor of response and prolongs the emotional state is generally accepted.

The adrenal cortex is different from the medulla in that it is not subject to direct neural regulation although it is regulated by a secretion of the anterior pituitary, the adrenocorticotropic hormone (ACT). It is this hormone that is responsible for the release of the steroid hormone (Nash, 1970). During stress some tissues, especially muscle tissues, seem to require increased amounts of the adrenal cortex hormones. Thus, it appears that large secretions of adrenal cortical hormones are essential for the maintenance of continued states of prolonged reactions to stress.

Evidence on the exact nature of adrenal cortical secretions is quite incomplete. The secretions of the adrenal cortex are quite intricate, since in the adult they contain twenty-five or more different steroids. And, although the adrenal cortex is essential to life, the essential functions are probably not dependent on all these steroids. In mature humans there is a direct relationship between stress and the output of 17-ketosteroids, the output increasing during stress. It is likely that the relative lack of the 17-ketosteroids in early childhood is one of the factors responsible for the differential emotional responses between the child and the more mature adult. These differences may be both quantitative and qualitative.

Neural Influences

The thalamus is an important center for mediating emotional behavior, as distinct from emotional experience. Bard (1934) pointed out that decorticate cats gave a "sham rage reaction" in which the behavior is a gross, automatic, poorly directed rage reaction. A human situation that is somewhat parallel may be observed in a patient after frontal lobotomy—surgery which renders a person partly decorticate. Such persons display immediate and often excessive responsiveness to external stimulation, although their emotional behavior tends to lack depth, as shown by introspective reports. Their responses are of short duration, may alternate quickly from one emotional state to another, and are less inhibited than those of normal individuals (Nash, 1970).

It seems, then, from research upon animals as well as upon man, that the cortex, especially the frontal lobes, is involved in both the inhibition of emotional responses and in the instigating and sustaining of them. Furthermore, the emotional behaviors of the mature organism, at least those higher up the phylogenetic scale, involve some sort of interaction between the thalamus and the cortex.

The Expression of Emotion

Within the trilogy—perception, action, emotion—emotion expresses the relationship between perception and action. The relationships have been described by Pribram (1967, p. 836) as follows:

> When the variety of perceptions exceeds to some considerable extent the repertory of action available to the organism he is motived to, i.e., attempts to extend this repertory. Whenever this attempt fails, is nonreinforced, frustrated, or interrupted, the organism becomes of necessity emotional, i.e., he must resort to mechanisms of self-regulation, self-control. Further, on the basis of experience, emotion is likely when the probability of reinforcement from action is deemed low.

This conception of the relationships between perceptions, emotions, and actions show that experiences, glandular processes, and neural processes are interrelated in the expression of emotion. Motivation and emotion occur when the organism tries to extend its control to the limits of what it perceives. To the extent that this attempt is regarded as feasible at a particular moment, the organism is motivated; to the extent that it is regarded as infeasible at the moment, the organism "gives up," or becomes of necessity emotional (Pribram, 1967). Thus, motivation and emotion go hand in hand and in some situations are so interrelated that they cannot be correctly assessed or separated.

The conception of emotions as neural processes as opposed to glandular (although the role of the endocrines must not be ignored) provides for the inclusion of "positive" as well as "negative" emotions. Emotion need not be disruptive, although a type of disruption of action usually initiates the emotion.

Stress and Behavior. The concept of the general "stress syndrome" has been one of the fruitful ideas of this era in biological and medical research. According to this concept the body of a mammal mobilizes a system of defensive reactions involving the pituitary and adrenal glands in response to stress. Concerning its operation, Levine (1971, p. 26) states:

> . . . Information concerning stress (coming either from external sources through the sensory system or from internal sources such as change in body temperature or in the blood's composition) is received and integrated by the central nervous system and is presumably delivered to the hypothalamus, the basal area of the brain. The hypothalamus secretes a substance called the corticotropin-releasing factor (CRF), which stimulates the pituitary to secrete the hormone ACTH. This in turn stimulates the cortex of the adrenal gland to step up its synthesis and secretion of hormones, particularly those known as glucocorticoids. In man the glucocorticoid is predominantly hydrocortisone; in many lower animals such as the rat it is corticosterone.

It is interesting to note that the system of defensive reactions can be evoked by all kinds of stresses including not only severe somatic stresses such as disease, bone fractures, burns, surgery, and drugs, but also by a wide range of psychological conditions such as fear, anxiety, a loud noise, and exposure to a novel environment. Indeed, many of the conditions and situations that activate the pituitary-adrenal system in man do not involve tissue damage. It seems, therefore, that these hormones have many functions in addition to the defense of tissue integrity.

Dynamics of Aggression. Although psychology is unable to offer definite statements about the nature of aggression, psychological research and theory can make a worthwhile contribution to an analysis of aggressive behavior. There is empirical evidence that the range of behaviors subsumed under the category of aggression differ in their dynamics. According to Feshbach (1971, p. 284), "Motivated aggressive acts can be further subdivided into instrumental aggression that is directed toward the achievement of nonaggressive goals and aggressive drive for which the goal response is injury to some animate or inanimate object." Killing a poisonous snake in defense of one's life and the defense of others is an example of instrumental aggression. On the other hand, the person who beats a barking dog because of his irritation at the dog is engaging in drive-mediated aggression.

There is much evidence based upon research that certain aggressive actions on the part of man or animals may be a result of conditioning and may be controlled through providing or withholding extrinsic reinforcers. Freud (1930) claimed that all aggressions are manifestations of the aggressive drive. Thus a number of psychoanalysts conceived of mob violence, riots, and war as manifestations of man's aggressive instinct. The concept of aggressive drive does not presuppose an instinct theory. This may be noted in the case of aggression among animals. For a given animal species, one can frequently observe the signal or behavior by one member of the species which will release or set in motion an aggressive response in another member of that species. A dog not wanting to fight or being the loser in a fight may simply back away from the fight without being pursued by the victor. A deer in the midst of an antler fight will stop or modify his movements when aimed at the unprotected flank of his opponent (Lorenz, 1966). Intraspecies killing in animals is much rarer than in humans, and the pursuit of a rival or enemy over space and time in order to inflict injury or kill him is a peculiarly human type of behavior. Feshbach (1971, p. 284) states:

> The ethological studies suggest that what may be innate or instinctive in human aggression is the evocation of aggressive responses by as yet to be specified stimuli. . . . However, the concept of an instinctive aggressive reaction is quite far from the notion of aggressive drive-mediated behavior, the goal of which is the infliction of injury.

Aggression has been associated with masculine characteristics, especially among preliterate societies and certain groups of contemporary lower-class societies. The warrior-fighting definition of the male image may be observed among certain groups today. The relationship between aggression and masculine characteristics may not be completely a matter of culture as revealed by comparisons of male and female infants. Studies of different primate species reveal that males have a stronger predisposition to aggressive motor responses than females (Harlow, 1962). Furthermore, the administration of the male hormone, testosterone, has been found to enhance aggressive behavior in very young female rats and female macaques (Young et al., 1964).

Brain Damage and Personality Structure

According to Dr. Frank Ervin, who heads a psychiatric research laboratory at Massachusetts General Hospital of Boston, "There are an estimated 10 million Americans with gross brain disorders—epilepsy, mental retardation, serious illness. There are probably another 10 million, unrecognized cases of minor brain disorders resulting from traumas or infections" (Rosenthal, 1970, p. 57). Chromosomal abnormalities, malnutrition during the prenatal period or infancy, maternal infectious conditions, poor infant care, serious diseases, and severe head injuries have been linked to brain-damaged condition. Brain-injured children may exhibit a variety of behavior. A survey of the literature more than a decade ago by Beck (1961) yielded a list of forty-three different behavior symptoms.

The physiological basis of behavior can be inferred from studies of changes in behavior and personality structure following brain damage. Eysenck (1967, p. 331) concluded from a review of studies:

> There is now a considerable body of evidence to show that the behavioral effects of injury or pathology of the brain are far from homogeneous. This is not to say that there are no behavioral changes which are common to all cases of brain injury, but rather that the observed effects on behavior are principally dependent upon the locus of injury and the nature of the neuropathology. . . . In addition to the variables referred to above as determining differential patterns of impairment, in many of these studies evidence was also found, of course, of some general impairment in behavior associated with brain damage as such, particularly in terms of some forms of lowered intellectual efficiency.

Neurochemistry of Intelligence

Although we are not directly concerned with the neurochemistry of intelligence and memory, it is important to know that much research is being conducted on the chemical basis of memory (Gurowitz, 1968). A number of studies confirm the role of ribonucleic acid (RNA) in memory storage and transfer and even the possibility of transfer from one donor to another through the donation of RNA from educated to naïve organisms (Faiszt and Adàm, 1968). Through the use of labelled nuclei acids to study protein synthesis, Gaitonde (1969) observed complex changes with age in the protein composition of the brain. Other studies of animals have correlated dietary deficiencies with abnormal brain development. With the vast amount of research in progress, we should be able to clarify the role of the biochemistry of the brain on intellectual development. These results may have a profound influence on our understanding and thinking about the nature and improvement of intelligence.

Studies of animals have shown that the effects of malnutrition on the growth and development of the nervous system are dependent upon the time, duration, and severity of the nutritional deficit (Widdowson and

McCance, 1963). Studies of animals also indicate that growth in all organs occurs in three phases: first, hyperplasia, during which the number of cells increase; second, hyperplasia and hypertrophy, during which the number and size of cells continue to increase; and third, hypertrophy, when growth occurs only in size of the cells. It appears from these studies that during the hyperplasia phase malnutrition can interfere with cell division, resulting in fewer cells in the brain, which seems to be a permanent effect, whereas malnutrition during hypertrophy results in a decrease in the size of the cells but not in the number of cells of the brain.

Malnourished at an Early Age Score Less on Intelligence Tests. A three-year study of Mexican children hospitalized at an early age with severe malnutrition found that they scored lower on intelligence tests in later life than did their siblings who had not suffered from the condition (Hicks, 1970). The study was conducted by Dr. Joaquin Cravioto and by Dr. Herbert G. Birch as a part of a larger study of the ecological factors in child growth and development. The investigators selected thirty-seven children to act as the experimental group. Each child had been hospitalized somewhere between his sixth and thirteenth month of life with kwashiorkor, a severe malnutrition condition. Each had recovered and was at the time of the study five years of age or older.

A brother or a sister of each experimental group member was selected as a control. Each sibling of the control group was within the years of age of his brother or sister in the experimental group and had never had severe forms of malnutrition. Both groups of children were taken to the Army hospital in Mexico City and given a standardized intelligence test.

The average intelligence quotient of the experimental group was 68.5, and that of the control group was 81.5—a difference of thirteen points. Only four of the kwashiorkor subjects scored above 90, while more than two-thirds of the siblings who had not suffered from severe malnutrition scored above 90. This shows that malnutrition during the early months has a lasting effect on its victims. (Nichols presents an extended discussion of the nature-nurture controversy on the topic of intelligence within another chapter of this book. It is a fascinating subject on which research continues today.)

Neurological Correlates of Reading Problems. Psychological correlates of many reading problems can be traced to neurological abnormalities or disorders. Kawi and Pasamanick (1959, p. 61) noted that "the relationship of . . . maternal and fetal factors to reading disorders is similar to that observed in stillbirths, neonatal deaths, cerebral palsy, epilepsy, and behavior disorders." Tuller (1966) found abnormal EEG patterns in children with reading problems. The results of a study by Boshes and Mykelbust (1964) furnished an impetus to other studies bearing on the relationships between neurological development and reading problems. In a more recent study (Mykelbust and Boshes, 1969, p. 4) it was noted: "When the brain involvement is on the right hemisphere, the EEG more often reveals dysfunction."

Age, Physiological Changes, and Mental Abilities

There is scientific evidence that the number of brain cells actually declines with age. Furthermore, there are significant physiological changes in the brain structure with certain diseases or changed physiological states. For example, in the case of arteriosclerosis we find a loss of memory and frequently other mental states, depending upon the severity of the physiological changes. This is, for many, the most depressing part of growing old.

Two researchers at Duke University, Carl Eisdorfer and his associate, Frances Wilkie (1971), suggest that the declines in mental abilities in elderly people have resulted from the presence of high blood pressure. The subjects of their studies consisted of 202 men and women in their sixties and seventies, observed over a ten-year period. At the beginning of their study the subjects were divided into three groups: those with normal, borderline, and high blood pressure. Every thirty months, each person underwent a thorough physical examination and completed a battery of psychological and intelligence tests. The results of their study were somewhat unexpected: "among patients who were in their early 60's when the study began, those who had normal blood pressure showed virtually no intellectual changes by the tenth year; those with high blood pressure dropped almost ten points in their test scores" (p. 40). In the case of those with borderline blood pressure, the majority actually registered an increase in their scores by several points, supporting an older theory that older people should have a slightly elevated blood pressure to support adequate circulation in the brain.

Violent Acts May Have a Root in Brain Abnormality

No doubt much of the violence that plagues our society goes unreported. President Nixon's Commission on Law Enforcement reports that violence is far more often an act among friends than among strangers (Rosenthal, 1970). It has been frequently observed that family squabbles, wife beating, and familial fights may never make the police records. Until recently, such factors as the criminal's family life and environment were considered the underlying causes. However, more recently, scientists have begun to give serious study to the theory that personal violence may have a physiological base. It was pointed out earlier that research with both animals and humans as subjects has shown that aggression, anger, and rage are closely associated with electrochemical activity in the brain. Rosenthal points out: "Genetic disorders, poorly developed central nervous systems, glandular secretions, brain diseases, and severe head injuries have been linked to aggressive actions" (1970, p. 57).

Frank R. Ervin (Rosenthal, 1970) notes that brain abnormalities take a variety of forms, but the aggressive behavior is a common pattern. This he refers to as the "syndrome episodic dyscontrol." The conclusion by Ervin that brain abnormalities may spark violent actions stems from his work with epileptic patients. He studied the fits of anger and destruction exhibited by patients with temporal lobe epilepsy—a disease that affects the limbic structure of the brain. The investigators at Boston City Hospital discovered that the violent attacks correspond to an erratic pattern of electroencephalograph (EEG). It was observed that electrical stimulation, through surgically implanted electrodes at certain points in the limbic system, could trigger violent behavior; electrical stimulation of other points could stop an attack that had started. Additional research with nonepileptic subjects showed that the same kind of activity occurs in persons with episodic dyscontrol as goes on in the epileptic. This finding has tremendous potentials for the treatment of "violent-prone" individuals.

Through detailed medical histories, the Boston investigators found that loss of self-control episodes often could be traced to childhood. In many cases they could be pinpointed from infancy or some period suffered from a bout with measles, prolonged high fever, or accident in which there was brain damage. Rosenthal (1970, p. 71) quotes from Ervin: "We find that violence-prone persons have a childhood history of hyperactive behavior, multiple fire-setting, prolonged enuresis (bedwetting), cruelty to animals, destructive activities generally out-of-keeping with their peers."

Summary

Neurological and physiological processes manifest themselves in a wide range of simple and complex ways. Research during the past two or more decades has shed much light on the relationship of these processes to adjustments, since it is generally recognized that every human behavior pattern depends upon connections between the receiving mechanisms (sense organs) and responding mechanisms.

A group of structures that has received much attention is the ductless glands, which were once regarded by many psychologists as the basis for personality differences. Each of these glands has its own peculiar function to perform, although they are closely interrelated as noted in the case of the pituitary glands and the sex glands. Malfunctioning of any of the glands creates special problems, if not corrected. Some of these problems have been discussed in this chapter.

The development of behavioral patterns depends upon the development of the nervous system and learning. During the past decade physiological psychologists have probed into the brain and learned much about its functioning. As a result of psychosurgery, the behavior patterns of patients with severe manic-depressive psychosis showed an improvement. Electrical stimulation of the brain and other forms of neurosurgery have been used to treat individuals with abnormal emotional manifestations. There would appear to be great potential in these techniques for the improvement of certain forms of emotional behavior. The complexity and interrelatedness of the glandular system and the autonomic nervous system make these studies more difficult, but much is being learned and a great deal accomplished in the improvements of behavioral patterns.

The integration of cognitive and physiological determiners reveals more about the complexity of motivators. Studies bearing on this interrelatedness are helping to answer questions that have existed for centuries about the relation of mind and body. This may be noted in particular in connection with the hunger and sex drives, both of which are further related to glandular secretions. A distinction was made between sexual drive and sexual arousability, with the sexual drive being closely bound up with sexual hormones—androgens and estrogens. On the other hand, sexual arousal in man appears to be mediated through the central and autonomic nervous system.

Sexual maturation produces behavioral changes as shown in comparisons of the behavior patterns of early- and late-maturing boys and girls. Thus, many of the behavioral activities characteristic of the adolescent period seem to have a physiological basis, although cultural factors operate to determine the nature and direction of certain behavior patterns. Even homosexuality seems to have a physiological basis, although we should recognize the influences of certain environmental situations and stimulations.

Thus, we find that emotions, stress, appetites, and perhaps aggression are deep-seated in man's physiological nature, although we should not overlook the role of learning, particularly conditioning.

The physiological basis of behavior has been studied through studies of personality structure following brain damage. Recent studies have revealed the importance of RNA to memory, transfer, and the possibility of transfer from one donor to another. They have also shown the effects of malnutrition, especially when it is properly timed. Even violent acts may have a basis in brain abnormality. Additional research involving the brain will reveal much information about the mind-body relationships.

REFERENCES

Bard, P. The neurohumorol basis of emotional reactions. In C. Murchison (ed.), *Handbook of General Experimental Psychology*. Worcester, Mass.: Clark University Press, 1934.

Beck, H. S. Detecting psychological symptoms of brain injury. *Exceptional Children*, 1961, *28*, 57–62.

Boshes, B., and Mykelbust, H. R. A neurological and behavioral study of children with learning disorders. *Neurology*, 1964, *14*, 7–12.

Brown, F. A. Living clocks. *Science*, 1959, *130*, 1535–1544.

Cannon, W. B. *Bodily changes in pain, hunger, fear and rage*, 2d ed. New York: Appleton, 1929.

Cofer, C. H., and Appley, M. H. *Motivation, theory and research*. New York: Wiley, 1964.

Eisdorfer, C., and Wilkie, F. A clue to senility, *Newsweek*, Aug. 23, 1971, p. 40.

Eysenck, H. J. *The biological basis of personality*. Springfield, Ill.: Charles C Thomas, 1967.

Faiszt, J., and Adàm, G. Role of different RNA fractions from the brain in transfer effect. *Nature*, 1968, *220*, 367–368.

Feshbach, S. Dynamics and morality of violence and aggression: Some psychological considerations. *American Psychologists*, 1971, *26*, 281–292.

Freud, S. *Civilization and its discontents*. London: Hogarth Press, 1930.

Gaitonde, M. K. Report on meeting of Neurochemical Group of the Biochemical Society. *Nature*, 1969, *221*, 808.

Gurowitz, E. M. *Molecular basis of memory*. Englewood Cliffs, N.J.: Prentice-Hall, 1968.

Harlow, H. The heterosexual affectional system in monkeys. *American Psychologists*, 1962, *17*, 1–9.

Hebb, D. O. Drives and the CNS (conceptual nervous system). *Psychological Review*, 1955, *62*, 243–254.

Hicks, N. Undernourished score less when intelligence is tested. *Atlanta Constitution*, February 26, 1970, p. 5B.

Jones, M. C., and Bayley, N. Physical maturity among boys as related to behavior. *Journal of Educational Psychology,* 1950, *41,* 137.

Kawi, A., and Pasamanick, B. Prenatal and paranatal factors in the development of childhood reading disorders. *Monographs of the Society of Research in Child Development,* 1959, *4.*

Kinsey, A. C. Homosexuality. *Journal of Clinical Endocrinology,* 1941, *1,* 424–428.

Krafft-Ebing, R. von. *Psychopathia sexualis.* Philadelphia: Davis, 1892.

Krech, D., Crutchfield, R. S., and Livson, N. *Elements of psychology,* 2d ed. New York: Alfred A. Knopf, 1969.

Levine, Seymour. Stress and behavior. *Scientific American,* 1971, *224* (1), 26–31.

Lorenz, K. *On aggression.* New York: Harcourt, Brace and World, 1966.

Margolese, M. S. Homosexuality: A new endocrine correlate. *Hormones and Behavior,* 1970, *1,* 151–155.

Markowski, B. Some experiences of a medical prisoner of war. *British Medical Journal,* 1945, *2,* 361–363.

Miller, N. E. Learning of visceral and glandular response. *Science, 163,* 434–445.

Money, J. Sex hormones and other variables in human eroticism. In W. C. Young (ed.), *Sex and internal secretions.* VIII. Baltimore: Williams and Wilkins, 1961.

Mykelbust, H. R., and Boshes, B. Minimal brain damage in children. Final Report, June 1969, U.S. Public Health Service Contract No. 108–65–142.

Nash, J. *Developmental psychology.* Englewood Cliffs, N.J.: Prentice-Hall, 1970.

Niremberski, M. Psychological investigation of a group of internees at Belsen camp. *Journal of Mental Science,* 1946, *92,* 60–74.

Pribram, K. H. The new neurology and the biology of emotion: A structural approach. *American Psychologist,* 1967, *22,* 830–838.

Probing the brain. *Newsweek,* June 21, 1971, 60–65.

Rosenthal, A. Violence is predictable. *Today's Health,* 1970, *48* (11), 56–57, 71–72.

Schachter, S. The interaction of cognitive and physiological determinants of emotional state. In L. Berkowitz (ed.), *Advances in Experimental Social Psychology,* Vol. 1. New York: Academic Press, 1964.

———. Obesity and eating. *Science,* 1968, *161,* 751–756.

———, Goldman, R., and Gordon, A. Effects of fear, food deprivation, and obesity on eating. *Journal of Personality and Social Psychology*, 1968, *10*, 91–97.

Schachter, S. Some extraordinary facts about obese humans and rats. *American Psychologist*, 1971, *26*, 129–144.

Stone, C. P., and Barker, R. G. The attitudes and interests of premenarcheal and postmenarcheal girls. *Journal of Genetic Psychology*, 1939, *54*, 27–72.

Stunkard, A., and Koch, C. The interpretation of gastric motility: I. Apparent bias in the reports of hunger by obese persons. *Archives of General Psychiatry*, 1964, *11*, 74–82.

Swyer, G. I. M. Homosexuality: The endocrine aspects. *The Practitioner*, 1954, *172*, 374–377.

Teitelbaum, P., and Campbell, B. A. Ingestion patterns in hyperplagic and normal rats. *Journal of Comparative and Physiological Psychology*, 1958, *51*, 135–141.

Tuller, D. Electroencephalograms of children who fail in reading. *Exceptional Children*, 1966, *32*, p. 637.

Whalen, R. E. Sexual motivation. *Psychological Review*, 1966, *73*, 151–163.

Widdowson, E. M., and McCance, R. A. The effects of finite periods of undernutrition at different ages on the composition and subsequent development of the rat. *Proceedings of the Royal Society of London*, B. 1963, *158*.

Young, W. C., Goy, R., and Phoenix, C. Hormones and sexual behavior. *Science*, 1964, *143*, 212–218.

Zuckerman, M. Physiological measures of sexual arousal in the human. *Psychological Bulletin*, 1971, *75*, 297–329.

5

Theories of Adolescent Development

E. Kuno Beller*

It will be evident, from the other chapters in this book and from the literature in general, that an abundance of empirical data has been accumulated and that adolescence has been accepted as a clearly delineated and important period. Yet, theory has taken a less central place in the research and discussions on adolescence than it has in the study of other phases of human development. One reason for this might be that the study of human development reaches its most complex stage during adolescence. In most societies, the onset of puberty is marked by pronounced changes in many areas of functioning. Although the rate of change varies from area to area and from individual to individual, by and large, the human being at this stage of development poses a problem to himself, to his family, and to the larger group of which he is to become a member. Biologically, intellectually, the adolescent approaches maturity at a rather rapid rate. Psychologically and socially, he often interrupts the course of gradual development and deviates in a variety of ways both from his somewhat younger peers and from his elders. This disparity in the rate and direction of change between adolescence and the other phases of development also presents special problems when one attempts

* E. Kuno Beller is Professor of Psychology at Temple University. Prior to this, he was the Director of Research of the Child Development Center in New York City. Dr. Beller has published a number of chapters and articles on child psychology, motivation, perception, and psychopathology. In addition he has written *Clinical Process*.

to integrate the data contributed from differing disciplines, such as biology, psychology, and sociology. However, the very difficulties that have interfered with the formulation of theories of adolescence point clearly toward the need for a theoretical framework which will make the disparities and deviations that characterize development during adolescence meaningful and predictable.

The different theories of adolescence to be discussed in this chapter will be grouped as follows: biological, psychological, psychosocial, sociological, psychoanalytic, and anthropological. Since the limitations of space do not permit an exhaustive discussion of the several theories (as in Ausubel, 1954; Blos, 1962; and Muuss, 1962), an attempt will be made here to reduce the overlap and repetition which exist in abundance from theory to theory, and to highlight instead the unique features of each.

Biological Theories of Adolescence

Practically all theories which we will undertake to examine accept adolescence as a unique phase in human development and agree on the central biological and physical changes of puberty which mark its onset. However, they differ widely with regard to the importance and influence of these biological changes on the psychological processes. Furthermore, there is a frequent use of the same, or very similar empirical facts, as evidence for, or illustrative of, quite different theoretical models.

Hall: Recapitulation

It is of historical interest that the father of a "psychology of adolescence," namely G. Stanley Hall (1916), was also the founder of the approach to adolescence as a separate and distinct phase in human development. Following Darwin's concept of evolution, Hall introduced a theory of recapitulation which assumed that the experiential history of the race becomes a part of the genetic constitution of the individual. According to this view, each individual passes through stages which repeat the history of mankind. The direction of development in general, and of adolescence in particular, is thus seen as essentially controlled by internal forces.

In animals, phylogeny is recapitulated before birth. In human beings, infancy represents a reenactment of the prehistoric stages of the human race. During infancy, the development of vegetative, sensory, and motor functions are dominant. The early part of middle childhood represents a reenactment of the cave-dwelling culture of early history. The later part, namely, preadolescence, which lasts from eight to twelve years of age, parallels that phase of early history at which discipline marked the major progress of mankind. At this stage of development, the child is amenable to mechanical training; that is, training which involves those skills necessary for sensory, motor, perceptual, and cognitive functioning. Adolescence itself is a period of rebellion which, in terms of recapitulation, corresponds to a time when the human race was in a transitional stage. Historically, Hall chose *Sturm und Drang* (storm and stress) as the model for temperament and mentality that characterizes adolescence. Furthermore, adolescence is frequently characterized by extremely contradictory tendencies which make this phase of development one of instability and one in which the individual may fluctuate between emotional, social, and ideological extremes. Thus, it is only in late adolescence that the individual begins to settle down and reach his maturity. This phase of development represents a recapitulation of the beginning of modern civilization.

Since Hall considered adolescence, as he considered all other stages of development, to be primarily biologically determined, there was little room in his system for environmental factors to influence adolescent phenomena. Consistent with this point of view, Hall considered it best not to interfere with the natural course of development, since he believed it to be inevitable and determined by inner forces.

Hall might be taken as a prototype of those later biological approaches to human development which assume, in a general way, that the direction of psychological development recapitulates the evolutionary development of the strata in the human brain. A common characteristic shared by these biological approaches is that they do not postulate basic psychological principles for predicting developmental changes. The only principles provided to account for such changes are drawn from biology and biogenesis. For the realm of psychological development, these theories provide descriptive concepts for the ordering of the experiences and behaviors that characterize each of the successive stages of development.

Gesell: Morphogenesis and Spiral Growth

Arnold Gesell is best known for his observational work on human development from birth to adolescence (1940, 1946b, 1956). His descriptions of age trends have been accepted by many parents in the United States as norms of what to expect in their developing children. Gesell's biological orientation, with respect to the predetermined stages of maturation, reflects rather clearly the points made in the previous paragraph. On a level of theory, Gesell offered the general formulation that mental growth is a progressive morphogenesis, that is, a process of differentiation and integration. According to this view, environmental factors may facilitate or inhibit growth; but the basic direction of growth is laid down by maturational forces. In order to account for changes between developmental stages, Gesell employs the model of a spiral (1946a). Growth consists of oscillation along a spiral course toward maturity. The child frequently reverts to earlier forms of behavior before he is able to surpass his previous performance. Thus, progression and partial regression, until further progression takes place, characterize the course of developmental change.

Like Hall, Gesell saw adolescence as a transitional period between childhood and adulthood. Unlike Hall he did not conceive of adolescence as a period of storm, contradictions, and extremes. However, in his generalizations which are derived from his empirical observations, Gesell does place stress on the differences which appear in the adolescent from year to year. This is really similar to Hall's *Sturm und Drang*—an aspect of development which Gesell had de-emphasized in his theorizing. The ten year old is described as stable, well-adjusted to his family, and altogether fond of company. At the same time, he is intrigued by secret societies and is supersensitive to the fairness of adult authority. With regard to peers, he prefers to associate with his own sex. In contrast to the ten year old, the eleven year old is moody, quarrelsome, rebellious, and argumentative. This turbulence has disappeared in the twelve year old who is more sensible and tolerant than he was at eleven. The twelve year old is concerned with social recognition and more interested in the opposite sex. This greater peace with social environment changes again at thirteen. The thirteen year old turns inward; he is more critical of himself and his family. In line with his rapidly changing body structure and body chemistry, he is more tense, more aware of himself, and less secure than he was in the preceding year. At fourteen, the adolescent goes through a phase of reversal toward extroversion and frequently becomes enthusiastic. He is self-confident and more at ease with himself. He has begun to make definite choices of his ego ideals, and he identifies closely with his heroes from folklore and from other sources. This trend is again reversed in the fifteen year old, who manifests increased tension, hostility, and rebellion against authority. He is again self-conscious and, in addition, perfectionistic. The rebellious trend at this age level makes the youth vulnerable to delinquency, particularly because he is eager to move away from home and to disassociate himself from family and authority. In sharp contrast to the picture presented by the fifteen year old, the sixteen year old gives evidence of emotional integration and balance, a high degree of social adjustment and self-control. He is friendly, outgoing, and independent in a self-confident sort of way.

The foregoing brief descriptions indicate that adolescence is conceived of as a phase of glaring contradictions within adjacent age levels with alternating stages of calmness and storm. They also reflect normative generalizations with regard to restricted age levels. These cannot be easily conceptualized in terms of the relative effects of biological, psychological, and cultural factors. It is for these reasons, together with the inferences that parents have drawn with respect to the meaning of their child's deviations from the norms, that Gesell came under the fire of considerable criticism. Notwithstanding such hazards, and in spite of the methodological criticism justly leveled against Gesell's work, he has provided us with a host of ideas which provide fertile ground for conceptual probing and empirical research.

Kretschmer: Body Types

A different biological approach to adolescent development has been formulated by the followers of Ernst Kretschmer (1951). They have employed his theory of body types to explain the direction of developmental change. Kretschmer focuses our attention on three basic body types: the pyknic, athletic, and asthenic. He held that each of the body types represents a predisposition to certain major psychological tendencies. For example, schizoid tendencies are said to appear more frequently in people with slender and tall or athletic body build, whereas manic-depressive or cycloid tendencies are said to appear more frequently in people with a stocky body constitution. Adolescence was characterized by Kretschmer's followers as a developmental phase with "schizoid" characteristics. Moreover, the degree of turbulence experienced by the adolescent was hypothesized to be correlated with his body type. This means that a youth with a lean and slender body type would already have a tendency toward a schizoid personality and would therefore experience adolescence as a turbulent period. A child with a stocky body constitution, who is inclined toward cycloid personality characteristics, would not experience adolescence as a very disturbing phase in his development. There is, as yet, very little empirical evidence to support or refute these speculative assertions.

Zeller: Body Gestalt

The approach of Wilfried Zeller, a follower of Kretschmer, is actually closer to the theorizing of Gesell since Zeller (1951) postulates relationships between changes in body constitution and changes in psychological functions. For each stage in psychological development, there is a specific *body gestalt* (body gestalt refers to the total structure and composition of the body) that corresponds to it. Although changes appear most clearly in one or another of the body areas, functions, or organs, Zeller emphasized that these changes only signify a total change of the body gestalt, which would also be reflected by a similar change in the psychological sphere. For example, children lose their first tooth and gain their first permanent tooth between five and one-half and six and one-half. Such a specific change is indicative of a much broader change in both the physique and personality of the child. This change also coincides with the child's introduction to formal schooling. Similarly, the appearance of secondary sex characteristics at puberty (see Garrison's discussion within this volume) involves a much broader, more comprehensive change of the body structure and hormonal dominance. The broader change in body structure is a beginning disharmony that occurs at the onset of the pubertal phase. In early adolescence this increased disharmony of the body gestalt is reflected in a sudden increase of impulsivity, nervousness, and a more critical attitude. This is directed at the adolescent's body, as well as toward his inner psychological world. Zeller presents a number of empirical observations in support of his theory. He maintains that changes in body gestalt cannot be measured totally by means of quantitative methods. Certain aspects of these changes are qualitative, and for that reason the observer has to rely on intuitive judgments to grasp changes in the gestalt quality. It is interesting to note in this context that Sheldon (1940) has made similar statements with regard to judgments of body types.

The application of typology to development represents one of the two major biological approaches to adolescence in contemporary Germany. The major biological approach is represented by a stratification theory of personality. This theory holds that psychological functions are embedded in layers of the brain. The more elementary affective functions are thought to have their root in the cerebellum, while the more cognitive and intellectual functions originate in the cerebrum. The stratification theory makes the assumption that a direct relationship exists between the evolution of the brain, its structure and stratification, and the development of personality.

Remplein: Personality Strata

Heinz Remplein (1956) has been singled out as a representative of this orientation because his approach is essentially a biological one. Remplein's theory of development follows closely a genetic concept of brain development. Innate dispositions determine the direction of development. They also determine the limits of influence that environmental forces can have on the development of personality. The lowest layer of personality, involving dispositions which are necessary for survival, is the most resistant to environmental influences. Those innate dispositions of development which are part of the higher layers of personality reflect the newer layers of the brain and are more open to environmental pressures.

Remplein emphasizes the need for psychological development to follow the structure of layers of personality and hypothesizes that premature pushing beyond the developmental levels expected may lead to such negative consequences as an arrest in development since the psychological energies are used up too early.

In Remplein's system, the lowest layer of personality consists of those psychological processes that are related to the body functions which preserve life, in body needs for comfort, and in the psychological functions that are closely related to body organs. The second layer of personality is the endothermic stratum which is the seat of emotions. The third and highest layer of personality is the personal stratum which is represented by ego functions, e.g., cognition and volition. This layer of personality organizes and directs the elements of the lower layers into specific forms of behavior.

Following closely his biological model, Remplein does not consider developmental change as continuous, but rather as the superimposition of new layers on older ones. The old layers do retain some autonomy, even though the conscious functioning of the individual is dominated by the new layers. A developmental source of maladjustment may result from a failure of the newly developing strata to integrate properly with the older one. This hierarchical process of integration is particularly vulnerable to maladjustment during the transition from early to middle childhood and from middle childhood to adolescence. These periods of transition are characterized by negativism. The first period of negativism occurs between two and four and involves the integration of the two lower personal strata (the vital needs stratum, and the endothemic stratum). This integration must occur before their subordination to the newly rising personal stratum. The child becomes conscious of his ability for self-determination and, through negativism, he facilitates the process by which the personal stratum acquires dominance over the two lower psychic strata.

The second period of negativism occurs during the transition from middle childhood to adolescence, that is, from ten to thirteen years of age. Changes in endocrinological secretion, brought about by the onset of puberty, lead to a resurgence of new drives. These take the form of adventure-seeking and the acting out of sexual and aggressive urges. The adolescent experiences these resurging drives as a desire for self-determination and independence while his environment perceives them as forms of negativism and rebellion. In reality, this negative phase, like its earlier forerunner, represents a transition which makes possible a new integration between the strata of personality (e.g., sexual impulse emanating from the lowest strata and love emanating from the second strata). In addition, there is a renewed attempt of the third personal strata to assert its leadership on a higher level of psychological functioning than was previously possible.

Since these periods of negativism are necessary for the restructuring of relationships between the strata of personality, it is important to be tolerant of the emotional instability, disobedience, and exaggerated self-assertion that are characteristic of these transitional periods in normal development.

Psychological Theories

We have selected Oswald Kroh, Edward Spranger, and Kurt Lewin as representatives of the psychological approach in the study of adolescence. Their theories represent a movement away from biological models. In spite of differences between these theorists, they all share a focal interest in the psychological processes as the central factor in adolescent development. Specifically, these three theorists concentrate on various aspects of experience, such as consciousness, perception values, inner conflict, and stress. They all build their theories on the basis of their study of individual human experience rather than on the structure of the brain.

Kroh: Phase Structure

Oswald Kroh's (1951) approach resembles, in some ways, the formulations of personality stratification theorists. In fact, his work and writings have influenced the thinking of Remplein. Kroh broke away from using the structure and evolution of the human brain as a model for his theory of psychological development. He was primarily concerned with the psychological aspects of consciousness at different stages of development. Kroh advanced the concept of *phase structure* which emphasized the wholeness of personality along the lines of Gestalt theory. Kroh's influence on Zeller can be seen in the latter's concept of body gestalt which was discussed earlier in this chapter.

Kroh formulated two major developmental trends. The first trend referred to the expansion of the child's concept of the world. In this, Kroh comes closer to Heinz Werner's (1940) concept of physiognomic perception. At first, the child expresses magical thoughts concerning objects in the external world. This is followed by a period of a more realistic perception of the world beginning with the elementary school years. The onset of adolescence marks the emergence of a theoretical view of the world which enables the individual to reach a deeper understanding of life. The second developmental trend bears some similarity to

Piaget's formulations. This developmental trend extends from reflex action to motor control and purposeful action, followed by foresight and planning, and finally reaches the point of causal cognition and creative production (see the chapters by Gallagher and by Piers).

Kroh was the originator of the idea of negativistic periods which separate the three main stages of development from one another. His formulations on the nature and function of negativism during transitional periods have been taken over by Remplein.

Spranger: Value Hierarchy

Edward Spranger (1955) also dissociates himself from biological speculations in formulating his theory of adolescence. He is entirely committed to a psychology of understanding which does not deny certain effects of endocrinological change, but maintains that psychological change cannot be explained by physiological states. Moreover, he proposes that the methods employed to study psychological change are not the same as the methods employed by natural science to investigate physiological change. His methodological approach is one of understanding rather than of causal explanation and prediction. Spranger emphasizes the totality of the psychic structure. This is more akin to Gestalt psychology and phenomenological psychology than to the structural psychology of Wundt and Titchener.

Adolescence is conceived of as a period of transition during which a hierarchy of values is established. This hierarchy of values is the basis of Spranger's theory of personality types. Differences in the value hierarchy will effect different patterns of change. Spranger distinguishes three such patterns of adolescent development. The first pattern consists of radical and dramatic changes which accompany a shift in the individual's perception of himself. The second pattern refers to a slow and continuous change in which the individual gradually adopts cultural values that are held by his society without basic alteration in his personality. The third pattern refers to a growth process in which the adolescent achieves his goals through self-discipline and active efforts.

The discovery of the ego as a self is a central concept in Spranger's formulation of structural change during adolescence. The ego is now experienced by the adolescent as separate from the external world. The result is in feelings of loneliness and a heightened need to experiment with the newly discovered self in the adolescent's search for a life plan and a definite identity. The adolescent begins to examine previously unquestioned ideas and relationships. This may result in rebellion against institutionalized traditions of society. It may also result in an increased need for social recognition and new interpersonal relationships. The predominance of one or another of these trends will be determined by the value hierarchy or typology that characterizes an individual adolescent.

Although Spranger had due regard for influences of social and environmental conditions on adolescent development, he was concerned primarily with inner determinants and with the individual's experience and perception. Spranger is essentially a phenomenologist for whom the primary task of the psychologist is the study of the content and structure of inner experience. In this he shared the preoccupation of a third important theorist, Lewin. Lewin's approach is also essentially psychological and phenomenological, although environmental determinants played a larger role in his theorizing than in Spranger's.

Lewin: Field Theory

Kurt Lewin (1935, 1939, 1948) was more interested in analyzing the subjective world of the adolescent than in the individual differences between adolescents. He applied his concepts of field theory to accomplish this task. The basic psychological law of field theory is that behavior (B) is a function (F) of the person (P) and of his environment (E) or $B=F(PE)$. The sum of all interacting environmental and personal factors is called the life space or the psychological space. Within the life space, there are positive and negative goals to which the individual feels either attracted or repelled. These goals are called *valences*. An individual moves either toward or away from the goals in his life space, and this movement is termed *locomotion*. A very important variable in this conceptual framework is the existence of barriers that interfere with the individual's locomotion and with his reaching his goals.

According to Lewin, the life space of the child depends on the stage of his development. The growing child is increasingly able to distinguish between the real and the unreal, hopes and realistic expectations, and falsehood and truth. Thus, a result of increased differentiation is the growing organization of the child's life space.

Several conditions in the development of a child will affect the degree of structure and organization of the child's life space. If the parents do not provide a sufficient amount of structure for the child in the early stages of development, his personality will lack integration. However, as the child grows older and as his life space becomes more differentiated, he needs freedom to advance into new regions and to have new experiences. Thus a reduction in the amount of direction as well as in the restrictions legislated by the parents is indicated.

Rate of change is a second condition that will affect the degree of increasing differentiation in the developing child. If change is gradual, it will facilitate organization. If changes are rapid and sudden, they are likely to result in periods of stress and crisis. Adolescence is characterized

by relatively rapid change in the structure of the life space and, therefore, results in stress and in disorganization within the life space. Lewin
does not attribute the stress which results from biological changes during
puberty to the amount of change that takes place objectively, but rather
to the central position of the body in the life space of an individual.
Thus, it is the subjective meaning of the body to the adolescent that
determines for him many of the consequences of the perceived changes in
the body at the time of puberty.

A third condition that will affect differentiation is the presence of
conflicting forces at various points in development. The conflicting forces
may originate in the child's organism, or in the environment as the child
perceives it. The analysis of the heightening of conflicting forces during
adolescence forms an important basis for Lewin's approach to the understanding of adolescence. For example, if the child has been highly
dependent on his family, then cultural demands for increased self-
sufficiency at puberty will conflict with the dependency, and puberty will
be experienced as a period of violent change. Another source of conflict
and stress for the adolescent in our society results from the ambiguous
way in which he is treated by adults. For instance, certain childish forms
of behavior and goals which still have strong positive valences for him are
no longer accepted as appropriate by adult society. However, the adolescent is not permitted to replace these childish behaviors with adult forms
of behavior such as driving a car, drinking liquor, and having sexual
relations which also have strong positive valences.

Lewin has compared the marginal position of the adolescent in
transition to the position of a minority group member who tries to dissociate himself from his background and to enter the majority group.
The adolescent wishes to dissociate himself from his childhood background and to enter the adult society which he perceives as the powerful
majority group. If the minority group member is only partly successful in
establishing relationships with the privileged group, he becomes a marginal man in both groups. This applies equally to the experiences of the
adolescent. Both are plagued by an increased amount of emotional
tension, and both are extremely sensitive to the shortcomings of the
background from which they try to dissociate themselves.

Lewin offers certain interesting formulations concerning the ideological instability and extremism that often characterize adolescents. The
adolescent experiences an expansion of his life space which is accompanied by uncertainty and by conflicting pressures, and therefore has the
consequences of emotional and ideological instability. Moreover, in
taking a radical position with regard to social ideology, the adolescent
moves through fewer regions than the adult. This is so because the perception of the political arena is much more differentiated for the adult
than it is for the adolescent. The adolescent distinguishes only between

the left and the right, whereas the adult distinguishes more steps between the extreme right and the extreme left. The ease with which adolescents take extreme positions is also a function of the lack of differentiation in the adolescent's political ideology compared to the differentiation that exists in the political life space of the adult individual. On this point, the Block, Haan, and Smith chapter within this book will be of interest to the reader. Still another reason for the adolescent being an easy prey for ideological extremists comes from changes in the fantasy-reality balance in development. The adolescent is increasingly under greater pressure from the adult society to relinquish his "lack of realism" in favor of the reality of the adult world. This often has the consequence of accentuating the conflict of the real with the ideal and of leading to an intensive desire of the adolescent to structure, or rather to overstructure, his field of values and ideals. It may account for the readiness of the adolescent to follow anyone who offers a definite pattern of values. Extremists, of course, have the least doubt and the least self-criticism with regard to the values they hold.

Lewin's position with regard to adolescence may be summed up as follows: The adolescent phase of development involves a widening of the life space, especially socially, and in time perspective. This change has the consequence of a sharp decrease in cognitive structure. The adolescent has less direction as well as more conflicting pressures for his behavior than either the child or the adult in our society. The adolescent occupies a position between the child and the adult similar to a marginal member of an underprivileged minority group in our society. Puberty, as a new experience of the adolescent with his own body, can be represented as a baffling change of a central region in the established life space. From these three postulated characteristics of adolescence follow certain predictions concerning social behavior and emotional experiences. The adolescent will be overly sensitive and will fluctuate between extremes of shyness and aggressiveness. The adolescent will experience extreme conflict between social and moral values, between ideologies, and between different styles of living. Finally, the experience of conflict will set up tensions which will throw the adolescent into positions of extreme attitudes and actions.

Psychosocial and Sociological Theories

The psychological theorists discussed in the previous section, particularly Lewin, did not ignore the importance of the social environment as a determinant of adolescent development. They merely placed their emphasis on intrapersonal psychological processes and on experience. Similarly, the social psychologist does not ignore or neglect the importance of personality mechanisms and intrapsychic factors. However, his emphasis is on the influence of the social environment and on the role of the interacting processes between the adolescent and his society.

Davis: Socialization

We find the concept of socialization the key concept employed by Allison Davis (1944). Davis approaches adolescent development as being a continuous process of social reinforcement and punishment. Society designates behavior as acceptable by reinforcing or rewarding it and designates other behavior as unacceptable by punishing it. Anticipation or fear of punishment, after repeated experiences, brings about "socialized anxiety," which then becomes a key factor in the socialization process. Socialized anxiety functions as a tool for the individual in his attempt to adapt to the demands of his culture. Once the child develops this anxiety, he will acquire behavior which mitigates or reduces it. It should be noted that socialized anxiety is different from neurotic anxiety since neurotic anxiety is irrational and not adaptive. Similarly, if socialized anxiety is too strong, or too intensive, it will have an inhibiting and disorganizing effect.

Society defines what goals, values, and behaviors are acceptable and to be acquired. In our society, socialized anxiety increases with the onset of adolescence, particularly in a middle-class youth. This is because he faces increased demands from society to accept social responsibilities and because society asks him to delay and generalize the gratification of such pressing needs as sex and aggression. With this increased pressure, and with the heightening of socialized anxiety, the adolescent becomes aware of the values of his culture and depends increasingly upon social acceptance, prestige, and status.

Lower-class adolescents have different experiences in the areas of gratifying sex and aggression. The basic difference in the lower-class adolescent is that he does not develop the socialized anxiety which, in turn, motivates him to achieve and to postpone immediate gratification for the sake of long-range goals. Amos and Wellford consider this point in their chapter on "The Culturally Disadvantaged Adolescent." Moreover, the lower-class adolescent learns that he is not likely to receive symbolic rewards such as status and social acceptance for inhibiting sexual and aggressive behavior.

Havighurst: Developmental Task

While Davis was primarily concerned with the role of social anxiety in adolescent development, Robert Havighurst (1951) formulated and investigated the concept of developmental tasks. These tasks are defined in relationship to those goals and criteria which society expects fulfilled or met at the different stages of development. Developmental tasks can be defined, then, as the skills, knowledge, and attitudes which a child has to acquire at successive points in his development. The mastery of these tasks depends on physical maturation, as well as on personal effort. Developmental anxiety is a motivational and reinforcement process which facilitates the acquisition and mastery of developmental tasks. The mastery of developmental tasks on any one age level prepares the individual for mastering new tasks at the next age level. Havighurst suggests that failure in a given developmental task will result in maladjustment, social disapproval, increased anxiety, and subsequently greater difficulty in mastering future tasks. Each developmental task has its critical period within which it must be learned. This emphasis by Havighurst should remind us of the formulations by the theorists of the German school. In particular, Kroh and the personality stratification theorists come to mind. However, Havighurst places a greater emphasis on the socializing agents and upon the methods of reinforcement which society uses in an attempt to help the individual at a given age level. He also emphasizes the cultural relativity that determines the nature of the developmental tasks. The more dominant the cultural element of the task is (over the biological element), the more likely it will differ from culture to culture.

Havighurst defines developmental tasks for each level. For adolescence, he defines such tasks as accepting one's physique and sex role, relations with peers of both sexes, emotional independence of parents, partial attainment of economic independence, making vocational choices, acquiring intellectual competence and socially responsible behavior, preparing for marriage and family life, and the building of values which are in harmony with the world picture of the society to which the adolescent belongs.

Sociological Theory

Sociological theories of adolescence focus clearly on social institutions and on the position of the individual in society; that is, on the adolescent's role and his status as the determiners of his development. Even though sociological theory is at the other end of the biological-social dimension, it is interesting to note that sociologists pay considerable attention to the interacting effects of biological, physical, and social factors in adolescent development. The same cannot be said for biological theorists who deal much less systematically with the social environment as a determinant of developmental change.

Kingsley Davis: Sociological Theory

We have selected Kingsley Davis (1960) as a representative advocate of sociological theory. Davis maintains that, in a complex Western society, adolescence represents a phase of development in which physical maturation and mental maturity move far ahead of social maturity. In terms of physical strength and mental capacity, full maturity is attained shortly after puberty.

Socially, the adolescent has a long way to go before he reaches a mature status. In most societies, power and status are dependent on social position and experience rather than on brute strength or even on mental capacity. However, social position and experience come with middle or old age rather than with adolescence. Thus, despite his physical or even mental equality to his elders, the adolescent is placed in a socially subordinate position. This presents a source of conflict between the generations. It is probable that the learning process would have a better chance if physical and mental maturity would come between thirty and thirty-five years of age instead of between fifteen and twenty years of age. As it is, especially in modern society, the individual must keep on learning after his capacity to do so has begun to decline. Knowledge, judgment, insight, and self-reliance are generally far from their peak when mental capacity has already reached its peak. In a physical sense, society does not utilize its great men until they are past their prime. However, in a social sense, society does utilize its men at the peak of their administrative or sociological maturity. That is to say, it utilizes them when they have hopefully accumulated the greatest know-how for making political decisions of far-reaching consequences.

From a sociological point of view, adolescence is the phase of development in which the lag of social development behind physical development first becomes pronounced. From this point of view, one might anticipate that as society becomes more complex, the lag will become greater and adolescence will be prolonged further into organic adulthood. Specifically, the position of adolescence is determined sociologically by four factors: occupational placement, reproductive control, authority organization, and cultural acquisition.

Occupational Placement. Selection of individuals for occupational placement may be made by conscription or by choice. If the selection is made by choice, it follows that the earlier the choice is made, the more intensive can be the training. The later the choice is made, the more it may rest on an accurate evaluation of personal talent and preference (see Hackman's chapter on vocational counseling with the adolescent). The more complex societies defer the final decisions until adolescence and provide most of the specialized training during that period. Primitive societies need not defer the decision until adolescence. They can make their choice much earlier and provide the training during childhood because division of labor is so slight. If training starts early, as is the case in a simple society, and extends through childhood, adolescence will not stand out occupationally as a period of any particular importance. By the time the individual reaches adolescence, he is practicing his occupation and is accepted by his society as an adult. If, on the other hand—as is the case in a complex society—occupational choice and training is centered in adolescence, the strain in this phase of development will be greater. Finally, if standards for occupational status are determined by achievement in the culture is raised, but the status of the adolescent is lowered by putting him at the bottom rung. This makes adolescence a period of strain and, in some societies, a period of deprivation.

Reproductive Control. In every society, reproductive capacity first appears at the inception of adolescence. However, the control of reproduction and of sexual behavior is exercised differently in different societies. Each society is confronted with three basic questions concerning reproduction and sexual gratification. First, whether the adolescent shall be permitted to enter normal heterosexual intercourse, or whether he should be forced or encouraged to postpone such behavior. Second, whether marriage should be permitted with the onset of sexual maturation. Third, whether marriage should be the result of free choice or whether it should be controlled by others. Also, should marriage establish a separate household or one that is merely an extension of the parental ménage? This last question is an issue which primitive and modern societies face together. Until recently, one common characteristic was shared by most societies. The adolescent was permitted to exercise both his sexual and reproductive functions; however, society carefully controlled the exercise of these functions.

In our society, the ideal of premarital chastity is upheld. The postponement of marriage, as well as the independence and separateness of the wedded couple, is also advocated. The adolescent is permitted to associate closely with the opposite sex, but is put on his honor to remain virtuous. The adolescent is permitted to choose his own mate independently, but his or her parents retain veto rights in many areas. Both Juhasz and Staton discuss these problems in separate chapters, so we will not consider them further here. Of course, the competitive struggle for status in the occupational area also gets entangled with the competitive system in the courtship and dating area. This does little to lessen the problems of the adolescent period.

Authoritarian Organization. The next major sociological issue concerning adolescence is that of the child's emancipation from the authority of his family. In our society, adolescents believe that obtaining a job and becoming married entitles a person to independence. In other societies, the authority of parents continues after adolescence, and adolescence does not stand out as a significant period of change in an individual's relationship to authority. In our society, in the absence of publicly accepted practices for emancipation from authority, wide individual variations exist from family to family and each family must settle the matter in its own way. In many instances the adolescent craves the protection of his family, but he rebels against its authority. He is torn by the conflict of dreading to leave the careless existence of childhood and of accepting the burdensome responsibility of adult life. The nature of this conflict and its possible consequences were discussed in some detail in the presentation of Lewin's theory. This whole issue will be taken up again when we turn to the psychoanalytic theory of adolescence.

Let us examine more closely some of the sociological determinants of the conflict between parental authority and adolescence. One of these determinants is the rate of social change. The more rapid the social and technological change in a society, the greater will be the difference in the cultural content experienced by two different generations at the same stage of development. The parent learns that his adolescent experiences are outdated when he assumes the responsibility of transmitting his background experience to his own child. The problem of cultural lag, on the parents' part, is aggravated in modern society by the fact that the child is exposed to competing authorities. Professional educators usually teach ideas which are in advance of their own culture, and, thereby, they widen the intellectual gap between parent and child.

It is interesting to raise the question as to why parental authority generates so much more conflict than other institutions of authority. One of the factors determining this difference is that society defines clearly those selective areas in which it assumes authority. In contrast, parental authority includes most aspects of a child's life. Often parents are glad to relinquish their authority over the adolescent child and to grant him independence. However, a child's social status is identified with parental status, and parental status is socially identified with the child's conduct. Therefore, parents often wish to insure proper conduct on the part of their offspring by prolonging parental authority.

A related phenomenon bearing on adolescent conflict is the combination of *concentration and dispersion* that characterizes our family system. The smallness of the family unit in our society makes for intensity of family feelings. Most of the day's schedule takes place outside the home and this makes for dispersion of activities. This dispersion of activities away from home isolates and increases the intensity of the affectional bonds within the home. The major share of the family sentiment is directed toward a few individuals who are so important to emotional satisfaction that complexes easily develop. There is less sentiment to go around, and, therefore, we are left with youth who are emotionally deprived.

Cultural Acquisition. A fourth issue that defines the adolescent period is that of cultural acquisition. The more primitive the culture, the earlier the child can be taught its rudiments. Highly civilized societies require specialized educational establishments. The universal and specialized school system, as we know it, becomes a necessity. However, the school system concentrates on teaching abstractions which are often divorced from the facts and experiences of real life. Thus, the adolescent emerges from his school with knowledge which does not help him to handle concrete everyday situations. This incongruence tends to produce problems of motivation. The existence of the long interval of time between learning and its vocational application also contributes to the problem of academic motivation. Davis (1960) suggests certain modifications in the school system which would reduce the problem it currently produces. The school system should make greater efforts to introduce inventions of new educational technology and to overhaul the incentive mechanism. For example, recent methods of improving reading habits may shorten the absorption of the same amount of knowledge.

The current incentive mechanisms might be greatly improved by introducing vocational and occupational training earlier. This would permit the adolescent to carry out rewarding functions in society simultaneously with his continued schooling.

Psychoanalytic Theory

Psychoanalytic theory is being presented separately because it cannot be put into any one of the previous headings without distortion. Biological, psychological, and social processes and concepts occupy equally central positions. In its early stages, psychoanalytic theory was heavily weighted toward biological factors and evolutionary ideas. Very early in its development, however, the clash between the biological-constitutional versus the social-environmental orientation was worked out by two psychoanalytic theorists who broke away and developed their own theories. Of course I am referring to Carl Jung and Alfred Adler. The former went in the direction of extreme emphasis on a constitutional typology and evolutionary recapitulation of human experience, whereas the latter elevated the family and other social factors to a position of central importance. As psychoanalysis developed, Freud (1936) himself shifted toward a greater emphasis on external reality. Later, Anna Freud (1948), in her concern with the educational process and particularly with defense mechanisms of the ego, anticipated the developments of ego psychology. Finally, studies in cultural anthropology carried out by psychoanalysts such as Abraham Kardiner (1939) and Erik Erikson (1950, 1959) have elevated culture and environment to central positions in psychoanalytic theory.

Infantile Sexuality

For many centuries, and until relatively recently, it was assumed that puberty marked the onset of sexuality. With the advent of Sigmund Freud (1953) the concept of infantile sexuality and of psychosexual development replaced the traditional concept of puberty. Infantile sexuality refers to those pleasurable experiences which are associated with the stimulation and gratification of the basic needs relating to food intake, elimination, and genital excitement. These occur prior to the onset of puberty. The organization and course of infantile sexuality during early and middle childhood determine how adolescence is experienced and expressed. Briefly, some of the structural formations of childhood may be described as follows.

Early Childhood

The psychic apparatus of the infant is dominated by the pleasure-pain principle. The dominance of this principle diminishes as a result of two important factors. First, as the infant develops trust in his mother's ability to allay his tensions, he becomes correspondingly less dominated. The second factor is the child's growing control over internal tension and his mastery of the stimulation from his external environment. This process contributes to a shift in the child's position from passivity to activity. The child learns to manipulate others and the physical world to gain his own ends.

The child's feelings of self-confidence derived from his mastery and from his shift to an active position are absorbed in the next phase of development, namely, the phallic phase. This is particularly true in the boy, in whom they take on the form of exaggerated fantasies of power. During the phallic phase, the child begins to develop fantasies of possession and intimacy toward the parent of the opposite sex; this period is the oedipal stage. The oedipal conflict is wrought with sexual and aggressive wishes that take on frightening proportions. The child resolves this conflict between forbidden impulses and authority by identifying with the authority figure and thereby erecting a built-in censor of his own forbidden impulses. This is the beginning of conscience and super-ego. The experience of this conflict and its resolution usher in the period of middle childhood which has been called the latency period.

Middle Childhood

The particular importance of the latency period for adolescence is the sharp increase on control over the impulses which occur during this period. The increased control is facilitated by the development of a conscience based on the internalization of, and the identification with, parental authority. With it, the child's respect for law and order assumes a dominant place. The internalization of parental authority has another consequence as well. The child's dependence on parental praise and approval for feelings of self-worth is replaced by those inner sources of assurance which we call self-esteem. Another important consequence is the child's greater independence from the parent. As a result of this greater independence, the child is less likely to be frustrated by the parent, and this lessens his mood fluctuations and produces more emotional stability.

The formation of the superego and the strengthening of the ego represent an increased differentiation of the personality. It is further facilitated by a separation of verbal and motor expression. This in turn permits rapid strides forward in the development of language and symbolic activity. This differentiation is particularly important in enabling the child to tolerate conflicting demands from within as well as from the external environment.

As mentioned earlier, the mother-child relationship is important for the development of the structural formations of childhood that survive and determine the course of adolescence. At first, the infant experiences both parents as dispensers of comfort or frustration. Mother's role is not primarily feminine, but rather that of an active person. The child is in a passive position of getting or not getting. By identifying with his mother as a source of nurturance, the child acquires not only some independence, but also some of his mother's active position.

For the boy, the mother continues through childhood to be the object of his affection. What changes in the little boy is his position from passive receptivity to active mastery. The latter reaches its first peak in the phallic phase of development. Here the little boy identifies his power with masculinity. Excessive masturbation, which may arise both during this period and in puberty, is interpreted as a defense against regressing to a passive position. The boy discovers sex differences, and in his fantasy he interprets the difference as an injury to the opposite sex. Psychoanalytic theory relates this interpretation to the contempt and fear with which our culture treats femininity in boys. The male's contemptuous attitude toward the female sex often harbors his deep-seated fear of regressing to his earlier passive receptive position in infancy. The boy's identification with his father helps him to combat this fear. Identification with the father is facilitated by the fear consequences of the boy's rivalry with his father for the affection of his mother. The fear is resolved by identifying with the father. These changes toward masculine identity-formation, or a failure of such changes and an alternative course of regression to a passive position, are of utmost importance as a background for the developmental trends which occur during adolescence.

The formation of feminine identity is different and equally important for the adolescent phase. At first, the girl shares with the boy a passive position toward her mother as a provider. When the girl enters a phase of independence and of an active position, unlike the boy, she not only changes her position toward her mother, but she also changes her love object from mother to father. Her continued identification with the mother as a provider will reinforce her active position and will conflict with the girl's imitation of her mother's passive position toward her father. The active position the girl takes persists for a long time throughout childhood. There are very strong psychological, social, and practical reasons for the persistence of this active position. The little girl is greatly rewarded for being self-sufficient; she envies boys for their physique and status; a girl is not criticized as much for being a tomboy as a boy is criticized for being a sissy; the active position is a satisfying one to any child regardless of his sex; finally, the role of the woman is that of a nurturant-giving person which certainly entails an active position. It is not until much later in the course of development that the girl begins to take a passive position toward men and to identify more fully with her mother in the mother's passive position toward the father. Thus, we find that the course of the development of masculine identity for boys is simpler than the development of the feminine identity for girls. The boy not only retains the same love object (the mother), he also develops in one direction, namely from passivity to activity. The girl, on the other hand, changes from a passive to an active position, then back again to a passive position. The latter must differ considerably from the early infantile passivity shared by boys and girls alike. These, then, are the structural formations of childhood which survive into adolescence.

Adolescence

At the onset of adolescence, both boys and girls give signs of experiencing stress and of giving up some of the accomplishments in education and social conformity that were achieved during the latency period. The degree and direction of regression will have common elements. It will also be greatly affected by preadolescent development, as outlined, up to this point. The adolescent manifests not only regressive tendencies but also a variety of defensive maneuvers to ward off the regressive pull.

An important development at the onset of adolescence, as seen by psychoanalytic theory, is the moving away from the love objects of early childhood. This is a continuation of the move in the same direction which occurred during latency. A certain amount of affection becomes liberated as a result of the dissociation from early love objects and goes in search of new love objects outside the family. With it occurs a weakening of the parental authority which formed the backbone for superego development. This weakening of the superego is further reflected in feelings of loneliness, inner turmoil, and depressed moods. Adolescence has been described as a phase in which mourning and being in love dominate the affective life of the young person. The rebellion against, and separation from, the parent involves a real loss and results in experiences of emptiness, grief, and sadness which are a part of all mourning. The working through of such mourning is an important task of adolescence.

Friendship acquires an enormous importance for adolescent boys and girls. Not only do friendships gain in importance but they also acquire a new quality, namely, an idealization of the friend. The idealized image of the friend supplements the earlier idealized image of the parent. The relationship between the loss of early love objects and the formation of intensive relationships, such as friendships and crushes during adolescence, can be seen in the reactions to the loss of an idealized friend when such a disappointment or loss results in depressions or in going on eating binges. The fact that these relationships are often transitory and of short duration betrays an ulterior purpose of these friendships. The friendship has been a search for a replacement of the abandoned parent.

Heterosexual Relationships. Now, turning to heterosexual relationships, psychoanalytic theory points to striking differences between boys and girls in their reactions to the opposite sex at the onset of puberty. The boy first turns away from heterosexuality and escapes into his male peer groups. He is preoccupied with defending himself against regressive tendencies and the feared consequences of such tendencies. The girl does not react in the same way at the onset of puberty. She goes through a stage of exaggerating her active position in life without turning away from heterosexuality. In contrast to the boy, her defense against regression (to an infantile passive position and to infantile sexuality) is an exaggeration of heterosexual interest and experience. She does not assume a feminine role, but acts as the active, aggressive partner in the pseudo-love game. Related to this turn of events is the fact that girls mature more rapidly than boys during this period and experience more violent and painful changes in their physiological functioning. Evidence from psychoanalytic therapy on the adolescent acting-out of girls suggests that the excessive active and aggressive role in the frantic attempt to relate to men represents an overcompensation in the adolescent girl. This is a counter against the strong regressive pull to be fondled in the same passive manner as the infantile girl was fondled by her mother. Instances of adolescent infatuation with much older men may represent a giving in to this regressive pull.

Defense Mechanisms. As indicated earlier, the adolescent employs a variety of defensive maneuvers in his reaction to the inner impoverishment he experiences, and to other sources of stress and conflict. One fairly common defensive reaction consists of a self-induced heightening of ego states. In this category belongs self-induced exertion. Pain and exhaustion are fairly common phenomena among adolescents. These self-induced ego states of affective and sensory intensity allow the adolescent to experience a heightened sense of self. They enable the adolescent to discharge tension which comes from the stress and conflict he experiences.

Sometimes specific defenses against anxiety and conflict function under an umbrella of a socially accepted form of behavior. An example of this may be seen in the sharing of a code of behavior which permits the adolescent to divorce his feelings from his actions. This may occur because the behavior is public and because he does not have to take the responsibility for it. Under such circumstances, the adolescent can act out, without having any strong feelings about his action. The specific defense mechanisms hidden in this type of socially sanctioned acting out are denial and isolation. The adolescent denies his feelings and isolates feeling and awareness. He is fully aware of what he does without having any feelings. Conversely, due to his submerging himself in the peer code, he may experience feelings of anger or act aggressively without any awareness of what the source and target of his anger is, or without awareness of the aggressive consequences of his behavior.

The Peer Group and Social Belonging. Erikson (1959) points toward the positive value of the gang for the adolescent and the ways in which the clique helps the adolescent form his ego identity. The adolescent who rebels against the dominance of his parents, against the dominance of their value system and their intrusion into his life, has a desperate need for social belonging. The peer group and the gang help the adolescent find his own identity. The adolescent relies on his peers for comfort by stereotyping himself at a time when his body image changes radically and when he is confronted with pressures which threaten to overwhelm him. This is one of the reasons why totalitarian systems are so attractive to the adolescent. They supply convincing and suitable identifications. Democratic identity involves freedom of choice and does not supply an identity as readily. The democratic group requires that the person have sufficient ego identity to tolerate ambiguity. The adolescent who has to question his own identity at every moment welcomes membership in the totalitarian peer group which relieves him of his painful search and provides emotional crutches until he can learn to stand on his own two feet.

Erik Erikson: Identity Formation and Adolescence

We have mentioned the name of Erik Erikson several times. It is now appropriate to consider his theory in greater detail. Erikson has taken the Freudian position and considered it in the light of anthropological cultural research. His major focus has been on the process by which the individual develops his ego identity. As we know, when puberty is reached, the individual's body grows rapidly and sexual maturity arrives on the scene (see Garrison's chapter). This may present problems for the adolescent, as his self-image may be in conflict with his views of the perceptions of others. Erikson believes that, for the youth of today, the development of one's ego identity has largely replaced the theme of sexuality that was so prevalent at the time of Freud. This is not to deny the importance of one's developing sexuality but rather that it is subsumed within the process of establishing the concept of self. For the adolescent this is accomplished initially through identification with popular figures such as movie stars, sports figures and representatives of youth movements. His own peer group is then used to find his identity within a social context. Erikson (1950) believes that there are eight stages through which each of us moves in our search for ego identity and that our progress depends on the satisfactory resolution of each of the previous stages. For example we begin with the stage of Trust versus Mistrust. The next stage is Autonomy versus Shame and Doubt, and so forth. The interested reader may wish to turn to the writings of Erikson himself (1950, 1959) or to read an excellent short presentation by Muuss (1962). In addition, the description of Spranger's theory that was given earlier in this chapter will give insight into Erikson, as Spranger was influential in the development of Erikson's thinking.

The total thrust of one's life, according to Erikson, is in the process of establishing ego identity. In childhood the relationships with parents are most important. In adolescence the focus moves to identification with peers and other important persons; and in early adulthood it moves to the area of vocational decisions and the falling in love. During these periods of life, the individual continually revises and redefines who he is or who he *perceives* himself to be. Satisfactory resolution of this task produces the healthy or adjusted individual. Conflict or unsatisfactory resolutions along the path to adulthood contribute to maladjustment. Block, Haan, and Smith discuss Erikson at some length in their chapter on activism and apathy at the collegiate level, and the introductory chapter by Adams will give the reader additional insights into the adolescent who is going through the process of identity formation. Hamachek's chapter on the development of the adolescent self, considered from the framework of Erikson's theory, will be particularly instructive.

Contributions and Modifications in the Theory of Identification and Identity Formation

As we have seen, psychoanalytic theory emphasizes the importance of the active and passive position of the mother, the formation of affectionate bonds between the child and his parents, and ensuing conflicts over rivalry. It also emphasizes ambivalent feelings, and fear of the consequences of infantile sexual and aggressive fantasies as essential processes influencing the direction of sexual development in both boys and girls. The emphasis in these formulations has been on intrapsychic processes, particularly of the developing child. Similarly, these formulations concentrated on the child's perception of parental roles and on changes in the child's identification with his or her perceived role of the parent. An important contribution to these formulations has come from recent attempts to conceptualize parental roles with greater emphasis on differences in actual, rather than merely perceived, parental role functioning. Theory and research have also gained through a further breakdown of the process of identification and identity formation into identification in areas which are relevant or unrelated to sex typing. A third contribution has come from a reformulation of the concept identification so as to make this concept more amenable to sociological and anthropological theory and research. This last attempt involved the notion of status envy as an essential process of identification and the distinction between attributed, subjective, and desired identity as a way of making the concept of identity less global and thereby more useful for precise formulation and research.

Expressive and Instrumental Role Functioning. Parsons (1958) considered the masculine role to be essentially instrumental and the feminine role to be essentially expressive. Instrumental role functioning is task-oriented rather than person-oriented. Expressive role functioning is oriented toward interpersonal attitudes and feelings, toward making and eliciting emotional responses in the immediate social interaction. Parsons proposes further distinction between fathers and mothers, in that fathers are capable of engaging in both instrumental and expressive roles while mothers are more committed to expressive role functioning. This distinction was further elaborated by Johnson (1963), who hypothesized that the mother is essentially expressive toward her sons and daughters during their first phase of identification in the life cycle. The second phase of the child's identification is determined by the father, who behaves differently towards daughter and son. The father rewards the daughter's expressive role functioning by commending her for being attractive and relating to her, essentially, in an affectionate context. In contrast, the father may make demands of his sons and stress an achievement orientation much earlier than with his daughter. This formulation implies that identification with the father will facilitate the development of appropriate sex roles in both boys and girls (i.e., masculine instrumental role functioning in boys and expressive role functioning in girls).

Parental versus Sex Role Identification. Regardless of the nature of the parent's own role identification, a child may identify with parental characteristics which are relevant to sex role functioning and with other parental characteristics which are not relevant to sex role functioning. Thus, a child may be strongly identified with parental functioning of the same or opposite sex without having internalized an appropriate or inappropriate sex role model. Moreover, the solidification of a child's sex role identity depends not only on the parent but also on the responses and expectations of other adults as well as peers in the child's culture.

A further complication in the relationship between parental identification and sex role identity comes from the parent's own sex role identity. For example, if the parent's own sex role identification is opposite to that of his or her own sex, the child's identification with the same sex parent will result in an inappropriate sex role identity formation.

Lynn (1966) points to another distinction which has important implications for the development of sex role identity. Although boys do not interact as much with fathers as with their mothers, boys develop a strong masculine identity. This results from the fact that the attitudes and activities which characterize a masculine role are communicated to the boy by other representatives of society and by cultural media. Moreover, boys receive rewards for typical masculine role behavior, and criticism or ridicule for attitudes and behaviors which are generally associated with feminine roles.

The fact that mothers interact more frequently and in more concrete situations with their children led Lynn to predict that both girls and boys will be more identified with those personality characteristics of their mothers which are culturally neutral with reference to sex typing. Concomitantly both boys and girls will be less identified with neutral characteristics of their fathers' personalities than of their mothers' personalities.

The development of masculine and feminine identity have each their own complexities and conflicts. Boys have to change first from their identification with mother to a masculine identification. In contemporary Western culture this change is complicated by the fact that the boy has to learn his masculine role largely in the absence of a concrete model, his father. Yet the culture punishes a child in a variety of direct and indirect ways for behaving in an opposite sex manner. Girls, on the other hand, experience complexity in their sex role development resulting from their need to assume both active and passive positions. This complexity is further compounded by the fact that in adult society the feminine role holds less prestige and privilege than the masculine role. These different sources of anxiety and conflict manifest themselves in a variety of ways, i.e., discrepancies between underlying sex role identification and overt sex role behavior of both male and females in our culture. In our culture males may be inclined to manifest a masculine sex role preference with an underlying (repressed) opposite sex role identification. In contrast, women may tend to show an opposite sex role preference with an underlying same sex role identification.

Status-Envy Hypothesis. Burton and Whiting (1961) emphasized two aspects of identification. Identification consists of learning a given role by rehearsal in fantasy rather than by actual performance, and identification of a given role is motivated by envy of the incumbent of a privileged status. In other words, life alone will not produce identification. The child identifies maximally with people who control access to resources because of their position (age, occupation, and other status characteristics). The child who wishes to have free access to the desired resources will aspire to identify with the person whose status enables him to control access to the desired resources.

Burton and Whiting distinguish between three kinds of identity: attributed identity, which refers to a status assigned to a person by other members of his society; subjective identity, consisting of the status the person sees himself occupying; and, optative identity, which refers to the desire to occupy a certain status. Most societies attempt to bring about integration between attributed, subjective, and optative identities through a process of socialization. Society wishes any member to see himself as others see him, and that he perceive himself as being what he wants to be. The process of *socialization* consists of an enforced sequence of experiences in which becoming an adult involves being first deprived of access to resources which only the adults in that society enjoy; and wanting to be a member of the class of adults. When society permits the individual to occupy this privileged status, the individual becomes what he wanted to be. In other words, the subjective and optative status become integrated.

Burton and Whiting apply their theory of identification to a wide range of anthropological data. For example, it is suggested that male initiation rites at puberty are associated with exclusive mother-child arrangements and long postpartum sex taboo. The initiation rights serve to bury the feminine identity the boy has established with his mother during early childhood and to replace this earlier identity with a secondary male identity. Another source of support for the status envy hypothesis of identification is seen in the gang membership of adolescents who reject femininity in every form. Miller (1958) interprets excessive concern with being "tough" as a reaction formation to cross-sex primary identification.

As I have indicated at the outset of this section, the formulations of Parsons, Heilbrun, Lynn, and Burton and Whiting are most valuable when seen as modifications, rather than replacements, of the theories of identification discussed earlier.

Anthropological Theories

Anthropology, more than any other discipline, has cast doubt on the validity of biological theories of personality development. Ruth Benedict (1950) has suggested that very few human traits are universal. Moreover, the universal existence of certain human traits would not represent scientific evidence that such traits must be biogenetically determined. Similarly, anthropologists do not consider many problems to be inherent in adolescent development. Cross-cultural studies have shown that a good many of the problems which have been described and discussed earlier in this chapter may not exist at all in some societies, and may be solved at different age levels in other societies. Even physiological maturing, such as the onset of puberty, will acquire different meanings in different cultures and, therefore, will result in different reactions and behavioral changes during adolescence. For example, as Margaret Mead (1952) has shown, it has been found in primitive tribes that menstruation may be interpreted as dangerous by one tribe because the menstruating girl could dry up the well, and as good in another tribe because the menstruating girl could improve the crops and increase the food supply. Instances have also been found in which no taboos and rituals are connected with menstruation. In such instances, the girls are not even forbidden to prepare food or to mix freely with other members at the onset of menstruation.

Cultural anthropology challenges the universality of the specific stages in human development which are an essential part of most of the theories discussed in this chapter. The majority of anthropologists hold that specific patterns of cultural conditions determine whether development takes place in stages or is continuous. Gradual and abrupt changes before and after adolescent development vary widely from culture to culture, and no single rate of change, within development, can be considered universal. The cultural prescriptions for age and stage grading in Western society may be contradictory, but they are definitely there, and they strongly reinforce stages in development.

Observers of adolescents in modern society are more likely to be impressed with the unique sources of developmental change that characterize adolescence than are the observers of primitive cultures. The rules, sanctions, and taboos for conduct in primitive cultures are more directly related to the patterns and changes of behavior during adolescence than is the case in our complex modern society. Thus, the role of the social environment in adolescent development emerges more clearly in primitive societies than it does in a modern society. This more direct and explicit influence of cultural conditioning on adolescence may well be related to the greater continuity between the parent and the growing child in the primitive society. Conversely, the more indirect and complex relationship between cultural conditioning and adolescent development, as well as the presence of the conflicting and ambiguous standards in modern society, may have facilitated the widening gap between the parent and the growing child. By comparison with primitive societies, it is clear that the adolescent in modern society conforms increasingly more to peer-group standards and has become less responsive to parental values and expectations. Other reasons for the widening gap between the generations have been discussed earlier in this chapter, particularly in the section on sociological theory.

Most anthropologists who have studied primitive cultures are impressed with the beneficial effects of gradual change and continuity in development, particularly for the period of adolescence. One anthropologist (Leta Hollingworth, 1928) , has gone so far as to describe the position of characterizing adolescence as a period of inevitable storm and stress, from which new and different personalities emerge, as a survival of the ceremonial rebirth of folklore which constituted the initiation of primitive youth into manhood and womanhood. She also describes those attempts to explain psychological changes during puberty as a result of biological and organic change, as a survival of the sudden change in social status that occurred as the result of puberty initiation rites among primitive people. The biological theorists have clung to their belief in the biological determinants of psychological changes during adolescence with extreme tenacity. Contrasting this with the extreme paucity of convincing evidence, Hollingworth's suggestion becomes even more intriguing. However, in fairness, it must be remembered that the more recent biological theorists have left ample room for individual differences in biological predispositions. This allows for a wide range of different effects of organic change on adolescent development. An example of this can be seen in the discussion of followers of Kretschmer, who have held that differences in body type will affect differences in the amount of storm and stress experienced by the adolescent.

Summary

The present writer shares some of the expressed concerns of the anthropologist with respect to biological theories of adolescence. The evolutionary speculations of G. Stanley Hall and the biological speculations of Remplein are post facto analogies which seem mainly an attempt to reconcile biological and psychological development. They are found lacking as a conceptual framework for the organization of the psychosocial phenomena of adolescence. This is particularly true when it comes to understanding, prediction, and control. Gesell's concept of spiral growth and of an oscillation between progression and regression in development may be useful and may have helped Gesell to organize his empirical observations. However, the validity of this concept, when applied to psychological change, does not hinge on demonstrating a direct link between oscillation in biological development and psychological development. Learning theory has found this fluctuation in conditioning and habit formation and has been quite successful in discovering psychological mechanisms and processes to account for these phenomena. Similarly, Piaget's concept of equilibration and Anna Freud's concept of the interaction between progression and regression in developmental change, provide models of oscillation in development without any reference to biological processes. As in the case of learning theory, both Piaget and Anna Freud use psychological mechanisms to account for this oscillation. These mechanisms are both plausible and testable.

Some of the biological variables and processes that have been suggested appear to have considerable promise for facilitating systematization of the psychosocial phenomena during adolescence. As indicated earlier, the concept of body build (proposed by Kretschmer) and the reference to endocrinological changes have considerable promise for understanding the fluctuations in mood and anxiety during adolescence. This is true because these particular psychological variables are more closely linked to biological processes than are many other aspects of human experience.

Finally, it should be apparent to the reader of this chapter that much fruitful thinking and many profitable ideas are to be gained from a greater familiarity with European theories. To the present time these theories have not received a receptive ear in the psychological circles of the United States. It is hoped that the brief introduction to adolescent theories provided in this chapter will encourage the student to continue to familiarize himself with the writings of Spranger, Kroh, Zeller, and the other psychologists who have much to offer toward an understanding of adolescence.

REFERENCES

Ausubel, D. P. *Theory and problems of adolescent development.* New York: Grune and Stratton, 1954.

Benedict, R. *Patterns of culture.* New York: New American Library, 1950.

Blos, P. *On adolescence.* Glencoe, Ill.: Free Press, 1962.

Burton, R. V., and Whiting, J. W. M. The absent father and cross-sex identity. *Merrill-Palmer Quarterly of Behavior and Development,* 1961, *7,* 85–95.

Davis, A. Socialization and adolescent personality. In *Adolescence: Yearbook of the national society for the study of education,* 1944, *43,* Part I.

Davis, K. Adolescence and the social structure. In J. Seidman (ed.), *The adolescent.* New York: Holt, Rinehart and Winston, 1960.

Erikson, E. H. *Childhood and society.* New York: W. W. Norton, 1950.

————. Identity and the life cycle: Selected papers. *Psychological Issues Monograph Series,* I: No. 1. New York: International Universities Press, 1959.

Freud, A. *The ego and the mechanism of defence.* Translated by E. Baines. New York: International Universities Press, 1948.

Freud, S. *Three essays on the theory of sexuality.* London: Hogarth, 1953.

Gesell, A., et al. *The first five years of life.* New York: Harper, 1940.

————. The ontogenesis of infant behavior. In L. Carmichael (ed.), *Manual of child psychology.* New York: Wiley, 1946.

————, and Ilg, F. L. *The child from five to ten.* New York: Harper, 1946.

————, Ilg, F. L., and Ames, L. B. *Youth: The years from ten to sixteen.* New York: Harper, 1956.

Hall, G. S. *Adolescence.* New York: Appleton, 1916.

Havighurst, R. J. *Developmental tasks and education.* New York: Longmans, Green and Co., 1951.

Heilbrun, A. B., Jr. An empirical test of the modeling theory of sex role learning. *Child Development,* 1965, *35,* 789–799.

Hollingworth, L. S. *The psychology of the adolescent.* New York: Appleton-Century, 1928.

Johnson, M. M. Sex role learning in the nuclear family. *Child Development,* 1963, *34,* 320–321.

Kardiner, A. *The individual and his society.* New York: Columbia University Press, 1939.

Kretschmer, E. *Korperbau and Character.* Berlin: Springer Verlag, 1951.

Kroh, O. Psychologie der entwicklung. In *Lexikon der Paedagogik,* Vol. II. Bern: A. Francke, 1951, 438–447.

Lewin, K. *A dynamic theory of personality.* New York: McGraw-Hill, 1935.

————. Field theory and experiment in social psychology: Concepts and methods. *American Journal of Sociology,* 1939, *44,* 868–897.

————. *Resolving social conflict.* New York: Harper, 1948.

Lynn, D. B. The process of learning parental and sex-role identification. *Journal of Marriage and the Family,* 1966, *28,* 466–470.

Mead, M. *Adolescence in primitive and modern society.* In G. E. Swanson, T. M. Newcomb, E. L. Hartley et al. (eds.), *Readings in social psychology.* New York: Henry Holt, 1952.

Miller, W. B. Lower class culture as a generating milieu of gang delinquency. *Journal of Social Issues,* 1958, *14,* 5–19.

Muuss, R. E. *Theories of adolescence.* New York: Random House, 1962.

Parsons, T. Social structure and the development of personality: Freud's contribution to the integration of psychology and sociology. *Psychiatry,* 1958, *11,* 321–340.

Remplein, H. *Die seelische Entwicklung in der Kindheit und Reifezeit.* Munich: Ernst Reinhard, 1956.

Sheldon, W. H. *Varieties of human physique.* New York: Harper, 1940.

Spranger, E. *Psychologie des Jugendalters.* Heidelberg: Quelle and Meyer, 1955.

Werner, H. *Comparative psychology of mental development.* New York: Harper, 1940.

Zeller, W. Ueber de Entwicklungstypus. *Psychologische Rundschau,* 1951.

6

Nature and Nurture in Adolescence

*Robert C. Nichols**

The nature-nurture issues, as they apply to adolescent psychology, concern the extent to which adolescent behavior is dependent on inherited characteristics, passed from one generation to the next by genetic mechanisms, and the extent to which they are dependent on the individual life experiences of the adolescent. The major dimensions of human behavior, those things that distinguish man from other animals, are obviously genetically determined; while the specific form they take (the particular language spoken, the type of clothing worn, the kinds of tools that are used) is, just as obviously, culturally determined. This seems to be true of the period of adolescence itself. The physiological changes and the growing capacity for independent action are dependent on maturation of genetically determined characteristics, while the specific behaviors resulting from these changes (e.g., rebellion, self-consciousness, peer orientation, and initiation rites) are conditioned by the culture. In this broad fashion heredity and environment are both necessary and interdependent determinants of all behavior.

The situation is much less obvious, however, when we consider the relative importance of heredity and environment as determinants of

* Robert C. Nichols is Professor of Educational Psychology at the State University of New York at Buffalo. He has written a chapter in *Methods and Goals in Human Behavior Genetics* and has published widely on such topics as the gifted, birth order and intelligence, academic aptitude and success, and the influence of hereditary factors.

individual differences in behavior within a given culture. The people in the United States, for example, compose a common cultural group that is becoming increasingly homogeneous with the increasing equality of educational opportunity and the increasing penetration of the mass media. Yet, there are great differences in the typical behavior of individual adolescents, all of whom have been exposed to this common culture. There are differences in abilities, differences in interests, differences in temperament and personality. What is the origin of these individual differences? To what extent are they due to genetic differences, and to what extent are they due to differences in experience?

In the first third of the twentieth century, psychologists were greatly preoccupied with this question. Individual psychologists tended to take extreme positions, and there were violent polemics between the hereditarians on the one hand and the environmentalists on the other. Like many arguments in the history of science, this issue was never resolved, but concern with it simply died away as the major combatants reached retirement age and younger psychologists became interested in other problems. Recently there has been a renaissance of interest in behavior genetics, and it has once again become a lively area of research and controversy. The current scientific concern is not so much with showing the preeminence of either hereditary or environmental factors, but with gaining an understanding of the way in which behavior is influenced by genetic mechanisms. The proportion of the variance (differences among people) of a trait that is attributable to genetic differences has no absolute validity, but instead is specific to a given population at a given time. If all people of a given group are exposed to the same environmental circumstances, any differences in behavior among the people in this group will be attributable to heredity. At the other extreme, any differences in behavior observed among people with the same genetic characteristics, such as identical twins, can be attributed to differences in experience. Since all behavior is affected to some extent by both heredity and environment, the *heritability* (the proportion of the total variation attributable to heredity) of particular traits perhaps tells more about the diversity of hereditary and environmental influences in the population than it does about the relative importance of heredity and environment in any absolute sense. Thus, heritability estimates are of relatively little enduring scientific importance, although they do contribute to the understanding of behavior patterns within a given culture at a given time. Our understanding of adolescent behavior will be enhanced by a consideration of the degree to which individual differences among adolescents in Western culture are due to differences in environmental experiences and the degree to which they are due to hereditary differences.

Since the first edition of this book (1968), there has been a considerable amount of public controversy concerning the degree to which behavioral traits—particularly intelligence—are dependent on genetic factors. This dispute has been motivated by the important implications of this issue concerning equality of opportunity for racial minorities and other disadvantaged groups. Although the resolution of this social problem is still a task for the future, the controversy has served to clarify the scientific issues and to bring about a more careful examination of the available evidence than might otherwise have occurred.

Intelligence and Academic Achievement

The trait that has received the most intensive study from the heredity-environment point of view is intelligence. This is due primarily to the fact that individual differences in ability are large and have pervasive influences on life and school success. There are also much better measures of individual differences in intelligence than there are of other behavioral characteristics. So we will first examine the evidence concerning the role of hereditary and environmental factors in bringing about differences in ability among adolescents. Students are usually keenly aware of the fact that there are great individual differences in measured ability, even among such relatively homogeneous groups as the student bodies of the more selective colleges. Some students seem consistently to make top grades with ease, while others are able to compete only by long hours of arduous study. What is responsible for these differences?

There are three main types of variables that seem likely to have an important influence on ability and school achievement. These are the *school factor* or organized educational influences, the *family factor* or all of the social influences of family life on a child, and the *genetic factor*. In addition to these three main influences, one might also distinguish nutritional factors, peer influences, and community influences, which we will consider as part of the family factor.

The separation of the effects of the major types of influences on ability has proved to be difficult, and all of the research so far has not resulted in unanimously accepted conclusions. This is due primarily to the fact that in human society most good things tend to go together. All other things being equal, the most intelligent parents, i.e., those with the best genetic potential, tend to provide the most comfortable and intellectually stimulating home environments for their children, and they also tend to send their children to the most affluent and well-equipped schools. Thus, the ubiquitous correlation between family socioeconomic status on the one hand and test performance and school achievement on the other is ambiguous in meaning, and isolating the independent contribution of the various factors involved is difficult. An additional complicating factor is that there are still strong emotionally motivated attitudes and vested interests concerning the heredity-environment issue that have tended to inhibit dispassionate, objective evaluation of the available evidence. Although no one line of evidence is conclusive, the recent controversy has revealed considerable consistency among the results of the various kinds of relevant studies.

The School Factor

It seems almost self-evident that there should be a large school effect on measures of ability and academic achievement. Obviously, universal education in the United States has been largely responsible for producing the highly literate and capable population we see today. Without continued educational efforts we would undoubtedly regress to more primitive levels. But the very fact that education is so widespread and so obviously successful may reduce its importance as a source of individual differences in ability in this country.

Recent studies of school effects have tended to emphasize that differences in school experiences have little relationship to differences in student performance after all the relevant background factors have been controlled. For example, there are large differences among colleges in such respects as the average Graduate Record Examination scores of their graduates, the proportion of their graduates planning to enter various careers, and the proportion later entering graduate school. Early studies tended to assume that these differences between graduates were mainly due to the different experiences of the students at the various colleges; and "Ph.D. Productivity," the proportion of a college's bachelor level graduates who eventually obtain a Ph.D., was widely considered to be an index of college quality (Knapp and Goodrich, 1952; Knapp and Greenbaum, 1953). However, subsequent studies (Astin, 1962) have shown that the differences between colleges in Ph.D. productivity are almost entirely due to differences in the characteristics of the students entering the colleges as freshmen. Similar dependence of college output on student input has been found for career choice (Astin, 1965), Graduate Record Examination scores (Nichols, 1964; Astin, 1968), and personality and interest scales (Nichols, 1967).

One might say that large school effects should not be expected for students of college age. By the time that a person is seventeen years old, the major influences have already been operating for a long time, and students have likely developed defenses against noxious stimuli and methods of compensating for environmental inadequacies. It seems reasonable to assume that we should look to earlier ages for substantial school effects.

A large-scale study of equality of educational opportunity by the U.S. Office of Education (Coleman et al., 1966; Nichols, 1966b) focused on the period from the first through twelfth grade, where school effects might more reasonably be expected. Over six hundred thousand students in a representative sample of more than four thousand public schools took tests of verbal and nonverbal ability and of school achievement. There were substantial differences in the average performance of students in the various schools, as might be expected; but these differences among schools were associated with measures of the students' home background rather than with characteristics of the schools, per se. When family background was controlled statistically, the students' ability and achievement scores were found to be correlated, not with measures of school quality, but with the socioeconomic characteristics of the other students in the school. This finding suggests that peer influences may be more important determiners of achievement than are school and teacher quality. These and other results led the authors to conclude that "variations in school quality are not highly related to variations in achievement of pupils. . . . The school appears unable to exert independent influences to make achievement less dependent on the child's background" (Coleman et al., 1966, p. 297) . Thus, the same rationalization of negative results that we used for colleges is also used here: The really formative influences have already taken place; enduring individual differences in ability are already established before students enter first grade.

Another indication of the relatively small influence of the school factor on individual differences in intelligence comes from the difficulty of producing substantial gains in ability by special educational effort. A number of compensatory education programs have been undertaken in the United States in recent years in an attempt to make up for educational disadvantage in selected groups of students. In reviewing the effectiveness of these programs the United States Commission on Civil Rights (1967) concluded "that none of the programs appear to have raised significantly the achievement of participating pupils, as a group, within the period evaluated by the Commission" (p. 138). Although defenders of compensatory education have rightly pointed out that intensive and prolonged educational intervention from an early age has not yet had a really fair trial, the fact remains that initial expectations of significant effects of special educational programs on measured ability have generally met with disappointment.

The largely negative results of studies of school effects suggest that in the United States, where some sort of education is available to everyone and the mass media continually bombard us with seductive conceptual material (in other words, where very few suffer really drastic educational disadvantage), the family factor and the genetic factor are likely the major sources of individual differences in ability. Within this book, Johnston and Bachman discuss the function of the school in adolescent development and touch on a number of these issues.

The Family Factor

Perhaps the best evidence for the importance of early experience for later intellectual development comes from studies of animals. Hebb (1949) suggested that animals reared in a stimulus-rich environment should show enduring superiority in adaptive response and perceptual capacity over animals deprived of this early stimulation. This hypothesis has been well substantiated in a variety of experiments (Denenberg, 1962). Even very brief handling experiences of infant rats, if they occur at fairly sharply defined critical periods, will affect the animals' learning performance in adulthood. It is interesting to note that infantile stress appears also to result in earlier sexual maturation (adolescence) in both animals (Morton, Denenberg, and Zarrow, 1963) and humans (Whiting, 1965).

The human situation is undoubtedly much more complicated than that of rats and mice, and it is dangerous to generalize from animal studies more than the gross principle that early experience can be very influential on later behavior, and perhaps that there are critical periods when certain experiences are more salient than they are at other times.

The literature concerning environmental effects on intelligence was reviewed by Bloom (1964), who concluded that the maximum effect on intelligence of extreme environmental differences was around twenty IQ points (about 1.25 standard deviations). It is interesting to note that twenty IQ points is the average difference found by Salzberger and Jarvik (1963) between pairs of identical twins when one twin had been deaf since early in life. Bloom also concluded that environmental effects appear to be greater early in life, particularly during the preschool years, than they are at older age levels.

One reason for this conclusion is that intelligence scores become increasingly more stable with increasing age. Bloom noted that about 50 percent of the variance in intelligence at age seventeen can be predicted from measures at age four. This does not mean that a child has attained half his adult intelligence at age four, as this fact has sometimes been misinterpreted, but merely that individual differences in ability are apparent early in life and that people tend to maintain roughly the same standing relative to others of their age as they grow older. This degree of predictability of adult intelligence at an early age is especially surprising when one considers the difficulties of measuring intellectual abilities in young children, who have not yet developed facility in symbolic reasoning that is such an important part of adult intelligence.

There is surprisingly little good information available about the effects of various early experiences on the development of adult intelligence in humans. Most writers who discuss such effects cite short-term studies (e.g., Greenberg, Uzgiris, and Hunt, 1968). Considering the importance of such knowledge for the future well-being of society, the lack of good research in this area is appalling.

One line of indirect evidence, studies of birth order, does suggest that there may be substantial effects of the family factor on intelligence, particularly on the development of verbal ability. Information about birth order (whether one comes first, second, third, etc., in order of birth among his siblings) can be obtained easily and reliably from adults, yet it gives some information about the early life experiences of the person. The family environment is quite different, for example, for two brothers two years apart simply because one has an older sibling and the other has a younger sibling with which to relate. Thus, differences between siblings of different birth orders may reflect the effects of these differences in family experiences. Unlike most other comparisons, birth-order differences are not confounded with possible genetic effects. Altus (1966) has reviewed the literature on birth order, which suggests that earlier-born (the older) siblings in a family tend on the average to be more intelligent, more likely to attend college, and more likely to achieve eminence than are later-born siblings. This difference shows up clearly when large numbers of cases are studied, but it is small in size so that it is not a very important factor in an individual case. Breland (1972) reviewed the recent birth-order literature and agreed with Altus' conclusion concerning birth-order differences in intelligence. In addition he analyzed birth order data for almost eight hundred thousand participants in the National Merit Scholarship Test and found the consistent birth-order effects shown in Figure 1. Additional analyses showed that the birth-order differences are more pronounced for closely spaced siblings than for siblings three or more years apart in age, and that the birth-order differences were mainly in verbal abilities. From these findings he speculated that the birth-order differences may be due in part to the older siblings' greater verbal interaction with parents.

The general cultural level of the community also seems to have an effect on ability. Wheeler (1942) tested over three thousand Tennessee mountain children and compared their scores with children of the same age living in the same area tested with the same tests ten years earlier. During the intervening ten years the TVA and other federal programs had brought about great improvements in economic conditions and educational and cultural opportunities in the region. The average IQ in

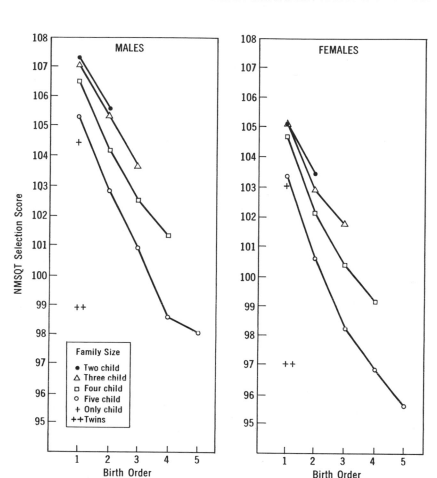

Fig. 1. Mean NMSQT Selection scores by birth order and family size for 794,589 National Merit Scholarship Test participants in 1965. Because of the large sample, all differences between successive birth positions in all family sizes for both sexes are statistically significant with the exception of the difference between the fourth and fifth birth positions for males in five-child families. Participants in familes of more than five children are not shown. The mean NMSQT score for all participants was 103, and the standard deviation was 21.

Source: H. M. Breland. *Birth order and intelligence.* Unpublished Ph.D. dissertation, State University of New York at Buffalo, 1972. Used by permission.

the area increased about ten points, from 82 to 92, over the ten years, apparently as a result of the environmental improvement.

Thus, there are clear indications that the family factor is an important source of individual differences in ability, but as yet we do not know just what the critical experiences are or much about their timing, except that the most important events occur early in life, probably before three or four.

The Genetic Factor

In contrast to the scant information about the family factor, there is fairly convincing evidence that the genetic factor is a major determinant of individual differences in ability. Erlenmeyer-Kimling and Jarvik (1963) have prepared the chart shown in Figure 2 to summarize the

Category		0.00 0.10 0.20 0.30 0.40 0.50 0.60 0.70 0.80 0.90	Groups included
Unrelated persons	Reared apart		4
	Reared together		5
Fosterparent-child			3
Parent-child			12
Siblings	Reared apart		2
	Reared together		35
Twins — Two-egg	Opposite sex		9
	Like sex		11
Twins — One-egg	Reared apart		4
	Reared together		14

Fig. 2. Correlation coefficients for "intelligence" test scores from fifty-two studies. Some studies reported data for more than one relationship category; some included more than one sample per category, giving a total of ninety-nine groups. Over two-thirds of the correlation coefficients were derived from IQs, the remainder from special tests (for example, Primary Mental Abilities). Midparent-child correlation was used when available, otherwise mother-child correlation. Correlation coefficients obtained in each study are indicated by dark circles; medians are shown by vertical lines intersecting the horizontal lines which represent the ranges.

Source: L. Erlenmeyer-Kimling and L. F. Jarvik. Genetics and intelligence: A review. *Science* 1963, *142*, 1477–1479. Copyright 1963 by the American Association for the Advancement of Science. Used by permission.

results of the fifty-two studies they were able to find in the literature concerning the relative similarity in measured intelligence of people with varying degrees of genetic relationship. The figure shows that the similarity in intelligence of pairs of people increases steadily as their genetic relationship increases. The orderliness of these results is all the more compelling when we consider that the studies were conducted over a period of several generations in several different languages on several different continents, and that results were included from studies with serious methodological defects.

Twins are of particular significance for the study of hereditary influences because they form a natural experiment in which the two kinds of twins are alike in the similarity of their environmental experiences but differ in hereditary similarity. *Fraternal or dizygotic* (DZ) twins develop from separate ova fertilized at about the same time by separate spermatozoa. The resulting two individuals have about half their genes in common, the same genetic relationship as ordinary siblings. *Identical or monozygotic* (MZ) twins, on the other hand, develop from a single ovum fertilized by a single spermatozoon that separates into two parts during the early stages of cell civision. Each part develops into a separate individual, both of which have identical genetic endowment. The *zygosity* of twins (whether they are MZ or DZ) is best determined by analyses of blood samples. There are a number of genetically determined characteristics of the blood which make almost completely accurate diagnoses possible. However, highly accurate diagnoses can also be made on the basis of similarity of easily observable external physical characteristics. Such characteristics as eye color, hair color and texture, facial features, shape of ear lobes, height, weight, and fingerprints have a large hereditary component. Nichols and Bilbro (1966) have shown that sets of twins who are similar in all these characteristics are almost always MZ, while twins with a substantial difference in any one of these characteristics are usually DZ.

To the extent that a trait is genetically determined, identical twins would be expected to be more similar than are fraternal twins. Table 1 shows the degree of similarity in intelligence of the two kinds of twins observed in several studies. The fact that the correlation for identical twins is less than the typical reliability of the tests used (which in most instances is between .90 and .95) suggests that differential environmental experiences of the twins have affected the development of ability. The fact that fraternal twins show considerably less similarity than identical twins suggests that the greater genetic similarity of identical twins is responsible for their greater similarity in ability. In an attempt to correct partially for the possibly greater similarity of experience of MZ twins, Nichols (1965) discarded from his analysis those sets of twins who re-

Table 1. Summary of Results of Studies of the Intellectual Resemblance of Twins

	MZ Twin Sets		DZ Twin Sets		
Study	*Intraclass Corre- lation*	*N*	*Intraclass Corre- lation*	*N*	*Test*
Holzinger (1929)	.88	50	.63	52	Binet IQ
Newman, Freeman, Holzinger (1937)	.91	50	.64	50	Binet IQ
Newman, Freeman, Holzinger (1937)	.92	50	.62	50	Otis IQ
Blewett (1954)	.75	26	.39	26	PMA Composite
Husèn (1959)	.90	215	.70	416	Swedish Military Induction Test
Husèn (1960)	.89	134	.62	180	Reading Achievement
Husèn (1960)	.87	134	.52	181	Arithmetic Achievement
Erlenmeyer-Kimling and Jarvik (1963)	.87	14[a]	.53	11[b]	Various Intelligence Measures
Nichols (1965)	.87	687	.63	482	NMSQT Composite
Snider (1955)	.83	152	.63	194	Iowa Tests of Ed. Devel. Composite
Schoenfeldt (1971)	.87	150	.43	53	Project Talent Verbal Knowledge (males)
Schoenfeldt (1971)	.95	187	.61	103	Project Talent Verbal Knowledge (females)

[a] Median of 14 studies.
[b] Median of 11 studies.

ported periods of separation, major illnesses, or other important differences in experience. The effect of discarding these cases was to increase both the MZ and the DZ correlations by about the same degree, indicating that differences in experience do not account for the greater similarity of MZ twins.

Several formulas have been proposed for calculating the heritability of a trait from twin correlations (Holzinger, 1929; Nichols, 1965; Jensen, 1968). Heritability is the proportion of variance attributable to genetic factors. When applied to the twin correlations in Table 1, these formulas yield estimates that approximately 70 to 80 percent of the variation in intelligence is attributable to hereditary factors.

Jensen (1970) has reviewed the four major studies of identical twins reared apart (Newman, Freeman, and Holzinger, 1937; Shields, 1962; Juel-Nielsen, 1965; Burt, 1966) consisting of a total of 122 sets of twins. To the extent that separated identical twins actually have unrelated environments, any resemblance between them can be attributable to their identical genetic endowment. Thus the correlation between identical twins reared apart is a direct index of heritability. Jensen reported a correlation of .82 between intelligence scores in the combined sample of 122 separated identical twin sets.

Studies of adopted children provide a different line of evidence relevant to the question of the relative importance of the family factor and the genetic factor in determining the widely observed family resemblance in intelligence. Intelligence test scores of children raised with their true parents show increasing correlation with their mothers' education (a good substitute for intelligence tests on the mother) as the children grow older. The curve starts with a correlation near zero at age one or two and levels off at a correlation near .35 at about age six or seven. There are at least two possible explanations for the child's increasing similarity to his mother with increasing age: greater length of exposure to the psychological influence of the mother; and, better measures of the child's true intelligence with increasing development of verbal skills. Adopted child studies offer a way to separate these two effects. To the extent that a family factor is important, the adopted child's intelligence should become increasingly similar to that of the foster parents with increasing age in a manner similar to that for children raised with their true parents. To the extent that the genetic factor is important, the adopted child's intelligence should increasingly resemble that of his true parents from whom he is separated. Honzik (1957) has brought together data from two longitudinal studies which show these relationships quite clearly. The correlation of adopted children's test scores with the education of their true mothers (whom they have never seen) follows a pattern identical to that just described for children raised with their true parents, and the curve also levels off at a correlation of about .35. The correlation of the adopted children's test scores with the education of their foster mothers (who actually raised them) never reached a point higher than .10. Similar results were obtained for the relationship of the child's intelligence with the education of their true and foster fathers. These findings suggest that the genetic factor plays a greater role than the family factor in producing the correlation between the ability of children and the socioeconomic status of their parents.

Still another line of evidence for the importance of the genetic factor comes from animal breeding experiments. If a behavioral trait is to some extent hereditary, selective breeding should produce strains that differ in regard to the trait. Tryon (1942) selected rats for their performance in running a maze, breeding together those with the best maze scores to produce a "maze-bright" group and those with the worst maze scores to produce a "maze-dull" group. After eight generations of such selection there was practically no overlap in the maze scores of the two groups.

Tryon's pioneering study was widely interpreted as showing the inheritance of "intelligence"; however, further studies of Tryon's "maze-bright" and "maze-dull" strains, which have been maintained as separate breeding populations, suggest that their differences in "brightness" are specific to maze-running and do not generalize to other measures of ability. Searle (1949) compared the two strains on a number of measures and concluded that the "maze-bright" strain was more strongly motivated by food and water deprivation and was less fearful of mechanical apparatus than was the "maze-dull" strain. Thus, Tryon seems to have produced strains that differ more in temperamental traits than in intelligence.

Figure 3 shows results of a breeding study similar to that of Tryon, and reported by Thompson (1954). There was rapid separation of the two strains so that after six generations the dull strain was making twice as many errors as was the bright strain. These findings are quite typical of breeding studies in general; however, the separation of the strains would not continue indefinitely in the same way with continued selection. The diverging curves would level off and become parallel as the two strains become homozygous for the genes relevant to the behavior being selected. Maze learning in rats is certainly not the same as human intelligence, but the fact that almost any behavioral trait will respond to genetic selection leaves little doubt that results similar to those shown in Figure 3 could be obtained with human ability in a similarly severe selection process.

We might summarize this discussion of factors producing individual differences in intelligence by making a rough ordering of the major factors in terms of the degree of their contribution to individual differences in ability among adolescents in the United States. The evidence seems to indicate that the genetic factor is responsible for the largest portion of variability, followed by the family factor, and that the school factor makes the smallest contribution to individual differences. It is interesting to note that this is exactly the reverse order from a ranking in terms of the amount of effort and attention devoted to these factors in attempts to improve the performance of young people in this country. Indeed, it is probably this very distribution of effort that has resulted in the findings we have discussed. The more we succeed in equalizing the effects of a particular factor in the population, the less important that factor will become as a source of individual differences.

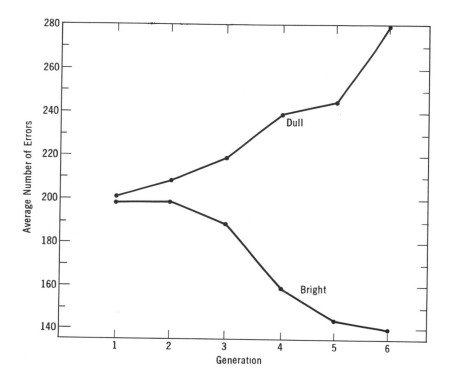

Fig. 3. Average error scores in maze learning for successive generations of selectively bred "bright" and "dull" strains of rats.

Source: W. R. Thompson. The inheritance and development of intelligence. *Research Publication of the Association for Nervous and Mental Disorders,* 1954, *33,* 209–331. Used by permission.

Components of Intelligence

So far we have considered intelligence as a unitary trait, which is a useful fiction, since almost all ability measures are positively correlated and verbal reasoning ability plays a large part in almost all cognitive tasks. However, factor analytic studies have shown that there are a number of components of ability that can be measured independently. Are these ability components the result of environmental experiences that facilitate the development of some abilities but not others, or are they due to independent genetic mechanisms? The evidence on this interesting issue is far from conclusive, but several studies suggest that there are a number of independently inherited abilities. Blewett (1954) and Vandenberg (1962) have studied the resemblance of twins on the Thurstone Primary Mental Abilities test, an instrument designed to measure separately several components of ability. Both studies concluded tentatively that more than one ability component is dependent in part on genetic factors. Nichols (1965) reached a similar tentative conclusion from studies of twin resemblances in the subtest pattern of the National Merit Scholarship Qualifying Test. Perhaps the best evidence on this point has been reported by Schoenfeldt (1968), who studied 523 sets of twins participating in Project Talent, a national survey of the abilities of approximately four hundred thousand high school students. By factor analytic studies of the sixty ability tests included in Project Talent, Lohnes (1966) developed a measure of general verbal ability and separate measures of ten specific abilities. The specific abilities were measured in such a way that they were uncorrelated with general ability and with each other. The heritability coefficients for each of Lohnes's eleven factors are shown in Table 2.

Table 2. Twin Resemblance in Specific Abilities Measured Independently of General Intelligence

	Heritability[a]	
Factor	*Males*	*Females*
General Intelligence	.55**	.62**
Differential Aptitudes		
Visual Reasoning	.35*	.43**
Perceptual Speed and Accuracy	.34*	.28*
Memory	.40**	.29*
Educational Achievements		
English Language	.36*	.28*
Mathematics	—.05	.32**
Special Knowledge		
Simple Information	.21	.01
Information about Hunting and Fishing	.15	.05
Information about Colors and Food	.24	.09
Information about Etiquette	.21	.15
Information about Games	.32*	.32*

Source: L. F. Schoenfeldt. The hereditary components of the Project Talent two-day test battery. Paper presented at the American Research Association Meeting, February 16, 1967. Used by permission.

[a] The heritability coefficient reported is an index of the degree to which MZ twins were more similar than were DZ twins, and is an estimate of the proportion of variability attributable to genetic factors.

* Differences in similarity between MZ and DZ twins statistically significant ($P <$ .05).

** Difference in similarity between MZ and DZ twins statistically significant ($P <$ .01).

Schoenfeldt did not report intraclass correlations, so his results for general intelligence cannot be compared directly with the results shown in Table 1. However, the coefficients in Table 2 provide a basis for comparing the relative heritability of the various factors. These results are consistent with previous studies in showing that general intelligence has substantial dependence on genetic mechanisms. What is new is the finding that differential aptitudes and educational achievements, when measured in such a way that they are independent of general ability, are also dependent in part on heredity. Special knowledges appear to have little, if any, genetic component. The data seem to indicate that the genetic component of differential aptitudes and educational achievements is smaller than that of general intelligence, but Schoenfeldt did not indicate the extent to which differences in the reliability of his measures could have produced the apparent differences in heritability.

Another, somewhat more indirect line of evidence concerning genetic influence on the components of intelligence is provided by Fifer's (1965) study of ability patterns of racial and ethnic groups. Since such groups are to a degree independent breeding populations, it is to be expected that they will differ on many genetically determined traits. However, it cannot be concluded that all behavioral differences between racial groups are genetic, because they also differ in typical child-rearing patterns, average socioeconomic status, and other environmental influences. In an attempt to separate the effects of these two influences on ability patterns, Fifer administered tests of four specific abilities to middle-class children and to lower-class children from four racial or ethnic groups. The samples of children were representative of all first-grade children in the New York City schools of the particular racial group and socioeconomic level. First-grade children were used because they were old enough to provide stable test results, but had not yet been exposed to common school experiences. It might be argued that if the ability profiles of these groups are due primarily to childhood experience, they would differ at the different socioeconomic levels, since child-rearing patterns are greatly influenced by socioeconomic status (Sears, Maccoby, and Levin, 1957). However, if the ability profiles are due primarily to genetic factors, they should remain relatively constant for each racial group at the two socioeconomic levels.

Figure 4 shows the mean ability profiles for the various groups. For each ethnic group the children from middle-class homes scored substantially higher than did children from lower-class homes, reflecting the well-known correlation between family socioeconomic level and a child's ability. Each of the four ethnic groups had a distinctive profile shape that held for both middle-class and lower-class children. For example, the figure shows that Jewish children were relatively high in verbal skills and

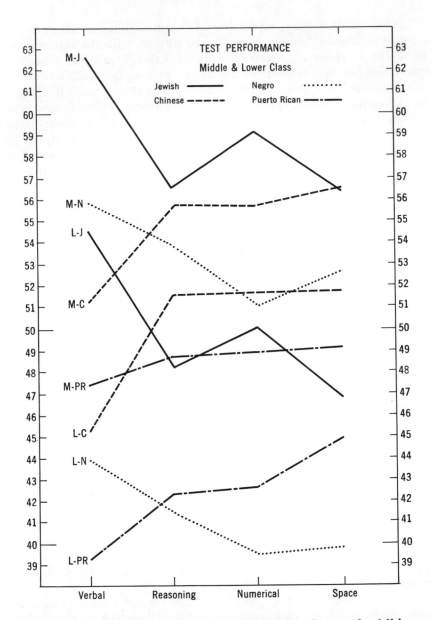

Fig. 4. Mean test profiles of lower and middle class first-grade children of four ethnic groups. Each profile is the average performance of twenty boys and twenty girls. The tests were specifically constructed to measure these specific abilities at this age level.

Source: G. Fifer. Social class and cultural group differences in diverse mental abilities. In *Proceedings of the 1964 Invitational Conference on Testing Problems.* Princeton: N.J.: Educational Testing Service, 1965. Used by permission.

relatively low in spatial perception, while Chinese children showed the reverse relationship. These patterns were little affected by socioeconomic status, even though the overall ability level varied greatly from one socioeconomic level to the other.

Group Differences—The Jensen Controversy

In 1969 Arthur Jensen published an article in the *Harvard Educational Review,* "How Much Can We Boost IQ and Scholastic Achievement?" (Jensen, 1969a), which resulted in considerable controversy (Edson, 1969; Neary, 1970; and fourteen critiques appearing in subsequent issues of the *Harvard Educational Review*). Jensen's paper reviewed much of the evidence cited above, which led him to conclude that the genetic factor is by far the most important determinant of individual differences in ability, accounting for about 80 percent of the variance. Most of Jensen's critics did not seriously challenge this conclusion, but focused their attention instead on two related propositions that have important practical and political implications: viz, the environment as a threshold variable, and the genetic basis for racial and socioeconomic group differences in ability.

Jensen proposed that environmental facilitation of intellectual development operates as a threshold variable in that below a certain threshold value, constituting a minimally adequate environment, variations in environmental facilitation have a pronounced effect on subsequent intelligence. Above the threshold, variations in environmental facilitation have relatively little influence on ability. Thus, Jensen suggested that the environment acts on intellectual functioning much as vitamins act on physiological functioning. Below a certain minimum requirement, variation in vitamin intake has a big effect. Above the minimum requirement, variations in vitamin intake make little difference. Jensen based this conclusion largely on the evidence showing little influence of the school factor and the family factor on intellectual development along with evidence of marked intellectual impairment in cases of really extreme environmental deprivation. Jensen suggested that the threshold seems to be quite low for effects on intelligence so that a child who is able to play freely out-of-doors receives the necessary minimum environmental stimulation. If true, this hypothesis has far-reaching implications for educational and environmental enrichment programs, and the main response of the critics was to point to instances in which environmental enrichment seems to have had a large effect. Some of the critics' arguments are persuasive, but they lack the necessary support of well-designed studies of the long-term effects of early environmental influences.

Table 3. Average Ability Test Scores of Children Enrolled in a Representative Sample of Schools in the United States

Group	Verbal Ability			Nonverbal Ability		
	Grade 1	*Grade 6*	*Grade 12*	*Grade 1*	*Grade 6*	*Grade 12*
Whites						
Metropolitan						
Northeast	53	54	55	54	55	54
Midwest	54	52	53	56	56	56
South	52	50	52	52	54	52
Southwest	54	50	52	56	54	53
Whites Non-metropolitan						
North and West	53	52	52	56	55	53
South	52	49	50	51	53	51
Southwest	54	51	52	53	55	53
Negroes						
Metropolitan						
Northeast	45	44	43	41	48	44
Midwest	48	44	43	47	49	45
West	46	43	39	45	46	43
South	45	42	39	42	45	40
Southwest	44	43	39	42	45	41
Negroes Non-metropolitan						
North and West	45	42	38	46	45	42
South	44	39	35	39	37	34
Southwest	45	42	38	42	41	37
Mexican-Americans	47	42	44	50	43	47
Puerto Ricans	45	37	43	46	38	45
Oriental-Americans	52	49	51	57	55	54
Indian-Americans	48	44	43	53	48	49
All Races and Regions	51	48	51	52	53	52

Source: Data obtained from J. S. Coleman et al. Equality in educational opportunity. Washington, D.C.: U.S. Government Printing Office, 1966.

Note: Both verbal and nonverbal ability tests were standardized to have a mean of about 50 and a standard deviation of 10 for the total sample at each grade level. The total sample involved over 100,000 children at each grade level.

The group-difference argument has centered around the most likely cause of the relatively large differences in measured intelligence of various racial, ethnic, and socioeconomic groups in the United States. The data shown in Table 3 are typical of the group differences usually found. Attention has focused on the Negro-white difference because these are the largest groups numerically and because the mean difference in test score is large. Negroes tend to score about one standard deviation below whites regardless of age and geographical region. This difference is large enough to have great practical consequences in terms of the modal performance of each group and in terms of the proportion of each group scoring above or below a given cut-off point. However, it should be kept in mind that there is overlap between the groups all along the scale so that one cannot judge the intelligence of a person on the basis of his group membership.

After reviewing the evidence indicating high heritability for intelligence of individuals, the relatively small impact of compensatory education programs, and the large group differences, Jensen concluded, "So all we are left with are various lines of evidence, no one of which is definitive alone, but which, viewed all together, make it a not unreasonable hypothesis that genetic factors are strongly implicated in the average Negro-white intelligence difference" (p. 82). The controversy resulting from this statement has shown that the hypothesis is not "not unreasonable" to a majority of psychologists, and the issue is far from resolved at this time. However, it is possible that future historians of psychology will count this as one of the more important sentences of our time. Not because it turns out eventually to be either right or wrong, but because of the stimulus it has provided for discussion and research on the origin of individual differences in ability.

Personality and Interests

The results of studies of hereditary and environmental influences on intelligence are relatively clear-cut and unambiguous when compared with studies of nonintellective traits. This discrepancy is due in part to the lack of satisfactory measures for temperament, and it may also be due in part to the sensitivity of personality traits to transient environmental influences.

Personality and Interest Scales

The researchers working with twins have consistently noticed that identical twins are quite similar in personality, temperament, and interests. Shields (1962), in studying identical twins reared apart, commented on the striking similarity of the twins in personality as perceived by the examiners.

Studies of twin resemblance in personality and interest have tended to find identical twins more alike than are fraternal twins on a great variety of scales and measures. Typical results from twin studies of interests are shown in Table 4. For the six major dimensions of interests, there

Table 4. Summary of Results of Typical Studies of Twin Resemblance in Interests

Study		MZ Twin Sets		DZ Twin Sets		
		Intraclass Correlation	*N*	*Intraclass Correlation*	*N*	*Test*
Practical Interests						
Carter (1932)		.74	43	.14	43	Strong Engineer
Nichols (1969)	Males	.39	220	.25	137	VPI Realistic
	Females	.27	296	.30	197	Orientation
Schoenfeldt (1971)	Males	.50	144	.44	49	Project Talent
	Females	.37	232	.32	122	Mechanical-Technical
Vandenberg and Kelly (1964)		.61	43	.30	34	Strong Engineer
Science Interests						
Carter (1932)		.65	43	.22	43	Strong Physicist
Nichols (1969)	Males	.48	220	.28	137	VPI Intellectual
	Females	.43	296	.32	197	Orientation
Schoenfeldt (1971)	Males	.58	150	.34	53	Project Talent
	Females	.42	187	.31	103	Science Int.
Vandenberg and Kelly (1964)		.62	43	.30	34	Strong Physicist
Business Interests						
Carter (1932)		.52	43	.49	43	Strong Life Insurance Salesman
Nichols (1969)	Males	.41	220	.18	137	VPI Enterprising
	Females	.40	296	.25	197	Orientation
Schoenfeldt (1971)	Males	.40	150	−.05	53	Project Talent
	Females	.43	187	.38	103	Business Interest
Vandenberg and Kelly (1964)		.54	43	.31	34	Strong Life Insurance Salesman
Clerical Interests						
Carter (1932)		.47	43	.31	43	Strong CPA

Nichols (1969)	Males	.35	220	.22	137	VPI Conventional
	Females	.35	286	.10	197	Orientation
Schoenfeldt (1971)	Males	.40	144	.28	49	Project Talent
	Females	.35	184	.21	104	Computational Int.
Vandenberg and Kelly (1964)		.45	43	.34	34	Strong CPA
Artistic Interests						
Carter (1932)		.44	43	.30	43	Strong Artist
Nichols (1969)	Males	.47	220	.20	137	VPI Artistic
	Females	.47	296	.35	197	Orientation
Schoenfeldt (1971)	Males	.52	150	.22	53	Project Talent
	Females	.63	187	.26	103	Cultural Interests
Vandenberg and Kelly (1964)		.39	43	.32	34	Strong Artist

is a consistent difference between the two kinds of twins, which suggests that the direction one's interests take is to some extent inherited. The correlations for interests tend to be lower than in the ability domain, more so than can be accounted for by the lower reliability of measurement of interests. This suggests that some of the major environmental determinants of interests operate differently on twins within the same family. This would point to rather specific experiences, which might differ for twins of a set, as the major environmental factors rather than gross variables, such as school, socioeconomic level of the family, etc.

A large number of twin correlations have been reported for a wide range of personality scales and measures. However, the great diversity of measures used, some with questionable reliability, and the relatively small samples of twins used in a majority of the studies has produced conflicting evidence that is difficult to summarize. Table 5 shows typical results of the larger studies for the two major second-order dimensions of personality, extroversion, and neuroticism. When these correlations are adjusted for the lower reliability of personality measures, they do not appear too different from the twin correlations for intelligence

Mental Disorder

Another line of evidence concerning the heritability of personality traits comes from the extensive body of research on the inheritance of mental

Table 5. Summary of Results of Typical Studies of Twin Resemblance in Personality

Study		MZ Twin Sets		DZ Twin Sets		Test
		Intraclass Correlation	*N*	*Intraclass Correlation*	*N*	
Extraversion-Introversion						
Carter (1935)		.50	55	.40	44	Bernreuter Introversion
Gottesman (1962)		.55	34	.08	34	MMPI Social Introversion
Nichols (1969)	Males	.56	207	.19	126	CPI Factor I
	Females	.59	291	.39	193	(Extraversion)
Schoenfeldt (1971)	Males	.71	150	.55	53	Project Talent
	Females	.81	187	.47	103	Sociability Factor
Bruun (1966)		.51	157	.26	189	Sociability
Neuroticism						
Carter (1935)		.63	55	.32	44	Bernreuter Neuroticism
Gottesman (1962)		.55	34	.20	34	MMPI Psychesthenia
Nichols (1969)	Males	.55	207	.28	126	CPI Factor II
	Females	.55	291	.34	193	(Neuroticism)
Schoenfeldt (1971)	Males	.45	181	.45	65	Project Talent
	Females	.63	178	.16	87	Mature Personality
Bruun (1966)		.28	157	.21	189	Neuroticism

disorder. Some theorists hold that the various mental disorders represent extreme forms of the motives and defense mechanisms that make up the personality differences between people in the normal range. To the extent that this is true, information about the heritability of mental disorder should also be applicable to the normal personality. However, it is also possible that mental disorders result from biochemical imbalances of a different order from the sources of normal variation in personality. This later possibility seems particularly likely in the case of schizophrenia, which is the mental disorder that has been most widely studied from the genetic point of view.

Table 6. Risk of Schizophrenia for Relatives of Schizophrenics
(after Kallmann, 1916, 1950)

Class	Percentage Risk of Schizophrenia
Children of two nonschizophrenic parents (general population)	0.9
Relatives of adult schizophrenic index cases—	
Not consanguineous— {Step sibs	1.8
Spouse	2.1
First cousins	2.6
Nephews and nieces	3.9
Grandchildren	4.3
Half-sibs	7.1
Parents	9.2
Full-sibs	14.2
Dizygotic co-twins	14.5
Dizygotic co-twins of same sex	17.6
Children with one schizophrenic parent	16.4
Children with two schizophrenic parents	68.1
Monozygotic co-twins	86.2
Monozygotic co-twins living apart for at least five years	77.6
Monozygotic co-twins not so separated	91.5

Source: J. Shields and E. Slater. Heredity and psychological abnormality. In H. J. Eysenck (ed.), *Handbook of Abnormal Psychology.* New York: Basic Books, 1961. Copyright Pitman Medical, London, 1960. Used by permission.

Kallmann (1953) has conducted extensive investigations of the mental health of relatives of hospitalized mental patients. A summary of his results for schizophrenia is shown in Table 6. The increasing concordance of schizophrenia in pairs of people with increasing genetic relationship is convincing evidence for the importance of the genetic factor in determining the incidence of this disorder. This conclusion is supported by the observation that the incidence of schizophrenia is relatively constant in all human societies, even those with widely varying child-rearing practices and sources of environmental stress.

Recent twin studies of schizophrenia using perhaps more complete samples of all twins in the population (Gottesman, 1966; Kringlen, 1966) have found lower concordance rates for identical twins than that reported by Kallmann, but the difference in concordance between the two kinds of twins was still substantial.

Most other mental disorders also show greater concordance for MZ than for DZ twins, as is indicated by the typical results of twin studies

Table 7. Summary of Typical Results of Twin Studies of Mental Disorders

Disorder and Reference	MZ Twin Sets		DZ Twin Sets	
	Concordance[a]	N	Concordance	N
Schizophrenia				
Kallmann (1953)	86	268	15	685
Manic-depressive Psychosis				
Fonseca (1959)	75	21	38	39
Epilepsy (without brain damage)				
Lennox and Jolly (1954)	88	51	13	47
Neurosis, Psychopathic Personality				
Slater and Shields (1955)	53	38	25	32
Alcohol Addiction				
Kaija (1957)	65	26	30	58
Juvenile Delinquency				
Rosanoff *et al.* (1935, 1941)	85	42	75	25

Source: Adapted from J. Shields and E. Slater. Heredity and psychological abnormality. In H. J. Eysenck (ed.), *Handbook of Abnormal Psychology.* New York: Basic Books, 1961. Copyright Pitman Medical, London, 1960. Used by permission.

[a] The concordance is the percentage of cases in which the disorder occurs in both twins of a set of all cases in which the disorder occurs in either twin of a set.

shown in Table 7. These results would lead us to believe that there is a substantial genetic component in most mental disorders. However, it is not at all clear whether or not this same genetic component is also a determinant of normal variation in personality traits.

For additional details about the heritability of mental disorders, see Fuller and Thompson (1960) and Shields and Slater (1961).

Animal Studies

The importance of genetic factors in determining temperamental traits of animals has already been suggested in the discussion of Tryon's selective breeding experiment. Hall (1938) performed a selection study, similar to Tryon's study of maze performance, in which rats were selected for twelve generations for high and low emotionality. A commonly accepted definition of emotionality in the rats was used: frequency of urination and defecation in a large, brightly lit open field. By the twelfth generation there was essentially no overlap in emotional response between the emotional and the nonemotional strains.

The temperamental differences typically found between different strains of animals are also evidence of the importance of the genetic factor. Inbred strains of rats and mice show large differences in activity level, emotionality, and sociability (Fuller and Thompson, 1960). Scott and Fuller (1965) have described differences among five breeds of dogs in some thirty major test situations that furnished data on emotional reactivity, dominance, aggression, motivation, problem-solving and special capacities. Dog fanciers will not need to be told that large breed differences were found.

Animal studies have also shown that experience, particularly events occurring early in life, are important determinants of temperamental traits. Denenberg (1966) has reviewed studies in this area which show that a major effect of early stimulation is to reduce emotional reactivity to stress later in life. This reduced emotionality may be either adaptive or maladaptive depending on the test situation.

It should be pointed out that, while animal studies offer important clarifications of the mechanisms by which behavior is determined, they are of little help in understanding the relative effects of nature and nurture on adolescent personality. They merely show what we assumed to be true at the beginning of this chapter: that both heredity and environment are essential determinants of all behavior. An assessment of the relative importance of nature and nurture in producing the individual differences in adolescent personality observed in Western culture must await better studies at the human level.

Heredity-Environment Interaction

We have so far considered heredity and environment as if they were independent influences on behavior; however, for many traits there is an interaction between hereditary and environmental factors. In other words, the way in which a given genetic characteristic will be manifested may depend on environmental circumstances, and the effect of a given environmental experience may vary depending on the genetic characteristics of the experiencing organism.

An example of the way in which the manifestation of a genetic characteristic may be influenced by the environment in which it develops is provided by the treatment of phenylketonuria, a type of mental deficiency, by a special diet. Phenylketonuria is a recessive genetic defect resulting in a reduced ability to convert phenylalanine, an essential amino acid, into tyrosine because of a lack of the appropriate enzyme, phenylalanine hydroxylase. Without special treatment the toxic effect of the accumulation of phenylalanine or some of its derivatives results in mental deficiency. However, Armstrong and Tyler (1955) have reported a greatly reduced degree of mental deficiency in cases maintained on a low phenylalanine diet.

A number of recent animal studies have shown that the effects of environmental experiences are different, and sometimes in the opposite direction in different strains of animals (McClearn, 1964). For example,

King and Eleftheriou (1959) found that early handling experience resulted in an *increased* number of responses in a shock-avoidance conditioning situation for one subspecies of deermice and a *decreased* number of responses in the same test situation for another subspecies of deermice.

Not a great deal is known as yet about the interaction of the hereditary and environmental influences that bring about the normal variation of intelligence and personality at the human level. The hereditary-environment interaction that has perhaps received the greatest attention from researchers is the possible differential effectiveness of different educational methods for students of differing ability, the so-called treatment by aptitude interaction. Such an interaction could have important implications for education; however, Cronbach and Snow (1969) reviewed the research on this issue and concluded that no good example of such an interaction had been definitely established.

Summary

Individual differences among adolescents are caused in part by differences in native endowment, in part by family and peer influences, and in part by differences in educational opportunities. The available evidence suggests that, in the United States, inherited differences are the most important and educational differences are the least important (of these three categories of influence) in bringing about individual differences in intelligence and academic achievement. Environmental experiences occurring early in life have greater effects than do those occurring later in life.

The various components of intelligence—in other words, the pattern of abilities—also seem to be determined in part by heredity.

The evidence concerning the relative importance of hereditary and environmental factors in bringing about individual differences in personality does not yet lead to a definite conclusion.

Both heredity and environment are important determinants of all behavior. In many instances heredity and environment interact in that the effect of the hereditary characteristics depends on the environment in which they develop; and the effect of environmental experience varies depending on the genetic characteristics of the experiencing organism.

REFERENCES

Altus, W. C. Birth order and its sequelae. *Science,* 1966, *151,* 44–49.

Armstrong, M. D., and Tyler, F. H. Studies on phenylketonuria. 1. Restricted phenylalanine intake in phenylketonuria. *Journal of Clinical Investigation,* 1955, *34,* 565–580.

Astin, A. W. "Productivity" of undergraduate institutions. *Science,* 1962, *136,* 129–135.

———. Effect of different college environments on the vocational choices of high aptitude students. *Journal of Counseling Psychology,* 1965, *12,* 28–34.

———. Undergraduate achievement and institutional "excellence." *Science,* 1968, *161,* 661–667.

Blewett, D. B. An experimental study of the inheritance of intelligence. *Journal of Mental Science,* 1954, *100,* 922–923.

Bloom, B. S. *Stability and change in human characteristics.* New York: Wiley, 1964.

Breland, H. M. *Birth order and intelligence.* Unpublished doctoral dissertation, State University of New York at Buffalo, 1972.

Bruun, K. F., and Partanen, J. *Inheritance of drinking behavior: A study of adult twins.* Helsinki: The Finnish Foundation for Alcohol Research, 1966. Cited by S. G. Vandenberg, The nature and nurture of intelligence. In D. Glass (ed.), *Genetics.* New York: Russell Sage Foundation, 1968.

Burt, C. The inheritance of mental ability. *American Psychologist,* 1958, *13,* 1–15.

———. The genetic determination of differences in intelligence: A study of monozygotic twins reared together and apart. *British Journal of Psychology,* 1966, *57,* 137–153.

Carter, H. D. Twin similarities in occupational interests. *Journal of Educational Psychology,* 1932, *23,* 641–655.

Coleman, J. S., Mood, A. M., Campbell, E. Q., et al. *Equality in educational opportunity.* Washington, D.C.: U.S. Government Printing Office, 1966.

Cronbach, L. J., and Snow, R. *Individual differences in learning ability as a function of instructional variables.* Final Report, U.S. Office of Education, Contract No. OEC 4–6–061269–1217. Stanford University, School of Education, March 1969.

Denenberg, V. H. The effects of early experience. In E. S. E. Hafez (ed.), *The behavior of domestic animals.* London: Bailliere, Tindall & Cox, 1962.

———. Animal studies on developmental determinants of behavioral-adaptability. In O. J. Harvey (ed.), *Experience, structure and adaptability.* New York: Springer, 1966.

Edson, L. Jensenism. *New York Times Magazine,* August 31, 1969.

Erlenmeyer-Kimling, L., and Jarvik, L. F. Genetics and intelligence: A review. *Science,* 1963, *142,* 1477–1479.

Fifer, G. Social class and cultural group differences in diverse mental abilities. In *Proceedings of the 1964 Invitational Conference on Testing Problems*. Princeton, N.J.: Educational Testing Service, 1965.

Fonseca, A. F. Da' Analise heredo-clinica das perturbacoes afectivas atraves de 60 pares de gemeos. Oporto: Faculdade de Medicina, 1959.

Fuller, J. L., and Thompson, W. R. *Behavior genetics*. New York: Wiley, 1960.

Gottesman, I. I. Differential inheritance of the psychoneuroses. *Eugenics Quarterly*, 1962, *9*, 223–227.

———. Schizophrenia in British twins. Paper presented at the Second Invitational Conference on Human Behavior Genetics, Louisville, Kentucky, April 30, 1966.

Greenberg, D., Uzgiris, I., and Hunt, J. McV. Hastening the development of the blink-response with looking. *Journal of Genetic Psychology*, 1968, *113*, 167–176.

Hall, C. S. The inheritance of emotionality. *Sigma Xi Quarterly*, 1938, *26*, 17–27.

Hebb, D. O. *The organization of behavior*. New York: Wiley, 1949.

Holzinger, K. J. The relative effect of nature and nurture influences on twin differences. *Journal of Educational Psychology*, 1929, *20*, 241–248.

Honzik, M. P. Developmental studies of parent-child resemblance in intelligence. *Child Development*, 1957, *28*, 215–228.

Husen, T. Psychological twin research, Vol. 1. *A methodological study*. Stockholm: Almqvist & Wiksell, 1959.

———. Abilities of twins. *Scandinavian Journal of Psychology*, 1960, *1*, 125–135.

Jacob, P. E. *Changing values in college*. New York: Harper, 1957.

Jensen, A. R. Estimation of the limits of heritability of traits by comparison of monozygotic and dizygotic twins. *Proceedings of the National Academy of Sciences*, 1967, *58*, 149–156.

———. How much can we boost IQ and scholastic achievement? *Harvard Educational Review*, 1969, *39*, 1–123.

———. IQ's of identical twins reared apart. *Behavior Genetics*, 1970, *1*, 133–148.

Jones, H. E. Perceived differences among twins. *Eugenics Quarterly*, 1955, *5*, 98–102.

Juel-Nielsen, N. Individual and environment: A psychiatric-psychological investigation of monozygous twins reared apart. *Acta Psychiatrica et Neurologica Scandinavica* (Monogr. Suppl. 183).

Kaija, L. Drinking habits of twins. First International Congress on Human Genetics, Part 5, *Acta Genetica*, 1957, *7*, 437–441.

Kallmann, F. J. The genetic theory of schizophrenia. *American Journal of Psychiatry*, 1946, *103*, 309–322.

————. The genetics of psychosis: An analysis of 12,232 twin index families. *Congress of International Psychiatry*, Paris: Hermann Rapports: 1950, *6*, 1–27.

————. *Heredity in health and mental disorder*. London: Chapman & Hall; New York: Norton, 1953.

King, J. A., and Eleftheriou, B. E. Effects of early handling upon adult behavior in two subspecies of deermice, Peromyscus maniculatus. *Journal of Comparative and Physiological Psychology*, 1959, *52*, 82–88.

Knapp, R. H., and Goodrich, H. B. *Origins of American scientists*. Chicago: University of Chicago Press, 1952.

————, and Greenbaum, J. J. *The younger American scholar: His collegiate origins*. Chicago: University of Chicago Press, 1953.

Kringlen, E. Schizophrenia in Norwegian twins. Paper presented at the Second Invitational Conference on Human Behavior Genetics, Louisville, Kentucky, April 30, 1966.

Lee, E. S. Negro intelligence and selective migration: A Philadelphia test of the Klineberg hypothesis. *American Sociological Review*, 1951, *16*, 227–233.

Lennox, W. G., and Jolly, D. H. Seizures, brain waves and intelligence tests of epileptic twins. *Research Publication of the Association of Nervous and Mental Disease*, 1954, *33*, 325–345.

Lohnes, P. R. *Measuring adolescent personality*. Pittsburgh: University of Pittsburgh, Project Talent Office, 1966.

McClearn, G. E. Genetics and behavior development. In M. L. Hoffman and L. W. Hoffman (eds.), *Review of child development research*. New York: Russell Sage Foundation, 1964.

Morton, J. R. C., Denenberg, V. H., and Zarrow, M. X. Modification of sexual development through stimulation in infancy. *Endocrinology*, 1963, *72*, 439–442.

Neary, J. Jensenism: Variations on a racial theme. *Life Magazine*, June 12, 1970.

Newman, H. H., Freeman, F. N., and Holzinger, K. J. *Twins: A study of heredity and environment*. Chicago: University of Chicago Press, 1937.

Nichols, R. C. Effects of various college characteristics on student aptitude test scores. *Journal of Educational Psychology*, 1964, *55*, 45–54.

———. The National Merit twin study. In S. G. Vandenberg (ed.), *Methods and goals in human behavior genetics.* New York: Academic Press, 1965.

———. The resemblance of twins in personality and interests. *NMSC Research Reports,* 1966, 2, No. 8. (a)

———. Schools and the disadvantaged. A review of J. S. Coleman et al., *Equality of educational opportunity. Science,* 1966, *154,* 1312–1314. (b)

———. Personality change and the college. *American Educational Research Journal,* 1967, *4,* 173–190.

———, and Bilbro, W. C. The diagnosis of twin zygosity. *Acta Genetica et Statistica Medica,* 1966, *16,* 265–275.

Rosanoff, A. J., Handy, L. M., and Plesset, I. R. The etiology of child behavior difficulties, juvenile delinquency and adult criminality, with special reference to their occurrence in twins. *Psychiatric Monographs,* 1941, No. 1.

Salzberger, R. M., and Jarvik, L. J. In J. E. Rainer et al. (eds.), *Family and mental health problems in a deaf population.* New York: New York State Psychiatric Institute, 1963.

Schoenfeldt, L. F. The hereditary components of the Project Talent two-day test battery. *Measurement and Evaluation in Guidance,* 1968, *1,* 130–140.

———. Intraclass correlations obtained by personal communication, 1971. Study described in Schoenfeldt (1968).

Scott, J. P., and Fuller, J. L. *Genetics and the social behavior of the dog.* Chicago: University of Chicago Press, 1965.

Searle, L. V. The organization of hereditary maze-brightness and maze-dullness. *Genetic Psychology Monographs,* 1949, *39,* 279–325.

Sears, R. R., Maccoby, E. E., and Levin, H. *Patterns of childrearing.* Evanston, Ill.: Row, Peterson, 1957.

Shields, J., and Slater, E. Heredity and psychological abnormality. In H. J. Eysenck (ed.), *Handbook of Abnormal Psychology.* New York: Basic Books, 1961.

Shields, J. *Monozygotic twins brought up apart and brought up together.* London: Oxford University Press, 1962.

Slater, E., and Shields, J. Twins in psychological medicine. Paper read to the British Association, reported in: Relation of genetics to population studies, *Nature,* 1955, *176,* 532–533.

Smith, R. T. A comparison of socioenvironmental factors in monozygotic and dizygotic twins, testing an assumption. In S. G. Vandenberg (ed.), *Methods and goals in human behavior genetics.* New York: Academic Press, 1965.

Snider, B. C. F. *A comparative study of achievement test scores of fraternal and identical twins and siblings.* Unpublished doctoral dissertation, University of Iowa, 1955.

Thompson, W. R. The inheritance and development of intelligence. *Research Publication of the Association for Nervous and Mental Disorders,* 1954, *33,* 209–331.

Tryon, R. C. Individual differences. In F. A. Moss (ed.), *Comparative psychology.* Englewood Cliffs, N.J.: Prentice-Hall, 1942.

U.S. Commission on Civil Rights. *Racial isolation in the public schools.* Vol. I. Washington, D.C.: U.S. Government Printing Office, 1967.

Vandenberg, S. G. Innate abilities, one or many? *Research Report No. 3 from the Louisville Twin Study,* University of Louisville, 1962.

———, and Kelly, L. Hereditary components in vocational preferences. *Acta Geneticae Medicae et Gemellologiae,* 1964, *23,* 266–277.

———. Contributions of twin research to psychology. *Psychological Bulletin,* 1966, *66,* 327–352.

———, and Stafford, R. E. Hereditary influences on vocational preferences as shown by scores of twins on the Minnesota Vocational Interest Inventory. *Journal of Applied Psychology,* 1967, *51,* 17–19.

Wheeler, L. R. A comparative study of the intelligence of East Tennessee mountain children. *Journal of Educational Psychology,* 1942, *33,* 321–334.

Whiting, J. W. M. Menarcheal age and infant stress in humans. In F. A. Beach (ed.), *Sex and behavior.* New York: Wiley, 1965.

Wolf, R. The measurement of environments. In *Proceedings of the 1964 Invitational Conference on Testing Problems.* Princeton, N.J.: Educational Testing Service, 1965.

7

Cognitive Development and Learning in the Adolescent

*Jeanette McCarthy Gallagher**

Adolescence is like a balance sheet with both debits and credits. The debits weigh heavy: self-consciousness, acne, uncertain legs, and an even more uncertain future. This chapter, however, will spotlight the adolescent's chief credit: his increasing ability to think on a new level, that of formal thought.

Progress in school is contingent on the student's capacity to think (Peel, 1960). When the student becomes able to explain processes, a new quality emerges in his thinking. Much of a student's thinking is explanatory, the kind most often described by Swiss psychologists Bärbel Inhelder and Jean Piaget, who trace the development of cognition or the acquisition of knowledge from childhood to adolescence.

The following explanation of cognitive development and learning in the adolescent, based on Piagetian theory, will be guided by these questions:

What distinguishes the thinking of an adolescent from that of a child?

* Jeanette McCarthy Gallagher is Assistant Professor of Educational Psychology at Temple University. She has been a Postdoctoral Research Fellow at Harvard University in the Center for Cognitive Studies. Dr. Gallagher's writing and interests have been focused largely on the cognitive development of children.

Is there research evidence to show that as the adolescent develops there is a qualitative change in his thinking?

What factors effect this change in cognitive development, and what are the relations to learning in the adolescent?

Is it possible, through improved teaching methods, to encourage the adolescent to use his thinking capacities on a more mature level?

Contrasts in Thinking between Childhood and Adolescence

Compare the behavior of an eight-year-old child to that of an adolescent after each is asked to solve a problem called Combination of Colorless Liquids (example modified from Inhelder and Piaget, 1958). The experimenter gives the subject four numbered flasks containing: (1) diluted sulphuric acid; (2) distilled water; (3) oxygenated water; and (4) thiosulphate, which acts as bleaching agent in this experiment. Because the four liquids are both colorless and odorless, the four resulting flasks appear identical except for the numbers on the bottles. The experimenter also presents a small bottle (labeled g) containing potassium iodide, and a dropper. Finally, two unmarked glasses are placed before the subject, one containing (1 + 3), i.e., sulphuric acid plus oxygenated water, the other containing (2), distilled water.

The experimenter tells the subject to watch while he adds a few drops from g to each glass. If you are a student of chemistry, you already know that oxygenated water oxidizes potassium iodide in an acid medium. Therefore, the mixture (1 + 3 + g) results in a yellow color, the "correct solution."

The experimenter then directs the subject to work until he can produce the yellow color. Remember that during the demonstration, the subject could have grasped only one key to resolve the problem: there is something about the colorless liquid in g that produces the final yellow color. What is not apparent is the combinatorial nature of the problem, i.e., which and how many combinations of liquids from flasks (1), (2), (3), and (4), together with g, result in the yellow color?

Our first subject is an eight-year-old child. He begins by trying, in no observable order, all of the following double combinations: (1 + g), (2 + g), (3 + g), and (4 + g). Of course, the resulting mixtures are colorless so the puzzled child asks: "What's wrong? I tried everything."

In answer the experimenter suggests that the child use liquid from the bottles plus g. The child tries in a random procedure, such combinations as (1 + 2 + g) and (2 + 4 + g). After several attempts, the child tries (1 + 3 + g) and is delighted with the final yellow color.

However, his trial-and-error method is costly because he fails to remember the correct combination. Later, when he refinds the "lucky" (1 + 3 + g) combination, he loses it again by adding (4), the bleaching agent. Puzzled, he looks at the experimenter and speculates, "Oh, maybe I added too much from the small bottle." But no test follows.

Several characteristics of a seven to eleven year old's thinking were exemplified in the described strategies when he was confronted with the Combination of Colorless Liquids problem. First, the child's method lacked an overall plan. After the somewhat systematic beginning of double combinations failed, the child proceeded in a random fashion that only accidentally led to a "hit." Secondly, the child's spontaneous method was elementary, i.e., associating each bottle, in turn, to the liquid in g or combining contents of four flasks at the same time. Only prompting by the experimenter led to a triple combination such as (1 + 2 + g). The child did not understand the importance of trying all *possible* combinations. Finally, the child became so centered on the importance of g that he could not decenter, i.e., realize that the addition of (4) took away the obtained color. The flasks became all important as objects or elements in themselves. Therefore, the child did not consider attributing the absence or presence of color to the *combination* of several elements.

In summary, the child's thinking, exemplified by his procedure or strategies, was: devoid of an overall plan or systematic trial of all possible combinations; elementary and therefore not sufficient because of the complexity of the problem; or it focused or centered on one element at a time instead of on the interrelationship of the elements that ultimately explained the final result.

Now focus on the strategies of an adolescent, approximately fifteen years old, when he is confronted with the Combination of Liquids problem. After the experimenter instructs the adolescent to produce the yellow solution, this subject also begins by combining each of the numbered flasks with g.

"Maybe I forgot to use each solution," he comments after no yellow color appears. "I'll write them down as I proceed."

After combining all the flasks successively with g and listing the results, the adolescent moves on to triple combinations, i.e., liquid from two flasks in combination with g. When he mixes (1 + 3 + g) : "Ah! It's turning yellow. You need 1, 3, and the drops."

The experimenter asks, "Where is the yellow? Is it in there (pointing to g) ?"

"No, they go together," the subject answers.

Next the subject is quizzed on the effects of solution 2 and 4.

He responds: "I don't think solution 2 has any effect, but I'll make sure. If it has no effect, the yellow color will remain after I add solution 2 to this (1 + 3 + g) ."

After proving his point, the adolescent adds: "I think solution 2 is water. Give me some water from the faucet and I'll make certain. After he adds the water, the subject concludes: "See, the new combination (1 + 3 + g + water) is yellow as before. So solution 2 must be water."

The adolescent also is able to make further observations: "Perhaps solution 4 is water, too. If it is water, no change will occur. [He adds (4) to (1 + 3 + g).] No, now the color is gone. I think something in (4) keeps it from coloring. Let me try (2) and (4) again." [He combines (1 + 2 + 3 + g) and (1 + 3 + 4 + g).] "Look! Solution 2 causes no change in color so it must be water, but 4 keeps it from coloring. Now I can complete my list."

What distinguished the thinking of the adolescent during the Combination of Colorless Liquids problem from that of the child? First, the adolescent systematically proceeded to explore the results of all possible combinations. Only a complete combinatorial system furnishes the total number of possibilities.

In addition, the adolescent attempted to determine the effect of one or more liquids upon another, i.e., their interrelationships. Relationships can be understood only when variables can be separated.

As an example, review the younger child's performance during the chemical problem. When the yellow color disappeared after the addition of solution (4), the child failed to devise a method of experimentation to determine why. The adolescent, however, established this hypothesis based on an implication or logical conclusion: "If (4) is water, no change will occur." The adolescent was able to suggest the possible effect of one liquid upon another, a relationship. At the same time he was able to separate mentally the effect of one variable upon another. The "if . . . then" statement is important because it manifested a deduction from the hypothetical or the possible. The adolescent is capable, then, of hypothetical-deductive thinking: suggesting possible relations even before the test in reality confirms the proposed possibilities. After the test in reality, he can return to the starting point to propose another hypothesis, therefore manifesting reversibility.

In summary, three interrelated characteristics of adolescent thought have emerged: the ability to determine possible combinations of variables that solve the problem; the ability to suggest mentally the possible effect of one or more variables upon another when a certain relationship is suspected among variables; and the capacity to combine and separate variables in a hypothetical-deductive framework ("if this is so, . . . this will happen") so that a reasonable possibility is recognized before the test is made in reality. The fundamental property of adolescent thought is this reversible maneuvering between reality and possibility (Piaget, 1957a; Inhelder and Piaget, 1958).

The Development of Thinking According to Jean Piaget

A brief overview of cognitive development according to Piaget will place the contrast between the child's and the adolescent's thinking in proper perspective. Piaget (1970a) is concerned primarily with the formation and the meaning of knowledge: how a person proceeds from a state of less sufficient knowledge to a state of higher knowledge.

By studying children's behavior in many problem situations, Piaget concluded that there is a parallel between progress in logical organization of knowledge and corresponding psychological processes such as reasoning, memory, and mental imagery. For example, in the Combination of Colorless Liquids problem, there was a qualitative difference between the logic of the adolescent who used the "if . . . then" hypothetic-deductive approach compared to the young child who did not. The analysis of the adolescent's behavior showed the level or quality of the adolescent's reasoning ability.

Piaget emphasizes that a person does not grow in knowledge by passively copying objects in the external world. A person must act upon objects to know them. This action may take various forms: direct manipulations, visual observation, or a mental or internal transformation or change such as comprehending an idea after combining new and old information (Piaget, 1959; 1970a) .

In the Combination of Colorless Liquids problem, the adolescent would not have reached a solution by passive combination of liquids. The answer was not in the liquids, nor in the adolescent, but, instead, in the actions that the adolescent performed with the liquids.

Sensorimotor Stage. Knowledge or knowing about objects has its origin, then, in interactions between the person and the object. Even before the advent of language, the infant manifests "intelligent" behavior when interacting with his environment. For example, an infant will draw a blanket toward himself to obtain an object placed on it. The period of development from zero to two years is labeled the sensorimotor stage (Piaget, 1957a) .

Preoperational Stage. At approximately eighteen months of age, the child uses the symbols of language with a certain facility. He also is able to interact symbolically with objects, by pretending that a box is a truck, for example. Because true thought or operations do not yet exist, this period or stage of development is called "preoperational."

Concrete Operational Stage. At the stage of seven or eight years, the stage of cognitive development called "concrete operations" begins. Here the first real mental operations exist. An operation can best be defined by an example. When water is poured from a wide, short glass to a narrow, tall glass, the preoperational child will think there is more water in the taller glass! He is at the mercy of his perceptions and functions on a figurative level of knowing. However, at around the age of seven or eight, he is able to *conserve*, i.e., to realize that no water was added or subtracted and that the quantity remained the same irrespective of the container's size. His operation becomes reversible because he can mentally reverse his action and realize that the same amount of water was previously in both glasses so it continues to be equal. The psychological criterion for the existence of the reversible operation is the ability to conserve (Piaget, 1966).

Not an isolated phenomenon, this reversible operation is linked to other operations. Knowledge is ordered into structures as elementary interactions with objects become integrated into higher level interactions (Piaget, 1970b; 1971a).

These operations, internal reversible actions, are *concrete* until the child is about twelve years of age. A child in the concrete operational stage acts directly or concretely on objects. This behavior was exhibited in the Combination of Colorless Liquids problem when the child dealt concretely with the liquids, but failed to understand possible relations between them. The child was limited by his mental structures or capacities to classify and order objects concretely.

Formal Operational Stage or Adolescent Thought. With the beginnings of adolescence, adultlike thinking slowly emerges. The stage is called *formal operations* or *formal thought.** Whereas the child in the concrete stage is concerned about relations between objects, classifying and ordering them according to his capacity for first-order operations, the adolescent is aware of alternative hypotheses from the possible to the real. His operations, therefore, are second-order because he is aware of relations between the various hypotheses. Because the adolescent is able to deal with relations between relations, he is able to grasp the meaning of proportions, correlations, and probability, all rooted in second-order relations (Inhelder and Piaget, 1958; Lunzer, 1965; Lovell, 1971).†

Describing formal thought as structuring relations between relations gives unity to this stage of thinking. The description makes clear that the

---

* The term *formal* is used because a person at this level of thinking possesses the ability to consider the possible and, therefore, is able to reason about the form of an argument apart from its content. (See Peel, 1960, p. 115.)

† Piaget stresses the combinatory system and the group of inversions and reciprocities (INRC Group) as the structures of formal thought. Proportions and other second-order relations, logically related to the concept of the INRC group, are stressed here, instead. (See Inhelder and Piaget, 1958, pp. 314–323.)

use of formal thought extends beyond the Inhelder and Piaget experiments based on science and mathematics to all curriculum areas.

There are two points of possible misunderstanding. First, formal thought does not house its power in verbal statements, but in the power flowing from the combinatory system from which possible hypotheses may be tested in reality (Inhelder and Piaget, 1958). Formal thought differs in *quality* from concrete thought rather than in quantity of information or verbal statements.

Secondly, the formal operations of the adolescent build upon those of the child in the concrete period. The existence of any stage of cognitive development necessarily depends upon the acquisition of the previous one (Piaget, 1970b). Cognitive structures are not isolated: the adolescent actively integrates new information to older information and, if necessary, makes mental changes. However, the stages of cognitive development are not "overnight" phenomena. The following section makes clear that in one area of cognition, an adolescent may function on a formal level while he approaches other problems at a concrete level.

Validity of Formal Thought

How valid is it to postulate that a separate level of thinking evolves during adolescence? How does a researcher supply evidence of it?

The researcher examining formal thought stands on only one side of a polygon. He must remind himself constantly that all facets of formal thought form an integrated whole. By relating his findings to those of his colleagues, the researcher adds another bit of knowledge to understanding adolescence. Therefore, formal thought research is most valuable when the findings can be generalized: i.e., extending the acquisition of an operational structure to related situations (Pinard and Laurendeau, 1969).

A major question is whether investigators have found evidence of formal thought structures described by Inhelder and Piaget. In other words, is it possible to place adolescents in problem-solving situations and find manifestations of abilities such as formulation of hypotheses and completion of analogies based on proportions?

Selected Research Studies

Kenneth Lovell of the University of Leeds, England, has been a key investigator and stimulator of valuable research in formal thought. He selected ten experiments reported in Inhelder and Piaget's *The Growth of Logical Thinking* (1958) for a replication study (Lovell, 1961). The replicated experiments included the Combination of Colorless Liquids, Conservation of Motion on a Horizontal Plane, Equilibrium in the Hydraulic Press, Equilibrium in the Balance, and Projection of Shadows. Each subject was examined individually on four experiments, but each experienced the Combination of Colorless Liquids problem. The stratified sample involved two hundred subjects, ranging in age from eight years to adulthood.

After examining the results, Lovell (p. 149) concluded: "The main stages in the development of logical thinking proposed by Inhelder and Piaget have been confirmed." The strategies of a majority of the subjects demonstrated much the same kind of reasoning as outlined by Inhelder and Piaget. By subdividing the concrete and formal thought stages, Lovell scaled the subjects' strategies. He, however, emphasized two points. First, Lovell noted that the school population investigated in Geneva by Inhelder and Piaget must have consisted of above-average children and adolescents because many of Lovell's slower subjects lagged three or more years behind the Genevan group in manifesting solutions that could be labeled "formal." In addition, Lovell criticized Inhelder and Piaget for forcing the findings to fit their theoretical framework. In some cases, Lovell suggested, the subject's performance was categorized into an existing substage of concrete or formal thought, that is, the subject was forced to match the model rather than the model adjusted to match the individuality of the subject.

Although four of the Lovell experiments were part of the secondary school sciences curriculum in Britain, and had presumably been performed before by many of the subjects, the level of thinking in these experiments was not much different from the level in untaught experiments. It seems, therefore, that if structures necessary for understanding instructions are unavailable to the subject, information is forgotten or remains merely at the rote level. In other words, the level of cognitive development controls the learning experience.

Hughes (1965), a student of Lovell, conducted one of the first longitudinal studies, investigating growth of formal thought over a four-year period. The forty subjects of average and below-average ability were selected from a secondary school in a declining area of a large industrial city. The boys were tested from age eleven to approximately fifteen. The four Piagetian tasks used included the Combination of Colorless Liquids. Results of the four experiments were interrelated, indicating that if a student did well in one task, he would do well in the others. In addition, as the boys grew older, the stability of formal thought increased, as indicated by interrelations between the results of the experiments and other measures of ability. For example, results of a numerical proportions test correlated with results of the classical Piagetian tasks.

The Lovell subjects found the Combination of Colorless Liquids a very difficult task. The four-year strategy analysis can be summarized:

First year. Very reluctant to continue if success not achieved in initial stage. No subject attained formal thought level. Several said: "You get the yellow color when you put them in a certain order." More difficult in this experiment than any other.

Second year. Two boys obtained the yellow color. Others showed improvement by a systematic approach. Did not explore the effects of liquids (2) and (4).

Third year. Progress similar to second year. One boy suggested a hypothesis; did not volunteer to test it.

Fourth year. Fewer subjects reached at least a substage of formal thought, compared to performance in the other experiments. Only seven of forty subjects demonstrated strategies indicating formal thought.

Hughes emphasized that especially in the Combination of Colorless Liquids experiment, his subjects lacked spontaneity. When prompted, several subjects suggested possible combinations. However, they failed to volunteer to implement the suggestion. Unless asked to do so, none of the subjects checked properties of all the bottles, thereby indicating the lack of an operation based on a combinatory system. Why was there such a lack of spontaneity? Several possible reasons were proposed by the researcher: a restricted "traditional" in previous education, rigid and authoritarian present education, limited facilities, cramped working conditions, frequent changes of staff, and the poor cultural environment of the neighborhood. These conditions, the report continued, were unlikely to produce an active zeal for experimentation found in a more favorable *Zeitgeist.*

On the surface, the proposed explanations seem to echo American inner-city school problems. The factor of social transmission outlined by Piaget seems a key one here; however, it also may be important to consider whether a four-year time period is adequate to explore the movement toward acquisition of formal thought. Many of Lovell's (1961) subjects were still at the concrete operational level at age fifteen. It may be difficult to trace a sample after the school transfers that occur in the British system, but it seems imperative to do so to unravel some problems related to effect of variations in experience on the emergence of adolescent-level thought. Neimark and Lewis (1967, 1968) have given evidence that the longitudinal results correlated with the cross-sectional picture when they tested aspects of formal thought. However, Inhelder (1971a,

1971b) stresses that cross-sectional experiments only rarely capture the subjects while they are in fleeting, transitional stage so important in understanding cognitive development.

A longitudinal study by Stephens at Temple University on the development of reasoning in normals and retardates is furnishing valuable data on the ages at which certain Piagetian concepts are achieved. In a preliminary report (Stephens, McLaughlin, and Mahaney, 1971), the performance of normals (IQ 90–110) and retardates (IQ 50–75), was compared using mental age (MA) intervals from six through nineteen. Task achievement was defined as the earliest MA interval at which 66 percent of the subjects in that interval attained satisfactory performance.

Transition to formal thought has been set to occur between ages eleven–thirteen with equilibrium or adequate functioning set at age fifteen (Inhelder and Piaget, 1958; Stephens, Piaget, and Inhelder, 1966). However, Stephens et al., in the current longitudinal study of average subjects, are finding that advanced MAs are required for achievement in some formal tasks. For example, the MAs for normals for achievement in the Combination of Colorless Liquids problem was fifteen, while the achievement age for the dissociation of weight and volume was sixteen. Lovell (1971) cites the research of Hallam which indicated that certain reasoning abilities in the study of history are not attained until approximately age sixteen. Recently, Piaget (1972) has stressed the need for the investigation of formal thought between the ages of fifteen and twenty when the individual is formulating a "life program."

As emphasized, formal thought cannot be defined in terms of a verbal criterion: it is a system of second-order operations, i.e., relations between relations, permitting reversal of direction between reality and possibility. However, verbal statements may be substituted for objects in formal thought (Inhelder and Piaget, 1958). Elkind' (1968) proposed that proficiency in dealing with symbols is a necessary condition for effective *utilization* of formal thought. Junior high school students, average in academic achievement, were matched in age, sex, and IQ with special students who were below grade level in reading and other subjects. This latter group shared an apparent "symbolic deficiency" manifested in their poor reading ability.

After demonstration, a test of combinatorial reasoning was administered to all subjects. They were told to combine four different-colored poker chips in as many ways possible. Responses were scored according to the number of combinations attained and whether systematic strategies were used. The adolescents with reading difficulty made fewer combinations and used less systematic strategies than the adolescents with comparable IQs in the regular classroom.

Larry Newman, a Temple University graduate student, recently completed a pilot study on reading ability in adolescents as it is related to the development of logical structures. A sample of very poor and advanced readers (ages thirteen–nineteen) was categorized by a standardized test. Formal thought was tested by Inhelder and Piaget's Balance and Pendulum problems.

The results showed very little differences in strategies of the two groups in the Pendulum problem, with most subjects operating on the formal level. In the Balance problem, however, the poor readers used concrete level strategies. Inhelder and Piaget (1958) emphasize that an understanding of proportions, the model for the Balance task, does not appear until the first substage of formal thought. It is puzzling why the Pendulum problem did not differentiate between the poor and the advanced readers. Perhaps the balance problem, and Elkind's poker-chip combinatory problem, tap formal thought more closely as second-order operations or demand more understanding of relations between relations (Lunzer, 1965; Lovell, 1971).

In a recent study by Simpson (1970), reading tests surpassed individual intelligence tests in ability to predict successful high school graduation of low achieving students. It is important, therefore, to investigate further the performance of adolescents at all levels of reading ability handling a variety of tasks designed to tap formal thought.

Formal Thought as Second-Order Operations

In a recent review of problems associated with formal thought and its assessment, Lovell (1971) upholds the position that formal thought is best characterized as second-order operations or the ability to structure relations between relations. This approach is an aid in integrating the research on the various facets of formal thought.

Because the structure of verbal analogies is identical to that of numerical proportions, Lunzer (1965) devised an analogies test to investigate whether a subject needed second-order relations or formal thought to reach a solution. Subjects tested were nine to over seventeen years. Items in the numerical and verbal sections were graded for difficulty, with some items containing "distractors." This item occurred in the most difficult section: "Leather is to (soft—shoe—hide) as (hard—clay—house) is to brick." The correct answer is "Leather is to shoe as clay is to brick." However, if the pairs are inverted, another answer is correct.

In the easier section, Lunzer predicted that the younger children would be able to solve the analogies using concrete reasoning. However, the age nine level of success fell far below the prediction. Lunzer concluded that analogies, whether verbal or numerical, demand a more complex process of reasoning, understanding relations between relations, than exists at the concrete level.

Conclusion to Research on Formal Thought

Research supports the Piagetian position that there is an adolescent-level thought organization different in quality from earlier stages of cognitive development. Formal thought, however, does not seem to exist evenly across all areas of experience. In the Hughes (1965) and Stephens et al. (1971) studies, formal thought appeared earlier in the brighter adolescents. However, Elkind (1968) has proposed evidence that a specific skill, such as reading ability, may be a factor affecting the appearance of formal thought.

A fruitful research approach is to view formal thought as second-order operations or relations. Preselected groups such as good readers and poor readers or high and low history achievers could be given a variety of formal tasks in a two-step study (Gallagher, 1969). Priorities of difficulty and interrelations to tasks could be established. In order to study the transition from concrete to formal thought, the longitudinal method should be used when possible. Look now at the forces or factors which Piaget proposes are responsible for this transition.

Factors in the Development of Cognition

Understanding adolescence is the aim of this text. Central to this understanding is the movement toward mature thought. It is imperative to explore the why and how of this transition from the concrete to the formal thought level.

The history of developmental psychology could be rewritten as the "history of the nature-nurture" controversy (see Nichols' discussion within this book). Linked to cognitive development, the controversy takes the form: Does maturation (nature) or experience (nurture) play the more important role in cognitive development? The insightful psychology student will answer: "This is a pseudo question. The two factors obviously interact." But what is this "interaction"? Piaget (1970b) labels this interaction factor *equilibration,* leading to self-regulation. Equilibration is the fundamental factor of development; without it other factors would never become coordinated.

Piaget (Ginsburg and Opper, 1969; Piaget and Inhelder, 1963) lists four forces or factors in cognitive development: maturation of the nervous system; physical experience; social transmission, including language and schooling; and equilibration.

Maturation

If the maturation of the nervous system, the biological base, were the key factor in cognitive development, then the operations, emerging in adolescence, ought to unfold in their entirety. Evidence is to the contrary. In Lovell's (1961) classic follow-up study of Inhelder and Piaget's *The Growth of Logical Thinking* (1958), the subjects were scattered widely over the various substage of thinking at the concrete and formal levels. For example, of twenty-six students in the age range twelve–fifteen, only twelve attained the highest level of formal thinking in the Combination of Colorless Liquids problem. Others were scattered in the substages of concrete operations and the remaining substages of formal operations. The longitudinal study by Hughes (1965), outlined in the foregoing section, also confirmed this unevenness in attaining formal thought.

Maturation of the nervous system, then, is a *condition* of cognitive development (Piaget, 1971b). The important consideration, especially relative to adolescence, is whether the possibilities will be realized. The biological factor should be viewed not so much as an innate, preprogramed condition, but as a *growth* potential. Therefore, neural connections affecting cognitive development should be considered not only as hereditary connections but also as increasingly acquired connections (Piaget and Inhelder, 1963).

Role of Physical Experience

There could be no development of knowledge without contact with objects in the environment. Again, a person gains knowledge, not by passively copying objects in the environment, but by *acting* upon objects. Piaget (1970a) repeatedly has cited the following example to clarify this. When a child of five or six years discovers, by experience, that in counting from left to right a dozen pebbles in a line, he obtains the same sum as if he had counted them from right to left or in a cyclical order. The child learns the law of commutativity: The sum is independent of the order. However, the new knowledge of commutativity was obtained from the *actions* carried out on the pebbles and not from looking passively at them or noting physical attributes such as hardness or weight. Put another way, the child did not discover a property of pebbles; he discovered a property of the action of ordering. The pebbles had no order; the child's action introduced the order. A person learns, then, from actions carried out on objects, or logicomathematical experience. When he learns from the perceptual properties of objects, by noting their weight, color, or hardness, it is physical experience.

The distinction between logicomathematical experience and physical experience is important to understand learning in the adolescent. The adolescent's capacity for formal thought directs his actions upon things and moves him toward understanding relations between relations. Therefore, the adolescent's level of cognitive development directs his learning experience.

Social Transmission: The Role of Education and Language

The third classical factor of cognitive development is the social factor or the role of education and language. However, there can be no effect from social or linguistic experience unless the adolescent is ready to assimilate and integrate this experience into his own cognitive structures. Here is another example of development leading the way and setting limits on learning.

Inherent in the social factor is the weight given the effect of culture on cognitive growth. The researcher asks: What does it mean, *intellectually,* to grow up in one cultural milieu and not another (Greenfield and Bruner, 1969) ? Havighurst, in this book, examines this question in some detail within a social context.

To investigate this question, Peluffo (1967) devised a clever experiment using combinations analogous to Piaget's Combination of Colorless Liquids problem. An electrical apparatus with five bulbs and five switches was devised. The subject had to determine which combination of three switches would light a red bulb. Subjects, aged from eleven years to adulthood, were selected from a variety of Italian educational and socioeconomic backgrounds. The strategy leading to the correct combination was used less frequently by those who had little education and/or who came from an underdeveloped district. However, those who moved to advantaged areas did better in completion of the task than did those who remained in the underdeveloped area. Peluffo concluded that the development of formal thought is inhibited strongly by an underdeveloped milieu and lack of schooling.

Flavell's (1971, p. 190) statement related to Peluffo's research, as well as to the importance of improved education in American junior and senior high schools, highlights the role of experience:

> Now we usually think that what's really important is the kind of stimulation a child gets in infancy, and that once that's taken care of, you don't have to worry so much about the rest of development. We think of infancy, in other words, as *the* critical period for cognitive development. But if you really look at the facts in the Piagetian domain, it turns out that it is far more certain, and I think more biologically guaranteed, that a child is going to achieve sensorimotor acquisitions than it is that he will

acquire formal operations. The evidence suggests that whether or to what extent you get formal operations will depend much more upon the specific encounters the child has with his milieu than would be the case for sensorimotor actions or even concrete operations.

When the adolescent formulates hypotheses, because he has attained the operative structures on the formal level, he obviously is aided by language. The adolescent's language becomes increasingly more adequate to allow expression of possible combinations (Inhelder and Piaget, 1958; Piaget, 1966). However, an elementary logic existed before the advent of speech in infants (Piaget, 1952). Moreover, Sinclair failed to improve the operational level of five- to seven-year-old children by verbal training (Inhelder et al., 1967; Sinclair, 1967). Language, then, is not the *source* of intelligence, but rather an instrument or tool in Bruner's sense (Bruner et al., 1966) in the service of intelligence itself (Piaget, 1970b).

Language as a tool is a crucial concept relative to formal thought. Furth (1966, 1970b) has supplied evidence that intellectual development is not substantially affected by deafness until the age of ten or eleven. "Verbal statements and propositions come into their own as primary nourishment of the child's intelligence as he is getting close to formal operational functioning. This means that once the intelligence has, as it were, grown-up—and not earlier, it then becomes ready to feed and expand on verbal material" (Furth, 1970a).

Formal thought, then, does not mean verbal thought. Understanding language does not guarantee high-level thinking (Furth, 1970b). However, formal thought may feed on and be triggered by verbal interchange so that group discussions and group problem solving take on added importance in the adolescent years.

Here a word of caution is in order. Because the stages of cognitive development follow the same sequential order in *any* environment, the social environment alone cannot explain everything. Experiences in a social environment are always *necessary* but not *sufficient* for the development of logical structures (Piaget, 1959b; 1970b). However, as Flavell (1971) has emphasized, the social environment may be more important in the transition from concrete to formal thought than it had been in earlier transitions. It is necessary to turn to the interaction factor of equilibration to clarify the passage to formal thought.

Equilibration—the Fundamental Factor of Cognitive Development

Maturation, experience, and the social environment, including language, then, are all vital to the adolescent's growth in knowledge. However, to explain this growth fully, there must be an organizing or coordinating factor to effect an *active* reaction to external disturbance when integrating new knowledge is difficult.

Living organisms are self-regulating. In early biological development, the embryo often "self-rights" or regulates itself when a piece is removed (Waddington, 1966; Piaget, 1971b). Growth in knowledge reflects, or is analagous to, this self-regulatory organization of living organisms.

This analogy can best be understood by considering what occurs when an individual attempts to assimilate conflicting or disturbing pieces of information into his cognitive structure. Morf (1957) investigated the relation between logic and language during the transition from concrete to formal reasoning.

By presenting short stories followed by conflicting questions to subjects from seven to fifteen years of age, Morf was able to analyze differences in answers between those subjects probably at the concrete level compared to those probably at the formal level. Morf selected stories and questions that would force the use of the logic of combinations, i.e., the ability to perceive all possible variables in reaching a solution. A version of the following story, modified here from the French, tested one of the combinations essential to formal thought: implication or the ability to draw out the inferences of possible statements in an "if . . . then" form (Morf, 1957, p. 175).

The Watchmaker Test. In a watch factory, complaints were received that some watches were being poorly made. The director sent a technician to the factory to discover the trouble. The technician examined the machines and spoke with the workers. After a while, he telephoned the director and said, "So far I have found that all the watches made in September are defective since they do not keep time." The director looked at several watches in front of him. (The standardized questions designed to test implication follow.)

> (a) First the technician looked at a watch which had been made in September and said to himself: "This one was made in September; therefore, it is defective."
> Q. Could he say that?
> (b) Then he took a second watch and said: "This one was made in July; therefore, it cannot be defective."
> Q. Could he say that?
> (c) Then he took a third watch which he knew was defective and said: "This one is defective; therefore, it was made in September."
> Q. Could he say that?
> (d) Finally, he took a fourth watch and said: "I know that this one

has no defect; therefore, it could not have been made in September."

Q. Could he say that?

Morf took extra precaution to make certain each subject understood the important facts of the story read to him. "No" answers to questions (b) and (c) were considered crucial to understanding the implications: If a September watch is examined, then it would probably be defective; but if a non-September watch is examined, then it *may* or *may not* be defective.

Before age twelve, little understanding of implication was in evidence; after age thirteen, over one-half, and after age fifteen, about three-fourths of the subjects gave evidence of reasoning based on implication. The typical error at the concrete level was to treat implication as an equivalence: the statement that "all the watches made in September were defective" was made equal or converted into "all the defective watches were made in September." Therefore, the erroneous conclusion followed: "A non-September watch could not be defective."

A common reaction to such research is to suggest training sessions to "speed up" the movement from one stage to another. Piaget (1971b) calls this the "American question." Morf's training or didactic intervention sessions led to some surprising results. In some cases, subjects seemed to move to an advanced logic only to shift back to the concrete level. Following is a modified section from the training session of a nine-and-a-half-year-old subject (Morf, 1957, pp. 196–197) :

> Q. We have said that all the September watches are bad (third re-asking of *b*). We do not know anything about the others (explicit!). This one is from July. Can we say that it is good?
>
> A. Yes.
>
> Q. Why?
>
> A. Because all those from September are bad.
>
> Q. (At end of the training session.) All those from September are defective. Can the others also be defective?
>
> A. Yes.
>
> Q. Why?
>
> A. Because we haven't said anything about them.
>
> Q. (Then questioning from *a* to *d* again and reasking of *b*.) Can we say that the July watch is good?
>
> A. Yes.
>
> Q. Why?
>
> A. Because all those from September are bad. (!)

Note what is happening. The child is comfortable with two concrete classes: "defective-September" and "nondefective-July." When the error is pointed out, the child momentarily is disturbed and then answers correctly. The effect, however, is transitory. Upon further questioning, the error reappears.

Morf discovers, however, that older subjects, especially those who functioned in the formal level for other problems, found the "conflict" questioning of the experimenter helpful so that some of the adolescents actually corrected their initial error. The disturbance created by the questioning was needed to focus on the deficiency in the reasoning process and to actualize the adolescent's ability to understand a *possible* classification such as "non-September–*possibly* defective." Therefore, for some adolescents, the training session became a *learning* experience.

Learning in Relation to Equilibration. Why didn't the younger children and some of the adolescents profit from Morf's training experience? The factor of equilibration, as a sequence of self-regulation, is the key to the relation between learning and cognitive development (Piaget, 1959a; 1972).

The adolescent must be able to assimilate or integrate new information into existing structures of knowledge. In other words, a well-developed system-structure or competence within the person is necessary in order to take in outside data. There is no learning without establishing relationships (Piaget, 1959a). The subjects who did not profit from Morf's training sessions in all probability did not possess the competence to be sensitive to the incoming stimuli. The adolescents who profited from the training, however, already had the capacity to understand all possible combinations and so could be led to comprehend the implications of the watchmaker story.

Improved instruction, trained teachers, adequate facilities—important though they may be to the adolescent's educative process—can have an influence *only* to the extent that the student can assimilate the offered knowledge into his own operational structures or capacity.

Assimilation, however, is never present without accommodation, i.e., the person's modification or change of a cognitive structure by the new information (Piaget, 1970b). When the rigid-concrete class "defective-September" was modified by a disturbance to include the possibility that defective watches may have been manufactured in other months, then an accommodation or modification had taken place. The individual reached an equilibrium or balance resulting from intellectual activity, compensating for the external disturbance.

Formal thought reaches equilibrium when a high form of reversibility is in evidence: the ability to shift from the possible to the real. This reversibility implies a decentering process, the ability to take the point of view of others. Therefore, the adolescent does more than associate or "pile up" facts in stimulus-response chains. The entire equilibration process of gradually emerging equilibrium between assimilation and accommodation is for the adolescent the result of many decenterings, often through discussion with others.

The stage of cognitive development, then, explains learning. The learning of the adolescent, based on his capacity to reason from possibility to reality, will be different from that of the child. The level of cognitive development limits what can be learned. As Inhelder and Sinclair (1969, p. 20) state: "Learning of the fundamental operations of thought means to understand." Moreover, verbal instructions may be an instrument leading to understanding. However, the learning capacity is not provided by this instrument, but by the student. Therefore, learning is subordinated to the laws of development.

Motivation in Relation to Equilibration. It follows, then, that the self-regulatory or self-righting aspect of equilibration must be emphasized in relation to learning in the adolescent. Self-regulation implies internal reinforcement or motivation. Because of already equilibrated structures, the adolescent is able to assimilate new stimuli; however, it is the unknown or a new problem which provides the disequilibrium by disturbance or conflicts. There is satisfaction in seeking a solution to the problem or "disturbance," leading to a new understanding. The only reinforcement involved, then, is a certain functional pleasure resulting from the search and discovery of solutions to the problem, thereby reaching another equilibrium. The whole process of equilibration is a continual search for a better and better equilibrium. Motivation, therefore, cannot be understood apart from the equilibration process because the adolescent's pleasure in using his cognitive capacities in interaction with the environment supplies his motivation (Piaget, 1957; Tanner and Inhelder, 1960).

The Model of Equilibration and the Education of the Adolescent

When high school students are asked to write down personal problems, whether their own or what they project their friends' to be, difficulties in academic work head the list (Adams, 1964). In the midst of a computer and moonwalk age, educators grope for methods to make the junior and senior high school years less frustrating for many adolescents.

In his chapter on reforming the high school, Silberman in *Crisis in the Classroom* (1970) has concentrated on changes in curriculum and the movement toward freer scholastic environments. Johnston and Bachman focus sharply on this area within their chapter contained in this volume. Concomitant with such external reforms is the need for an "internal" reform whereby teachers understand the process of the acquisition of knowledge.

Equilibration, as the fundamental factor of development and the basis for Piaget's learning theory (Montpellier, 1964; Gallagher, 1972), suggests a conflict or disturbance model of instruction. Development cannot take place unless the individual is in a state of conflict. The equilibrium of intelligence is not a state of rest but an equilibrium of mobility; in the presence of a conflict the student tends to compensate or adjust and, therefore, is motivated to seek a solution. In a sense, intellectual appetite is motivated by discordant information (Piaget and Inhelder, 1963; Presseisen, 1971).

Conflict in the Educational Setting

The self-regulating process of equilibration provides, then, the internal reinforcement for eliminating contradictions and conflicts (Palmer, 1968). In the educational setting, conflict is introduced by probing and follow-up questions which challenge a student's stated position. Gall (1970) has noted, however, that 60 percent of teachers' questions require students to *recall* facts. About 20 percent require them to think, and the remaining 20 percent are procedural! Gall described an in-service teaching program that assisted teachers in dramatically improving their questioning behavior, and such programs should be fostered to improve the types of questions that adolescents ask one another in classroom interactions.

It is also possible to introduce conflict by the method of small-group discussions. Conflict questions could be presented to the adolescents which pose various problems: selecting the best evidence from several research readings, comparing one point of view with another, criticizing a commonly held opinion, or proposing solutions to a contemporary issue. Piaget (1972) has recently highlighted the value of group discussion. Because the adolescent is able to formulate hypotheses, he can adopt the point of view of an adversary in a discussion without necessarily incorporating the adversary's belief system. In addition, the adolescent has the capacity to construct his own theories to provide ideal solutions to problems. This capacity follows from reflecting on and analyzing his own thinking, i.e., second-order thoughts. Through the discussion interplay, moreover, the adolescent actually enters the society and ideology of adults.

Learning experiences, as we have noted previously, will have an effect according to the capacities of the student. Adolescence, as a time of proposing ideal solutions to real problems, is ripe for profiting from well-planned group discussions which are the setting for growth in knowledge through conflicts (Lovell, 1968).

The formulation of hypotheses is, to the adolescent, a process of invention, a bringing forth of something new (Piaget and Inhelder, 1963). The adolescent seeks acceptance of his proposed solutions, while at the same time he respects the competence of a teacher who can lead him to understand his errors in reasoning. It follows, then, that the adolescent needs opportunities to invent by seeking relations between relations, going beyond discovery of relations between things. Bruner (1966) suggests that such invention could take the form of writing a third act to a play after the first two acts had been studied. Group discussion could follow on whether or not the actors in the adolescent's "invented" third act manifested behavior that was logically consistent with the character as portrayed in the first two acts.

From the Possible to the Real World of Adult Society

By invention of solutions and reduction of disequilibrium, the adolescent gradually formulates a life program based on a scale of values of affective organization (Piaget, 1962). It is in this life program, corresponding to the aptitude of the adolescent, that the merging of the cognitive and emotional aspects of personality appears. Therefore, an understanding of growth in personality is aided by a grasp of the meaning of formal thought, the movement from the proposing of the ideal, possible solution to a testing in the real world of adult society (Elkind, 1970; Piaget, 1972).

Summary

In this chapter, adolescent-level thinking was proposed as formal thought according to the cognitive theory of Jean Piaget. The adolescent becomes capable of reasoning on different hypotheses—on the possible, on the probable—and not just on the real, the concrete. Formal thought may be viewed as second-order, whereby the adolescent reflects on his own thinking, seeking relations between relations. Cognitive development is controlled by the factors of maturation, physical experience, social transmission, and the coordinating or interacting factor of equilibration. The self-regulating process of equilibration defines learning in the adolescent. When the adolescent is faced with conflicting information, he is motivated to seek a solution according to the cognitive capacities he possesses. Instructional techniques that pose conflicts, therefore, provide the adolescent with situations for growth in knowledge.

REFERENCES

Adams, J. F. Adolescent personal problems as a function of age and sex. *The Journal of Genetic Psychology,* 1964, *104,* 207–214.

Bruner, J. S., and Clinchy, B. Towards a disciplined intuition. In J. Bruner (ed.), *Learning about learning: A conference report.* Washington, D.C.: U.S. Government Printing Office, 1966, 71–83.

————, Oliver, R., and Greenfield, P. M., et al. *Studies in cognitive growth.* New York: Wiley, 1966.

Elkind, D. *Children and adolescents: interpretive essays on Jean Piaget.* New York: Oxford University Press, 1970.

————, Barocas, R., and Rosenthal, B. Combinatorial thinking in adolescents from graded and ungraded classrooms. *Perceptual and Motor Skills,* 1968, *27,* 1015–1018.

Flavell, J. H. *The developmental psychology of Jean Piaget.* New York: Van Nostrand, 1963.

————. Comments on Beilin's paper. In D. R. Greene, et al. (eds.), *Measurement and Piaget.* New York: McGraw-Hill, 1971.

Furth, H. G. *Thinking without language: psychological implications of deafness.* New York: Free Press, 1966.

————. *Piaget for teachers.* Englewood Cliffs, N.J.: Prentice-Hall, 1970. (a)

————. On language and knowing in Piaget's developmental theory. *Human Development,* 1970, *13,* 241–257. (b)

Gall, M. D. The use of questions in teaching. *Review of Educational Research,* 1970, *40,* 707–721.

Gallagher, J. Research in cognitive development; some methodological consideration. Unpublished manuscript, Department of Educational Psychology, Temple University, 1969.

————. Equilibration—sources for further study. In C. F. Nodine, J. M. Gallagher, and R. H. Humphreys (eds.), *Piaget and Inhelder: On equilibration.* The Jean Piaget Society, Philadelphia, Pa., 1972.

Ginsburg, H., and Opper, S. *Piaget's theory of intellectual development: An introduction.* Englewood Cliffs, N.J.: Prentice-Hall, 1969.

Greenfield, P., and Bruner, J. S. Culture and cognitive growth. In D. A. Goslin (ed.), *Handbook of socialization theory and research.* Chicago: Rand McNally, 1969.

Hughes, M. M. *A four-year longitudinal study of the growth of logical thinking in a group of secondary modern school boys.* Master's thesis, University of Leeds, 1965.

Inhelder, B. Developmental theory and diagnostic procedures. In D. R. Green, et al. (eds.), *Measurement and Piaget.* New York: McGraw-Hill, 1971. (a)

―――. Information processing. Paper delivered at First Annual Meeting of the Jean Piaget Society. Temple University, Philadelphia, Pa., May 26, 1971. (b)

―――, and Piaget, J. *The growth of logical thinking from childhood to adolescence.* New York: Basic Books, 1958.

―――, Bovet, M., and Sinclair, H. *Developpement et apprentissage. Revue Suisse de Psychologie,* 1967, *26,* 1–23.

―――, and Sinclair, H. Learning cognitive structures. In P. H. Mussen, et al. (eds.), *Trends and issues in developmental psychology.* New York: Holt, Rinehart, and Winston, 1969.

Lovell, K. Developmental processes in thought. *Journal of Experimental Education,* 1968, *37,* 14–21.

―――. A follow-up study of Inhelder and Piaget's *The growth of logical thinking. British Journal of Psychology,* 1961, *52,* 143–153.

―――. Some problems associated with formal thought and its assessment. In D. R. Green et al. (eds.), *Measurement and Piaget.* New York: McGraw-Hill, 1971.

Lunzer, E. A. Problems of formal reasoning in test situations. In P. H. Mussen (ed.), *European research in cognitive development. Monograph of the Society of Research in Child Development,* 1965, *30,* 19–46.

Montpellier, G. L'apprentissage: La théorie de l'équilibration de Piaget. In Jean-François le Ny, Gérard de Montepellier, Geneviève Oléron, et César Florés, *Traité de psychologie expérimentale: Apprentissage et mémoire* (Vol. 4). Paris: Presses Universitaires de France, 1964.

Morf, A. Les relations entre la logique et le langage lors du passage du raisonnement concret au raisonnement formel. In L. Apostel et al. (eds.), *Études d'espitémologie génétique.* Vol. 3., *Logique, langage et théories de l'information.* Paris: Presses Universitaires de France, 1957.

Neimark, E. S., and Lewis, N. The development of logical problem-solving strategies. *Child Development,* 1967, *38,* 107–117.

―――, and Lewis, N. Development of logical problem-solving: a one-year retest. *Child Development,* 1968, *39,* 527–536.

Palmer, E. L. The equilibration process: some implications for instructional research and practice. In I. J. Athey and D. O. Rubadeau (eds.), *Educational implications of Piaget's theory.* Waltham, Mass.: Ginn-Blaisdell, 1970.

Peel, E. A. *The pupil's thinking.* London: Oldbourne, 1960.

Peluffo, N. Culture and cognitive problems. *International Journal of Psychology*, 1967, *2*, 187–198.

Piaget, J. *The origins of intelligence in children.* New York: International Universities Press, 1952.

———. *Logic and psychology.* New York: Basic Books, 1957. (a)

———. Logique et équilibre dans les comportments de sujet. In L. Apostel, B. Mandelbrot, and J. Paiget, *Logique et équilibre. Études d'épistémologie génétique.* Vol. 2. Paris: Presses Universitaires de France, 1957.

———. *Apprentissage et connaissance* (première partie). In P. Gréco, and J. Piaget (eds.), *Études d'épistémologie génétique.* Vol. 7, *Apprentissage et connaissance.* Paris: Presses Universitaires de France, 1959. (a)

———. *Apprentissage et connaissance* (seconde partie). In M. Goustard et al. (eds.), *Études d'épistémologie génétique.* Vol. 10, *La logique de apprentissage.* Paris: Presses Universitaires de France, 1959. (b)

———. Three lectures: The stages of the intellectual development of the child; The relation of affectivity to intelligence in the mental development of the child; Will and action. *Menninger Clinic Bulletin*, 1962, *26*, 120–145.

———. A theory of development. In D. L. Sills (ed.), *International Encyclopedia of the Social Sciences.* New York: Macmillan Co. and Free Press, 1966.

———. *Genetic Epistemology.* New York: Columbia University Press, 1970. (a)

———. Piaget's theory. In P. H. Mussen (ed.), *Carmichael's manual of child psychology.* Vol. 1. New York: Wiley, 1970. (b)

———. Intellectual evolution from adolescence to adulthood. *Foneme*, Third International Convention, Milan, Italy, 1970. (c)

———. The theory of stages in cognitive development. In D. R. Green et al. (eds.), *Measurement and Piaget.* 1971. (a)

———. *Biology and knowledge.* Chicago: University of Chicago Press, 1971. (b)

———. Problems of equilibration. In C. F. Nodine, J. M. Gallagher, and R. H. Humphreys (eds.), *Piaget and Inhelder: On equilibration.* The Jean Piaget Society, Philadelphia, Pa., 1972.

———, and Inhelder, B. Les opérations intellectuelles et leur développement. In P. Oléron, J. Piaget, B. Inhelder, and P. Gréco, *Traité de psychologie expérimentale: L'intelligence* (Vol. 7). Paris: Presses Universitaires de France, 1963.

Pinard, A., and Laurendeau, M. "Stage" in Piaget's cognitive-developmental theory: Exegesis of a concept. In D. Elkind and J. H. Flavell (eds.), *Studies in cognitive development.* New York: Oxford University Press, 1969.

Presseisen, B. Z. *Piaget's conceptation of structure: Implications for curriculum.* Unpublished doctoral dissertation, Temple University, Philadelphia, Pa. 1972.

Silberman, C. E. *Crisis in the classroom.* New York: Random House, 1970.

Sinclair. H. *Acquisition du langage et développement de la pensée.* Paris: Dunod, 1967.

Simpson, R. L. Reading tests vs. intelligence as predictors of high school graduation. *Psychology in the Schools,* 1970, *7,* 363–365.

Stephens, W. B., Piaget, J., and Inhelder, B. Application of theory and diagnostic techniques to the area of mental retardation. *Education and Training of Mentally Retarded,* 1966, *1,* 75–87.

———, McLaughlin, J. A., and Mahaney, E. J. Stages at which Piagetian concepts are achieved. *Proceedings of the 79th Annual Convention, American Psychological Association,* 1971, 203–204.

Tanner, J. M., and Inhelder, B. (eds.). *Discussions on child development.* Vol. 4. Geneva, New York: International Universities Press, 1960.

Waddington, C. H. *Principles of development and differentiation.* New York: Macmillan Co., 1966.

8

Adolescent Creativity

Ellen V. Piers*

Interest in and speculation about creativity is not new, but efforts to approach it scientifically have expanded vigorously in the past twenty years. It is an area where there are far more questions raised than answers given: yet, it is in raising questions that the scientist frequently pinpoints the problem. Before we focus on adolescent creativity, let us take a brief look at the current status of the field as a whole. This will give us the background to understand the major problem when we narrow the focus to the adolescent himself.

The Status of Creativity

One way to cover the field of creativity is to ask the questions that the psychologist asks; or, for that matter, the questions that the reader might ask. Such a plan might be more useful than presenting another review of the literature, a task which has been carried out by Barron (1963), Golann (1963), Taylor (1964), Mackler and Shontz (1965), and Dellas and Gaier (1970). So, let us begin at the beginning and raise the issue of:

* Ellen V. Piers is Associate Professor of Psychology at Pennsylvania State University and a supervisor in their Psychological Clinic. Dr. Piers has written a chapter in *School Psychological Services: Theory and Practice* and has authored a children's self-concept test as well as several articles on the self-concept and on creativity.

What Is Creativity?

Regression in the Service of the Ego. Theories and definitions of creativity have been legion. Only a few of the most influential will be dealt with here, beginning with the psychoanalytic conception of regression in the service of the ego. This oft-quoted phrase was presented by Kris (1952) and elaborated by Schafer (1958). It is described as a momentary, at least partially controlled, level of psychic functioning, where constructive use is made of more primitive, drive-dominated, nonlogical (primary process) modes of thought. According to this view, the inspirational phase of creativity involves regressive thought processes, but in the service of final production so that control is not lost (as in psychotic thinking). In the elaborative phase of creativity the more conventional and logical (secondary process) modes of thought prevail. Considerable research has been carried out more or less related to this concept, and other theoretical statements have been made, supporting the idea that the creative process involves both more primitive and more realistic types of thinking.

Self-Realization. In contrast to this psychoanalytic view is the position of Carl Rogers. Creativity for Rogers is self-realization, and the motive for it is the urge to fulfill oneself. In his words, it is "the tendency to express and activate all the capacities of the organism, or the self" (1961, p. 351). The three inner conditions of creativity are: openness to experience, which implies flexibility and tolerance of ambiguity; an internal locus of evaluation; and an ability to "toy with" elements and concepts.

Rogers is using the term *creativity* in two senses here: what Maslow has designated as "special talent creativeness" and the broader "self-actualizing creativeness" (1959, p. 85). This latter sense implies a sound and integrated personality or one moving toward that state under the proper conditions, one of which might be psychotherapy.

Effective Surprise. Bruner (1962) takes as the hallmark of a creative enterprise an act that produces effective surprise. He describes some of the conditions that affect the creative process, but which, when taken together, may seem paradoxical. These include such conditions as detachment along with commitment, passion as well as decorum, a freedom to be dominated by the object, and immediacy along with deferral. He feels that what he calls the "internal drama," the working out of the conflict and coalition within the set of identities composing the person, is the source of much creativity.

Recent Definitions. Many definitions have been used in the recent attempts to study creativity scientifically. Taylor reported that the

Fourth National Research Conference on Creativity at the University of Utah found two definitions most useful: Ghiselin's proposal that "the measure of a creative product be the extent to which it restructures our universe of understanding," and "the extent of the area of science that the contribution underlines," used by Lacklen of the Space Agency. Taylor also quotes Stein's definition that a process is creative when it results in "a novel work that is accepted as tenable or useful or satisfying by a group at some point of time" (1964, p. 6).

These definitions are social and stress the contribution or solution to a problem. Accepted by some, but not all, is the additional concept of individual creativity. From this point of view, the individual who makes something that others, unknown to him, have made before, should also be called creative.

Guilford (1965), who deals in factors involved in creative thinking, focuses more on the abilities themselves, such as fluency, flexibility, and originality. He does not require that creative output be socially useful or desirable, since science does not deal with values in this sense. His critics point out that by omitting this social aspect, the usual distinction between creative productions and pathological productions (which are frequently original but not often useful) becomes lost. Barron (1969) also seems to be ignoring social usefulness when he says: "Creativity may be defined, quite simply, as the ability to bring something new into existence."

Part of the confusion in definition lies in the fact that students of creativity have emphasized one or another of its various aspects: the product, the process, or the person. Kagan (1967), for example, says categorically: "Creativity refers to a product; if made by a man, we give him the honor of the adjective." He feels that a rich reservoir of knowledge is mandatory for a creative invention, and that the novelty which is the defining attribute in creativity owes its allegiance to two forces—the availability of diverse possibilities and, equally important, the desire to surprise. The creative person has the freedom that permits "generation of possibilities." Such freedom, Kagan feels, is not born, but made.* The fear of being incorrect is the greatest enemy of this fluid process.

Wallach (1970) most recently has chosen to focus on the creative process, because research with young people has dealt primarily with process, whereas the work on products and persons has been done mostly with adults. He is primarily concerned with showing that these processes are: different from usual thinking, and have face validity.

Jackson and Messick (1965) deal primarily with properties of the

---

* While the freedom to utilize creative potential may be "made," this does not imply that the potential itself is "made."

creative response. They describe four criteria of creativeness, namely, unusualness, appropriateness, transformation power, and condensation. The latter two criteria are more difficult to judge, and each is dependent on the criteria which precede it. They also describe the judgmental standards used to evaluate the response properties and the aesthetic responses which are elicited from others. Finally, they describe the predisposing cognitive styles and the personal qualities which would result in creative responses. Their whole conception is summarized in Table 1.

Table 1. Categories in Creativity

Predisposing Cognitive Styles	*Personal Qualities*	*Response Properties*	*Judgmental Standards*	*Aesthetic Responses*
Tolerance of incongruity, of inconsistency, etc.	original	unusualness	norms	surprise
Analytic and intuitive	sensitive	appropriateness	context	satisfaction
Openminded	flexible	transformation	constraints	stimulation
Reflective and spontaneous	poetic[a]	condensation	summary power	savoring

Source: F. W. Jackson and S. Messick. The person, the product and the response: Conceptual problems in the assessment of creativity. *Journal of Personality,* 1965, *33,* 309–329.
    [a] In the sense of concentrated, imaginative and powerful.

In trying to determine what creativity is, it is also important to establish what it is *not.* Taylor (1964) says that it is necessary to distinguish between creativity and productivity, since productivity implies quantity and creativity implies high quality of a particular kind. Research findings suggest that they overlap at least to a limited degree, but the mistaking of one for the other should be avoided, particularly where a group such as research scientists are rating each other. Arastek (1968) likewise says the essential factor in creativity is not production, but the challenge of the assumption.

Flanagan (1963) goes one step further and distinguishes creativity from both productivity and ingenuity. In his definitions *productivity* is shown by bringing forth many ideas and solutions. It emphasized both quantity and contribution. *Creativity* is shown by bringing something new into being. The emphasis is on the newness and lack of previous existence of the idea or product. *Ingenuity* is shown by inventing or discovering a solution to a problem. Here the emphasis is on the existence of a problem, and the demonstration of a quality of genius in solving it in an unusually neat, clever, or surprising way. It is thus a more limited concept than creativity. Most investigators would probably include ingenuity as an aspect of creativity, and assume productivity as a frequently predisposing but not sufficient condition for creativity.

In general, the concepts of novelty and originality (or a novel rearrangement) and resulting social contributions are the most frequently mentioned in connection with creativity. But some, like Taylor, are content to say we do not yet know what creativity is, and that the definition need not come first. As with intelligence, construct validity for measures of creativity must be built up slowly by exploration and examination. Of course, the choice of a criterion measure or measures, which is conceded to be the current major problem in creativity research, requires some type of definition.

Two other questions are related to the definition of creativity. The first is the issue of whether creativity is a demonstrable unique construct and different from intelligence. The other issue deals with the specificity or generality of the construct.

Specific or General?

The specificity-generality issue can be looked at in two ways. One attempts to answer the question of whether there are critical factors in the creative process which are common to individuals across different areas of creative endeavor. These are most usually compared in the artistic versus scientific areas, and results of studies (Barron and Welsh, 1952; Gough, 1961; MacKinnon, 1962; Cashdan and Welsh, 1966) generally confirm the idea of some general characteristics and modes of operating. They also indicate some characteristics specific to the various areas. The other way of examining the issue focuses on the generality of the creative approach within an individual across various modes or dimensions. Here the evidence is more conflicting. Mednich (1962), for example, has suggested that people may be "visualizers" or "verbalizers" and that their associational productivity will vary according to whether a task is cast in visual or verbal terms. Wallach and Kogan (1965), however, feel that a creativity dimension should cut across this distinction, and they found comparable results in their sample for both visual and verbal tasks. This was confirmed for the Wallach-Kogan tests by Cropley and Maslany (1969). Renner (1970) likewise demonstrated that training effects (in art) could generalize to influence complex responses to another class of stimuli (music). But on the basis of a comparison of results on the Remote Associates Test (verbal) and the Barron-Welsh Art Scale (visual), Mendelsohn and Griswold (1966) suggest that creativity may not be a unitary phenomenon. Piers and Kirchner (1971) likewise found no significant correlation between these two tests, and Piers and Morgan (1970), using the Wallach and Kogan measures, found no transfer of verbal training to visual tasks. Dellas and Gaier (1970) are among those who suggest that perhaps different types of creative talent exist. While some of the difficulties may lie in the adequacy of the measures themselves, the conflicting results indicate that we need further clarification of the question. I think it highly likely that we shall eventually resolve the generality-specificity issue in creativity the same way we have (after many years of argument) in the area of intelligence, i.e., acknowledge the presence of both general and specific factors.

What Is the Relationship Between Creativity and Intelligence?

This question is of particular concern to those who work with children and adolescents, and it has led to considerable research and controversy. Unfortunately, the interpretations and generalizations which have sprung from some of the work in this area have been accepted much too uncritically, and valid criticisms have been ignored. Let us consider some of the issues.

Guilford, who began analyzing intellectual abilities in general through his Aptitudes Project several years ago, soon included systematic studies of creative abilities. As he developed his *Structure of Intellect* model (1959), he differentiated two productive operations: convergent thinking and divergent thinking. Convergent thinking involves the giving of a well-determined answer as in a routine mathematical problem, while divergent thinking involves the generation of a variety of things, where there is no one correct answer. (One aspect of this is thinking of "what might be" rather than "what is.") Within the context of this model, Guilford found that most of the abilities that (presumably) contribute to creative thinking or performance fall into the divergent production category. As such, he considers that they are a form of intellectual ability, but of a much broader concept of intelligence than is usually held. They are not included, as others have also noted, in most intelligence or achievement tests, which stress only a few kinds of intellectual abilities such as cognition, memory, or other types of convergent thinking.

The question, then, is, To what extent are convergent and divergent thinking independent abilities? Are they sufficiently so to justify speaking of intelligence *and* creativity, or intelligence *versus* creativity?

Many of the studies have reported little or no correlation between the two. MacKinnon (1962), for example, at the Institute for Personality Assessment and Research (IPAR), found very low correlations with intelligence in his group of creative architects. Holland (1961) concluded that intelligence has little or no relationship to creative performance in arts and science at the high school level (also see Welsh, 1966). Yamamoto (1964) obtained a correlation of .30 in high school between IQ and an index of creativity. Getzels and Jackson (1962) reported low correlations with their individual measures and based most of their (unfortunately) widely quoted study on similarities and differences between their High IQ–Low Creative groups (mean IQ 150 on a variety of tests) and their Low IQ–High Creativity groups (mean IQ 127). Torrance (1960) did eight partial replications of the Getzels and Jackson study. In all of these, by emphasizing only two groups, the impression was given of different, almost mutually exclusive, abilities.

Barron (1963), also reporting on the IPAR work, suggested that the relationship between intelligence and creativity might depend on the type of creativity being considered. He felt that creative writers who produce original work in large quantities have mean IQs around 140 or higher. Also where the subject matter itself requires high intelligence for the mastery of its fundamentals, as in mathematics or physics, he felt that correlation with creativity is probably higher than it is for artists. Over the total range of intelligence and creativity he first estimated the correlation as about .40. More recently (1969) he has quoted an average in the .20s, although this may not reflect the whole range. In any case, beyond an IQ of 120 or so, measured intelligence seems a negligible factor in creativity, and motivational and stylistic variables become more important.

The most vocal critics of the conclusions relating to intelligence from these and other studies have been DeMille and Merrifield (1962), Ripple and May (1962), Thorndike (1963), McNemar (1964), and Wallach and Kogan (1965). Rather than going through their individual criticisms, perhaps we can summarize the main points:

Restriction of Range. Any restriction of range, such as is found when "highly intelligent" and "highly creative" groups are used, will automatically lower the correlation between them. This is an elementary statistical fact of which many people seem to remain blissfully unaware. While we can assume that most authors who report the low correlations in these cases are aware that the range has been restricted (and in some cases say so), the fact nevertheless remains that the correlations are picked up by other people, and incorrect generalizations to the whole range are made.

Instruments Used. Any attempt to separate *intelligence* and *creativity* into two relatively independent domains requires that the tests used to measure intelligence be more highly correlated with each other than they are with the tests used to measure creativity. Many of the tests originated by Guilford and adapted by Getzels and Jackson, Torrance, and others, have not fulfilled these requirements. We find that, in case after case, some divergent thinking tests correlate as highly with the intelligence measures, on the average, as they do among themselves.

Pooling of Scores. The question is also raised whether we are justified in pooling divergent test scores, which may have an average intercorrelation as low as .18 or .24, and calling the results "creativity." (I did it myself once . . . see Piers, Daniels, and Quackenbush, 1960.) These low inter-correlations, as opposed to averages of .50 and .60 obtained from traditional intellectual measures, argue either that the divergent thinking tests used are too diverse to be brought together under the general term "creativity" or that the domain itself is too diffuse to be considered as a unit.

Groups Utilized. The separation of groups into "highs" and "lows" (sometimes at the mean, sometimes as in the Getzels and Jackson study on the basis of the top 20 percent) can be very misleading, unless the relativity of these terms is stressed. We can agree that a mean IQ of 150 is high, but how many would agree that a mean IQ of 127 is low! Exaggerating the problem has been the emphasis on "Low-Highs" and "High-Lows," to the exclusion of the other two possible groups, particularly the "High-Highs," from whom we might ultimately expect the greatest contribution. Characteristics reported for the High Creative–Low Intelligence groups are thus becoming generalized to High Creative individuals in general, which may or may not be justified.

Having made many of these points, Wallach and Kogan (1965) published an extensive study with fifth-grade children, designed to establish definitively the degree to which the domains of creativity and intelligence can be separated meaningfully. Concluding that time limits and a testlike atmosphere interfere with creative responses and blur the distinctions, they eliminated these, and used visual and verbal tasks of good internal consistency in a playlike atmosphere with no time limits. The average intercorrelation among the creativity measures was .41; among the intelligence (and achievement) measures it was found to be .51; and between the creativity and intelligence measures it was .09. They thus achieved the separation they were seeking, and established that the creativity measures could legitimately be pooled to yield a creativity index score.

The authors then divided their groups at both means (for each sex), obtaining the familiar High-Lows and Low-Highs, but also using the remaining cells of High-Highs and Low-Lows, and compared the four groups on the many personality measures they had also obtained. Results of the analyses of variance at first seem rather random and uninterpretable; but the authors managed, quite ingeniously, to pull together the results into the following generalizations:*

High Creativity–High Intelligence. These children exercise within themselves both control and freedom, both adultlike and childlike kinds of behavior.

High Creativity–Low Intelligence. These children are in angry conflict with themselves and with their environment and are beset by feelings of unworthiness and inadequacy. In a stress-free context, however, they can blossom forth cognitively.

Low Creativity–High Intelligence. These children can be described as "addicted" to school achievement. Academic failure would be perceived by them as catastrophic, so that they must continually strive for academic excellence in order to avoid the possibility of pain.

Low Creativity–Low Intelligence. Basically bewildered, these children engage in various defensive maneuvers ranging from useful adaptations such as intensive social activity to regressions such as passivity or psychosomatic symptoms (Wallach and Kogan, 1965, p. 303).

In a more recent major publication, Wallach (1970) has attempted to refine his position and define more clearly how creativity and intelligence can differ. After considering the research literature, he concluded that such factors as flexibility, word fluency, cleverness, and elaboration correlate significantly with intelligence and that their inclusion in so-called creativity tests has led to the confounding of the two constructs. The tasks which seem most clearly independent of intelligence are those characterized by ideational (associational) fluency. Wallach defines this as a person's ability to generate, in plentiful number, ideas that are appropriate to a given task constraint. The ability involves both response productivity and uniqueness. He accepts an associative basis for the creative process and attempts to explain it in terms of flatter (response probability) associative gradients, and broader (nonevaluative) attention deployment. He also reports evidence linking associative creativity with elicited fantasy and presumes this might be extended to spontaneous fantasy.

Wallach recognizes that showing that a given set of abilities do not correlate with intelligence is not enough to show that they do reflect

---

* It should be remembered that once again these Highs and Lows simply refer to above and below the mean of the group, which was largely upper-middle class.

creativity. However, he feels that he has presented evidence which provides at least face validity for these processes and says the next step
should be the study of how these processes are implicated in the attainment of products which are judged creative. Others (Jacobson, Elenewski, Lordahl, and Lieroff, 1968) do not agree with the interpretation of
creativity in terms of traditional associative and mediation processes, so
the argument will probably go on.

After examining the research evidence, what can we say in general
about the relationship between intelligence and creativity? In this connection I like Freehill's (1961, pp. 83 and 103) distinctions between:
genius . . . "Superlative and recognized achievement . . . an exalted
kind of mind which leads to original work of such quality that it is
permanent and has nearly universal influence"; *talent* . . . "remarkable
ability falling short of the superlative . . . narrower cleverness . . .
may or may not have universal effect, and is of notably less transcendent
proficiency"; and, *giftedness* which is used as a general term for all
superior performance as well as more specifically for high intellectual
ability (high IQ).

By definition then, geniuses are our most creative individuals, and
from Cox (1926) and others we estimate that they are also of very high
intelligence. Johnson (1955) says there is little doubt that virtually all
the persons who have made major creative advances in science and technology in historic times have possessed very great problem-solving powers.

The intellectually gifted may or may not be creative. One of the
better accepted facts is that many people with high IQs who learn easily
and who may be productive and successful are not necessarily original.

The talented also may or may not be creative in the sense of marked
originality which makes a lasting social contribution, but they are probably more creative than the average person. The intelligence of the
talented has been estimated as being above average, but not necessarily
very superior.

To sum up, creativity and intelligence are not synonymous. They
are positively correlated, but the degree of correlation apparently varies
from slight to substantial, depending on the range and type of creativity.
They *can* be separated, with some individuals scoring relatively higher or
relatively lower on one or the other. High intelligence as measured by
our traditional tests is certainly no guarantee of creativity, but many of
our greatest contributions have come, and probably will continue to
come, from those few who are high on both.

Is Creativity Inherited, and Normally Distributed?

The assumption among psychological researchers is that most people have
creative potential but that there are wide individual differences in

degree. This differs from the idea of many lay people who feel that one either has or has not the potential to be creative. Gardner Murphy wrote: "We know from watching children in progressive schools that the desire to create must be almost universal, and that almost everyone has some measure of originality which stems from his fresh perception of life and experience, and from the uniqueness of his own fantasy, when he is free to share it" (1947, p. 453). And Fliegler says: "All individuals are creative in diverse ways and different degrees" (1961, p. 14). Lowenfeld (1959) distinguishes between actual and potential creativity, the former being that potential which is already developed and functioning. But Kneller (1965) warns against the assumption that variations in creative achievement represent simply the degree to which it has been expressed or developed. As with intelligence, we must assume that variations are primarily due to a wide range of potential. In another chapter, Nichols discusses the influence of heredity on measured intelligence and achievement. Because of the measurement difficulties, remarkably little definitive work has been done on the relationship between heredity and creativity. Even how closely creativity follows the normal probability curve has not been established. But Wallach (1970), in his discussion of the relation between fantasy and associative creativity, suggests that the role of hereditary factors in fantasy is probably greater than has been assumed. Barron (1969) also lends support to the influence of heredity in aesthetic judgment and adaptive flexibility through his study of monozygotic and dizygotic twins in Italy, in which he found markedly greater concordance for the monozygotic.

Can Creativity Be Developed?

Many people feel that creativity can be developed. But from some of the statements in the preceding section, it would seem that this development can take place only within the limits of an individual's potential. In other words, a child with limited potential will probably not become extraordinarily creative even with considerable stimulation and training, although he may do better than he did before. The point that is usually stressed is that our educational efforts have emphasized convergent thinking for all ranges of potential. The assumption is that, if we do emphasize divergent thinking, we can achieve enormous increase in the actual creativity of all levels of the population.

Courses in creative thinking are now multiplying rapidly, and research in developing creativity is going on at many universities. One of the most extensive group of studies has been conducted at the University of Buffalo (Parnes, 1962), results of which seem to warrant the postulate that the gap between an individual's innate talent and his lesser creative output can be narrowed by deliberate education in creative thinking.

The Creative Education Foundation at Buffalo holds regular Creative Problem Solving Institutes and has recently launched the *Journal of Creative Behavior*.

In other experimental studies, Maltzman (1960) found that he could increase originality through training. His studies involved the repeated presentation of a list of stimulus words in a modified free association situation accompanied by instructions to give a different response to each stimulus. This training also resulted in an increased number of responses to the Unusual Uses Test, whereas specific training in unusual uses did not. Piers and Morgan (1970) found that free association training with fifth-grade children increased productivity and uniqueness on a verbal creativity task (Alternate Uses), but the effect did not transfer to a nonverbal measure (Pattern Meanings). Examples of other successful efforts to stimulate creative responding are studies by Davis and Roweton (1968) and by Taylor (1970).

Studies on training for creativity have also taken place in industrial settings, and report at least some positive results. There are still many unanswered questions, however, including what training is best for what areas, how long effects last, and how much change can actually be effected.

A question of critical importance today is the impact of the so-called mind-expanding drugs on creativity. Many young people justify taking these drugs on the grounds that it will enable them to be more creative. But long before the practice reached its present proportions, Vornoff (1941) discussed the influence of stimulants and excitants (hashish, opium, alcohol) on cerebral activity as related to the creative product. He concluded that these drugs initially act as stimulants, but not for long, and that they ultimately inactivate the creative power of the individual. Arastek (1968) concurs and feels that Barron (1963) did not deal with long-range effects when he recognized the expansion of consciousness through drugs. We obviously need considerably more controlled research, particularly with regard to LSD, since the issue comes down to whether the oft-reported intense personal experiences do result in any more creative products.

How Can We Identify High Creative Potential?

It would be helpful if we could identify early the individuals who have the greatest potential. Such identification involves the establishment of predictors of future creativity. Considerable research has been done in this area, although it is recognized that in order for these characteristics to have true predictive validity, they should be used in longitudinal or follow-up studies in which they are compared with actual creative performance. Since the criterion problem of what constitutes creative performance is still not settled, and very few longitudinal studies have been made, we cannot assume that long-range predictive validity has been established for many of our indicators. Instead we have been forced, in the main, to rely on factorial or concurrent validities. In too many cases, the problem of validity has been ignored entirely, and conclusions are drawn from results with measures which have no claim to be measuring creativity other than the author's intent.

We do know that some of our traditional measures have not worked. Such things as school grades, traditional IQ tests, and sheer mastery of knowledge are not efficient predictors. So we have turned to many other sources of information in our efforts to identify the potentially creative person. The person himself has been asked to perform on certain tests, to do certain tasks, or to fill out forms on which he describes or rates himself in various ways. Teachers, peers, supervisors, and family members have been asked to rate him. Tangible products or accomplishments have been noted.

Modes of approach have also varied. Some (Cox, 1926) have looked at the early lives of individuals who later proved to be geniuses. The IPAR investigators and Anne Roe (1951, 1953a, 1953b) have studied the characteristics of groups who currently are rated as creative. Guilford attempted to devise tests which had factorial validity, that is, which consistently clustered together in his divergent thinking areas.

These Guilford aptitude tests have attracted so much attention and have been adapted by so many other investigators that they should be discussed in some detail. They were developed in the 1950s and represented one of the first efforts at validation of creativity measures. Guilford and his coworkers regarded the establishment of factorial validity as the preliminary step in validational procedures, the second being the correlation of factor measures with practical criteria. By making up many tests designed to fill the squares of his Structure of Intellect model, and by refining these through successive factor analyses, Guilford believed he had found the basic traits in creative thinking. These included, for verbal tasks, three fluency factors (ideational, associational, and expressional), two flexibility factors (spontaneous and adaptive, earlier called originality), and an elaboration factor. These all fall under divergent production. Guilford feels that creative thinking, though primarily divergent, also includes some convergent production abilities.

Examples of divergent thinking tests are Alternate (or Unusual) Uses, where the subject is asked to give, in a given time limit, all the uses he can think of for a newspaper or other object; Consequences, which asks the subject to consider what would happen "if . . ."; Plot Titles, which asks the subject for titles to a narrative paragraph; and many others involving figural and symbolic information as well as verbal. Most are scored for both quality and quantity.

As was mentioned in the section on creativity and intelligence, the Guilford tests have not all fulfilled their promise of being separate from intelligence, or of correlating with practical criteria. As a result, they are now being used with somewhat more discrimination than formerly. Guilford himself (1970) still incorporates all of them within his Structure of Intellect model.

Another frequently mentioned measure of creativity is the Barron-Welsh Art Scale (Barron and Welsh, 1952), a nonverbal test, and the Revised Art Scale developed from it. These tests seem to measure primarily a preference for complexity and have been found to differentiate between more and less creative groups in both the arts and sciences. Mednick's Remote Associates Test (1962), which calls for three-way associations, has been reported by its author and others to show promise, but has been dismissed by some as more a measure of convergent than divergent thinking, because it calls for one correct answer. Wallach (1970), however, supports the author's claim that it reflects divergent thinking, because the items in each question are linked only associatively, rather than by elaborate rules of logic or problem-solving. Examples of other tests purporting to measure creativity are the Myers-Briggs Type Indicator (Myers, 1962), The Preconscious Activity Scale (Holland and Baird, 1968), the Minnesota Tests of Creative Thinking (discussed under "Creativity in Childhood"), and innumerable operationally defined one-time measures based on projective techniques, stories, etc. The main difficulty with almost all these instruments is not only the lack of evidence for predictive validity, but also the fact that they rarely correlate with each other (Ohrmacht, 1970), or with other indices of creative performance (Dellas and Gaier, 1970). Exceptions to this are Eisenman's (1969, 1970) findings of significant correlations between his polygon measure of complexity-simplicity and the Barron-Welsh Art Scale.

Personal Opinion Survey and Unusual Uses

Taylor (1964) reviewed the results from the various classes of measuring devices and felt that enough research had been done to enable a crude ordering to be made in terms of predictive efficiency. He ranked the various classes tentatively as follows, noting at the same time some individual exceptions:

1. Biographical items and past achievements.
2. Self-rating and direct expression of goals and aspirations.
3. Originality and personality inventories.
4. Aptitude and intelligence measures.
5. Parental attitudes.

Ratings by teachers appeared to have little value for predicting creative performance, but ratings by supervisors and peers seemed to show promise in some settings. No evidence for the validity of other special devices and tests, or of physical measures, is currently available.

If Taylor is correct, the personality inventories—and especially the creative aptitude measures which attract so many investigators—are running a poor third and fourth on the above list. Until we have better evidence of their usefulness we should regard with a great deal of caution the conclusions drawn by the investigators using them. Meanwhile, we should continue to try to improve our selection of biographical items, past achievements, and other more promising predictors. The recently developed inventories by Schaefer and Anastasi (1968), described in the section on "Creativity in Adolescence," are a step in this direction.

What Are the Characteristics of Creative People?

Too many characteristics of creativity have been enumerated to be very meaningful. In part this has been a function of the wide variety of measures used. It has also been a function of the confusion created by adding those characteristics uncovered by the sometimes doubtful measures purporting to identify *potential* creativity, to those which are characteristic of persons judged currently creative, or creative historically. We shall try to concentrate on those characteristics which have been reported fairly consistently.

There appear to be many more or less distinct intellectual components of creativity. Guilford's several divergent thinking factors, which he feels operate along with convergent thinking in creative work, have already been discussed. In other studies, physical scientists who were judged creative rated themselves high on cognition, discrimination of value, flexibility, academic achievement, and intuition. They were also characterized by early interest in intellectual activities and above-average breadth of interest.

Nonintellectual factors are also important for all types of creativity and may play a greater part than do the intellectual in some of the more artistic forms. Motivation, for example, seems to be one of the important nonintellectual components. Most studies mention high drive, involvement, curiosity, persistence, and dissatisfaction with the status quo.

Other personality characteristics frequently mentioned are high self-sufficiency, autonomy, and independence of judgment; self-confidence; self-acceptance; humor, intuition, desire for complexity; and tolerance of ambiguity. Creative males score toward the feminine side in some of their interests and in characteristics such as awareness of their impulses and sensitivity.

Characteristics which have been found to be negatively related to creativity include attitudinal rigidity, premature judgment, and defensiveness. More low creative people describe themselves in terms such as contented, gentle, conservative, patient, virtuous, and concerned for others.

Some characteristics seem relevant to different types of creativity. Type of interaction with parents, liking for ideas versus people versus things, tendencies toward socialization and interpersonal involvement, introversion versus extroversion, and suppression versus expression of impulses may vary according to different fields of interest. For example, Roe (1953b) reported that social scientists' interaction with their parents involved overprotection, whereas physical and biological scientists developed early a way of life not requiring personal interaction.

In some areas there have been conflicting findings. One which has consistently sparked great controversy is the relationship of creativity to psychopathology. We do see evidence of unhappiness in childhood, maladjustments, neurosis, and even psychosis in reports of some creative individuals. The important questions are, whether the incidence of maladjustment is any greater in this group than in the general population, and whether they are creative *because* of the maladjustment or *in spite* of the maladjustment. MacKinnon (1967) found his group at the Institute for Personality Assessment and Research to earn higher scores on tendencies to psychiatric disturbances, but interpreted this not as psychopathology, but as good intellect, richness and complexity of personality, and general lack of defensiveness. In those with clearer evidence of psychopathology, there was also evidence of adequate control mechanisms. Because they did not repress or suppress as much, they might experience more anxiety, but they also had stronger egos.

Taft and Gilchrist (1970) drew a distinction between arts and architecture students who were high or low on creative interests and on ratings of productivity. Those that were high only on productivity rated themselves as more unhappy and had had medical attention for emotional problems. The authors speculate that in this case the productivity might be an attempt to solve problems. Those high on both creative interest and productivity showed the usual creative personality traits. In contrast to MacKinnon's findings of high anxiety, others have found high creatives to be extroverts and low in anxiety as contrasted with neurotic introverts, who are anxious and rigid. Dellas and Gaier (1970) come to the conclusion that the empirical evidence demonstrates no basis for the assumption of a relationship between creativity and neurosis.

The few studies on sex differences in creativity present the usual equivocal findings. Helson (1961, 1966, 1967, 1968), who has done the most work in the area, indicates that different factors may be involved in the operation and emergence of creativity in women. Almost all studies acknowledge the effect of cultural sex-typing as an inhibitor of female creativity (look back at the self-description of low-creative people!). Maier (1970) found that under encouraging, ego-enhancing instructions, females improve their performance on creative problem-solving more than males do.

To sum up, let us describe the personality attributes that Crutchfield (1961) feels tend to characterize creative individuals in general. In cognitive areas they are more flexible and fluent; their perceptions and cognitions are unique. In their approach to problems they are intuitive, empathic, perceptually open, and prefer complexity. In emotional-motivational spheres they are free from excessive impulse control, achieve through independence rather than conformity, are individualistic, and have strong, sustained, intrinsic motivation in their field of work.

What Do We Know about Creativity in Childhood?

Until recently there has been very little research on creativity in young children. Our knowledge has come chiefly from anecdotal accounts of the outstanding creative achievements, at an early age, of many of our geniuses. One of the few specific investigations was that of Andrews (1930), who studied the development of imagination in the preschool child. Using a variety of methods and observations, she came to the conclusion that total imaginative scores are highest between four and four and a half, with a sudden drop at age five when the child enters kindergarten. Griffiths (1945) also studied young children and felt that fantasy had an important function in helping to solve developmental problems. From various investigations it would appear that two of the most powerful inhibitors to creativity in early childhood are premature attempts to eliminate fantasy and the "holding-back operations" that keep children from learning until they are "ready" to learn.

At the elementary school age, greatest attention traditionally has been given to manifestations of creativity such as creative writing and art. Recently there have been developed a few more materials and attempts to measure creative capacities systematically, but it is difficult to say just where we stand. Much of the work at this level has come from Torrance and his associates at the University of Minnesota. Starting with adaptations of Guilford's tests, they soon left his measurements of single factors for more complex tasks, and developed the Minnesota Tests of Creative Thinking. While many of these tests seem ingenious and attractive to children, it is not always clear what type of validity they claim to take the place of the factorial validity they gave up. Torrance himself states that the most urgent research need in relation to the elementary school years is the standardization of one or more batteries of tests for assessing creativity. Standardization implies, of course, further evidence of validity.

Besides test validity, there exists the question of whether results using these same tests can be replicated by others. Wodtke and Wallen (1965), for example, in testing the validity of some of the generalizations made by Torrance concerning the classroom behavior of "creative" students, found that teacher and observer ratings of fourth and fifth-grade students did not correlate, the teacher ratings always being correlated with intelligence. In addition, high scorers on the Torrance tests exhibited no more "objectionable" behavior than did low scorers, and behavior of children under low and high control teachers did not differ on the dimensions rated. The authors concluded that too many recommendations for teachers of "creatives" have been made without systematic research to support them.

The relative effects of IQ and creativity on achievement could be minimized except that Torrance continues to make a great deal of it, and has adopted the so-called *threshold hypothesis,* which he attributes to J. E. Anderson. In this instance, the concept suggests that below some critical point (estimated to be at about 120 IQ), differences in IQ are considered to be the major determiners of differences in academic achievement. Above this critical point, differences in creativity may be more closely related to differences in achievement.

Both Getzels and Torrance apparently interpret their work as supporting the hypothesis. However, several studies have failed to confirm their results. Edwards and Tyler (1965) found that ninth-grade groups high on both creativity and intelligence scored no higher on achievement tests than did those high on intelligence. They concluded that a scholastic aptitude test like the SCAT is still a more dependable predictor of school achievement than are creativity tests. A more extensive study by Cicirelli (1965), working with the Minnesota tests and sixth-grade pupils, also failed to support the hypothesis either for a minimum or maximum IQ threshold, except for the possibility of a maximum IQ threshold at IQ level 130–139 in the case of language achievement. While the relationship between creativity and achievement was a weak one, Cicirelli found that the form of the relationship was such that IQ and creativity were additive and linear in their effect on academic achievement.

Wallach (1970), from his review of the evidence, concludes that the *threshold hypothesis* has not been supported.

Other approaches to the measurement of creativity in children have typically involved attempts to adapt Guilford or other adult instruments (such as the Myers-Briggs Type Indicator, 1962) to younger age levels. Besides their work on creativity and intelligence, Wallach and Kogan

(1965) have opened up several new areas with their studies of the effects of anxiety and defensiveness on creative performance, as well as their emphasis on a playlike atmosphere and extended time limits. Their finding of anxiety at an intermediate level in their creative groups is somewhat discrepant from that of Reid, King, and Wickwire (1959), who found creative children less anxious than noncreative.

Pankove (1967) found a positive relationship between risk taking and creativity in fifth-grade boys, with low defensiveness enhancing the relationship and high defensiveness attenuating it.

To sum up, systematic research on creativity in childhood is in a very preliminary stage. It would be unwise to draw conclusions or make generalizations at this point. The criterion problem is especially evident at this level, and only longitudinal studies will definitively answer the question of whether adult creativity can be predicted with any degree of accuracy during the early school years.

Creativity in Adolescence

It has taken us a long time to get to the specific subject of this chapter, and now that we are here, it will be discouraging to find that while encouragement in such areas as creative writing and art have been present for a long time, and such projects as Science Fairs have become increasingly popular, the high school years have been, until recently, the most neglected of all the age levels when it comes to systematic research on creativity. Many of the publications have dealt with the intelligence-creativity controversy, starting with the Getzels and Jackson (1962) study and followed by replications or modifications which supported or failed to support their position.

A more useful approach is the attempt of Guilford and his colleagues (1961) to establish whether the same factors appear in samples younger than his original groups of Air Cadets. Apparently sixth- and ninth-graders do show essentially the same factors, although a few specific tests should be carefully watched, since they tend to change in nature over the different age levels. It is fortunate that Guilford confirmed the general similarities, as many investigators were already using his tests for junior and senior high school groups. Results of the studies with these tests, however, have not added a great deal to our knowledge so far perhaps because, as was suggested before, they are inappropriately used.

A departure from the usual pencil and paper measures of creativity was the judging of pictures by children three to eighteen years enrolled in a municipal art program. (Trowbridge and Charles, 1966). The judges found that while technical competence increased gradually and steadily, creativity remained relatively constant from three to fifteen years with a sharp rise from fifteen to eighteen years. In contrast to this, the Torrance and other tests of creativity usually find a fairly steady rise in creativity with age, although some have attributed the correlation to the confounding within the tests, of creativity with intelligence.

Predictive studies have been relatively short-term. Best known of these have been the studies by Holland (1961), Holland and Astin (1962), and Nichols and Holland (1963), etc., on National Merit Scholars. In the 1963 study, predictors of academic achievement and extracurricular achievement in science, art, writing, dramatics, music, and leadership during the first year of college were studied with a sample of 1033 Merit Finalists. One hundred fifty-four potential predictors were used, including aptitude scores, originality scales, self-ratings, life-goals, personality and interest scales, home background variables, and child-rearing attitudes of the students' parents.

With so many measures being correlated, it is difficult to summarize results. The authors concluded that a variety of nonintellective predictors exist. Measures of creativity, originality, interests, personality factors such as extroversion and social dominance, and measures of past performance related to a variety of artistic and leadership criteria. Scholastic aptitude was, of course, nonpredictive in this very selected sample. The best predictor of creative achievement in college was creative achievement in the same area in high school.

A similar high-aptitude sample was used in the Parloff and Datta (1965) study of male high school entries in the Westinghouse Talent Search. The group that was highest in judged and potential creativity differed from the lowest in capacity for status, ambition and drive, independence, autonomy, self-reliance, efficient use of intelligence, and perceptiveness.

Another large-scale study which should eventually yield much valuable data is J. C. Flanagan's Project Talent, in which background information is being gathered on thousands of high school students along with results of an extended battery of tests. As these students are followed, important variables can be identified which will be used to predict later criteria of creativity.

One of the most active researchers in creativity with adolescents recently has been Charles E. Schaefer. Following up on the National Merit Scholarship Corporation results, he and Anne Anastasi (1968) worked with a large sample of high school boys in New York City to develop a more standardized biographical inventory that would identify creativity. Creative and control groups were formed in both artistic and scientific areas, based on a double criterion of teacher nomination and scores on the Guilford Alternate Uses and Consequences tests. Inventory questions dealt with physical characteristics, family history, educational history, leisure-time activities, expressions of preference, objective facts, and some plans and goals. Items significantly differentiating between creative and control groups formed the final inventory. Anastasi and Schaefer (1969) then developed a similar inventory for girls, though here because of a shortage of girls in scientific areas, the creative and control groups were in writing and art. Allowing for this variation, many biographical correlates were similar for boys and girls. There were some clear differences between areas, but creative groups in general were characterized by continuity and pervasiveness of interest in their chosen field, prevalence of unusual, novel, and diverse experiences, and educational superiority of family background.

Although, as mentioned previously, teacher nominations have not always proved a useful method of selection, the care with which these inventories were developed would seem to make them a significant contribution to our identification measures.

Other measures had been administered to the same sample. Schaefer reported on results from the Revised Art Scale (1968), where significant differences were found only between boys in the artistic creative group and their controls, although there was a trend for all creative groups to score higher. The Gough Adjective Check List (Schaefer, 1969a) was used to identify the self-concept of creative adolescents with confirmation of some previously-found characteristics such as preference for complexity and novelty, impulsivity, autonomy, and self-assertion. A hypothesized higher incidence of imaginary companions in the creative group was investigated (Schaefer, 1969b), and confirmed for both sexes for those who produced works of a literary nature but not for other groups. Finally, Schaefer reports (1970) on the development of an effective originality scale using the Frank Drawing Completion Test.

Individuals and groups are also focusing on the development of creativity in this specific age group. Davis (1969), for example, has recently reported on methods of training creativity in adolescents and has put out a guide (Davis and Hautman, 1968) describing his program.

It is encouraging to see an increase in the number of studies and materials devoted to creativity in adolescence. Since one of the major findings so far relates to the continuity of interests and behaviors at least between high school and college, we should be able, by extending the same type of investigations to younger and older age groups, to determine how early we can identify and encourage the characteristics and patterns of our truly creative adults.

What Can the Schools Do to Foster Creativity?

In spite of all our unanswered questions concerning the nature, development, and measurement of creativity, there is a consensus that our schools can and must do more to foster it. In the past, we have concentrated on the transmission of information as one of the chief goals of education. While this is still a necessary goal, it is too often transmitted in a way which stifles creativity. Johnston and Bachman make some interesting comments on school curricula in this volume.

Anderson (1965) contrasts *Open* and *Closed* systems in education. The Open system is a system of relating which is both stimulating to the person and accepting of uniqueness in his perception and his thinking. Examples are found in the seminar, the class discussion, the term paper, the original experiment, or the student project. To Anderson this system constitutes a propitious environment for creativity.

The Closed system has two types. In the *Personally Closed* system one individual tends to restrict the expression of uniqueness, obstruct or inhibit creative interaction. Domination and usurpation are involved, which use force, threat, or the symbolic expression of force in shame, guilt, and other techniques for the stifling of individual differences and for producing conformity. Children and adolescents are still victims of these practices, both at school and at home. The *Impersonally Closed* system refers to the limiting of education to the experience of others, without leaving enough room in the curriculum for individual discovery, individual rearrangement, or reorganization. Both Closed systems constitute an unpropitious environment for creativity, according to Anderson. Kagan (1967) feels that because of this emphasis in the past, a child views the purpose of education as being "to learn" rather than "to think." He goes on to say that to know is not to think, and to think is not to act.

Wallach (1967) comments on the effects of teaching machines and automated learning. Their emphasis on facts and analytic systems may only increase students' severity with regard to error. This method of learning rarely permits conceptual possibilities, so should not be used to the exclusion of other methods.

Rogers (1966) maintains that today the most important conceivable goal of education is learning how to learn or learning how to change, and to adopt new goals in our present-day world situation. This, he thinks, rates far above any type of static knowledge. To do it will require increased flexibility of thinking.

Although we know very little about how to accomplish this goal, several types of suggestions have been made. Guilford (1966) says we need to decide what has to be learned, what it takes to be creative, and which contributing qualities respond best to training. Since there is always some degree of transfer in every act of creative thinking, he recommends that the general aspects of information be emphasized, and strategies be learned that have general application in connection with new information. An assumption, verbalized by Guilford and others, is that in whatever field of information the individual aspires to be creative, it is important to have a good fund of information of that kind in his memory storage. MacKinnon (1966) puts it that the more items of information the person has, the more likely it is, on purely statistical grounds, that he will be creative. So the approach certainly does not argue for less information, but rather for more and for different ways of using it.

The teacher, of course, is held to be the most important single influence. In the life history of their creative adults, the IPAR group repeatedly found subjects testifying to the importance of some one teacher in the nurturing of their creative potential. Provus (1966) says that teachers, not materials or media, produce (or fail to produce) creative learning. But when given opportunities to construct creative learning materials, he found that only about 2/5 of the teachers became involved, while 1/5 fled from the experience and 2/5 remained passive. Even those who were interested took many months to change their style of teaching.

Although what constitutes a creative teacher has not really been defined, it is assumed that a creative teacher fosters creativity in children. This assumption may be mistaken. In the one or two studies which have been conducted, there seemed to be no correlation between the creativity of the teacher and the creativeness of the children. Perhaps there is a difference between a teacher being creative *personally* and knowing how to teach *creatively*.

Wallach and Kogan (1965), who emphasize learning in a spirit of associative play, feel that Bruner's "inductive teaching" or the "discovery method" holds promise. A variation of this was conducted by Crutchfield and Covington (1963) with an autoinstructional training program consisting of simplified detective stories which the children solved by being given successively more clues and information.

Finally, while it is felt that all children would profit from training in creative thinking, we may need different methods for different groups, and there is some disagreement about which groups to concentrate on first. Wallach and Kogan (1965) maintain that their high intelligence–low creativity child would be the most promising, while MacKinnon (1966) states that special attention should be given to groups who do not do well verbally or on verbal intelligence tests. In any event, he would deemphasize group participation with its demand for conformity and provide maximum opportunity for potentially creative students to work out their own interests. He reminds us that his most creative adults were not "well-rounded" but had "sharp edges" to their personalities. They did not all have particularly smooth childhoods, and some suffered much anxiety and confusion. MacKinnon feels that many students who will eventually be identified as creative adults, will, as adolescents, be troubled and disturbed, experiencing conflicts of roles, possibly crises in religious beliefs, uncertainty with respect to a multiplicity of life goals, and so on. For these he recommends casual and inconspicuous guidance toward more and more sources of knowledge out of which the students can find the answers they need. The general role of educational institutions in adolescent development has been discussed in detail by Johnston and Bachman in the next chapter, so we will not carry the topic further here.

Summary

Creativity is usually defined in terms of novelty and originality (or a novel rearrangement) and resulting social contributions. It can be studied as a process, a product, or a person. All people possess creative potential but in different amounts and of different kinds. Creativity is related to, but different from, intelligence as we ordinarily measure it, and very bright people may be creative or noncreative.

Work on the identification of creative potential in children and adolescents is just beginning, and only longitudinal studies and more definite criteria will tell us whether our present measures are in fact predicting who will be a creative adult.

Since we feel that creative thinking can be developed to a much greater extent than it is at present, there is much to be done to modify our present system of education so that more creative potential will be realized.

REFERENCES

Anastasi, A., and Schaefer, C. E. Biographical correlates of artistic and literary creativity in adolescent girls. *Journal of Applied Psychology,* 1969, *53,* 267–273.

Anderson, H. H. On the meaning of creativity. In H. H. Anderson (ed.), *Creativity in childhood and adolescence.* Palo Alto, Calif.: Science and Behavior Books, 1965.

Andrews, E. G. The development of imagination in the pre-school child. *University of Iowa Studies of Character.* 1930, *3* (4) .

Arastek, A. R. *Creativity in the life cycle. Vol. II. An interpretative account of creativity in childhood, adolescence and adulthood.* Leiden: E. J. Brill, 1968.

Barron, F. *Creativity and psychological health*. Princeton, N.J.: Van Nostrand, 1963.

———. *Creative person and creative press*. New York: Holt, Rinehart and Winston, 1969.

———, and Welsh, G. Artistic perception as a possible factor in personality style: Its measurement by a figure preference test. *Journal of Psychology*, 1952, *33*, 199–203.

Bruner, J. E. The conditions of creativity, In H. E. Gruber, G. Terrell, and M. Wertheimer (eds.), *Contemporary approaches to creative thinking*. New York: Atherton, 1962.

Cashdan, S., and Welsh, G. S. Personality correlates of creative potential in talented high school students. *Journal of Personality*, 1966, *34*, 445–455.

Cicirelli, V. G. Form of the relationship between creativity, IQ, and academic achievement. *Journal of Educational Psychology*, 1965, *56*, 303–308.

Cox, C. M. The early mental traits of three hundred geniuses. In *Genetic studies of genius: Vol. II*. Stanford, Calif. Stanford University Press, 1926.

Cropley, A. J., and Maslany, G. W. Reliability and factorial validity of the Wallach-Kogan creativity tests. *British Journal of Psychology*, 1969, *60*, 395–398.

Crutchfield, R. S. The creative process. In *Conference on the creative person*. Berkeley: University of California Institute of Personality Assessment and Research, 1961.

———, and Covington, M. V. Facilitation of creative thinking and problem solving in school children. Paper presented at the AAAS convention, Cleveland, Ohio, 1963.

Davis, G. A. Training creativity in adolescence: A discussion of strategy. In R. Grinder (ed.), *Studies in Adolescence II*. New York: Macmillan Co., 1969.

———, and Hautman, S. E. *Thinking creatively: A guide to training imagination*. Madison: University of Wisconsin, Wisconsin Research and Development Center for Cognitive Learning, 1968.

———, and Roweton, W. E. Using idea checklists with college students: Overcoming resistance. *Journal of Psychology*. 1968, *70*, 221–226.

Dellas, M., and Gaier, E. L. Identification of creativity: The individual. *Psychological Bulletin*, 1970, *73*, 55–73.

DeMille, R., and Merrifield, P. R. A review of J. W. Getzels and P. W.

Jackson, *Creativity and intelligence: Explorations with gifted students. Educational Psychological Measurement,* 1962, *22,* 803–808.

Edwards, M. P., and Tyler, L. Intelligence, creativity and achievement in a nonselective public junior high school. *Journal of Educational Psychology,* 1965, *56,* 96–99.

Eisenman, R. Creativity, awareness and liking. *Journal of Consulting and Clinical Psychology,* 1969, *33,* 157–160.

———. Creativity, birth order and preference for symmetry. *Journal of Consulting and Clinical Psychology,* 1970, *34,* 275–280.

Flanagan, J. C. The definition and measurement of ingenuity. In C. W. Taylor and F. Barron (eds.), *Scientific creativity: Its recognition and development.* New York: Wiley, 1963.

Fliegler, L. Dimensions of the creative process. In M. Andrews (ed.), *Creativity and psychological health.* Syracuse, N.Y.: Syracuse University Press, 1961.

Freehill, M. *Gifted children.* New York: Macmillan Co., 1961.

Getzels, J. W., and Jackson, P. W. *Creativity and intelligence.* New York: Wiley, 1962.

Golann, S. E. Psychological study and creativity. *Psychological Bulletin,* 1963, *60,* 548–565.

Gough, H. G. Techniques for identifying the creative research scientist. In *Conference on the creative person.* Berkeley: University of California, Institute of Personality Assessment and Research, 1961.

Griffiths, R. *A study of imagination in early childhood.* London: Routledge, 1945.

Guilford, J. P. Three faces of intellect. *American Psychologist,* 1959, *14,* 469–479.

———. A psychometric approach to creativity. In H. H. Anderson (ed.), *Creativity in childhood and adolescence.* Palo Alto, Calif.: Science and Behavior Books, 1965.

———. Basic problems in teaching for creativity. In C. W. Taylor and F. E. Williams (eds.), *Instructional media and creativity.* New York: Wiley, 1966.

———. Creativity: Retrospect and prospect. *The Journal of Creative Behavior,* 1970, *4,* 149–169.

———, Merrifield, P. R., and Cox, A. B. Creative thinking in children at the junior high school levels. *Reports of the Psychological Laboratory,* No. 26. Los Angeles: University of Southern California, 1961.

Helson, R. Creativity, sex and mathematics. In *Conference on the creative person.* Berkeley: University of California, Institute of Personality and Assessment, 1961.

————. Personality of women with imaginative and artistic interest: The role of masculinity, originality and other characteristics in their creativity. *Journal of Personality,* 1966, *34,* 1–25.

————. Sex differences in creative style. *Journal of Personality,* 1967, *35,* 214–233.

————. Generality of sex differences in creative style. *Journal of Personality,* 1968, *36,* 33–48.

Holland, J. L. Creative and academic performance among talented adolescents. *Journal of Educational Psychology,* 1961, *52,* 136–137.

————, and Astin, A. W. The prediction of academic, artistic, scientific, and social achievement of undergraduates of superior scholastic aptitude. *Journal of Educational Psychology,* 1962, *53,* 132–143.

————, and Baird, L. L. The preconscious activity scale: The development and validation of an original measure. *The Journal of Creative Behavior,* 1968, *2,* 217–225.

Jackson, P. W., and Messick, S. The person, the product and the response: Conceptual problems in the assessment of creativity. *Journal of Personality,* 1965, *33,* 309–329.

Jacobson, L. I., Elenewski, J. J., Lordahl, D. S., and Lieroff, J. H. Role of creativity and intelligence in conceptualization. *Journal of Personality and Social Psychology,* 1968, *10,* 431–436.

Johnson, D. M. *The psychology of thought and judgment.* New York: Harper, 1955.

Kagan, J. Introduction. In J. Kagan (ed.), *Creativity and learning.* Boston: Houghton Mifflin, 1967.

Kneller, G. F. *The art and science of creativity.* New York: Holt, Rinehart, 1965.

Kris, E. *Psychoanalytic explorations in art.* New York: International University Press, 1952.

Lowenfeld, V. Creativity and art education. *School Arts,* 1959, *2,* 2–15.

MacKinnon, D. W. The nature and nurture of creative talent. *American Psychologist,* 1962, *17,* 484–495.

————. Instructional media in the nurturing of creativity. In C. W. Taylor and F. E. Williams (eds.), *Instructional media and creativity.* New York: Wiley, 1966.

————. The study of creative persons: A method and some results. In J. Kagan (ed.), *Creativity and learning.* Boston: Houghton Mifflin, 1967.

Mackler, B., and Shontz, F. C. Creativity: Theoretical and methodological considerations. *The Psychological Record,* 1965, *15,* 217–238.

Maier, N. R. F. *Problem solving and creativity in individuals and groups.* Belmont, California: Brooks Cole, 1970.

Maltzman, I. On the training of originality. *Psychological Review,* 1960, *67,* 229–242.

Maslow, A. H. Creativity in self-actualizing people. In H. H. Anderson (ed.), *Creativity and its cultivation.* New York: Harper and Row, 1959.

McNemar, O. Lost: Our intelligence? Why? *American Psychologist,* 1964, *19,* 871–882.

Mednick, S. A. The associative basis of the creative process. *Psychological Review,* 1962, *69,* 220–232.

Mendelsohn, G. A., and Griswold, B. B. Differential use of incidental stimuli in problem solving as a function of creativity. *Journal of Abnormal and Social Psychology,* 1964, *68,* 431–436.

Murphy, G. *Personality.* New York: Harper and Row, 1947.

Myers, I. B. *Manual of the Myers-Briggs Type Indicator.* Princeton, N.J.: Educational Testing Service, 1962.

Nichols, R. C., and Holland, J. L. Prediction of the first year college performance of high aptitude students. *Psychological Monographs,* 1963, 77 (7, whole 570).

Ohrmacht, F. W. Personality and cognitive referents of creativity. A second look. *Psychological Reports,* 1970, *26,* 336–338.

Pankove, E. *The relationship between creativity and risk taking in fifth-grade children.* Unpublished doctoral dissertation, Rutgers State University, 1967.

Parloff, M. D., and Datta, L. E. Personality characteristics of the potentially creative scientist. *Science and Psychoanalysis,* 1965, *8,* 91–106.

Parnes, S. J., and Harding, H. F. (eds.). *A source book for creative thinking.* New York: Scribner's, 1962.

Piers, E. V., Daniels, J. M., and Quackenbush, J. F. The identification of creativity in adolescents. *Journal of Educational Psychology,* 1960, *51,* 346–351.

———, and Morgan, F. T. Free association as creativity training in children. *Proceedings of the 78th Annual Convention, American Psychological Association,* 1970, 303–304.

———, and Kirchner, E. P. Productivity and uniqueness in continued word association as a function of subject creativity and stimulus properties. *Journal of Personality,* 1971, *39,* 264–276.

Provus, M. M. Some personal observations on creativity. In C. W. Taylor and F. E. Williams (eds.), *Instructional media and creativity*. New York: Wiley, 1966.

Reid, J. B., King, F. J., and Wickwire, P. Cognitive and other personality characteristics of creative children. *Psychological Reports*, 1959, *5*, 729–737.

Renner, V. Effects of modification of cognitive style on creative behavior. *Journal of Personality and Social Psychology*, 1970, *14*, 257–262.

Ripple, R. E., and May, F. B. Caution in comparing creativity and IQ. *Psychological Reports*, 1962, *10*, 229–230.

Roe, A. A psychological study of physical scientists. *Genetic Psychology Monographs*, 1951, *43*, 121–239.

————. A psychological study of eminent psychologists and anthropologists and a comparison with biological and physical scientists. *Psychological Monographs*, 1953, *67*, No. 2. (a)

————. *The making of a scientist*. New York: Dodd, Mead, 1953. (b)

Rogers, C. R. *On becoming a person*. Boston: Houghton Mifflin, 1961.

———— (participant). In C. W. Taylor and F. E. Williams (eds.), *Instructional media and creativity*. New York: Wiley, 1966.

Schafer, R. Regression in the service of the ego: The relevance of a psychoanalytic concept for personality assessment. In G. Lindzey (ed.), *Assessment of human motives*. New York: Rinehart, 1958.

Schaefer, C. E. The Barron-Welsh Art Scale as a predictor of adolescent creativity. *Perceptual and Motor Skills*, 1968, *21*, 1099–1102.

————. Self concept of creative adolescents. *Journal of Psychology*, 1969, *72*, 233–242. (a)

————. Imaginary companions and creative adolescents. *Developmental Psychology*, 1969, *1*, 747–749. (b)

————. Development of an originality scale for the Frank Drawing Completion Test *Perceptual and Motor Skills*, 1970, *31*, 402.

————, and Anastasi, A. Biographical inventory for identifying creativity in adolescent boys. *Journal of Applied Psychology*, 1968, *52*, 42–48.

Taft, R., and Gilchrist, M. B. Creative attitudes and creative productivity. *Journal of Educational Psychology*, 1970, *61*, 136–143.

Taylor, C. W. (ed.). *Creativity: Progress and potential*. New York: McGraw-Hill, 1964.

Taylor, I. A. Creative production in gifted young (almost) adults through simultaneous sensory stimulation. *Gifted Child Quarterly*, 1970, *14*, 46–55.

Thorndike, R. L. Some methodological issues in the study of creativity. In *Proceedings of the 1962 Invitational Conference on Testing Problems*. Princeton, N.J.: Educational Testing Service, 1963.

Torrance, E. P. Educational achievement of the highly intelligent and the highly creative: Eight partial replications of the Getzels-Jackson study. (Research Memorandum BER–60–18). Minneapolis: Bureau of Educational Research, University of Minnesota, 1960.

————. Education and creativity. In C. W. Taylor (ed.), *Creativity: Progress and potential*. New York: McGraw-Hill, 1964.

Trowbridge, N., and Charles, D. C. Creativity in art students. *Journal of Genetic Psychology*, 1966, *109*, 281–289.

Vornoff, S. From cretin to genius. New York: Alliance Book Corp., 1941.

Wallach, M. A. Creativity. In P. H. Mussen (ed.), *Carmichael's Manual of Child Psychology*, 3rd ed. Vol. I. New York: Wiley, 1970.

————. Creativity and the expression of possibilities. In J. Kagan (ed.), *Creativity and learning*. Boston: Houghton Mifflin, 1967.

————, and Kogan, N. *Modes of thinking in young children*. New York: Holt, Rinehart, 1965.

Welsh, G. S. Comparison of D–48, Terman CMT and Art Scale scores of gifted adolescents. *Journal of Consulting Psychology*, 1966, *30*, 88.

Wodtke, K. H., and Wallen, N. E. Teacher classroom control, pupil creativity and pupil classroom behavior. *Journal of Experimental Education*, 1965, *34*, 59–63.

Yamamoto, K. Role of creative thinking and intelligence in high school achievement. *Psychological Reports*. 1964, *14*, 783–789.

9

The Functions of Educational Institutions in Adolescent Development

Lloyd D. Johnston and Jerald G. Bachman[*]

As you watch the educational enterprise going through its interminable routines, it is hard to avoid the impression that the whole affair is mostly a complicated ritual in which the vast majority of participants—pupils, teachers, administrators, policy makers—have never given a thought to the question *why*, in any fundamental sense, they are going through the motions they think of as education. In spite of the tardy recognition in a few quarters that there are some ugly situations in the schools of the urban ghettos and rural slums, the general attitude still seems to be that if we are spending 50 billion dollars a year on the education of 50 million children, and if over 40 percent of those are now getting to go to college, as compared with less than 20 percent a few years back, then "we must

* Lloyd D. Johnston is Study Director at the Institute for Social Research at the University of Michigan. He has coauthored (with Jerald G. Bachman et al.) *Youth in Transition*, Volume I, and his book *Drugs and American Youth* will soon be released. His articles have been written on such topics as the high school, drug use, and job and career satisfaction in teachers.

Jerald G. Bachman is Senior Study Director at the Institute for Social Research and a Lecturer in Psychology at the University of Michigan. He has authored or coauthored *Youth in Transition*, Volumes II and III; *Youth Look at National Problems;* and has written a number of articles on organizational processes, youth, and schools.

be doing something right," even though we haven't the remotest idea of what it is. This blind faith in quantity as proof of quality is precisely the faith that, in the long run, could be our undoing.*

It is a widely held belief among students of education that the American educational establishment aspires to and accomplishes much less than it might or should. In this chapter we shall be dealing with three general questions which relate to that belief. We shall begin by exploring the general functions the schools can potentially serve, both for the individual students and for the society at large. Then we shall present survey data from students and teachers on what they think the functional objectives are in American high schools at present, and what they should be ideally. Finally, we shall review the existing evidence on the actual effects high schools seem to be having.

It should be noted that in this chapter the focus is on schools, although there are a number of other institutions which have as their mission the education and socialization of young people. Most important of those, perhaps, is the family; but churches, youth clubs, youth agencies, the media, and even correctional institutions play a role in adolescent development. Space simply does not permit any thorough discussion of such a comprehensive array of institutions, but it is important to keep in mind that the school is but one of a number of institutions through which a society influences its young.

Functions for Students and Society

Society can be served by its schools in many ways. Cultural values, beliefs, and traditions can be transmitted to its newest generations. Future citizens can be given the knowledge and skills necessary to fill needed roles in the society. Less obvious, perhaps, are the custodial and channeling functions of educational institutions. The schools, particularly under a system of compulsory education, structure the time and activities of those members of the society who have not yet been given the rights and responsibilities of adulthood. The young are kept occupied, "out of trouble," and under control. Finally, schools select and channel young people for later educational and career patterns through their systems of tracking, grading, and certification. Thus they make many of the "tough decisions" for society; decisions about who will go how far in the educa-

* H. S. Dyer, The discovery and development of educational goals. In *Proceedings of the 1966 Invitational Conference on Testing Problems*, 1967, p. 4. Copyright 1966 by Educational Testing Service. Used by permission.

tional and occupational structure. Ostensibly, the decisions are made in a way which is best for society as a whole.

The functions which the school can serve for the individual student are at least as diverse as those it serves for the society. They might be thought of as of two general types: those relevant to the student's experience during the school years and those which are relevant to later happiness and success. The former are seldom treated as important in their own right—our conception of education seems to have a future-payoff orientation—but for the student the fulfillment and satisfaction experienced during the school years are important, too. The school provides a structuring of time as well as a set of alternative activities and associations. In so doing, it is serving important functions for the adolescent.

There are other benefits, however, which relate less to the intrinsic experience of the school years and more to future opportunities and experiences. At the most superficial level, the high school diploma provides the individual a credential which he may need to achieve future goals such as getting into college or securing a desirable job. The credential may or may not reflect the skills and achievement it is assumed to represent. The skills which it is intended to reflect are some other important benefits which the individual may derive from his schooling: general intellectual capacities as well as specific skills and knowledge which are important for succeeding in a particular career or in higher levels of education. Finally, the school potentially offers the student the skills and knowledge he will need to function successfully in the many adult roles which lie ahead of him: citizen, spouse, parent, worker, and so on. In other words, we assume that the schools have a considerable potential for equipping the student to achieve his own goals successfully in these many domains, however he may define them.

What we have enumerated here are potential functions of the school, both for the society at large and for the individuals who attend them. It is not clear that all these functions are currently being fulfilled. There may not even be a reasonable consensus in the country regarding which functions schools should serve. Controversies have raged in recent years, for example, over what role the public school should have in the transmission of religious beliefs and practices. Whether sex education (see chapters by Staton and Juhasz) and the control of personal dress and grooming belong within the school's domain are also questions which have been receiving extensive debate. Whether political issues and viewpoints should be discussed in school is another familiar subject of contention.

There is also a question of whether all of these functions can be served simultaneously, or whether there are some inherent conflicts among them. For example, there is a serious question of whether an institution can serve a custodial function (through compulsory attendance, etc.) and at the same time provide an optimally conducive climate for cooperation and learning. It is similarly questionable whether the school can serve its gatekeeping function (through the use of grading and elaborate degree requirements) and still attain optimal conditions for learning.

Nevertheless, the fact remains that a broad array of functions *can* be served by schools. In the next section we will be examining the issue of which ones seem to be receiving top priority from American educators at the present time.

Goals in American High Schools

Until quite recently, very little empirical research had been done on the subject of school objectives, although there was an endless flow of rhetoric on the subject. Several years ago, the area came under scrutiny as a part of the Youth in Transition project, a nationwide study of young men in high school (Bachman et al., 1967). Because the role that the schools are *trying* to play in the adolescent's development is so integrally related to the role they are playing or could play, we believe this information is worth some consideration. We shall begin by providing a brief description of the study, followed by a summary of the findings on school objectives.

The Youth in Transition Project

The project began in 1966 with a representative sample of 2,227 tenth-grade boys located in eighty-seven public high schools throughout the United States. Follow-up data collection took place in 1968 (N = 1890), 1969 (N = 1800), and 1970 (N = 1620); thus, the study followed the young men in the initial sample through high school (most graduated just after the 1969 data collection) and into the several worlds of higher education, jobs, and military service.

Samples of high school teachers in each of the eighty-seven participating schools were contacted in the spring of 1968 and asked to complete a mail questionnaire; 2100 (approximately 70 percent of those invited) returned completed questionnaires. This sample of teachers approximated a representative cross-section of American high school teachers at that time.

One segment of the teacher questionnaire dealt with school objectives. A similar segment was included in the final (i.e., 1970) data collection from the sample of young men and was administered to those who had remained in the same high school through the first three data collections (N=1300).

Measurement and Conceptualization

The page from the teacher questionnaire dealing with school objectives is presented in Table 1. The high school students answered an almost identical set of questions. The list of objectives in the two questionnaires is the same, permitting the comparison of teacher and student answers. Both groups were asked to deduce from the actual behaviors of administrators (the boys reported on administrators and teachers collectively) what objectives were being emphasized. In addition, the respondents were asked to describe their own feelings about how important each objective should be.

Selecting the objectives to be rated was not an easy task: certainly more could have been included, but available space set an outer limit. The problem was one of covering enough of the important domains without becoming so vague as to have meaningless objectives (a condition colorfully labeled by Dyer as "word magic"). The reader must judge the success of this effort for himself. As can be deduced from the introduction to the question set, we chose to define objectives as the purpose of individuals, not of organizations. Unfortunately, it has become common practice to anthropomorphize organizations and to speak of them as if they had intentions. This is unfortunate because it suggests either that organizations somehow have goals independent of those held by the people who are in them or that all members of an organization agree on the objectives of their collective behaviors. We would argue that the former is impossible and the latter is so rare as to be virtually nonexistent. Although some schools may have their objectives written down in a dust-covered volume, it is unlikely that they bear any resemblance to the purposes teachers and administrators have for their own organizational behavior. Unless, in fact, such written objectives are given life through the intentional behavior of those who make up the school, they are of no consequence to the dynamics of the school as a social system.

National Findings

The average responses of both teachers and students to these questions on school objectives are summarized in Figure 1. The fourteen objectives have been reordered to produce a smooth descending order based on the teacher reports of the actual situation. In other words they are rank-ordered according to the average importance that the teachers say they actually receive across the schools.

Table 1. Page from Teacher Questionnaire

Below are listed several possible long-term objectives that might be held by a high school. We would like you to make two ratings of each objective: (A) how much importance do you think the administrators in your school (principal, assistant principal, etc.) attach to each of the following objectives for your school? Make your judgment based on what *you* think your administrators are *actually trying* to do; and (B) how much importance do you think *should* be attached to each objective in your high school?	(A) Apparent Importance to Your School Administrators *Low* 1　*Moderate* 2　*High* 3　*Very High* 4　*Extremely High* 5	(B) Importance You Think Should Be Given *Low* 1　*Moderate* 2　*High* 3　*Very High* 4　*Extremely High* 5

1. Transmitting a thorough knowledge of subject matter　☐ ☐ ☐ ☐ ☐　☐ ☐ ☐ ☐ ☐
2. Preparing students to assume the family roles of spouse and parent　☐ ☐ ☐ ☐ ☐　☐ ☐ ☐ ☐ ☐
3. Preventing dropouts　☐ ☐ ☐ ☐ ☐　☐ ☐ ☐ ☐ ☐
4. Developing students' interests in political processes and social issues　☐ ☐ ☐ ☐ ☐　☐ ☐ ☐ ☐ ☐
5. Maintaining order and quiet in the school　☐ ☐ ☐ ☐ ☐　☐ ☐ ☐ ☐ ☐
6. Increasing students' motivation and desire to learn　☐ ☐ ☐ ☐ ☐　☐ ☐ ☐ ☐ ☐
7. Improving students' social and psychological adjustment　☐ ☐ ☐ ☐ ☐　☐ ☐ ☐ ☐ ☐
8. Developing students' concern for others　☐ ☐ ☐ ☐ ☐　☐ ☐ ☐ ☐ ☐
9. Developing outstanding athletes and athletic teams　☐ ☐ ☐ ☐ ☐　☐ ☐ ☐ ☐ ☐
10. Increasing student understanding of occupational opportunities and of the necessary skills, training, and interests　☐ ☐ ☐ ☐ ☐　☐ ☐ ☐ ☐ ☐
11. Responding to the *individual* academic needs of students　☐ ☐ ☐ ☐ ☐　☐ ☐ ☐ ☐ ☐
12. Getting a high proportion of students into college　☐ ☐ ☐ ☐ ☐　☐ ☐ ☐ ☐ ☐
13. Achieving outstanding academic performance　☐ ☐ ☐ ☐ ☐　☐ ☐ ☐ ☐ ☐
14. Giving non-college-bound students vocational skills　☐ ☐ ☐ ☐ ☐　☐ ☐ ☐ ☐ ☐

School Objectives

Develop Athletics (9)

Transmit Subject
Matter (1)

Maintain Order and
Quiet (5)

High % to College (12)

Achieve Academic
Performance (13)

Prevent Dropouts (3)

Increase Occupational
Knowledge (10)

Motivate to Learn (6)

Give Vocational
Training (14)

Respond to Individual
Needs (11)

Improve Social/Psych.
Adjustment (7)

Develop Concern for
Others (8)

Develop Political/
Social Concern (4)

Prepare for Marriage
and Parenthood (2)

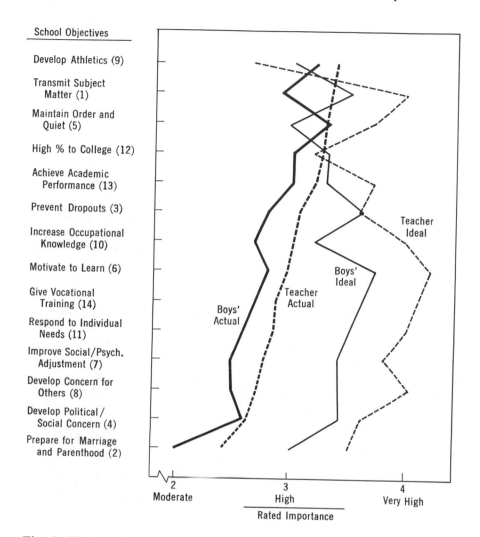

2
Moderate

3
High

4
Very High

Rated Importance

Fig. 1. Ideal and actual objectives as reported by teachers and boys.

Actual Objectives. Focusing for a moment on just that one line (Teacher-Actual), the reader will discover some surprising facts. The most startling is that teachers report athletics to be the area receiving most emphasis in our nation's schools! Then come the concerns traditionally related to academic achievement, i.e., subject matter, order and quiet, high percentage to college, and outstanding academic achievement. By contrast, the objectives having to do with socialization—the transmission of values and of knowledge which is related to the taking of adult roles (particularly those of citizen and family member) —come last. Teachers report that these get the least emphasis from administrators.

Turning next to the average ratings assigned to the fourteen objectives by the boys, we find that, despite a slight difference between the heights of the teacher and student curves, there is a strong positive relationship between them (Rho = .94) .* In other words, the students pretty much agree with their teachers about the priorities existing in our high schools. Such a finding was not necessarily expected, particularly given the lack of open discussion of objectives in schools. This amount of agreement suggests rather strongly that there are in fact differential priorities given to the fourteen objectives listed and that the student and teachers know pretty much what they are. They clearly agree that athletics and academic achievement are being emphasized a good deal, while objectives more directly related to psychological and social development get the least emphasis. It is rather disillusioning to find that students see the maintenance of order and quiet in the school as the top priority of administrators and teachers.

Teacher and Student Preferences. Turning next to the way that teachers and students would like to see things ideally, we discover some other rather surprising facts. The first is that the Ideal curves for both groups show much higher importance ratings overall than do the Actual curves. In other words, with a few notable exceptions, students and teachers would like to see most of the objectives here receive *more* emphasis than they are now getting. This finding could be interpreted in at least two different ways.

On the one hand, in reporting the emphasis they think *should* be given to each objective, teachers and students may not be taking into account the reality constraints faced by administrators: such things as limited time and financial resources, the availability of curriculum materials or qualified staff, conflicts among power groups about school purposes, etc. In other words, they may not be taking into account the

---

* Agreement is also found at the school level of analysis where the correlation between the average rating given to an objective by the teachers in each school can be correlated with the average rating given the same objectives by the students *in the same schools*. Across the fourteen "actual" objectives, we found an average product moment correlation of .23. We interpret this level of agreement as indicating validity in the measures, particularly given the small samples in each school and the fact that a two-year interval separated student and teacher responses.

Rho is a measure of agreement of the rank orders of the fourteen objectives provided by teachers and students. It is a correlation of the ranks with a maximum possible value of 1.00, which would indicate that both groups ranked the fourteen actual school objectives exactly the same. Rho in this case is .94, indicating very high rank order correspondence.

limitations and tradeoffs which must be faced in the real world. Although there may be some validity to this interpretation, we do not think it provides the full explanation.

The other interpretation, which we think probably accounts for most of the difference between the two curves, is that teachers and students are saying that they would like schools to be more purposeful institutions; more goal-oriented generally than they now are. Charles Silberman (1964), in his book *Crisis in the Classroom,* argues the same point most dramatically. Henry Dyer (1967), in a short essay on school objectives, provides another eloquent statement of the problem. (See opening quotation in this chapter.)

The overall differences between the heights of the Actual and Ideal curves are only part of the story. Even if those who run our schools did not aspire to greater overall accomplishment, students and teachers indicate a preference for a different set of priorities than they see existing now, and they show a considerable amount of agreement among themselves as to what those new priorities should be.

Despite the differences in the height and variability of the two Ideal profiles in Figure 1, students and teachers show a marked similarity in the rank order of their preferences (Rho = .73). Both groups felt that of the fourteen broad objectives offered, "increasing students' motivation and desire to learn," should receive the most emphasis. We interpret this objective to say in essence that learning should be a rewarding experience; that the behaviors normally involved in active learning (reading, questioning, seeking out information, integration, differentiating, etc.) should be reinforced in school. The fact that teachers and students rated this objective first suggests that they view such reinforcement as *more* important than learning a particular subject matter; or learning the skills for a particular trade; or learning the skills required to be a good athlete; or maintaining order and quiet in the school. It would also mean that when forced to choose between these objectives versus reinforcing the process of learning itself, they would choose the latter. In the contemporary education literature there is virtual unanimity that schools fall far short on this count. America's teachers and students, as illustrated by the data in Figure 1, seem to agree. They are saying, in essence, that "the powers that be" in our schools are simply not setting their sights high enough in this area.

The answers given to some other questions in the Youth in Transition survey add further evidence of our lack of success in the reinforcement of active learning. When asked, "How interesting are most of your courses to you?" only 6 percent gave the most favorable responses, "Very exciting and stimulating." Another 36 percent said, "Quite interesting." On another question, which asked how often they were interested enough

to do more reading (or other work) than the course required, only 21.
percent said "often" or "most of the time." Only 30 percent thought that
the things they were learning in school would be "very important" for
their later lives. Finally, only 18 percent answered "very true" in response to the statement: "My school work gives me a good chance to use
my skills and abilities."

Teachers and students both give athletics their lowest average rating,
dropping it from the top priority position it now holds. Both also assign a
second-place rank to "giving non-college-bound students vocational
skills." In fact, of the fourteen objectives there were only two which
received rankings from teachers and students which differed by four
positions or more. ("Maintaining order and quiet in the school" received
the rank of 13 from boys and 8.5 from teachers. "Preventing dropouts"
received the high rank of 2.5 from boys but only 10.5 from teachers.)

Implied Changes in Priorities. Given that teachers and students agree
pretty much on what the priorities in schools are and should be, it is
worth noting the areas where they indicate the greatest changes are
needed. We have already seen that a substantial downgrading of athletics
is being called for. The areas deserving the greatest increase in emphasis,
according to both groups, are those having to do with the social-psycho-
logical growth and development of students: increasing students' motivation to learn, preparing students to assume the family roles of spouse and
parent, developing students' interest in political processes and social
issues, developing students' concern for others, improving students' social
and psychological adjustment, and responding to the individual academic needs of students.

Another area which both groups agree should receive substantially
more emphasis is "giving non-college-bound students vocational skills."
Students feel that this area deserves more attention despite the fact that
roughly half of them go on to college and would not personally benefit
from such a change.

One interesting area in which there is some disagreement between
students and teachers is "maintaining order and quiet in the school."
Teachers would like to see a bit more emphasis here, while students
would like to see less. Since the objective implies a type of control (perhaps coercive control) of one group over another, it is not surprising that
the group being controlled would like less and not more. However, it
should also be noted that students do not, on the average, believe that
emphasis on this objective should be greatly reduced. Like the teachers,
they must view some semblance of order and social control as necessary to
the accomplishment of the other objectives they value. In summation,
neither group felt that the objective of "order and quiet" should receive

a substantially different emphasis than it is now receiving, but they do differ in the direction of the small changes they would prefer.

Other high school objectives which students and teachers perceive as receiving about the right amount of emphasis are "getting a high proportion of students into college" and "achieving outstanding academic performance." Both of these objectives are seen as receiving strong emphasis in the schools already, and while teachers would like to see somewhat more emphasis on academic excellence, both groups generally appear to be fairly satisfied with the relative importance currently being given to these objectives.

Given that students and teachers seem to be in fairly high agreement about what the priorities are in American high schools at present, as well as in the ways that they feel those priorities should be changed, it is worth considering briefly the dynamics which have given rise to the current state of affairs. In the process, we are likely to discover some forces which will create resistance to attempts to change things from the way they are now.

Social Forces in the Development of Objectives

If one reads the letters-to-the-editor column of almost any newspaper in the country, he will know beyond any doubt that there are deep and serious disagreements within our population concerning the appropriate functions of schools. Administrators are not immune to these controversies; therefore, the more controversial the area, the more reticent they are to push for a forceful curriculum in the area. This reticence may well explain why "preparing students to assume the family roles of spouse and parent," which would imply sex education and child-rearing education, is rated currently as receiving the least emphasis of all fourteen objectives.

Moreover, the general public (and parents specifically) evaluate the school administration on the basis of what is measurable and observable to them. The number of football games won, the number of fights in the school, the number of Merit Scholars produced, the proportion of students going to college, and the dropout rate—all are publicly observable and measurable. They also correspond to the objectives perceived as receiving top priority at present. In addition, getting students into college and its concomitant, academic excellence, are particularly important to the social elites (from whom most school boards are drawn) and the middle class (who often comprise most of the active voters). These facts, no doubt, explain in large part the relative emphasis at present on "getting a high proportion of students into college" versus "giving non-college-bound students vocational skills." The recipient populations for these two objectives vary greatly in their political strength and representation in school governance, and school administrators respond to the power being exercised.

The teachers are, of course, also affected by a set of social forces. Simply because they endorse a different set of priorities and emphases than they attribute to administrators does not mean that they are actually able to translate their ideal priorities into personal actions. Teachers also experience considerable pressure to avoid controversial areas, emphasize academic achievement (measured in terms of test scores), and so on. Administrators have powerful tools at their disposal with which to exact compliance as do parents and other groups. The observability of an outcome also has a lot to do with whether it will be weighed in the evaluation of an individual teacher, just as it does for the school as a whole. If a teacher's class has come to enjoy the process of learning, probably no one but that teacher and his (or her) students will know it. However, administrators and perhaps teachers will know precisely how much the class advanced on some standardized test of subject achievement. Similarly they will have an idea of just how "noisy and obtrusive" the class was. These outcomes are observable.

Another kind of social force, however, obtains somewhat uniquely at the level of teachers, and it derives from the way they are organized. Some of the fourteen objectives we have been discussing have organizational subunits within the school charged with their accomplishment. It is probably no accident that the best example of this matching between structure and purpose—athletics—is the area which is reported to receive more emphasis than any other. Virtually every school has a physical education department and (sometimes separately) department of athletics. It is the explicit and primary mission of every instructor in that department to develop students' athletic skills. Furthermore, the fact that there is an organizational unit sharing that same goal means that the instructors can collaborate, help each other, develop a coordinated curriculum, and lobby as a unit for a share of the school's resources. The goal of "increasing students' motivation and desire to learn" has no similar group working on its behalf nor does "improving students' concern for others."

Some of the most important functions a school might serve do not have a single person charged with their accomplishment or even with designing *ways* to accomplish them, no matter how large the school. The traditional division of labor around academic disciplines simply does not reflect many of the ostensible purposes of schools (in particular those having to do with personal growth and socialization), and it is precisely these areas which are now receiving the least emphasis.

Of course, it can be argued (and often is) that every teacher has the responsibility to accomplish these other objectives in the process of teaching a particular discipline. But when these objectives are clearly secondary and their accomplishment goes unnoticed, it should be apparent that they will suffer in the real world of forced choices between alternative payoffs. The social forces on the teachers are stacked in favor of academic and athletic achievement above all else by virtue of the way their labors have been defined, divided, and integrated.

Psychological Forces in the Development of Objectives

There are some psychological, as well as social, forces which help to explain priorities reported in our schools. For example, the fact that a teacher's accomplishments are not easily measured for many of the objectives discussed means not only that it is hard for others to evaluate a teacher's performance in those areas but also that it is hard for the teacher himself to evaluate it. Many a teacher leaves a class not knowing whether he had a dramatic impact on his students or none at all. This means that it can be hard for a teacher to derive a sense of achievement from attempting to accomplish such objectives, and it is hard for him to know whether and how to change what he is doing.

While such difficulties in measuring progress can limit the teacher's intrinsic rewards for such efforts, there are other factors which may actually negatively reinforce his attempts to contribute to students' social and psychological growth. If one does not know what to teach or how to teach in an area, the idea of even attempting to teach can be most anxiety-provoking. This is particularly true about teaching in such areas as sex education, child-rearing, political participation, etc., which involve more of the total personality than cognitive knowledge. It ultimately involves exposing more of one's self, one's attitudes, values, personal behaviors, fears, inconsistencies, etc. The anticipation of such "unmasking" is anxiety-provoking, even to the teacher who knows what he plans to do in the area and has spent some time examining the relevance of his own values and such. But to a teacher who has had no training, has no social support from colleagues, and has done little planning or relevant self-examination, to enter into such topics means to risk great embarrassment, to risk loss of control of the situation, to risk losing "face" and self-esteem. These are very painful outcomes, ones which will be strongly avoided, and these avoidance forces will very likely make many of the areas we have been discussing (socialization, personal development, etc.) unapproachable in the traditional classroom. Therefore, to argue that such objectives will get adequate emphasis under the traditional system is to ignore some very powerful forces which work in the wrong directions. To deal with such issues effectively requires a somewhat different role relationship between students and teachers (a different mutual level of exposing of self), and there are some very strong resistances which must be dealt with in order to bring it about.

For administrators there is considerable risk attached to trying to change the school from "what everyone has come to expect," and very little in the way of training and relevant information to help him minimize the risk. Experimentation with traditional institutions in the society is not yet a course of endeavor which enjoys widespread popular support.

Are Schools Effective?

This deceptively simple question has turned out to be a very difficult one to answer. We do not propose to give anything like a complete answer, but we can look at some of the evidence which bears on the question and, perhaps more importantly, examine the logic which is used in interpreting the evidence.

Education and Success Go Hand in Hand

It is well known that the more education a person has, the more likely he is to be successful—particularly in the world of work. Not only is education linked to lifetime income, it is also closely related to many other job characteristics such as high status, attractive working conditions, opportunities for personal development, and the like (Trent and Medsker, 1968; Withey et al., 1971). The relationship is far from a perfect one, of course. Some highly successful individuals have very little formal education, and some highly educated people have had little vocational success. Nevertheless, the positive relationship between education and vocational success is generally quite strong, and it has influenced a lot of popular thinking about education.

One of the ways in which the education-success relationship has influenced our thinking is that we have come to attach a cash value to education, especially higher education. Figures are presented to show lifetime earning differentials between those who do and do not complete college. Another widespread belief derived from the education-success relationship is expressed in the anti-dropout commercials that are run as a public service on radio and television: "When you drop out of school, you double your chances of not finding a job."

These notions about the payoff value of education make an assumption about cause-and-effect that needs to be examined carefully. The assumption is that the greater success of educated people is pretty much the direct result of their education—so if it worked for them it ought to work for others. Of course, it is also true on the average that successful people tend to come from successful parents (Blau and Duncan, 1967), but we tend to place less emphasis on that relationship because it is beyond an individual's control. An individual cannot change his genetic endowment or his early childhood experiences, but he can make his own choice (up to a point) about the extent of his education. For this reason there is great emphasis placed on the role of education. Educated people are more successful; therefore, education is the pathway to success.

This simplistic cause-and-effect interpretation of the education-success relationship tends to view educational institutions as "skill and knowledge factories" which take in raw materials (students) and somehow process them so that they emerge a few years later transformed into more finished "educated" products. And if the education factories do so well with the people they are presently processing, why not assume that they could do an equally good job with others? The answer is obvious: Individuals who seek extensive amounts of education start out more able, ambitious, and advantaged on the average than those who do not. Those who go on to college are relatively high in intelligence, past scholastic performance, and family socioeconomic level, to name just a few important dimensions; those who drop out of high school are usually below average on each of these same dimensions (Bachman et al., 1971).

To put it more dramatically, we could not take the typical high school dropout, get him through the rest of high school, put him through four years of Harvard, and expect him to come out with the same intellectual skills as the other Harvard graduates. In fact, such an experience would probably be a total disaster for him.

But this all seems so obvious—why have we belabored the point? Because the "education leads to success" message so often ignores the fundamental fact that individuals who seek further education are *already* high in the kinds of ability and ambition which lead to later vocational success. Conversely, those who drop out of high school are below average in success-related ability and background factors. In the Youth in Transition study, for example, it was found that unemployment was substantially higher among dropouts than among young men who had finished high school; however, this difference in employment rate was largely attributed to differences in ability and family background (Bachman et al., 1971).

Should we conclude from all this that education makes no difference at all and that background and abilities are all that matter? Surely that would be jumping to another equally simplistic conclusion. Our point is merely that education and success go hand in hand for a variety of complexly interrelated reasons. Formal education undoubtedly plays a part in vocational attainment, but it is certainly not the only factor and perhaps not even the primary factor.

Research on School Difference and School Effects

In the chapter in this volume on the roles of nature and nurture in adolescent development, Nichols states: "Recent studies of school effects have tended to emphasize that differences in school experiences have little relationship to differences in student performance after all the relevant background factors have been controlled." Students in some colleges and universities score high in tests and later vocational outcomes, but upon closer examination these differences turn out to be almost completely predictable from input characteristics—characteristics of the students before they entered college. In short, the "better" colleges get the "better" students. The same general conclusion was reached by Coleman in his study of students in grades one through twelve; pupil achievement was predictable to a considerable degree from family background, and there was little evidence of school effects—differences in pupil achievement attributed to differences in schools (Coleman et al., 1966).

The conclusions of the Coleman Report have been discussed and debated extensively, and the data have been subjected to a number of further analyses; nevertheless, in our view the basic conclusion remains sound. But perhaps pupil achievement in the form of standardized academic tests is not the only place to be searching for school effects. Perhaps some schools are more effective than others in influencing nonacademic factors such as self-esteem, values and attitudes, or occupational and educational aspirations; and perhaps the most effective way to verify school effects is to use longitudinal designs in which students are followed for several years so that *changes* along such dimensions can be noted. The Youth in Transition project, described earlier, did use a longitudinal design and dealt primarily with nonacademic effects of different high school environments.

It would be satisfying to be able to say at this point that the results clearly indicate differential school effects along these nonacademic dimensions. And it would be even more satisfying to describe the major characteristics of the most effective schools so that other schools might emulate them. Alas, our efforts to isolate school effects have been notably unsuccessful. After several years of intensive analysis, we are forced to a conclusion similar to Coleman's. There are differences between schools, to be sure, in terms of educational and occupational aspirations, test scores, values and attitudes, affective states, and so on. But when we ask what produces these differences, we find almost invariably that they can be attributed to individual differences in background and basic abilities. The differences appear to be due to input characteristics rather than genuine school effects. (A detailed reporting of these findings will be provided in forthcoming publications in the *Youth in Transition* monograph series.)

What shall we conclude from this rather consistent inability of carefully controlled research to uncover differential school effects? One possibility, of course, is that schools simply do not do much of anything for (or to) their students. Another more likely explanation is that our efforts toward universal education and equality of educational opportunity are more successful than we realized, and that public schools throughout the nation are more similar than they are different. As Nichols put it in his discussion of nature and nurture: ". . . the very fact that education is so widespread and so obviously successful may reduce its importance as a source of individual differences in ability in this country."

Much policy and practice are directed toward making educational environments equally effective. If an educational technique shows promise in one school, there is a strong tendency to try it in other schools. Indeed, had the Youth in Transition project been able to isolate some particular practices which characterized effective schools, there would have been an effort to encourage other schools to adopt the same effective practices, and the result would have been a further leveling of school differences.

Additionally, the educational environment of adolescents today is certainly not limited to schools. To the extent that other institutions in the society contribute to the education and socialization of young people —the media, churches, youth organizations—the ability of the school to create substantial individual differences is diminished. This is even more true if students are able to compensate for experiences which are not available in their particular schools by finding them elsewhere. Thus, for example, if a cutback in the school budget wipes out a program in individual instrumental music, at least some of the students affected will compensate by taking private lessons; if the art budget is reduced, more students may take art at the "Y." All these factors operate to level out some of the differences and deficiencies which may occur in formal school settings.

In retrospect, the overall lack of differential school effects is not necessarily proof that schools are generally ineffective. It could just as well indicate that our schools, in conjunction with aspects of our culture, are succeeding in making equally rich educational opportunities available to nearly all who desire them. Perhaps a more realistic conclusion involves a balance between these two interpretations. Public schools show a great deal of similarity with one another, and this applies both to their areas of strength (e.g., academic preparation for college) and their areas of weakness (e.g., vocational preparation and placement). Thus, it is not so much a matter of which schools are the effective ones, but rather a case of discovering the *areas* in which schools in general are effective and (more urgently) those in which they tend to be ineffective.

Dropouts

Any discussion dealing with the flaws or failures of American education almost invariably turns to the "problem" of the high school dropout. That some young people choose to leave school before graduation is usually taken uncritically as evidence of a bad decision on their part, and the failure of the schools to be "relevant to their needs." We think that both of these interpretations of dropping out are oversimplified and need more careful examination. But, first, it is worth noting that if the dropout rate is taken to be a sign of school success or failure, then we should acknowledge that schools have become increasingly successful in recent decades; the dropout rate has been steadily declining and for males is only about 20 percent at the end of the 1960s (Bachman et al., 1971).

Dropping out of school is overrated as a *problem* in its own right—it is far more appropriately viewed as the end result or symptom of other problems which have their origin much earlier in life. The difficulties experienced by the dropouts we studied, the low aspirations and accomplishments, and even the limitations in self-esteem and self-concept, were already present or predictable by the start of tenth grade, and there is little evidence that dropping out made matters worse.

Some of the problems which dropout-prone individuals display by the time they reach high school are limitations in academic ability, past scholastic failure, and patterns of delinquent behavior. Persuading someone to stick it out for the last year or two of high school will not overcome these already manifest difficulties. If these problems of dropouts are to be affected by the schools, it will have to be in their earlier years of schooling, perhaps even in the preschool years.

But even if we could avoid most of the limitations imposed by deficient educational opportunities in the early developmental years, it would still be worth asking whether our current notions about high school education are entirely sound. Our research on dropouts led to the conclusion that some young men can manage reasonably well on the basis of one or two years less formal education than our present system prescribes. In fact, an examination of a wide variety of personality and behavior dimensions revealed very few changes of any consequences, and virtually none that would support the argument that dropping out damages a young man's mental health or his commitment to society's values. On the whole, the dropouts were in most respects not dramatically different from those non-dropouts who did not go on to college. (One major exception was delinquent behavior; dropouts were much higher in delinquency measures both before and after dropping out.) The relatively small differences between these groups were just as clear at the start of tenth grade as they were three or four years later. Unemployment was higher among dropouts, but, as we noted earlier, this can be attributed largely to preexisting differences in ability and family background. The majority of dropouts were employed, and their level of job satisfaction and income were virtually identical to those of high school graduates who entered the work force.

In short, the dropouts in the Youth in Transition project apparently suffered very little loss as a result of leaving school a year or two early, at least on the short-term basis for which we now have data. And that may well represent evidence that the typical high school is presently rather ineffective *for those young men who are not preparing for college*. In the next section we return to this point and consider its implications.

Implications for Change

Our review of some of the objectives and effects of educational institutions certainly does not suggest that the system is fully effective and should continue essentially as is. On the contrary, there seem to be clear implications for change, and in this section we discuss a few of them.

In the earlier discussion of school objectives it was suggested that what was being called for was not only a different set of priorities but also a greater overall purposiveness in the schools. If the deduction is correct, then a number of changes can be suggested to move schools in that direction. Almost all involve a greater emphasis on the *process* of developing, refining, and renewing objectives.

Schools of education could work on training future teachers and administrators in ways of developing operational and meaningful objectives for their schools, in building support for those objectives both inside and outside the schools, in implementing them, and finally in evaluating the success of such efforts. The required skills do not come "naturally": They require considerable thought, knowledge, and training. In the process, schools of education may need to reexamine exactly what skills and knowledge they intend to impart, and to evaluate the appropriateness of their own curricula for imparting them. The discipline divisions within high schools mirror to a considerable extent the organizational divisions in our schools of education: The very objectives which fall between the cracks in high school curricula have met a similar fate in the curriculum structures of our education schools. For example, how many schools of education include course offerings on how to prepare adolescents for their adult roles of spouse and parent?

School boards and administrators should provide their schools with sufficient staff, free time, and supplementary resources to develop thoughtful operational objectives, to undertake the planning and coordination necessary to accomplish them, and to assess their own effectiveness. Such activities take a great deal of time, particularly in the beginning, but surely the potential payoff far overshadows the cost.

There must be student (see comments by Adams in the introductory chapter) and community involvement in processes of goal-setting. Citizen involvement in the goals of schools has not generally been great. For educators, this has sometimes provided more latitude to do as they please, but it has also meant that the community has not been committed to and involved in many of the schools' goals. Therefore, when bonding or millage issues must be passed, voters are much less ready to make the sacrifices necessary to meet them.

While they historically have lacked much "say" in their schools, students are enhancing their power position considerably through group action. (At the collegiate level see the chapter by Block et al.) It is predictable that they will have to be involved in the establishment of school goals in the future. Ironically, this change may well turn out to be among the most important innovations in this century—even though it seems to be happening in spite of (rather than because of) our professional educators. The investment of the student himself in the socializing and educating goals of his school may be half of the battle in achieving them; particularly given the extent of agreement found between students and teachers on what they think their schools should be accomplishing. In this connection we should note two exciting books by Postman and Weingartner in which they set out to enlist both teachers and students in the process of "turning schools around"—*Teaching as a Subversive Activity* (1969) and *The Soft Revolution* (1971). These authors take the view that it is possible, and indeed essential, for students and teachers to help achieve new educational alternatives, and to do so "without contributing to the destruction of their society or themselves" (Postman and Weingartner, 1971, p. vii).

It seems clear from the responses of teachers and students that they feel some areas are in need of greater emphasis than they presently receive (note the gaps between "actual" and "ideal" in Figure 1). Because these same areas are among the most difficult for teachers, they are the ones in which ideas, plans, and support materials are most needed. Curriculum specialists and social scientists from a number of disciplines surely have an important contribution to make in providing such resources. It is simply unrealistic to suppose that individual teachers, or even schools, can create them themselves.

Educational and social scientists can also contribute in the separate but related area of assessment. There is a great tendency to focus attention on *measurable* outcome such as dropout rates or percentages of high school graduates entering college. The current public clamor for accountability in education is likely to increase this tendency further. Therefore, we need to develop a wider range of measures of nonacademic outcomes. For example, two major longitudinal studies recently had to invent their own tests of occupational knowledge (i.e., knowledge about "the world of work") because no existing standardized measures could be found in this area. It seems likely that the mere presence of assessment instruments will create a considerable pressure for schools to be more purposive and effective in the areas measured. (One major effort is already under way in this area—the National Assessment of Educational Progress. See Womer, 1970.) Additional efforts which focus more on the nonacademic impact of the school are still needed, however.

Broader Educational Opportunities for Youth

We noted earlier the findings from the Youth in Transition that dropouts apparently did not suffer serious disadvantages as a result of leaving school a year or two before graduation, and this implies that the typical high school may be rather ineffective for those young people who are not preparing for college. Does this mean that we should change high schools so that they are better suited to the non-college-bound as well as those in college prep? Yes, no doubt we should. There is much room for improvement in vocational preparation and placement, and in other areas as well. But before we fix firmly on the ideas that the comprehensive high school must once again provide the whole answer, let us reconsider what seems to be a fundamental assumption in the current American educational system—the idea that everyone needs at least twelve years of uninterrupted formal education between the ages of six and eighteen.

What if high school ended a year or two earlier than it presently does? Young people wishing to enter college might spend the years equivalent to grades eleven and twelve in publicly supported college preparatory schools. Others might enter one-year or two-year vocational training or work-study programs. Still others might choose to go directly into the world of work with the option of returning to one of the above programs on a part-time or full-time basis after one or two years, or even a longer interval. The main effects of these arrangements would be to remove the stigma which is now attached to leaving school before grade twelve and to provide a more diverse assortment of educational alternatives to young people than now exists. The recent growth of community colleges with their wide-ranging course offerings, flexible time schedules, generous enrollment policies, and low tuition rates indicates the growing need for this sort of educational freedom of opportunity.

In a world of rapidly changing technology with its emphasis on continuing education and periodic retraining, there is less and less reason to maintain the traditionally sharp boundary between the role of student and the later role of worker. Shortening the prescribed minimum period for full-time uninterrupted schooling might be a positive step toward new patterns of lifetime education in which individuals can choose for themselves among a wide range of "educational life styles."

Summary

We began this chapter by discussing the functions which schools can serve for both the society and the individual, noting that some functions may be in direct conflict with one another. We then turned to a study of the actual administrative objectives or purposes in the American high school, as reported by teachers and students.

There we found a rather amazing amount of agreement between high school teachers and male high school students about the relative importance that is actually being accorded to a number of different objectives in our nation's schools. There was also a very great similarity between teacher and student beliefs about what the relative emphases should be ideally. This latter finding will probably come as a surprise to many, including the students themselves.

Both groups feel that athletics should be downgraded from first to last place; that the objectives traditionally concerned with academic achievement (academic excellence, high percent to college, order and quiet in the school, teaching of subject matter) should get roughly the same emphasis that they now get; and that objectives related to the social and psychological growth and socialization of the student should receive substantially more emphasis. Imparting vocational skills to the non-college-bound was also seen as an objective deserving of considerably more concern.

The "ideal" profiles for both groups of respondents were substantially higher than their "actual" profiles, suggesting a need for a greater overall sense of purposefulness and goal orientation in our schools.

A number of factors were discussed in an attempt to explain the priorities which were reported to exist currently: the high observability of some outcomes, the varying political efficacy of recipient groups, the public controversy surrounding certain issues, the absence of organizational or curriculum structure to support some objectives, the lack of certain types of teacher training, the dangers involved in social experimentation, and so on. It was argued that both psychological and social forces must be taken into account in any attempt to change things.

The question of whether or not schools are effective was addressed at some length. The fact that success seems to go hand in hand with educational attainment does not necessarily mean that the education is the major cause of the success. Findings from the Youth in Transition study indicate, for example, that dropping out is more a symptom of previous problems than the cause of any subsequent problems.

In studies comparing the impact of different schools it has been found that, although some high school characteristics systematically relate to academic performance and other student outcome, the relationships tend to disappear once individual background characteristics are taken into account. This fact suggests that the vast majority of American high schools may be rather similar in their impact (or lack of it) on students.

This sameness of impact suggests a relative sameness of form and content in schools. Therefore, whatever strength or weaknesses they have, they tend to be widely shared, suggesting that experimentation with educational institutions on a much larger scale than we have previously seen may be what is needed to determine how things can really be improved.

A number of possible changes have been suggested based on the findings reviewed in the chapter. One is to grant the high school diploma at a younger age and to offer a broader range of educational alternatives than now exists. Another set of recommendations is aimed at increasing the purposive nature of schools—to increase people's awareness of why, in Dyers' words, "they are going through the motions they think of as education."

REFERENCES

Bachman, J., Green, S., and Wirtanen, I. *Youth in transition, Vol. III: Dropping out—problem or symptom?* Ann Arbor: Survey Research Center, Institute for Social Research, 1971.

———, Kahn, R. L., Mednick, M. T., Davidson, T. N., and Johnston, L. D. *Youth in transition, Vol. I: Blueprint for a longitudinal study of adolescent boys.* Ann Arbor: Survey Research Center, Institute for Social Research, 1967.

Blau, M., and Duncan, O. *The American occupational structure.* New York: Wiley, 1967.

Coleman, J. S., Campbell, E. Q., Hobson, C. J., McPartland, J., Mood, A. M., Weinfeld, F. D., and York, R. L. *Equality of educational opportunity.* Washington, D.C.: U.S. Government Printing Office, 1966.

Dyer, H. S. The discovery and development of educational goals. *Proceedings of the 1966 Invitational Conference on Testing Problems.* Princeton, N.J.: Educational Testing Service, 1967.

Postman, N., and Weingartner, C. *Teaching as a subversive activity.* New York: Delacorte Press, 1969.

————, and Weingartner, C. *The soft revolution.* New York: Delacorte Press, 1971.

Silberman, C. E. *Crisis in the classroom: The remaking of American education.* New York: Random House, 1964.

Trent, J., and Medsker, L. *Beyond high school.* San Francisco: Jossey-Bass, 1968.

Withey, S., Coble, J., Gurin, G., Robinson, J., Strumpel, B., Taylor E., and Wolfe, A. *A degree and what else?* New York: McGraw-Hill, 1971.

Womer, F. B. National assessment says. *NCME Measurement in Education,* 1970, 2, 1.

10

A Cognitive Approach to Sex Education

Anne McCreary Juhasz*

Today's children are growing up in an age of transition; transition from earth to space orientation, from family-oriented life to individualistic life style, and from person-to-person contact to multimedia, mass communication. The rapidity of this change and the inability of society to keep pace emotionally and psychologically with the technological and scientific advances have resulted in insufficient time to observe and contemplate, to evaluate, and to plan accordingly. Long-established rules and mores of church and society are diminishing in power, and the security that they provided has not been replaced by modern inventions. In addition, our culture insidiously presents sex as a stolen sweet, commercial asset, fun, weapon, status symbol, cure for loneliness, and as the crowning expression of romantic love. At the same time, our culture still officially labels it sin—outside the bonds of matrimony (N.Y. Academy of Medicine, 1965). In this situation, there is no single, stable, credible interpreter of life as the child sees it, in its many contradictory and confusing aspects.

Equally important is the obvious lack of consistency in the manner in which adults apply their value systems to daily life. Verbalized codes

* Anne McCreary Juhasz is Professor of Educational Foundations at Loyola University of Chicago. She has authored, coauthored, or edited *Language Experience Reading Program, Effective Study, Adolescents in Society,* and *Interpersonal Relationships and Human Sexuality.* She had also published a number of articles on sex education, reading, and mental health.

of behavior may be mere theories; in actual practice behavior often differs radically. In addition, time, place, person, or situation may determine the extent to which one follows the code. In many instances the deed itself is not considered bad but being caught in the act brings disapproval. Many adults feel no sense of wrong if they occasionally drive across an intersection when the traffic light is red; only if caught do they feel guilty. When adolescents learn that corruption, evasiveness, and dishonesty permeate business and political life and that social relationships are used as a means of obtaining desired positions, promotions, or contracts, it is difficult for them to believe that a different code of ethics should govern personal relationships.

Kardiner (1954) points out that in a competitive, success-oriented society, where failure is automatically accompanied by loss of self-esteem and increase in anxiety, hostility, and egocentricity, one can expect that sex activity will be torn out of the context of social usefulness and will be carried on without concern for the welfare of the person with whom it is achieved. He feels that it is unrealistic to expect sex morality to follow a course that differs from the morality that prevails in a society at large, and that sexual activity will thus become reckless and destructive.

In the realm of sexual relationships, the developing adolescent is charged today with the responsibility of determining meaningful behavior patterns and deciding upon a course of action and a personal value system from among the many which he observes. He is no longer satisfied to accept, unquestioningly, the dogma of the church, the standard of the middle class, the advice of parents, or the pressure of peers. Nor does he swallow, indiscriminately, the propaganda of the entertainment and news media. In all fields of education there is a massive movement toward relevance and understanding. Relevance is related to human and social needs; understanding is based on knowledge. There is no doubt that human sexuality, in terms of interpersonal relationships between two or more human beings, is an individual's most pressing concern. In order to understand how people feel about different kinds of human sexual behavior, and why they feel as they do, accurate information is essential. Facts are the raw materials used in problem solving, and if young people are to come to grips with the uncertainties, their anxieties, and their hostilities, it is essential that objective, unbiased information be provided.

However, facts about sexual organs and functions are not sufficient. Discussion of varied sexual behavior and different attitudes toward sexuality is also necessary. In addition, it is imperative to recognize the fact that education in sexuality is taking place from the moment of birth. The infant is continually learning about what it means to be male or female. Not only the facts but also the actions and the attitudes of those with whom he comes in daily contact, provide some form of instruction. While it is important to transmit knowledge, it is also important to recognize that, at any stage of life, the child does have some sexual knowledge and accompanying sexual feelings and emotions. It is also necessary that each individual be familiar with the most important phases of his psycho-sexual and socio-sexual development and with some of the factors which have shaped these in the past and which continue to influence them in the present. Finally, he needs to be aware of the variations in sexual behavior which he will encounter, which he must evaluate, and from which he may choose in deciding upon a personal life style.

The Need

I have pointed out earlier that today in America, formal moral codes have largely disappeared and that, actually, only operational codes remain. Rubin (1965) outlines six major competing value systems and points to the problem of selecting and indoctrinating in any single one, since adolescents will observe, in real life, as well as in fictions and film, examples of all six. The first of these systems he names *traditional repressive asceticism.* This sets forth an absolute standard based on *thou shalt not have any kind of nonmarital sexual relationship.* This includes a grudging acceptance of sex within marriage, and the linking of sex with procreation. His second system is *enlightened asceticism,* which accepts the basic point of view in system one and includes self-control, discipline, and mastery of sexual urges at a time when codes are crumbling. He feels that the way to develop this enlightened asceticism is the open forum where issues can be discussed and evaluated. *Humanistic liberalism* is the third system, and it emphasizes the concept of interpersonal relationships where the consequences of the act are of prime importance. The fourth system, *humanistic radicalism,* supports the idea that society should be restructured to enable young people to have relatively complete sexual freedom. Number five, *fun morality,* as espoused by Albert Ellis, characterizes sex as fun, and specifies that the more the better. The final system, six, is *sexual anarchy,* espoused by René Guyon, where anything may be included except injury or violence to one's fellows.

Affluence has resulted in increasing numbers of children freed from supervision by the automobile and the motor bike, released from parental control at college and at war, relieved of fear of pregnancy by the pill and of V.D. by penicillin. Bombarded by nudity and sex on all sides, for them, selecting a moral code for sexual relations is a confusing and difficult task. There is no doubt that young people are seriously and eagerly trying to find a kind of life style that incorporates and demonstrates their concern for one another and their search for identity. The growth of communal life and interest in the Jesus Movement attest to this. So does the increasing participation in sensitivity training and group drug use.

There is ample evidence to suggest that students do not have adequate information, and do hold misconceptions about sex which cause anxiety and interfere with the process of making informed, logical decisions. The following questions which junior high school, lower socioeconomic, ghetto children asked Kleinerman (1971, pp. 30–31) illustrate this:

> Can you get pregnant if a boy touches you on top? What does God have to do with getting a baby? Where does a boy touch you when you have a baby? If you sit on a boy's lap will you become pregnant? How many times do you have to intercourse to have a baby? How does Kleenex work to stop pregnancy? Should a girl have sex when she is menstruating?

Lack of adequate information about human sexuality is not restricted to the lower socioeconomic groups. Greenbank (1961) reported that half of the 1959 graduates of a Philadelphia medical school believed that mental illness is frequently caused by masturbation. Moreover, one out of every five faculty members also believed this. Mudd and Siegel (1969) indicate that medical students still feel a need for sex education both for personal and professional reasons. In a study of Canadian university students, Juhasz (1967) found no relationship between self-ratings on adequacy of sex knowledge and actual scores on a test of sex knowledge. Males overestimated greatly their knowledge of structure and function of the sexual organs and of venereal disease; females overestimated their knowledge of masturbation, conception, and venereal disease.

There is also evidence that learning about sex and getting answers to questions about sexual behavior does not necessarily lead to preoccupation with sex. Juhasz (1971) found that when students in Anaheim, California, had received factual information and answers to their questions about sexual organs and reproduction, they became bored by repetition of this material. They were much more interested in learning how to understand their own feelings and actions and those of other individuals. For example, the most pressing concern for a seventh-grade girl was how to get a boy to ask her to sit in a booth rather than at a counter in a restaurant. Another girl expressed disillusionment on finding out from a panel of boys that when a boy holds a girl's hand it does not necessarily mean that he feels affection for her. It may just be the thing to do. *Making out* with members of the opposite sex was not the major concern of early adolescents. Their main problem was getting along with parents and siblings.

In the same evaluation, students overwhelmingly expressed the desire for longer courses in sex education and increased opportunity for discussion. At the junior high school level, students were interested in future adjustment and success as marriage partners and parents.

Simon and Gagnon (1967, p. 74), discussing the fact that some people assume that sex education will lower rates of illegitimacy, venereal disease, and promiscuity, note that "the more viable assumption behind an interest in sex education is that it should work to make sex a more rewarding part of people's lives—to make sex education serve competence and not necessarily restraint." They point out that the content of sex education is rarely presented as something that is experienced or thought about, but rather as something that one does or that happens to one. The reader gets the idea that content often deals with actions which should be avoided in order that the individual will not suffer undesirable consequences rather than with the type of experience which will result in a happy, rewarding relationship.

The Philosophy

The philosophy underlying my approach to education in human sexuality rests on five basic assumptions. *First,* I agree with Reiss (1968b) that education is not indoctrination and does not teach people *what* to think. Rather, it teaches them how to think. For example, in relation to sex education, he suggests that instead of teaching that either abstinence or permissiveness is the best behavior, one should teach how sexual relations occur and then analyze this to increase the student's ability to think calmly and rationally so that he may better handle problems when they arise. This emphasis on thinking is justifiable. Atkinson (1965, p. 109) points out that "children can be encouraged to address themselves to moral issues, to consider the things said, reasons given on one side and another, and helped to assess their truth, consistency, and cogency." He warns that there is no guarantee that children's conclusions will be the same as those of adults, but he does feel that one can expect that moral positions thought through and arrived at by the individual are more likely to influence the adolescent's conduct more than those imposed upon him by others. Thus, in teaching the adolescent to think through any moral dilemma, adults are providing a more effective problem-solving method than in offering principles to be automatically accepted and used.

Second, I believe that sexuality enters into any human interaction. Every human is sexual and must learn to live in a sexual world. Not only must he satisfy individual drives in order to live in harmony with himself and with his self-concept, but, at the same time, he must learn to control his biological urges, when necessary, in order to contribute positively in the society to which he belongs. Living, in the fullest sense of the word, involves participating in human relationships which are rewarding and satisfying, which add stature to those involved, and which satisfy individual needs and contribute to society. In order to participate in such relationships, knowledge, understanding, and appreciation of oneself and of others is necessary. This is true of all types of personal interaction including sexual relationships. However, while this aspect of living should be a part of man's interest and of his life, it should not be his chief preoccupation. Only by understanding oneself and developing feelings of self-respect, trust in one's judgment, certainty in one's values, and appreciation of one's strengths, is the individual able to express and demonstrate feelings toward others. Only through such self-development can the individual allot to sexuality the proper perspective in the whole complex of living.

Third, it is my opinion, that, provided with adequate information, young people are capable of making decisions about their sexual behavior and accepting responsibility for their actions. Kilpatrick and Nagel (1957) have set forth the following core values of a democratic society which apply to adolescents as well as to adults:

> Faith in the free play of critical intelligence and respect for truth as a definable moral value; respect for the basic worth, equality, and dignity of each individual; the right of self-determination of each human being; and, the recognition of the need for cooperative effort for common good.

In writing about adolescents I recognize that the adolescent is a capable individual of unconditional worth, involved in the full range of human emotions, experiences, and problems. As such, he is entitled to trust, honesty, cooperation, and respect. He is the bridge between the present and the future, the architect of society, the decision-maker who will determine the shape of the world to come, the parent who will raise tomorrow's children.

Fourth, it is my contention that many disciplines can contribute knowledge of the basis of present-day sexual behavior and attitudes. Anthropology, history, medicine, philosophy, psychology, and sociology all shed light upon the present and provide a broad interdisciplinary basis for discussion of human sexual behavior today. Such a basis can facilitate skills in understanding, evaluating and coping with varied sexual feelings and in developing a guiding value system. The most common type of training in human sexuality now open to the adolescent involves observation and imitation, but this training leaves many gaps in his essential preparation for mature adult life. If we accept the premise that an adolescent is a responsible, valuable human being in his own right, then we must agree that, as such, he is entitled to the basic facts about the heritage of the past which have been preserved and which have stood the test of time. It is also his right to have information on the full range of ideas, behaviors, philosophies, and values held by man—to know the results of alternative actions and to be aware that knowledge of cause and effect is basic for decision making. The next step is the realization that it is the carefully thought-out decision that determines the choice of action when a problem situation arises.

In providing the adolescent with basic knowledge, with freedom to think and act, and with encouragement to question, reflect, and evaluate, we give him the opportunity to develop a system of values. We enable him to plan a way of life wherein he can use his vast potential both to shape his own life and to build the future of mankind.

The *fifth* and final assumption is that conception of the problem and method of approach supercede content in importance. Content and knowledge are constantly increasing, and it can be expected that the individual who has a broad basic background and is skilled in processing the facts in an intelligent manner will be able to utilize new knowledge and transfer previously learned skills and abilities in order to cope with change constructively. Thus, discussion and problem solving, rather than memorization and regurgitation of facts, should best serve the student of human sexual behavior.

Developing Normal Heterosexual Patterns of Behavior

It has been established that education in sexuality is a constant process beginning at birth, and thus any discussion of the sex education of adolescents must begin with early sex role learning. The second section in this part of the chapter will deal with preadolescent and adolescent heterosexual behavior. This will be followed by a short section on other common types of sexual experience.

Early Sex Role Learning

It is part of popular belief that sexual instinct and behavior first occur at the time of puberty and that, therefore, adolescence is the period of most concern in this respect. However, we know that human sexuality, as an integral part of healthy normal development, first assumes importance at birth. The work of the Harlows (1965) with infant rhesus monkeys demonstrated the importance of normal mothering in the development of heterosexual behavior. Mating behavior and maternal response were inadequate in monkeys who were reared with wire-mesh, surrogate mothers who were incapable of normal reactions.

Brown and Lynn (1966, p. 155) differentiate between three major components of human sexual development and behavior: The biological-constitutional component, i.e., heredity, congenital, and maturational factors; sex role, the individual's identification of himself with one sex or the other; and, genital–sex object preference, the source, aim, and direction of sexual simulation, desire, activity, and satisfaction (masturbation, homosexuality, exhibitionism, etc.).

Agreement is lacking on the extent and kind of influence exerted by biological and anatomical structure. Sherfey (1966, pp. 121–123) reports:

> . . . recent embryological research has demonstrated conclusively that the concept of the initial anatomical bisexuality or equipotentiality of the embryo is erroneous. All mammalian embryos, male and female, are automatically female during the early stages of fetal life. In humans the differentiation of the male and female forms, by the action of fetal androgen, begins about the sixth week of embryonic life and is completed by the end of the third month.

Diamond (1965), on the other hand, thinks that prenatal genic and hormonal influences result in a definite predisposition at birth to a male or female gender orientation. Money and Hampson (1957) believe that gender role is undifferentiated at birth and that it is firmly imprinted by the age of two and a half. They also think that sex assignment as given by the parents or parent substitutes is the single most significant factor in establishing gender identity. Most authorities would agree that gender role is undifferentiated at birth, but many would argue that the process of imprinting has not yet been firmly established in human beings. Most studies have dealt with animal behavior and the results cannot be applied to humans.

Although more research has been conducted on sex role learning, the findings are not in agreement, nor are they any more conclusive than those related to sex role determination. Kagan (1958) feels that identification is important in the development of the ability to enact appropriate sex roles. However, certain specifications must be met: The model must be conceived as being in command of desired goals, especially power, love from others, and task competence in areas the child regards as important. The model must be perceived as naturant. The child must perceive some objective basis of similarity in external or psychological properties between himself and the model.

However, there is lack of agreement about which parent serves as the most influential model of identification. Johnson (1963) concludes that the father has the greatest influence upon the sex-role learning of both male and female children since he treats differently children of different sexes, and in this way girls learn the complementary sex role. Lynn (1966), on the other hand, feels that women are the most important influence in sex-role learning for both boys and girls. He bases his conclusion on the fact that children spend much of their early life, first with the mother and then with the female teacher. Children of both sexes imitate the female models. For girls, this is acceptable. However, for boys, mothers and female teachers lay down negative sanctions for imitative behavior which do not fit the stereotyped, socially accepted, male role. Thus, the boy uses problem-solving methods in reasoning that, if certain behavior is feminine and unacceptable, then the opposite behavior must be masculine. For example, boys are commonly admonished that boys do not cry (implying that it is acceptable for girls to do so). As a result, the male learns to suppress his tears and uses some other form of release such as aggression. Thus, through a kind of trial-and-error type of problem solving, based on negative admonition, the boy learns a masculine role which may or may not fit that of his male parent. (Hamachek discusses this topic in greater detail in an earlier chapter.)

The development of normal heterosexual patterns of behavior, and positive attitudes toward them is the third aspect of human sexual learning. It is commonly agreed that the foundations for later heterosexual attachment are laid in early childhood in the interaction between the child and his parents. Parents hand down to their children purposefully or unconsciously, their anxieties, prohibitions, attitudes, and feelings about sex. Parental attitudes toward elimination, modesty, masturbation, sex play, and body contact will determine the extent of guilt and anxiety which accompanies the mastery of bodily control. This is important in learning to accept oneself as a sexual human being, and in developing the capacity to enjoy heterosexual relationships in adult life. Researchers have shown that the amount of warmth, love, affection, and relaxation displayed by the mother toward the infant is reflected in the child's ability to be an affectionate, uninhibited adult.

Preadolescent and Adolescent Dating Behavior

It has been established that the preschool child has already formed a conception of married life based on his parents' behavior toward one another. The quality of the parents' marriage continues to affect the child as he reaches adolescence and begins to put into practice the skills of heterosexual interpersonal relationships. Landis (1963) asked three thousand college students to rate their parents' marriages as happy or unhappy and then noted the following differences between the dating patterns of children from happy marriages and those from unhappy ones: Children from happy marriages had a more active dating history, dated earlier, and dated more different people; their self-evaluation indicated that they would be able to establish an earlier satisfactory heterosexual relationship than children from unhappy marriages. The latter had more steady dating with fewer partners, more serious dating, more trouble making friends with the opposite sex, and more doubts about their own ability to have a successful marriage.

Douvan (1966) reports that dating is a way of learning sex roles and is a social relationship rather than a courting relationship. At that time the normal age for beginning dating was fourteen for girls and fifteen for boys. By seventeen, virtually all American girls dated, and almost a third had formed a relatively steady relationship with one boy. Girls appear to experience less difficulty in mastering appropriate heterosexual behavior patterns. For boys, early sexual experience with girls is a vital ingredient in attaining a satisfactory sex-role identity. Even though females, as a group, mature sexually (anatomically and physiologically) earlier than males, nevertheless, sexual activity rises more sharply for boys entering puberty than for girls. Kagan (1964) feels that early sexual activity among males is motivated, not by overwhelming biological urges, but by desire to strengthen masculine identification. Douvan (1966) explains the more restricted pattern of sexual behavior for girls entering puberty as a result of a higher level anxiety. It is interesting to note that young male teenagers rarely date girls much younger or much older than themselves. This means that they are in constant competition with older boys for girls their own age (Loeb, 1959).

More recently, Offer (1970) reported on a seven-year study of seventy-three normal adolescent boys who were followed through high school from thirteen or fourteen years of age up to nineteen or twenty years of age. They were interviewed and given tests and questionnaires. He found that by the end of the third year in high school 10 percent had had intercourse at least once; by the middle of the third post–high school year, 50 percent had had intercourse. Those who had not, listed the following reasons for abstinence: environment (no car, no apartment, etc.); lack of time; no need now; and, inhibitions (for example, one boy said that "he couldn't unless he loved the girl, but if he loved her he wouldn't take advantage of her, therefore he didn't," p. 920).

Broderick (1961) has conducted several studies on the patterns of relationships among adolescents and preadolescents. He investigated the behavior of fifth-, sixth-, and seventh-grade children, ages ten to thirteen years in a southern urban center. He found that most of the children in each grade claimed to have a sweetheart, most expected reciprocation, and most keep their feelings secret. In a 1949 study, 15 percent of the boys and 20 percent of the girls thirteen years of age dated. In 1958 the following figures indicate a rise in dating incidence: For ten and eleven year olds, 45 percent of the boys and 36 percent of the girls dated. For twelve and thirteen year olds, 70 percent of the boys and 53 percent of the girls dated. Seventy-four percent of all boys and 69 percent of all girls said they had been kissed. Seventy-four percent of the boys and 36 percent of the girls said that they had kissed a member of the opposite sex. Children in the sixth and seventh grades were most interested in members of the opposite sex as companions for walks and movies.

In a later report on the behavior of more than 1500 eleven and twelve year olds in Pennsylvania and Missouri, Broderick (1968) arrived at the following pyramidally structured set of stages through which most preadolescent boys and girls move in pursuit of social-heterosexual maturation: recognizing the heterosexual nature of marriage; viewing marriage as an attractive element in one's own projected future; setting an objective of affection or being *in love* with a member of the opposite sex (not necessarily reciprocal) ; and, choosing cross-sex companions for movie dates.

These reports of dating behavior of children of different ages during different decades have reflected both stability and change. While the movie date may not be the most common form of cross-sex companionship dating today, still Broderick's stages do have relevance. His structure points to the early importance of the home and the marriage relationship observed there.

Promiscuity, Masturbation, and Homosexual Behavior

Without rigid guidelines or training for mastery in heterosexual skills, adults and adolescents alike tend to be apprehensive and anxious if the developing teenager displays either too little or too much interest in heterosexual behavior, especially if this variation in interest results in masturbation, promiscuous behavior, or homosexual activity.

In discussing promiscuity in adolescence, Walters (1965) points to the fact that, in general, young women, basically, want a close relationship with a man. While they do not see chastity as a necessary virtue, they agree that fidelity in terms of *emotional openness, trust, and agreement on life's goals* is necessary for development into responsible adulthood. Promiscuity involving intercourse concurrently with more than one man or moving too rapidly from one sexual relationship to another is frowned upon. He feels that promiscuity may be due to several causes: lack of selectiveness resulting in a type of fickleness, mate selection based on narcissistic needs, or choice based on reenactment and maintenance of infantile ties to parents, especially the mother.

Gadpaille (1968) points out that in the normal body there is a biological tendency for the release of sexual tension or the gratification of sexual desire and that different modes of release may be selected by the individual. Before puberty, sexual curiosity and activity are present. This playful experimentation with the genitals or masturbation is not necessarily habit-forming. Nor is it dangerous. It is merely a developmental stage. However, in adolescence, the developing reproductive and hormonal system intensifies the sexual urge and sexual awareness. This development is accompanied by anxiety and self-consciousness about oneself and relationships with members of the opposite sex. Comparison with others of the same sex can provide reassurance of normalcy, and homosexual contacts can be viewed as a logical step toward heterosexual relationships.

Thus, there is no need to be unduly worried about this phase in the behavior patterns of young people. Based on his work with adolescents, Gadpaille feels that they are placed, by society, in an untenable situation. At a time when the biological sex drive is first felt, society is warning the youngster against heterosexual activity, thus cutting him off from the normal outlet for his tensions. His choice of a substitute will reflect his fears, anxieties, hostilities, and methods of coping with the adult world and with his own individual problems. Gadpaille (1969, p. 67) points out that "transient homosexual activity could be considered phase-appropriate only in cultures with sexually repressive child rearing, and in which guilt-free heterosexual experimentation post puberty is denied."

Thus, some degree of both masturbation and homosexual activity can be considered normal for the developing adolescent. Each may play an important part in the establishment of normal heterosexual patterns. The reactions of adults to this behavior will be the crucial factor in determining whether this early experimentation becomes either a negative or a positive influence on the young person.

Influences from the Past

The attitudes and behavior patterns of the adolescent will be shaped throughout the course of his development by his parents and his home surroundings. However, these have been inescapably influenced by religious and social forces which have affected generations of his forebears throughout preceding centuries. While attitudes and behavior patterns have changed throughout time, it is interesting to note that vestiges of former thinking still remain in many parts of America today.

Our heritage has been transmitted from the ancient Hebrews, largely through the Old Testament. This inheritance includes the traditions of male dominance, respect for women who are members of the same class or caste, and the double standard in sexual morals. We have also inherited some rules pertaining to incest and sexual perversions (Queen, Habenstein, and Adams, 1961). Early writings found in the Talmud instructed people to increase and multiply; thus marriage and children were valued highly. In early Greece and Crete male offspring were important for inheritance purposes and monogamy was established. The ancient belief prevailed that sexual enjoyment was a good thing; that it was every man's right and that it was essential to his health. At this time, the double standard for men and women emerged and so did prostitution. For the Romans, children were also the main reason for marriage. As Christianity became a powerful force, Man was considered superior, and Woman merely another possession. Sex and sin became synonomous. Sexual intercourse, even in marriage, was thought to be unhealthy, and wicked, and thus all children were born in sin, and all women were considered evil and dangerous. By the fifteenth century, rebellion against the church's attempts to regulate moral behavior led to a reformation movement and the new religious groups known as Protestants came into being. This was accompanied by declarations of leaders like Martin Luther, which acknowledged the right for all to marry, recognized woman's sexual needs, gave approval of limited sexual intercourse within marriage, and considered sexual impotence and frigidity as grounds for divorce.

During the centuries which followed, sex continued to be a taboo subject, something that nice people neither discussed nor indulged in. By the nineteenth century, the ostrich approach toward sex and the double standard for sexual behavior had set their indelible stamp on Western culture. However, by the late 1800s, women were beginning to agitate for equal rights and the feminist movement gained strength. At this time, the first journal of sex, *The Adult,* was published in Britain. Articles included "How Can Free Lovers Be Happy Though Married" and "Dress in Its Relationship to Sex." However, in America, Puritans, landing on the Mayflower, had imported the *sex is sin* doctrine which remained prominent for the century (Juhasz and Szasz, 1969).

The twentieth century, punctuated by wars, flooded with technological innovations, and geared to experimentation and travel, brought rapid change in many varied aspects of interpersonal relationships.

Today's adolescent is surely influenced by his parents and by their parents who, themselves, spent their adolescent years in periods of change. However, even though these older people still retain some of the attitudes and behavior patterns learned in youth, at the same time, members of each generation have incorporated into their value systems those newer ways and beliefs which they could accept without arousing anxiety or guilt feelings. As a result, they have passed on to successive generations a conglomerate of the new and the old. Inconsistency in expectations for suitable behavior and conflicting pressures have contributed to the adolescent's difficulty in mastering the heterosexual sex role.

The twentieth-century culture has been described as the teenage culture. One of the most unpredictable results of the emphasis on youth has been the growth of a new consumer market provided by exploiting the adolescent's need for independence, group acceptance, steady work, and material possessions. As early as the 1950s, advertisers managed to install false standards for selecting dating and marriage partners. Turner (1954, p. 223) decried this fact when he wrote:

> So long as a girl has her teeth white and her bowels free, so long as she is freshly (or sultrily) scented, glamorously shampooed and wears her breasts high and divided, she deserves a mate, even though she cannot read, sew, cook, and has never heard of God.

In addition to changes in values, there have been important changes in the role of the family, which now has little control or authority over its members and few useful tasks for the child. Thus, the home can no longer provide for the basic needs. At a White House Conference on Children and Youth in 1960 Margaret Mead stated: "Identity search through special clothes, special vocabulary, and special postures toward the rest of the world, once confined to the deprived and semicriminal groups, now pervades the entire high school population." Clothing, vocabulary, and body language can all reflect sexual attitudes and can all play an integral part in interpersonal relationships. An analysis of the lyrics of popular songs reflects changing trends and provides clues to courtship patterns. The following differences were noted in a comparison of 1955 American lyrics with those of 1966. In 1955, love had a permanent quality, there was deep romantic involvement, and the female evidently had the power to control the male. In 1966, there was permissiveness without affection and no expectation of a permanent relationship. Choice was important, women were no longer on a pedestal, a wider range of behavior was included, and there was a quick break when a relationship was finished—all these aspects of interpersonal relationships were reflected prominently in song lyrics of the sixties. An active search for an affair and the breakup of relationships were also among the most frequent themes (Carey, 1969).

This brief review of the influences of the past upon the attitudes and values of today's adolescent should lead to a better understanding of the problems faced by the teenager in his attempt to master the appropriate heterosexual role. The final part of this chapter deals with some of the specific adolescent problems within the social context.

Problems of Heterosexual Development

One of the most pressing questions facing the adolescent has been whether or not to engage in premarital sexual intercourse. For earlier generations of young people, fear of sinning against the church, of becoming pregnant, or of disgracing parents and family acted as strong deterrents and at the same time provided a justifiable excuse when peer pressure was exerted. Now that the hold of the church has weakened and the young people view love and loving as basic values, now that the pill is readily available, and parents are themselves often engaged in extramarital affairs, decision making is more often the responsibility of the involved individuals alone. Also, with prolonged education resulting in postponement of marriage, the psychological pressures for intercourse build up over a prolonged period of time.

An additional complication arises from the fact that young people can no longer evaluate and decide on the bases of the standards set forth by their home or by the social group of their childhood. Today these are not the only available models. The mass media portray both true and highly glamourized patterns covering a wide range of sexual behavior by various socioeconomic and ethnic groups. Young people travel more extensively and leave home to attend military or educational institutions where they receive different information and misinformation about sexual behavior and functions, and also come into contact with varied kinds of sexual activities.

People talk about the sexual revolution, the new permissiveness, and the generation gap. In actuality, patterns of sexual behavior are in a state of evolution and not revolution. This is evidenced in the gradual acceptance of wider variations of human sexual activity rather than total rejection of the past and rebellion against tradition. The idea of sexual revolution is tied to the idea of the generation gap. This gap is probably most evident in the area of communication rather than of action. Increasing discussion about sexuality and attempts to bring out from under cover what has been present but concealed in the past, merely result in an honesty and openness among young people which is difficult for adults to accept and to cope with. The shotgun marriage of the past was usually common knowledge, but everyone pretended that brides in these instances were virgins and that their infants were born less than nine months after conception.

Actually, this system worked very well in a society which accepted Malinowski's *Principle of Legitimacy* (1966, p. 35). He set this forth as the most important moral and legal rule concerning the physiological side of kinship and defines it as follows: "No child shall be brought into the world without a man—and one man at that—assuming the role of sociological father, that is guardian and protector, the male link between the child and the rest of the community."

Nevertheless, it is the female who bears the child, and in America today she is the one who is held responsible for obtaining the necessary male to provide legitimate status for the child. She has several alternatives at her disposal. The most socially acceptable of these, at this time in history, is to refrain from bearing children until after marriage. However, figures indicate that this solution is, yearly, becoming less frequent and that both attitudes and actions are changing.

Much of the research on sexual behavior of young people has been conducted with university students and with girls in homes for unwed mothers. Even though the older students may no longer be categorized as adolescents, one can extrapolate from the research in meaningful manner in order to understand adolescents and their behavior. A study by Symonds and Jensen (1961), extending over a thirteen-year period and beginning when individuals were teenagers, showed that there was no change in behavior patterns or personality traits over the thirteen-year period. Basically, what each individual was at thirteen or eighteen he remained at twenty-six or thirty-one.

Bell and Buerkle (1961) asked Temple University coeds and their mothers to answer this question: *How important do you think it is that a girl be a virgin when she marries?* Of the mothers 88 percent said that it was *very wrong* not to be a virgin, 12 percent *generally wrong,* and none circled *right in many situations,* compared to 55, 34, and 13 percent for their daughters. Asked, *Do you think sexual intercourse during engagement is: very wrong, generally wrong, right in many situations,* mothers responded *very wrong* 83 percent, *generally wrong* 15 percent, and *right in many situations* 2 percent, compared with their daughters' responses of 35, 48, and 17 percent. Only 37 percent of the daughters, compared to 83 percent of the mothers, felt that girls should freely answer mothers' questions about attitudes toward sexual intimacy.

In a national sample, Reiss (1968a) found that high school and college students of all socioeconomic classes were generally more permissive than the adults questioned at the same time. Sixty-three to sixty-eight percent of the students felt that their sexual attitudes were similar to those of their parents. He also found highly permissive attitudes in both the upper- and lower-class segments of society.

Figures over the past decade reveal the trends in actual behavior of young people. In 1953 Kinsey found 20 percent nonvirgins in a national sample of college women. In 1959 Ehrman reported that 13 percent of the university students in his study of girls eighteen to twenty-two years of age were nonvirgins. In 1965, Freedman reported that over 75 percent of the unmarried undergraduate college women were virgins. Those who were not virgins said that either emotional involvement or engagement were necessary before they would consider sexual intercourse with a man. A 1968 report in *Education Digest* indicated that 85 percent of thirteen to nineteen year olds polled were virgins. For the same year, the National Council on Illegitimacy provides the following figures: 77,000 babies were born to unmarried girls under fifteen years of age, 158,000 to unmarried girls between fifteen and nineteen years of age (Yurding, 1968). Vincent's 1969 figures on illegitimate children born in the United States indicate an increase in each succeeding generation of black females, specially among the poverty-level, and lower-middle income, fifteen- to twenty-four-year-old subjects. Figures from the National Council on Illegitimacy indicate that the rate of illegitimacy for nonwhites doubled between 1957 and 1968. However, there was also an increase for white females. In 1957, the ratio of illegitimacy for nonwhites was 12 times that of whites; in 1968, it was only 6 times that of whites.

The fact that many of the reported illegitimate births to teenagers are for blacks has given rise to the popular conception that they are promiscuous and morally, mentally, and socially inferior, or else that they have been exploited by irresponsible males. However, this stereotype is not true. Increasingly, research on the unmarried father reveals that the father, in many cases, has a real affection for the mother, that he does feel responsible, and in many instances is willing to help to support the child. Often the father is the steady boyfriend and the mother continues to see the father after the birth of the child. It is true that many of the girls on whom reports are based are lower working-class blacks, often from broken homes. Furstenberg (1969) reports on a group of 169 such unmarried girls in their middle teens. They had had their first sexual relationships from two to three years after menarche; by the age of fifteen, only 39 percent were still virgin; 85 percent became pregnant the same year as their first intercourse to a single boy, and 85 percent continued to see the father.

There is some evidence that children, in adult life, will repeat the pattern set by their parents, in increasing numbers. In many cases, lack of knowledge of birth-control methods is a major factor of unwanted pregnancy. In some subcultures, use of birth control is unacceptable, just as it is in some religions. There is an increasing movement among counselors of unmarried mothers to provide information on contraception as well as contraceptives in an effort to cut down on repeat illegitimate births. Often the parents of the unmarried partners are included in the program which covers sex education and interpersonal relationships as well as contraceptive information.

Both ethnic background and religious training influence the teen-ager's chances of becoming an unmarried parent. Several representative studies are reported here as examples of the wide diversity that exists in America today. Rosenberg and Bensman (1968) studied the sexual pattern of three American ethnic subcultures, all recent migrants to large cities, all living in poverty. The groups consisted of white Appalachians living in Chicago, blacks in Washington, D.C., and Puerto Ricans in New York. They found that sexual patterns are related to general life styles and reflect the social milieu of the ghetto and the short-range, hedonistic goals of the groups studied. They noted that the lower-class sexual mores differ from those of the American middle class, but not more than they differ from each other among the three ethnic groups. For example, for Chicago boys in the study, a car is essential in order to *have sex*. It is means of picking up a date and getting to a drive-in movie. It serves as a mobile bedroom and facilitates double-dating which is neces-sary for safety from menacing gang members. Sex, violence, and liquor go together. The code of ethics of these boys would certainly appear strange to many Americans. The Chicago boy in this study is careful not to have intercourse with a girl whom he might want to marry. However, he would consider it quite proper to beat up a fiancée or a wife who did not submit to his authority in nonsexual matters. He would feel a minimum of anxiety about the consequences of sexual intercourse and a strong disinclination to take any responsibility for what happens. Again, the car is essential. If the girl becomes pregnant and pressure or trouble may be expected, the boy can just hop in the car and take off for another town or state.

For the Puerto Ricans in New York City *scheming* is initiated at large parties or *sets* at someone's apartment where some drinking and quite a lot of pot smoking takes place. Violence is not a part of this sexual scene. The Puerto Rican boy worries about impregnation since he feels responsible for the support of the child and also is aware that parents might force marriage. In Washington, the school is the pivotal point for sexual behavior. The blacks in this study begin dating classmates whom they meet at school. Also, the school provides some sex instruction. These children have some information about sexual organs and functions and can use correct terminology. Boys in this group feel no obligation to marry girls just because they happen to make them pregnant.

This study dealt only with poverty-level, ethnic subcultures. However, undoubtedly, many variations in behavior and attitudes could be found in the heterogeneous structure of American society. This example illustrates the influence of socioeconomic factors on sexual behavior.

A second powerful influence is religion. Religious training and background have served as inhibiting factors in sexual relationships for many young people. Reiss (1964) studied a teenage sample of 903 students ages sixteen to twenty-two. He found blacks more permissive than whites toward premarital sexual behavior. Bell and colleagues (1970) found that patterns of premarital coitus, according to religious background, remained the same from 1958 to 1968. Protestant girls had the highest rate, next the Jewish girls, and lowest were the Catholic girls. Regardless of religion, those with the highest rate of church attendance had the lowest rate of premarital coitus and the greatest feelings of guilt afterwards.

Juhasz (1969) noted that Canadian students evaluated moral teaching about sex as positive when either religious training in the church or strict upbringing in the home kept the student out of trouble by establishing limits for his behavior, and when the student indicated that the resulting sense of security was a positive force. Moral teaching about sex was judged to have negative effects under the following circumstances: When sex was considered a taboo topic and the act something that good girls and boys did not do, but no explanation was given; when there was a Puritanical outlook or a Victorian attitude at home but, nevertheless, approval of forced marriage; or when any type of moral training, such as booklets having a moral outlook, resulted in repelling the student rather than having a positive effect.

Fear and anxiety were mentioned by Canadian students who indicated that they had had insufficient information about sexual function and behavior. This lack of information caused many problems in interpersonal relationships at the college level, and students resented the fact that their parents and teachers had neglected to discuss this topic with them. These feelings are general among people in the United States also. Many studies lend support for the inclusion of some kind of education and assistance for children as they pass through the stages of heterosexual development on the way to maturity. The question will be one of the method and content.

Summary

The following statement by Rubin (1965, p. 187) summarizes a basic philosophy which is relevant for education in human sexuality:

If we indoctrinate our young people with an elaborate set of rigid rules and ready-made formulas, we are only insuring the early obsolescence of these tools. If on the other hand, we give them the skills and attitudes, the knowledge and understanding that enable them to make their own intelligent choice among competing moral codes, we have given them the only possible equipment to face their future. This type of guidance does not deny that a dilemma exists whenever choices must be made. Each choice commands a price, and the individual must weigh the price to be paid against the advantages to be gained.

The purpose of sex education should be to provide the type of guidance outlined above and, in so doing, to clear the clouded glass, to define more sharply the events in the *happening* that is life. First, honest accurate information should be provided which will place sexuality in its proper perspective and bring it out in the open where it can be discussed. Second, it should provide the basis on which adolescents can examine different types of behavior and the consequences of such behavior to themselves and to society. Finally, this information and discussion should help individuals to develop an acceptable way of life in harmony with their goals and ideals for themselves, their children and their society.

REFERENCES

Atkinson, R. *Sexual morality*. London: Hutchinson and Co., 1965.

Bell, R. R., and Buerkle, J. V. Mother and daughter attitudes to premarital sexual behavior. *Marriage and Family Living*, 1961, *24*, 384–388.

————, and Chaskes, J. B. Premarital sexual experience among coeds. *Journal of Marriage and the Family*, 1970, *32*, 81–85.

Broderick, C. B., and Fowler, S. E. New patterns of relationships between sexes among preadolescents. *Marriage and Family Living*, 1961, *23*, 27–30.

————, and Rowe, G. P. A scale of preadolescent heterosexual development. *Journal of Marriage and the Family*, 1968, *30*, 97–101.

Brown, D. G., and Lynn, D. B. Human sexual development: An outline of components and concepts. *Journal of Marriage and the Family*, 1966, *28*, 155–162.

Carey, J. T. Changing courtship patterns in the popular song. *The American Journal of Sociology*, 1969, *74*, 720–731.

Diamond, M. A critical evaluation of the ontogeny of human sexual behavior. *Quarterly Review of Biology*, 1965, *40*, 147–175.

Douvan, E., and Gold, M. Modal patterns in American adolescence. In M. L. Hoffman and L. W. Hoffman (eds.), *Review of child development research*. Vol. 2. New York: Russell Sage Foundation, 1966.

Facts about sexual freedom. *Education Digest,* 1968, *34,* 12–15.

Freedman, M. B. The sexual behavior of American college women. *Merrill Palmer Quarterly,* 1965, *2,* 33–48.

Furstenberg, F., Jr., Gordis, L., and Markowitz, M. Birth control knowledge and attitudes among unmarried pregnant adolescents: A preliminary report. *Journal of Marriage and the Family,* 1969, *31,* 34–42.

Gadpaille, W. J. Homosexual experience in adolescence. *Medical Aspects of Human Sexuality,* 1968, *10,* 29–38.

―――. Homosexual activity and homosexuality in adolescence. *Science and Psychoanalysis,* 1969, *15,* 60–70.

Greenbank, R. K. Are medical students learning psychiatry? *Pennsylvania Medical Journal,* 1961, *64,* 989–992.

Harlow, H. F., and Harlow, M. K. The effect of rearing conditions on behavior. In J. Money (ed.), *Sex research new developments.* New York: Holt, Rinehart and Winston, 1965.

Johnson, M. Sex role learning in the nuclear family. *Child Development,* 1963, *34,* 319–333.

Juhasz, A. M. How accurate are student evaluations of the extent of their knowledge of human sexuality? *The Journal of School Health,* 1967, *37,* 409–412.

―――. Background factors, extent of sex knowledge and source of information. *The Journal of School Health,* 1969, *39,* 32–39.

―――, and Szasz, G. *Adolescents in society.* Toronto: McClelland and Stewart, 1969.

―――. Student evaluation of a high school sex education program. *The California Journal of Educational Research,* 1971, *22,* 144–155.

Kagan, J. The concept of identification. *Psychological Review,* 1958, *65,* 295–305.

―――. Acquisition and significance of sex typing and sex role identity. In M. L. Hoffman and L. W. Hoffman (eds.), *Review of child development research.* Vol. 1. New York: Russell Sage Foundation, 1964.

Kardiner, A. *Sex and morality.* New York: Bobbs-Merrill, 1954.

Kilpatrick, W. H., and Nagel, E. Liberalism and intelligence. *Fourth John Dewey Memorial Lecture,* Bennington, Vt.: Bennington College, 1957.

Kinsey, A. C., Pomeroy, W. B., and Martin, C. E. *Sexual behavior and the human male*. New York: W. B. Saunders Co., 1948.

Kleinerman, G., Grossman, M., Breslow, J., and Goldman, R. Sex education in a ghetto school. *The Journal of School Health*, 1971, *41*, 30–31.

Landis, J. T. Dating maturation of children from happy and unhappy marriages. *Marriage and Family Living*, 1963, *25*, 351–353.

Loeb, M. B. Sex role and identity in adolescence. *Casework Papers*. New York: Family Service Association of America, 1959.

Lynn, D. B. The process of learning parental and sex role identification. *Journal of Marriage and the Family*, 1966, *28*, 466–470.

Malinowski, B. Parenthood—the basis of the social structure. In R. W. Roberts (ed.), *The unwed mother*. New York: Harper & Row, 1966.

Money, J., Hampson, J. G., and Hampson, J. L. Imprinting and establishment of gender role. *American Medical Association Archives of Neurology and Psychology*, 1957, *77*, 333–336.

Mudd, J. W., and Siegel, J. Sexuality: The experience and anxieties of medical students. *New England Journal of Medicine*, 1969, *281*, 1397–1403.

New York Academy of Medicine, Committee on Public Health. *Health education: Its present status*. (Prepublication copy.) New York: NYAM, 1965.

Offer, D., Marcus, D., and Offer, J. L. A longitudinal study of normal adolescent boys. *American Journal of Psychiatry*, 1970, *126*, 917–924.

Queen, S. A., Habenstein, R. W., and Adams, J. B. *The family in various cultures*. New York: J. B. Lippincott, 1961.

Reiss, I. L. Premarital sexual permissiveness among negroes and whites. *American Sociology Review*, 1964, *29*, 688–698.

————. How and why American sex standards are changing. *Transaction*, 1968, *5*, 26–32. (a)

————. Sex education in the public schools: Problem or solution? *Phi Delta Kappan*, 1968, *40*, 52–56. (b)

Rosenberg, B., and Bensman, J. Sexual patterns of three ethnic subcultures of an American underclass. *The Annals of the American Academy of Social Science: Sex and the Contemporary American Scene*, 1968, *376*, 61–75.

Rubin, I. Transition in sex values—implications for the education of adolescents. *Journal of Marriage and the Family*, 1965, *27*, 185–189.

Sherfey, M. J. The evaluation and nature of female sexuality in relation to psychoanalytic theory. *Journal of American Psychoanalytic Association,* 1966, *14,* 28–127.

Simon, W., and Gagnon, J. H. The pedagogy of sex. *Saturday Review,* 1967, *50,* 74–91.

Symonds, P., and Jensen, A. R. *From adolescent to adult.* New York: Columbia University Press, 1961.

Turner, E. S. *A history of courting.* London: Michael Joseph, 1954.

Vincent, C. E., Haney, A., and Cochrane, C. M. Familial and generational patterns of illegitimacy. *Journal of Marriage and the Family,* 1969, *31,* 659–667.

Walters, P. A. Promiscuity in adolescence. *American Journal of Orthopsychiatry,* 1965, *35,* 670–675.

White House Conference on Children and Youth, Inc. Problems of the late adolescence and the young adult. *Children and Youth in the 1960's.* Washington, D.C.: White House Conference on Children and Youth, 1960.

Yurdin, M. O. Recent trends in illegitimacy—implications for practice. *Child Welfare,* 1970, *49,* 373–375.

11

The Emotions and
Sex Education for Adolescents

*Thomas F. Staton**

Little research, in the academic sense of the word, has been done on sex education. The subject, indeed, is one that does not lend itself, under the limitations of our cultural standards and mores, to conventional methods of scientific investigation. Most reports involve the number of instances in which this is done or that is done in a program of sex education. The reports by Kinsey and his colleagues (1948, 1953), Masters and Johnson (1966a), and dozens of other researchers give us voluminous information on physical occurrence of sexual behavior, but Dorothy Rogers' (1962) observation that little study has been made of the *emotional* aspects of sex still holds true. Ehrmann (1957) states that there are relatively few actual knowns of sexual behavior in human beings in general, and Americans in particular. Significantly missing are studies of the emotional aspects of sexual behavior. It is possible to cite opinions, but conclusions reached must be viewed as tentative.

It is reasonable to consider, however, that the opinions of clinical psychologists, psychiatrists, and counselors, based on years of experience in psychotherapy and counseling, possess some validity; so such opinion is

* Thomas F. Staton is Professor and head of the Department of Behavioral Sciences at Huntington College. He has written *Dynamics of Adolescent Adjustment, How to Instruct Successfully, How to Study, Psychology for Managers,* and numerous articles on applications of psychology to various aspects of human development, business, and industry.

often cited in this chapter as evidence as to the psychosexual dynamics active in some area.

Objectives of Sex Education

The subject of sex education cannot be treated meaningfully apart from value judgments. Education on the *physical* aspects of sex can; but when we enter the area of education regarding sexual behavior, it is unrealistic to teach other than in terms of behavioral objectives. Then the question of values arises: *Whose* objectives?

It seems to me to be reasonable to teach for the behavioral objectives that seem to maximize the likelihood of good mental health and social adjustment and to minimize the likelihood of emotional trauma or social injury. I suggest that a marriage in which partners can enjoy their sexual relations uninhibited by feelings of conflict or anxiety arising from earlier sexual experience, or psychic scars from past episodes, is a worthy aim. The enjoyment of sexual relationships with one's wife or husband is not only a solid pillar for a marriage but one of its greatest pleasures. This should not be jeopardized by earlier sexual activities that might injure the married relationship. It is most difficult to adduce research data of the conventional type to substantiate the implication of the last sentence that premarital sexual relations do in fact lessen the likelihood of optimum marital happiness. But I recently was privileged to read a letter from a prominent psychologist to his college-age daughter, written in response to a query from her for some reasons he believed that virginity was important for the adolescent. Where the life and happiness of his own daughter was involved, he wrote as follows:

> As a psychologist I have observed, as have many others, that sexual relationships, prior to marriage, tend to destroy one's ability to develop a satisfactory relationship in marriage. This is true for both males and females. Because intercourse is such an intimate relationship between a man and a woman, that is the emotional relationship that should accompany intercourse, it is also a most fragile part of love. When one shares this relationship with a number of individuals, one's ability to concentrate in one individual is lessened. If marriage should be viewed as an exclusive relationship between two individuals, then the best way to heighten the probability that this will occur is to wait until marriage to develop this relationship.

I will grant that in the United States today there is a considerable divergence between the lip service rendered the traditional standards of sexual morality and the sexual behavior of the nation. Nevertheless, it seems to me that the behavioral objectives taught in a program of sex education for adolescents should be in consonance with the professed moral ideals of the society in which the adolescents will live.

A recent poll of people over twenty-one revealed that 77 percent regarded premarital coitus as a violation of the social norm and that "many people hold this view with sufficient intensity to place such behavior outside their tolerance limit" (Reiss, 1970, p. 78).

The fact that some adolescent subcultures offer rewards in popularity and position for a girl's granting sexual favors, and that others are tolerant of all degrees of sexual license, should hardly be taken into consideration in deciding what standards of sexual behavior and values should be the objective of a program of sex education. After all, it is a sad but well-known fact that many of our adolescent subcultures exert group pressure on members to experiment with drugs and to participate in tests of daring such as driving automobiles recklessly on busy streets. The realistic adult recognizes the difficulties involved in attempting to dissuade adolescents from these behaviors which are undesirable from his viewpoint, when those behaviors are not only tolerated but actually rewarded within the adolescents' peer group. This does not call for abandonment of standards that are perhaps higher than those of the age group we are trying to educate. Rather, it calls for the most effective use of education, adult authority, and the helpful elements of peer group values to bring boys and girls through to maturity. Hopefully, this maturity will contain standards and values that are more in keeping with the professed mores of society than the ones they and their peers would have developed if left alone.

I agree with Cannon and Long (1971, p. 40) that premarital sexual activity, which is to a large degree adolescent sexual activity, is on the increase. They have this to say: ". . . in more recent studies much higher proportions of premarital coitus have been reported for college females. . . . Apparently there is not a single major study that has been made in the late sixties that has found premarital coitus rates that were the level of those found in the late 1950s and early 1960s."

But to me this implies that more, not less, emphasis in a sex education program should be placed on premarital chastity. Despite this change in premarital behavior, a very large number of Americans still hold the Judeo-Christian ethic of sexual continence outside of marriage as one of the proper objectives of any program of sex education for adolescents. This is true even though the people believing in this code may not comprise as overwhelming a majority as they have at some times in the past, and even though they may be less severe in their criticism of those who violate the code than they would have been a number of years ago.

A realistic consideration of the objectives and problems of conducting a sex education program for adolescents requires facing and evaluating the changes wrought regarding pertinent aspects of sex by changing public attitudes, and due recognition of aspects left unchanged. The winds of change in public attitudes of the past few years have not altered the way girls become pregnant. They still become pregnant in exactly the same manner in which girls did when public opinion more strongly condemned premarital sexual activity. The moral rightness or wrongness of extramarital sexual activity has not been changed by shifts in public acceptance of it, in the standards and values of people who respect the Judeo-Christian code of life. The danger of contracting venereal disease has changed at the same time as the change in public attitude. This danger has increased a great deal, according to widely cited figures on the prevalence of venereal disease among both boys and girls.

Thus arguments against premarital sexual experience among boys and girls, based on its intrinsic relation to pregnancy and on Judeo-Christian moral standards, are as valid now as they ever were. Arguments based on the possibility of contracting venereal disease are greatly strengthened. But reasoning against adolescent premarital sex based on the basis of its injurious effect on the self-concept of the girl, and, to a lesser extent, its desensitizing effect on the boy, has much less substantiation now than it had a few years ago. The effect of premarital exploitation on the girl's self-concept was a fact strongly emphasized in the chapter I wrote for this text some five years ago. While the effect on her self-concept of being sexually used has not yet been eliminated in the case of the adolescent girl, it probably has been lessened. The present treatment of the subject, therefore, will place less emphasis on devaluation of the girl's self-concept as a reason for premarital sexual continence among adolescents. This probably diminished effect, however, does not invalidate the point of view presented in the earlier chapter that sex education for unmarried adolescents should have as one of its objectives indoctrinating them in attitudes that will deter their engaging in premarital sexual activities.

My frame of reference regarding sex education can be briefly sketched as follows: Good sex education maximizes the likelihood of married partners achieving greatest happiness in their sexual relations with each other; and, in current American society, premarital promiscuity, or even occasional premarital experience, produces effects on the personalities of boys and girls that lessen their likelihood of optimum marital adjustment.

Any adequate program of sex education must be designed to provide instruction and understanding in two major areas: the physical aspects of sex and the psychological aspects. These areas and instruction intertwine and overlap. Nevertheless, the program should make conscious provision for each as a distinct element.

Education in the Physical Aspects of Sex

In an education program for adolescents on the physical aspects of sex, content should include instruction on the reproductive system and process, the nature and bases of heredity, chemical and glandular functions related to sex, and anatomical differences in the sexes. In addition, boys and girls should learn of the changes that take place in their bodies as they grow from childhood to adulthood, and the causes and effects of these changes. All this should be taught not as subject matter to be learned as an academic discipline, but from the standpoint of developing in adolescents an understanding and appreciation of the significance and implications of these phenomena for their lives and functions as men and women.

Most textbooks in elementary psychology contain excellent expositions of heredity. In books on child psychology can be found discussions of the reproductive processes and systems that are suitable as a basis for this aspect of sex education for adolescents. Elementary texts in physiology, biology, and anatomy provide adequate source material for instruction in the anatomy and physiology of sex; and most textbooks on adolescent psychology present substantially what an adolescent should know about the changes taking place in his body during adolescence (see Garrison's chapter).

Education in the Psychological Aspects of Sex

Although innumerable articles and texts are available presenting the physiology of sex in a form easily adapted to a program of adolescent sex education, much less of practical value on the psychology of sex has been published for the sex education of adolescents. To convince yourself of this, pick up at random a dozen textbooks on adolescent psychology and see the extent to which the authors explore such topics as: dominance–submission in boy-girl relationships; the role of love in sexual desire in the girl as opposed to the boy; and, the influence of conversation on sexual behavior. In the area of psychosexual education there is a notable dearth of readily available material covering facts and concepts that are essential to a program of sex education if it is to equip boys and girls with the knowledge and understanding they require. With the stipulation, therefore, that education on the physical aspects of sex is an essential part of any program of sex education, the remainder of this chapter will be devoted to an exploration of psychosexual factors which also are an essential, but often neglected, part of any adequate program. The psychosexual dynamics postulated in the chapter are drawn from the writings of many clinical psychologists, psychiatrists, sociologists, and counselors, substantiated by my own clinical and counseling experience.

Sexual Desire in Humans

The simplest, most elemental and universal manifestation of sexual differentiation is the mating urge. In lower animals, the mating drive generally becomes urgent only when the male is stimulated by the female's periodic condition of sexual receptivity called estrus or "heat," and the female is only receptive during that period. In humans, the male's mating urge, his sexual desire, is unrelated to the biological condition of the female, and her receptivity is little (although somewhat) dependent upon the stage of her fertility cycle. In humans, sexual desire, while it has its origin in bodily chemistry (as it does in the lower animals), arises and becomes intensified not primarily as a result of biological conditions but of psychological factors. These factors are principally attitudinal and emotional.

The fact that human consciousness of and reaction to sexual stimuli are primarily emotional rather than having their origin in chemical changes, or even in the objective fact of the stimuli themselves, is easily confirmed by dozens of examples. A brother typically is not stimulated sexually by his sister under circumstances that would produce arousal if another girl were involved. A physician typically is not sexually excited by seeing or touching a female patient whom he is examining or treating. And, although more exceptions may be found to this example, it is still a matter of record that male artists characteristically look on nude female models without sexual arousal. If the reaction were fundamentally biological and chemical, sexual arousal of the males in the foregoing illustrations would be universal. It is universal among the male animals of lower species when bodily chemistry decrees it.

The fact that the mating urge, manifested as sexual desire, is primarily psychological rather than precipitated by biological conditions is vital to any intelligent treatment of the subject of human and sexual affairs. In educating adolescents to adhere to desired patterns of sexual behavior, it means that we must think in terms of their mental and emotional lives; of the experiences which will have one or another effect on their emotions at a given time; of their desires, aspirations, and fantasies; and of the invisible but terrific force of peer group opinion and behavior. We have to consider, and lead them to understand, how their imaginations can trigger their endocrine systems to action under certain conditions. All these factors are more important than the objective conditions of the situation in which the adolescent is involved.

Thus, in considering and in leading adolescents to consider *realistically* anything pertaining to sex, we must think and show them how to think in terms of the psychology of a situation. The same portion of a girl's leg may be visible as a result of wearing shorts or of having her skirt become disarrayed. Objectively speaking, the part of the leg seen is the same in both situations. The effect on a boy seated beside her at a drive-in movie may be vastly different. Whether this is the first or the fifth time it has happened also will influence the boy's reaction, although it would not alter the objective, physical situation of the moment. The mind of the boy or the girl does as much to determine the sexual significance of an act, statement, or circumstance as does the actual nature of the act, statement, or circumstance. It is important for boys and girls to appreciate the implications of this fact. Some of these implications will emerge in our further exploration of the needed content of psychosexual education, and still others will be noticed frequently by the perceptive adult working with adolescents.

In the last analysis, sexual behavior depends principally on the attitudes held by the individual involved. As pointed out by McKinney (1960), the biological sex urge is seldom so powerful that it seizes control of the adolescent and dominates his behavior without its first being stimulated by psychological factors and, or, deliberate physical manipulation. When fanned to a fever heat by prolonged petting, sex-oriented conversation, infatuation on the part of the girl, or wish fulfillment fantasies on the part of the boy, the sex urge can, indeed, become temporarily overwhelming. But it was built to this pitch of influence by the minds and emotions of the people involved. It did not become so as an inevitable biological process. The intensity of the sex urge, and the extent to which it controls behavior, are infinitely more influenced by the emotions aroused by the attitude-directed behavior of a boy or girl than by the biological nature of either.

A program of sex education should especially emphasize information on sex that boys and girls will not receive in the process of everyday living but that they need to have in order to know how to manage their social relationships wisely and constructively. Each course should feature those aspects of most concern to the sex involved. Thus, girls need receive only brief instruction on the phenomena of erections and nocturnal emissions, but considerable instruction on the menstrual cycle. The emphasis for boys would be reversed. In the succeeding discussion, the relative need of each sex for different topics will be apparent.

Meanings Attached to Premarital Sex

One example of male-female behavior dramatizes a social attitude and a psychological fact that are basic to the philosophy of an effective program of sex education. Characteristically, boys feel proud and boast of sexual conquests, while girls often suffer loss of self-respect and incur feelings of anxiety or guilt from having engaged in sexual intimacies outside the marriage relationship. This fact reveals a fundamental difference in male-female relationships to premarital sex and carries with it profound implications for a program of sex education for adjustment.

Except in an occasional subculture (usually in unsavory ones), the girl who engages in premarital sexual activities loses status and respect if the fact becomes known. Not only does general observation of society indicate this to be a fact, but research and professional observation as well. Kaats and Davis (1968) found 45 percent of the males they polled at the University of Colorado felt that a girl's virginity would be an important consideration in their evaluation of her as a prospective mate. Only 17 percent thought their own virginity or absence of it was a significant factor in their own suitability.

Bell (1970, p. 183) states: "Since the male often wants the girl to whom he is committed to be 'good,' he may redefine her as 'bad,' if his relationship with her becomes sexual." Lucky and Ness (1969), in a poll covering several representative colleges throughout the United States, found that only 30 percent of the men polled felt that it would not influence their evaluation of a girl as a suitable mate to find that she had intercourse with someone else at an earlier time. In my own clinical practice I have encountered cases where a woman's premarital intercourse with her present husband was cited by him as evidence of her unreliability and lack of proper moral standard. Thus, the case for sex education stressing girls' avoidance of premarital intercourse is strengthened by the injurious effect of such activity on her marriageability and her status in the eyes of her husband after marriage.

The boy who is known (or thought) to have achieved sexual relations with many girls is not correspondingly derogated by his peer group. Why? Because the boy has mastered, he has made a conquest, he has demonstrated his masculine appeal and virility. These are causes for pride, if altruistic values are ignored. The girl, on the other hand, has not conquered or seduced by her irresistible femininity. (It is commonly understood that a girl does not have to possess fascinating femininity to make her desired sexually by a male—she only has to be female.) In another generation, she was said to have "fallen." Today, she has "been had," given in, submitted, been used, or surrendered. The whole language of sexual intercourse (scientific, colloquial, and slang) emphasizes that the boy wins and the girl surrenders or is defeated in the contest that ends in their having sexual intercourse. Thus, sexual promiscuity by the adolescent girl has a diametrically and fundamentally different effect on her ego and self-concept from what it has on the teenage boy. To him, it is a source of pride. To her, it is having been used, having let herself be conquered and exploited.

Kinsey (1953) reports that 18 percent of unmarried women who reported having had sexual intercourse admitted more than minor regret for their actions, and 13 percent minor regret. Bell and Chaskes (1970) reported a much larger percentage of girls who felt they had gone "too far" in degree of intimacy with boys they dated, but the percentage of girls reporting such feelings in 1968 was much lower than of those reporting in 1958. Sixty-five percent of the 1958 group made such an evaluation and only 36 percent of the 1968 group.

Stratton and Spitzer (1967, p. 441) found that "permissive sexual attitudes are associated with an unfavorable self-concept" on the part of girls. (It may be noted, however, that conclusions reached earlier by Maslow and Sakoda [1955] do not support these findings.)

Clinical psychologists and psychiatrists find frequent instances of *unconscious* as well as *unadmitted* anxiety and guilt deriving from premarital sex experiences. They have repeatedly commented on the number of girls encountered in their clinical practice who, underneath a veneer of sophisticated emancipation from the double standard, were suffering from severe feelings of guilt and loss of self-respect as a result of having let themselves be "used" sexually. "I'm only a body to him," is the bitter remark often heard in such circumstances and such a feeling is destructive to self-respect and pride.

Eventually, of course, the girl may overcome such feelings and regard her sexual submission as merely her contribution to a social relationship, analogous to the boy paying for the theater tickets. Such sophistication, however, is rarely encountered in adolescents. It is more typically a defense gradually built up as a girl grows older, in an attempt to rationalize her degraded self-esteem back into self-respect. Kinsey (1953) reports that the more a girl had engaged in premarital intercourse, the less likely she was to regret her actions. This is hardly surprising.

Because of social attitudes and a girl's frequent emotional reaction (totally apart from any moral considerations or the danger of disease or pregnancy), therefore, much can be said in favor of sex education designed to encourage chastity in the adolescent girl. It is important to her self-concept, self-respect, self-esteem, and mental health. (It should be noted that this chapter is concerned with optimum sex education for adolescents, not for adults who presumably might have greater experience, greater capacity for self-restraint, and self-discipline, and superior capability of intelligent self-determination.)

Aside from the disapproval that they, too, will encounter from some segment of society, boys do not escape completely unscathed from sexual promiscuity. The sexually promiscuous male develops the attitude of exploitation, or self-centeredness, and of disregard for the welfare and happiness of members of the opposite sex as long as his own pleasure is achieved and his own desires are satisfied. This attitude is not a good background on which to build a happy family life. It will inevitably affect his adjustment with the girl he marries. One cannot exploit others—deliberately subject them to injury and, or, danger—without injury to one's own integrity and mental health. Penal reformers have claimed, and psychologists substantiate their claims, that floggings ultimately injure the man who gives them as much as they injure those who receive them. The effect of service as guards in concentration camps (or even repeated observation of humiliation inflicted on others) on the natures of men has been generally recognized, and vividly described by Frank (1963). The ruthless, the inconsiderate, the opportunists and exploiters, as seducers or otherwise, are undergoing damage less obvious but as real as that which is suffered by the other parties in the relationship.

Even an initially reluctant girl, her inhibitions broken down, may be cooperative and experience pleasure in the throes of sexual passion. This fact does not alter the effect on the boy's nature of having used his powers to persuade another to act in a manner potentially harmful to her, for his own momentary pleasure. The adolescent boy who uses his assets and desire for personal pleasure to overcome the moral resistance of girls is building a pattern of attitudes and values that may cripple him in all of his relationships with humanity. The self-centeredness and ruthless using of others, frequently developed by a boy in sexual promiscuity, are not likely to limit their scope to the girls he enjoys. They may also be transferred and reveal themselves in his activities in the community, on the job, and in his home.

I believe, from many years of clinical experience, that the effects of sexual promiscuity on boys' and girls' personalities, and on their prospects of good mental health and marital adjustment, constitute more than adequate grounds for making continence prior to the marriage relationship a valid and desirable objective of sex education.

The investigations conducted by Kinsey and his staff (1948, 1953) substantiate the clinical judgment I expressed in an earlier treatise (1963) on adolescence that males and females are quite different in their psychosexual constitutions. This is important for boys and girls to learn. It is human nature to assume that others think and feel much as we do, and attach much the same significance to things that we attach to them. The fact is that sexual desire in boys has a vastly different emotional base from sexual desire in girls; and an act or circumstance often has completely different sexual implications to members of the different sexes.

Knowledge of some of these instances of difference can spare the girl the embarrassment of having a boy attach different meaning than she intended to an act of hers. It also will spare the boy the embarrassment of seeming to be crude and vulgar. The Kinsey (1948, 1953) studies confirm the common observation that masculine nudity does not characteristically serve as a sexual stimulant to, or arouse sexual desire in, a girl. The sight of feminine nudity, on the other hand, is usually all that is necessary to arouse sexual desire in a boy. Any movement suggesting nudity (e.g., taking off a dress under which a swimsuit is worn, unfastening the back of the halter to sun while lying face down on the beach, adjusting a stocking with hands hidden under the skirt) may have erotic significance to boys, even though it may be done quite innocently by girls, with no consciousness of their erotic significance.

There is, of course, considerable psychological evidence to suggest that bikinis, miniskirts, hot pants, and like attire, while ostensibly worn innocently and with no self-consciousness, in reality represent unconscious if not conscious attempts to attract erotic attention. But there *are* such things as completely unintentional actions by girls (especially adolescent girls who lack extensive social experience and sophistication) that hold much erotic significance to boys. The girl not sophisticated in the psychology of sex may assume that boys' responses to sexual stimuli are essentially the same as hers, and she, as Simon and Gagnon (1969) report, experiences sexual arousal as a result of romantic words and actions rather than erotic ones.

Romance, Love, and Exploitation

One area of psychosexual difference in boys and girls is in the emotional bases of their sex urge. Ehrmann (1959) succinctly summarizes his research in this area as follows: Males are erotic; females romantic. The emotional roots of the boy's sexual desire seem to lie in the desire to possess, and the feeling of mastery and strengthening of his self-concept that accompanies his achieving intimacy with a girl. This fact has been commented on by clinicians such as Deutsch (1944), and their observations substantiated by the research of Lindzey and Goldberg (1953) and by Ehrmann (1959).

Also the boy's physical desire is aroused early in circumstances of physical intimacy, or even in the intimacy of conversation about sexual matters. This physical desire spurs on his attempts to achieve more intimacy, and the greater intimacy achieved in turn increases the intensity of his physical desire. Love plays a minor and incidental part (if any at all) in the arousal, intensification, and satisfaction of his sexual desire. His sexual desire is erotically oriented, not romantically oriented (Grant, 1957), although he may cultivate the trappings of romance because of their appeal to the girl.

On the other hand, as Stone and Church (1957) point out, a girl's sexual desire springs primarily from a feeling of love for the boy. It is compounded by a desire to make him happy, which appears to be absent in the boy's feeling of sexual desire for the girl. Rarely does her physical desire for sexual relations become a driving force in her behavior, and then only after extensive preliminary psychological and perhaps physical stimulation. The fondling and kissing, snuggling and caressing, are to her things of pleasure, and, more often than not, satisfactory ends in themselves. To her they signify love and romance. They give her pleasure, and she is happy in the belief that she is giving equal pleasure to the boy. Her sexual nature is attuned to love and romance. Physical appetite usually makes an appearance late, if at all, and dominates her behavior only in the last stages of love play.

Failure to understand and appreciate these vast psychosexual differences often leads to frustration and unhappiness for both boy and girl. Interestingly, both boys and girls seem slow to comprehend the truth from personal experience. A boy often feels that girls are "teases." They lead him on, raise his hopes of achieving intercourse, excite him to the point of agony, and then unreasonably stop him or even become offended when he attempts to carry the intimacy to what is (for him) the only possible rational conclusion.

The naïve girl, however, has thoroughly enjoyed what was to her the romance of shared lips and caresses. She has been happy in the thought that she is affording equal happiness to the boy toward whom she feels, at least at the moment, so tender, if not actually loving. Now she finds that he is pressing for an intimacy she never intended, which shocks her, in which she perceives danger to herself and a violation of her code of behavior. Unlike the boy, she had not considered the petting a prelude, a means to an end that was inevitable if satisfaction was to be achieved. To her the kissing, caressing, and whispered endearments were ends in themselves, inducing a state of supreme happiness and contentment. Suddenly, as in a case described by Kanin (1957), her sweet companion is no longer a sweet companion but a wolf, and a slavering, snapping one at that! She does not know why he "changed" so. She does not realize that he considers that *she* is the one who suddenly changed, suddenly contradicted her former behavior. The boy is frustrated and angry, feeling he has been led on and made a fool of. The girl is shocked, angry, sometimes hysterical. She did not know her behavior was, in the eyes of the boy, giving a clear go-ahead signal.

Sex education has failed when misunderstandings such as this arise. The *situations* may arise despite good psychosexual education (although it is probable that they would arise less often), because adolescent boys and girls occasionally will get themselves into such fixes. But the bafflement, the misunderstanding, the outrage and feeling of being cheated can be prevented. Through understanding on both sides of what has happened, the boy and girl are better equipped to avoid developing a harmful distrust or contempt for the opposite sex, and a recurrence of such a contratemps.

Closely related to the erotic-romantic relationship just described is the different relationship between love and sexual desire in boys and girls. An old saying sums up the situation succinctly and with only moderate distortion: "A gentleman will try to seduce every girl except the one he loves, but a nice girl will not be seduced by any man except the man she loves." Every clinical psychologist working with adolescents has heard girls say, "I *loved* him . . . that's the only reason I did it. I thought he loved me, too. Why did he want to do it if he didn't love me?" Blood (1962, p. 131), interpreting research data, concludes: ". . . it seems fair to say that *most* of the premarital intercourse of college men is exploitive in nature rather than an expression of love." Reiss (1961, p. 6) puts it even more strongly, saying, "One finds very often an inverse relation, in that boys prefer to have coitus with girls they do not care for, because they regard the girls they do care for as 'too good' for such behavior."

Knowledge of this fundamental sex difference in the relationship between love and sexual desire will not change the behavior of all girls. People tend to believe what they very much want to believe, even though the rational portion of their mind tells them it is not true. The girl who loves a boy wants his love to equal hers. Therefore, when he uses the claim of his love for her as a device to assist in seduction, she often will believe him because she so desperately *wants* him to love her. She disregards evidence in order to believe that he does. Knowledge of this fact, too, is a proper part of a girl's sex education.

The different relationship between love and sexual relations is logical, not mysterious or paradoxical, but rational and reasonable, when we further examine the psychosexual structure of males and females. Both from the standpoint of biology and society, a girl runs a greater risk of inconvenience, embarrassment, and tragedy for engaging in sexual relations outside of marriage. It is natural that if she is of normal emotional and social adjustment she would be reluctant to accept such a risk and inclined to do so only to bring happiness to one she loved. Ideally, a boy should be unwilling to subject any girl to such eventualities for his pleasure. Certainly, if he is emotionally mature, sensible, and responsible, he would be reluctant to subject a girl he genuinely loved to possible social censure and personal tragedy. In a momentary surrender to blind sexual fury he might do so, but at such a time he would not be an emotionally adjusted and rational being.

Thus it seems fair to say that in consenting to premarital sexual relations a girl is, at least in many instances, "proving her love" (although, of course, she may feel just as strong a love but nevertheless refuse to violate her self-concept and standard of behavior). On the other hand, the boy's insisting on sexual intimacies suggests a lack of mature love rather than its presence.

Understanding all these things enables a girl to understand the psychodynamics of her attitudes and actions and those of the boy. Properly appreciating these factors allows her to choose her course of action accordingly. That is to say, she does not act on a gross misinterpretation of the motives and attitudes of her partner.

Dominance and Submission

Another psychosexual difference between boys and girls that Ehrmann (1959) discusses is worthy of note. Boys characteristically possess the male urge to dominate, while girls have the characteristic female tendency toward submission. This distinction is well nigh universal among lower animals, and shows itself prominently in primitive cultures. As man becomes more humane, develops a greater grasp of the concept of social justice, masculine domination of the female declines. In contemporary American culture, the decline of masculine dominance has progressed to a degree where there are so many exceptions in individual person-to-person contacts that it cannot be applied accurately as a generalization. This decline in masculine dominance, however, is conspicuously greater among adults than among children or adolescents. In other words, masculine dominance tends to exist until social maturation diminishes or eliminates it. This tendency of the male to dominate and the female to submit is often responsible for the common situation of a girl persisting in her infatuation with a boy who pointedly humiliates, neglects, and socially misuses her. Perhaps this is more often the correct explanation than is her having a feeling of genuine affection for the boy. It is an atavistic tendency of the weak (or merely insecure) to seek security through submitting to the strong, and rudeness or brutality is easily confused with strength by the insecure.

This dominance-submission tendency, not yet "socialized" out of adolescents, accounts for much of the trouble parents have in preventing their teenage daughter from running frantically to the street when summoned by a peremptory blast on the horn by her current boyfriend. The male summons and the female comes. Even when the girl seems to take the initiative, to be the aggressor in the relationship, it almost always is apparent to the observant adult that in actuality she is trying to maneuver the boy into a position of displaying possessive behavior toward her. An understanding of these mechanisms of the two sexes will help the girl to combat her submissive tendencies consciously when they may lead her into dangerous situations. It may also help the boy who is basically good-hearted to understand himself and his girl and to refrain from importunities exploiting his strength and her weakness.

Controlling the Situation and Environment

Separation of the sexes for instruction in sexual matters (which is discussed in more detail in the chapter) serves as an example in giving boys and girls a comprehension of the relationship between sexually oriented conversations or discussion of sexual topics and sexual arousing and desire. Kinsey (1963) found that adolescent boys, and many adolescent girls, have experienced the arousal of sexual excitement, if not passion, as a result of reading accounts of sexual activity or participating in discussions of sexual topics. With such sexual arousal mutually experienced, there is greater difficulty in a girl's controlling her own behavior as well as the advances of her companion. Experienced boys and men often employ suggestive and subsequently more directly sexually oriented conversation as a means of arousing sexual interest in a date and gradually lessening her inhibitions. The girl who engages in sexually oriented conversation to show her emancipation, or for a thrill, is encouraging the development of urges and passion in both herself and her date that almost inevitably leads the boy to attempt physical intimacy. The adolescent girl should know that unless she wants to lead her date into sexual intimacies on the physical level, she had better not engage in suggestive or sexually oriented conversation with him. Words may be as effective as signs, or even physical contact, in arousing and intensifying erotic urges.

In this connection, it may be noted that Ehrmann's (1952) depth interviews with girls on the psychodynamics of petting revealed that the crucial point at which limiting further physical intimacies became most difficult was when the girl permitted caresses beyond a simple embrace. Psychologists had theorized that probably the degree of intimacy which made it most difficult for a girl to call a halt to the progression of erotic activities was after she had permitted the boy's hand to caress her inside her clothing. From interviews with adolescent and late-adolescent girls, Ehrmann found that the girl permitting the boy's hands to caress her below the shoulder level, even caressing her breasts outside her clothing, triggered the erotic forces in each party that were most likely to constitute the point-of-no-return. Failure to comprehend this can result in a girl letting her relationship with her companion get out of her control before she realizes she has entered the danger zone of sex play.

The mother who admonishes her child not to get wet, but does not warn him away from an inviting stream beside the picnic grounds has not effectively guided his behavior. Similarly, a program of sex education that fails to acquaint adolescents with circumstances that get them into situations where unwise behavior is likely to take place is not as effective as it should be.

Robert Burns summarizes the ingredients of a situation leading to sexual indiscretions as follows: "A well-loved lad, convenience snug, a treacherous inclination." When a boy and girl find themselves in a situation of privacy for a considerable period of time, and most especially if it follows an experience encouraging feelings of romance in the girl or erotic arousal in the boy (such as a dance, a party, a romantic movie, or any emotion-arousing activity), the temptation to follow the urgings of psychological and biological nature is strong.

"If you drink, don't park—accidents cause people" is a paraphrase I have heard young people use to express two other factors promoting sexual activity among adolescents. The lowering of moral and other inhibitions under the influence of alcohol are too well known to merit elaboration. Both psychologists (Wattenberg, 1955) and sociologists (Kanin, 1957) have noted that an automobile parked in a secluded place promotes sexual intimacy. Adolescent girls should be aware of the difficulty they may have in handling a situation that can develop when an automobile ride eventuates in the boy parking the car in a place of undisturbed privacy. It is hard to get away from such a spot if the girl finds she is the only one who wishes to leave. It would have been more effective for her to object to going there in the first place. The same opportunity and temptation exist, often intensified, when adolescents are permitted prolonged privacy in the home or at a party. In fact, Kinsey (1953) reports the girl's home as the prime location for premarital intercourse, the boy's home and automobile being major secondary locations.

Parental requirements that dating adolescents come home within a short time after leaving a scheduled activity or group function, and prohibitions against late dating hours or extended periods of privacy for a couple in the home, seem wise. The adolescent who protests, "If we were going to do anything wrong, we could do it in ten minutes as well as in an hour," either does not know the dynamics of sexual intimacy on dates or is pretending ignorance. Except in the case of the boy and girl who have become habituated to sexual intimacies from long practice with each other, boy-girl sexual behavior almost invariably follows a well-defined and time-consuming course, from kissing to necking to petting to intercourse, with considerable time spent in each activity. Kinsey (1953) found that even an interruption is likely to terminate the progression (through one person becoming alarmed or self-conscious) or at least "set back" the progress that had been made.

Extended time in considerable privacy is conducive to the development of intimacies. This is true even though the couple has not deliberately sought for and planned these intimacies. The boy or girl who winds up engaging in sexual activities that were not premeditated usually has spent a considerable time working up to the level of involvement. Without the prolonged erotic and romantic play, final intimacy would not have taken place.

Earlier in the chapter it was said that the biological urge for satisfaction of the sex drive seldom becomes overwhelmingly powerful unless cultivated by prolonged petting or conversation of an erotic nature; however, the sheer biological urge to mate is capable of becoming so powerful in both sexes that few adolescent boys and girls have the mature self-discipline to resist it. Given sufficient help and cooperation, nature can, indeed, establish a point-of-no-return in the relation of an adolescent boy and girl. Both time and privacy, in considerable quantities, usually are required for this point-of-no-return.

The time a boy and girl spend in intimacies has a cumulative effect. That is to say, they carry over from one date to the next. This is one of the dangers (although probably not the chief one) of adolescents "going steady." A boy and girl who think enough of each other to be together repeatedly, especially to the exclusion of dating other people, become increasingly familiar with each other's bodies as well as personalities. Increasingly intimate physical contact comes to be taken for granted. For them, the starting point for romantic or erotic activities becomes petting of greater and greater intimacy, with little or no time being spent in the preliminary conversation and kissing by which a boy and girl not thoroughly familiar with each other gradually achieve greater physical intimacy. You can almost say that every romantic interlude takes up where the last one left off and goes on from there.

Sex and Sexuality

Masters and Johnson (1966b) draw an interesting and valid distinction between sex (by which they mean an aspect of physiology) and sexuality (which involves the whole complex of personality factors and social relationships having their origin in the reproductive drive). Sex is innate in the human being. Sexuality must be learned. As far as is known, the learning of sexuality follows the same principles of learning as does the learning of other attitudes and habits. Learning theory, as well as common sense, suggests that a pleasurable reaction once given is more readily given in a subsequent, similar situation. Thus, it is an unusually safe prediction that the more a boy or girl has taken part in sexual intimacies, the less likely he or she is to refrain from similar actions when another opportunity or temptation occurs. A very real danger of what is euphemistically called "a single mistake" is that from all that is known of learning theory, it predisposes repetitions. Certainly, it is my own view that the danger of premarital sexual intimacies between a boy and girl in love with each other lies as much in the fact that habit patterns thus formed will have a tendency to prevail in other situations involving other people as in the fact that such premarital intimacies may injure their own future relationship. Perhaps all this can be summarized as follows: Premarital intercourse is not necessarily promiscuity, but it certainly increases the likelihood of promiscuity developing.

How Should Sex Education Be Conducted?

Sex education, like education in correct grammar or good manners, is not something that can be satisfactorily achieved through formal teaching. It must be accompanied by general life experiences that support and reinforce the more formalized portion of education. Adults in every area of adolescents' lives (parents, teachers, clergy, coaches, counselors, scout or recreational leaders) should be alert to seize every opportunity to enhance the boy or girl's sex education. Noteworthy news events, situations encountered in the study of literature or history, current civic happenings, or circumstances in the adolescent's own experience can make important concepts in sex education more real and of greater practical significance to boys and girls.

Certainly, in the average family it is good for parents to give their children as much instruction in all aspects of sex education as they are capable of giving. Statements of Drucker (1952) and Lee (1952) are representative of the opinions of psychologists on this point. The intimacy existing between a parent and young child affords ample natural opportunities for instruction in these fields to be given gradually and naturally, in the normal procession of family living. Information and guidance can be given in response to the child's question or other expression of curiosity about his body or the bodies of others. This would cover reproduction or other directly sexual topics. The amount of information and degree of detail can be adjusted to the child's level of interest and understanding. Finally, the intimacy existing between parent and child can be used in the process of imparting information on sex to emphasize that this is not a topic one discusses casually in social conversation.

In the normal and wholesome family environment, this basic information on sex will have been given by the parent before the child reaches adolescence; but, as Rogers (1962) points out, the amount of information regarding the physiology and psychology of sex that the average parent *can* give is extremely limited. It usually is confined to the most elementary explanations of the simplest facts of sexual structure and reproduction, because few parents retain (even if they once learned) the degree of knowledge of psychology and biology required to give the adolescent a clear understanding of the psychological and biological aspects of sex. It is even more important and more difficult to build an appreciation of the significance of this information in the lives of people.

It is both practical and in keeping with the modern concept of the responsibility of our schools for the school to assume considerable responsibility for giving the adolescent an understanding and appreciation of the anatomy, physiology, chemistry, and biology of sex. This should also include the psychology of sex and the significance of sex in a person's life.

As may have been inferred from earlier statements, I take what I fear is very much a minority position on how sex education should be presented in the school. My position, however, is based on many years of working with boys and girls in both clinical and school settings. It is my conviction that sex education in the school should not be scheduled primarily in groups where both sexes are present. Sex education will be more effective, and assume its more appropriate place in the thinking and value systems of boys and girls, if given to separate groups. Physical education classes seem to me one logical answer.

I completely agree with those who contend that segregation of the sexes for purposes of sex education makes sex something of a taboo, something that is not accepted and dealt with matter-of-factly (e.g., the circulation of the blood or the hunger drive). But it seems to me that the people advancing this contention miss the whole point of sex education; or, perhaps, their objectives are different from mine. Sex is *not* just another physiological process, *not* just another craving. It is a most unique thing, carrying with it wonderful as well as dangerous potentialities. Treating it as an impersonal thing like the function of the liver, or just another emotion such as sibling jealousy, is unrealistic. This is true because the psychological forces (social sanctions and taboos, the potential for emotional satisfaction or disturbance, and social adjustment or maladjustment) associated with sex are so much greater, more complex, and more contradictory than in the case of other physiological and psychological functions.

The mode of sex education should recognize the uniqueness of its subject and assist the adolescent to develop the concepts of privacy and reserve properly associated with sex. It is difficult to teach such reserve by admonition in a setting that contradicts the admonition. The fact is that our attitudes and feelings tend to follow the patterns of our thoughts and speech about as much as our thoughts and speech follow the patterns of our feelings and attitudes. I believe any serious student of semantics will agree that lessening the inhibitions in discussion of a subject will lessen the inhibition of the majority of discussants in their behavior regarding the subject discussed. Adolescent boys and girls cannot discuss with true inner (as opposed to apparent) scientific detachment a subject that exercises on them such profound, provocative, titillating emotional stimulation as does sex. Therefore, unless the objective of sex education is to lower the barriers of reserve between adolescent boys and girls, segregation for sex instruction and especially for discussion of sexual topics and problems is essential.

The Self-concept and Sex Education

In my own experience I have found one approach to influencing adolescent sexual behavior notably more effective than any other. It is my observation that the boy or girl who has a strong self-concept and who recognizes a type of behavior as inconsistent with that self-concept characteristically will avoid that behavior. This is congruent with Stagner's (1961) emphasis on the role of the self-image and self-respect in bringing consistency into behavior. I have found that a girl who thinks of herself as master of her behavior, who takes pride in being a person who cannot be manipulated by others, and who feels that being used for someone else's pleasure is beneath her dignity and standard, is unlikely to indulge in behavior that would injure that self-concept. Similarly, the boy who thinks of himself as a responsible person of honor and integrity, who feels contempt for preying on weaker or less knowledgeable people, who takes pride in the honesty of his dealings with everyone, is unlikely to attempt to persuade a girl to engage in activities that might expose her to injury or criticism.

Consequently, my approach to influencing behavior through sex education is principally an attempt to get boys and girls to form self-concepts of themselves as people who are above anything that would lessen self-respect (especially for girls), or would take advantage of another to that person's possible hurt (especially for boys). Adolescent boys and girls respond amazingly well to discussions that help them acquire firm, clear pictures of themselves as people of pride, honor, and integrity, as people who will not act out of character with the self-concept they develop and want to maintain.

In this respect, society lends us a helping hand. Although society is tolerant of immorality (of other kinds, as well as sexual), as was noted earlier in the chapter, sexual misbehavior becoming known lessens the respect a girl is accorded in all societies (save a few subcultures). Even in the case of the boy, investigators have found that adult society, as a whole, possesses values such that he cannot trespass them morally without some injury to the respect and regard in which he is held. This lessened respect will result in injury to the boy or girl's self-concept. Adolescents are not independent of prevailing social values and standards. They are influenced by them and are unable to avoid evaluating themselves to some extent in terms of them. Stagner (1961), indeed, states that self-respect appears to be chiefly our introjected conception of the respect of others; and Gordon (1963) emphasizes the self-concept as including the individual's response to the evaluation placed on him by society. Boys' and girls' self-concepts are injured if they fall below those standards. Make an adolescent sufficiently conscious of a good self-concept, and you will influence his behavior profoundly. The self-concept approach to teaching morality ties powerful emotional pressures within the boy and girl to certain modes of behavior, rather than giving them only an intellectual concept with which to resist the emotions and pressures toward promiscuity that they will encounter. Hamachek devotes a chapter to the topic of the self-concept elsewhere in this book. While his focus is not on the role of sex, the reader will find it rewarding to consider his presentation in conjunction with mine.

The best way I have found to help adolescents develop strong self-concepts is through group discussions. Where sex is not the *primary* subject involved, mixed groups may be used under some circumstances. Self-consciousness minimizes the expression of values and standards violating good morals and ethics in such a group and maximizes exploration of positive values and behavior. Thus, participants get a feeling of group endorsement of high moral standards and sound values, and tend to accept them. Accepting them, they can be motivated to try to live up to them to avoid degrading their self-concepts or tacitly admitting their inferior standards.

Much of the content of a sex education program has to be presented first as lecture or reading assignments, to get the requisite information to boys and girls. Some elements of it (such as the physiology of sex and the biological processes) may need nothing more than a lecture or reading assignment and a period in which questions can be asked if clarification is needed.

Where attitudes regarding sex are to be developed, however, or behavior is desired, use group discussion to explore the significance and implications of the facts and concepts within the subject. By going through the process of thought on a topic himself, by putting his thoughts into words, by hearing himself talk about a subject, and by attempting to follow and understand the thoughts of his peers, the adolescent boy or girl achieves a relationship to facts and concepts that is infinitely more effective in crystallizing attitudes or producing behavior change than is reading or hearing a lecture on the topic. Particularly when the group reaches conclusions on pertinent issues, shows substantial agreement on certain standards and values, those conclusions, standards, and values are much more likely to be incorporated into the self-concepts of the boys and girls participating than if they were formulated and handed out by an adult.

If boys and girls can be found who are capable of leading the discussion, this is all the better. A good role for the teacher or counselor in such a discussion is that of resource person, one who can supply facts and guide reasoning when needed. Because, of course, the discussions must in fact result in sound conclusions and establish sound values and standards, to be effective. If we can assume that high moral values and standards *are* sound, it follows that sound reasoning will reach them, and the teacher should not hesitate to volunteer information or concepts that set straight a discussion that is straying into invalid patterns of thought and reasoning. This, of course, should be done as briefly, unobtrusively, and nondictatorially as possible.

As an example of what is meant here, I sat with a group of college men and women who were discussing a philosophy, propounded by a widely known writer, of complete sexual freedom, with mutual consent and pleasure the only criteria of morality. Discussion was centering on the advantages of such a moral system, substantiating the man's reasoning and challenging the reasons usually advanced in support of conventional morality. I asked how the writer's system operated in his own heterosexual relations. In fact, as some members of the group had read and brought out, he apparently used a girl as a convenience and status symbol. By reason of his personality, virility, position, or all three, he had no difficulty in getting attractive girls to live with him on his own terms. When he tired of one, he terminated the relationship and sought another. The girls involved seemingly had little to say about anything pertaining to the relationship other than their original acquiescence to it. The group quickly determined that, in fact, the "mutual consent" involved was more apparent than real, and proceeded to a discussion of whether mutual consent could reasonably be dependent on as the sole regulator of an association such as the extremely closely knit and emotionally charged relationship between two people that tends to develop along with complete and prolonged intimacy. A question had started the group on a line of thought that led to more realistic perception and accurate reasoning than the one they were pursuing.

Summary

Sexual behavior in the human being is regulated more by attitudes than by biological forces. Sex education, therefore, should aim more at attitude formation than at a simple imparting of knowledge. The developing of a strong self-concept, or seeing one's self as a self-disciplined, responsible, and honorable person, is a relatively effective means of controlling behavior. It is thought that the desired attitudes are more likely to be produced by group discussions (generally with only one sex participating) than by other formal educational procedures.

The sexes differ radically in their psychosexual makeup and dynamics. Girls are romantic and boys are erotic. Girls' self-concepts tend to be injured by sexual relations outside marriage and their social standing somewhat compromised if their sexual activities become widely known. Boys' self-concepts are more likely to be enhanced by their sexual "conquest," and they incur much less social disapproval if their sexual activities become known. Both the boy and the girl, however, are likely to suffer psychological injury through sexual behavior that violates the professed standards of society.

REFERENCES

Bell, R. R. *Marriage and family interaction.* Homewood, Ill.: Dorsey Press, 1970.

————, and Chaskes, J. B. Premarital sexual experience among coeds, 1958 and 1968. *Journal of Marriage and the Family,* 1970, *32,* 81–84.

Blood, R. O., Jr. *Marriage.* New York: Free Press of Glencoe, 1962.

Cannon, K. L., and Long, R. Premarital sexual behavior in the sixties. *Journal of Marriage and the Family,* 1971, *33,* 40.

Deutsch, H. *The psychology of woman: A psychoanalytic interpretation.* New York: Grune and Stratton, 1944.

Drucker, A. J., Christensen, H. T., and Remmers, H. H. Some background factors in socio-sexual modernism. *Marriage and Family Living,* 1952, *14,* 334–337.

Ehrmann, W. W. Student cooperation in a study of dating behavior. *Marriage and Family Living,* 1952, *14,* 322–326.

————. Some knowns and unknowns in research into human sex behavior. *Marriage and Family Living.* 1957, *19,* 16–22.

————. *Premarital dating behavior.* New York: Holt, 1959.

Frankl, V. E. *Man's search for meaning.* New York: Washington Square Press, 1963.

Gordon, J. E. *Personality and behavior.* New York: Macmillan Co., 1963.

Grant, V. E. *The psychology of sexual emotions: The basis of sexual attraction.* New York: Longmans, Green and Co., 1967.

Kaats, G. R., and Davis, K. E. The dynamics of sexual behavior of college students. Mimeographed. University of Colorado, 1968.

Kanin, E. J. Male aggression in dating-courtship relations. *American Journal of Sociology*, 1957, *43*, 197–204.

Kinsey, A. C., Pomeroy, W. B., and Martin, C. E. *Sexual behavior in the human male*. Philadelphia: W. B. Saunders Co., 1948.

Lee, M. R. Background factors related to sex information and attitudes. *Journal of Educational Psychology*, 1952, *43*, 467–485.

Lindzey, G., and Goldberg, M. Motivational differences between male and female as measured by the Thematic Apperception Test. *Journal of Personality*, 1953, *22*, 101–117.

Luckey, E. B., and Ness, D. A comparison of sexual attitudes and behavior in an international sample. *Journal of Marriage and the Family*, 1969, *31*, 369.

McKinney, F. *Psychology of personal adjustment*. New York: Wiley, 1960.

Maslow, A. H., and Sakoda, J. M. Volunteer error in the Kinsey study. In J. Himelhoch and S. F. Fava (eds.), *Sexual Behavior in American Society*. New York: W. W. Norton & Co., 1955.

Masters, W. H., and Johnson, V. E. *Human sexual response*. Boston: Little, Brown and Co., 1966. (a)

————. A defense of love and morality. *McCall's*, November, 1966, 102–103, 173. (b)

Reiss, I. L. Premarital sex as deviant behavior: An application of current approaches to deviance. *American Sociological Review*, 1970, *35*, 78.

————. Sexual codes in teenage culture. *The Annals*, 1961, *338*, 53–62.

Rogers, D. *The psychology of adolescence*. New York: Appleton-Century-Crofts, 1962.

Simon, W. and Gagnon, J. Psychosexual development. *Trans-action*, March, 1969, 14.

Stagner, R. *Psychology of personality*. New York: McGraw-Hill, 1961.

Staton, T. F. *Dynamics of adolescent adjustment*. New York: Macmillan Co., 1963.

Stone, L. J., and Church, L. *Childhood and adolescence*. New York: Random House, 1957.

Stratton, J. R., and Spitzer, S. P. Sexual permissiveness and self-evaluation: A question of substance and question of method. *Journal of Marriage and the Family*, 1967, *29*, 434–441.

Wattenberg, W. W. *The adolescent years*. New York: Harcourt, Brace, and Co., 1955.

12

The Need for Involved Youth

*George S. McGovern**

When I was asked to contribute a chapter on the role of youth in the political arena of today, I gave serious thought to what I should include and exclude. Certainly there are numerous issues worthy of discussion as being of interest and pertinence to youth. A number of the chapters of this book consider such timely topics as the culturally disadvantaged, drug use and abuse, the counterculture, and the activism and apathy of university students. I have decided that I could make my greatest contribution by focusing on the need for involved youth in the process of reordering our national priorities. Since I have been a senator in the United States Congress, I have spoken on these issues time and time again and my conviction as to their importance has not decreased.

It is relatively easy to list the problems and weaknesses facing our country and our world. What we are all desperately searching for, is the answer or answers as to how we might cope with these problems and weaknesses and ultimately to solve them. Without the involvement, constructive criticism, and dedication of our nation's youth, the situation is indeed hopeless.

Our national purpose is threatened by such problems as poverty,

* George S. McGovern is a United States senator from South Dakota and was the Democratic presidential candidate in 1972. He received his Ph.D. in history from Northwestern University and has written such books as *War Against Want, Agricultural Thought in the Twentieth Century*, and *A Time of War, A Time of Peace*. He has written numerous articles for various scholarly journals, popular magazines, and newspapers.

violence, racism, economic inequities, pollution, housing, and health. Yet, elected officials are, in many cases, unwilling to take the action necessary to alleviate these problems. We cannot stop here; it is not enough to point our finger at the problems and at the elected officials whom we would, and perhaps should, label as the villains. In the last analysis, it is the masses of the American people, you and I, who allow these same elected officials to neglect their responsibilities. The people still have the most powerful force of all: *the ballot*. With the voting franchise, we have the power to elect men and women who will take courageous and wise action; and when we forfeit that franchise, we invite reactionary officials to lead us down the path to the destruction of the United States of America.

The Issues

It is not enough, of course, to vote. We have both the responsibility and the opportunity to help shape and make public debate on the issues; to work for candidates and for or against key issue questions on the ballot; to engage in all the nonelectoral projects which are so important: to counsel addicts, to work with homeless teenagers, and to lobby for consumer protection rights and legislation. Let us consider, in more detail, the key issues facing our country today.

Vietnam

I doubt that there is any rational man or woman in this country who would not list the war in Vietnam at the top of the list. After fifteen years of struggle, 55,000 American lives, and billions of dollars from our nation's income, that cruel slaughter goes on. Every poll indicates that the overwhelming majority of the American people want the war to end *now*. Yet the Congress and the president ignore these sentiments.

When the war is over, we will have a responsibility to deal with those whom it has ravaged: the Vietnam war veteran and those tortured young men who went to jail or abroad rather than fight in a war they believed to be wrong. In that connection, we have a responsibility to provide generous educational and job opportunities for our veterans and amnesty for those men who follow their conscience and choose not to fight. It is shameful that unemployment among Vietnam veterans stands at 10.8 percent; and that only a handful of our "leaders" have had the courage to stand up for a policy of amnesty and forgiveness for those who have followed their consciences.

Military Budget

Next, we must drastically reduce our bloated military budget which takes two out of every three tax dollars. I have proposed that we make specific cuts of 33 billion dollars over the next few years and turn the money and manpower into the areas of health, education, job training, pollution control, and prison reform and housing, which we need so badly. Even as I write this, the president and members of his administration call for an increased defense budget, although our inner-city schools, for example, do not have enough money to continue. We must reduce the money we spend on death and weapons and increase the money we spend on life and hope in this country.

We also face enormous challenges in harnessing the powers of our wealthy corporations and individuals. We must reform our tax policies, crack down on industry which pollutes, and impose strict consumer protection standards so that wealthy individuals and corporations do not receive the status of privileged characters in our society.

Tax Reform

In the area of tax reform, I have proposed that we eliminate mineral depletion allowances, accelerated depreciation write-offs, and investment tax credits. We should increase gift and inheritance taxes and impose a minimum income tax so that the 301 families in the United States who last year made over $200,000, but paid no taxes, will pay their fair share.

Pollution

We must deal with the destruction of our environment. To illustrate this point we could use numerous examples. To select one, in Santa Barbara, California, in 1969, the Union Oil Company spilled 250,000 gallons of oil into the ocean; and this spill, seen around the world, damaged beaches and wildlife in the surrounding areas. This is one reason why I have introduced legislation to give individuals the federally guaranteed right to sue polluters.

Consumer Protection

We must also make some changes in the area of consumer protection. Several years ago, a famous baby food company advertised their products as "nutritious." A Ralph Nader investigation discovered that instead of meats, vegetables and fruits, the products contained monosodium glutamate, starches, and sugars. When the company discovered that a baby's saliva destroyed the product, they invented another phony starch which was resistant to saliva. None of these additives was in the food except for economic reasons. None had been proven safe for consumption by babies. My introduction of the Truth in Advertising Act of 1971 would insure the consumer the legal right to obtain documentation and certification of advertisers' claims. It is just one more step we must take to make sure that the special and large interests do not run the United States and that the country and its resources truly belong to the people.

Poverty and Racism

We still must come to grips with the moral curses of poverty and racism in our land. One possible way would be to establish a minimum income floor for each family. I would also propose a drastic increase in low cost, racially mixed housing in the suburbs; strict enforcement of equal employment opportunity regulations; massive new funding for our ghetto schools; a tenfold increase in job training centers in our ghettos; more minority-group police and prison employees; more minority-group history and culture courses in our schools; as well as a large increase in government loans to minority businesses and especially minority banks. Most of all we need a Congress and a president who will speak out loudly and unequivocally for understanding and compassion between us all whether we be black, white, or Spanish-speaking in our cultural heritages.

Our Constitutional Democracy

Our ability to address these problems depends directly on the way our elected officials carry out their functions. Our government was set up as a constitutional democracy. Yet today, we face the danger of drifting into a one-man rule. There is no clearer example of this tragedy than in the case of the war in Vietnam. The conduct of that war has been carried on by a handful of impetuous chief executives and a few advisors, *without* the consent of Congress—the elected representatives of the American people. The war-planners have carried on secret bombing missions, secret deals, and secret invasions of Laos and Cambodia without seeking the consent, counsel, and guidance of the Foreign Relations Committee whose direct responsibility it is, under the Constitution, to work with the president in planning our global policies and strategies. So while the war in Vietnam is indeed a tragedy, the way in which it is carried out is also a tragedy. While we have specific problems in this country, the overriding one is that the processes of government, masterfully woven in the Constitution and in the Declaration of Independence, have been ignored to the point where two or three men plan the decisions for a country and a world.

It is fair to say that the need to restore constitutional government is among our most urgent national needs. Down through the centuries, wise people have always realized that good government required balance. This balance only comes when the consent of the largest number of people possible is given to a policy, and when the considered judgments of our elected officials are taken into consideration.

Article I, Section 8, of the Constitution provides for the Congress to "declare war." We have a war going on in Vietnam, but the Congress has never been asked to declare it. Abraham Lincoln stated that the:

> . . . provision of the Constitution giving the war-making powers to the Congress was dictated, as I understand it, by the following reasons: kings had always been involving and impoverishing their people in wars and pretending generally, if not always, that the good of the people was the object. This our Convention understood to be the most oppressive of all kingly oppressions, and they resolved to frame the Constitution so that no one man should have the power to bring oppression upon us (Shaw, 1950, p. 60).

How right Abraham Lincoln was. But today, the president and a small band of advisors, closed off from the fresh breeze of public debate and discussion, unilaterally decide to support dictatorship in Vietnam, Greece, Spain, Pakistan, and in other areas. They continue to destroy most of Southeast Asia even though the vast majority of the American people decided long ago that this war was wrong.

The responsibility does not belong to the president and his advisors alone. All along the Congress has had the power to reverse this trend. The Congress had several opportunities through the McGovern-Hatfield Amendment, and similar proposals, to discontinue funds for the Vietnam war and to set a date for a complete pullout of all Americans. It has failed to do so. The men and the women who serve the United States Senate and House of Representatives are powerful people. They have access to the media. They are respected by their constituents. Most important, they control the purse strings. The president cannot ignore a congressional request, backed up with firm control over the funds available, that the Congress be allowed to participate fully on all major decisions of foreign and domestic policy.

The Power of the People

This brings us to the last and most important point of this brief review of our nation's problems. The American people do have the power to turn presidents and senators and congressmen in or out of office, and thus to profoundly influence the direction of the country. The funds to build and deploy the Anti-Ballistic-Missile, for example, were granted by a paper-thin one-vote margin in the United States Senate several years ago. This means that if just one more anti-ABM senator had been elected in 1968, instead of the ABM we might now be able to spend those funds on health, housing, or jobs. Several senators who lost reelection by margins of less than three thousand votes in 1968 would have voted against the ABM. Think of the difference in our future if all the students at one large university, in that senator's state, had turned out to vote for him. There would be no ABM today, and the welfare of the American people would have been advanced considerably.

Today, with the advent of the eighteen-year-old vote, which extends the franchise to an additional twenty-five million new voters, young people do truly have the power to vote into office men and women who will bring about progressive change in this country. The voters of this nation have the power to change the course of history if they will only vote. Yet, in 1972, only 55 percent of the eligible voting age population voted in the presidential election. In the average presidential primary, the turnout is only 20 percent of all registered voters. We have a long way to go; and if our society does not change, that failure will be directly traceable to those who sat on the sideline while the crucial elections were taking place.

It is transparently simple to see the point which I am making. The president and the Congress control the purse strings for federal government programs. They can determine whether money is spent for missiles or day-care centers, for bombers or housing, for death or life. And the voters have the power to elect men and women who will stand for either the right or wrong priorities. We must look to this new generation of new voters to provide the margin of difference on the side of the priorities of life and hope.

Involvement in Government

I am arguing that young people should become involved in the decision-making process of their government. There are certain steps which I believe the government must take to maximize the potentials for such participation. In this vein I have suggested five proposals for increasing the participation of young people in the political process. Two of the proposals are indirect; they seek to maximize the educational and employment benefits for young people so they can be prepared and economically able to participate fully in governmental and societal enterprises.

Maximizing Voting Rights

It is hypocritical for us to tell young people to get involved when we restrict their right to vote. For example, in the majority of states, students are denied the right to vote where they attend college. They are told that they are not residents of those towns. This is absurd since students pay local sales taxes where they attend college; since the average length of residency of all Americans in any given town is 4.3 years; since students provide revenue for local merchants; and since students are counted in the town's census figures which determine the amount of revenue a town receives from the state. Students participate in the life of their college town or city. They are clearly residents when it comes to voting rights. They should be allowed to vote where they attend college, and I have introduced a bill in the United States Senate to give them that right.

Moreover, in twenty-nine states, there are no provisions for absentee balloting in primary elections. This means that the student faces the distinct possibility that he will not be allowed to vote either at home or at school. This is an outrage, and it must change because the very essence of democracy is that all that can possibly be done to maximize one's participation in the life of one's country is done.

Presidential Appointments for Youth

There should be a substantial number of presidential appointments to federal boards and commissions to persons under thirty years of age. The record of the Nixon Administration in the first three years of office is discouraging in this regard and we must do better. Out of 2,780 presidential appointments to federal boards and commissions in this period, only 3.8 percent have gone to persons under thirty years of age. There were no students or young people on the Commissions on Higher Education, in All-Volunteer Army, marijuana and drug abuse, Vietnam Veterans, and Youth Opportunity. There was only one student on the Commission on Campus Unrest and Vice-President Agnew publicly called for his resignation. This generation of young people is intelligent and idealistic, and we need them at the highest levels of government to give our decision-making bodies some badly needed diversity.

A President's Youth Council

I would advocate a President's Youth Council made up of young people —students, nonstudents, young housewives, and young laborers—who would meet once a month with the president to give him their ideas and input as to what young people are thinking and as to their ideas for the country. We need to have our government officials open themselves to the ideas of young people, and this would be an institutionalized way to accomplish this goal.

Educational and Work Opportunities

We need to improve the educational and work opportunities for young people so they can participate to the fullest possible degree in the life of their country. Youth unemployment stands at 15 percent. Unemployment among black youth is at 40 percent. Unemployment among Vietnam veterans is at 10.8 percent. In the first month of President Nixon's Phase II economic policy, 100,000 additional young people were out of work as compared to the month before. The solution to this problem is increased funding of public-works job bills; government job-creation in the areas of health, education, welfare, law enforcement; and increased funding of summer youth unemployment funds.

Scholarship Assistance

Lastly, we need to increase scholarship assistance so that more young people can have the benefits of a higher education. I have proposed that we take the one billion dollars which some wanted to spend on a super-sonic airplane, to take the rich to Paris, and use it to create 200,000 five-thousand dollar scholarships to send poor students to college. This would certainly enrich the life of our nation to a far greater degree.

A Change of Priorities

We can change the priorities of this nation if young people will sense the need for this change and get involved. Exerting pressure on legislators does work. All one need do is to look at the example of the Super-Sonic-Transport. Consumer groups and millions of citizens wrote letters to their congressmen and senators and asked them to vote against the funding for the SST because the money could be better spent elsewhere and because the SST posed a threat to the environment. The SST was defeated and a number of senators stated publicly that they had voted "no" because of the large volume of mail which they received asking them to vote against the bill. This is an excellent illustration of a lobbying effort which worked. It proves that it can be done.

There is no greater challenge to me than public life, than politics. I hope that this will become increasingly true for the youth of our nation. For this to occur, we must make politics an "honorable profession" again.

To do this we need to create an open government: a government which systematically declassifies its documents; a government in which the president holds cabinet meetings which are open to the press, and press conferences twice a month. This should be a government in which all the elected officials disclose their earnings, their financial resources, and their campaign contributions; a government in which elected officials tell the truth!

Houses will not be built, the poor fed, and the sick made well unless the government directs its enormous resources and talents toward that end. These problems will not be solved if we drop out. Suffering does not go away because we forget it. The promised land takes a long time to find, and it will not be found by those who use tactics which alienate the very people whose minds we seek to change. In that connection, I believe that the single greatest need today is for those of us who seek to end poverty, war, and racism, to convince those who need to be convinced to come along with us; that we too are interested in the issues which interest them: crime, taxes, violence, welfare, and the problems of senior citizens. A true humanitarian is interested in all of the issues which bother all of the people; not just the issues which concern him and his generation. We need to become more broadminded and determined to talk to those with whom we disagree. We can change the direction of this country, if only you and I have the courage to stay involved. It is not changing today because too many people are uninterested, uninvolved; too many of us have given up.

The question which faces all of us today, young and old, is whether we will put our own pleasure first or whether we will focus on the needs of those who suffer. The question is whether we will only carry signs and employ slogans or whether we will actually do the work—the registering of voters, the canvassing, the writing of flyers—which will elect men and women who will control the purse strings of this government for the sake of life and hope.

Summary

Albert Camus (1961, p. 73) once wrote: "Perhaps we cannot create a world in which no children suffer. But we can reduce the number of suffering children. And if you do not help us do this, who in the world will help us?" That is the crisis we face today. We cannot afford the luxury of an absolutistic frame of mind which despairs when we cannot solve every problem immediately. There is no room for absolutists who drop out after a couple of defeats in a democracy. A fruit-bearing democracy requires patient people. People who above all else have what the

Romans called *Gravitas,* that is, patience and courage. For only these values can enable us to persist until justice and compassion prevail. Each of us can work to improve one life, or two or three, and those acts taken together can build a meaningful life for our time and for generations to come.

The people are not centrist, or liberal, or conservative; rather, they seek a way out of the wilderness. But if we who seek their trust, trust them; if we try to evoke the better sides to our nature, the people will find their own way. We are the children of those who built a great and a free nation, and we are no less than that. We must now decide whether our courage and our imagination are equal to our talents. If they are, as I believe, then future generations will continue to love America; not simply because it is theirs, but for what it has become; for what, indeed, we have made it.

We can live in the kind of world we want if human beings will learn the most important psychological and spiritual truth there is. This truth is that absolutism, or the desire to have one's life and society be perfect and easy, is a pipe dream. Also we must realize that nihilism, or giving up on trying to improve one's life and society because they cannot be made perfect, is denying what it means to be a human being. For what it means to be a human being is to realize that, despite the imperfections, despite the failures, despite the lack of wholeness in the world, one man or one woman can still make a difference in the life of one human being; and in that difference in one life is the kind of contribution from which a decent world will someday be found.

REFERENCES

Camus, A. *Resistance, rebellion and death.* New York: Alfred A. Knopf, 1961.

Shaw, A. H. (ed.), *The Lincoln encyclopedia.* New York: Macmillan Company, 1950.

13

Activism and Apathy in Contemporary Adolescents*

Jeanne H. Block, Norma Haan, and M. Brewster Smith†

In the early 1970s, it is still too early to gain an adequate perspective on the wave of political protest and of "countercultural" disengagement that swept American campuses during the 1960s, or on the altered mood that appears to be supplanting it—no replica of the apathetic, conform-

* This chapter was prepared in connection with our Institute of Human Development study or the moral orientations of student activists, supported by grants from the Rosenberg Foundation and the Foundations' Fund for Research in Psychiatry. We gratefully acknowledge the support of these organizations which, of course, are not responsible for our assertions and judgments here.

† Jeanne H. Block is Research Psychologist in the Institute of Human Development at the University of California (Berkeley). She has published a number of articles in the areas of personality development, psychosomatic medicine, schizophrenia, and cross-cultural research on child raising.

Norma Haan is Associate Research Psychologist in the Institute of Human Development and Lecturer in Social Welfare. She has coedited *Readings in Professional Education: An Interdisciplinary Approach*, and collaborated with Jack Block in *Lives Through Time*. She also has published on moral development, coping mechanisms, and personality correlates of changes in IQ.

M. Brewster Smith is Professor of Psychology and Vice Chancellor for Social Sciences at the University of California, Santa Cruz. Formerly he was Director of the Institute of Human Development at Berkeley. He has written *Social Psychology and Human Values* and coauthored *Opinions and Personality*. His other contributions to the literature are on such topics as attitudes, values, mental health, and psychological competence.

ing, success-oriented mentality about which complaint was frequently voiced during the "Eisenhower era" of the 1950s. A large research literature on political and social protest in the 1960s had just been synthesized into some coherence (see Sampson and Horn, 1970; Lipset and Schaflander, 1971; and Horn and Knott, 1971) when the scene changed. The nature of the change itself is a matter for debate; surely the public's perception of the recent change toward peace and quiet on the campus has been heightened by journalistic selection and exaggeration just as was its perception of the disruption of the 1960s.

In revising a chapter written before the campus conflicts reached their peak, we are thus faced with puzzles about both past and present, and with a plenitude of theories and conjectures, many of which are already clearly inadequate. We can already be sure that explanations of what happened in America in the 1960s that ignore the worldwide sweep of student alienation and protest—explanations that focus only on the civil rights struggle, the Vietnam war, and the draft—cannot be complete. Accounts that interpret the campus crises of the 1960s in broad social-historical terms as a watershed in the history of youth in modern postindustrial society (e.g., the "revolutionary" and "counterrevolutionary" views of protesting students discussed by Keniston, 1971) also run into trouble in the face of more recent developments. At this point in emerging history, we should do well to be modest in our aspirations. While we shall avail ourselves of recent findings that suggest what may become the trends of the 1970s, our main concern will be to discuss selectively what has been learned about the political and social orientations of campus youth in the 1960s, when campus protest captured the attention of social scientists and the public alike.

Political and social protest in the 1960s, as previously, was carried out by a minority of students. But this committed and protesting minority was distinctive, in comparison both with the privatistic, conforming majority (who held the center of the stage relatively unchallenged in the Eisenhower years), and also with the activist minority of the depression 1930s. Ethos and action—sincerity, authenticity, purity of gesture—seemed in the 1960s to count for more than achievement and success (goals of the 1950s) or ideological correctness and consistency, so valued in the 1930s. The recent reactions of young people to American political and social institutions have some genuinely new elements. This chapter attempts to identify the nature of recent protest, to provide a coherent conceptualization of the several varieties of activism and apathy and to summarize the results of major empirical studies regarding the origins, correlates, and consequences of societal involvement or uninvolvement. We begin with a brief historical excursion to compare activism during the Great Depression and activism in the Affluent Society.

Activism in the Thirties and in the Sixties

In both the depression era and the recent past, student radicalism arose from the background of an immediately preceding period in which political apathy, concern for security, and passive conformity were pronounced. These complacent periods, in turn, followed the two most calamitous wars in history. During the depression, large numbers of young people were actively involved in radical organizations. The American Student Union, an amalgamated group encompassing most radical student groups of the time, claimed a membership of 100,000 students in a college population that then numbered one and a half million (Lipset, 1966). Student protests of that time were oriented around two themes: radical revision of the social and economic order, and pacifism. Many of the activities in which radical students then participated were similar to those of today: They organized associations of the unemployed, picketed, demonstrated, signed the Oxford Pledge refusing to bear arms for the United States, and designated Army Day as an annual day of protest on which rallies were held and strikes conducted in the cause of peace. It has been estimated that more than 200,000 students took part in the antiwar parades of that period (Lipset, 1966).

As of 1966 the combined memberships of the Student Non-violent Coordinating Committee, the Congress of Racial Equality, Students for a Democratic Society, and the Student Peace Union were estimated to have involved only between twelve thousand and fifty thousand students in a college population of six million students (Munk, 1965; Peterson, 1966; Braungart, 1966). For activists of the recent generation civil rights and peace were the two consuming issues. Each of the activities of the 1930s has a counterpart in today's protests: community organizations of the poor in urban ghettos, picketing, demonstrating, burning of draft cards, anti-Vietnam Days of Protest, and peace marches. By the time of the reaction to the U.S. invasion of Cambodia and the subsequent killing of students at Kent State University in confrontation with National Guard troops, in the spring of 1970, destructive and violent actions had become more common. But even in 1969–70, the peak year, only about 8 percent of U.S. four-year colleges and universities experienced protests in which property was damaged, and only about 5 percent ones in which there was physical violence. Arrests were reported in connection with incidents on 12 percent of the campuses (Astin, 1971).

In their status as minorities of their student generation, in their antiwar commitments, and in some of the strategies of protest employed, these two generations of student activists—separated by thirty years—have important features in common. There are significant differences, however, that distinguish their preferred modes of protest and have led to different reactions on the part of the adult community.

The depression years were a time when dissent was flavored and polarized in one way or another by Marxist ideology. Ideology and theory were often so important that differences of opinion within a particular organization could not be resolved. As a result, many splinter groups were formed, each homogeneous ideologically. In contrast, the radical youth groups of the 1960s began as relatively nondoctrinaire; they were oriented to specific issues or particular injustices. Concerned as they were with immediate moral tasks, they were not inhibited by ideological dogma from cooperating with groups whose values might be widely different from their own. The largest radical student organizations in the 1930s were campus derivatives of adult political organizations of the so-called "Old Left" whose programs were determined and dominated by the older membership. In contrast, most radical student organizations of the recent generation had no affiliation with adult-sponsored organizations and operated autonomously. But factionalism and ideology developed in the later 1960s, with a splintering of the movement reminiscent of the earlier generation.

Still another difference between these two generations is that recent protest occurred at a time when, for large segments of the population, material affluence and financial security were at unprecedented levels. In this time of affluence, the leaders of youthful revolt came primarily from families in the upper economic and educational strata; as children they were financially secure; they had enjoyed material comforts and educational opportunities and could look forward to successful careers in high-status professions. Protest was more understandable and acceptable to society in the 1930s, when poverty, unemployment, hunger, disenchantment, and fear were rife. Greater countenance was given to the radical causes of that time by the New Deal government itself, which was modifying its doctrines and policies along liberal lines to accord with economic and social realities. In the 1930s, then, student radicalism was closer to the mainstream of opinion than it has recently appeared to be.

The most dramatic difference, however, between the student activists then and in the 1960s is not so much with respect to ideological emphasis as in strategy, specifically in the use of civil disobedience. Recent activist students learned their most valued technique from the civil rights demonstrators in the South, who successfully used tactics of civil disobedience to fight segregation of buses, restaurants, parks, and other public facilities. Student activists extended the use of civil disobedience, especially sit-ins, into other areas of dissent. Ordinary citizens find civil disobedience disconcerting. The tactics employed by recent activists estranged many in the adult world who, as the activists saw it, value security, image, and conformity; but who, in their own eyes, value order, due process, and civility. Estrangement turned to indignant opposition, not only in the adult world but also on the part of many previously sympathetic students, when destructive violence became an explicit tactic of certain extremist groups, such as the Weatherman faction of Students for a Democratic Society (SDS). Many observers felt that in resorting to violence, the extremists discarded the movement's most potent moral weapon.

The attention drawn by young activists—in public anxiety, in controversial articles, and in research—has been disproportionate to their actual numbers, since a rather small minority of students on a relatively few campuses were centrally involved in protest. But to dismiss this small, vocal group as atypical is to miss the point. They spoke for many not so articulate as themselves, as was shown on the Berkeley campus during the by-now-famed sit-in at Sproul Hall. During the "free speech" rebellion, for every student sitting in, there were twenty-one sympathetic students who approved—either mildly or strongly—of the Free Speech Movement (FSM) (Gales, 1966). The university, particularly the selective campus that aspires to intellectual leadership, provides one of the few institutional bases in American society for cultural criticism and social renewal. What happens on campuses, therefore, matters very much, particularly when it is realized that the most selective universities have been the scenes of greatest student unrest and protest. In the campus microcosm, as in the larger world, it takes only a minority to set the spirit of an age.

The Scope of Student Activism

Almost all research studies of social action and protest among youth have limited their inquiry to the college population. The findings we cite, therefore, do not deal with younger adolescents nor do they reflect the majority of young people in the late teens who do not continue their education. The studies of Coleman (1961, 1965) and of Musgrove (1965) indicate that in the United States, and in England, secondary school youth for the most part have not been conscientious critics of society. Held off by adult society from full participation in it, teenagers have participated instead in a youth culture that is, in good part, an exploitative adult creation. Aspects of the youth culture might be seen as implicitly critical of the adult world of "square," respectable values. But even though conscientious protest spread to many high schools by the late 1960s, and the downward spread of drug use had become a national problem (see chapter by Jalkanen), the phenomena with which we will be concerned primarily involve college students, not teenagers. Note, also, that we shall not discuss the important but very different wave of black and Chicano campus protest that began after the political protests discussed here. This wave has been concerned with gaining opportunities for disadvantaged minorities that the white activists could take for granted for themselves, as well as with distinctive symbolic issues of the ethnic identity.

The earliest thorough study assaying the scope of organized student protest is that of Peterson (1966a), who surveyed deans of students in all regionally accredited four-year colleges in the United States in the fall of 1965. Peterson found that local issues of civil rights were most apt to provoke student protest. Complaints about food service and parietal rules governing personal conduct were cited as the next most frequent causes of student dissent. The Vietnam war ranked next, while educational reforms and issues of academic freedom were the categories least often cited as student concerns. Only the off-campus issues of civil rights, the Vietnam war, and disarmament showed variation in protest by type of institution. Private secular universities and liberal arts colleges and large public universities tended to report student protests involving these issues more frequently while public liberal arts colleges, religiously sponsored institutions, and technical and teachers' colleges reported little student activity in these spheres. A positive relationship was found between institutional quality as indexed by the proportion of faculty with doctorates and the frequency of protest over off-campus issues. Colleges in the South report substantially less student protest over off-campus issues: civil rights and American foreign and military policies. In Peterson's study, only one in four deans reports the presence of any radical student groups on their campuses, and only six of the 849 colleges included estimated the number of student radicals as exceeding 5 percent.

Peterson (1968), Bayer and Astin (1969, 1971) and Astin (1971) carry the account up to the beginning of the 1970s. In 1970–71, about 20 percent of U.S. campuses of all kinds and sizes experienced violent or disruptive protest—this in a year commonly regarded as "quiet" on the campus. (Data collected on the same basis for 1968–69 gave a comparable figure of 22 percent.) But in the private universities that had been the primary scene of protest, the percentage experiencing severe (violent or disruptive) protests dropped from 70 percent to 52 percent over this two-year period. In general, the relationship between institutional selectivity or quality and campus size, on the one hand, and severe protest, on the other, seemed to be flattening out. By 1970–71, protests focused on war-related issues occurred at 46 percent of the institutions where any protests took place, protests focused on issues concerning services to students at 51 percent, ones focused on minority group issues at 19 percent, ones focused on student power issues at 62 percent, and ones focused on ecology-pollution issues at 16 percent. The data for "severe" protests are much the same with the exception of minority-group student issues, which were more frequently involved (Bayer and Astin, 1971).

Peterson (1966) and Braungart (1966) agree in estimating the number of *organized* students *actively* engaged in social protest at fewer than 1 percent of the total college student population. However, when the definition of activism is broadened to include politically unaffiliated students participating in social protest, a far larger percentage of students is included. In a national sample of college students polled by *Newsweek* magazine (1965), 18 percent said they had participated in picket lines, presumably for civil rights. Katz and Sanford, in their research on the Stanford and Berkeley campuses, concluded that the number of socially involved students totaled about 15 percent of the student body. (See Katz et al., 1968.)

What, then, of the majority of students on the campuses today? The most suggestive picture of the changing scene is given by Yankelovich (1972), on the basis of interview surveys of representative cross-sections of the national college population conducted from 1968 to 1971. Yankelovich finds that, although political protest has declined over this period, disaffiliation from the dominant cultural values—or attraction to the values of the "counterculture" (see Roszak, 1969)—has continued to increase. Changing cultural values, in regard to marriage, authority, religion, work, sexual morality, and other aspects of the Puritan Ethic have become more marked year by year, while political beliefs have moved away from the radical peak of 1970.

> For example, students in 1971 were less critical of our major institutions —the two-party system, business, the universities, the unions, the Supreme Court, etc.—than they were in the previous year. . . . Three out of four [now] believe that desirable social change can best be effected within the system. In 1970, two-thirds of the student body thought that·student radicalism would continue to grow. A year later a majority believed it is leveling off or declining (Yankelovich, 1972, p. 7).

But for the 11 percent who remained identified with the New Left in 1971, the life styles of the counterculture and of radical politics continued to go together.

The prevailing mood as it emerges from the Yankelovich surveys is increasingly privatistic. While six out of ten think things are going badly in the country and three out of ten think they might prefer to live in another country, students describe themselves as confused about the future (55 percent) but personally happy (50 percent). Their key self-ascribed values are love and friendship. In 1971, for the first time, a majority (not a minority) would welcome more acceptance of sexual freedom, and a minority (not a majority) would welcome more emphasis on technological improvements. For 43 percent there is some appeal to the idea of living off the land for at least a year or so; over a third express interest in living in a commune for at least a short term. Are we witnessing the early stages of a profound cultural change, as Reich (1970) claims in *The Greening of America?* Or is the mood rather a protective response to prolonged political frustration? It is far too soon to say. As this is written, we can only be confident in noting that the momentum of change in values seems to be continuing as the wave of activist political protest fades.

Although the common concerns of young people center around a search for personal identity, this search takes many different forms. Some direct themselves quite determinedly toward future goals and the achievement of adult roles and status; others take a tortuous, circuitous path as they attempt to challenge the values of a society whose goals do not conform to their sense of humanity or insistence upon justice. In the next section of this chapter, we explore the development of activism and apathy in terms of the tasks of adolescence, the parental values that have been inculcated, and some socio-moral discrepancies that affect youth as they seek to establish an authentic place for themselves in a complex and sometimes compromising adult world.

The Development of Political-Social Sensitivity

To construct a firm sense of identity and to fashion a set of values consistent with the self, consonant with one's history, and worthy of commitment are the work of adolescence (Erikson, 1963). The young person entering adolescence has not only to respond to the changes occurring in his physical state and stature, but also to encompass a rapidly expanding world as his psychological life space and his actual, geographic environment enlarge in diverse ways. New, extended perceptions of the world, the development of complex cognitive skills, and the emergence of different, intense affects typify the experiences that are to be integrated during adolescence.

The scope of the physical environment enlarges because newly acquired competencies and mobility permit the early adolescent to range beyond the boundaries of his immediate neighborhood into the larger, outlying world. Junior and senior high schools widen the range of his encounters with students and teachers and confront him with subject matter that now leaves room for opinion and interpretation. The greater freedom to discover and explore presents the middle-class adolescent with a diversity of situations, people, and ideas from which he was earlier insulated (geographically or by parental prohibitions). The adolescent needs to digest these new perceptions and awarenesses in a way that is consonant with his own sense of emerging integrity. However, marked discrepancy with his own earlier values and attitudes and those of the significant people in his childhood are likely because the adolescent is confronted with the contemporary values of a world that has dramatically shifted during his and his parents' lifetimes.

The adolescent period is marked not only by a broadening of experiences and a heightening of awareness, but by an increased capacity for dealing with cognitive complexity so that hypothetical, reflective, abstractive, future-oriented thinking become possible. According to Piaget, most children prior to the age of eleven conceive of themselves in concrete, definitional, empirical given terms and have not yet developed abstract notions of self or ideals. Beginning between the ages of about thirteen to fifteen, a new effective component enters when the adolescent becomes able to experience feelings about himself relative to certain abstract ideals (Piaget and Weil, 1951). The development of an ideal concept is possible only when the individual is capable of future-oriented reflective thinking, thinking about thoughts, and when he is able to differentiate between the real and what could possibly be true (Inhelder and Piaget, 1958). With the development during adolescence of propositional, hypothetical thinking it becomes possible to articulate a set of ideals based upon what could be real for one's self and one's society and to evaluate oneself relative to those ideals (see Gallagher's chapter).

As the young person becomes capable of hypothetical thinking and begins to anticipate the character and qualities of his own and his generation's future within the society, he may come to find it wanting. He begins to think in terms of daring possibilities, often dedicating himself to effecting changes in societal values and institutions. Inhelder and Piaget (1958) call this developmental juncture the "idealistic crisis," and suggest that commitment to concrete cognitive attainments by taking a job or starting professional training turns the idealistic reformer to the realities of the adult world, leading him away from the dangers of purely formalistic, hypothetical thought.

The cognitive capabilities emerging during adolescence are accompanied, influenced, and sometimes exaggerated by other, future-oriented necessities. The adolescent aspires to define himself as a person who knows himself, not only in terms of what he is but, equally emphatically, in terms of what he is not. Individuation of one's self cannot occur in an unpeopled vacuum, and the future adult and citizen-to-be frequently casts his self-examination in terms of comparative similarities and contrasts between himself and his family, and between himself and his society.

This scrutiny of self in relationship to historically significant mentors and previously unquestioned and unexamined social institutions is a daring maneuver emotionally that is not handled with skill or grace by many adolescents. Some do not even venture to probe at all. Some may parry the hazards and gambles that self-definition entails by avoidance, either by not thinking or only thinking concretely of the next best thing to do—with little occasion for criticism of self or society. They define their roles and goals without serious self-examination.

Questioning adolescents, however, are in a stage—aptly described by Erikson (1963, 1964) in rich detail—that involves a central and essential preoccupation with establishing a sense of *fidelity*. Fidelity concerns the articulation of ideals, interpersonal and social values, and qualities of particular human relationships worth the devotion of one's self. In constituting a sense of fidelity, the adolescent wonders whether he can trust himself to behave reliably, that is, predictably and consistently. He tests to see whether he can esteem himself in terms of his own humanity, veracity, courage, or other components of his ego-ideal. If he is to persuade himself to enter his society as a full-time participant, he must examine his past, his forebears, his society, and its institutions to determine what they imply for himself and his generation. His scrutiny involves at least a three-sided question: Can I find fidelity within myself; can I find it in my parents in spite of our generational differences; and can I find it in my society? Adolescence is thus a time for examination and testing of self, parents, and society. If all goes well between the adolescent and his elders, the emergent adult knows who he is, who he is not; and he has made differentiated, informed commitments to some aspects of his society and selected those causes which he will continue to support. Adams develops this theme in the first chapter.

Constituting a sense of fidelity is both an internal matter for one's self and an external matter for one's society, one's parents, and one's own generation. The adolescent's choice in committing himself to the making of his own generation's history depends upon the tolerance of his society for dissent and also upon the adaptive strength of his personality for dealing with dissonance. Some societies and some parents cannot afford, and will not allow, the scrutiny involved in establishing fidelity. Some adolescents cannot pose the questions, protecting themselves with the shared code of peer group uniformism (Blos, 1962), or conformity. Other young people pose their questions in a nonnegotiable manner so that the answers are merely self-fulfilling prophecies. In these instances, growth may be impaired since, as Erikson (1964) suggests, fidelity is a matter acutely relevant to the ego's adaptive strength; essential for continued growth and greater personality differentiation. Young people who cannot manage this difficult task constructively, either because their own resources are insufficient or because their social predicament is too formidable, not only foreclose their own potentialities for growth; they also deprive society of one of its major sources of creative change: the push from each new generation to make society more responsive to its needs.

In the favorable case, the outcome in late adolescence is a shift in emphasis from experiencing, questioning, and experimenting to *integrating*. In Erikson's terms, such a resolution involves the development of a *historical perspective* that relates to an understanding of the irreversibility of events and the significant cause-and-effect relationships in society. Adolescent ideals become tempered by the knowledge of the intransigencies of reality. The adolescent adjusts to outer reality as he comes to recognize aspects of his own self and life that cannot be changed or helped. The realistic integration comprised in such a historical perspective does not merely represent compromise with the world as it has always been. Rather, the maturing person's efforts to effect social change become more differentiated as they are directed toward making society more responsive to the needs of each new generation of youth.

The development of political and social sensitivity is, for the individual adolescent, a derivative of his confrontation with life and of the disparities and contradictions that he notices and has to integrate between the professed values and ideals of society and the actual societal context. The adolescent's reactions to the societal context may, however, take a variety of forms, which we will now consider.

Adolescent Reaction to the Societal Context

To avoid the terminological confusion that seems to prevail in much discussion of adolescent political-social behavior, we need to introduce some conceptual distinctions. Young people engaged in protest against contemporary social institutions have been variously termed *protesters, rebels, radicals, activists, demonstrators, beatniks,* or young people engaged in *pro-social action.* These terms obviously vary in the extent to which they are pejorative. They also confuse degree of social involvement with acceptance or rejection of social institutions, ideological orientation, and the pro- or anti-social nature of the protest. Similarly, in the descriptions of uninvolved youth, important differences are obscured when such labels as *alienation, lack of commitment, passivity, disaffiliation,* and *resignation* are used interchangeably. Two dimensions seem useful to us in conceptualizing the political stances and social reactivity of the adolescent. The first dimension is the *degree of involvement* with contemporary political-social issues. At one extreme we find uninvolved, socially indifferent, or apathetic youth, while at the other end of the continuum we see the involved, active, dedicated young person with a sense of instrumentality. In the political-social sphere this dimension is reflected in the degree to which an individual feels that he can make a difference, can be an instrument of change in his society.

The second dimension relates to the degree to which the adolescent *accepts or rejects the traditional values and the institutional authority of the society.* At one end of this dimension we encounter the young person who accepts the prevailing values of society and conforms readily to its institutions. At the other extreme is the young person who rejects traditional societal values and flouts legitimate authority.

How involvement or uninvolvement is conjoined with acceptance or rejection of traditional values and authority has widely different implications for the quality of adolescent behavior. Before we attempt to coordinate these two dimensions, the reader should note that we are maintaining *ideological orientations* as a conceptually independent dimension. Although there has been a tendency to equate social involvement and political activism with liberal politics, we have been impressed by the existence of an active protest group with a conservative political philosophy. The continuing presence of such individuals requires that activism be defined independently of political ideology if we are to extricate the correlates of activism per se from those of liberalism per se.

In the discussion that follows, we talk of adolescent political-social behaviors in terms of typologies for reasons of expository convenience. It should be understood, however, that continua are presumed.

Politically Apathetic Youth

Young people in this group are distinguished by their lack of political-social involvement and their readiness to accept the societal status quo. Judging from the studies of Katz et al. (1968) on the recent college generation, this group represents the majority of contemporary youth. These young people have identified with and accepted the values of their parents, which are largely within the mainstream of societal opinion. They have tended to handle whatever conflicts may have arisen from perceived discrepancies between their own and the larger world by minimizing the discrepancy and by retreating to their own small portions of society in which career, success, marriage, family, and financial security are the overriding considerations. They tend to accept the status quo, perhaps with a pessimistic attitude about the possibility of change. Focusing primarily on their own individual lives, these young people are little concerned with the long-term problems of society. We may describe these young people as politically apathetic. The Yankelovich (1972) data suggest that both the apathetic majority and the activist minority have recently yielded ground to the next group to be considered.

Alienated Youth

Adolescents in this group have rejected the traditional values of society, rebel against institutional authority, and are uninvolved nonparticipants in the political-social arena. Unlike the youth described above, these young people do not accept the prevailing *leitmotifs* of the culture. They reject its values, refuse its roles, and elect to escape from the culture by "opting out." This was the "beat" or "hippie" position, well described by a Berkeley student in the campus newspaper:

> "If you radicals see the disgusting nature of present society and see how unlikely it is that anything you do will change it, why waste your time trying? We agree with you that no sensitive human being wants to be a part of that society, but why worry about changing it at all? All that will happen is that you yourselves will waste your youth in an impossible struggle that may well leave ugly blemishes on your soul. Give up the struggle, try to love as much as possible, take a few trips and forget about it all" (Lerner, 1966) .*

These young people have much in common with those described by Keniston (1965), who studied alienated Harvard students in the late 1950s. Keniston's alienated students had an approach to life that was primarily egocentric and aesthetically oriented. They concerned themselves with a search for adventure, the creation of experiences, and the pleasures of sentience and unmediated responsivity. The alienated are relatively unideological. They live in the present, and their personal present may have little continuity with their personal history. They value their individuality and freedom, and distrust commitments that imply submission of the self to long-range, compromising goals. Their regard for self-expression, their pessimistic evaluation of society, their concern with existential experience, and their patent refusals to accept the hypocrisies they project into adulthood combine to produce an adolescent subculture bent on escape from the conventional society and deeply involved with experiencing. It is not surprising that "consciousness-expanding" drugs and other forms of mystical experiences are sought by many of these adolescents who feel estranged from society and judge issue-oriented protests to be meaningless. We confine the term *alienated youth*

---

* Quotation marks are Lerner's: This is Lerner's characterization of the "hippie" position and not an expression of his own position.

to include young people who are both uninvolved and rejecting of societal values.

Individualist Youth

Young men and women who are involved with political-social issues and accept the traditional American values and authority structure are our concern under this rubric. The political-social commitments of these adolescents are directed to maintaining the status quo or even to reestablishing an era of unhampered individualism. Their activities may include petitioning, letter-writing campaigns, active support of conservative candidates and policies, and techniques of counterprotest as they seek to reinforce the positions of traditional institutional authority. Although participants in demonstrations or members of picket lines, these young people confine their activities to legal forms of protest, rejecting the notion of civil disobedience.

This group is not ideologically homogeneous. Some present-day conservatives have been influenced crucially by the writings of Ayn Rand (1957, 1964) in which individualism and autonomy are stressed. These young people may endorse seemingly radical causes requiring only that they be consistent with individualistic principles. Less extreme student groups, influenced by the politics and morals of the conservative position, direct their energies toward maintaining the traditional values that they see as responsible for America's growth. Both conformity and the strong political involvement of these active conservatives are suggested in the term *obedient rebels* that has been given them by Schiff (1964). We call them *individualists*.

Constructivist Youth

As we move to another point along the acceptance-rejection continuum, we encounter a cluster of adolescents that overlaps with the activists still to be considered. These actively committed adolescents occupy an intermediate position on acceptance or rejection of authority but are highly involved with political-social problems. They devote themselves to restitutive work in volunteer activities: in mental hospitals, in work with physically handicapped, in tutoring children from urban ghettos, and so on. Enlistment in the Peace Corps, Vista, or Teacher Corps also represents a kind of commitment to effect social change in ways that involve working *within* the existing framework of society. Although these young people may have formulated an ideological position for themselves, they show little homogeneity except in their common altruistic concerns. They lack the zeal of the revolutionary but feel committed to work constructively to alleviate the ills of society. They are prepared to undergo discomfort, physical hardship, isolation, or even physical danger in order to contribute to the betterment of the human condition. They differ from the activists and dissenters primarily in that they tend to be task-oriented, do not categorically reject authority, and work in ways that do not necessarily challenge the institutions of society. Young people falling in this group we will call the *constructivists.*

Activist Youth

These young people share with the constructivists a history of involvement in "good works"; but, unlike them, they have rejected major values of contemporary society and have dedicated themselves to fight, demonstrate, and protest actively against policies and institutions of mainstream American society that violate their sense of humane justice. Heterogeneous in ideology, they unite for action on common causes. Their rejection of authority extends to their selective willingness to engage in civil disobedience in the face of possible arrest and incarceration. These young people reject "liberalism" as misguided. They are not optimistic about the effects their protests will have on society. Although their protests seek to dramatize social issues, their behavior is based on a concern for personal integrity and authenticity. They feel compelled by their need for fidelity to speak out forcibly on issues they view as morally wrong; not to do so would be to participate in what for them is common hypocrisy. They deplore the dehumanizing forces of a technological society and reject authoritarianism and centralism in favor of a commitment to "participatory democracy" in which political power is placed in the hands of those affected by decisions. Unlike the apathetic, conforming adolescent for whom social concerns are irrelevant, a substantial part of the lives of the young activists is regulated and determined by the issues of current concern. Although sharing the disenchantment with American society and influences of existential philosophy that characterizes the alienated, the activists are more concerned with the existential *act* as a way of achieving integrity, whereas the alienated have been more concerned with existential *perception* as a route to a sense of oneness. This difference in orientation toward the outer or the inner world fundamentally separates what we here call the *activists* from the alienated.

Dissenters

A final group of active protesters needs to be distinguished: young people who share the preceding group's commitment to radical action, but lack any history of involvement in constructive social effort. They are specialists in protest. As we will see, there are indications that the dissenters may arrive at their posture of antagonism by a psychological route that is quite different from that of the activists. As angry rebels, they may correspond more closely than the activists to popular conceptions.

Having made these conceptual distinctions, we are now ready to consider the findings of relevant research studies in these terms.

An Overview on Research on Activism

Most studies have been concerned with the activists and dissenters, the involved, rejecting students—usually without making the distinction. This emphasis began with an interest in the participants in the Free Speech Movement (FSM) on the Berkeley campus and was impelled by the incidents of protest at other major universities. Most of the studies have been conducted on the elite university campuses of America where intellect, inquiry, and criticism are valued. Their findings are largely consistent but may not hold for other college environments. Quite other relationships might be expected in the case of minority group protest. The research reviewed below far from exhausts the considerable volume of studies that have appeared in recent years.

Student Activists and Dissenters

Activists and dissenters have been studied at Berkeley in several investigations. Watts and Whittaker (1966) collected biographical and questionnaire data from students who sat in at Sproul Hall and examined the academic records of a sample of FSM participants. These researchers compared the academic status and questionnaire responses of FSM students with a sample of randomly selected students on the Berkeley campus. Heist (1965) compared a sample of students actually arrested in Sproul Hall with a randomly selected cross-section of Berkeley students in terms of their backgrounds and responses to a personality inventory. His research focused on the intellectual dispositions and academic history and achievement of his subjects. The present authors began a study a year after FSM crisis erupted. This study contrasted a sample of arrested FSM students with a randomly selected sample of Berkeley undergraduates and with samples of politically active students representing different ideological positions who were on campus during the FSM crisis. The study was subsequently extended to Peace Corps volunteers and to comparison groups on another campus (San Francisco State College). Biographical information including political-social activities, descriptions of actual and ideal self, evaluation of ethical principles, used in resolving moral dilemmas, and descriptions of the students' perceptions of their parents' child-rearing practices were obtained from each of the several hundred participants in the study (Haan, Smith, and Block, 1968; Block, Haan, and Smith, 1969; Smith, 1969; Smith, Haan, and Block, 1970; Haan, 1972).

At the university of Chicago, Flacks (1967) compared activist with nonactivist students, defining activism by the extent and nature of participation in particular political-social causes. Some of the subsamples are matched on a number of social characteristics (socioeconomic class, sex, religion, and type of college attended). The research has been extended to include some parents of activist and nonactivist students as well.

At Pennsylvania State University, Westby and Braungart (1966) compared members of the "left" (Students for Peace) and the "right" (Young Americans for Freedom). Membership in either organization was the sole criterion for inclusion, and degree of participation in social or political causes was not taken into account.

Braungart (1966) extended the research on membership in extreme "left" and "right" student organizations by collecting questionnaire data from delegates to two national conventions, the Students for a Democratic Society and Young Americans for Freedom. The questionnaire data, obtained from more than three hundred activists, provided information about social, political, attitudinal, and other background factors that might relate to activism.

Solomon and Fishman (1964) obtained questionnaire responses from a large, randomly selected sample of participants in the 1962 Peace March on Washington. Interviews in depth were conducted with a small sample selected from the larger group to provide more information about personological characteristics of these young pickets for peace. Counterprotest demonstrators who were picketing in support of administration policies were also included in the research. A more intensive, qualitative study of participants in the "Vietnam Summer" of 1967 was reported in rich detail by Keniston (1968).

In a careful attempt to distinguish the correlates of activism from those of ideology, Kerpelman (1970) studied left, middle-of-the-road and right activists and nonactivists in three northeastern institutions (a small private liberal arts college, a medium-sized private university, and a large public university), focusing on measures of intelligence, personality, attitudes, and values. Activism was defined in terms of membership in specified organizations, but validated in terms of a pencil-and-paper scale of political activism.

Family Background. The origins of student activists were in the economically, educationally, and socially privileged strata of American society. Whether measured by family income, occupational prestige of parents, socioeconomic indices, or the amount of education of parents, the families of actively committed students were more advantaged than those of other college students (Braungart, 1966; Westby and Braungart, 1966; Flacks, 1967; Smith, Haan, and Block, 1970).

The parents of activist students themselves tended to be politically liberal (Solomon and Fishman, 1964; Flacks, 1967; Keniston, 1968). The radical positions of these youth can thus hardly be interpreted simply as a rebellion against parental values, as is required by Feuer's (1969) Oedipal theory of intergenerational conflict. Committed students may have chided their parents for failing to act in accordance with their political beliefs; they may have accused the older generation of having "sold out" to the Establishment and the comforts of suburbia. However, the political values of parent and child had much in common, so it is essential to distinguish two facets in contemporary rebellion. Rejection of major *societal* values does not necessarily imply rebellion against *parental* attitudes. Although they placed themselves squarely in opposition to many of the prevailing views and practices of the culture, the activists identified with and accepted many of their parents' values (Block, 1972).

Many young people engaging in protest described themselves as nonreligious. In terms of parental religious traditions, a higher number of Jewish students were involved in protest than might have been expected. Different investigators estimate that from 20 to 37 percent of student activists were Jewish (Solomon and Fishman, 1964; Watts and Whittaker, 1966; Flacks, 1967; Smith, Haan, and Block, 1970). The over representation of Jewish student activist organizations and the preponderance of immigrant parents among activist groups found by Flacks may relate to the emphasis on intellectual values in the Jewish culture as well as to a historically determined identification with the oppressed.

Academic Achievement. Not only did the parents of student activists achieve higher educational levels, but the students themselves had strong intellectual orientation and superior academic records in their colleges and universities (Heist, 1965; Flacks, 1967). Heist found in his thorough studies of intellectual disposition and academic achievement among the FSM participants at Berkeley that the FSM sample scored higher on the intellectual scale in the Omnibus Personality Inventory than did the random sample. He found also that the cumulative grade point averages of FSM participants, computed after the semester in which the FSM had preempted much student time and energy, exceeded the all-university undergraduate grade point average. Heist concludes that the students arrested in Sproul Hall were well-qualified young people with strong commitments to intellectual values who maintained excellent academic records at a highly competitive university.

This view of activist students is challenged by Kerpelman (1970), who used two objective measures—a vocabulary test and a measure of "academic ability"—and found no significant differences between students who belonged to activist organizations of the left or right and those who did not. But the issue is not clearly drawn. Intellectual orientation and good academic performance are not identical with tested intelligence, and Kerpelman's organizational criteria of activism cannot be equated with the criteria employed in the studies cited in which participation in *actual protest* figures more largely.

Personality Characteristics. In terms of questionnaire responses on the Omnibus Personality Inventory, the FSM students at Berkeley presented themselves as intellectually committed, esthetically reactive, expressive young people who were independent and relatively free from their cultural and institutional past (Heist, 1965). Specifically, Heist found that FSM members received significantly higher scores on scales reflecting nonauthoritarian attitudes and independence of authority, skepticism about conventional religious beliefs and a tendency to reject them, tendency to express feelings and impulses directly; and four intellectual dispositions: Theoretical Orientation, Thinking Introversion, Estheticism and Complexity.

In our own study (Smith, Haan, and Block, 1970), the FSM men described themselves as significantly more critical, curious, idealistic, individualistic, impulsive, informed, moody, perceptive, rebellious, and restless than did those in the randomly selected sample. In contrast, self-description of males in the random sample indicated greater concern with conventionality and achievement, as suggested by their higher scores on the following adjectives: conventional, optimistic, practical, responsible, ambitious, reserved, foresightful, considerate, self-controlled, and orderly.

Essentially similar results are obtained when the FSM women were compared with women in the randomly selected sample. FSM girls described themselves as significantly more informed, perceptive, loving, doubting, rebellious, and restless. In contrast, the women students in the random sample described themselves as significantly more conventional, ambitious, competitive, self-controlled, foresightful, orderly, responsible, and feminine.

These findings appear to be congruent with Heist's. The activists saw themselves as less conforming and conventional, admitted to restlessness and rebellion; valued knowledge, interpersonal perceptivity; and tended to be idealistic. At the same time, they were less concerned about achievement and success. No important differentiation in the picture results from applying our distinction between activists and dissenters.

Value Systems. In our study at Berkeley, FSM participants differed substantially from the randomly selected students in their value systems as reflected in the adjectives with which they described their ego-ideals. The so-called Protestant ethic is spelled out strongly by the items more characteristic of the ego-ideals of the randomly selected students: ambitious, self-denying, conventional, competitive, self-controlled, foresightful, orderly, responsible, and so on. In contrast, the FSM participants were more likely to proclaim values that are concerned with self-expression, intellectual orientation, and a sense of community with and responsibility for one's fellowman: curious, idealistic, altruistic, creative, impulsive, tolerant, perceptive, rebellious, empathic, responsive, restless, and so on. Again, there are no important differences between our activist and dissenter types.

Using a ranking procedure, Flacks (1967) found, similarly, that dedication to work for national and international betterment and interest in the world of ideas, art, and music were ranked as most important personal values for his activist students. Those scoring low on activism tended to place marriage and family and career in the highest ranked positions of importance.

Moral Reasoning. If the distinctive value perspective of student activists was much as one might expect, research on qualitative features of their moral reasoning reveals relationships that are less obvious. A major purpose of our Berkeley study was to throw light on these relationships (Haan, Smith, and Block, 1968; Smith, 1969; Haan, 1972). We adapted the methods of Kohlberg (1963, 1964) to classify the quality of students' moral reasoning about a set of ethical dilemmas into three broad levels: *premoral* (characterized by egocentric, opportunistic thinking), *conventional* (by concern with stereotyped role expectations or with acceptance of established authority), and *postconventional* (by concern for the reciprocal necessities of the common welfare, or for self-accepted abstract principles). Striking relationships emerged. The clearest contrast was between FSM arrestees and the comparable cross-section. Among the cross-section, 74 percent of the men and 90 percent of the women fell at the conventional level—as compared with only 22 percent and 34 percent of the arrestees. Substantially more of the arrestees reached the postconventional level (55 percent and 58 percent for men and women, respectively, as compared with 20 percent and 6 percent). But more of the arrestees also fell at the premoral level (23 percent and 8 percent versus 6 percent and 4 percent), which for college youth must be interpreted in Kohlberg's scheme as reflecting some kind of regression in moral thinking rather than retarded or arrested development. We get a hint here that participation in disruptive protest may follow from self-centered impulsiveness or opportunism as well as from commitment to principles. Similar comparisons between our pure types of political-social orientation make it clear that participation in acts of public protest is the important differentiating factor. Those who were inactives, conventionalists (who belonged to fraternities or sororities and had not engaged in social service protest or activities), and constructivists differ little from one another in their distribution across the three Kohlberg levels, and activists differ little from dissenters.

More recent research by Fishkin and Keniston (1972) undertaken in May, 1970 (the time of the Cambodia–Kent State crisis) shows that radical versus conservative ideology as such is related to the quality of moral thinking as indexed by the Kohlberg dilemmas. While their data are based on a rather inadequate sample, they find a strong association between political conservatism and conventional moral reasoning, and an overall positive relationship between a radicalism versus conservatism factor and both premoral and postconventional reasoning. The premoral students were especially likely to endorse violent radical slogans; the postconventionals, to *dis*agree with conservative slogans (but not necessarily to agree with radical ones, whether violent or peaceful). Since these relationships strikingly parallel our own for the behavioral criterion of FSM arrest, they suggest that the behavioral relationships we observed may be ideologically mediated.

Parental Child-Rearing Practices. Many young activists in contemporary America were reared under the influence of Benjamin Spock (1946) who, as an articulate pediatrician, led a revolt against the more authoritarian, rigid, constraining child-rearing practices characteristic of an earlier generation of American parents. The Spock-oriented mothers of the 1940s substituted inductive reasoning for insistence upon blind obedience, corrective discipline for punitive discipline, flexible responsiveness for rigid scheduling, and reasonable limits for arbitrary prohibitions. It may be argued that the emergence of a dedicated spontaneous generation concerned with humanitarian values and personal authenticity is a triumph of Spockian philosophy and principles. Others have suggested, in a less benign interpretation, that activism is the consequence of excessive parental permissiveness, a failure to teach respect for authority, and an unfortunate submission to the needs and feelings of the child. What do research data tell us about the relationship between activism and permissiveness?

The parents of activist students do appear to have been more permissive than those of nonactivist students. Parents of activists were described by their children as more lenient, less intrusive into the lives of their children, and milder disciplinarians than those of the nonactivists (Flacks, 1967). Confirmatory data were obtained from the parents themselves: Parents of activists rated themselves as more permissive than did parents in other groups.

In our study (Block, Haan, and Smith, 1969; Smith, Haan, and Block, 1970), FSM participants as compared with the randomly selected sample described both parents as less authoritarian and more permissive. They perceived their parents as having a closer effective relationship with their children and as placing less emphasis on prohibitions, restrictions, and punishment.

The most characteristic parent-child relationship described by FSM students was, however, complex. White attributing closeness and warmth to the relationship, the FSM students also admitted conflict with parents. While subscribing to many of their parents' values and views, they were less likely than the randomly selected students to rate themselves as in agreement with their parents with respect to choice of occupation, religion, politics, and friends.

In this instance, our distinction between purer activist and dissenter types is helpful. Parents of the activists encouraged their children to be independent and responsible. Unlike the parents of conventionalists, those of the activists were described as encouraging the child's differentiation and self-expressiveness, with discipline per se being less critical. They were unaccepting of aggression. The picture is not one of laissez-faire permissiveness as the lay public understands the term, but of responsible, nonpunitive parenthood: Spock interpreted with sophistication. Parents of the dissenters, on the other hand, were described in terms that correspond more closely to the popular stereotype. They made rather minimal demands for independent, mature behavior and self-control. The overall picture is one of inconsistency between indulgence and intrusiveness, leading to a conflicted, unsatisfying relationship, a plausible dynamic basis for rebellion. And the evidence in regard to reported parental attitudes is in accord with the suggestion that dissenters were indeed in greater rebellion against parental attitudes than were activists.

Summary. The results of the studies that we have reviewed yield quite consistent results. These position-taking young people tend to have been superior students from socially and educationally advantaged homes. To a large extent, their political values and social ideals were consonant with the values of their parents, who themselves were politically liberal. They were nonconventional in their moral judgments, whether from the basis of a principled postconventional morality or (to a lesser extent) from an opportunistic, premoral orientation. The activists described their parents as permissive and stressing a rational approach in their child-rearing practices. Perhaps because they had been reared in child-centered homes where communication and understanding were important, these young people came to value dialogue and to expect that social institutions, like their parents, would listen and be responsive to their concerns. Mostly, they felt supported by their parents as they challenged the values of modern society. A subgroup of dissenters, however, seems to have been carrying to the larger world a personal rebellion that had roots in their relations to their parents.

The Individualists

The research findings on individualist students actively engaged in conservative causes have been somewhat inconsistent. Fewer studies have concentrated on them, and the samples on which conclusions are based have sometimes been small. The groups have been defined in several ways: by actual participation in counterprotest demonstrations (Solomon and Fishman, 1964; Flacks, 1967), by membership in conservative activist organizations (Schiff, 1964; Westby and Braungart, 1966; Kerpelman, 1970), or by delegate status to national conventions of student conservative organizations (Braungart, 1966). There have been differences, also, in the ideological positions of the conservative groups studied. Schiff (1966) reports that students who were converted to conservative causes early in adolescence reflect primarily a search for meaning, while those converted later are rather seeking to escape from and to deny the possibility of real change as they encounter the adult world. Finally, some inconsistencies in findings may relate to the nature of the groups against which the individualist is contrasted, a normative group or an activist group.

Family Background. Apart from agreement that active conservative students tend to come from Republican families who are predominantly Protestant (Solomon and Fishman, 1964; Braungart, 1966; Westby and Braungart, 1966; Flacks, 1967), there is little consistency in findings and no conclusions can be presently drawn.

Personality Characteristics. Few investigators have systematically assessed the personality characteristics of young people actively committed to conservative causes. There is some evidence that these students are more submissive to authority and tend to exert greater control over expressions of impulse and anxiety (Schiff, 1964). Interestingly, and contrary to stereotype, no evidence of greater prejudice or ethnocentrism was found by Schiff in his evaluations of student conservatives. We found at Berkeley that the individualists (as contrasted with the random sample) described themselves in ways that emphasized their independence, unwillingness to compromise, egocentricity, and unconventionality, traits highly prized in Ayn Rand's (1957, 1964) individualistic philosophy that influenced many conservative activists at Berkeley.

More recently, Kerpelman (1970) has found that right activists (and nonactivists) were the highest of his comparison groups on a factor identified as "authoritarianism" (left activists were lowest). Right activists resembled left activists in being high on a second major factor, "autonomy." *All* activists—left, middle, and right—were found to need less support and nurturance, to value leadership more, to be more socially ascendant and assertive, and to be more sociable than their ideological counterparts who were not politically active. (Remember Kerpelman's organizational criterion of activism.) In Kerpelman's study, there were no differences between groups classified independently by activism and ideology in regard to measures of emotional stability or responsibility and restraint.

Value Systems. The values of the individualists studied at Berkeley, as reflected in their distinctive characterizations of their self-ideals, were oriented to matters of personal integrity and individualism. These students ascribed less value to interpersonal relationships and were less oriented to altruistic or humanistic values than were other groups. But the sample was small. Flacks (1967) found that his counterprotesters ranked *marriage and family* and *career* as first and second in order of personal importance, while giving low ranks to interest in the arts, abstract ideas, or involvement in improving world conditions.

Parental Child-Rearing Practices. The parents of individualists appear to have expected much of their children and to have placed high value on achievement and characterological "goodness," according to our results and those of Schiff (1964). When parental expectations were not fulfilled, the mothers of conservative activists tended to react with anger and disappointment, while their children responded to the pressures with feelings of resentment and failure. Particularly for the male in the conservative sample, there was an emphasis on the mother's use of guilt-arousing techniques of control. The mother-son relationship was described as more impersonal, less affectionate, and less appreciative than that depicted by the randomly selected sample. The father-son relationship appeared to differ little from that typical of the random sample. However, our sample was small, and these findings obviously need corroboration.

Summary. We know less about the individualists than about the activist group and the information is less consistent. Any conclusions about active conservatives must be very tentative. One apparently clear finding is greater parental pressure in the direction of achievement, in a child-rearing context that relies on authoritarianism and is relatively lacking in emotional warmth. The values expressed by the conservative students reflect an emphasis on individualism, integrity, and consistency. The nature of the conservative movement itself may satisfy the adolescent's needs for structure, certainty, and reliance on authority.

The Alienated

Alienated, estranged, politically apathetic adolescents have stimulated relatively little systematic research beyond the intensive study conducted on a small scale of Harvard students by Keniston (1965) in the 1950s. This is in part because the alienated, by inclination and conviction, are antipathetic to quantitative research. On the basis of psychological test responses, Kenniston selected twelve disaffected and disaffiliated Harvard undergraduates who manifested the "alienated syndrome"—rejecting the dominant values, roles, and institutions of contemporary American society—and studied them intensively over three years. He became well acquainted with these young men and has provided an incisive portrayal of them and of their cultural and familial heritages, with an insightful analysis of the social context that predisposes young people toward alienation. His analysis remains relevant a decade later.

Of course, Keniston describes the alienated syndrome in a very atypical group of young people, upper middle-class students at one of the most prestigious private universities. The fact that most of these young people were able to remain students for the three years of the research indicates that their rejection of traditional American achievement values was discriminating rather than total.

The alienated young man, according to Keniston, regarded his mother as a talented woman whose career had been sacrificed to marriage and family. He expressed a special sympathy for his mother's unrealized potentials and identified with her unhappiness. His desire for a close, dependent relationship with his mother was countered, however, by his resentment of her domination, possessiveness, and neuroticism. The father image portrayed by the alienated Harvard students is of an inhibited, constricted, cold, withdrawn man oriented to success, status, and security. Fathers of the alienated were pictured as men who, in their youth, had visionary dreams and idealistic hopes. Under the stress of parental and societal pressures for achievement, the fathers of the alienated abandoned these dreams and, as their sons saw it, "sold out" their noble aspirations to the demands of the marketplace. Keniston's alienated young men were not overtly hostile toward their fathers but were condescending and accorded them little respect.

In early childhood, the alienated described themselves as shy and reserved and were oriented to the intellectual world of books and ideas. The adolescence of the alienated was marked by turmoil accompanied by strong negative feelings about sexuality. During mid-adolescence, these alienated-to-become began questioning the values of their parents and of society at large. It was not until later adolescence, however, that they overtly rejected parental, community, and cultural values.

The rejections of the alienated were many. They refused to orient themselves and their lives toward long-range goals because of an inherent pessimism about the future. They rejected the Puritan virtues of self-control, self-denial, order, responsibility, insisting on the values of spontaneity, expression, intense confrontation with experience, and personal freedom. They rejected the conventional adult role with its attendant responsibilities, inevitable compromises, and the expectation of adult sexuality. Their positive values were in experiencing—deeply, freely, and appreciatively.

In a more recent essay, Keniston (1971) distinguishes between two types of alienation, the activist (similar to our conception) and the disaffiliate. The disaffiliate is nonpolitical, culturally alienated, and rejects societal offerings and values. The demonstrations of disaffiliates, according to Keniston, are private rebellions manifested in beatnickism, bohemianism, or psychedelic withdrawal from the mainstream of public life. Keniston finds little political participation in this group but occasional peripheral involvement in protest movements. Their rejection of American society is based less on idealism and outraged indignation, Keniston postulates, than upon temperamental opposition to the requirements and rewards of American society—and to their fathers who epitomize this society for them. The disaffiliate is estranged from both family and society. If and as countercultural values become more prevalent among the young (Yankelovich, 1972), the *deviant* aspect emphasized by Keniston should change in respects that will be interesting to follow.

Estrangement from family and friends was also found by Watts and Whittaker (1968; see also Whittaker and Watts, 1969), who studied disaffiliated nonstudents living on the fringes of the Berkeley campus. These investigators recruited their research volunteers from the coffeeshops and bookstores adjacent to the University. The group included a heterogeneous range extending from students temporarily out of school in order to work for one semester, to others who never were students and were unemployed. Nevertheless, the sample did not differ from Berkeley students in socioeconomic background. For this sample, rejection of contemporary society, personal isolation, estrangement from family, and experimentation with drugs were more frequent than in the contrast sample of students Watts and Whittaker studied. They were equal to the contrast sample, or better, on a vocabulary index of intelligence. In terms of their scores on the Omnibus Personality Inventory, both males and females (whose profiles were closely similar) were very high in scores for psychological complexity and impulse expression, strong in intellectual orientation and in aestheticism, low in authoritarianism, and high in socioemotional maladjustment, in comparison with the student sample.

The importance of distinguishing subtypes within the alienated student syndrome was demonstrated in a study by Block (1972), who identified two patterns of alienation that differ in their personal and familial concomitants. In a study focused explicitly on the question of generational continuity-discontinuity, Block compared two groups of Berkeley students: students actively rejecting societal institutions and values as well as parental value orientations—the Discontinuous individuals—and students actively rejecting societal institutions and values but accepting of the basic value orientations of their parents—the Continuous individuals. Comparisons of the two groups revealed that the Continuous group described themselves and asserted personal values for themselves that might be considered, comparatively, more "straight," e.g., responsible, practical, informed, foresightful—while the Discontinuous group proclaimed a "counterculture" orientation, e.g., rebellious, free, artistic, playful, loving. Differences in socialization emphases, replicated in a second study that included the parents of Continuous and Discontinuous students, revealed that parents of the Continuous students were described as more "responsibly responsive." They encouraged individuation, reflectivity, assumption of responsibility, and discussion of issues and problems. These parents also indicated a feeling of greater satisfaction in their parental roles. Parents of the Discontinuous students displayed a greater adherence to authoritarian child-rearing orientations. They placed greater emphasis on achievement, conventionality, control, and attempted both to circumscribe and prestructure the experiences of their young. Generational continuity was found to be associated, also, with greater agreement between parents with respect to their child-rearing values, a factor that might be expected to contribute to a more consistent, coherent learning matrix for the growing child.

Summary. The alienated, like the activist, is engaged in a repudiation of traditional societal values. He differs from the activist, however, in a passive pessimism, in keeping with which he concerns himself with the extension and intensification of subjective experience rather than with active protest. Another basic difference between the alienated and the activist is in terms of attitudes toward parents and family. The activist tends to identify with many of the values of his parents. The alienated, however, has developed a disparate set of values, inconsistent with those of his parents, that are likely to elicit disapproval and strain communication.

The Constructivists

Young people directing their energies to constructive programs of action *within* existing societal institutions have not been the object of much research inquiry. Gelineau and Kantor (1964) assessed a number of Harvard and Radcliffe student volunteers in a large public mental hospital and found them little different in social background from the typical Harvard or Radcliffe student. The only distinguishing features were: A larger number had attended public schools, and a disproportionate number of volunteers were from Jewish backgrounds while Catholics were somewhat underrepresented. Gelineau and Kantor found the volunteers to be intelligent, secular, sophisticated, idealistic, and valuing of creativity. They were motivated by their interest in human contact and an altruistic desire to be helpful to others.

In a study of an early contingent of Peace Corps volunteers, Smith (1969) suggested three main factors as motivating enlistment. A "psychosocial moratorium" (Erickson, 1956), providing time out for self-discovery and evaluation of life goals, was important to the volunteers. They required, however, that this moratorium be constructively earned by devotion to something intrinsically worthwhile. The opportunity in the Peace Corps for direct personal action toward good ends was an important motivational component. Opportunities for adventure and experience in foreign cultures was a third, but lesser, reason for the appeal of the Peace Corps. Volunteer service contributes to the adolescent's need to establish an identity for himself and to test his skills and competence in a way that does not directly confront or challenge authority. Altruism, in this context, provides a safe outlet for the expression of doubts about the adult society and a channel for the adolescent's idealistic desires to effect changes in that society.

In our Berkeley studies, constructivists, especially the men, came from less affluent socioeconomic backgrounds than had the activists and dissenters. They were distinctive in describing themselves as responsible, practical, and tolerant (males) and helpful (females). Their values, as indexed by traits they would distinctively like to have, emphasized being empathic and helpful (men) and optimistic and argumentative (women)—though the last trait was little chosen by any group and should therefore be discounted. We have already noted that they did not differ appreciably from conventionalists and inactives in the quality of their moral reasoning, according to Kohlberg's scale. In regard to their reported experience of the parent-child relationship, which they evaluated positively, they resembled the conventionalists in emphasis on punishment and restriction of self-expression, though they reported less emphasis on achievement and competition. There was little suppression of physical aggression. Parental control relied on anxiety rather than on guilt. The family pattern seemed congruent with their altruism, which was achieved at the expense of spontaneous expressiveness.

Our survey of research findings will not include politically uninvolved young people who accept most of our prevailing societal values. This group includes the typical adolescent whose developmental and personological characteristics have been described in other chapters of this book. We proceed now to consider briefly some of the factors predisposing to the activism of the 1960s and some explanations that have been offered for its emergence.

Sociocultural Factors Predisposing to Activism

The unpredicted change in the ethos of youth from the "silent" generation of the 1950s to the "protesting" student of the 1960s, now followed by the equally unpredicted apparent decline of protest and disruption in the 1970s, has challenged sociologists and social psychologists for explanations. The traditional historical forces previously associated with the emergence of radical youth movements—limited occupational and economic opportunities, the breakdown of traditional authority under the impact of industrialization—seem an insufficient explanation for the development of recent protests. Several hypotheses that have been offered will be summarized.

Sociological Explanations

Keniston (1965) has posited that intensification of technological change in our country and in much of the modern world has been at the expense of human values. Our technological society stresses empiricism, pragmatism, efficiency, and production. The absence of articulate social goals and the deification of technological progress at the expense of social concerns has dehumanized society. The very rapidity of change makes the past irrelevant to the present, and the continuity with history that eases the task of identification and adaptation is weakened. The "generational gap" is widened by accelerating changes so that communication between generations becomes increasingly difficult. Patterns for the solution of today's problems cannot be found in the experiences of the past. The protest of youth against this "dehumanization" process is a part of their struggle for identity and integrity. This line of reasoning has the merit of applying to the worldwide situation as well as to the United States. Insofar as alienation and protest are alternative responses to dehumanization, the recent decline of protest does not present special difficulties for this explanation.

Psychosocial Factors

Feuer (1969), in a scholarly but tendentious historical analysis of youth movements that is colored by his early embitterment with student protest at Berkeley, combines a psychoanalytic view of inevitable underlying generational conflict (as a corollary of the Oedipus complex) with the hypotheses that romantic and destructive youth movements erupt when the adult generation has become "de-authoritized" for historical reasons. There is indeed good reason to believe that when the established generation is discredited, the grounds for protest or alienation are laid. But Feuer's theory ill accords with the evidence that many activists sought to realize parental values, far from rebelling against them; and it can hardly account for the collapse of the movement with the turn of the decade.

Bettelheim (1969), another caustic critic of the activists, saw paranoid trends in many of those whom he encountered clinically, and was perhaps unduly preoccupied with parallels with the youth movements that heralded Nazi Germany. But he suggests an underlying dynamic that warrants careful attention: the frustrations of modern young people in their prolonged dependent status and delayed adult responsibility, when they have little opportunity to deal with consequential matters of the real world. Certainly, this situation of youth is conducive to romantic activism, to apocalyptic politics—or to dropping out. How to involve the young more consequentially in the affairs of society, how to bridge the discontinuity between youth and adulthood that the American educational system has so much accentuated, *is* a serious problem for American society.

Flacks (1967) based his interpretation of youth protest in terms of an extension of Eisenstadt's (1956) and Parsons' (1963) analysis of the disjunction between the values and expectations of the traditional nuclear family and those prevailing in the occupational sphere of society. Although discrepancies between familial and societal values are inevitable in modern industrial society, Parsons suggests that these differences are lessening in middle-class America. Flacks goes on to propose that within middle-class society there is a segment of well-educated families whose stress upon democratic, egalitarian principles, on permissiveness, on values other than achievement, does not accord with the prevailing values and expectations in the occupational sphere. Young people reared according to these precepts should find it difficult to accept the traditional social values that require submission to authority, competition, ambition, and self-control. Their questioning of the social norms, instigated by their parents, has been reinforced by their selectively chosen friends, by their experiences in progressive schools or camps, and by their reading. The customary rewards and incentives of the occupational sphere have only limited effectiveness for these young people who have already achieved status and affluence by virtue of their family origins. Flacks suggests that the abstract concern with democratic and egalitarian values of the parental generation, expressed in their child-centered approach to rearing, has become embodied in their children as personality traits. Adolescents who engaged in protest were thus not rebelling in a conventional sense but were expressing the values according to which they have been reared. Further, the nonauthoritarian stance of their parents released these young people to react to the problems and significant people of their time. This explanation, too, has no difficulty in accommodating to alternatives of protest and alienation.

The Existentialist Attitude

The young people of today have been reared at a time characterized by the omnipresent and ominous pressure of the nuclear stalemate. Many cogently wonder, along with their elders, whether mankind will be able to get by "by the skin of its teeth." These bleak uncertainties, as the voice of traditional religion wanes, have made many youth responsive to the existentialists' call for individual commitment and responsibility—or absurd defiance. At first or second hand, the existentialist formulations of Sartre, Camus, and Kierkegaard have served to crystallize attitudes that differentiate thoughtful youth of the present generation.

The existentialist call to "being," "actualizing," or "becoming" appeals to many. In an age of mass society and impersonal technology, its emphasis upon an enlarged and acute sense of personal responsibility is refreshing. Sartre (1957) holds that man is responsible for himself, for his own individuality, and is responsible also for all men. He emphasizes that the future will be as man decides it is to be. He exhorts man to involve himself in the decision making that will determine his future.

If the existentialist posture in its version of human dignity repudiates the cosmic reassurances of traditional religion, it has equally little use for the rationalism of the scientific world view. In its romantic subjectivism, it offers no guidelines, no criteria for meaningful choice in a world of "absurdity." All depends on inner conviction, on freely willed choice. What is chosen in full consciousness and freedom is "authentic," and authenticity is a principal virtue. Depending on one's personal bent, one may seek authenticity in the intensification of inner experience and spontaneity (as do the alienated) or one may, like the activists, find meaning in the existential act of making a stand against injustice and hypocrisy. To the extent that youthful protesters conceived of their activism with a generally existentialist outlook, they felt no need for rationally elaborated or logically consistent theory. By the same token, they become the less accessible to rational dialogue with their elders. The alienated version of the existentialist posture is just as estranged from rational discourse.

Retreat of the Protestant Ethic

With the increasing secularization of America, religion has declined as determinant of behavior. Psychoanalysis, existentialism, and the influence of the scientific method have encouraged the development of a more humanistic ethical system concerned with honesty, authenticity, and personal responsibility for one's acts. Freed from the taboos of the Victorian era and impelled by the dictates of a rational conscience, today's youth find that their struggles for authenticity often require dissent. At the same time, the consumption-orientated values of an affluent society have further eroded the foundations on which the traditional future-oriented achievement-centered ethos of Benjamin Franklin rested (Riesman, 1950).

Child-Rearing Factors

Flacks has stressed the importance of permissive, democratic child-rearing practices in the development of the young activist. It is not just with matters of respect for the child and encouragement of self-regulation that we are concerned in this section. It seems to us that the very *techniques* used by parents who have rejected authoritarian methods of control encourage the development of empathy and concern for others. When categorical enforcement of arbitrary rules by implacable authority is abandoned in favor of more rational methods of discipline, several things happen. First, the reasons behind parental demands are explained to the child so that they no longer appear quite so arbitrary. Second, these reasons are usually based on welfare concerns. The mother prohibits the child from actions, not because they are inherently "bad," but because they are potentially harmful to himself or others. Third, the child is encouraged to see the relationship between his own actions and their subsequent effects on other people. These "other-oriented" mechanisms of discipline are associated, along with affection, with the development of a "humanistic conscience" (Hoffman, 1964). The development of empathy and humanistic orientation make it probable that a young person will concern himself with the plight of others. The relationship between activism and humanism is supported by our results on value systems reported earlier.

Child-training practices viewed in this way highlight the continuity between parent and child generations, explain to some extent the support accorded to protest by parents of activists, and rationalize the frustrations felt by activist youth when confronted by arbitrary authorities who refuse their invitation to dialogue.

But the considerable degree of discontinuity between generations, especially in matters of discipline in child-rearing, has left difficult problems concerning authority in its wake. Parents who try to raise their children at least partly in contrast to the way they themselves were raised do not have the assurance of established models, of having learned their own parental role from the reciprocal position of being a child. They are more likely than traditional parents to be uncertain, and inconsistent, and inept even when they mean well. No wonder they depend upon Spock or his equivalent. Under these circumstances, it is not surprising that neither parents nor their children, nor modern society generally, have been able to keep consistently clear Erich Fromm's (1941) important distinction between rational authority and inhibiting or arbitrary authority. And it is not surprising that "hang-ups" about authority continue to plague contemporary youth. Thus, according to Yankelovich (1972, p. 33), "the major barrier students see standing in the way of securing desirable work is their attitude toward authority. No obstacle comes even close to this one, including political views [or] style of dress. . . ."

Summary

In this chapter we have discussed and examined the activist and the apathetic adolescent who raises his voice, or who does not raise his voice, in political and social protest. Our focus has been mainly on youth in the 1960s from the perspective of the different, but as yet confusing, scene of the early 1970s. The activist youth has voiced his dissatisfaction with contemporary society. This has produced tensions. Toward the end of the 1960s these tensions too often led to violence, to consequences that were destructive, however pure the motive. However, tensions between generations and between youth and society are inevitable because the older generation stands as gatekeeper to the opportunities and aspirations of the young, and because the choices and commitments of youth have the power to either confirm or negate the values of their elders and of their society. If man and society are to change and grow, the adult world not only has to provide guidance for its youth, but also must be able to hear and profit from youth's perceptions, indignations, and insights. The "rejuvenations" (Erikson, 1962) of society and the older generation come from the vitalism, idealism, and dedication of the young.

REFERENCES

Astin, A. W. New evidence on campus unrest: 1969–70. *Educational Record,* Winter, 1971, 41–46.

Bayer, A. E., and Astin, A. W. Violence and disruption on the U.S. campus: 1968–69. *Educational Record,* Fall, 1969, 337–350.

———, and Astin, A. W. Campus unrest, 1970–71: Was it really all that quiet? *Educational Record,* Fall, 1971, 301–313.

Bettelheim, B. Obsolete youth, *Encounter,* 1969, *23* (No. 3) , 29–42.

Block, J. H. The child-rearing practices report. Institute of Human Development, University of California, Berkeley, 1965 (Mimeo) .

———. Generational continuity and discontinuity in the understanding of societal rejection. *Journal of Personality and Social Psychology,* 1972, in press.

———, Haan, N., and Smith, M. B. Socialization correlates of student activism. *Journal of Social Issues,* 1969, *25,* 143–177.

Blos, P. *On adolescence: A psychoanalytic interpretation.* Glencoe, Ill.: Free Press, 1962.

Braungart, R. G. SDS and YAF: Backgrounds of student political activists. Paper presented to the American Sociological Association, August, 1966.

Campus '65. *Newsweek,* March 22, 1965, 54.

Coleman, J. S. *The adolescent society: The social life of the teenager and impact on education.* Glencoe, Ill.: Free Press, 1961.

———. *Adolescents and the schools.* New York: Basic Books, 1965.

Eisenstadt, S. *From generation to generation.* Glencoe, Ill.: Free Press, 1956.

Erikson, E. H. The problem of ego identity. *Journal of the American Psychoanalytic Association,* 1965, *4,* 55–121.

———. Reality and actuality. *Journal of the American Psychoanalytic Association,* 1962, *10,* 451–474.

———. Youth: fidelity and diversity. In E. Erikson (ed.) , *Youth: Change and challenge.* New York: Basic Books, 1963.

———. *Insight and responsibility.* New York: W. W. Norton, 1964.

Feuer, L. *The conflict of generations.* New York and London: Basic Books, 1969.

Fishkin, J., and Keniston, K. Moral development and political ideology, 1972 (unpublished manuscript).

Flacks, R. The liberated generation: An exploration of the roots of student protest. *Journal of Social Issues,* 1967, *23,* 52–75.

Fromm, E. *Escape from freedom.* New York: Farrar and Rinehart, 1941.

Gales, K. E. A campus revolution. *British Journal of Sociology,* 1966, *17,* 1–19.

Gelineau, V. A., and Kantor, D. Pro-social commitment among college students. *Journal of Social Issues,* 1964, *20,* 112–130.

Haan, N., Smith, M. B., and Block, J. H. Moral reasoning of young adults: Political-social behavior, family background, and personality correlates. *Journal of Personality and Social Psychology,* 1968, *10,* 183–201.

Haan, N. Activism as moral protest: Moral judgments of hypothetical moral dilemmas and an actual situation of civil disobedience. In L. Kohlberg and E. Turiel (eds.), *The development of moral judgment and action.* New York: Holt, Rinehart and Winston, 1972.

Heist, P. Intellect and commitment: The faces of discontent. In O. W. Knorr and W. J. Minter (eds.), *Order and freedom on campus.* Boulder, Colorado: Western Interstate Commission for Higher Education, 1965.

————. The dynamics of student discontent and protest. Paper presented to American Psychological Association, September, 1966.

Hoffman, M. L. Techniques and processes in moral development. Mimeographed report, 1964.

Horn, J. F., and Knott, P. D. Activist youth of the 1960's: Summary and prognosis. *Science,* 1971, *171,* 977–985.

Inhelder, B. and Piaget, J. *The growth of logical thinking from childhood to adolescence.* New York: Basic Books, 1958.

Katz, J., et al. *No time for youth: Growth and constraint in college students.* San Francisco, Calif.: Jossey-Bass, 1968.

Keniston, K. *The uncommitted: Alienated youth in American society.* New York: Harcourt, Brace and World, 1965.

————. *Young radicals: Notes on committed youth.* New York: Harcourt, Brace, and World, 1968.

————. *Youth and dissent: The rise of a new opposition.* New York: Harcourt Brace Jovanovich, 1971.

Kerpelman, L. C. Student activism and ideology in higher education institutions. Final Report, Project No. 8–A–028, Bureau of Research, Office of Education, March, 1970.

Kohlberg, L. The development of children's orientations towards a moral order. I. Sequence in the development of moral thought. *Vita Humana,* 1963, *6,* 11–33.

———. Development of moral character and moral ideology. In M. L. Hoffman and L. W. Hoffman (eds.), *Review of child development research,* Vol. I. New York: Russell Sage Foundation, 1964.

Lerner, M. Hippies and radicals. *Daily Californian,* October 27, 1966, 6.

Lipset, S. M. Student opposition in the United States. *Government and Opposition,* 1966, *1,* 351–374.

———, and Schaflander, G. *Passion and politics: Student activism in America.* Boston: Little, Brown and Co., 1971.

Munk, M. New left: Background of young radicals. *National Guardian,* September 18, 1965, 3.

Musgrove, F. *Youth and the social order.* Bloomington, Indiana: Indiana University Press, 1965.

Parsons, T. Youth in the context of American society In E. Erikson (ed.), *Youth: Change and challenge.* New York: Basic Books, 1963.

Peterson, R. E. *The scope of organized student protest in 1964–1965.* Princeton, N.J.: Educational Testing Service, 1966. (a)

———. Organized student protest in 1964–1965. Paper presented to American Psychological Association, September, 1966. (b)

———. *The scope of organized student protest in 1967–1968.* Princeton, N.J.: Educational Testing Service, 1968.

Piaget, J. and Weil, A. M. Le développement chez l'enfant de l'idée de patrie et des relations avec l'étranger. *Bulletin International des Sciences Sociales* (UNESCO), 1951, *3,* 605–621.

Rand, A. *Atlas shrugged.* New York: Random House, 1957.'

———. *The virtues of selfishness.* New York: New American Library, 1964.

Reich, C. *The greening of America.* New York: Random House, 1970.

Reisman, D. (with R. Denney and N. Glazer). *The lonely crowd: A study of changing American character.* New Haven: Yale University Press, 1950.

Roszak, T. *The making of a counter-culture.* Garden City, N.Y.: Doubleday, 1969.

Sampson, E. E., and Korn, H. A. *Student activism and protest.* San Francisco, Calif.: Jossey-Bass, 1970.

Sartre, J-P. *Existentialism and human emotion.* New York: Philosophical Library, 1957.

Schiff, L. F. The obedient rebels: A study of college conversions to conservatism. *Journal of Social Issues,* 1964, *20,* 74–95.

———. Dynamic young fogies, rebels on the right. *Trans-action,* 1966, November, 30–36.

Smith, M. B. Explorations in competence: A study of Peace Corps teachers in Ghana. In M. B. Smith (ed.), *Social psychology and human values.* Chicago: Aldine-Atherton, 1969. (a)

———. Morality and student protest. In M. B. Smith (ed.), *Social psychology and human values.* Chicago: Aldine-Atherton, 1969. (b)

———. *Social psychology and human values.* Chicago: Aldine-Atherton, 1969. (c)

———, Haan, N., and Block, J. H. Social-psychology aspects of student activism, *Youth and Society,* 1970, *1,* 261–288.

Solomon, F., and Fishman, J. R. Youth and peace: A psychosocial study of student peace demonstrators in Washington, D.C. *Journal of Social Issues,* 1964, *20,* 54–73.

Spock, B. *The commonsense book of baby and child care.* New York: Duell, Sloan and Pearce, 1946.

Watts, W. A., and Whittaker, D. Free speech advocates at Berkeley. *Journal of Applied Behavioral Science,* 1966, *2,* 41–62.

———, and Whittaker, D. Profile of a nonconformist youth culture: A study of Berkeley non-students. *Sociology of Education,* 1968, *41,* 178–200.

Westby, D., and Braungart, R. Class and politics in the family backgrounds of student political activists. *American Sociological Review,* 1966, *31,* 690–692.

Whittaker, D., and Watts, W. A. Personality characteristics of a nonconformist youth subculture: A study of the Berkeley non-student. *Journal of Social Issues,* 1969, *25,* 65–89.

Yankelovich, D., Inc. *The changing values on campus. Political and personal attitudes of today's college students.* New York: Pocket Books, Washington Square Press, 1972.

14

Youth and the Counterculture

*Herbert J. Cross and E. Lansing Pruyn**

The counterculture and its relationship to youth in our society is difficult to write about because the phenomena that must be reported and analyzed are all controversial. While for most people the controversy may not be intense or even articulate, many adults and most youth in our society have strong feelings about the world they live in. The decade of the 1960s was filled with many newsworthy events that documented areas of difference between youth and the established order.

In the spring of 1968, student unrest was great enough to require concerted police action in every major European nation, plus Japan and the United States. Campus demonstrations became usual events (see Block, Haan, and Smith's chapter), and the great student strike of 1970 seemed to mark a zenith in student unrest. The spring of 1970 was the first time student demonstrators were fired at and killed in the modern United States; and it was the first time that demonstrations halted a substantial proportion of higher education. The traditionally solemn ceremonies of graduation were marked by disturbance and unscheduled student speakers throughout the nation.

* Herbert J. Cross is Associate Professor of Psychology at Washington State University. He has written a number of articles on such topics as the influences of personality development, the generation gap, and alternate life styles.

E. Lansing Pruyn is Executive Director of Perception House of the Eastern Connecticut Drug Action Program and is Instructor in Sociology at Eastern Connecticut State College. His interests are in political and social change, humanistic psychology, and in encounter groups.

Active protest is only one form in which youth flouts the established values of his society. A more subtle but intense, and perhaps more significant challenge to tradition comes from what is now called the counterculture. The counterculture embodies myriad forces, almost all youthful, that are either trying to change the older generation's rules for living or, if change is not seen as being possible, to ignore them.

A frequently asked question is whether or not current generational conflict is more intense than that seen by previous generations. Mark Twain's salty comment about how much one's father learns between the offspring's eighteenth and twenty-first birthdays still seems relevant. However, it seems to us that generational conflict is more intense and more meaningful for the general society than it has been at any time in the past. In the United States youths are becoming a political and economic force by sheer presence, for they are greater in numbers than ever before (see McGovern's chapter).

Why, then, has conflict between the generations emerged as such a potent phenomenon in our society at this particular time? We can only speculate, but it would seem that adolescent rebellion is new because the adolescent himself is a relatively new and unique invention of an economically comfortable and rapidly industrializing society. In societies where everyone has to work, fight, or hunt for his survival, the social attitude toward childhood is different and young people develop into adulthood without the limbo imposed on them by our modern world. As our society has become more technologically complex, it has required an increasingly well-trained labor force to maintain itself. The long period of training required necessitates a trainee-student status for a number of years, and the youthful members of society learn how to satisfy the requirements of tradition during this time. However, as our society has become increasingly industrialized, urbanized, and technologically complex, youths have reacted against what they regard as dehumanizing forces; and, instead of learning the requirements of tradition, they learn to counter tradition. Mass education not only trains workers, it informs them of traditions and values as well.

The social value system which is taught by the educational institutions seems ambivalent and, at times, even confused. We have maintained that our society is based on an ethic which guarantees "life, liberty, and the pursuit of happiness," yet, in our official policy toward some people and nations, economic necessity seems to have been the only guiding force.

These diverse factors, which we will have more to say about later, have resulted in the counterculture. The antecedents of the counterculture, and its effects, are difficult to define because of this diversity. To gain a better focus, we shall quote several authorities and discuss their contributions to the topic.

Goals of Counterculture

Simmons and Winograd (1966) were among the first to put together in book form a summary of the youth culture. Their account is written in a popular style, and they attempt to define who they are talking about by answering the question, "Who's happening?" by stating who is not. Some of the people and institutions they mention as "not happening" are Texas oilmen; the Pasadena senior prom; the senior chamber of commerce; the junior chamber of commerce; the "man of the year" in Waukegan, Topeka, Vicksburg, Council Bluffs, or *Time;* Pearl Buck, Edna Ferber, Doris Day, the University of California budget, Lyndon Johnson, society's censors, selective service boards, steel industry, yachtsmen sipping drinks off Florida's Gulf Coast, Oakland's police force, Walt Disney, or the Cartwrights or McNamara or Ky; New York's stop and frisk law; California's anti-riot bill; the city council; the Christmas industry; the Johnny Carson show.

Presumably the list could go on *ad nauseam* arousing consensus from some readers. We agree with Simmons and Winograd but cannot specify the dimensions on which these individuals and institutions are alike and different from the counterculture. Our inability to specify and Simmons and Winograd's choice to define negatively, by stating what's *not* happening, illustrates the difficulty of defining the counterculture.

Roszak (1968, p. 48) states:

> If the counterculture is, as I shall contend here, that healthy instinct which refuses both at a personal and political level to practice such a cold-blooded rape of our human sensibilities, then it should be clear why the conflict between young and adult in our time reaches so peculiarly and painfully deep. In an historical emergency of absolutely unprecedented proportions, we are that strange, culture-bound animal whose biological drive for survival expresses itself *generationally.* It is the young, arriving with eyes that can see the obvious, who must remake the lethal culture of their elders, and who must remake it in desperate haste.*

Thus, Roszak identifies the counterculture by stating its goals and equating it generally with the youth movement. Further, he says that "it is scarcely so disciplined a movement (as to be entirely youthful). It is something in the way of procession constantly in flux, acquiring and losing members all along the route of march" (1968, p. 48).

Slater, a caustic social critic, states:

* From *The Making of a Counter Culture,* by Theodore Roszak. © 1968, 1969 by Theodore Roszak. Reprinted by permission of Doubleday and Company, Inc.

The old culture, when forced to choose, tends to give preference to property rights over personal rights, technological requirements over human needs, competition over cooperation, violence over sexuality, concentration over distribution, the producer over the consumer, means over ends, secrecy over openness, social forms over personal expression, striving over gratification, Oedipal love over communal love, and so on. The new counterculture tends to reverse all of these priorities (1970, p. 101).

For his definition, Slater had to state the goals of both the dominant culture and the counterculture as polarities. The polarity notion has also been suggested by Yablonsky (1968), who notes that the hippie phenomenon is the first social movement completely opposed to the mainstream society's values. Weakland (1969) also noted this polarity in his excellent paper on hippies, pointing out how many hip values were mirror images of the dominant culture values. For example, the hippies "turn on," i.e., smoke marijuana as an aid to pleasure seeking, whereas the "straight" world abhors pleasure seeking for its own sake and keeps marijuana illegal. Representatives of the straight society steadfastly maintain that they will never "turn on," while the counterculture youths maintain that no one can understand them without "turning on." The unfortunate outcome of these two polarities is that each side is left with a nonnegotiable position. One cannot understand the other, and neither can retreat from its ideological stand because its very integrity and self-definition would have to be questioned.

Yablonsky (1968) is the only writer intrepid enough to offer a classification of hippies and an estimate of their numbers. He divides half the hippie world into high priests and novitiates and the other half into four categories of "plastic" hippies. (*Plastic* is the counterculture term for cheap substitute, which is what plastic often was when it was first introduced.) High priests and novitiates are truly committed, or sincere hippies. High priests have generally used LSD or similar drugs and maintain that they have reached a level of awareness wherein they understand man's basic godlike nature. This is a pantheistic view which promotes the love ethic and is strongly antiviolent. The priests see it as their duty to inform the world of their message and to envelop the distrusting establishment with their attitude of love and trust. Haley (1969) also discusses this attitude among "true" hippies.

Following this group are the novitiates who seem even more enthusiastic about being different from the establishment and are striving to maintain that difference. They are not totally "dropped out," however, and have not achieved the inner peace of the high priests, who are stoic in the face of establishment adversity while the novices are struggling and hostile. For example, a novice would be paranoid about using marijuana; whereas, a high priest would be more relaxed because he sees the laws and possibilities of arrest as foolish and he is literally above them. Yablonsky estimates that about 10 to 15 percent of the true hippies are of the high priest variety, with the remainder being novitiates. The other half of the hip world consists of teeny-boppers, drug addicts, and severely disturbed people, plus an impossible to classify group. Teeny-boppers are teenagers who are not ideologically committed to being hip, but who are attracted by the drugs, music, and self-indulgent freedom of the street life. Another distinguishable group are drug addicts, many of whom are addicted to or dependent on amphetamines or heroin (Davis and Munoz, 1968), who use the instability and freedom of the hip life to maintain their self-destructive habits. Another of Yablonsky's categories is the severely emotionally disturbed, who benefit from the tolerance and acceptance of their peers to keep out of trouble with the law or the psychiatric community. Yablonsky further proposes a group of unidentifiable, miscellaneous hangers-on (Hell's Angels, social scientists, curious tourists, and criminal addicts) who cannot be easily differentiated from the hippies.

The plastic hippies are found mainly in metropolitan areas, whereas the more totally committed priests and novices are found in more rural areas and isolated communes. As of 1967, Yablonsky estimated a total of 400,000 true and plastic hippies and "perhaps several hundred thousand" "Clark Kent," or invisible, hippies who maintain jobs or student status but who manifest many hippie values and behaviors. Further, there are millions of sympathizers, mostly in colleges and universities. We expect that Yablonsky's estimates were somewhat liberal at the time he made them (1969); however, they are probably gross underestimates today.

The Intangible Nature of the Counterculture

It seems that each authority we have cited is talking about a relatively intangible thing as he describes the counterculture, the youth movement, or even the highly visible hippies. Each writer offers something of value, but none seems to have captured the essence of the counterculture. To us, it seems that the counterculture consists of people who are intensively questioning the dominant culture and concluding that many drastic changes are needed—or else. Many of the questioners need to be away from the dominant culture. Others are able to negotiate social space within the framework of the dominant culture such that they can work for the actualization of their alternative value system. They are generally aware that their value system is in almost total opposition to that of their social environment (but, their colleagues are often unaware of this division in values). Many of them are former dropouts, drug users, etc., who have gone through an experience similar to Kesey's "Acid Test Graduation" (Wolfe, 1968). They tend to be highly mobile, working in a fringe position in an established institution for a relatively short period of time, and then moving on—either dropping out once again, or moving to a different fringe position in a different institution. These people are most frequently younger, more intelligent, and better educated than those who do not question the mainstream cultural values. We think counterculture refers to an extremely diverse group of people: hippies, activists, many college and high school students, and their sympathizers who regard themselves as different from the mainstream.

Sources of the Counterculture

We cannot write about how people become counter to the mainstream culture without stating their motivations, which are collectively the counterculture message. Nevertheless, we shall discuss the sources here and more specifically focus on the message in the next section. Two general questions should be answered about the source of the movement: How did it start, and what is the process whereby it acquires members, viz., how do people become converted?

Origins. It is generally thought that the hippie movement was an outgrowth of the beat movement of the 1950s (Berger, 1967). While this is hard to document, it seems likely that many beat writers, e.g., Kerouac, Ginsberg, were important influences. The "beats" of Greenwich Village (Polsky, 1967) began using LSD and marijuana in greater numbers in the late 1950s and early 1960s. Probably the benign California weather attracted many of the young people who traveled there in the early 1960s from New York. Many others were dropouts or students at Berkeley, and hence began to congregate in the Bay area.

Smart and Jackson (1969, p. 286) offer the following brief history:

> The hippie community increased rapidly as a result of the Kesey Acid Tests held in Big Sur, California, in August of 1965. Ken Kesey, novelist and author of two bestsellers, held gatherings at which the refreshments, mostly punch, contained LSD. It is thought that as a result of these gatherings 10,000 people experienced an LSD adventure ("trip"). In the early part of 1966 the Haight-Asbury district, near Golden Gate Park in San Francisco, became the mecca for hippies. From different parts of North America young people headed for the "Haight," having heard of it in folk rock and acid rock music; from mass media and word of mouth.

The fascinating story of Kesey's early attempts at an alternate life style is beautifully chronicled in Tom Wolfe's best-seller, *Electric Kool-Aid Acid Test*. Briefly, Kesey and friends (called the Merry Pranksters) toured the country in a psychedelic-colored, electronically sound-equipped, LSD-supplied bus. Reading about their adventures is a painless way to acquire information about the beginning of the hippie movement and about the LSD experience.

Dr. Timothy Leary was for several years a tireless advocate of LSD and the dropout life style. He did a great deal of research with hallucinogens, attempted to found a religion based on LSD, and toured the nation lecturing on beneficial effects of drugs. *High Priest* (1968) is an autobiographical account of his change in consciousness and change in status from a Harvard psychology professor to a guru of the drug world. Leary has been one of the most simply direct of all critics of the dominant American culture. He has preached that young people should "turn on, tune in, and drop out." "Turn on" means to turn your inner self on by experiencing the internal stimulation of LSD or a similar drug. "Tune in" means to tune in to the message of the drug proselytizers (Leary himself). "Drop out" means to discontinue contributing to the establishment of the American society. Leary has been unpopular with law-enforcement agencies and has been arrested several times. His life style and ideas about influencing others to follow it are so intolerable to the dominant culture that he has been branded as unacceptably deviant. It is ironic that Leary has called himself a high priest and Yablonsky's term for the most sincere hippies is "high priest." Leary makes it clear that he understands the *double-entendre* in "high."

Allen Ginsberg may have been even more influential than Leary in spreading the message that drugs are good and the established society is bad. Ginsberg has for years advocated the legalization of hallucinogenic drugs, free love, and a noncapitalistic free economy. His successes at proselytizing have come because of his fame as a poet and as a colorful figure. He is clearly newsworthy and it seems that every chance he gets to speak through any organ of the mass media, he promotes his own alternative to the establishment life style. Instances of his effective press agentry have been documented (Toffler, 1970).

Conversion to the Counterculture. The process of changing from "straight to hip," or from mainstream culture to the counterculture, must be a complex one and probably varies greatly for individuals. Many members of the mainstream have heard both Leary's and Ginsberg's message and were not converted, and certainly all of the alleged ten thousand "turned on" by Kesey's acid tests did not become hippies.

An interview with an articulate young man who had once been a heavy cannabis and peyote user, and a dropout, produced the following:

Individuals become aware of their alienation from society by a process of radicalization-alienation that goes something like this: They are living their lives with some awareness of the system's faults but they are really not aware of the value split in the system. That is, all of the system's values are not the same as its manifest values. They might think that the SDS and other protesters are wasting time but they are sort of sympathetic. Then something happens to affect them, personally. Some event, usually, or some way they get personally hooked in and pissed-off, this is the key thing. Then there is some kind of head flip, a something that flips in their head and instead of feeling powerless and frustrated some sense of personal power is regained. Then they might get into a situation, or a demonstration or occupy a building or something. Then they begin to think about themselves and the system in a different way. Being personally affected and the head-flip is the key thing.

A similar and beautifully described process is chronicled by James Simon Kunen (1969). He talks about his passage from a conforming undergraduate to an activist in the Columbia uprising of 1968. He describes the extremists on both sides and details each step in his change in allegiance. Jerry Rubin (1970) describes the same process from the point of view of a revolutionary field general who has the goal of changing sympathetic moderates into activists.

Robert Houriet (1971), a promising young writer who was once a night editor of the *Camden Courier-Post,* describes this dropping out as stemming from a conflict with the *Courier-Post's* owner over the hair length of a reporter. Houriet, as night editor, felt that the reporter did a creative and enterprising job, even though he wore mod clothes and had long hair. The owner thought differently and exerted pressure. The reporter got his hair cut, deposited it on the owner's desk, and departed the premises. Houriet shortly left the editorship and traveled to the 1968 Democratic Convention in Chicago, half-intending to do a free-lance story on the idealistic McCarthy supporters. The demonstrations, police actions, and accompanying events dismayed him, as well as others there, and he set off to do a story on the many young people who populate the communes. The story of Houriet's dropping out and growing discomfort at working within the system seems representative of many other individuals.

So far we have been talking mainly about radicalization, the process which applies more directly to *activists* in particular than to counterculture members more generally. This topic is covered in greater depth elsewhere in this book, but what seems to happen to many activists who feel that their political activity yields no change is that they become increasingly disaffected. Some give up the struggle and allow themselves to become co-opted back into the dominant culture. Others begin to ignore both the establishment and those who work so hard to change it. Many of them are able to transcend both the dictates of the dominant culture and the mirror image of it represented by much of the activist movement. In effect, they reach a new level of consciousness (Reich, 1970), as we shall refer to later.

Simon and Trout (1967) offered observations of college hippies at Michigan State University and defined a group called "Skuzzies," who had been strong political activists. When no tangible change was produced by their political activity, they became more hedonistic, less involved, and embraced the "hang-loose" ethic (Suchman, 1968). Jay Haley (1969) also sees hippies as different from activists and writes of them expressing their alienation with different patterns of behavior and goals. Hippies are trying to ignore the structure of the mainstream society, while activists are trying to change it. Yippies (Hoffman, 1970; Rubin, 1970) combine many elements of hipness and activism and have emerged as a third force in the counterculture.

Drugs and the Counterculture

There is widespread agreement that the use of the illegal drugs plays some part in the process of young people becoming counterculturists. Erich Goode (1969) has classified marijuana as a sociogenic drug, i.e., it has some stimulating influence on social activity. Typically, marijuana is used in a group of intimate, or potentially intimate people, who share the same values and regard themselves as apart from and somewhat superior to others who have not shared their experience. Smoking marijuana is also illegal, so that the activity must be carried on in secrecy, which adds to the in-group solidarity of the participants. Since the dominant culture continues to punish marijuana users severely, many users are suspicious and hostile toward people that they cannot trust. In fact, all illegal drug users can be thought of as potential allies or sympathizers to the counterculture cause. They are violating a major dominant culture prohibition and at the same time embracing an activity that is quite acceptable to the counterculture.

The following are excerpts from two interviews (fall, 1969) of students who regularly smoked marijuana (one to four times per week):

Q. Have there been any effects on you, say psychologically, from using drugs?

A. When you say drugs, you have to separate. Like, grass has no effect, but in the past year since I've been trying, I think so, I think I've gotten to know myself better and seen through myself a lot. It's helped me psychologically to kind of balance my head out somewhat . . . things

I think are more important than money, status, class, or prestige and
all that rot.

Q. Has the use of drugs affected your goals; has it alienated you away
from any jobs?

A. Yes, sure. Since two years, since we got into majoring in sociology. Right
then, I was yea, rah, rah, revolution type shit. Gonna change the world;
very idealistic. I think that drugs didn't make me any less idealistic,
it just made me. . . . I'd like things to be ideal but I realized that they're
not going to change if I run out and cause a big hassle; go fighting for
this cause and that cause. I've become a lot more passive toward some
goals that I had held.

Q. What part do you think drugs play in the counterculture, or the differences between the generations?

A. Well, it's spurring the counterculture on. Because the counterculture
has gone to the point where they're rejecting a good many of the
culture values the country holds now. And drugs happen to be one of
the things the current value system looks down on, and therefore the
counterculture is picking up on it. Maybe going on with it to emphasize
it. It's like you say, we can't have it but, here, here, we're going to do
it, a lot, because it's fun. It's an attention-getter for the culture.

Second Interview

Q. What part do you think drugs play in the counterculture or the differences between generations?

A. I think that it's definitely changing; making a bigger gap between the
generations, between people that do it, and people that don't do it. It's a
definite line being drawn and definite attitudes being developed. People
that take drugs think differently from people that don't, for the most
part. And it's a culture type thing, and there are changes because of it.

Q. Do you think it is a reactionary or a constructive thing?

A. I think it's going to be constructive, like, maybe when it gets down to
the new culture, maybe drugs won't be used that much because they
won't be needed. But they're needed now, in the basic things, to make
people become aware that they need a new way. Maybe once the
new way is here, drugs won't be needed anymore.

The following are excerpts from interviews of a member (twenty-
eight-year-old male, unemployed) and a peripheral member (twenty-five-
year-old female schoolteacher) of a tribal community in Coventry, Connecticut. They were done in the spring of 1968.

Chuck on the Topic of Drugs

After the Army I got a job, and a friend and I got an apartment. I smoked
a lot of grass and took a lot of acid, and I'd taken acid about three years
ago—between the time I left college and came back from New York and

studied art. Yeah, that's when I took my first acid trip, and I didn't dig it much. Then I took a couple more in there somewheres. It wasn't really till I got out of the Army that I started digging acid.

Q. Bad trips or something like that?

A. No, when I got out of the Army I started liking it and started taking a lot of it.

Q. Does it seem to have changed you?

A. I really don't think so. I don't. What it has done is sort of wiped out my past. My past doesn't matter to me anymore. I don't get hung up over my past anymore. At least I don't think I do. I sort of dropped everything that I'd clung to that had any value. I used to be fairly literate. I can't read anymore.

Q. Can't or won't.

A. Won't, won't. I'll sit down and try to read a book now and then. And I will read one, but it just doesn't get me up like it used to.

Q. Are there any other changes that are kind of noticeable?

A. Now, I have a little hope. For a long time, I was a bitter cat. I saw no hope for anything or for anyone. I figured everything was doomed. Now, I've got a little hope, and it makes me groove to myself a little more because I see a reason for myself being around. And the tribe has just made it such a beautiful experience to live and every day I'm just finding out more and more about myself and dropping a lot of the things that made me mad, that made me scared.

Irene on the Topic of Drugs

Very important was turning on because I'd always been inhibited and I had a great deal of difficulty making new friends. I'm usually very slow at it but when I started to turn on, I got a great deal more confidence.

Q. This is pot?

A. Yes,—I noticed that immediately, the first thing. It also relaxed me more, I was a very high-strung person. It tends to relax me more, as far as academics went. My record in school here—my first semester I did very poorly. Then two semesters after that I got only about twenty-five cubes or something like that. I was just all wound up. I couldn't study properly. Then I started turning on and since then I made the dean's list every time. I just unwound. I became more relaxed, I became more involved in other things. It introduced me to the whole world of music, which I had never really paid much attention to before.

Q. How often are you on the stuff?

A. On pot? Oh, I turn on at least once a day. I usually turn on on the way home from work.

Q. Are there aftereffects or while you're turned on can you do these things?

A. Now, I can do them both ways. It's perfectly normal. I can do it either way. Like I can function. I've gone to work stoned, I done things stoned like perfect normality.

Q. When did you start?
A. Four years ago, second semester of my sophomore year.
Q. What about LSD?
A. Yeah. I took my first trip that summer. I've taken about twenty-five or thirty.
Q. Has that made any big difference?
A. Yes—it, let's see, I don't consider it, er, I have an aversion to people who consider it a sacrament or a religious experience. Maybe I'm childish, I don't know. That's the impression I get from the "tribe" people, but I'm meeting a lot of new people now and they use their drugs like I do, to get high, usually. That's my first initial thing. I want to get high, I want to experience it. And quite a few times after taking trips I've had some very good experiences. I've learned something about myself and I've felt very calm and at peace with the world. I've had one really bad trip but I recovered from that immediately, because I realized what had caused it and I put myself back together, and quickly. See, all the trips I've taken have been with Sean (husband) and he usually ends up over at _____ getting thorazine. I never understood why he even bothered taking them if he was so frightened of them. And—the funny thing is, I've noticed recently, I've been thinking back about it, are the parts when I've left Sean and gone off by myself. I'm glad I've taken it. I don't regret anything.

The first three interviews rather graphically illustrate the process of slowly building alienation and distrust within users of illicit drugs. All four, especially the last one, suggest strong subjective benefits which are meaningful to the users. Allen and West (1968) have stated that there is a relationship between becoming a hippie and using drugs, and have even outlined four stages of progression toward hippiedom: dissatisfaction and impotence in dealing with society's demands, a search for personal meaning and relevancy, association with other searchers, and drug taking and dropping out of the competitive society.

On March 22, 1972, an official presidential commission reported on its year-long evaluation of marijuana laws and usage and recommended that **marijuana** be decriminalized. Decriminalization consists of maintaining the prohibition on marijuana commerce and production but allowing private usage. The drug itself would be considered contraband and could be confiscated by law-enforcement agents. The commission's recommendations reflect a melange of popular and political values, and are curiously ambivalent. If it becomes legal to possess marijuana privately, but not publicly, the likelihood of inequity before the law seems increased by this double standard. Furthermore, if it is legal to possess but not to buy or grow marijuana, how will it be possible to obtain it? Can the sale of a legal substance be illegal? The official government policy about marijuana has been so severe that the commission's attitude probably represents a step toward reducing generational conflict, but it has hardly been a bold or even a clear-cut step.

Since alcohol is officially sanctioned, it might be useful to consider some of its properties versus those of marijuana that are frequently mentioned by youthful marijuana users. Marijuana produces no harmful physical aftermath; alcohol carries a built-in punishment-hangover for heavy indulgers. Marijuana users frequently search for an intoxicated state, a high; whereas social drinkers flirt with such a "high," but more often attempt to control it. Long-term use of alcohol has self-destructive implications, while long-term effects of marijuana are unknown and presumed by users to be benign. Experienced smokers report that they can be "stoned" and still perform most of their daily activities. So, if these are real properties of the drug, it would be possible for marijuana pleasure seekers to be "high" on the job, to be drugged with no hang-overs, and actively to seek pleasurable alterations in their own conscious-ness without suffering from the experience. The idea that anyone can seek and obtain a gratifying pleasurable state, with little effort and few negative consequences, is difficult for an achieving society to accept. Grinspoon (1971) has suggested that the establishment's fear of mari-juana may be based on a fear that the motivation for socially useful work will be eroded by its use.

Another perspective on the generational conflict about marijuana might be gained by looking at patterns of use and possible meanings of use to the users. Marijuana is illegal, and users must be officially deviant since they are admitted lawbreakers. Keniston (1968–1969) has stated that young drug users are seeking an identity or seeking experiences to help them explore themselves, and that drug use is an accepted and normal (within the peer group) manner of doing this. So, they are deviant in one respect but ordinary in another. Deviance may be re-garded as an attempt to satisfy frustrated expectations, just as heroin use is likely to be associated with the frustration of poverty and inner-city life.

In an investigation of college student marijuana users, Dufresne (1972) found no evidence that frustrated expectations were associated with use. He did find that students who were adamant about not using marijuana were more traditional and more similar to their parents than users were. In another survey with 178 Connecticut students, Cross and Davis (1972) found that moderate marijuana use was not associated with self-reports of adjustment. The overall results of both these studies tend to support Keniston's hypothesis that marijuana use among the college population is not deviant.

The social phenomena of marijuana use and its illegality is a great issue between young and old. Communication difficulties, hypocrisy, and fear have prevented useful dialogue and legal reform. One of the major contributing factors to this conflict is that official government policy has failed to differentiate between different drugs and different patterns of use. Marijuana has been legally classed as a narcotic, and penalties for use have been as severe as they have for heroin, yet heroin is clearly a greater social problem. The failure of drug education programs is a related phenomenon, because drug education is commonly approached from the perspective of discouraging all drug use. When an "establishment" drug educator condemns marijuana and opiates in the same message, youths who are already using marijuana interpret what he says as propaganda. The relative success of former users as drug counselors may be partly attributable to their unique ability to discriminate both drugs and issues that the establishment cannot.

Two recent books, *Marihuana Reconsidered,* by Lester Grinspoon, and *Marijuana: The New Prohibition,* by John Kaplan, convincingly document that marijuana laws and their selective enforcement criminalize, radicalize, and serve to alienate thousands of young people every year. The response of the young to the pleasures of drugs and the fear and hatred of the old eventuate in many converts to counterculture. For a detailed description of the various drugs which are used today, the reader should turn to the chapter by Jalkanen on this topic.

The Message of the Counterculture

Of course, much of the message of the counterculture has been touched on in the preceding sections. In order to present this message, we must look realistically, without jaundice, at the mainstream society in order to recognize its faults. Perhaps we can assess why its own youth are evolving new and counter values. Several writers (Roszak, 1968; Reich, 1970; Slater, 1970) make the point that counterculture values are mirror-image values to the mainstream culture.

It seems to us that the current mainstream value which most broadly captures what the counterculture is fighting against is a kind of economic exploitation of people and resources. It might be called productive-consumerism, and it seems to lead to production and consumption at all costs. This ethic incorporates a lack of reverence for life and a glorification of industry and technology. The basis of this propensity to produce and consume comes from a deeply rooted economic premise labeled the "scarcity assumption" (Slater, 1970), i.e., there is a scarcity of goods needed to maintain a comfortable existence so that more must be produced.

People must be efficient workers and must be motivated to produce goods which will overcome the scarcity. The fear of hunger, discomfort, and even death which were once associated with scarcity of food and other staples, has lingered on, even though it is not relevant in a technologically advanced society.

The counterculture message which is the antithesis of productive consumerism is a rehumanization which places its major priorities on a glorification of life. Humanism and the fullest development of human potential is more important than work, efficiency, or production. Many slogans which had their origin in the counterculture, i.e., "make love, not war" and "celebrate life," reflect this humanism. Hedonistic drug intoxication and sexual pleasure are pursued with little thought to the responsibility with which they are invested by the dominant culture. In the counterculture, it is acceptable to get high and make love for the fun of it; whereas the dominant culture allows intoxicated states (alcohol induced) only if one accepts the responsibility of hangovers, and sex is supposedly confined to marital or at least committed partnership. Further manifestations of the humanistic counterculture focus may be seen in contemporary art, music, and even styles of dress.

The fullest development of human potential, enjoyment of life, and tolerance of human frailty are all parts of the counterculture message. One route to understanding this message is through the underground and quasi-underground press. There are a plethora of publications now that aim at promulgating counterculture values and presenting items of interest to counterculturists and their sympathizers. An unquestionably fine publication was the *Whole Earth Catalogue,* the brainchild of Steward Brand, one of the intellectuals of the movement and heroes of counterculturists on the West Coast. The *Whole Earth Catalogue* has inspired other publications, among them the *Mother Earth News,* published by John Shuttleworth.

Shuttleworth reflects the rehumanization message in stating the goal of his magazine in an interview format. The magazine is dedicated to two things: Giving people back their lives and stopping the rape of the planet.

Q. What do you mean by "giving people back their lives"?

A. Just that. I want everyone to be their own man—everybody to have control and direction of their own lives. Abraham Lincoln said it best. "Just as I would not be a slave, I will not have one." I want to be free; therefore I am interested in helping others be free.

Q. Everyone?

A. Everyone and everything. Black, white, red, brown, and yellow people. Men, women, children, animals, birds and fishes. Plants, every living thing. All life is sacred and of God. We've got to take the broadest possible view.*

Humanistic intent is perhaps also apparent in the statement released by the yippies at the Chicago Democratic Convention of 1968. Some of the demands have been taken over by congressmen, and there is discernible movement toward many points. We present the demands here because of our construction of them (most of them!) as relatively representative of the counterculture message, even though they were issued by the most active of the activists.

1. An immediate end to the war in Vietnam and a restructuring of our foreign policy which totally eliminates aspects of military, economic, and cultural imperialism. The withdrawal of all foreign based troops and the abolition of the military draft.

2. Immediate freedom of Huey Newton of the Black Panthers and all other black people. Adoption of the community control concept in our ghetto areas. An end to the cultural and economic domination of minority groups.

3. A prison system based on the concept of rehabilitation rather than punishment.

4. A judicial system which works toward the abolition of all laws related to crimes without victims. That is, retention only of laws relating to crimes in which there is an unwilling injured party, i.e., murder, rape, assault.

5. The total disarmament of all the people beginning with the police. This includes not only guns, but such brutal devices as tear gas, MACE, electric prods, blackjacks, billy clubs, and the like.

6. The abolition of money. The abolition of pay housing, pay media, pay transportation, pay food, pay education, pay clothing, pay medical help, and pay toilets.

7. A society which works toward and actively promotes the concept of "full-employment." A society in which people are free from drudgery of work. Adoption of the concept "Let the machines do it."

8. A conservation program geared towards preserving our natural resources and committed to the elimination of pollution from our air and water.

9. A program of ecological development that will provide incen-

* *The Mother Earth News,* 1970, No. 2, p. 6. Used by permission.

tives for the decentralization of our crowded cities and encourage rural living.

10. A program which provides not only free birth control information and devices but also abortions when desired.

11. A restructured educational system which provides the student power to determine his course of study and allows for student participation in over-all policy planning. Also, an educational system which breaks down its barriers between school and community. A system which uses the surrounding community so that students may learn directly the problems of the people.

12. The open and free use of the media. A program which actively supports and promotes cable television as a method of increasing the selection of channels available to the viewer.

13. An end to all censorship. We are sick of a society which has no hesitation about showing people committing violence and refuses to show a couple fucking.

14. We believe that people should fuck all the time, anytime, whomever they wish. This is not a program demand but a simple recognition of the reality around us.

15. A political system which is more streamlined and responsive to the needs of all the people regardless of age, sex or race. Perhaps a national referendum system conducted via television or a telephone voting system. Perhaps a decentralization of power and authority with many varied tribal groups. Groups in which people exist in a state of basic trust and are free to choose their tribe.

16. A program that encourages and promotes the arts. However, we feel that if the Free Society we envision were to be fought for and achieved, all of us would actualize the creativity within us. In a very real sense we would have a society in which every man would be an artist.*

We recognize that it may be repetitious for these several counterculture spokesmen to speak their version of the message, and we will close this section with two final statements of members of Brotherhood of the Spirit, a commune in Northfield, Massachusetts. They were answering a question about the purpose of their community's existence:

"To teach men how to express goodwill to one another; that the earth once again be resplendent with the flowers of: order, balance, harmony, growth, spiritual love, god-perception, and the greatest of all these—compassion."

A twelve-year-old member of the same community in answer to the same question said simply, "We want to save the world."

Counterculture Values: Some Research Studies

A group of inventive social scientists (Rappaport, Bernstein, Hogan, Kane, Plunk, and Sholder, 1970) at the University of Illinois compared people from a communal living center with fraternity and sorority members. All the subjects were Illinois undergraduates, but twenty-four of them had chosen to live communally, sharing work, responsibility, and sex.

The two groups rated sixteen concepts on semantic differential scales. The concepts were chosen to reflect congruence with traditional values, or the opposite. The fraternity-sorority were significantly more favorable on *corporation, profit, contest, security* than were the commune members. They were significantly more unfavorable on the nontradition congruent concepts—*extreme, revolution, communal, sharing, collective* —than were the commune members.

When the two groups were compared on whether or not they would choose to be cooperative or competitive in a competitive game situation, significantly more of the commune members ($p < .005$) chose cooperation. The addition of a cash reward made no difference in whether or not commune members would be cooperative, but money tended to make fraternity-sorority members more competitive.

There has been one investigation (Cross, Doost, and Tracy, 1970) which attempted to define value differences between a group of hippies who had dropped out of the academic community and a group of middle-class students. The hippies lived communally, called themselves hippies, and referred to their group as "the tribe." They were matched in age with a group of students who were pursuing degrees and both groups were given the Rokeach value scale (1969). The scale consists of eighteen alphabetically arranged terminal values presented on one page, and eighteen instrumental values presented on another. Terminal values refer to ends, e.g., a comfortable life, a world of peace; whereas instrumental values refer to means, e.g., ambitious, broadminded, capable. The subject is instructed to rank the values in order of their importance as guiding principles in his life. Each value is on a gummed label with a short definition in parentheses. The subject's task is to peel it off, place it in box 1, find the next most important value, place it in box 2, etc., until he has ranked all values. The labels are easily movable and rearrangeable should the subject change his mind.

The hippies valued the end state of inner harmony more than any other terminal value. After inner harmony, they regard wisdom, freedom, world of peace, mature love, equality, and beauty as most worthwhile. Least worthwhile were national security, salvation, social recognition, a comfortable life, pleasure, a sense of accomplishment, an exciting life, family security, and self-respect. Hippies were significantly higher than students on end states of inner harmony, wisdom, world of peace, and world of beauty; whereas students valued self-respect, family security, sense of accomplishment, and national security significantly higher.

On instrumental values, the hippies ranked honest and forgiving significantly higher than the students, while the students ranked responsible, intellectual, capable, logical, and ambitious significantly higher than the hippies. Hippies were also more homogeneous in their rankings than students. The students' most valued end states are seen as rather conventional and traditional, while their strong instrumental values are all related to achievement. The hippies seem to be more humanistic and less standard oriented. The difference in the achievement-related cluster, plus the hippies' higher rankings of honesty and forgiveness, are consonant with their dislike of academic values. It could be that the hippies represent an extreme reaction to many faults of the multiversity. What many young people complain about in the institution is precisely what the hippies drop out of and get away from.

One of the major concerns of the counter vis-à-vis the dominant culture revolves around trust and honesty. Haley (1969) relates an anecdote about a hippie hitchhiker who offered a joint to the driver who had picked him up. When questioned about the possibility that the driver could be a narcotics agent, the hippie replied that the trust between them was more important than what could happen to him from violation of drug laws. That is, trust is more important than the protection of one's own welfare. This kind of true altruism is representative of the humanistic ethic of the counterculture.

Rotter (1967) has studied trusting behavior of college students since 1964 with a scale designed to assess interpersonal trust. One of his major findings, with large numbers of subjects, was that levels of trust are sharply declining. With five different samples, totaling over 2700 cases, interpersonal trust scores declined every year in a strongly significant drop. If this is a true finding, then either the youthful counterculture comprises an extremely small part of the college population or openness and trust are not part of the youth movement. Neither proposition is true, as shown in an inventive dissertation by Roberts (1970), who reanalyzed all the previously gathered trust data into items that purportedly assessed interpersonal trust (between peers) and political trust (in institutions). The political trust subscale appears to assess trust (or in this case, distrust) in the U.N., the judiciary, news media, big-time sports contests, international politics, and public officials. Roberts' re-analysis shows clearly that trust in peers has not declined between 1964 and 1970, but trust in these institutions has plummeted. The most obvious interpretation is that college students have become strongly critical of society's institutions.

Counterculture Adjustment Patterns

We believe that there are three patterns of coping with the dominant culture's demands which are seen in individual youths in the countercul-ture. Just as Yablonsky had difficulty classifying counterculture types, we feel that these patterns are not always mutually exclusive. Nevertheless, we believe they are sufficiently general to talk about.

Individual Mechanisms of Adjustment

Escapism. One frequently seen pattern is escapism. Many youths use the counterculture to escape from demands of parents, mates, social norms, etc., with which they cannot effectively cope. It seems easier to "drop out" than to maintain financial solvency enough to eventually pay the mort-gage, the pediatricians, and the fuel bill, and to achieve upward social mobility in the meantime. The escape may take the form of removing oneself physically from the demanding environment, or removing oneself psychologically via changing belief systems, or drugs. Escapism has been discussed so frequently (Yablonsky, 1968; Weakland, 1969) that we need do little more than recognize it exists. Some adjustment data on heavy drug users (Mirin, 1970) suggests strongly that there is an escapism factor operating in their continued and heavy consciousness alteration.

Psychopathology. The individual youthful pattern, which we believe exists, we will label *traditional psychopathology*. By this we mean that there are many counterculture youths who might be classed within one of the traditional psychiatric categories if they were subject to diagnosis (see Yablonsky, 1968). For example, we have talked with individuals who manifested several "classical" schizophrenic symptoms; from loose associa-tions to bizarre thought patterns that seem like delusions. Some of the more extreme counterculture groups find it much easier to accept odd and eccentric individuals than do most mainstream society communities at this point in time. There are few systematic data on adjustment among counterculturists from a more traditional point of view. Smart and Jones (1970) found that heavy drug users (who were very likely Yorkville hippies) show up on the MMPI as more emotionally isolated and to be more likely to think bizarre thoughts than did a sample from Ontario schools and colleges.

Whittaker and Watts (1969) were able to get 151 "street people" in Berkeley to take the Omnibus Personality Inventory. They were compared with a sample of students at the University of California, Berkeley. The street people were higher on aestheticism, complexity, autonomy, impulse expression, and lower on personal integration. Scale patterns analyses suggested that approximately 10 percent of the street people were hostile, rebellious, and withdrawn enough to be considered as socially maladjusted. Another 10 percent were socially aggressive, anxious, and rebellious enough to be classed as "angry young men." Another 20 percent were extremely impulsive and showed a propensity to pursue "deviant activities." The authors stressed that these patterns should not be interpreted as psychopathological, but as indicative of "normal" alienation. Whittaker and Watts seem uncomfortable in labeling their hippie subjects as more maladjusted than students, but they do point to a fairly consistent set of trends.

Consciousness. Another youthful adjustment mechanism we will call adaptive change in consciousness. Various of the patterns which we have classed under "traditional psychopathology" might be considered changes in consciousness, but they are less easily defined as adaptive. An adaptive change in consciousness is more flexible than a change that merely permits adjustment, and there should be a subjective feeling of at least moderate satisfaction. Reich (1970), in a most provocative book, *The Greening of America,* speaks of three different types of consciousness which are the dominant thought patterns of society.

Consciousness I is the most traditional; it is committed to defensive individuality, believes hard work is the key to success, and that moral virtue is its own reward. Further, human weakness and deviation from the norm can be trained away if the strong are stern enough and certain enough of their position. It is a state of mind that served America well when it was an underdeveloped nation, needing pioneer spirit.

Consciousness II follows the thinking of the New Deal Democrat. Present social ills will be ameliorated by greater commitment of individuals to the public good. There is a belief in the usefulness of society's institutions, and an individual subordinates himself to the good of all through committing himself to the institution. Consciousness II is the consciousness of most professionals, whose achievements have come from meritorious service. Meritocracy is perhaps the best single descriptive term for the kind of society to which Consciousness II leads.

Consciousness III is the most recently evolved state of mind, which is held mainly by the young in our society. It is a consciousness devoted to responsibility to self, to an enjoyment of whatever one is doing, and a sharing with one's fellows. It reacts against alienation from self and from others by focusing on the worth of every human being, self included.

Consciousness III does not measure others or compete with them, but it accepts them because there are enough commodities in the world for all; therefore, competition is meaningless. The world is a community and all men are brothers, so that no one should ever manipulate, coerce, or force anyone else to do anything. Reich speculates that Consciousness III has evolved because of the contradiction of the promise of the good life, the American dream, and the dissonant threat of urban blight and a cancerous war which precludes the good life. These opposing promises, so to speak, are continually presented by the mass media, and it is reasonable to believe that their juxtaposition arouses questions which become disquieting and are not easily answered. Finally, a nagging sense of discomfort results in the belief that something is basically wrong, and the prospect of being part of such a system is not attractive.

A change in consciousness such as this probably has some elements in common with achieving insight in some psychotherapies and enlightenment in some religions. It may also have some elements in common with the natural high that former "heads" describe that they can attain through meditation. We cannot adequately detail this change in consciousness, for it is probably never quite the same in any two people. For some, it approaches the power of seeing the entire world on a theretofore undiscovered dimension (see, for example the description of Baba Ram Dass's enlightenment told by Houriet, 1971). For others, it is probably closer to a decision like changing one's occupation, or deciding to embark on an adventure.

The change of consciousness has great adaptive value because it allows the individuals who achieve it a flexibility and possibility of varied life styles that have survival value.

Counterculture Institutions

Perhaps the best way of judging a culture is by the institutions it evolves. We are fully aware of our grandiosity in suggesting what these are, but still offer some that we think are important: sensitivity to and appreciation of other people's individuality, honest business ethics, rock music, supernaturalism, group marriage, free schools, and communes.

We think that one of the major positive features of the counterculture is the trend toward appreciating individuality. One of the most difficult of man's cosmic problems has been communicating with other men and finding someone outside himself with whom to communicate. One of the effects of the counterculture has been to revive the humanistic focus.

Anti Rip-off. We have already talked about honesty and trust as being part of the counterculture philosophy. This "anti rip-off" ethic (*rip off* means "to steal or exploit"), as we will call it, seems to exist along with recognition that everyday business ethics are exploitative and tend toward being mercenary and dishonest. There is a good deal of genuine trust and fair dealing in the counterculture, especially between those who seem hip by their appearance. The value of money is different in the counterculture. Jerry Rubin and friends once caused a furor by distributing dollar bills at the New York Stock Exchange. Many counterculture publications have a unique policy towards ads, for example. *The Whole Earth Catalogue* printed no ads but is a collection of items which the editors deem useful—at no cost to the manufacturers of the items! *The Mother Earth News* occasionally publishes a free "plug" for a merchant who is deemed to be honest. This kind of economic friendliness has been seen frequently, but does not always extend to business institutions. For example, the following ad from the *Last Supplement to the Whole Earth Catalogue* (1971, p. 126) illustrates one well-known counterculturist's dislike for banks:

> I want to sell my house in La Honda, a great house and five acres of redwoods seven miles from the ocean. It'd be nice to do it straight across without the banks getting a finger in it. You can take a look at it by asking anybody in La Honda, and call me in Oregon if you're interested. It'd make a fine boy scout camp or home, complete with creek, trees, and memories [name and phone number given].

There are many members of the counterculture, however, who regard stealing from the establishment as entirely acceptable. Ripping off the establishment is viewed as "liberating" goods and is justified by the argument that by liberating merchandise the exploitative profit system is aborted in midstream. We have no quantitative data but know of hippie shoplifters whose particular targets are supermarkets. One twenty-two-year-old dropout city dweller describes his mealtime as entering a large supermarket, shopping for one or two items to take out, and eating everything he could while in the store. He had survived for over a year with no other source of livelihood. So, while the anti rip-off ethic is strong and seems to be a necessary counterweight to the pervasive profit motive of the dominant culture, there is considerable theft within the counterculture.

Rock Music. This music so completely occupies many youths and it has so strongly influenced the dominant society that we will regard it as a counterculture institution. It seems to have two real attractions: It encourages the flaunting of forbidden content, particularly about sex and drugs, and it allows dramatic social protest. Although young people do not always attend to the profundity of the message of their music (Robinson and Hirsh, 1969), it is frequently profound enough to arouse one's social conscience when played over and over. James T. Carey (1969) studied rock lyrics and concluded that they generally state that the listener should think for himself, that the choice is for him to maximize his freedom, or drop out of a society that is impersonal and resists change.

Rock music is the medium through which young people air their grievances and praise the way things might have been. There are many artists and groups which are really important to listen to in order to understand the youth culture. Friedenberg (1969) mentions the following as examples of high art: Bob Dylan, The Beatles, Simon and Garfunkel, Donovan, and Jefferson Airplane. As low art, he offered the Mothers of Invention and the Rolling Stones. We would like to add Crosby, Stills, Nash and Young to the former category and the Doors to the latter.

Many of the individual artists are genuinely idealized and, in fact, are the most likely cultural heroes generated by young people. The generations polarize quickly around rock, for the older agents of the dominant culture see it as obscene and decadent; while the counterculture seems to especially enjoy these aspects. The Federal Communication Commission and other regulatory agencies have ruled that pieces referring to drug use may not be broadcast. Such a regulation is difficult to enforce because of the enormous number of drug-related pieces, and the fact that the lyrics are in the street argot which is not understood by enforcement agents.

The rock festival was a short-lived institution with which the counterculture displayed and reveled in its life style. Great crowds of young people gathered to experience each other's company, listen to the music, and flout the drug laws. A great many municipalities and some states have legislated against any large gathering so that rock festivals are now difficult to stage. Rock concerts, however, continue to draw overflow crowds, and the music industry seems to be growing at a faster pace than most of America's economy.

Supernaturalism. Another counterculture institution is a new appreciation for supernatural-mystical explanations. We will call it transrationality, for it seems to transcend rational thought. The current popularity of mysticism goes far beyond the counterculture, but much of the impetus has come from the amulet-wearing, astrology-conscious hippies. The dominant culture used science and technology to become a coldly efficient operation which alienates many of its members. Science has become so intimately associated with technocratic control (computer-filled dossiers, wire taps, etc.) that it has become an object of scorn. Rational thought has led us to the moon but has not helped to eradicate racism, or urban blight. Roszak (1968) states that objective consciousness is a myth that has a peculiar power over those who believe in it. Our scientific world has taught that the only knowledge, the only reality, is arrived at by objectivity. Maintaining objectivity necessitates being free of subjectivity, and even being coldly removed and uninvolved. One must conceptualize and not experience.

Counterculture transrationality goes in the opposite direction. It laughs at objectivity and resists conceptualization in favor of feeling and experience. Experiencing is accepted without the necessity of typing or rational labels. Meaning does not depend on verifiability but upon unexplainable "grocking," "grooving," or "digging," which are all roughly translatable as understanding and liking. Just as rationality was the watchword for the dominant culture, karma has become important to the counterculture. Transrationality is much more flexible than the well-worn rationality because, by its very nature, it does not have to be related to specifics. Indeed, it puts suspicion on the process of specifying itself. The spirituality in Eastern religions has become quite attractive, as well as a general pantheism, and lately a return to a kind of hip fundamentalism. The popular press has recently chronicled the story of thousands of "Jesus-freaks," who are preaching salvation with a Jerry Rubin appearance but a Billy Graham text. Most cities now have some kind of community center whose major function is emergency aid from bad drug trips to saving confused runaways. At almost any of these centers, some of the staff will be Jesus-freaks, proselytizers of hip Christianity.

Mystical experiences have a major function in common with intense drug experiences, which frequently play a part in conversion from dominant culture attitudes; that is, "blowing one's mind," or "burning out the circuits" of the old way of thinking. A strong experience which is outside the realm of explanation of science, say a vision of oneself reincarnated or a communication with God, has the effect of making it unrewarding to return to the former mode of thought. Often this comes with LSD. Just as real acid would burn out electrical circuits of solder and wire, "acid" can burn out memory circuits of old ways of life.

Many theorists have argued that people construe reality in whatever way meets their needs. We maintain that the dominant culture legitimizes a mode of construction that is overly analytic, reductionistic, formally logical, and structurally rigid. McLuhan (1967) has said that this mode of organizing reality is based on a linear manipulation of abstract concepts.

The counterculture, on the other hand, has the flexibility to accept new modes of construing reality without being bound by the dominant culture. To date, it has evolved several modes, all of which tend to be experiential rather than conceptual; wholistic rather than reductionistic; multilinear rather than linear; and immediate rather than goal-oriented. Since it is the least powerful of the two cultures, the counterculture cannot lay claim to the legitimizing symbol of "rational" for its modes of construction.

However, counterculturists never seem to tire of pointing out examples of insanely absurd behavior based on the rational premises of the dominant culture. For example, destroying a Vietnamese village by artillery bombardment in order to "save" it, might be contrasted to a spontaneous gathering of hippies celebrating the spring equinox. If the destruction of the village is based on rational premises while the equinox "happening" is irrational, perhaps a reevaluation of the concept is in order. The importance of one's mode of constructing reality lies in its survival value. While we cannot be sure about the survival value of counterculture modes, there seems to be ample evidence that the dominant culture mode has lost considerable survival value. One critic (Slater, 1970) suggests that it has within it the seeds of destruction of life on this planet. Transrationality, pantheism, Zen, or hip Christianity seem particularly adaptive at this time for the counterculture.

Sex and Marriage. Intimacy between people, sex included, is one of the enduring problems of all societies, but it seems to have evolved in a particularly maladaptive pattern in American society. If we are indeed a nation of individualists (Slater, 1970), we express it nowhere better than with our interpersonal-sexual behavior. The yippie manifesto at Chicago recognized the sexual nature of human beings, as well as their reaction to society's unrealistic demands. One of the dominant culture's institutions that seems under the greatest strain is marriage (Mead, 1971). Marriage is certainly not unpopular, but is simply not as necessary as it once was. While young women (women are the guardians of morality) are only slightly more promiscuous then they were a decade ago, they are considerably more likely to form out-of-wedlock sexual alliances (Reiss, 1967; D'Augelli, 1971). Furthermore, divorce no longer contains the same stigma of maladjustment, and the real difficulties of long-term marital dyads are being openly questioned (Mead, 1971). The women's liberation movement has contributed to young people's examination of the desirability of dyadic marriages.

Larry and Joan Constantine (1970a, 1970b) have provocatively outlined some of the difficulties of group marriages. They believe that groups larger than six adults are unlikely to become real intimate marriages and that communal living is not always marital. Agreements, contracts, and rules between a complex network of adults, all married to each other, must be in constant flux and, therefore, tend toward instability. Half of the groups studied by the Constantines broke up during the first year. Houriet (1971) reports in detail on Harrad West, a six-member group marriage in an upper-middle-class section of Berkeley, California. Harrad West is obviously named after Rimmer's *The Harrad Experiment* (1967) and is patterned on his idea of polygamy as a route to full self-acceptance. Harrad West owns an eight-bedroom Tudor colonial, where all have separate bedrooms except one couple. In addition to the six adults there are three children. Partners shift around according to a schedule, much as the household chores are divided up. Members maintain separate incomes and property, but share expenses, which gives them quite an economic advantage over people living noncommunally. Harrad has survived for about a year and a half now, even though it is illegal in California and is beset with internal problems. That is, all the members do not get along with one another. They remain engaged in an ongoing therapy group, both for self-understanding and aiding with group problems. As another visitor (Joy Francoeur, 1970) to their group remarked: "These people don't just sit around and hope their group marriage will work, they work at making it work."

It is impossible to determine what the ultimate social importance of group marriages may be, but they will surely continue to attract a great deal of interest and attention.

Communes. These groups represent an extreme counterculture reaction in the sense that they are an absolute alternative life style to that of the dominant culture. While other counterculture institutions are separate on one or two dimensions, communes are separate on several. We cannot generalize about all of them, but most are communal in the sense that work and property are actually shared and there is close interaction between members. The characteristically American intense individuality is, therefore, incompatible with communal living.

In the last six years, approximately 2,500 communal living groups were founded (Houriet, 1971). They were predominately isolated, rural, small, and relatively unstable in membership. Great impetus was given to "getting back to the land" in the mid-sixties, especially in San Francisco's Haight and other urban hippie colonies where street people began to feel that their movement was being soured by tourists, aggressive motorcyclists, insincere thrill seekers, and police harassment. *Getting Back Together* (Houriet, 1971) involves getting closer to nature and away from urban conflict.

Communes have had varying degrees of success. It is probably fair to state that a beginning group has a 50–50 chance of survival, but a group that makes it past two years should have worked out most growing pains. There are some communities that have been in existence for decades and appear to be really permanent. Houriet (1971) makes a distinction between communes and communities. The former are composed mainly of hip young people who are strongly identified with the hedonistic subculture of drugs and rock, and who are usually anticapitalistic. Their government tends to be laissez-faire, and they generally have little focus other than trying to achieve a life style that is different from the dominant society.

Communities, on the other hand, tend to be more specifically organized around a craft, art, or religion and attract a more diverse group of people than the hip young. More elaborate rule structure is likely, and, of course, they are more stable. Some communes have developed a specific purpose and have made the transition to communities. Many communes have gone through open-ended phases where they accepted all prospective members and lived in relative anarchy, with dangerous conflicts and competition between members. Some broke up, and others managed to weather difficult periods and even develop the specific purpose needed to unite and strengthen them. One sociologist (Kanter, 1970) has made an analysis of successful nineteenth-century communes and concluded that group commitment is the single most crucial element of a commune's longevity. Commitment is shown by signing over all personal property at joining, group rituals, and shared labor. Modern communes frequently make decisions via group meetings, and most hold periodic encounter sessions to reduce intragroup conflicts.

A great number of communes seem to be founded around the striving for intimacy and sharing that has received a great deal of impetus from the human potential movement. Many T-group leaders live in communes, and several communes are composed of human relations consultants who market their talent as group leaders. The linkage between the human potential movement and communal living is that both are counter to the dominant culture in striving to transcend the defensive individuality so characteristic of Americans.

A community with which we are most familiar is the Brotherhood of the Spirit of Northfield, Massachusetts. It is one of the most successful of modern communes. Its leader and founder is Michael Metalica, a twenty-one-year-old high school dropout who thought that he was odd and crazy throughout his childhood. He revamped his ideas of self-esteem after meeting Elwood Babbit, a local medium and follower of Edgar Cayce, who convinced Michael that his visions and strange thoughts were supernormal rather than abnormal. By this time Michael, who lived in a tree house and worked for local farmers without pay, had attracted half a dozen or so compatriots who decided to found a commune. Their early history was rough indeed, but they now number over 250 members and in four years have acquired two large homes, one three-story dormitory, and seem to be gaining strength every day. They encourage visitors and attempt to preach their message of brotherhood and spiritual enlightenment to whomever will listen. Although they have suspended the admission of new members from time to time, their policy is to turn no one away if he seems earnest. A prospective member's commitment is determined by a two-month living-in period. At being admitted, which occurs if the community has no objection that is voiced in a group meeting, the prospect commits all his property to the group. Perhaps the most unusual thing about the brotherhood is the organization around their religion and their total commitment to it, plus a tolerance for those who have not fully understood or fully accepted the spiritual laws.

Members of the brotherhod believe that they must follow seven "immutable laws of the universe," which were revealed to them by Elwood Babbit in full trance. The laws deal with order, balance, harmony, growth, and growth of the universe; as well as with God perception, spiritual love, and compassion. Brothers believe that they must master these laws, which correspond to seven energy centers of the body, mind, and spirit, even if it takes several lifetimes—hence they believe in reincarnation. The notion of reincarnation focuses on the spirit of the members and gets their attention away from their carnal selves. A good deal of the activity within the community involves talking about spiritual communication, former lives, the spiritual negativity of the dominant culture, and related issues. Most visitors who take the time to listen earnestly to brotherhood members are impressed with their immersion and involvement in their beliefs. Ironclad laws forbid drugs, alcohol, tobacco, and sexual promiscuity, thus emphasizing the society's spiritual focus.

Considered on the dimensions of a group versus individual commitment, spiritual versus carnal emphasis, simple poverty versus property, and brotherhood versus competition, the Brotherhood of the Spirit is thoroughly distinct from the dominant culture. Members believe that they are destined to save the world from selfish carnality and negativity, and to help others attain the seven immutable laws of the universe, culminating in compassion and love.

Educational Institutions. One counterculture response to the establishment system is the counterculture educational institutions. Free schools and colleges have sprung up all over the nation, and many have lasted four or five years now. Much impetus has come from youth's reaction to the dominant culture's influencing agents, i.e., its educational institutions. Critics of the educational system have detailed so many faults that it seems hardly necessary to recap them here. A few of the most trenchant critics are Paul Goodman, Edgar Z. Friedenberg, John Holt, Kenneth Keniston, Ivan Illich, and A. S. Nell. The criticisms most frequently center around schools and colleges' training toward consumerism, conformity, and supplying the labor and leaders to continue ongoing economic institutions—all at a cost of neglecting emotional and social development of young people. In other words, society's schools treat young people as if they had no voice, rights, aims, or intentions worth listening to, and, most of all, as if they had no feelings.

Free schools have existed for decades but have never really been part of the counterculture as they are now. Even Summerhill, the most famous of all, was antiestablishment only in a traditional educational sense. Many of today's free schools are staffed by people who have alternative ideas about life, not just education. One good example of a counterculturist educator is Jerry Friedberg, who with seven others organized the Lorillard Children's School. The founders had studied education together for two years, and wished to apply their innovative ideas. They meshed with a parents' group who had run a day camp and nursery school and found space in a local church. Staff size grew to fourteen, and they started with thirty-three children three to seven years old. They developed a child-centered program with its major focus on personal growth, honest communication, and noncoercive persuasion. Learning emerged spontaneously, and they were able to do without stated rules, schedules, assignments, or work rotations. The free atmosphere was conducive to personal growth of both students and staff. The disquieting idea for some of the staff was the unsettled question of whether they were doing enough—discharging their responsibility. Evidently they were, for Lorillard prospered and became a model free school. Friedberg and three others of his staff, however, felt that removing children from adults and placing them in specialized environments to educate them was less desirable than educating them in their community, and so they started an educational community. Their Arrakis commune has been relatively successful as a learning center, Gestalt therapy influence group, and alternate life style influence group.

We shall relate the story of a visit to one other free school by quoting from the journal of Joy Francoeur, a Connecticut student who traveled over the country visiting communes and schools:

> The name of the school was New Directions Community School, and it's located in Richmond, California. The school is pretty small; it has approximately 30 students in grades 7 thru 12. Classes average about 5 students. And, school policy is made twice weekly at meetings of all the students—as one of their pamphlets states "since students started the school

it was only natural that they should run it." We wandered around in the school for an afternoon; no one was uptight at all. We sat in on one of their classes on primitive weaving—it was really interesting. It sure was better than the typical home economics sewing classes in most high schools where everyone learns to make a skirt that looks like everyone else's skirt. Some of the other courses that are taught there and differ a little from those taught in most high schools are the following: ceramics, jewelry, leather work, photography, ecology, community organizing and new politics, encounter groups, black literature, modern protest novels, film-making, Chicano history, Black history, Black Panther party, model cities and city planning, Japanese language and culture, jug band, guitar, violin, and women's liberation. Plus, they teach all the typical subjects that are taught in most diploma high schools to seniors; however, they are not accredited. I really dug this school and realized how healthy the freedom was that they allowed their students. When I think back on all the time I wasted on some of the crap I took in high school, and then think of how much happier I would be now if I knew how to play jug band or create some really wild jewelry. Harry was in complete ecstasy at the school; he just had this look all over his face that said "Wow, I want to be a kid again and go to a school like this. The kids in this school also spent a lot of time in encounter groups, group therapy, one to one counseling, etc. In other words, the school helps the kids put their heads together instead of fucking them up. (At least that's my opinion, I'm sure the majority of American parents wouldn't agree.) I'm really serious, I think if I had a kid I'd send him to a school like this."*

Both her description of the school and her comparison to her own school experience are instructive.

Experimental colleges and free universities are most often staffed by graduate students and undergraduates from nearby colleges. The students generally come from the same nearby colleges. The curriculums are almost entirely composed of revolutionary interpretations of history and economics, humanistic psychology, existential philosophy, various types of sensitivity groups, astrology, and drugs. There are no requirements, grades, credits, or degrees. People study because they are interested, and the teachers teach for the same reason. It is little wonder that both teachers and students seem to enjoy their roles. Traditional universities frequently seem to be exactly the opposite, in that neither teacher nor students are interested, and only requirements, credits, and degrees keep them working.

A dominant culture compromise with the free university has incorporated some free university elements, such as student autonomy and

---

* J. Francoeur. Personal journal written for the Inner College. Unpublished manuscripts, University of Connecticut, 1970. Used by permission.

more "relevant" courses, into flexible educational programs within the traditional institution. The University of Connecticut Inner College program, for example, has now graduated seventeen students, all of whom were able to determine their own course of study to some extent. Like most attempts at alternative approaches to education within the traditional educational structure, the Inner College has been forced to walk the fine line between servility and loss of accreditation. Although many concessions to the norms of the established institution have been forced upon the Inner College, students in the program have the opportunity to learn in ways that are not usually open to regular undergraduates.

Experiments such as the Inner College serve two main functions. From the perspective of the educational establishment, they serve as a pressure relief valve. They channel the energies of disaffected students into marginally acceptable avenues of learning. From the standpoint of the counterculture, they offer a semilegitimized route of escape from the demands of the dominant culture. They are islands of free territory within the confines of the larger institution. Only time will tell whether or not these experiments will lead to real changes or to the siphoning off of energy for educational reform.

Summary

Our presentation has largely focused on the adaptive value and positive factors of counterculture institutions. There have also been rather ominous trends toward violence, some of which, e.g., the Weathermen, are representative of counterculture extremists. Violent deaths, apparently from heroin, have come to Janis Joplin and Jimi Hendrix, two of rock music's greatest artists. The tendency for transrationality to shade over into black magic and satanism (Vachon, 1971) seems to be a return to fear and ignorance, which are hardly useful. We cannot present all the faults of the counterculture, but can point out that its mechanisms break down in some cases, and are clearly maladaptive in others.

The counterculture has brought many new trends to the dominant society. Personal styles of appearance, recreation, sex, child-rearing, and education seem particularly affected. In fact, almost every facet of the mainstream society has been affected in some way by counterculture adjustment mechanisms. The alternative life styles presented by the counterculture are being attended to, and some changes are therefore occurring in the dominant culture.

The counterculture is serving to change emphases and priorities of many talented young people, so that fewer are being attracted by business and technological occupations, and more are entering social sciences and applied fields. At most colleges, sociology and psychology courses are booming in popularity, as are fine arts and the humanities. Fewer of the very best students, however, are going into business and the physical sciences.

Berger and Berger (1971), in a provocative paper entitled "The Blueing of America," suggest that business, government, and technical occupations will be filled by the newly educated children of the blue-collar working class. If the Bergers' analysis is correct, the counterculture will continue to grow at small cost in personnel to the technocracy. Its major impact will continue to be psychological.

As Reich (1970) has suggested, we believe that the counterculture's major adjustment mechanism represents a change in awareness of young peoples' modes of construing their world: involvement, as well as changed awareness, in the prescription to overcome the pathological alienation of the dominant culture.

The counterculture looks so diverse and inconsistent at this early stage because it represents the initial attempts of individuals to adjust to different dimensions of their alienation. Some are focusing on personal growth, trying to cure alienation from self; others on social action, trying to cure alienation from other men; and, finally, on environmental action, trying to change man's exploitative relationship with his physical environment. What it will become in the future we shall have to wait to see.

REFERENCES

Allen, J. R., and West, L. I. Flight from violence: Hippies and the green rebellion. *American Journal of Psychiatry,* 1968, *125,* 364–370.

Berger, B. M. Hippie morality, more old than new. *Trans-action,* 1967, *5,* 19–27.

Berger, P. and Berger, B. The blueing of America. *Intellectual Digest,* 1971, *2,* 25–27.

Carey, J. T. The ideology of autonomy in popular lyrics: A content analysis. *Psychiatry,* 1969, *32,* 150–164.

Constantine, L., and Constantine, J. How to make group marriage. *The Modern Utopian,* 1970, *4,* 33–37. (a)

———, and Constantine, J. Where is marriage going? *The Futurist,* 1970, *4,* 44–45. (b)

Cross, H. J., Doost, R. M., and Tracy, J. J. A study of values among hippies. *Proceedings of the 78th Annual Convention, American Psychological Association,* 1970, 449–450.

————, and Davis, G. L. College students' adjustment and frequency of marijuana use. *Journal of Counseling Psychology*, 1972, *19*, 65–67.

D'Augelli, J. *Moral reasoning, sex-guilt, sexual attitudes, and parental behaviors as related to women's premarital sexual behavior.* Unpublished master's thesis, University of Connecticut, 1971.

Davis, F. Why all of us may be hippies someday. *Trans-action*, 1967, *5*, 10–18.

————, and Munoz, L. Heads and freaks: Patterns and meanings of drug use among hippies. *Journal of Health and Social Behavior*, 1968, *9*, 156–163.

Dufresne, J. *On the applicability of the deviance hypothesis to student drug use.* Unpublished master's thesis, University of Connecticut, 1972.

Francoeur, J. Personal journal written for the Inner College. Unpublished manuscripts, University of Connecticut, 1970.

Friedberg, J. Beyond free schools: Community. *The Mother Earth News*, No. 6, Nov. 1970, 82–86.

Friedenberg, E. Z. Current patterns of generational conflict. *Journal of Social Issues*, 1969, *2*, 21–38.

Fromm, E. *The sane society.* New York: Holt, Rinehart and Winston, 1955.

Goode, E. Marijuana and the politics of reality. *Journal of Health and Social Behavior*, 1969, *10*, 83–94.

Grinspoon, L. *Marijuana reconsidered.* Cambridge, Mass.: Harvard University Press, 1971.

Haley, J. The amiable hippie. In *The power tactics of Jesus Christ, and other essays.* New York: Grossman Publishers, 1969.

Harris, T. G. A conversation with Margaret Mead. *Psychology Today*, 1970, *4*, 58–76.

Hinkle, W. The social history of the hippies. *Ramparts*, 1967, *5*, 9–26.

Hoffman, A. *Revolution for the hell of it.* New York: Dial Press, 1970.

Houriet, R. *Getting back together.* New York: Coward, McCann, and Geoghegan, 1971.

Kanter, R. Communes: Why and how they are formed and which are likely to make it and why. *Psychology Today*, 1970, *4*, 53–57.

Kaplan, J. *Marijuana: The new prohibition.* New York: World, 1970.

Keniston, K. Heads and seekers. Drugs on campus, countercultures and American society. *American Scholar*, 1968–1969, *69*, 97–112.

Kesey, K. *The whole earth catalogue supplement, the realist,* 1971.

Kunen, J. S. *The strawberry statement: Notes of a college revolutionary.* New York: Avon Books, 1969.

Laing, R. D. *The politics of experience.* New York: Ballantine, 1967.

Leary, T. *High priest.* Cleveland: World, 1968.

McLuhan, M., and Fiore, Q. *The medium is the massage.* New York: Random House, 1967.

Mead, M. Future families. *Trans-action,* 1971, *8,* 50–54.

Mirin, S. M. Casual versus heavy use of marijuana: A redefinition of the marijuana problem. Unpublished manuscript, Psychopharmacology Laboratory, Boston University School of Medicine, Boston, Mass., 1970.

Polsky, N. *Hustlers, beats and others.* Chicago: Aldine, 1967.

Rappaport, J., Bernstein, D., Hogan, M., Kane, J., Plunk, M., and Sholder, M. Fraternal and communal living: Values and behavior on the campus. Unpublished manuscript, University of Illinois, 1970.

Reich, C. A. *The greening of America.* New York: Random House, 1970.

Reiss, I. L. *The social context of premarital sexual permissiveness.* New York: Holt, Rinehart and Winston, 1967.

Rimmer, R. *The Harrad experiment.* New York: Bantam Books, 1967.

Roberts, M. D. *Changing patterns of college students trust.* Unpublished dissertation, University of Connecticut, 1970.

Robinson, J. P., and Hirsh, P. It's the sound that does it. *Psychology Today,* 1969, *3,* 42–45.

Rokeach, M. *Beliefs, attitudes and values.* San Francisco: Jossey-Bass, 1969.

Roszak, T. *The making of a counter culture.* Garden City, N.Y.: Anchor Books, 1968.

Rotter, J. B. A new scale for the measurement of interpersonal trust. *Journal of Personality,* 1967, *35,* 651–665.

Rubin, J. *Do it!* New York: Simon and Schuster, 1970.

Shuttleworth, J. The plowboy interview with John Shuttleworth. *The Mother Earth News,* No. 2, March 1970.

Simmons, J. L., and Winograd, B. *It's happening: A portrait of the youth scene today.* Santa Barbara, Calif.: McNally and Loftin, 1966.

Simon, G., and Trout, G. Hippies in college—from teeny-boppers to drug freaks. *Trans-action,* 1967, *5,* 27–34.

Slater, P. *The pursuit of loneliness: American culture at the breaking point.* Boston: Beacon Press, 1970.

Smart, R. G., and Jackson, D. *The Yorkville subculture: A study of life styles and interactions of hippies and non-hippies.* Toronto: Addiction Research Foundation, 1969.

Smart, R. G., and Jones, D. Illicit LSD users: Their personality characteristics and psychopathology. *Journal of Abnormal Psychology,* 1970, *75,* 286–292.

Suchman, E. The "hang-loose" ethic and the spirit of drug use. *Journal of Health and Social Behavior,* 1968, *9,* 146–155.

Toffler, A. *Future shock.* New York: Random House, 1970.

Vachon, B. Witches are rising. *Look,* 1971, *35,* 40–48.

Weakland, J. H. Hippies: What the scene means. In R. H. Blum and Associates (eds.), *Society and Drugs.* San Francisco: Jossey-Bass, 1969, 342–372.

Whittaker, D., and Watts, W. A. Personality characteristics of a nonconformist youth subculture: A study of the Berkeley nonstudent. *Journal of Social Issues,* 1969, *25,* 65–89.

Wolfe, T. *The electric kool-aid acid test.* New York: Bantam Books, 1968.

Yablonsky, L. *The hippie trip.* New York: Pegasus, 1968.

15

Drug Use and the Adolescent

*Arthur W. Jalkanen**

National statistics indicate that as many as twenty-six million Americans may use various forms of inappropriate drugs. Further, analyses of the data indicate that up to 4 or 5 percent of our young population, from ages of fourteen to twenty-one may have tried heroin. These are alarming statistics and cause widespread concern in every part of our nation. Perhaps the basic concern results from an inability to look at the phenomenon of drug abuse from a consistent viewpoint, and that the multiple perceptions create even more concern and problems.

One perception for understanding drug use in adolescence can be borrowed from the medical profession. Dr. Abraham Kantrowitz, a noted heart surgeon at Sinai Hospital near Detroit, Michigan, has developed a "patch booster" concept in understanding heart problems. Rather than using the "heart transplant theory" with heart problems, he has designed a "booster pump" to help the existing weak heart. One can view adolescent drug use, most of which is growth experimentation, as a system in need of a patch booster. Basically, if we as educators, youth, or relevant adults, develop a "booster education program," we can assist the adoles-

* Arthur W. Jalkanen is Dean of Students, Director of the Center for Drug and Alcohol Studies, and Associate Professor of Social Science at Oakland Community College (near Detroit, Michigan). He has been consultant to numerous school districts in Michigan, is currently on the Department of Justice Bureau of Narcotics and Dangerous Drugs Project Staff, and has studied the drug use patterns of American soldiers. He has written a number of articles in various periodicals on the topics of drugs, counseling, etc.·

cent through some possibly turbulent years. The normal growth process will then prevail, whereby the large majority of young adults solve their growth and developmental problems through maturation and education. To develop necessary educational and experiential programs that can act as "booster pumps" to the normal growth process in the adolescent years, it is helpful to become familiar with the scope and range of drug abuse. Let us begin with a historical review of the problem.

Epidemiology of Drug Abuse

Drug abuse is not a new phenomenon. People, attitudes, motivations, and drugs themselves have changed, but the use of drug substances has been with us forever. One could say that the use of drugs evolved from the awareness of their purposes and effects. Five thousand years before Christ, the Sumerians wrote on clay tablets of the cultivation of a plant to extract its juice. The plant *gil,* meaning "joy or rejoicing," was the opium poppy. In addition, the prophet Ezekiel wrote, "And by the river upon the bank thereof shall grow trees; and the fruit thereof shall be for meat, and the leaf thereof shall be for medicine." Furthermore, in the tenth century, Arab traders took opium to China where it was used medically as a specific for diarrhea. With continued experimentation with the drug, however, it was found that opium could be used as a substitute for food. When increased numbers of people began using opium, the drug soon became a social disease, and by the beginning of the twentieth century mass addiction had spread through China.

By 1900 opium smoking had spread to other countries, including the United States, where many drug problems already existed by that time. Addiction to morphine, an opium derivative, was common due to its uncontrolled use in military medicine during the American Civil War of 1861–65. Diacetylmorphine, also, had been introduced by 1900 and was heralded by many as a cure for morphine addiction. It was used quite freely until 1908 when it was realized that it produced an addiction even graver than morphine. Diacetylmorphine is commonly called heroin today. In 1878 another drug, known as cocaine (from the land of the Incas), was acknowledged and its introduction coincided with the invention of the hypodermic needle. The result of this was an addict population of 150,000 by 1900 (U.S. Department of Justice). After 1909 the smoking of opium ceased to be a problem in this country, as importation for other than medical purposes was prohibited. Our problems with morphine and heroin, on the contrary, continued to grow until 200,000 addicts were reported in 1914. One out of every four hundred people in the country at that time was addicted. Recognition of the problem brought legislative action in 1914 with the passage of the Harrison Act, and the addict population began to decline. The Harrison Act controlled domestic distribution by, among other things, establishing a federal tax on narcotic drugs, requiring registration and registration tax on all legal dispensers of narcotic drugs, making it illegal to sell narcotic drugs not in a stamped package, and making sales pursuant to a legal order form.

Many important changes and discoveries relating to drugs were observed during the years 1914 to 1947. It should be noted, however, that the number of addicts declined steadily during this period. One of the most significant changes was the addition of marijuana to the abuse scene in the 1930s. Although there was evidence of marijuana use in this country prior to that time, "Even the most lurid journalists did not claim that marijuana seeped into society at large until the 1930's and usually the mid-1930's" (Mandel, 1966, p. 149).

Marijuana is rooted in history, and much of the legend surrounding its use is responsible for the controls and myths perpetuated to this day. Here is one account by Harry Anslinger (1937, p. 37), first Commissioner of the Federal Bureau of Narcotics:

> In the year 1090, there was founded in Persia the religious and military order of the Assassins, whose history is one of cruelty, barbarity, and murder, and for good reason. The members were confirmed users of Hashish, or Marijuana, and it is from the Arabic "hashshashin" that we have the English word "assassin."

That marijuana has become a classic drug of abuse should be obvious to every reader. It has advanced from its use in the early 1930s by a few jazz musicians to estimates of use by 16–20 percent of high school students in major population areas, and, in some large universities, surveys indicate that 10 to 30 percent of the students have smoked marijuana at least once.

The problem with marijuana exploded so rapidly that controls came quickly with the passage of the Marijuana Tax Act of 1937 (patterned after the Harrison Act). Additionally, it should be mentioned that, in 1930, the Federal Bureau of Narcotics was established. The interested reader will wish to turn to the chapter by Cross and Pruyn on the counterculture for additional information and the introspections and feelings of marijuana users. For a more detailed history of the development of marijuana, Bloomquist (1971) is an excellent source.

In the same decade (in 1938) there was yet another important occurrence at the Swiss Laboratories of Sandoz. It was here that Dr. Albert Hofman isolated d-lysergic acid diethylamide (LSD-25). Later, in 1943, Hofman accidentally ingested some of the fine, white powder and discovered the hallucinogenic properties of LSD. What the LSD experience is like is manifest in the following description by Cohen (1968, p. 34) of its effects:

> In general the mood tends to be euphoric and expansive, but labile mood swings are notable. The euphoria can mount to bliss, serenity, elation and joy. This aspect of the state is attractive to those who seek a chemical high. Extremely negative affectual responses are less common. These include tension, panic, fears of going mad or of an unknown, impending doom. A few subjects have remarked that their LSD encounter was marked by a complete absence of emotion, a sort of catatonic inability to feel anything. The feeling tone is reflected onto the other aspects of mental activity. Perceptual beauty is associated with pleasure and gaiety; flatness, drab colors and fearful imagery with dysphoria.

Thus the fortuitous discovery of the illusory properties of LSD introduced a new drug which promised hallucinations and other mental distortions.

The third major change during this time period (1914–17) was a gradual one. While at the turn of the century the addicts had been predominantly Chinese and Caucasian, by 1945 the majority were Negro and Puerto Rican (U.S. Department of the Treasury, 1967). The classic traffic drugs of that time—heroin, cocaine, and marijuana—were therefore being trafficked in the country's ghetto areas, which were financially lucrative spots for the operations of organized crime.

To understand more completely the harshness of our drug laws, at this point in time, it is necessary to realize that, at their inception, they dealt with organized crime. The traffickers who were exploiting the ghettos were indeed criminals. However, as our society has evolved, the characteristics of drug traffic have changed so drastically that use is no longer confined to so-called classic "criminal" types. The average marijuana dispenser now is the young adult involved in drug use rather than the organized criminal. Unfortunately our drug laws have failed to reflect these critical changes.

In 1947, a most important trend began. After reaching a low of approximately 19,000 addicts (U.S. Department of the Treasury, 1967), the decline being witnessed for twenty-five years ceased and the total number of addicts began to rise.

A crucial factor contributing to this change was, of course, the increasing use of psychedelic drugs. With the use of these mind-altering drugs, the ethnic identification of the user began to change. Drug use first became occasional, then casual, and finally prevalent in social areas other than the ghetto. It was the upper-middle class that constituted the greatest number of the users of these drugs. It also became apparent to many by that time that the nation had become, or was fast becoming, a drug-oriented society. Drug use in many forms had become a way of life for most Americans. Along with the great American dream of having a pill for everything came another abuse problem.

As early as 1951, the Subcommittee on Narcotics of the House Committee on Ways and Means, under the chairmanship of Congressman Hale Boggs, explored the problems created by illegal sales and abuse of barbiturates and considered action to correct the situation (U.S. Congress, 1951). In 1954, during the 84th Congress, the House Subcommittee on Narcotics again held hearings to consider the need for additional federal legislation in this area. By that time, the illegal distribution of amphetamines had become a more widespread problem and the hearings considered them as well as barbiturates. The "Ups and Downs" pills were prevalent and the issues of their use had to be confronted (Russo, 1968).

This form of abuse spread with such rapidity that in 1965 Senator Thomas Dodd of Connecticut estimated there were approximately 200,000 seriously dependent "pill heads" in this country. In that same year the Food and Drug Administration (FDA) estimated that over ten billion amphetamine and barbiturate capsules were produced during the year (enough to supply four dozen to everyone in the country), and that up to half of those had been diverted to illicit use, representing an income to the black market traffickers of some 500 million dollars annually. One outcome of this was the passage of new federal legislation—H.R. 2, the Drug Abuse Control Amendments of 1965—which, among other things, gave birth to a new federal enforcement agency, the Bureau of Drug Abuse Control, operating out of the Food and Drug Administration. The Bureau of Drug Abuse Control and the federal Bureau of Narcotics have since merged and now operate as the Bureau of Narcotics and Dangerous Drugs, under the Department of Justice.

The present scope of the drug situation is rather difficult to assess. Figures published early in 1969 (U. S. Department of Justice) indicated 62,057 heroin addicts alone, but conservative estimates place that figure closer to 200,000. The most cautious student of the marijuana scene estimates seven million marijuana users, and factual estimates on the number of "pill heads" and hallucinogen abusers are just not available at this time. From my knowledge of this area, it would not be an unreasonable estimate to suggest that eight to nine million Americans are involved in the drug scene.

Furthermore, illicit drug use and sale are rising among all sectors of the population, not just the young. All forms of drug abuse and the corresponding crimes against persons and property are also rising at an alarming rate. The state, using traditional deterrents of jail sentences and fines, is not maintaining even a holding action in preventing drug abuse and drug dependence (Warner, 1969).

With the onset of a new decade there are many suggestions as to what should or could be done once again to alter this problem's course in history. These suggestions must be evaluated and applied wherever practical. We must also consider the attitudes of society, for, as Warner (1969, p. i–iii) has said:

> . . . The attitude of society and the governmental agencies through which society acts may be fairly characterized as one of vengeance and vindictiveness toward the drug dependent person who is treated as an evil person. In the years to come, we will look back at the superstitions and cruel reaction of our society to drug dependence with the same horror and disgust we now reserve for the way another generation misunderstood and abused its mentally ill and, more recently, its victims of alcoholism.
>
> The present attitude of society and its governmental agencies cannot be condemned too strongly. We must undertake a radical policy change with appropriate governmental innovations that will realistically characterize and treat the drug dependent person as an ill person—not an evil person. Governmental agencies must regard drug abuse as a complex illness and a health problem, not an invitation to exact extra-legal and statutory penalties, while ignoring the psychological and physiological causes leading to drug abuse, thereby compounding the personal and social problems attendant on drug abuse.

Pharmacological Effects and Descriptions of Different Drugs

Having considered in some detail the evolution of the drug problem from the original use for medicinal purposes to the gradual exploitation of the effects of various drugs, it now seems appropriate to focus upon the descriptions and pharmacological effects of the different drugs. In order to comprehend more fully the issues of drug use and misuse, we must become familiar with the types of narcotic drugs that are commonly used in society today.

Before proceeding, however, with the classification of the types of drugs which are typically used, certain terms relevant to drug use and abuse should be defined. Drug addiction, as explained in the seventh report of the World Health Organization Expert Committee on Addiction-Producing Drugs (1957), is a state of periodic or chronic intoxication produced by the repeated consumption of a drug (natural or synthetic). Its characteristics include an overpowering desire or need (compulsion) to continue taking the drug and to obtain it by any means; a tendency to increase the dose (tolerance); a psychic (psychological) and generally a physical dependence on the effects of the drug; and, lastly, a detrimental effect on the individual and on society.

In its seventh report the Committee sought also to differentiate addiction from habituation. *Drug habituation* (habit) is a condition resulting from the repeated consumption of a drug. Its characteristics include a desire (but not a compulsion) to continue taking the drug for the sense of improved well-being which it engenders; little or no tendency to increase the dosage; some degree of psychic dependence on the effect of the drug, but absence of physical dependence and, hence, of an abstinence syndrome; and the detrimental effects, if any, focus primarily on the individual. These definitions have gained some acceptance, but a great deal of confusion in the use of the terms *addiction* and *habituation* has continued. This has been especially true with the emergence of new agents and the changing patterns of drug use.

Additional clarification was sought, therefore, in the Committee's thirteenth report. The World Health Organization Expert Committee on Addiction-Producing Drugs (1964) recommended substitution of the term "drug dependence" for both of the terms *drug addiction* and *drug habituation*. Drug dependence is a state of psychic or physical dependence, or both, on a drug, arising in a person following administration of that drug on a periodic or continuous basis. The characteristics of such a state will vary with the agent involved, and these characteristics must always be made clear by designating the particular type of drug dependence in each specific case; for example, drug dependence of the barbiturate type, or heroin type, or amphetamine type, etc. The description of drug dependence as a state is a concept for clarification and not, in any sense, a specific definition (Eddy et al., 1965).

Now that three most fundamental terms—addiction, habituation, and dependence—relating to drug use have been examined, the description, classification, and pharmacological effects of popular drugs will be considered.

Soft Drugs

Soft drugs are those usually referred to as nonaddictive. Although these drugs may be habit-forming, physiological withdrawal is not experienced upon termination of their use.

Marijuana. The term *marijuana* used in the Western Hemisphere refers to a preparation of pulverized leaves, stems, stalks, seeds, and flowers of the cannabis plant. A collection of the active resin (tetra-hydrocanabinol) obtained from the leaves and flowering tops of the cannabis plant is referred to as hashish, which may vary from five to ten times greater in potency than marijuana.

By law, *marijuana* is defined to mean all parts of the cannabis plant except the stalks and sterilized seeds. These preparations are referred to by the user as "pot," "grass," "weed," "hemp," "Mary Jane," "joints," "sticks," and "reefers."

Individuals are affected by cannabis derivatives on a continuum ranging from a benign intoxicating "high" to a frank schizophreniclike psychosis. The marijuana smoker generally finds the experience pleasant and nonthreatening. The degree of intoxication and subjective effects, however, will vary with the individual's personality, setting of the drug experience, emotional set before and after, and the amount of the active resin THC. Adverse reactions to marijuana use may include anxiety, fear, depression, suspicion, dissociation, depersonalization, disorientation, confusion, delusions, and auditory hallucinations (Talbott, 1969).

Mescaline (3, 4, 5–trimethexyphenylethylamine). Mescaline is derived from the buttons of the peyote cactus. It has also been synthesized in clandestine laboratories and appears on the illicit market as a white crystalline powder which, when put into solution form (by mixing with water) may be injected. Mescaline may be placed in gelatine capsules, or mixed with other substances (orange juice, alcohol, tea, etc.) for oral ingestion. A dose of 350 to 500 milligrams has reportedly produced reactions similar to those produced by LSD (Ludwig, 1965; Long, 1968; Louria 1969). Nicknames that generally refer to this drug are: "Mesc," "green saucers," "Chocolate Mesc," and "Strawberry and Orange Mesc."

Hallucinogens. *Hallucinogenic, psychotominetic, psychedelic,* and *psychotropic* are terms referring to a class of drugs capable of producing hallucinations, illusions, or distortions of perception and thinking, of the various senses. Included in this class of drugs are LSD-25 (d-lysergic acid diethylamide), Mescaline (peyote), Psilocybin, Psilocyn, DMT, Bufoteinine, Ibogaine, DET (diethyltryptamine), DOM, STP, THC, and marijuana.

There is a wide variability of response to the hallucinogens. Responses may vary from mild euphoria obtained from smoking marijuana to an acute psychotic episode following the ingestion of LSD.

LSD, referred to by the user as "acid," is derived from the ergot fungus of rye, a disease of the rye grain. Manufactured in clandestine laboratories, LSD can be found and prepared as a liquid or fine white powder. A dose of 50 to 100 micrograms (comparable to a speck of dust) will send the user on a "trip" for approximately eight to twelve hours depending upon the individual's physical and psychological profile. A variety of complications have been reported including the following: reappearance of the hallucinated, disorganized state without further ingestion; uncontrollable panic; extended periods of psychosis; personal invulnerability; and permanent organic damage.

Stimulants. This group of drugs acts directly on the central nervous system. Mild stimulants, such as the nicotine in cigarettes and the caffeine in coffee, are listed to suggest that an understanding of the problem and the treatment of compulsive drug misuse is perhaps best developed by studying similar compulsive acts in those who do not regard themselves as "drug users" (Myers et al., 1965).

The most potent stimulants are the amphetamines, destro-amphetamines, and methamphetamines. The amphetamines are referred to by the abusers as: "ups," "eye-openers," "bennies," "dexies," "speed meth," and "Crystal meth."

The toxicity of amphetamines and other stimulants includes irritability, slurred speech, ataxia, tooth-grinding movements, dry mouth, tremor, hyperreflexia, nausea, paranoia, and occasionally a toxic confusional state. Medical admissions are usually for hepatitis, trauma, confusion, or occasionally for self-induced injury resulting from an attempted suicide consequent to severe depression which may accompany withdrawal from excessive stimulant use (Louria, 1969).

Cocaine may appear in the form of large crystals, flakes, or fine white powder and is referred to by the abusers as "cokc" or "snow." Cocaine is not generally considered to produce physiological dependence or toxic reactions similar to those of the amphetamines.

Depressants (Sedative Hypnotics). The sedative class of drugs, exemplified by the barbiturates, depress the central nervous system, and are prescribed for the relief of anxiety and the induction of sleep. The barbiturates (some 2,500 have been synthesized), depending on the dose, can depress practically every system in the body. Therefore, this classification of drugs can be used as tranquilizers, sedatives, and hypnotics. Depressants are referred to as "Downers," "Barbs," "Yellow Jackets," "candy," "Nunbies," and "Red Birds."

The symptoms and signs of chronic barbiturate intoxication may include impairment of mental abilities, confusion, poor judgment, depression, and psychotic changes. Without proper medical attention an overdose of barbiturates, particularly when taken in combination with alcohol, may result in unconsciousness and death (Kales et al., 1969; Carr, 1970).

Hard Drugs

Hard drugs refers to those drugs which result in physiological addiction. Since these drugs are addictive, the individual experiences physiological withdrawal if the drugs are not taken regularly.

Opium. Opium is obtained from the milky exudate of the incised unripe seed capsules of the plant *papaver somniferum.* This activate or latex is taken from the opium poppy by making an incision into the poppy capsule and allowing it to bleed. The milky exudate is originally white in color but upon exposure to the air turns a dark brown. This is allowed to harden in the form of sticks, bricks, cakes, or balls.

The pharmacologically active constituents (alkaloids) and products of opium are many. There is powdered or granulated opium, opium seeds (used for pastry), tincture of opium (laudanum), camphorated tincture of opium (paragoric), pantopon, thebaine, morphine, codeine, papaverine, narcine, nucodan, numorphan, noscapine, heroin, etc.

Generally opium is smoked and, while burning, has a very sweet odor. Despite their dependence-producing liability, opium and its pharmacologically active constituents have continued to be among the most useful drugs available to the physician.

Morphine. Morphine, the alkaloid that gives opium its analgesic actions, remains the standard against which new analgesics are measured. The principal derivative of opium, morphine is a white crystalline powder, bitter in taste, and is used generally as a medicine in the form of a sulphate or hydrochloride salt. Morphine is marketed in the form of powder, tablets, and in multiple-dose vials.

The major effects of morphine are on the central nervous system and are manifested by analgesia, drowsiness, changes in mood, and mental clouding. The invention of the hypodermic needle and the parenteral use of morphine rather than curd opium has tended to produce a more severe variety of addiction (Jaffe, 1965).

Heroin. Heroin (diacetylmorphine) is a synthetic derivative of morphine. The abuser refers to heroin as "H," "Jones," "Harry," "Joy Powder," and "Horse." Heroin, the most frequently abused narcotic of the American addict, was introduced about the turn of the century as a nonaddictive substitute for morphine. However, this proved erroneous. A process of acetylation using simple and inexpensive equipment will produce a high quality product more potent than morphine.

Heroin may appear as a white, off-white, or light brown crystalline powder that is usually fine in texture. The differentiation in color may be explained by the use of crude equipment, contaminated reagents, weak anihydrades, or impure morphine. Because of its powerful (euphoric) effect, heroin is almost always adulterated with milk, sugar, quinine, or lactose.

Heroin is generally sold in one-ounce or smaller-size glasine bags by a "wholesaler." The "retailers" handle heroin in paper "decks," "bindles," and clear or red number-five capsules. Since heroin is usually adulterated at each step of the distribution process, 100 percent pure heroin originating in France typically reaches the addict "junkie" in the United States between 1 and 4 percent pure.

Major medical complications of heroin addiction are abscesses, endocarditis, hepatitis, death from overdose, pneumonia, septic pulmonary embolism, tetanus, and thrombophlebitis. General physical examination might reflect slowed breathing, apnea, needle marks, constricted pupils which respond sluggishly or not at all to light stimulation; drowsiness (on the nod) ; decreases in respiration, blood pressure, and temperature; running nose; loss of appetite; and bloodshot and watering eyes (Louria, 1969).

Codeine. Codeine is a drug synthetically manufactured from curd morphine. It is used in medicine generally as a sulphate or a phosphate possessing a lesser degree of potent analgesic properties than morphine.

Codeine occurs as odorless white crystals, as crystalline powder, or in the form of tablets. It is used extensively in combination with such drugs as aspirin or aspirin compounds and is contained in exempt cough preparations, which is the most commonly abused form. Table 1 further summarizes this information and provides related information about these drugs.

Alternatives for Action

The use of drugs is a threateningly common phenomenon in our society today. John F. Ingersoll (1969) indicates that drug abuse is increasing in epidemic proportions and has become a fact of life, if not a way of life, to a sizable segment of our youth and population. Though we may have techniques through police contact procedures to estimate the size of our heroin-addicted population in various metropolitan centers, the widespread increase of drug use has antiquated most, if not all, accurate statistics. To compound further the complexity of assessing the number of drug users, one must think of the "respectable drug users." *The New York Times* (1968) reports "there are no statistics on respectable drug (middle-class) users, but many apparently seek escape from boredom born of affluence . . . others look for God or self-revelation." On March 4, 1968, Dr. Helen Nowlis mentioned the lack of reliable data on the use of drugs by high school students. Dr. Nowlis further indicated that the data are extremely difficult to come by, since school systems are not anxious to have anyone survey their students. Since 1968, there has evidently been a steady increase in drug use by high school students, and school districts are now participating in some basic research on drug use. In the *Detroit Free Press* (1970) , a study of a school district near Detroit

Table 1. Drugs and Related Information

Name	Slang Name	Chemical or Trade Name	Type of Stimulus	Medical Use	How Taken	Initial Symptoms	Long-Term Symptoms	Possible Physically Addicting	Possible Mentally Addicting
Amphetamines	Bennies, Happy Pills, Dexies, Meth, Speed, Hearts, Jolly Beans	Benzedrine Dexedrine Dexamyl Methedrine	Stimulant	Curb Appetite, Relieve Mild Depression, Combat Fatigue	Swallowed or Injected	Alertness Nervousness	Depression upon Withdrawal, Hallucinations	No	Yes
Barbiturates	Barbs, Goof Balls, Reds, Yellow Jackets, Purple Hearts, Blue Heavens	Nembutal Seconal Amytal Luminal Butisol	Depressant Short-Acting, Fast-Starting Long-Acting Slow-Starting	Sedation, Help Minor Insomnia	Swallowed or Injected	Drowsiness, Muscle Relaxant	Addiction with Severe Withdrawal Symptoms, Possible Convulsions, Delirium	Yes	Yes
Cocaine	Corina, Coke, Gold Dust, Flake, Star Dust, Cecil Speedball (combination injection of cocaine & heroin)	Methyl-Benzoylecgoine	Stimulant	Local Anesthetic	Sniffed, Swallowed, or Injected	Excitation, Talkativeness, Tremors	Depression, Convulsions	No	Yes
Codeine: Opium Derivative	Schoolboy Pop (cough syrup)	Methyl-morphine	Depressant	Ease Minor Pain and Coughing	Swallowed	Drowsiness	Addiction	Yes	Yes
DMT	Businessman's High	Dimethyltryptamine	Hallucinogen	None	Injected, Smoked	Excitation	?	No	?
DET		Diethyltryptamine	Hallucinogen	None	Injected, Smoked	Excitation	?	No	?

Drug	Slang Names	Chemical Name	Classification	Medical Use	How Taken	Effects	Dangers		
Heroin: Semi-Synthetic Derivative of Morphine	"H," Junk. Horse, Skag, Smack, Snow, Joy Powder	Diacetyl-morphine	Depressant	Pain Killer	Injected or Sniffed	Lethargic, Drowsy	Addiction, Loss of Appetite, Convulsions in Overdose	Yes	Yes
LSD	Acid, Cubes, Trips, Big D	Lysergic Acid Diethylamide	Hallucinogen	Treatment for Alcoholism under Strict Gov. Control	Swallowed	Excitation, Rambling Speech	Hallucinations, Panic, Psychosis	No	?
Marijuana	Pot, Grass, Mary Jane, Joint, Tea, Gage, Reefers, Bhang, Brick, Stick	Tetra-Hydra Cannabinol	Hallucinogen	None in U.S.	Smoked, Sniffed	Euphoria, Alteration of Perception and Judgment, Bursts of Laughter	Usually None	No	?
Mescaline	Mesc, Cactus, Payola	3-4-5 Trimeth, Oxyphenylethyl-amine	Hallucinogen	None	Swallowed, Sometimes Injected	Anxiety		No	?
Methadone: Synthetic Opiate	Dolly	Dolophine Amidone	Depressant	Pain Killer	Swallowed or Injected		Addiction	Yes	Yes
Morphine: Opium Derivative	Morf, Miss Emma, White Stuff, M., Dreamer	Morphine Sulphate	Depressant	Pain Killer	Swallowed, Injected	Drowsiness, Euphoria, Itchiness	Addiction	Yes	Yes
Psilocybin	Mushrooms	Ortho Phosphoryl, 4-Hydroxy, N-Di-methyl-tryptamine	Hallucinogen	None	Swallowed	Nausea, Vomiting, Headaches		No	?
STP	Serenity, Tranquility, Peace	4 Methyl-2 5-Dimethoxy Alpha, Methyl	Hallucinogen	None	Swallowed		Possible Severe Mental Complications	No	?

Source: *The Pontiac Press*, Pontiac, Michigan, January 12, 1970. Used by permission.

indicated 50 percent of the high school students were using drugs. This figure may be judged high by experienced professionals involved in drug abuse programs, but certainly similar professionals would place drug use somewhere near 30 or 40 percent. These professional workers further indicate that drug use is not unusual in junior high schools, with the greatest usage occurring in grade nine. The students in grade ten appear to use less drugs, with grade eleven again showing an increase and, perhaps, the greatest use. Students in grade twelve appear to curtail use significantly as compared to students in grade eleven.

Accurate statistical data of drug use as reported by courts and police departments also indicate variances. If one were to study the number of cases of actual drug contact, as opposed to cases of court action on drug traffic, each precinct would illustrate the variance.

The Typical Teen Addict

Unfortunately neither research nor experienced workers in drug use agree that there is such a concept as a typical teen drug user. However, we can make some general descriptive statements about these young people. Approximately three-fourths of them are males. Workers in this area would tend to agree that the drug user is a quiet youngster, likeable, conservative, polite, easily influenced, and quick to want pleasure. They have few if any deep friendships. They have the facility to talk their way out of many problems. Once these adolescents become trapped and dependent upon narcotics, they are likely to withdraw from society. If they are in school, their grades drop. Ambition is lost and they are restless, moody, and quite secretive. Heroin users lose sexual interest in the opposite sex although there is some evidence that marijuana may increase sexual interest for some individuals (Lewis, 1970). When drug dependency becomes a way of life, the adolescent fades from the real world to spend his time in fantasy, dimly lit rooms, and mood music. This pattern can be seen in the conversations of the drug-using young. Home conflicts, alienation, lack of meaningful activities appear to surround the novice user, until the use of drugs becomes an end in itself. When society loses the potential of its young (see the introductory chapter by Adams) for any reason, it is a sad occurrence. Losing that potential because of drug dependence is even more tragic.

Theories Relative to Drug Use

Social scientists have not articulated specific theories for understanding drug use. Rather, there has been an attempt to modify or interpret theories and models developed in social science to apply to drug use. It is quite apparent that as drug abuse has become an increasing problem, we need a new theory for understanding drug use. A general review of the major theories further demonstrates this conclusion. The reader may also wish to attempt to tie in the chapter by Beller to this topic.

Sociology Theory of Drug Use

This theory was developed in conjunction with drug studies since 1900. Basically it concludes that drug use is an urban problem: that of New York blacks and Puerto Ricans, as well as Chinese in California. The theory of sociology in drug use during the 1970s explains and tries to define the affluent white middle class as exploring new activities (such as drug abuse). This theory of sociology is useful perhaps in understanding drug abuse but provides little more than "understanding." As a prescriptive study or discipline, sociology has not yet come of age in this area. If educators wish to intervene in the adolescent drug world, sociology theory will provide very limited help, and this help is in understanding, but not in what can be done about drug use.

Personality Theory of Drug Abuse

Here theories would speculate that there are normal personalities and abnormal personalities. Further, the subtle assumptions imply that drug abuse is not normal; therefore, the drug user has not a normal personality. This approach would react through state mental institutions, outpatient mental health services and, basically, the personality theory modalities of interaction. A study of this approach can raise serious questions for the entire profession of mental health services. It is known to all researchers that there is no measurable personality variable in drug users. This is to say, that the use of personality theory in drug abuse may be inappropriate, since the understanding of drug abuse provided by personality theory does not differentiate the user from the nonuser. In other words, drug users measure out as normal on a personality test. The procedures used with mentally ill people do not affect the drug use patterns of the drug users.

Self-Concept Theory of Drug Use

This theory postulates that a person with a low self-concept may use drugs to enable him to deal with reality. The theory further posits that "one does not need drugs" if he has a good self-concept. When this theory is tested, particularly with young adults, we find no difference in the self-concept of the drug user and the nonuser. If we had to make a significant observation in this area, we would need to say that the drug users have a somewhat higher self-concept than the nonuser. It is further demonstrable that programs designed to improve the "self-concept" do not in any manner affect decrease patterns of drug use. If anything, they may tend to make a drug user a drug advocate or drug seller. In summary, then, self-concept theory appears to add little in understanding drug use, and even less as a prescriptive program to decrease drug use.

Typology Theory of Drug Use

From Sheldon's (1940) body typologies to Holland's (1966) vocational personality types, we have induced typology theory into drug use. Though not as formalized, we use body characteristics to relate to the drug-using individual. The following categories briefly introduce a few of the more common typologies:

> *Pot Head.* A slovenly, lethargic, individual.
>
> *Acid Head.* One with hypertension, excessively overactive, usually with electric hairdo.
>
> *Speed Freak.* Parallels Acid Head, but usually an older person in later teens.
>
> *Junkie.* A term applied to a continual heroin user.
>
> *Addict.* Term applied to a long-term heroin user.
>
> *Pusher.* One who professionally sells drugs (term has subcategories such as "nickle man," "bindle man," etc.) .

These typologies were gleaned from current literature, and sampled on fifty-six adults. The mean score was 90 percent, indicating that almost everyone knows and agrees with the typology concepts of drug use.

Basically typologies are of little value and have even less validity. This concept or theory adds very little to understanding drug use, and is of no value to the prescriptive nature of drug programs.

Accident Theory of Drug Use

This theory considers drug use as an accidental phenomenon. Though it may be totally accurate, the use of this theory will provide little insight for understanding or prevention. Educators can even use the accident theory in preventive educational programs, and should a person have the opportunity to experience drugs by accident, the preventive program will "booster" the nonuser probability. Accident theory, then, provides little basic understanding of drug use, but can be helpful to a structured program premised on accident theory.

Law-Enforcement Theory of Drug Use

This theory posits drug use as illegal or legal. Illegal drug use is a violation of the law, and the violators must be prosecuted when apprehended. As a model for understanding and prescription, this theory is quite clear. The people must be educated as to what is legal and illegal; large-enough law-enforcement agencies must be maintained to apprehend violators, and prosecution must punish those who violate. Though this theory may exist in some parts of our nation, most law-enforcement personnel collectively feel that law enforcement alone will not suffice. It is clear that more than the law-enforcement theory is necessary to relate meaningfully to the drug abuse phenomenon.

Developmental Concept of Drug Use

Table 2 depicts a model for understanding the developmental nature of drug use. This model is designed as a continuum upon which one can view substance use. I have built this model through research on drug use: initially with fifty-six individuals, then validated with a population of 544 individuals. The following expansion of Table 2 should aid the reader in understanding the concepts involved.

Awareness. Awareness pertains to the activities or socialization processes involved in human interaction. An individual may become aware of the drug use dimension as a child, adolescent, or adult. Immediately upon awareness, various cognitive processes begin, after which decision-making processes intercede and evoke further action. *Nonparticipation* is a dimension of activity that may result from awareness of drug use. Because of social constraints, legal control, social taboos, or numerous other definable reasons, individuals do not have further drug use activities either in process or actual participation.

Fraternization. This concept pertains to the individual fraternizing with the drug using culture. It is an actual socialization process which results in group affiliation, participation, and events where drugs are used, or friendship pattern continuations with one involved in drug use. The individual herein continues group affiliations with those already involved in drug use. *Nonparticipation:* As previously described, individuals may continue from awareness to fraternization; and, after continued socialization and fraternization, an individual may again choose not to partici-

Table 2. Developmental Stages Precipitating Drug Use

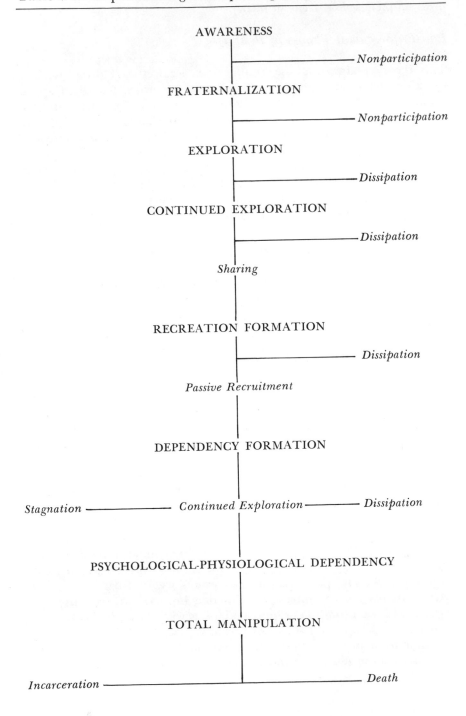

pate with the group culture involved in drug use. The dimensions for determining the nonparticipation of the individual involved in the drug use culture are definable constructs which can be tested for authentication. The rationale for nonparticipation, however, may vary and has been found to be manifested in particular personality constructs or the social mores present in the individual's cultural growth and development.

Exploration. Exploration pertains to the activity usually followed by fraternization within the drug culture. The exploration usually relates to the initial experience with drugs that results from the continued presence of an individual in a drug subculture. *Dissipation* is a term applied to a recurring dimension that becomes manifest when individuals try certain forms of drugs and then decide not to explore further or to use any kind of drugs. The individual dissipates from the drug culture and the drug use dimension, and he readily identifies himself as one who will no longer continue in any form of drug use.

Continued Exploration. In continued exploration the individual remains in the drug culture, trying various new forms of drugs. This might mean the continuation of one drug or moving to another or to one which is available at any given time. A phenomenon of the continued explorations is that of *sharing*. Sharing relates to the providing of drug materials to friends or others in a recruitment form of activity. This may be present in blatant distribution of marijuana cigarettes or the giving of various pills and substances to friends. Seldom, if ever, in this dimension is cost mentioned. As mentioned beforehand, *dissipation* results from some phenomenal experience in the drug use dimension. Either by social constraint or a self-identified process, the individual determines not to continue in drug use activity.

Recreation Formation. This is a stage concept of drug use in which the use of drugs and peer affiliations becomes an end in itself and becomes a recreation activity. In this stage of development the individual looks forward to the peer group meeting at which time numerous activities are ongoing, one of which is drug use. The culture effect has taken place, and the individual is tightly aligned with the entire group involved in drug use. *Passive recruitment* as an activity pertains to the form of recruitment of new drug users or passing of materials to other individuals. At this point, a trust dimension is developed within the group so that recruitment activities can take place with little concern for social retaliation. This recruitment makes itself manifest in driving others to pick up drugs, assisting in the distribution of material, holding material for another so that he is not associated with drugs, and in other such deceptive activities to assist friends in distribution of drugs or related paraphernalia. *Dissipation* occurs continually and may result from a bad trip, or some new group affiliation. At this point, the individual decides not to continue in the drug culture.

Dependency Formation. Dependency formation describes a stage in individual behavior. At this stage, the individual is dependent on the drug culture for recreation and continued existence. The dependency on the drug becomes manifest through the peer group, and friendship patterns are predominant at this stage. During this stage all activities planned result in the involvement of the peer group and the drug culture. *Stagnation* identifies a stage of continued drug use, wherein the individual depends on the group and centers his behavior around the drug culture group. A careful investigation of this stage shows that the individual does not experiment with other new drugs already known to the individual; no new group affiliations are made, and the individual is dormant in new activity relationships with drug use. Once again, *dissipation* is an activity wherein the individual may decide to withdraw from the drug cult and cease using drugs. For some unique reasons individuals *continue to explore* new drugs and at this point become familiar with intravenous injection procedures. It may well result from the use of speed or hard amphetamines, if one so classifies them, and a continual drive for further new drug experiences. At this stage the individual becomes affiliated with active recruitment in the drug movement. The nature of the traffic at this stage is quite extensive, and the individual now seeks, in many cases, small agents to distribute the material. It is common to see individuals in this stage with several hundred dollars of materials, much of which they move for profit or living expense maintenance. A common occurrence is that an individual will move drugs to pay rent and other bills after which he may stop recruitment activities until again in need of financial assistance.

Psychological-Physiological Dependency. This stage refers to the totally dependent person who has experienced the depth of drug use and now spends continuous time in drug use activities. It may well be that the dependency makes itself manifest from the monetary profit, the physiological need, or the psychological peer-group participation. If the individual is psychologically involved in the group, he is *manipulating* the group or the group activities pertaining to drugs and his own drug use. Physiological drug use might mean the individual must raise funds throughout the day hours and maintain a habit. The dependency is now so great that it involves all the individual's time. *Dissipation* again pertains to the individual's decision process not to participate in the drug use dimension. At this point, external help is usually necessary for the individual to effectuate this decision.

Death or Incarceration. These two phenomena are the eventual result of an individual's behavior that is totally manipulated in the drug culture. Death occurs as a product of substance use or as a result of behavior in the drug culture. Incarceration refers to a behavior controlled–environment, be it a state hospital, a jail, or a program such as Synanon that demands total involvement, either voluntarily or involuntarily.

The conceptual model that I have described should help to build a common understanding of the developmental stages precipitating drug use. What the helping person may do with this understanding presents yet another problem!

A Substance Abuse Program

The function of a substance (drug) abuse program is to create resilience in the normal institutions. If the substance abuse program is effective, the end product will be effective institutions including the family, school, work, and other such institutions. This can be further explained by reviewing the problems inherent in these institutions. In school, for example, when a young person is under the influence of a drug, or is apprehended with some in his possession, he is summarily dismissed from school. When a substance abuse program is begun in a school, the school has alternatives to dismissal, one of which is participation in a structured program designed to curtail substance use. The same phenomenon occurs in institutions, such as courts, the family, the hospitals, and law-enforcement agencies. Basically, it means that structured programs need to be designed to deal with new problems, one of which at this time is drug use and abuse. By establishing a special program, or a "support system" to the normal institutions, the normal institution can interact meaningfully with the new problem.

The Value of a Model for Understanding Drug Abuse

It is most central for social science systems to have a well-organized model upon which to design programs and to test hypotheses. The absence of a model naturally results in unsystematic programing and lack of consistent research and data in studying the problem.

If we use the model for understanding drug abuse which I have suggested, namely the developmental stages of drug abuse, this model should facilitate our understanding of drug abuse.

One of the things we might learn, for example, relates to the use of time in drug abuse. This simply means that the greater the drug involvement of the individual, the more time he takes from other possible activities. Whereas, little time is involved in substance use in the initial stages, substance use is a twenty-four-hour-a-day activity at its final stages. Further, the individual's time to use substance is taken from work, school, recreation, and other such established institutions.

Another value of viewing drug use along a continuum, as in the developmental stages presented in Table 2, is that it enables prescribing various treatment modalities. This is to say, it is easier to relate intervention activities on a continuum, and thereby approximate the needs of the individual involved in the drug culture. For example, we might decide that Phase I should relate to curricular learnings in school programs, as well as learnings from unstructured events as occasional observations, experiences or visits to "Drop-in Centers." Individuals involved in a Phase I activity have only explored drug use and are easily assisted.

Phase II would relate to recreational and depending activities in drug use; and the intervention activity might be more intensive and structured. Individuals at this stage usually spend numerous hours, regular nights (or days) in drug use, and are more than just exploring drug use. To assist the individual from the drug culture in this stage demands structured programs with intensive learnings.

Phase III would demand referral service to an area with heavy intervention techniques. People in this phase usually have large drug habits. Body physiology is affected by the drug use syndrome. The modality for intervention may take the form of medical maintenance (methadone) or drug absence with physical limitations, such as Synanon or Phoenix House programs, or state hostitals' activities with limited freedoms.

Drug Abuse Treatment Modalities

Drug abuse is a serious problem in the world, as in America. To relate to the number of drug using individuals in America today, somewhere between eight thousand and sixteen thousand organized programs have evolved. These programs service from a few individuals on a volunteer basis, to populations of several hundred, each week, in others. At the current time no one agency or department knows exactly how many functional programs exist in a large community, state, or nation. The figures established are estimates of the writer who has visited over eight hundred national programs in thirty-seven states. The program modalities for intervention can further be defined in four distinct categories.

The Rap House—Drop-in Center

From its early origins, this activity was very unstructured. Individuals could visit a center and talk or "rap" as the new world evolved. The entire continuum of service initially was talking. As the year progressed and public awareness of drug use increased, the programs in these houses or centers became more structured. Though many fundamental rap houses exist today, most of these houses have highly structured programs, with professional help available. Perhaps the one great improvement is the trained staff, that exists in almost every house of this nature.

The Crises Center Programs

Initially taking the form of a "crash pad" where overdose victims gathered, the crisis centers have improved and strengthened their structure. Today vagrant youngsters seek housing here; V.D. adolescents privately seek treatment, as do drug-using young adults. Legal service work, leisure time, and educational programs are organized by the crisis units. This form of program has perhaps witnessed the most growth of any drug abuse program.

Structured Programs

The structured programs were perhaps the first to arise in the problem scene. The Synanon houses, Phoenix Houses, Daytop homes, The Seed, all relate to stages of growth and development of intervention into the drug scene. Initially only relating to the heroin addict, these programs now handle hundreds of clients, own millions in property, and service a great need in American society. Their activity relates primarily to the person who is heavily involved with drugs.

Professional Models

The professional models include treatment in state hospitals, private practice, and family service systems. Initially these were the agencies who received the first wave of referrals of drug using individuals. The pressure brought about by these agencies increased the funding to new agencies and programs designed to deal with drug abuse. Today these professional models and agencies still receive cases, but the great number of active cases (some would estimate as high as 80 percent) are treated in nonprofessional agencies.

Options to Minimize Drug Abuse

Clearly the options to minimize drug abuse are in education, rehabilitation, and law enforcement. Any of the three options become futile if the expectation for meaningful action is premised on one activity alone. Furthermore, the normal agencies and communities responsible for the activity must cooperate closely by community, region, state, and nation. The development of rapid transit, transportation weekend flights out of town, and parcel post accentuate this necessity.

Educational Options

The educational options are premised on a need for communication. The typical guidance worker, teacher, judge, or parent will be able to communicate with a drug user only when there is a basic familiarity with the language of drug use (see Table 3). The language, primarily developed for deception, is the vehicle for authenticity that bonds one user to another. Unless one has at least a working knowledge of this language, he will be completely unaware of the communication (also see Bloomquist, 1971). It is in this entire area of drug use where education is desperately needed. Information concerning the user, the language of the user, and the effects of common drugs on the user are paramount requisites for the person working with youth today. Unfortunately, our graduate universities have neglected to provide these educational programs for us. To date, no formal graduate courses appear to exist in this area, and guidance workers and other school personnel must depend on in-service training programs usually organized by persons other than educators who do not tend to focus primarily on the student as a learner.

Though national coordination for drug education is the ideal, it is apparent that regional or community coordination is most feasible. State agencies can be helpful, but few states have moved rapidly enough to assist other than major metropolitan centers. The reality for educational activity may well rest with a regional committee that can provide direction and coordination for a drug education program.

The complexity of a program of this nature is most profound. Not only are schools faced with a sparsity of curriculum materials for drug education, but it also appears that the generation gap has disabled even the parent of the user who is familiar with drug abuse. Clergy, policemen, druggists, and judges are all seeking alternatives, and understand-

Table 3. Terminology

ACAPULCO GOLD	High grade of marijuana (female flowering parts)	MAIN LINER	Addict who injects directly into the vein
ACID	LSD	MAKE A BUY	Purchase drugs
BARBS	Barbiturates		
BREAD	Money	NARC	Cop or someone who helps the cops
BRICK	Kilogram of marijuana	NICKEL BAG	A $5.00 purchase of narcotics
BUSTED	Being arrested		
BUY	Purchase of narcotics by an undercover agent or informer	ON A TRIP	Under influence of hallucinogen
CAP	Capsule of powdered drug	POT	Marijuana
		PUSHER	Narcotic trafficker
		ROACH	Butt of a marijuana cigarette
CRYSTAL	Methedrine (Speed)		
DIME BAG	A $10.00 purchase of marijuana	SCORE	Buy
		SHOOT	Inject liquid drugs
GRASS	Marijuana	SMACK	Heroin
HARD STUFF	Heroin	SPEED	Cocaine or Methamphetamine
HASH	Hashish	STONED	Under the influence of drugs
HIGH	Under the influence of drugs, extreme euphoria	STRAIGHT	Off drugs
		TRACKS	Marks left on veins from repeated injections of drugs
JOINTS	Marijuana cigarettes		
JUNK	Heroin		
KILO	One kilogram of 2.2 pounds or 35 ounces	TRIP	LSD experience
		TURNED ON	Under the influence of a drug
LID	One ounce of marijuana		
		WORKS	Equipment for injection by hypodermic needle

ing, to this problem. The need, it appears, is for a standing task force of knowledgeable professionals with funds and time to sort out a program of action. A successful program will entail curriculum materials for every grade level, ongoing workshops for educators, clergy, policemen, judges, parents, and students. A direct frontal attack is necessary, if we wish to develop an effective educational program. If such an activity as massive drug use education were undertaken, one would expect to see the development of the appropriate media, as well as the use of experts in various disciplines. Perhaps the most significant concept pertaining to education drug use is that the education must encompass all constituents of a given community, region, or area, if it is to be effective. Furthermore education may be most effectual in curtailing experimentation, or in decreasing the number of "new users," and yet it may have little impact on the "addict" or "pusher." These two anomalies need further assistance.

Options in Rehabilitation

Rehabilitation programs pertain primarily to the novice user or the addict. Recognizing that these programs have educational value to the general public as well as to the person to be rehabilitated, their primary focus is on the individual proposed for rehabilitation. These programs must include medical, mental, and social (vocational-educational) activities. Each has a distinct role, and must support each other if the program is to be effective.

Medical. The medical activity needs to diagnose the current physical condition of the drug user. This involves a rapid identification of the substance that has been used, as well as the effect the drug (or drugs) have had on the body system. It can be expected that the prescriptive treatment resulting from a medical examination will detail the client's treatment including methadone (when possible or desirable), dietary needs, and continual medical supervision. It is during this process that identification of serum or infectious hepatitis will occur, and the plan for daily or weekly medical supervision, also, will be developed. This activity will enable a continual evaluation of the treatment as well as the rehabilitation.

Mental. The process of mental rehabilitation of the drug user may vary from "rap sessions" with the user on the road to recovery, to total incarceration of the user who has "flipped." In every case, however, it is most important that appropriate psychiatric or psychological supervision be given. Beginning with an intake psychological review, a decision can be made as to the prescribed rehabilitation process—whether in-patient treatment or out-patient therapy sessions with group leadership is required. As in medical activities, it is most important that professional leadership is continually available for client initial evaluation, as well as ongoing supervision.

Social (Educational-Vocational). This aspect of drug-user rehabilitation may be the most significant aspect of any total program planned to reduce drug use. Assuming that the goal of drug use rehabilitation relates to restructuring the user's life for meaningful life participation, it is most important that educational and vocational life planning is present. As mentioned previously, the drug user has frequently withdrawn from normal life activities and most often has difficulty in school programs or regular work activities. The role of guidance workers becomes paramount, both as counselors for life adjustment and as guidance workers in creating new opportunities that will provide meaning to the "user" on a road to recovery. Opportunities to continue education, training, work-study, or outright employment are most necessary. A well-structured program of educational-vocational growth should be developed with the "user" in mind and may well be the fastest road to recovery for all "drug-users."

Law Enforcement. The prudent use of law enforcement is a difficult problem for the helping professional to envision. The usual reluctance to relate to police and courts disables many effective drug program operations, and often the programs not coordinated with law-enforcement agencies have little lasting effect. This difficulty in relating to legal agencies is a new dimension. Communications and understandings need to be developed before each agency can begin to assist each other. A counselor that permits a "pusher-user" to continue proselytizing in a school may, in fact, be encouraging drug use rather than being of any assistance. An expectation that a counselor can "counsel" a user out of the habit (from the experience of many professionals dealing with the problem) seems to be an assumption which is quite unwarranted. In certain cases, particularly that of a pusher, the use of law-enforcement agencies is most helpful. Not only does legal action focus the problem on the pusher and begin to curtail the supply, but it also enables the pusher to begin receiving professional help. Since the laws pertaining to drugs may vary from one state to another (and from one precinct to another), communication with the juvenile court and area police is paramount. The expectation of involvement with law enforcement is that collective action by all agencies will support the individual action of any one agency.

Drug Commissions. President Nixon has proposed a national office (committee structure H.R. Bill No. 9312) for drug and narcotic abuse. Various governors have indicated that a commission in their state will be established for the same purpose. These beginnings move the energies of the nation and states in the direction of coordinating established drug-use programs. It would appear most logical that each county, each city, each community, each school, and similar agency identify persons and personnel who will be responsible for designing and coordinating the implementation of comprehensive drug abuse programs. These individuals would provide the leadership for civic organizations and other interested groups that desire to assist in the drug abuse activities. It can clearly be understood that when a problem so serious as drug abuse faces as large a population as it does today, only a total concentrated effort in every area will move us in the direction of the wise and appropriate use of drugs.

Summary

Drug use is a new phenomenon to much of America today. Being aware that up to twenty-six million Americans may be using some form of drug substance is not enough. It appears that we must actually become involved in the educational processes relative to drug use, particularly with our adolescent population. The research studies do support that many young adults will try some form of drugs, and most will stop using the substance by themselves. That more should not become involved, and that those using drugs would become knowledgeable about the assistance they can receive, is a realistic educational goal for our nation. In this goal we need to develop "patchboosters," a supportlike system of education and intervention to assist in the process of drug abuse prevention.

To carry out these objectives meaningfully, it is necessary to use a meaningful model for understanding the phenomenon of drug use and for constructing realistic programs. One such model is premised on developmental psychology, and is called the developmental stages involved in drug use. Using this model, it is possible to identify drug-using individuals on a continuum and thereby become able to prescribe meaningful modalities for intervention. The use of models not only encourages effective programs, it also provides a design for research and additional insight into the dynamics of drug abuse.

REFERENCES

Anslinger, H., and Cooper, C. R. Marijuana: Assassin of youth. *American Magazine,* July 1937, 37.

Bloomquist, E. R. *Marijuana: The second trip.* Beverly Hills, Calif.: Glencoe Press, 1971.

Carr, C. J. Man and drugs. *Archives of Environmental Health,* 1970, *20,* 77–83.

Cohen, S. A quarter century of research with LSD. In J. R. Ungerleider (ed.), *The problems and prospects of LSD.* Springfield, Ill.: Charles C Thomas, 1968.

Eddy, N. B., et al. Drug dependence: Its significance and characteristics. *World Health Organization Bulletin,* 1965, *32,* 721–727.

Holland, J. L. *The psychology of vocational choice.* Waltham, Mass.: Blaisdell Publishing Co., 1966.

Ingersoll, J. F. Director, Bureau of Narcotics and Dangerous Drugs, U.S. Department of Justice, Washington, D.C. Mimeographed speech, December, 1969.

Jaffe, J. H. Narcotic analgesics. In L. S. Goodman and H. Z. Gilman (eds.), *The pharmacological basis of therapeutics,* 3rd ed. New York: Macmillan Co., 1965.

Kales, A., et al. Drug dependency. *Annals of Internal Medicine,* 1969, *70,* 591–614.

Lewis, B. *The sexual power of marijuana.* New York: World Publishing Co., 1970.

Long, R. E., and Penna, R. P. Drugs of abuse. *Journal of the American Pharmaceutical Association,* 1968, *NS8,* 12–14 and 22–27.

Louria, D. B. Medical complications of pleasure-giving drugs. *Archives or Internal Medicine,* 1969, *123,* 182–187.

Ludwig, A. M., and Levine, J. Patterns of hallucinogenic drug abuse. *Journal of the American Medical Association,* 1965, *191,* 92–96.

Mandel, J. Hashish, assassins, and the love of God. *Issues in Criminology,* 1966, *2,* 149–156.

Meyers, F. H., Janetz, E., and Goldfien, R. *Review of medical pharmacology.* Los Altos, Calif.: Lange, 1965.

Russo, J. R. *Amphetamine abuse.* Springfield, Ill.: Charles C Thomas, 1968.

Sheldon, W. H. *Varieties of human physique.* New York: Harper, 1940.

Talbott, J. A., and Teague, J. W. Marijuana psychosis. *Journal of the American Medical Association,* 1969, *210,* 299–301.

U.S. Department of Justice. Bureau of Narcotics and Dangerous Drugs. *Drug abuse and law enforcement statistics.* Washington, D.C.: Bureau of Narcotics and Dangerous Drugs. Undated.

U.S. Department of the Treasury. Bureau of Narcotics. *Prevention and control of narcotic addiction.* Washington, D.C.: U.S. Government Printing Office, 1967.

U.S. Congress. House. Committee on Ways and Means. *Subcommittee on narcotics report on the illicit distribution of narcotics, barbiturates and amphetamines in the United States.* May 10, 1951.

Warner, D. In *Drug dependence in Michigan.* Lansing, Mich.: Special House Committee on Narcotics, 1967.

16

The Culturally Disadvantaged Adolescent

William E. Amos and Charles F. Wellford*

It has been frequently noted that our conception of the characteristics and problems of those whom we define as disadvantaged shifted significantly during the 1960s. During that period the focus of our attention shifted from individualized to collective problems. The treatment of the disadvantaged became not the problem of delivering services to clients, but rather the change of structural conditions (inequality, poverty, etc.) in order to eliminate the "root cause" that manifests itself in individual problems. The culturally disadvantaged emerged during this period as a newly recognized category of citizens who were to be saved by the War on Poverty. In the area of the lower-class adolescent, these efforts were guided by a theoretical model of the causes of the problems facing this

* William E. Amos is a member of the United States Board of Parole and is also Professorial Lecturer at George Washington University. He has held a number of governmental and educational positions. He has authored or edited such books as *Counseling the Disadvantaged Youth, Managing Student Behavior, Juvenile Delinquency: Theory and Practice, Action Program for Delinquency Prevention*, and *Readings in the Administration of Institutions for Delinquent Youth*. In addition, he has written many articles in the same topical areas. The views he expresses in this chapter are personal, not as a board member of the U.S. Board of Parole, and are not necessarily the opinions of the Department of Justice.

Charles F. Wellford is Associate Professor of Criminology at The Florida State University. He has coedited *Juvenile Delinquency Prevention* and has written several articles in the areas of criminology and delinquency.

segment of the disadvantaged: the *theory of differential opportunity structures* (Cloward and Ohlin, 1960). Either directly or indirectly the War on Poverty for youth operated as if this model were an accurate presentation of the root causes. In this chapter, we shall draw upon the research and experience that have been directed by that model to assess its usefulness. We shall then offer a modified description of the disadvantaged youth that we think is more relevant to the understanding of the problems he faces and the problems we face in our interactions with him. Finally, we will attempt to identify what now appear to be crucial research issues in order to better understand the disadvantaged youth and the delivery of services related to moving the youth toward a less disadvantaged status.

Differential Opportunity Structure Theory: Ten Years Later

The central element in differential opportunity structure theory is as follows:

> The disparity between what lower-class youths are led to want and what is actually available to them is the source of a major problem of adjustment. Adolescents who form delinquent subcultures, we suggest, have internalized an emphasis upon conventional goals, and unable to revise their aspirations downward, they experience intense frustration; the exploration of nonconformist alternatives may be the result (Cloward and Ohlin, 1960, p. 86).

This variation on the Mertonian model of structural sources of deviance (1939) offered two basic approaches to social reform: the stratification of aspirations, or the rejection of what Merton called the democratization of values; and the opening of legitimate opportunity structures (most notably via education, employment, and residence). Because a rejection of the "democratization of values" would be politically disastrous, it was decided that programs would be developed to change the rate of access of lower-class youth to legitimate opportunities, and in the process "solve" what were considered to be direct (e.g., under education and employment) and indirect (e.g., delinquency) consequences of blocked opportunity.

If we were to define the disadvantaged from this culturally relative position, we would say that they are those youth who have heavy liabilities which lessen their chances for competing successfully with their fellow citizens in all phases of life. Disadvantaged youth may be found living with their families in a world where day-to-day survival takes all their thoughts and energies. Keeping a roof over their heads and getting food and clothing pose daily problems. Many American youth are disadvantaged from birth because they are of a minority race and must make their way in a society still riddled with discrimination. Other youth are severely disadvantaged because of a physical environment which isolates them from opportunities for education and social experience in keeping with the requirements of modern life. These are the youth of city ghettos, of migrant farmworkers, or of played-out rural areas.

Many disadvantaged tend to be members of a transient society. They make frequent moves within a city and often to other cities and regions. This results in not really belonging to a local community, interruptions in education, and lack of access to, and knowledge of, desired social agencies. Many of the new registrants in local employment service or welfare offices are in-migrants. Lack of medical care, lack of proper training, and conditions of poverty often result in uncorrected physical and mental handicaps. Many appear to have mental disorders, but may be pseudoretardates or cultural retardates who appear to be retarded because of conditions which have prevented them from developing mentally.

Characteristics of Disadvantaged Youth

From these limiting experiences some very obvious characteristics seem to apply to a substantial number of such youth:

Potential. They may function below their potential due to various deficiencies or because they do not know of the various employment opportunities to which they could aspire. They may have such low self-esteem that it is difficult for them to see themselves as able to acquire or hold jobs for which they are otherwise capable. They may even be reluctant to train for better jobs in the belief that they will find nothing open to them.

Interpersonal Relationships. They may be socially undeveloped, act impulsively, and have difficulty getting along with coworkers and employers. They may not understand how to accept supervision, to develop and learn under it, or to tolerate any implied criticism. They may be irresponsible, and lacking in middle-class standards of reliability. They may not show up on time for interviews, may be late for work, or may not show up at all for several days. Punctuality is often not expected or practiced in their home environments. Some may be bitter and disillusioned, with hidden or obvious hostility. Others will have a sense of powerlessness in the face of overwhelming obstacles. Others will compensate with an overaggressive manner, but more will be inarticulate and withdrawn from adults.

Educational Deficiency. A major and most obvious characteristic is a pattern of educational deficiency. A youth may even be a high school graduate and still lack the ability to read or comprehend basic English, or to handle figures competently. This may be frustrating to him and bewildering to his parents. For many parents believe that no matter how much a child is disadvantaged, if he once gets to school and manages to stay there, he can expect automatically to make his way when grown and to rise economically and socially above his early environment. Various studies have shown that the parents of the disadvantaged, in both city and country, may place a high value on education for their children, though they themselves are largely undereducated. Yet, in spite of this respect for education per se, a majority of these parents cannot or do not give their children adequate support and encouragement either to attend school regularly or to study at home. This lack of family support places an extraordinary responsibility on the school system. Yet these youth generally go to schools which have the poorest facilities, the most crowded classrooms, and overburdened teaching staffs. When these youth enter the labor market, the lifetime tradition of disadvantage is continued, and their deprived background is manifested in their unemployability (Amos, 1964).

The success of efforts to develop reform programs based on this model has been negligible at best. The Coleman Report, the Westinghouse—Ohio University evaluation of Head Start, and the Job Corps evaluation have documented the failure of our efforts to translate this model directly into effective service systems. For example, today there are over one million youth between the ages of sixteen and twenty-one out of school and out of work. There are approximately 350,000 more that are in school but looking for part-time work. In addition, there are between 500,000 and one million who are not only out of school and out of work but are not even in our statistics. They simply exist around the fringes of society and might well be called the "young retired." Furthermore, the direct research on the model during the 1960s raised serious questions concerning its adequacy.

Evaluation of Blocked Opportunity Theory

As Klein (1971) has recently observed, the Cloward and Ohlin rendition of the blocked opportunity theory has been the most tested of all major theories on both minor and major scales. The work of Short and Strodtbeck (1965) certainly stands, along with Klein's, as the most comprehensive and rigorous attempt to subject this model to an evaluation. At each major point, we observe gross inadequacies in the Cloward and Ohlin model.

The Existence of Three Types of Subcultures. Short and Strodtbeck found no evidence for the postulation of criminalistic, conflict, and retreatist subcultures. This lack of evidence has also been observed by Cohen (1966).

The Process of Normative Alienation. Cloward and Ohlin suggested that the perception of opportunity blocking as "external" (i.e., not related to abilities of the subject) would lead to rejection of socially approved means to goal acquisition. Elliott (1962), Gordon (1965), and Empey (1969) have demonstrated that the gang delinquent in fact *does* internalize prescriptive norms.

The Perception of Opportunity. There has been little consistent evidence relating class differentials in the perception of degree of access to legitimate means and delinquency. In fact, there appears to be little relationship between class position and relative perception of legitimate means availability (Elliott, 1962).

Other sociological models for the behavioral problems (Cohen, 1955; Miller, 1958) of lower-class youth have proven to be equally irrelevant to the explanation of the deviance of lower-class youths. In summary, as Klein has observed: "Many of the theoretical statements about gangs currently so widely accepted as fact are nothing of the sort. Rather they are undemonstrated, undemonstrable, or actually demonstrated to be in error" (1971, p. 28).

If, as now seems more clear, these models grossly oversimplify the conditions of disadvantaged youth and the consequences in terms of deviance of these conditions, and if, as we are, also aware that the translation of even these simple models was grossly mismanaged (e.g., Moynihan, 1969), we should not be surprised by our relative failure to achieve "maximum feasible amelioration."

This is not merely to arrive at the banal conclusion that the causes of social conditions are "complex," and that more research is needed. At this point, our conceptions of the disadvantaged are so limited by the theoretical models in which we attempt to organize "relevant data" (and thus disregard or fail to find "irrelevant" data); and the reliance on ideological commitments rather than the results of recent research is so great, that we find little direction for future research in existing models. Instead, we seem compelled to suggest a suspension in theorizing until we have a better representation of what we are trying to explain and change. In the remainder of this chapter, we will provide what we think are some clues to a better understanding of the problems of the lower-class disadvantaged youth. We do not intend to repeat the various descriptions and characteristics of disadvantaged youth that fill the literature. We feel that at this time it is more important to discuss factors which influence efforts to understand and work with such young people, than to add to the demographic description of the disadvantaged (Kohrs, 1968).

Criminal or Delinquent Behavior

It is important to note that a persistent problem characteristic of disadvantaged youth is their involvement in criminal behavior. While we have come to realize that law violation among youth is a fairly general phenomena (studies of hidden delinquency), the overrepresentation of lower-class youth in labeled criminal behavior continues, with the problem for disadvantaged nonwhite being most acute. In terms of arrest rates, nonwhite rates are generally eight to ten times greater than whites, controlling for age, for all serious offense categories (Turk, 1969). This reflects class distributional differences between these racial categories; and, when class controls are introduced, the differences become significantly reduced. It is usually observed that the highest rates of delinquent behavior are to be found among lower-class blacks, followed by lower-class whites; however, the variation between classes is usually greater than the variation between races at the same class level. The important focus, then, in considering the delinquency of the disadvantaged is the class dimension.

In recent years a new pattern of youthful criminality has been imposed on this traditional finding: *the increase in violent crime*. It has been recently reported (Block and Zimring, 1971) that the rate of murder among the younger age categories has increased by as much as 700 percent in the last ten years, with the increase occurring mostly in stranger to stranger, cross-racial homicides. Wellford (forthcoming) has also observed significant increases in the age-specific rate of violent crime during the period 1958–1970 for the age categories fifteen to twenty-one. Thus, violent crime, though still a minor part of the crime problem, is increasingly becoming a behavior of youth and, most frequently, disadvantaged youth. This condition, as well as the more traditional one of high rates of official crime in this segment of the population, offers a continuing significant challenge and impetus to our ability to respond to the disadvantaged.

Some Critical Issues

The disadvantaged adolescent of today is not the disadvantaged adolescent of yesterday. He may or may not look the same, but he does not speak, react, or perform in the same manner. We are primarily speaking of the urban black youth. However, the points that we hope to make have meaning for all races and nationalities.

Hostility and Hate

A presidential commission in recent years pointed out that white racism was a principal factor in the racial problems of this country. We are sure that this is true. We are also sure that black racism has, or will, become an equal partner. The racial hatred in many major urban areas, as exhibited by blacks, has not only precluded those areas from becoming a part of the larger society but has forced many of the social agencies in the areas to close, or to function at a bare minimum of efficiency. The schools, industry, manpower, and welfare programs all have become bastions of racial hatred. In many instances this hatred is veiled with such descriptions as self-pride, black awareness, black power, etc. Such a climate makes it almost impossible to develop programs to prepare young people to enter a society that is beginning to open its doors to all people. This atmosphere of black racism is nationwide, and we see little being undertaken to combat it. Black leaders, for the most part, will not speak against it, for it is political or administrative suicide. White liberals support it either for political reasons or personal feelings. Everyone condemns white racism, but few condemn black racism. Let us hope both black *and* white racism can be eliminated before the country completely separates or meets in the streets.

Black Separatism

As far as the current authors are concerned, integration of races and cultures is perhaps the only long-term hope in our society. We do not base this on a moral consideration (although this country since its beginnings has been a "melting pot" and has been strengthened by this mixture), but on an economic consideration. From a practical standpoint, how can blacks with limited financial resources, inadequate proportions of administrative and technical skills, and constant conflict within their own ranks, hope to separate physically and economically from this society? Such preaching may sound exciting and enticing to a ghetto youth; but, after the romance is over, what has he learned or acquired in the way of skills and attitudes that will allow him to find a rewarding position in the marketplace? In a speech to the Annual Convention of the NAACP, Dr. Wilson Riles observed that it was self-defeating to teach black kids black English. He went on to say that what disadvantaged children need is training in basic English, not in "black nonsense." Such searches for identity only tell the youngster that he is not capable of competing and that success can come only when he is in competition with his own kind. What could be more harmful to a child's concept of himself and of the world?

Educational Conflict

William Raspberry, a young black columnist for the *Washington Post,* recently wrote (1971) an article entitled, "Can Slum Pupils Be Educated?" In his discussion he made the following statement:

> Is there something about life in big-city slums that renders most slum children incapable of academic success?
>
> No one in a position of educational authority is willing to answer yes. Nor does anyone seem to have sufficient factual data to support an unequivocal no.*

Those who have worked in an educational or training setting with such children have perhaps on various occasions wondered the same thing. We have seen the pattern of a slum child entering the first grade with little noticeable intellectual difference between himself and other children. By the time he has reached grade three, he is a year behind; by grade six, two years; and by age sixteen, he drops out, about three years behind. This same pattern is found with mountain whites, reservation Indians, and other "ghetto groups."

From our experiences, the one outstanding identifiable element is the child's inability to read. Educators have known for some years that progressive educational development is based on the ability to read at the appropriate grade level. We have also seen the high correlation between behavior problems and delinquency and the inability to read. Kenneth Clark has proposed that the Washington, D.C., school system make a concentrated effort to overcome the problem by giving extra emphasis to reading and arithmetic for at least one year. Opposition to this plan has so far kept it from being implemented.

In our opinion, more could be done to aid the disadvantaged by a nationwide, intensive, reading program in schools having a high number of disadvantaged youth. This is not to be interpreted as a panacea. We realize that it has limitations, but in our judgment it has more merit than does any other single program of which we are aware. It would hopefully do more to provide a meaningful base to understand and work with disadvantaged youth than does any other current program.

Work

The confusion between the dignity of work and dignified work has become a major issue when understanding or working with disadvan-

* *Washington Post,* April 22, 1971, A19. Used by permission.

taged youth. The dignity of all work and the merit in doing a good job has become a minor point of emphasis in counseling youth of all socioeconomic levels today (see the chapter by Hackman and Davis on vocational counseling).

We feel that the efforts for overcoming racial stereotypes and providing motivation for upward mobility are among the most important elements in counseling disadvantaged youth. However, we also feel that in many cases, absolutely unrealistic views of work and requirements for job success have been offered. Many youngsters who are school dropouts, with limited job skills or experience, expect to be placed well up the occupational ladder. But they may not be equipped with attitudes or goals that allow for vocational improvement and maturation. Even if they are, if rapid promotion is not forthcoming the only excuse the youth may offer is racial prejudice on the part of the supervisor. There is very little self-analysis or insight, and the climate of their environment supports their interpretation.

For several years, one of the current authors was Chief of the Division of Youth Employment Services in the U.S. Department of Labor. One of the real problems noted in the various youth employment or training projects for the disadvantaged was their unrealistic interpretation of what it takes to succeed on a job. "Any white youngster was promoted only because he was white and every black kid failed only because he was black."

We can well understand the basis for these feelings after years of rejection, actual discrimination, inadequate educational systems, and, in many instances, family disorganization. However, understanding these feelings *and* using them as a blanket excuse are two different things. Many people today equate understanding with excusing. In working with the disadvantaged, we do not need to provide them with excuses, but with hope, encouragement, the opportunity for success, and the realization that they, as unique persons, can produce and succeed. It is about time that we stopped equating the problems of the disadvantaged youth with what happened three hundred years ago. Let us equate them with today, and the opportunities and resources of today. Granted that opportunities and resources are not currently adequate for the social ills that our country faces, but they are more adequate than ever before, and all indications are that they will continue to improve.

Recent Observations on the Disadvantaged

Our previous comments raise certain issues that we feel have been neglected in recent discussions of the disadvantaged. Now we will turn to a review of some characteristics that have been stressed in the recent literature on the disadvantaged.

Lack of Motivation

It has been commonly accepted that minority youth are lazy, that they lack motivation. This, of course, is a generalization which would be as true of youth at all social levels, not just disadvantaged youth. However, from our observation in recent years, we see a positive pattern developing. Many such young people have a new concept of themselves and the world about them, and this is reflected in their behavior. The experiences of the past have conditioned many youngsters to feel that they cannot succeed, that a person of their color or race has no hope of success—so why try? The overwhelming repression of poverty has each day provided added proof that they will live and die as their parents did. We feel that in a few short years a rather remarkable change has occurred. From our conversations with youth workers around the country, there comes an optimism that a change is beginning to take place. Some youngsters from the poverty culture seem to have more hope, motivation, and an improved self-concept. Whether this is the beginning of a major transformation we do not know, for it is too early to tell, but it is a hopeful sign. One must note, however, that this positive sign is clearly related to the black separatism movement discussed earlier. The balance between these themes will be a major problem confronting social policy makers in the near future.

Lack of Long-Term Goals

One of the more negative effects of poverty is that it precludes adequate "models" with whom young people may identify and from whom they may pattern their behavior. In our opinion this has been a major reason why so many youngsters from the poverty culture have been unable to plan for the future and hold long-term goals. Of course, the pressures of day-to-day living also preclude relying on future rewards.

However, we again sense a change. It may be related to the various opportunities that have been provided in recent years, particularly in the educational and manpower areas. It may also relate to the considerable number of minority group members who are more visible in the programs and institutions that affect their lives. Whatever the reasons are, there seem to be an increased number of young people from the poverty and ghetto cultures who are developing and holding long-term plans and goals for the future.

Interestingly enough, there seems to be something of a switch in the black-white youth groups. More affluent white youth seem to be dropping out and rejecting long-term goals of the past, and more minority youth seem to be picking them up. More black youth are getting involved in the system and using their energies in bringing about constructive change. It seems that many such youth have seen what involvement can do and sense that, at last, they have a chance to be a part of society. The next step, of course, is planning for the future and the development of longer-term goals.

Mental Health

Many authorities have long felt that the rates of mental illness are higher in poverty areas. The incidences of psychoses, drug addiction, and alcoholism are not only more visible but also seem to be more prevalent. We may say, on the one hand, that much of the behavior which is interpreted as being irrational is very rational in the ghetto setting where the pressures of life are so overwhelming. It becomes negative behavior only when compared to behavior and values outside the ghetto. On the other hand, there is a great need for positive mental health efforts in poverty areas. When one relates good mental health to fully functioning or self-actualized people, then the great discrepancy can be seen. Not "fully functioning" does not mean that persons are mentally ill, but it does mean that their mental health needs improvement in relationship to self-understanding and day-to-day living.

Middle-Class Values

In recent years, the middle class and the values of the middle class have become the accepted cause of most of the ills of our society. The stereotype of materialism, competition, and lack of sensitivity that has been hung around the neck of "Middle-Class America" has been used to explain why the disadvantaged were "frozen out of the marketplace" and why society's interpretation of ghetto life was so biased, prejudiced, and wrong. It has been said often and forceably that the values of the middle class have no meaning for disadvantaged youth and that it is inappropriate to use them in any way. This is not entirely true. Any person who has worked intimately with such young people knows that the values they strive for and that many even assimilate at the present time are values that have to be called middle-class. Some of the strongest defenders of such values are the persons who are products of the ghetto who have risen to middle-class status. They not only believe and accept these values but they also reject many of the persons they have left behind because they have not embraced these values.

Many deprived youth have moved beyond the middle class in their values on clothes, cars, status, and other ego tools. They may "make out" with any available female, but when picking one for marriage or other long-term relationship, we have seen the same values (e.g., chastity) as attributed to the middle class dominate their behavior. The lower socio-economic levels of society have long emphasized education as a status symbol beyond what many middle-class patrons have done. This same overemphasis can be seen in religion, home buying, and the search for status.

We are not saying that disadvantaged youth should be judged or understood from a frame of reference dictated by middle-class values. We are saying that these values have merit in working with such youth; that these values are not *all* useless and improper in understanding the disadvantaged, and that many youngsters from poverty cultures strive for such values and honor them. It is so easy to stereotype all people from a given culture and forget that people are unique and that values are reflected in behavior.

The Administration of Social Change

If the "War on Poverty" and related social service programs have not had the desired impact, why not? From the senior author's extensive involvement in these programs, the following observations seem pertinent:

A Morass of Programs

There were and are simply too many programs and too few capable staff in too many agencies. The Departments of Labor; Health, Education and Welfare; Housing and Urban Development; Interior; Agriculture; and, the Office of Economic Opportunity are glutted with offices and programs designed to provide services to the same people. Bureaucratic defensiveness, uncoordinated repetition, and just plain administration allow the agency to grow with little impact on the individual client. As new programs are founded, staff are lured away from other programs by higher salaries; and it is not unusual to see a person at a meeting representing one agency when at a previous meeting he represented another. So, a very average person steadily rises in the professional world, and eventually his limited creativeness, ability, and insight will seriously limit the effectiveness of some program. Old government workers never die; they just transfer to another program.

Limited Factual Knowledge

That many programs are based on assumptions which are simply not true is common knowledge. We are the first to admit that the poor quality of research which has been flowing from the various universities and other institutions in the past ten years has not really provided the answer to many of the major questions concerning disadvantaged youth. However, we must note that much of the effort in the 1960s was politically motivated and failed to allow for effective participation by qualified social scientists in policy-making efforts.

Theories of Personality Development and Their Impact

In recent years, the academic community has also been concerned with the frames of reference that we use in training youth workers and related personnel. We have particularly been concerned with what theories of personality seem to work in relationship to services provided to the disadvantaged. In fact, it has reached the point in some instances that a particular theory is necessary if your grant or program is to be approved. We have identified three broad areas which may be listed as the psychoanalytic school, the self school, and the neobehavioristic school. For a number of years, the psychoanalytic schools were the principal framework upon which the helping disciplines were built. The schools of social work were influenced by analytical thinking, and, of course, this carried over into the other disciplines such as psychology, guidance, and counseling in schools of education. The reader may turn to the chapter by Beller for an extensive discussion of theories as they relate to the adolescent.

In the last two decades, the self-theories have gained considerable respect, particularly with those who are serving the more disadvantaged client. The works of Rogers, Maslow, and others have given us the understanding with which we can assist in bringing about changes in how a person sees himself and his world.

Also in recent years the neobehavioristic theories have come to the front. A significant number of programs that were funded under the Manpower Development and Training Act were programs that had their philosophical base in behaviorism. The lesson that we have to draw from this might be summed up in this way: "If your particular theory of personality is not popular today, simply wait a few years and it will be." We have overemphasized specific schools of thought to such a degree that we have forgotten that positive impact on people is usually the impact which occurs as a result of the relationship between the counselor and the client, and not because of the philosophical frame of reference that is used. What research we have shows that approximately two-thirds of those persons counseled benefit from the counseling regardless of the theoretical framework, if any, that the counselor was using (Amos and Williams, 1971).

We feel that the above observations are critical for any understanding of program development for the disadvantaged. Without capable supervisory staff, a factual philosophical base and good administration, an army of bright, involved people will have little impact.

Future Research Issues

The past decade has often been referred to as the "decade of understanding." The urge to understand has become the rallying cry of the antipoverty efforts. As a result, one has the feeling that it has become more important to understand than to develop effective preventive and remedial programs. In fact, an explanation has become an excuse, and, as a result, good programs have fallen in the crack somewhere between explanations and excuses. So what we have are many programs, great quantities of exhausted funds, and many disillusioned people—this includes the disadvantaged and their helpers.

It seems to us that what has come out of the efforts of the last ten years has been to show actually, how little we know about how to deal with the massive urban ills that we face in our society. Contrary to some, our opinion is that the behavioral sciences have been given an "unleashed" life in recent years. Never in history have the funds been available for research and consultation that were available during the 1960s, and, we might add, with so little positive results. It seems that the questions of real importance in understanding and working with disadvantaged youth have not been answered or even attacked. Unfortunately, there does not even seem to be a willingness to make the effort. Because of the nature of the problem, most of the issues have a negative flavor. Regardless of their flavor, or how unpalatable they may be to certain groups and philosophies, they must be studied and answered. The few meaningful efforts to approach these issues have been made by private groups with very small and very selective samplings for the most part. We feel that cooperative national backing is necessary to find answers that will guide the large comprehensive national programs; will be professionally acceptable to all groups and races; and will have the funds and staff to do the necessary long-term and in-depth studies required. Of course, the various national societies and professional organizations which have expertise or interest in the areas concerned should be partners in the effort. Because of the controversial nature of many of the studies, the most respected and competent people available should be involved.

Areas of Major Concern

Research efforts should be focused on investigating such perplexing areas and questions as these:

The Evaluation of Social Agencies. Given the relative failure of public service agencies to provide significant services to the disadvantaged, we must continue studies of these agencies. Their contribution to the perpetuation of the problems that they are established to alleviate must be determined. Furthermore, we must explore ways to make these agencies more accessible to public evaluation and control, particularly by those who are the recipients of services. The analysis of the changing of service delivery systems may be the most fruitful in improving our ability to affect the conditions of the disadvantaged.

Age and Learning. At what age can a disadvantaged child's environment be stimulated most effectively? Most educators agree that age six is too late to start remedial programs to create an environment more conducive to intellectual development. We need to know more about the quality and quantity of both staff and experiences that are most effective. We feel that this is one of the more promising areas for helping disadvantaged youth escape the effects of a limiting environment.

Stabilization of Family Life. How can the family life of many disadvantaged children be stabilized so that the experiences, support, and guidance so necessary for human development can occur? In the years since the Moynihan Report, it has not been popular to see this area as one of major concern, and yet the evidence continues to mount supporting the notion that family coping behavior is extremely varied among the disadvantaged. How unfortunate. Until this major social undertaking can be materially effected, then the causes of limited intelligence, behavior problems, delinquency, and other social ills will not be attacked effectively.

Race and Intelligence. This issue is one that has constantly been before the public, in some form, for many years. It has such political and emotional implications that it is almost impossible to discuss it even in professional circles. Even though many authorities will agree that there are a number of unanswered (and unasked) questions concerning race and intelligence, any individual or group that proposes studying the issue is branded racist. This is unfortunate.

In recent years, however, a number of scientists of international reputation have been willing to speak out and propose that long-range research be conducted. One such proposal was before the National Academy of Sciences. This resulted from the recommendation of an eight-man committee, led by Dr. Kingsley Davis, who had been given the charge of making a recommendation. The committee had been established as a result of the urgings of Dr. William Shockley. The Academy rejected the recommendation but unfortunately did nothing to resolve or clarify the issues. More recently, Hans J. Eysenck, in *Race, Intelligence and Education* (1971), has reopened the issue. One cannot dismiss men like Jensen (1969), Shockley (1971), and Eysenck as racists or opportunists. The argument boils down to one point—you have to know what the problem is before you can provide a remedy.

We hope in the near future that resources will be made available to study this major issue in depth, and that a racial climate will develop which will permit scientific research of such importance to be conducted.

Summary

In this chapter, we have attempted to provide a description and analysis of the lower-class youth, not by reviewing or reanalyzing the many demographic descriptions of this segment of our society, but rather by trying to identify some critical issues that we have observed emerging in the last few years. This personalized analysis reflects the problem areas that we suggest researchers and practitioners must acknowledge and confront in order to extend our ability to ameliorate the conditions of the disadvantaged.

Our analysis has led us to focus on three categories of factors affecting the disadvantaged: the theoretical model underlying our efforts to reduce the number in disadvantaged condition; the agencies that have attempted to translate this model into action programs; and the characteristics of the disadvantaged that we see as most important, or, neglected. We have suggested that the model, while ideologically useful, has not been able to explain the data developed by research prompted by the model. The agencies that have been evaluated have consistently been characterized as failing in their accomplishment of primary goals. The numbers of disadvantaged have increased, become more difficult to reach and work with, and have become justifiably hostile toward a society that promises social change but perpetuates structural inequality. The re-emergence of intense public concern with the disadvantaged must be preceded, we suggest, by an examination of the most basic conditions (the structure of change agencies and the psychological and sociological conditions of the disadvantaged) before we can hope to move to more effective programs for the amelioration of this problem.

REFERENCES

Amos, W. E. Disadvantaged youth: Recognizing the problem. *Employment Service Review*, 1964, *18*, 44–46.

———, and Williams, D. *Community counseling*. St. Louis, Mo.: W. Green, 1971.

Block, R., and Zimring, F. Homicides in Chicago. Paper read at American Sociological Association Annual Meeting, 1971.

Cloward, R., and Ohlin, L. *Delinquency and opportunity.* Glencoe, Ill.: Free Press, 1960.

Cohen, A. K. *Delinquent boys.* Glencoe, Ill.: Free Press, 1955.

———. *Deviance and control.* Englewood Cliffs, N.J.: Prentice-Hall, 1966.

Elliott, D. Delinquency as perceived opportunity. *Sociological Inquiry,* 1962, *32,* 216–227.

Empey, L., and Lubeck, S. Conformity and deviance in the situation of company. *American Sociological Review,* 1968, *33,* 760–774.

Jensen, A. R. How much can we boost IQ and scholastic achievement? *Harvard Educational Review,* 1969, *39,* 1–123.

Klein, M. *Street gangs and street workers.* Englewood Cliffs, N.J.: Prentice-Hall, 1971.

Kohrs, E. V. The disadvantaged and lower class adolescent. In J. F. Adams (ed.), *Understanding adolescence: Current developments in adolescent psychology.* Boston: Allyn and Bacon, 1968.

Merton, R. Social structure and anomie. *American Sociological Review,* 1939, *3,* 672–682.

Miller, W. B. Lower class culture as a generating milieu of gang delinquency. *Journal of Social Issues,* 1958, *14,* 5–19.

Moynihan, P. *Maximum feasible misunderstanding.* Glencoe, Ill.: Free Press, 1964.

Raspberry, W. Can slum pupils be educated? *Washington Post,* April 22, 1971, A19.

Shockley, W. Negro IQ deficit: Failure of a malicious coincidence model warrants new research proposals. *Review of Educational Research,* 1971, *41,* 227–248.

Short, J., and Strodtbeck, F. *Group process and gang delinquency.* Chicago: University of Chicago Press, 1965.

Turk, A. *Criminality and legal order.* New York: Rand McNally, 1969.

Wellford, C. Age composition and the increase in recorded crime. (In preparation.)

17

Career Development in Adolescence
*Henry Borow**

The economic state of any society, primitive or advanced, provides serviceable cues as to how that society views its adolescent members and to certain of the cultural roles it assigns them. A people who have achieved only marginal consumption of goods and services or who require that all its available manpower be used to build a rapidly expanding economy may curtail the period of childhood dependency of its young and move them into the labor force at an early age. A technologically sophisticated and stable society, on the other hand—one which has been able to marshal its resources and knowledge toward the attainment of a high per capita production rate—is not likely to regard its younger members as economic assets, and it may institute policies to delay early entry into the occupational world. Thus, the length of psychological adolescence and the experiences and values which are cultivated in this major life stage are conditioned to a significant degree by the way in which the controlling adult society organizes its human resources for work.

* Henry Borow is Professor of Psychological Studies at the University of Minnesota. Books with which he has been involved as editor or author include *Vocational Planning for College Students, General Education for Personal Maturity, Man in a World at Work,* and *Career Guidance for a New Age.* He has written numerous articles on topics such as counseling, occupational psychology, career development, nonintellectual factors in academic performance, and psychological testing.

Youth and Work: A Historical Note

Until the recent past, society's preoccupation with survival needs and minimum acceptable material comforts dictated a view of the child as an essential element in the family as an economic unit. In hunting tribes and agricultural societies alike, the rites of passage into manhood were closely linked to the young individual's demonstration that he could fulfill the obligations of a competent and productive worker. Work skills were frequently taught to the young by fathers and elders through a deliberate process of occupational transmission. It was not the formal tasks of the job alone which were inculcated but also the related folkways and mores which made each trade a distinct way of life. Social custom and institutional policies affecting the management of youth have often been bound to their roles as workers. We may remind ourselves, for example, that the establishment of the fall-to-spring school year in early agrarian America was mainly dictated by the need for young hands to assist with the all-important soil preparation and planting at one season of the year and with harvesting and grain storage at another. Later on, resistance in predominantly farm states to the enactment both of minimum-wage laws governing compulsory schooling, and the licensing of motorized vehicle operators, was motivated in part by the need for a large pool of young workers to help with the crops and livestock and to drive farm tractors and trucks.

The coming of the Industrial Revolution in the latter part of the eighteenth century placed a premium upon children as a source of manpower and ushered in a prolonged period of callous and inhumane exploitation of youth. Before industrialization, the "cottage system" had been an important part of England's textile economy. Virtually every child in the household helped with the spinning and cloth-making. With the appearance of textile machinery and factories, the work site for tens of thousands of children shifted away from the home. It became the practice to collect pauper children from the poorhouses and orphanages and bind them out without compensation to factory owners. Others were sent to the mills by parents who had no regular means of livelihood. In similar vein, young boys were placed in the coal mines and in the cities as chimney sweeps. Young children in Pennsylvania were used in full-time employment as slate sorters. Many young boys entered the British coal mines at age eight or earlier and worked incredibly long hours. Work weeks of seventy and eighty hours were not uncommon. Similar practices were in effect in the United States.

Gradually, there emerged a rising sense of revulsion and a spirit of active protest over child labor exploitation. The widespread abuse of very young workers was one of Karl Marx's prime targets in his attack upon the English industrial system. Novels like Dickens' *Oliver Twist* dwelt on the same theme. The plight of working children was a driving force in the social reform movements which swept over Great Britain and America toward the close of the nineteenth century. One significant result of this moral reaction took the form of a series of protective laws, the first of these being enacted in Massachusetts as early as 1836. The National Child Labor Committee, founded in the United States in 1904, has consistently promoted legal measures to safeguard the health and improve the working conditions of younger workers. This organization was responsible for the early sponsorship of youth job training programs and minimum working-age laws. While economic exploitation of children still exists as a national problem, all states now have enforceable child labor laws. It is estimated that American children whose parents are currently in violation of such laws constitute less than 5 percent of the relevant young population.

Beginning at about the time of the Great Depression of the 1930s, the vocational problem of youth took on a far different character. It was for most adolescents no longer a matter of too much work, of the wrong kind, too early in life; rather, it was one of a widening breach between the experiential life space of youth and the external world of work. Initially, the shrinking job market during the economically depressed years posed a formidable obstacle for young job seekers. School-leaving youth were often seen as a threat to older, established workers, and the job experience requirements and other personal qualifications which they found difficult to meet denied them ready access to full-time employment. Later, the rapid rise in national affluence which marked the post–World War II years brought with it a growing belief that working youth were no longer necessary for the maintenance of a comfortable standard of living in an increasingly leisure-oriented society. It became progressively more difficult for adolescents to envision a meaningful place for themselves in a psychologically remote world that seemed to be so completely and efficiently managed by adults.

The general effect of the new climate has been to strip adolescence of much of its earlier critical functions as a testing ground and apprenticeship for adult autonomy. Friedenberg (1959) has provided a penetrating analysis of this loss in potency of the adolescent period as it relates to the maturing process. Most young adults will, of course, make vocational decisions, find their way into the labor market, and play out their career histories. Given the broad personal freedom which today's youth exercises, however, we may seriously question whether the restricted opportunities for self-exploration and trial which their preadult experience typically affords prepare them to deal appropriately with the realities of a fearsomely intricate occupational universe.

The specific nature of youth's alienation from work will be treated later in this chapter. It may suffice at this point simply to observe that the vocational planning and adjustment problems of contemporary adolescents are complex and that obstinate challenges confront parents, educators, and counselors who propose to offer guidance.

Theories of Vocational Choice and Career Development

It has been only comparatively recently that serious attention has been given to the questions of how young people arrive at occupational preferences and how careers unfold. Since the range of occupations in simpler, nonindustrial societies was quite restricted, and movement from one field of work to another was the exception to the rule, problems of vocational choice and career mobility were not serious barriers to adjustment for the majority of young people. Furthermore, one's work was typically determined by social heredity, even in democratically oriented communities. The social class position of the family and its accustomed occupation quite generally defined the area of vocational opportunity for boys. In England and America, family names like Farmer, Fisher, Carpenter, Fletcher, and Cooper denoted the ancestral trades to which youths were drawn.

The late nineteenth century was marked by expansion, accelerating urbanization, and large-scale immigration. Such conditions combined to diversify the American occupational structure and, correspondingly, to make problems of vocational choice and training matters of central importance for young individuals seeking to find their place in adult society. Social workers, educators, and, most importantly, psychologists turned their attention to these problems. Out of their efforts a number of theories of vocational choice and career development emerged. Descriptions of four influential theories follow.

Matching and Trait-Measurement Theory

The earliest systematic attempts to give vocational guidance to American youth, dating from about the early 1900s, assumed that those preparing for the job market either would or should gravitate toward occupations commensurate with their interests and abilities. A rationale for vocational choice emerged based upon the matching of individual traits and assets with job opportunities and requirements. This concept of vocational choice draws upon the psychology of individual differences and is commonly referred to as *trait-measurement theory*. It assumes that humans differ from one another in their physical and mental makeups, that these trait differences tend to be stable over time, that such differences can be reliably measured, and that the possibility of occupational success increases with the degree to which the individual's trait profile matches the worker trait requirements of his chosen field of work.

The trait-measurement approach is historically linked to the so-called "matching" rationale for vocational guidance. Originally proposed and used at the Vocation Bureau of Boston by Frank Parsons (1909), the matching method called for: helping the individual develop a clearer understanding of himself and his relevant circumstances; helping him acquire a knowledge of entrance requirements, working conditions, and opportunities in different fields of work; and relating the facts about self and the occupational world by what Parsons termed the method of "true reasoning." The trait-measurement approach, which added the techniques and tools of psychological measurement to the matching concept, has provided the dominant strategy for vocational guidance since the early years of this century not only in the United States but in virtually every nation where trained guidance practitioners exist. Its strength and widespread acceptance lie in its straightforward logic and relatively simple application. However, the trait-measurement approach embodies a number of limitations which have led growing numbers of authorities since about 1950 to question its effectiveness. Chief among these drawbacks are its failure to relate vocational aspirations and choices to the psychology of motivation and human development. It furnishes fundamentally a static picture of how vocational choices are made.

Career Decisions as Attempts at Optimizing Satisfactions

Eli Ginzberg (1951), an economist, originally proposed a theory of vocational choice as a developmental process covering a minimum of six or seven years, and, more typically, at least ten years falling mainly in the adolescent period. From interview research on subjects ranging in school status from sixth graders to graduate students, Ginzberg concluded that individuals move through three principal psychological periods as part of the process of making vocational choices: *fantasy* period, *tentative* period, and *realistic* period.

During the *fantasy* period, which characterizes children up to about age eleven, the child's thinking about choices is not qualified by such practical considerations as needed ability, training, entrance requirements, and available employment opportunities. There is little distinction between what the child wants to be and what he believes he can be. He does not think in terms of the limiting conditions of the actual world.

During the *tentative* period, covering most of the adolescent years, the individual begins to consider the conditions and demands he must satisfy to make an appropriate choice of occupations. He considers ini-tially his interests, beginning at about age eleven or twelve. At successive ages, according to Ginzberg, the youth considers the relevance of aptitude and education (ages thirteen and fourteen) and personal values and goals (ages fifteen and sixteen). About age sixteen or seventeen, the adolescent attempts to integrate the facts relating to his interests, compe-tence, and personal values in reflecting about his vocational potential-ities. At approximately age seventeen, he enters a transition stage between the *tentative* and *realistic* periods of the vocational choice-making process.

It is during the *realistic* period, beginning typically toward the end of the seventeenth year of life, that the youth begins to work more directly on the resolution of his vocational choice problem. During this period, he becomes more sensitive to the opportunities and limitations of the external social and economic world, and he attempts to accommodate his motives and personal qualifications, as he perceives them, to the requirements and conditions of the real world. Ginzberg originally inter-preted this phase as involving a process of compromise with the demands of reality, but he now contends that the optimizing of personal satisfac-tion through career decisions is a more appropriate formulation. The individual tests himself out vocationally through competitive life experi-ences, such as school courses, then delimits his choice of occupation within the broader field in which it lies, and, eventually, takes the action signifying at least a provisional commitment to the occupation.

Ginzberg's conceptual account of the process of vocational choice is based largely on his observation of adolescent boys. He believes, however, that his descriptions of *fantasy* period and *tentative* period behavior hold reasonably well for girls, although he concedes that, as considerations of marriage and home life enter their thinking, the *reality* period may assume a different and more complex form for girls. Today's changing social and economic role of women further complicates the descriptive picture of their occupational career. Several recent studies have given some support for Ginzberg's contention that adolescents tend to move from fantasy to reality-based behavior as they advance in age. However, it is important to bear in mind that, even for boys, the history of occupa-tional choice-making does not always take place in the straightforward, uniform manner that Ginzberg's generalized picture suggests.

Ginzberg (1972) has recently reformulated his theory in several respects. We have already noted that he now views the individual's attempt to arrive at a career decision as the optimization of personal satisfaction rather than as a compromise with reality. Ginzberg now also concedes that the individual may continue to be involved in lifelong occupational choice behavior clearly beyond his specification of a vocation in the *realistic* period. This revision in theory acknowledges that the career pattern does not end with the first job and that occupational mobility may extend over the entire career history. Finally, Ginzberg now gives greater prominence to environmental and situational factors in vocational choice. While all individuals have a range of options available when they make their decisions, economic and social disadvantages constrict the possibilities open to certain groups, particularly minorities and the poor. Despite the constraint of reality, however, Ginzberg (1972, p. 175) believes that "the individual remains the prime mover in the decision-making process."

Vocational Choice and Development as the Implementation of a Self-concept

Donald Super (1957a), whose writings and research have had a pronounced influence on contemporary thinking about vocational life, regards occupational behavior as a sequence of developmental experiences culminating not only in a vocational choice but in a lifelong career pattern as well. Thus, Super speaks both of vocational choice and of *vocational development,* the latter being a process which includes the former and which he describes in terms such as *ongoing, continuous, orderly, patterned,* and *dynamic.*

For Super, adolescence is a critical period for revamping and building a more stable picture of oneself, a new self-image or self-concept. Striving to make an appropriate choice and to adjust to one's occupation are mainly matters of finding and assuming an occupational role in which one can express himself in a manner consistent with his concept of self. During the initial developmental stages, *formation* of the self-concept is shaped by one's social experiences and one's perceptions of the meanings of those experiences. With passing time, the adolescent finds himself in social situations which make it possible and, indeed, necessary for him to *translate* his maturing self-concept into occupational terms. Thus, his experiences with certain school subjects, part-time jobs, and active leisure-time activities help him progressively to understand these work potentialities more clearly and to build his vocational self-image. Ultimately, the individual *implements* his concept of self by tentatively selecting an occupation and, if successful, entering the field and moving through it (Super et al., 1963).

Super believes that the vocational counselor should be guided in his work by the foregoing theoretical interpretation of career development. He accordingly defines vocational guidance as "the process of helping a person to develop and accept an integrated and adequate picture of himself and of his role in the world of work, to test this concept against reality, and to convert it into a reality, with satisfaction to himself and benefit to society" (Super, 1957a, p. 197) . Super interprets the vocational decision making which occurs within the individual's developmental sequence as a type of personal problem solving. Borrowing from psychological work on the analysis of the thinking process, he proposes the following series of steps as a general model for understanding how vocational choices are made (Super, 1973) :

Anticipation
> Awareness of the Need to Choose among Alternatives
> Acceptance of Responsibility for Choice
> Awareness of Factors to Be Considered
> Knowledge of Sources and of Resources

Crystallization
> Use of Resources for Exploration and Information

Clarification
> Awareness of the Consequences of Choice

Specification
> Synthesis of Information in a Choice

Implementation
> Action on the Choice

It is Super's position that the problem-solving sequence outlined above holds promise for application in guidance. He offers it as a frame of reference for understanding the use of computer systems in support of vocational counseling (Super, 1973) .

Matching Model Personal Orientations to Occupational Environments

John Holland (1958, 1964, 1966) has proposed a conception of vocational behavior which is an updated and somewhat more sophisticated version of trait-measurement theory. He reasons that, out of a wide set of cultural and personal experiences, the individual develops well-established dispositions to deal with environmental tasks in certain preferred ways. These personal coping styles form the basis of Holland's personality classification scheme, and consist of six model personal orientations: Realistic, Intellectual, Social, Conventional, Enterprising, and Artistic. Each model-orientation is actually a broad complex of personal traits, abilities, aspirations, and coping mechanisms. But an individual's pattern of personal orientations may be determined in a number of ways, including the use of the six scales of Holland's Vocational Preference

Inventory (the name of each scale representing one of his personality types). Scores on this personality instrument are derived from the individual's responses, positive and negative, to a lengthy list of occupational titles. Holland believes that such responses are revealing since individuals tend to stereotype occupations by their labels and thereby disclose the type of environment with which they prefer to cope. Thus, the individual who is striving for a suitable career choice seeks out those environments which are compatible with his pattern of personal orientations, and he exhibits these inclinations through his responses to personality test items.

Six occupational environments exist within the American work structure, according to Holland, and these generally correspond in their characteristics and requirements to the six model personal orientations in Holland's personality typology. It is possible, then, to match preferred personal styles to occupational environments. Holland's research suggests that, to some degree, types of personal orientation, as measured by the Vocational Preference Inventory and other instruments, are indeed indicators of the curricular and occupational aspirations and choices of students. Thus, he believes that functional occupational categories reflect broad personality types and that it becomes "possible to talk about vocational choice, vocational behavior, and achievement in terms of personal variables" (Holland, 1964, p. 273). To the extent that this may be true, counselors can help adolescents gain insight into their personalities on the basis of their vocational perceptions and, conversely, can assist in clarifying their career options in terms of personality types. Whether career choice theories such as Holland's possess much practical utility in fostering realistic behavior remains, however, a matter to be more fully demonstrated.

Strengths and Limitations of Career Development Theory

The values of all serious theoretical accounts, including those of Ginzberg, Super, and Holland, are that they: provide a meaningful way of portraying occupational choice as a developmental process; suggest that the making of occupational decisions is more complex than commonly believed; identify many of the personal, social, and economic factors that influence thinking about occupational life; show that vocational choice can be profitably conceived as a multistage task in which the individual strives to link his evolving personal aspirations with the demands of the real world; and, point to significant new questions which can be framed as hypotheses and put to the test of research. On the debit side, most occupational theories have overstressed the question of how specific vocational choices are reached. They are as yet limited in interpreting the psychological processes in the *development* of vocational behavior. More-over, they are still highly speculative and provide at best only miniature and incomplete accounts of how vocationally relevant tendencies emerge in children and adolescents.

Concepts of Career Development

To move beyond the limits of any single specific theory and understand better the processes by which children grow into adolescence and estab-lish a vocational identity, we find it useful to borrow several principles from developmental psychology and the psychology of personality. Such concepts permit a wider framework both for research on career develop-ment and for vocational guidance practice. We shall identify and briefly describe several of these concepts.

Vocational Development Tasks

Borrrowing both from the psychological life stages concept (Buhler, 1933) and the notion of developmental tasks (Havighurst, 1953), the study of career development has moved from fixed preoccupation with the act of vocational choice toward an identification of the motives and related problem-solving behavior which typify the individual at each life stage in his particular social setting. When we shift our focus in this manner, we appreciate that it is not necessary to delay the study of occupational behavior in the youth until he confronts his first, formal choice-point in the decision chain, as, for example, the choice between the business, industrial arts, and college preparatory tracks at the end of the ninth grade. We can study with considerable profit the occupation-ally relevant behavior exhibited in younger subjects; and we can consider its lessons for the vocational guidance of youth, including the improved uses of occupational information. Examples of vocational development tasks in the preschool child are acquiring the ability for self-help, identi-fying with the like-sexed parent, and increasing one's ability for self-direction. Other examples, appropriate to the elementary school child, would include the ability to undertake cooperative enterprises, the assumption of responsibility for one's acts, and the performance of simple chores around the house. Illustrations of typical vocational development tasks of the high school adolescent are the choice of a curriculum, the acquisition of appropriate work attitudes and habits through a part-time job, and the development of increased personal and economic indepen-dence from family (Super et al., 1957a).

Havighurst (1964) has presented an interpretation of how normal developmental tasks at each successive age level are associated with the learning of an occupational role. The following outline includes the first four life stages in Havighurst's six-stage version of vocational development. It is apparent that, in his earlier psychological life stages, the individual is confronting experiences and learning to master developmental tasks which have an important bearing on his later vocational choice and adjustment behavior.

> Identification with a Worker (five–ten years of age)
>   Father, mother, other significant persons.
>   The concept of working becomes an essential part of the ego ideal.
> Acquiring the Basic Habits of Industry (ten-fifteen years of age)
>   Learning to organize one's time and energy to get a piece of work done. School work, chores.
>   Learning to put work ahead of play in appropriate situations.
> Acquiring Identity as a Worker in the Occupational Structure
>   (fifteen–twenty-five years of age)
>   Choosing and preparing for an occupation.
>   Getting work experience as a basis for occupational choice and for assurance of economic independence.
> Becoming a Productive Person (twenty-five–forty years of age)
>   Mastering the skills of one's occupation.
>   Moving up the ladder within one's occupation.

Career Pattern Concepts

Despite a durable popular myth, most individuals do not make a single, fixed career choice. They make several. Industrial sociologists such as Miller and Form (1964) have traced what is called the career pattern of industrial workers, that is, the movement from position to position within the career sequence. The career pattern concept is related to the study of occupational mobility but goes beyond it in that it assumes a causal chaining of the decisions in the pattern. This includes causes that are both internal (psychological) and external (socioeconomic). Moreover, the career pattern concept furnishes a perspective on the individual's occupational history and the character of his occupational adjustment which the study of isolated job choices does not afford. Vocational development theorists have extended the concept of the career pattern downward in time to include the tentative and often unstable choices and aspirations of childhood that may long precede the subject's formal entry into the labor force.

The Taking of Occupational Roles

In the complex, time-extended process by which the child becomes socialized with respect to the values, customs, and expectations of his subculture and the general culture, he must learn his behavior modes from those around him. As he grows, he imitates the behavior of older children and of adults who thus become his role models. In part he is learning to master his developmental tasks, and in part he is exploring roles and experiences in order to learn both the kind of person he is and the kind he aspires to be. Some of these role-taking experiences become important in shaping his emerging concept of self as a potential worker.

Occupational Role Modeling

It appears quite likely that the manner in which the developing child acquires perceptions and attitudes relating to work and to specific jobs comes under the influence of the significant adults in his life, such as parents, older siblings, relatives, neighbors, and teachers. While both the modeling of occupational behavior and the child's assimilation of attitudes and information about it are often incidental and unconscious, the effects upon developing behavior are thought to be pervasive and durable. For this reason, advocates of behavior modification techniques and reinforcement learning principles recommend that counselors arrange the child's environment to include the deliberate modeling of successful occupational behavior (Krumboltz and Thoresen, 1969; Krumboltz and Krumboltz, 1972).

Reality Testing

Most of the foregoing principles of career development can be understood in relation to a kindred concept, namely, the striving of the adolescent to establish his psychological autonomy and to discover himself by means of trying out a variety of personal roles and then experiencing society's reactions. In contrast to his earlier child self, the adolescent has built an improved critical capacity to judge his own capabilities and limitations in terms of the "feedback" he gets from those about him, such as parents, teachers, part-time work supervisors, and especially his peers. Accordingly, many of his acts are instances of self-exploration in which he measures his varying successes by the verdicts and standards of the significant persons in his life. He is, in short, testing himself out as an adequate person. In the process, he acquires a set of feelings about his potentialities not only as a family member and as a member of an adolescent culture, but also as a future worker.

Vocational Maturity

Super (1955) introduced the notion that psychologists and counselors can go beyond the mere observation and descriptive reporting of the normative behavior in children and adolescents, which has implications for vocational life, and can attempt to apply qualitative standards to such behavior. Super locates a basis for his reasoning in the principles of biological and psychological maturation. Individuals acquire an expanding repertoire of perceptions and responses as they develop, and these mechanisms permit them to manage their needs and to deal with environmental realities in more suitably adaptive ways. This, the evolution of behavior which has relevance for vocational exploration, decision making, and performance can be viewed as *vocational maturity*.

Super (1957a) and his associates propose that vocational maturity be assessed either by comparing the individual's attained vocational life stage with his expected life stage, based on chronological age, or by how well he is mastering his vocational development tasks, "regardless of whether they are tasks considered appropriate for his age and expected life stage" (Super, 1957a, p. 57). The latter definition is commonly used to construct measures of vocational maturity. Such instruments have been used predominantly to assess the occupationally relevant behavior of adolescent boys and girls at several age-grade levels. These measures have also been applied to the question of how vocational maturity changes progressively with age during adolescence.

Working with ninth-grade boys in the longitudinal *Career Pattern Study* at Teachers College, Columbia University, Super (1960) and his associates identified four indices of vocational maturity which were psychologically meaningful at this age level: the subjects' expression of personal concern about the problem of working out a vocational choice; his disposition to assume personal responsibility for the tasks of choice and planning; the specificity of information which he has about his preferred occupational field; and evidence of the specificity and amount of planning that he has already undertaken with respect to his preferred field. Gribbons and Lohnes (1968) used the concept of vocational maturity to develop their *Readiness for Vocational Planning Scales*. The eight scales are derived from a detailed interview schedule by which means the observer may assess such factors as those related to the subject's choice of curriculum and occupation, the accuracy of the picture he has of his own educational and vocational assets, and his awareness of interests and values in relation to the making of occupational choices. Many of the findings on the vocational behavior and adjustment of adolescents which are reported later in this chapter have been gathered by means of vocational maturity measures such as those described here.

Childhood Socialization: Antecedents of Adolescent Career Development

For many years, the concerns of the vocational psychology and guidance fields about the work role were narrowly focused upon the act of occupational choice itself rather than on the broad spectrum of merging fantasies, motives, perceptions, attitudes, values, and other manifestations of work-related behavior. Since it is not ordinarily until adolescence that students face formal decisions involving curricula and occupations, the serious study of the vocational implications of childhood experiences was largely neglected. It has become increasingly clear, however, that we cannot adequately understand the origin of the vocational thinking and decisions of adolescents without reference to their earlier history.

Members of the young child's immediate family, who comprise his primary reference group, are the most significant individuals in his socialization. It is in his interaction with them that he experiences sex typing and learns his earliest concept of self and his repertoire of coping techniques. The family establishes the "cultural timetables" by which he meets new social experiences, acquires new skills, and becomes aware of what the world expects from him stage by stage (Slocum, 1967). The implications for later vocational life of his early socialization is noted by Super (1957b, p. 248) when he states, "Habits and expectations of success in the childhood family constitute a basis for later vocational success. The person who grows up in a home in which he is given experiences of success (and) in which his successes are rewarded . . . develops habits of success which carry over into school, social life, and work."

The school soon enters the scene as the second main institutional agent under whose influence the child learns his cultural perceptions and practices. Complying with rules, carrying out assignments, performing competitive tasks, and relating to other people are all part of the learning experiences of the child in school. Out of these the child forms concepts of success and failure, acquires an awareness of what he can and cannot do, and develops the roots of his educational and vocational aspirations.

Underlying the aforementioned growth in the child's ability to deal with his home and school environments are certain foundational adjustment tendencies and coping styles. Each of these is generally learned early, becomes internalized as a habitual response mode, and operates as a potentially important determinant of how effectively the adolescent will subsequently enact task-oriented social roles, including those of student and worker.

Four of these behavioral characteristics will be briefly identified. They are highly interdependent and may, in fact, represent somewhat different emphases and interpretations involving the same broad dispositions and competencies.

Personal Autonomy in Meeting and Handling Everyday Tasks

Increasingly, since about the 1940s, the goal of hygienic child-rearing in America, particularly in middle-class society, appears to have been training for psychological independence. We want the child to be equipped to take over ever larger domains of task attainment and personal choice-making so that, in effect, he learns to draw on his own understandings, resources, and skills to meet and solve new problems. This expanding capacity for self-reliance will later serve the individual both in his generalized interpersonal relations and in competitive, task-centered settings such as the classroom and the place of work.

Internal Controls on One's Own Behavior

Young children vary in the rate with which they learn impulse control. The ability to delay gratification of a desire until one feels he has earned it or until it becomes socially appropriate is widely accepted as an index of growth in personal maturity. We see an example in the behavior of a child who delays his playtime activities until he has completed his home work assignment or a parentally assigned household chore. The rate at which the child progresses in his developmental tasks and in making an outward, productive attack on his problems will depend significantly on the early and successful establishment of internal controls on his own behavior. Implications for attaining readiness to contemplate and assume vocational roles seem clear.

Competence: Effectance Motivation

A number of observers have described the virtually universal tendency of healthy infants and young children to explore their immediate environment and to strive for mastery in dealing with it. Laura Murphy (1962) calls this "coping" behavior, which she states is to be seen in the young child's persistent efforts to satisfy curiosity, to participate in what is going on around him (rather than to avoid it), and to increase his manipulation and control of his delimited surrounding world. Robert White (1959), whose work in this area has been influential, uses the terms *competence* and *effectance motivation* in his account of how the child learns to deal successfully with his environment. Effectance motivation, White states, is commonly exhibited in the play and exploratory activities of young subjects. Gardner Murphy (1973) relates notions of coping and developmental mastery behavior in children to "work and the productive personality." While it remains for longitudinal research to provide greater empirical evidence of the relationship between early effectance motivation and later vocational adjustment, it seems reasonable to assume the existence of a significant causal connection between them.

Achievement Motivation

Early training in independence and the effective rewarding of independent behavior in solving problems appear to nourish the child's need to achieve at a superior level. Parental modeling of successful behavior, as we have already seen, also strengthens the child's drive to achieve. The concept of achievement motivation is thus used to refer to the tendency to set for oneself high standards of excellence and to act in a manner conducive to the attainment of these standards. Mussen, Conger, and Kagan (1963) have noted the consistency of achievement-oriented behavior as a personality trait, and they assert that the child who enters school with a desire to do well is likely to develop into the adult who is concerned with intellectual competence. Their conclusion is influenced by findings based on Fels Research Institute data, which suggested that the strength of intellectual goals in young pupils may be a useful index of later achievement in adolescence and adulthood (Moss and Kagan, 1961).

Youth on the Threshold of Work: The Occupational Outlook

The world of work which today's school-leaving youth confront is one of bewildering diversity and complexity. *The Dictionary of Occupational Titles* (U.S. Department of Labor, 1965) defines and codes almost twenty-two thousand separate American occupations, many of them with unfamiliar or multiple titles—specialized, technical, and frequently hidden from public view. Dramatic changes have occurred and continue to occur in the national occupational structure in the twentieth century. A nation composed mainly of farmers, miners, domestics, casual laborers, and small business owners and operators has been transformed into one whose economy is dominated by large-scale corporate enterprises and in which professional personnel, technicians, and skilled tradesmen have replaced, most of all, the small farm owner and the unskilled worker.

Since about midcentury, America has had predominantly a white-collar, rather than a blue-collar, work force. Moreover, the efficiency of sophisticated, high-speed machinery and new sources of industrial power have so boosted the nation's production capacity as to allow a massive shift in the direction of service jobs and away from goods-producing jobs. Stated in other terms, advanced manufacturing and distribution techniques have allowed us to produce far more goods than heretofore with far fewer workers. This circumstance has opened the way for the emergence of many new types of positions and specialities in the information sciences, arts, education, the health fields, and human services. In recent years, a new class of workers has emerged, technically trained but not at the baccalaureate level, and working closely with, and generally under, the supervision of professionals. Falling under the broad occupational label of "paraprofessionals," such workers include a variety of allied health personnel (paramedicals, such as laboratory technicians), engineering assistants, teacher aides, psychiatric aides, paralegal workers, and others.

It is not only the variety of work but also the brisk and uncertain pace of change in the world of work which makes the task of vocational planning among American school youth difficult. Even federal agencies which monitor economic developments and shifts in labor force supply-and-demand ratios have not always been able to make accurate forecasts of significant changes in occupational opportunities and requirements. Immediately following World War II, schools and their counselors typically cautioned young men about an expected surplus of engineers which failed to materialize. In the late 1960s and early 1970s, colleges failed to counsel new students about the near-glut in teaching, aerospace science, and other professional fields. We can, however, identify a number of significant and stable trends which characterize today's world of work and which have implications for the career planning and prospective work adjustment of adolescent youth.

Occupational Trends

Work Week. For most Americans, work no longer commands the major portion of their waking hours. At the turn of the century, the average worker spent sixty hours a week at his job, typically laboring six ten-hour days. The length of the average work week is now estimated at about thirty-six to thirty-eight hours. For statistical purposes, the U.S. Department of Labor defines full-time employment as work requiring a minimum of thirty-five weekly hours. Vacations are longer, retirement provisions are a common condition of work contracts, and national holidays are being set on Monday to allow more three-day weekends. It is currently estimated that perhaps more than four hundred American firms are operating on four-day work weeks, although the total weekly hours spent at their jobs by employees in these companies have not necessarily declined. Overall, however, we have become a more leisure-oriented nation; we have less work-committed time.

Leisure Time. The trend toward increased leisure has not affected all categories of work equally. Industrial workers have been the chief beneficiaries of the shorter work week. Many professionally trained workers, scientists, college professors, and managerial personnel, on the other hand, spend more hours at work than they did formerly. Surprising, too, is the fact that an average American today spends more years at work, this despite more schooling, later entrance into the labor force, and greater prospects for retirement than his grandfather experienced. The explanation is found in the sharp rise in life expectancy. A male child born in 1900 had a life expectancy of only 48.2 years and a work-life expectancy of 32.1 years. By 1960 the life expectancy for males had risen to 66.6 years and the work-life expectancy to 41.4 years (Wolfbein, 1968). Thus, young workers who enter the labor force will need to find satisfying and useful ways of organizing their time around both work and leisure roles. They will continue to find their identity through the work role, in part, but will need to find it increasingly in nonwork activities as well.

Part-Time Work. This has become an increasingly important factor in the national economy (U.S. Department of Labor, 1970). In 1970, approximately 12 percent of nonagricultural employees held part-time jobs. Assuming the continuance of the current trend, one of seven American workers in 1980 will be holding employment on less than a full-time basis. Part-time workers come chiefly from the ranks of older employees, married women, and young persons in late adolescence and early adulthood. Many in the latter group are secondary school and college students who are at least partially self-supporting through their work. While such job experience can be of potential value in establishing useful work habits and attitudes, there appears to be little evidence that most youthful part-time work experience, with the notable exception of school-based programs of cooperative vocational education, has a maturing effect on career behavior.

The Economy. The uncertain state of the economy was reflected in a national unemployment rate of about 6 percent in 1971 and 1972. This figure was half again as high as the rate in 1967. While increased joblessness occurred among almost all classes of workers, the burden fell with particular force among the poorly educated, the ethnic minorities, and the young. Whereas the 1960 ratio of youth unemployment (ages sixteen–nineteen) to adult unemployment (age twenty-five and above) was

3.3 to 1, the gap widened seriously to 5.5 to 1 at the end of the decade of the 1960s. This condition points to a major difficulty faced by present-day young people in the period of transition from school to work.

Education. The trend toward more years of formal education continues; and, in general, the relationship between years of education, employment rates, and earnings remains strong. Among white youth, those now leaving school as high school graduates probably exceed 80 percent; the corresponding figure for black youth is about 70 percent. These graduates generally fare better in the labor market than do dropouts. However, it may no longer be true that the chances for full-time employment increase constantly with years of education. Relative to job requirements and opportunities, we may as a nation be becoming an overtrained people or, perhaps, trained for the wrong fields. American colleges and universities turned out over 800,000 graduates in June of 1971, the highest total in history (*Time*, May 24, 1971). Each year brings an increase in new college matriculants, although the rate in increase may be slowing down. While the professional and technical occupational groups are expected to grow faster than other categories during the 1970s, an estimated 80 percent of U.S. jobs today could be satisfactorily handled by candidates with no academic training beyond high school. If the career education needs of youth are to be better served, it seems clear that the prestige and social pressures that are responsible for swelling college enrollments will have to be counterbalanced by attractive opportunities in the post-secondary vocational and technical schools and in the occupationally oriented two-year community colleges.

The Changing Occupational Status of Women

The enlarging social and intellectual roles of women are attended by changes in their economic status and career opportunities. The trend toward fuller and more active participation by women in the labor force actually dates from the early part of the century and has been clearly discernible since World War II. In addition, progress has accelerated with the emergence of the women's liberation movement.

It has been a common misunderstanding that, because young women have marriage and families as personal life goals, they are only lightly committed to occupational careers and tend to spend only a comparatively few years at work. Actually, one-half of women between the ages of eighteen and sixty-four are now in the labor force. By 1960, the percentage of women between the ages of thirty-five and sixty-four who held employment grew to three times what it had been in 1900. By 1968, 42 percent of all working-age women were in the full-time labor force. In addition, almost 30 percent of adult women were at work on a part-time basis. Of the total population of employed women, one-half have attained the age of forty or beyond; almost three-fifths are married (Wolfbein, 1964, 1968).

A major task of the schools and the home is to furnish adolescent girls with a realistic conception of their imminent role and function as workers in the economy. At one time or another, nine out of ten girls will be employed outside the home. The typical high school girl of today may expect to spend about twenty-five years of the remainder of her life in paid employment. Furthermore, for women vocational horizons are expanding; they are not so confined as previously to so-called "female occupations." Women workers were to be found in all 479 occupations enumerated in the 1960 national census.

The Alienation of Youth from Work

The introductory section of this chapter noted some significant historical changes in society's conception of the place of young persons as workers. We saw that, as technology advanced and our country became more affluent, we progressively devalued the potential contribution of children and adolescents to the economy. In the inventory of the family occupational resources, youth became, as it were, "excess baggage." The net effect of this depreciation, as the discussion which follows strongly suggests, has been to deprive the adolescent experience of much of its former utility in preparing young people to assume responsible work roles.

Societal barriers increasingly wall youth off from early, full-time labor force participation. The principal restrictive mechanism is the demand for more education, but the related qualifications of age and previous work experience are also involved. Thus, early and direct experience with work is open to fewer youth than was true in previous generations. Even indirect and vicarious contact with work seems more difficult for them to establish. Increasing numbers of jobs are either more intricate and complex than hitherto, or they have become fragments of larger work operations. In addition, large-scale organizations, having an inscrutability and impersonality not found in the small, intimate setting of work, account for increasing proportions of employees. The result has been that the work of parents becomes less visible to their children. There are fewer opportunities than formerly for children to witness parents firsthand at work or to talk with them comprehendingly about their work, much less the opportunity to work alongside them, as for example, in the case of the farm youth or the son of a small shopkeeper.

Ironically, the broadened freedom which is available to youth today for personal decision making obligates them to assume increased responsibility for choice concerning vocational plans at the very time when the options have become more numerous and puzzling and when the rising divorcement of youth from work has left them with comparatively limited acquaintance with the essential elements of choice. Knowing this, we are better prepared for the findings of several recent studies in which substantial proportions of high school graduates express uncertainty about their futures and report the retrospective wish that their school had provided more career guidance.

There is also an emotional detachment from work which may well be affecting increasing numbers of young people. Elsewhere, I have reviewed studies (Borow, 1966) which suggest that, through some not very well-understood perversity in the process of occupational socialization, many children shift from predominantly positive images and attitudes of work to negative ones. As they move through middle childhood and early adolescence, they appear prematurely and unconsciously to reject entire categories of work, a phenomenon which unnecessarily narrows the range of potential vocational choices and biases the exploratory experience in counseling.

The emotional rejection of work in general as an acceptable human activity can be more directly and clearly observed in the statements and choices of some adolescents and young adults. What percentage of the youth population is involved is not known, but it is probably still relatively small, yet growing. The declarations of advocates of the antiwork position range from charges about growing unemployment and diminished occupational opportunities, through dour assessments of the unfulfilling, restrictive, and dehumanizing character of most jobs in the economy. They may make energetic attacks on all conventional work as an instrument by which the self-serving "establishment" maintains itself in power at the expense of both human and natural resources (see the counterculture chapter by Cross and Pruyn). Moral values, such as altruism, and other personal ideals are motivating considerations of many who embrace the foregoing position. While some youth who dissent prefer to remain entirely aloof from work, at least for a time in their lives, others seek meaningful experiences through alternative life styles and alternative jobs. Examples of such positions are draft counselors, work in a crisis intervention center, selling in an organic foods shop or cooperative store, creating and selling homemade arts and crafts products, teaching in a free school, or joining the ACTION Corps (VISTA/Peace Corps). Thus far, the rejection of conventional work and the search for alternative jobs within the counterculture appears to hold attraction for adolescents and young adults mainly from upper-middle class family backgrounds rather than those who come from blue-collar families.

Work Disjunctions in Disadvantaged Youth

Amos and Wellford's chapter in this volume describes some of the developmental problems which exist among lower-class adolescents. While, as we have seen, alienation from work may be a general problem for American adolescents, it is nonetheless appropriate to identify here some of the special correlated behavior tendencies which compound adjustment to occupational roles among younger persons from lower-class and ethnic minority families.

Since 1960, the unemployment rate for blacks leaving high school—graduates and dropouts combined—has remained about double the rate for white youth. In 1968, the rate of joblessness among recent black school-leavers was 23 percent, nearly double the rate for the comparable white school-leaving population and approximately four times that for the nation's work force as a whole. While average annual earning levels for blacks and other minorities have improved, the level attained by those with an eighth-grade education is about 70 percent as high as the level for whites with a comparable education. For minority group members with four years or more of college, the economic improvement has been somewhat more encouraging. Their average annual earnings, taken as a percentage of the earnings of comparably educated whites, are now close to 80 percent (U.S. Department of Labor, 1970).

For many youth who are disadvantaged by socioeconomic or minority ethnic status, negative experiences with neighborhood, school, and work have often created serious obstacles to the growth of vocational maturity and adjustment to work. Distrust of education, meaningless social reward systems, lack of recognition for intellectual promise, the absence of effective occupational role models in the home environment, and poor school and guidance facilities have been typical conditions with which disadvantaged children and adolescents have had to contend. For many, these have been factors too difficult to circumvent and which, when combined, have militated powerfully against the prospects for adequate career development. The consequences are to be seen in the behavior of those boys and girls who may hold negative self-images as potential workers; lack realistic pictures of the world of work; display an inability or unwillingness to undertake long-range planning; seek immediate or short-term payoffs on their efforts; and fail to comprehend the conventional work etiquette which employers appear to expect from those seeking work. It was to deal with such noxious conditions of personal and social disadvantage that functional programs of compensatory education and work training have been established in recent years, and increasingly since the mid-1960s.

Occupational Aspirations and Motives

Most adolescents are upwardly aspiring in their vocational ambitions and choices. In a nationwide sampling of about one thousand boys between fourteen and sixteen years of age, Douvan and Adelson (1966) found that over one-half preferred professional and semiprofessional jobs. Fewer than 30 percent chose manual occupations, largely in the skilled trades and crafts. Only one in six boys chose a job lower in status than his father's. Douvan and Adelson's corresponding sample of girls in the same age range expressed interest in occupations linked to traditional feminine goals and values. Their expressed preferences were more ambiguous and less consistent than those of boys. More than a fourth showed preferences for the helping professions, such as nursing and medicine, while about 40 percent named jobs in the conventional female groups, such as sales clerk, secretary, and bookkeeper. Nearly all the girls planned to finish high school, and 60 percent intended to pursue further training.

Since studies do not generally distinguish between the preferences (involving less definite personal commitments) and the actual choices of adolescents, the findings are sometimes difficult to interpret. In general, there is little disparity between the preferences and the choices of middle-class boys. They appear reasonably confident that they can realize their ambitions. Girls and minority group subjects, on the other hand, tend to name expectations or probable choices below the level of their initially stated ambitions.

Vocational Motives

We have already seen that the search for a satisfying vocational goal can be linked with the adolescent drive toward increased personal autonomy and with the attempt to find a life role which is consonant with the image the young person projects of himself. In more specific terms, preference for one type of occupation over another can be viewed as an expression of the particular values which become clarified and ascendant during the adolescent years. As noted earlier in the chapter, Holland's six clusters of personal orientations are premised on this rationale. Rosenberg (1957) has identified three broad constellations of values about which vocational decisions tend to cluster. These involve the individual's orientation toward: helping people; earning extrinsic rewards, as, for example, high income or fame; and, self-expression, as exemplified by the writing professions and the performing arts.

The Douvan and Adelson (1966) survey identified the drive for achievement as an undergirding theme in the fantasies of boys. Thus, achieving behavior, perhaps in the sense of power, is seen as a prime masculine motive which may be linked with vocational aspirations. Like boys, the personal decisions of adolescent girls show a serious concern with educational and occupational planning; but their fantasies dwell on femininity, personal attractiveness, and social acceptance, and they are less closely tied to educational and vocational success. Their occupational plans are, as a rule, more strongly prompted by altruism than are those of boys.

When senior high school students are asked to specify the occupational conditions which they consider most important in the selection of a career, they typically name "interest in the work" with greatest frequency (Powell and Bloom, 1962). The desire for security is also prominently mentioned as a motive for choice. In comparison with adults, high school seniors—girls in particular—also identify interest in people and the opportunity to be of service to others as significant conditions of occupational choice.

There is doubt, however, that the majority of younger adolescents are themselves clear about their interest and value systems or that they consciously evolve vocational plans with their personal values sharply in mind. Brighter youth and those who are academically and socially more successful are generally better able to provide a more rational and explicit account of their vocational choices in terms of values. Yet, on the whole, it does not appear that a deliberate and calculated concern about implementing a set of personal values strongly governs the particular choice. Furthermore, many fortuitous and situational circumstances appear to affect vocational decisions in ways that are not always predictable. Thus, many youth, particularly those of lower socioeconomic class status and those with limited education, appear to "fall into" their job fields. It is out of consideration of such unplanned occupational behavior that contemporary vocational guidance has tended to center more directly on the need to assist young people over an extended period of time with problems of career development and, especially, with the need to clarify their own goals and to set rational vocational plans consistent with them. Hackman and Davis discuss the process of vocational counseling in the following chapter.

It is becoming clear that, as part of the continuing socialization experience, children and adolescents internalize powerful stereotypes of many occupations which are related both to the prestige they command and the life style they open up to those who enter them. Upper elementary school children appear to value occupations in terms of how they see their contribution to society. But among seventh graders, the notion of a social status hierarchy applicable to occupations has apparently been acquired, and they tend to rank jobs on a prestige criterion.

The process of social assimilation continues, and tenth graders are able to rank-order the status of occupations in almost precisely the same manner as adults (Gunn, 1964). Among college students, the perceived prestige of occupations is an important determinant of choice (O'Dowd and Beardslee, 1960). Entering a high status occupational field—business management or medicine, for example—may be seen as a way of attaining and insuring an enviable way of life extending to a high standard of personal living, a rich variety of leisure adventures, and attractive friends. Among some adolescents, including upwardly aspiring liberal arts college students, knowledge of the status-conferring power of an occupational field may be more accurate than knowledge of how one enters the field or of the specific duties one is expected to perform.

Stability of Adolescent Occupational Goals

Because society attaches considerable importance to the making of vocational decisions as a precondition of educational and personal plans, high school students sense considerable pressure to state their occupational choices. Among entering college freshmen, compliance with this social expectation comes in the form of selecting rather specific curricular fields or academic majors. Indeed, studies over many years have repeatedly demonstrated that newly admitted college students single out the occupational choice and preparation functions of the college experience as major factors in their decision to pursue higher education.

Evidence bearing on the foregoing point is provided by a study of approximately eighteen thousand college-bound high school students. These subjects constituted a representative 3 percent sample of a population of 612,000, tested under the American College Testing Program between November 1964 and October 1965. When asked to choose from a list of ten options the one which represented their most important goal in attending college, slightly over half (51 percent) chose, "To secure vocational or professional training." The alternative showing the second highest frequency was, "To develop my mind and my intellectual abilities" (Baird, 1967).

Those naming vocational goals as the primary motivating factor in their decision to enter college also tend, in substantially greater numbers, to cite the availability of a special curriculum as an important reason for their particular choice of college. Of course, valuing the occupational preparation function of college above other goals and having a particular vocational objective in mind at the time of entrance does not insure that the choice of occupation will remain fixed. The emergence of new curricular and occupational interests resulting from initial exposure to new courses in college or from the failure to earn satisfactory grades in required courses (e.g., freshman mathematics course in engineering) illustrates how vocational goals might undergo change. In the United States, the frequency of such shifts is substantial, even among entering college students who enroll in comparatively specialized curricula. It is nonetheless true that the persistence of stated occupational goals during adolescence increases with age. In this regard, the vocational goals of college students are appreciably more stable than those of high school students.

To the younger high school student, the problem of making a vocational choice often appears fearsomely complex and bewildering. Work motives and interests are in a relatively early stage of clarification, and knowledge of the external economic world, as we have seen, is seriously limited. It is not surprising, then, to discover that the occupational preferences and choices of younger adolescents tend to be transitory.

Seventh- and eighth-grade students express a great deal of uncertainty about their vocational plans. Even among the small minority (well under 25 percent) who are able to specify a definite career field, considerable fluctuation will occur in the occupation named over the next several years of their lives. Douvan and Adelson (1966) found that the majority of fourteen-to-sixteen-year olds view their vocational aspirations only as tentative and exploratory choices. Only 5 percent of boys in this age range report a feeling of certainty about continuing to work toward the career goal they have named. More than one-half of the stated occupational goals of tenth-grade boys are likely to change in the interval between their sophomore year and six months following graduation from high school (Schmidt and Rothney, 1955). Even among high school juniors it has been shown that a substantial majority will shift occupational goals over the next two years of their life.

Realism of Vocational Choice

As they mature, children in increasing numbers are able to specify vocational objectives, and they become generally surer about their choices. However, vocational psychologists and school counselors are likely to look beyond the fact of choice itself and to inquire about the appropriateness of the choice. The question of whether an adolescent's vocational plan is realistic generally rests on three considerations: the degree to which he has related his personal characteristics to the requirements and demands of his preferred occupation; the current and projected employment supply-and-demand status as it applies to his preferred occupation; and the adequacy of the educational plan by which he intends to implement his career choice. Given these criteria, how realistic are the occupational preferences and choices of adolescents?

Inadequate Information

The occupational information possessed by adolescent youth, especially those of junior high school age, is both sharply limited and of questionable accuracy. As previously discussed, the increasing complexity and diversity of the occupational structure has made it more difficult for present-day youth to develop proper familiarity with the world of work. Owing to cultural restrictions, the range of occupations about which a rural youth has knowledge is even more limited than for an urban youth. In practical terms, this difference is manifested in the expression of preferences among rural youth for a slender array of unimaginative occupational preferences reflecting a comparatively low level of aspiration.

Occupational Supply-and-Demand Disparity

Because of the attractiveness of high-status occupations and the parental and social pressures that lead youth toward these fields, a marked discrepancy often exists between the availability of such jobs in the economy and the expectations of the youth who seek them. An estimated 14 percent of jobs in the labor force are now classifiable as professional or technical. Yet the extensive Project Talent study found 62 percent of high school senior boys and 52 percent of high school senior girls naming occupations in these competitive categories (Flanagan et al., 1964). This study substantiates the findings of a number of earlier research reports on this question. By contrast, only 4 percent of early teenage boys (ages fourteen to sixteen) plan to take training in trade-level occupations (Douvan and Adelson, 1966).

Inappropriate Training Plans

It is not uncommon to find a high school student with measured abilities commensurate with the requirements of his chosen occupation but with education aspirations far too modest to permit qualification for entrance into the field. In Super and Overstreet's (1960) research, only about one-third of the ninth-grade boys studied revealed high school and post–high school plans appropriately related to their preferred occupations. By contrast, the findings of Douvan and Adelson (1966), based on far larger samples of adolescent subjects, show vocational plans to be more realistically based.

Evidence for Vocational Choice Realism

Perhaps the soundest evidence of realism in the vocational planning of adolescents comes from comparative studies of career development. Such research is demonstrating that high school seniors are generally more aware of the need for rational planning for vocational life and that they more clearly understand the factors to be considered than is true of sophomores and juniors. Compared to young adolescents, older adolescents name fewer glamour choices and tend to base their occupational selections and plans more directly on the distinguishing characteristics and requirements of the career field in question. Furthermore, O'Hara and Tiedeman's (1959) findings strongly suggest that a process of progressive clarification of self-concept may occur, between the ninth and twelfth grades, which prepares the individual for more reality-based personal planning and decision making. Students during this period develop increasingly accurate estimates of their own abilities, interests, and personal values. Because they become capable of conceiving of choices less in terms of interests alone and more prominently in terms of personal attributes and competitive requirements, it seems reasonable to suppose that they are better prepared for counseling that has as its objectives the making of educational and vocational plans.

Unfortunately, society and our schools often obligate adolescent youth to narrow their occupational choices prematurely and to commit themselves to specific career goals before they are capable of doing so and, indeed, before they generally need to do so. Society's aim should be less concerned with the forcing of early choice and more concerned with creating opportunities for occupational exploration so that the process of vocational development can be nourished and facilitated.

Summary

In view of what is now known about the nature of vocational development in American culture, a number of recommendations may be set forth as guides to educational policy and practice. I shall use them to summarize the points I have been making in this chapter.

The curricular choices and work-related experiences of adolescents should be kept open-ended and treated as necessary means for reality testing and self-exploration. While students should be encouraged to make plans and decisions, their course and curricular choices should not be allowed to restrict unduly the range of their future options.

The career guidance aims of the schools, and of counselors in particular, should balance traditional concerns about problems of vocational choice with the challenge of helping youth find ways of investing their lives meaningfully through work. Specifically, the future objective of vocational guidance should focus more clearly on promoting the value of work as a social institution and of cultivating a deepened regard for the world of work, including, especially, the work of others. These aims must, of course, supplement the fundamental one of promoting a sense of planfulness regarding one's educational and vocational future.

Supervised part-time work experiences, work-simulation units, and career gaming techniques will need to be more systematically developed as ways of combatting the divorcement of youth from occupational experience. Their application is particularly relevant to students whose learning strengths do not lie with highly verbal and conceptual approaches to instruction and guidance.

Because interpretations of the meaning of work for modern man and significant concepts of the world of work can be introduced at many points in the school experience, it is likely that career development in the future will be increasingly fostered through the formal curriculum as well as through individual counseling contacts. The boundary between vocational guidance through counseling and through classroom experience will become less sharply delineated. Improvements in current policy and practice in this developing synthesis will require that the school counselor play an initiating and catalytic role as a strategically placed member of the professional school staff. Some schools have already begun to move in this direction.

Finally, closer cooperation must be established between curriculum planners and counselors at different educational levels (elementary, secondary, college) and also between school counselors and those in other settings (public employment service, social work agencies, rehabilitation centers). While adolescence is a crucial period for vocational development, it is a continuous process and is not confined to one particular life stage or institutional setting. To the extent that there is general recognition of this principle, a broad-gauged and coordinated program of guidance-related experiences can be provided with the objective of promoting the career development of youth.

The foregoing recommendations are compatible with the recent stance of the U.S. Office of Education which calls for wholesale reforms in the objectives and curriculum of the public schools within the framework of *career education*. Commissioner Marland (1972) has charged that the schools have failed to provide experiences which are relevant to the realistic life options of many youths. Assigned a high priority in the support system of the Office of Education, the thrust of career education is to structure subject matter at all levels, kindergarten through the adult years, around the world-of-work theme. The aims are to develop appropriate attitudes about the psychological, social, and economic meanings of work and to help each student leave school with at least entry-level job skills (Hardwick, 1971). Thus, a national policy now exists which recognizes the importance of the career development needs of school youths and which provides active support for an ambitious educational plan to foster their vocational maturity and career competence. It remains to be seen how widely the plan is accepted by local school systems and how successful it will be.

REFERENCES

Baird, L. L. *The educational goals of college-bound youth.* Iowa City, Iowa: Research and Development Division, American College Testing Program, 1967.

Borow, H. Developmental of occupational motives and roles. In L. W. Hoffman and M. L. Hoffman (eds.), *Review of child development research.* Vol. 2. New York: Russell Sage Foundation, 1966.

Buhler, C. *Der Menschliche Lebenslauf als Psychologisches Problem.* Leipzig: Hirzel, 1933.

Douvan, E., and Adelson, J. *The adolescent experience.* New York: Wiley, 1966.

Flanagan, J. C., et al. *The American high school student.* Pittsburg, Pa.: University of Pittsburg, 1964.

Friedenberg, E. Z. *The vanishing adolescent.* New York: Dell, 1959.

Ginzberg, E., et al. *Occupational choice.* New York: Columbia University Press, 1951.

Ginzberg, E. Toward a theory of occupational choice: A restatement. *Vocational Guidance Quarterly,* 1972, *20,* 169–176.

Graduates and jobs: A grave new world. *Time,* May 24, 1971, 49–59.

Gribbons, W. D., and Lohnes, P. R. *Emerging careers.* New York: Teachers College Press, 1968.

Gunn, B. Children's conceptions of occupational prestige. *Personnel and Guidance Journal,* 1964, *42,* 558–563.

Hardwick, A. L. Career education—a model for implementation. *Business Education Forum,* May 1971, 3–5.

Havighurst, R. J. *Human development and education.* New York: Longmans, Green, 1953.

———. Youth in exploration and man emergent. In H. Borow (ed.), *Man in a world at work.* Boston: Houghton Mifflin, 1964.

Holland, J. L. A personality inventory employing occupational titles. *Journal of Applied Psychology,* 1958, *42,* 336–342.

———. Major programs of research on vocation behavior. In H. Borow (ed.), *Man in a world at work.* Boston: Houghton Mifflin, 1964.

————. *The psychology of vocational choice.* Waltham, Mass.: Blaisdell, 1966.

Krumboltz, J. D., and Krumboltz, H. B. *Changing children's behavior.* New York: Prentice-Hall, 1972.

————, and Thoresen, C. E. *Behavioral counseling: Cases and techniques.* New York: Holt, Rinehart and Winston, 1969.

Marland, S. P., Jr. Career education now. *Vocational Guidance Quarterly,* 1972, *20,* 188–192.

Miller, D. C., and Form, W. H. *Industrial sociology.* New York: Harper, 1964.

Moss, H. A., and Kagan, J. Stability of achievement and recognition seeking behavior from early childhood through adulthood. *Journal of Abnormal and Social Psychology,* 1961, *63,* 504–513.

Murphy, G. Work and the productive personality. In H. Borow (ed.), *Career guidance for a new age.* Boston: Houghton Mifflin, 1973.

Murphy, L. B. *The widening paths of childhood, the paths toward mastery.* New York: Basic Books, 1962.

Mussen, P. H., Conger, J., and Kagan, J. *Child development and personality.* New York: Harper & Row, 1963.

O'Dowd, D. D., and Beardslee, D. C. *College student images of a selected group of professions and occupations.* Cooperative Research Project No. 562. Middletown, Conn.: Wesleyan University, 1960 (Mimeographed).

O'Hara, R. P., and Tiedeman, D. V. Vocational self-concept in adolescence. *Journal of Counseling Psychology,* 1959, *6,* 292–301.

Parsons, F. *Choosing a vocation.* Boston: Houghton Mifflin, 1909.

Powell, M., and Bloom, V. Development of and reasons for vocational choices of adolescents through the high school years. *Journal of Educational Research,* 1962, *56,* 126–133.

Rosenberg, M. *Occupations and values.* Glencoe, Ill.: Free Press, 1957.

Schmidt, J. L., and Rothney, J. W. Variability of vocational choices of high school students. *Personnel and Guidance Journal,* 1955, *34,* 142–146.

Slocum, W. L. *Occupational careers.* Chicago: Aldine, 1967.

Super, D. E. The dimensions and measurement of vocational maturity. *Teachers College Record,* 1955, *57,* 151–163.

————, et al. *Vocational development: A framework for research.* New York: Bureau of Publications, Teachers College, Columbia University, 1957. (a)

Super, D. E. *The psychology of careers.* New York: Harper and Brothers, 1957. (b)

————, and Overstreet, P. L. *The vocational maturity of ninth-grade boys.* New York: Bureau of Publications, Teachers College, Columbia University, 1960.

————, et al. *Career development: Self-concept theory.* Princeton, N.J.: College Entrance Examination Board, 1963.

————. Computers in support of vocational development and counseling. In H. Borow (ed.), *Career guidance for a new age.* Boston: Houghton Mifflin, 1973.

U.S. Department of Labor. *Dictionary of occupational titles:* Vol. 1, *Definitions of titles,* 3d ed. Washington, D.C.: U.S. Government Printing Office, 1965.

————. *U.S. manpower in the 1970's: Opportunity & challenge.* Washington, D. C.: U.S. Government Printing Office, 1970.

White, R. W. Motivation reconsidered: The concept of competence. *Psychological Review,* 1959, *66,* 297–333.

Wolfbein, S. L. Labor trends, manpower, and automation. In H. Borow (ed.), *Man in a world at work.* Boston: Houghton Mifflin, 1964.

Wolfbein, S. L. *Occupational information: A career guidance view.* New York: Random House, 1968.

18

Vocational Counseling with Adolescents

*Roy B. Hackman and Jerry L. Davis**

Among the most important problems that the adolescent has to face are those of choosing a future occupation and the making of the decisions which ultimately lead one into that occupation. Counselors do not subscribe to the notion that a student can or shall pinpoint an occupation and choose his life work once and for all. However, a start must be made during adolescence, and it will be made with or without help from the adult world. Whether the choice is realistic or even satisfying, only time will tell.

Crucial questions are: Can we as counselors, teachers, or parents be of any real assistance to young people in the vocational area? Can we do this without dictating to them or making their decisions for them? Will they seek and accept our help, or will we again find ourselves on the periphery of a mystifying teenage world, which we do not understand and to which we simply close our eyes, our ears, and our minds?

Our answer to the first question is yes. Vocational counseling can be

* Roy B. Hackman is Professor of Psychology and Educational Psychology at Temple University. He is coauthor of the Hackman-Gaither Vocational Interest Inventory and has written a chapter in *Counseling and Guidance: A Summary View*. He has published a large number of articles on such topics as counseling, vocation choice theory and decision making, and psychological testing.

Jerry L. Davis is Associate Professor of Psychology and Educational Psychology at Temple University. His articles have focused mainly on the counseling area.

and usually is very helpful to the adolescent. However, we immediately open ourselves (and all other counselors) to the demand—prove it! In answer to this, we do not intend to attempt a survey of the professional literature which purports to deal with this problem. While there is positive evidence that bears on the issue, the techniques of scientific experimentation are extremely difficult to apply to counseling. This is due in part to the complexity of the problem, and in part to the selection of techniques that are frequently irrelevant to the issue.

Thus, our answer to the first question is clearly in the affirmative, although we cannot point to any large-scale, long-term investigation which proves or disproves the validity or utility of vocational counseling. Perhaps the best proof of its value is the fifty years of vocational counseling which has pragmatically demonstrated its worth with an untold number of young people and adults. The next and equally important question is whether or not adolescents will seek our help. The answer here depends on *what* we have to offer and *how* we offer it.

The early emphasis in guidance was primarily on skillful interviewing, some job information, and a kind of unsystematic matching of personal qualities with job demands. It then progressed to a heavy reliance on the measurement of individual differences (by means of tests) to predict job success. Finally it evolved into a more systematic matching of people with jobs (the so-called Parsonian model of vocational guidance). This has changed. The modern approach is more dynamic, although we are still concerned with the vocational adjustment of people, whether it be in the present or in the future.

To give perspective to its use with adolescents, we shall attempt to define the objectives of vocational counseling. Further, we shall describe some of the techniques utilized by vocational counselors in attempting to assist young people in their efforts to make vocational decisions. But first, let us consider some of the special considerations that need to be taken into account when working with adolescents.

The Setting

Sometimes one wonders if there really is such a thing as late childhood or adolescence. The world is rushing on and by us at such a rapid pace that there seems to be little time for a young person to be truly young and carefree and full of the zest of life. In a way, he is being forced into becoming a frustrated, miniature twentieth-century man or woman.

In effect, society, or at least individuals within it, has been tampering with the process of maturation in many ways. The process has been telescoped, redirected, and channeled (the fashionable term today would be "programed" or possibly "shaped") in ways that surely interfere with the psychological growth and development of young people. This in turn will shape their lives and affect the future course of our society (Parson, 1964).

We have been preoccupied with such problems as: the discovery of "talent," which usually means bright, middle-class, educationally oriented, but not necessarily creative or really talented students; the elimination, or at least reduction, in the number of dropouts (or "pushouts") from our schools, usually without changing the curriculum to fit their needs; technological change, automation, and programed instruction; the "new curriculum" or delinquency, LSD and "pot"; and the myth of the powerful (which it is, commercially speaking) and terrifying teenage culture which "turns" adults "on" and "off." All this has had a deleterious and indeed shocking effect on our attitudes toward real people who happen to be in the age bracket we refer to as adolescence. We must somehow shift the emphasis away from these things which cause so much fear, anger, anxiety, frustration, and, above all, abortive and ill-conceived "programs" for dealing with the so-called teenage or adolescent problem. While we cannot ignore them completely, they must be put into the proper perspective. We must, instead, focus our attention on boys and girls as individual human beings (Tyler, 1964, 1965), and not as members of an alien teenage culture in our midst.

We forget that in a way we are looking backward through a darkened mirror at ourselves. This is particularly true if we happen to be viewing our own children. We hold up goals and ideals which many of us never have attained and probably never will. Nonetheless, we still seek fulfillment for ourselves through our young people. In so doing, we always run the danger of forgetting them and thinking only of ourselves. We also forget that with a minimum of adult intervention and even well-intentioned advice or instruction, a great many young people will achieve within the limits of their own capacities and according to their value system. After all, growing up does not occur in a vacuum, but within the framework of a society of which we are also members and which we certainly had, and continue to have, a part in shaping (Wrenn, 1962).

We are not trying to convey that there is no teenage problem, but rather that these are individual boys and girls, some of whom do have problems and need special help from teachers, parents, friendly and interested adults, counselors, or other members of the helping professions. We should be prepared to offer whatever special assistance is needed and at the appropriate time. Hopefully, the individual boy or girl wants help and can profit from it. We should never force it upon him or her. In a way, it is perhaps unfortunate that professional counselors tend to believe that you cannot assist a person who either does not want help, or is indifferent to it, or becomes hostile when it is offered to him. This leaves counselors with a very difficult and somewhat embarrassing question. What should we do with an adolescent who obviously needs counseling but is not about to seek it out or accept it? Should we let him "go down the drain," or should we put pressure on him to achieve and, in so doing, conform to the demands of society? This is an unresolved dilemma for which we offer no solution. However, the application of the principles of learning as employed in behavior therapy (e.g., operant conditioning) eventually may be of great assistance in bridging the gap between the completely permissive and the completely directive point of view. Also, it is time that the lay public realizes that we should not use punitive methods to control behavior in the name of helping the individual involved. This is of paramount importance in dealing with the disturbed, antisocial, delinquent, hostile, or aggressive teenagers who are such a problem in our schools and communities.

We live in an ambivalent culture. On the one hand, it is permissive and it seeks to promote self-actualization and the good life for everyone. This is particularly true if middle-class values are accepted and followed. On the other hand, it is preoccupied with economic and technological problems which require manpower (see Borow's chapter) if they are to be solved, regardless really of whether the individual desires to be part of such efforts or not. Here the *establishment* is in control. The individual is, at best, secondary. It is quite apparent that a great many adolescents hate the establishment; most adults learn to tolerate it; hardly anybody really likes it.

Most successful adults have somehow learned to live with this dilemma. Not so with teenagers. They do not see the problem clearly, and they certainly are ambivalent. They want freedom and yet they want limits. They are constantly being accused of being nonconformists because they fight the particular establishment in their lives; yet, they want conformity and togetherness and as a result conform to their peer group or some other value-loaded system. This sometimes gets them into serious difficulties. There are tremendous pressures put upon them (e.g., to go to college), and the decisions which they have to make are made earlier and are, in many cases, irreversible. Their problem is more acute today than it was in their parents' or grandparents' time. These are the paradoxes that must be reckoned with in vocational or any other kind of counseling.

It is no wonder that our young people complain that they have difficulty in finding some purpose in life at a time when it is questionable if they are mature enough to do so. Many adults have never found a real purpose in life, and yet they expect and even demand that young people know what they want to do. For example, they ask adolescents what occupation or type of work they want to go into after they finish school and become adults. It is strange how many parents, teachers, and administrators want an adolescent to make a firm vocational choice because they think that having done so, he is now motivated to grow up and be successful in school and in the occupational world. Unfortunately, the mere act of stating a vocational choice often fails to motivate the person at all or it leads to failure and frustration because of its lack of realism.

We really must permit our young people to grow up. This takes time and varies from person to person. Too frequently, in our opinion, we try to force-feed them with all sorts of psychological, social vitamin pills (sometimes called reinforcers by psychologists) and special diets (such as programed or computerized instruction). Sometimes we offer, as incentives, synthetic and shallow rewards which are completely uninteresting to adolescents (e.g., grades in school). We fail, and we wonder why.

Vocational Choice

A process of vocational choice and career development does not begin or end in adolescence (Super, 1957). Whether they want to or not, adolescents often have to make conscious and deliberate (not necessarily rational) choices when they and their parents are faced with curricular decisions. These are intimately related to a wide spectrum of occupational goals. They also must make choices when they are dropping out of or leaving school and seeking to enter the occupational world because they "need a job." On the other hand, they may passively float or drift like jetsam in the ebb and flow of events of their own life stream, never making decisions and getting nowhere. They become locked into a chain of events over which they have no control, or understanding, or even interest. They do not fight the "establishment" that life seems to be. Why fight the impossible? Why not seek some degree of satisfaction elsewhere, regardless of whether or not it is acceptable to the adult world?

However, the choice process is developmental (Nicholas, 1963) with many turning or branching points along the way. It begins in very early childhood, and the forces which shape children's lives exist in powerful forms. The bulk of these forces and determinants are not subject to individual or family control or manipulation. In fact, the individual usually is not aware of them. It is no wonder that vocational choice is often viewed as accidental in nature and as a blind trial-and-error process. This is true because it is held that the individual has to respond to the realities of his life situation, regardless of his desires. Thus, for example, one could hold that the accident of birth determines the occupations of a large number (perhaps the majority) of workers, since it establishes family, race, nationality, social class, and, to a large extent, cultural and educational opportunity. If carried to the extreme, this would be a devastating point of view which would immobilize education and the helping professions. We would prefer to take the position that these are important variables (some are irreversible) which must be reckoned with in counseling. But they should not establish the worth of an individual, nor should they shut the doors of opportunity to him.

Without succumbing to a deterministic or fatalistic philosophy, one cannot help but conclude that many young people fall into occupational niches or slots without much rational consideration on their part. Of those who do not, many will become members of a classless and faceless society composed of individuals who do not work or reap the benefit of our so-called affluent society.

If the environment (family, school, and community) is benign and reasonably economically favored, the chances are good to excellent that adolescents will achieve some sort of occupational success. Members of this group (the advantaged) have excellent work potential, and vocational counseling is very effective with them. At the middle to upper level of these adolescents are those described by Johnstone and Rosenberg (1968).

According to one point of view, the normal person, if left alone, will make an adequate vocational choice, since he is impelled toward certain occupations because of his basic impulses, If, in addition, the adolescent is compliant (otherwise known as motivated, educationally oriented, well-adjusted, etc.), all will be well and he will automatically grow up to be a useful and happy citizen. It would follow, of course, that something must be basically wrong with the personality of the teenager who does not make a realistic choice at the appropriate time. It is felt that he must be abnormal or maladjusted or difficult or even that most horrible accolade of all, a *nonconformist*. This may be true in some cases, but mostly it is a dangerous myth which should be eradicated from our thinking. There are, in fact, many reasons why adolescents do not made vocational choices, not the least of which is that they are simply not ready to make them.

Alas, many normal boys and girls have difficulty in making and implementing curricular and vocational choices, as witnessed by the large number of dropouts in college (approximately 50 percent on the average) and by the considerable number of bright students who drop out of high school or who do not continue their education and training beyond high school. Johnston and Bachman have some pertinent comments on this topic in an earlier chapter. It has been our experience that people (including employers) tend to think of dropouts as stupid, nonconformist, emotionally disturbed, or delinquent, and thus want no part of them. No wonder they have little confidence in teenagers, and no wonder that teenagers want no part of adults. Worst of all, the facts do not warrant such assumptions.

Why do we insist that adolescents continually strive upward and onward toward the professions, technology, and the higher reaches of government and industry? Certainly status is closely tied to the work one does, but happiness is not necessarily synonymous with job success. The authors have worked with a large number of clients who were successful vocationally, but who certainly were not happy in any true sense of the word. Ultimately each adolescent must seek his own happiness, using his own frame of reference and his own value system. For some this may be job success; for many others it is not and cannot be attained through work since many types of jobs in our economic world are purely *instrumental*. That is, in no discernible way do they lead to self-fulfillment. We talk to our young people about the dignity, not the joy, of work, but we do not help them to see that in all probability other areas of their lives will have to furnish satisfaction and self-fulfillment.

If the environment that adolescents live in is impoverished or malignant, their chances of occupational success are very poor indeed. For these adolescents there is often no hope and no striving, because at best their expectancies of success are minimal and at worst completely negative. Here again, the adolescent who grows up in an urban or rural slum did not just get that way. One might say that his environment has trained him from birth. Of course, not all boys and girls from the "slums" fit into this category. It is also true that many innovative and creative programs are in existence to work on this problem. However, one conclusion seems inescapable: We must start long before adolescence to help these young people. They are extremely difficult to work with because they have experienced only failure in our schools. They need orienting and counseling that is not the traditional formal approach, and they also need help from counselors and teachers who can relate to them and somehow forget their own middle-class, tradition-bound values. These boys and girls are often referred to as the "hard-core" group. This term has two bad connotations: first, that they are nasty and we really cannot do anything with them short of institutionalization or incarceration, and, secondly, that they are the root and the cause of all our troubles with the adolescent world. In both cases, nothing could be further from the truth. These boys and girls, if left without help, become alienated from our middle-class culture (not their own culture) and then go on to swell the ranks of the poor and the other disengaged segments of our society. It is true that we have done very little, really, for these adolescents via vocational counseling. The basic problems which exist in the individual's life require massive remediation and intervention before vocational counseling can become more effective. As Amos and Wellford discuss these groups and their problems in another chapter, we shall not carry it further here.

Still another group of adolescents live in a different kind of environment. These are boys and girls who grow up in homes and in communities which have a laissez-faire attitude toward the adolescent. The community is neither hostile nor loving and really, to all intents and purposes, does not care (at least so it seems to the teenager). If you ask a father what he hopes for his son or what he would like him to do, he will say something like "anything he wants to"; or a mother might say, "I just want him to be happy." There is no attitude of concern expressed, and, in short, no apparent love. This happens very frequently with teenagers who do nothing bad or good to distinguish themselves, e.g., they are neither mentally retarded nor bright. To make matters worse, many of the same parents are themselves not interested in education, and they give no encouragement to their children. They have obtained self-satisfying life from skilled and semiskilled jobs and have no desire for anything else. Why should their children be different? No wonder so many boys drop out of school to work and so many girls get married and start families. Vocational counseling is difficult here because these boys and girls are frequently not educationally oriented; they have no special aptitudes or interests and they are not particularly interested in working. In the future the employment possibilities for this group are going to be more and more limited because of increasing automation. They are simply not suited for the increasing number of technical jobs in our society.

Young children are subject to all types of environments, and they learn to react in fairly predictable ways. Many things in their environments bear on vocational choices and are thus important in vocational counseling. When we meet these children later as adolescents, we are already looking at the end results of many forces which have "programed" their behavior without their knowledge or consent.

As counselors and teachers and parents, we need not expect to undo all the deleterious effects of an adolescent's early environment. Some of its effects have very little harmful carry-over into the adult world. Not everything that happens to a child cripples him emotionally for life. He may even thrive. Also, as counselors we have very little control over the adolescent's present environment. We can make only educated guesses as to what the adolescent's future environment will be. Of one thing we can be sure, however, and that is that there will be change. Counseling would be a hopeless task were it not for the inner strength, the flexibility, and the growth potentialities of young people. The die is not cast at six, nor at sixteen, nor at forty-six. We start with the teenager where he is, and we accept him and we listen to him and we help him learn to make sensible choices from among the alternatives available.

Vocational Counseling

Vocational counseling may be carried out in formal or informal settings, with individuals or with groups. It assumes that the adolescent is able and ready to begin the process of making a vocational decision, but may not know how to proceed and therefore needs and wants assistance. It also assumes that there are no other serious problems in the person's life (such as emotional problems) which override the vocational problem and require prior help. The process of vocational decision making is considered to be a rational one, and we therefore assume that the person is rational enough and intelligent enough to make this decision.

Counseling Relationship

A discussion of vocational counseling would be incomplete without a brief perusal of the essential conditions which must be present for counseling of any nature to be productive. To be effective with an adolescent—or a client of any age for that matter—the counselor must create a counseling relationship which promotes mutual trust between him and his client. The counselor must communicate feelings of acceptance, understanding, and sincerity to the client (Tyler, 1969).

The acceptance of the client must in no manner be a conditional feeling. The counselor must be willing to accept the adolescent as a totally unique human being with personal values, goals, and beliefs. Rogers (1957) refers to this total acceptance of the client as a feeling of unconditional positive regard. The accepting counselor does not judge his client in terms of other people or standards. He respects the basic right each person possesses to develop his own life style.

To communicate understanding, the counselor does not attempt to convey that he totally comprehends the uniqueness of his client, for one perhaps never completely understands another human being. However, the counselor does listen carefully in a sincere effort to grasp the unique goals and aspirations of his client. He must be tuned in not only to the cognitive thoughts being expressed by the client but also to the attitudes and feelings which underlie the verbal expressions. A counseling relation is not, therefore, simply a cognitive, intellectual discussion between two people.

If the counselor is sincere in the relationship, he is experiencing no differences between how he is feeling at any given moment and what he is communicating to the client. Sincerity is simply the ability to be real in a relationship; thus, his feelings and actions are in no way phony. Sincerity has been described as congruence (Rogers, 1957) and as genuineness (Carkhuff and Berenson, 1967) on the part of the counselor.

The research evidence to support the necessity of relationship conditions such as empathic understanding, respect, and genuineness is strong (Berenson and Carkhuff, 1967; Carkhuff and Berenson, 1967; Truax and Carkhuff, 1967). If the adolescent perceives his counselor as being accepting, understanding, and genuine in the counseling relationship, positive growth as a result of counseling is more likely to occur. These conditions allow the client to free himself and to mobilize his inner strengths to make vocational decisions. The client is provided with a nonthreatening environment which permits him to gain insight into his own need and value systems and self-concepts.

The purpose of this chapter is not to discuss counseling per se but rather vocational counseling; thus, we shall say no more about the counseling relationship. It is crucial to keep in mind, however, that "techniques" are of little or no value to the vocational counselor who is unable to establish accepting, understanding, sincere relationships with his clients.

Process or Outcome?

A major objective of vocational counseling with adolescents is to be of assistance in the making of wise vocational decisions. Vocational counselors thus have placed considerable emphasis upon encouraging adolescents to explore occupational goals and educational planning. No one promoting the importance of wise decision making would likely be critical of attempting to encourage youth to examine the complex world of work. It has been noted, however, in listening to young people that they appear too often to interpret this emphasis narrowly and to look upon the choice as a career commitment. As a result, adolescents, as well as their parents, are subjected to unnecessary anxieties and misconceptions.

Counselors appear to agree that youth need assistance to develop adequate, realistic decision-making behaviors regarding vocational and educational planning. Perluss (1963) reported that too few possessed sufficient sense of direction, too few had enough knowledge about the world of work, and too many had unrealistic goals—inadequate, vague ideas of what to expect after high school. Upon considering the vocational needs for a rapidly changing society, Wrenn (1965) stressed the need for helping youth to be prepared for making realistic vocational decisions over the span of career development, recognizing that young people would, on the average, change jobs five times during their work career.

The authors have counseled with numerous adolescents expressing vocational uncertainty. Based upon these experiences, it appears that youth too frequently make decisions rather haphazardly with little regard to the *process* involved. Some adolescents appear to jump to conclusions based on little or no information. Others seem to vacillate from one alternative to another, unable to make any kind of a choice which may be crucial to further vocational planning.

Despite consensus that youth should be prepared to implement vocational decision making and educational planning over a span of two to three decades of career development, there appears to be a lack of agreement as to how to accomplish this goal. There does seem to be support for the opinion that to make sound career decisions, youth need to be able to gather relevant information about themselves, the world of work, and educational training programs. Adolescents apparently require assistance in relating information about themselves to information regarding occupational opportunities and to weigh alternatives, considering consequences of competing choices in arriving at vocational decisions and making educational plans.

One approach to assisting adolescents in making decisions is to provide a sequence of steps in problem solving. Krumboltz (1966) defined the following specific steps which adolescents might learn as decision-making behaviors:

> Learn how to gather feasible alternatives to consider;
>
> Learn how to gather relevant information about each alternative;
>
> Learn how to estimate his own chances of success in each alternative;
>
> Learn how to consider his own purposes and values in relation to various occupations under consideration;
>
> Learn how to deliberate and weigh the various values, possible outcomes, and facts in relation to each alternative; and
>
> Learn how to formulate a tentative plan of action subject to new developments and new opportunities.

The goal of vocational counseling, therefore, would be to assist adolescents in learning to use the above sequence of problem-solving steps as a process for vocational decisions. The same process, however, might well generalize to making wise decisions other than just vocational ones.

Youth are continuously confronted with situations which require choosing alternatives. Vocational counselors have placed too much emphasis on what an individual wants to be rather than on what one is willing to invest to reach personal goals. It is time counselors evaluate vocational planning of adolescents in terms of the *process* utilized in arriving at decisions rather than attempting to evaluate the wisdom of any given decision per se. Too frequently, counselors have "judged" whether an adolescent should pursue a specific career objective in mathematics, or baseball, or engineering, etc. What right do counselors have to make such judgments? Vocational counselors must address themselves to the more important question; that is, what process did the adolescent utilize in arriving at his vocational decision? An examination of process rather than outcome is suggested in that in the next moment, hour, and day, there will be other important decisions to be made regarding a variety of alternatives.

The process is intended to give the person, be he adolescent or adult, a more comprehensive and accurate view of the world of work over a wide spectrum of jobs and occupational milieu. The process illuminates the wide range of choices open to him as well as that of his own range of potentialities for achievement and satisfaction. It assists him to understand and use the decision-making process for choosing alternative courses of action under conditions of uncertainty and risks, where the consequences of his actions cannot be fully specified in advance. Moreover, it takes into account the person's self-concept, his value system, his needs and motivation, and relates them to the world of work (see Borow's chapter). Above all, it places the responsibility and the freedom of choice on the counselee. It is a developmental process which extends over a period of time, thus permitting revision and elaboration as needed.

Adolescents appear deeply concerned with making vocational plans. Evidence of this is the large number of youth who seek counseling because they have no vocational goals. It further becomes evident that adolescents have either vague or no ideas as to how to make progress in resolving their dilemmas. This would clearly suggest that one must *learn* to be a decision-maker just as one must *learn* to be an effective vocational counselor.

As youth appear motivated to explore vocations, vocational counselors should seize the opportunity to help them learn how to make these decisions in such a manner that they can generalize the process to decision making of any nature. It seems obvious that adolescents have not learned in the classroom how to gather and synthesize relevant information about themselves and the world of work. A major task, therefore, confronting counselors is to develop a variety of procedures appropriate to making wise decisions.

The concept of developing realistic decision-making behavior as a counseling goal received considerable support in the literature of the 1950s (e.g., Ginzberg, 1952; McDaniel, 1956; Super, 1957; Rothney, 1958). Only recently, however, have experimental studies been conducted which were designed to shed light regarding procedures counselors might use to accomplish this counseling goal. The investigators (Krumboltz and Thoresen, 1964; Krumboltz and Schroeder, 1965; Thoresen, Krumboltz, and Varenhorst, 1967) have demonstrated that model-reinforcement counseling can be employed effectively to motivate students to seek and utilize information prior to making crucial decisions. Adolescents apparently can learn the process of making decisions by observing appropriate social models who effectively utilize a problem-solving sequence. Research evidence, however, suggesting systematic means of helping youngsters to learn how to consider their own values and purposes in relation to various alternatives remains wanting.

The decision-making process seek to help adolescents to answer basic questions about an occupation, such as:

> Can I do it? or learn to do it? (Aptitude)
> Will I like it and be satisfied? (Interests)
> How can I decide between this and some other job? (Decision making)
> Will I amount to something? (Status)
> Will I be worth anything to myself and others? (Self-concept)

Assisting in Decision-Making Process

For any particular teenager, there are many possible vocational choices. Of the occupations he knows, some are questionable possibilities but should be realistically investigated. For various reasons, others are out of the question and should be eliminated from further consideration. Still others seem to be realistic and desirable and should be retained for consideration and possible choice. Here we are referring to those occupations which are visible, i.e., those of which he has some knowledge. Since this is usually a very small number of occupations (out of many thousands of different jobs in our economy), his range of choice is very narrow and it may not include many which ought to be considered (Hopke, 1967).

The answer to this problem lies in furnishing occupational information (e.g., job duties, employment outlook, etc.), beginning very early in adolescence, or even sooner (Hoppock, 1963; Baer and Roeber, 1964). In so doing, job information should first be presented and considered in terms of broad fields of work, such as Business Contact or Technical work. While it is true that there are jobs which cut across fields, most of them fall within one or another of the major areas. Each group of jobs has some important characteristics which are common to all of its members.

The student should first make a tentative choice in terms of the major field of his interest and how he sees himself as a future worker, i.e., his overall "vocational identity." Each major occupational field includes many different types of jobs which differ in terms of the ability needed, essential personal characteristics, and the extent and level of training needed for entrance.

Next, the student should focus his attention into one or more major subareas. These, in turn, can be narrowed down into specific jobs to be investigated further. This last step requires detailed occupational information, which can be found in the various briefs, monographs, pamphlets and books available in most school libraries.

The process goes from the general to the specific. It is sequential and entails study and making choices at each major point mentioned above. Also, it involves determining a field of interest and the types and levels of specific jobs within it. As an example of how this might be done, let us start with some major occupational fields or groupings of jobs from which an adolescent might first consider and choose:

Physical Science, e.g., occupations in Mathematics, Astronomy, Chemistry, Physics, Geology, and Meteorology.

Biological and Agricultural Science, e.g., occupations in Zoology, Botany, Agronomy, Physiology, Entomology, Bacteriology, and Genetics.

Social Sciences, e.g., occupations in Psychology, Sociology, Anthropology, Economics, Political Science, and History.

Medicine and Health, e.g., such major occupational groups as Physician, Dentist, Veterinarian, Pharmacist, Chiropractor, Osteopath, Optometrist, Nurse, Dietician, Medical Technologist, Dental Hygienist, Physical Therapist, and Occupational Therapist.

Engineering and Technical, e.g., such major occupational groups as Engineer (with many specialities), Architect, Metallurgist, Surveyor, Draftsman, and Laboratory Technician.

Business, e.g., such major occupational groups as Accountant, Auditor, Purchasing Agent, Sales Manager, Public Relations Man, Personnel Manager, Job Analyst, Credit Manager, Office Manager, Store Manager, Appraiser, Foreman, Salesman, Bank Teller, Bookkeeper, and Business Machine Operator.

Education, e.g., such occupations as College Professor, School Superintendent, School Principal, High School Teacher (specializing in various subjects), Primary and Kindergarten Teacher, Industrial Arts or Vocational Education Teacher, and Special Education Teacher.

Social and Welfare Work, e.g., such occupations as Social Case

Worker, Social Group Worker, Marriage Counselor, Director of Social Welfare, Parole Officer, Clergyman, and Recreation Leader.

Special Talent, e.g., such occupations as Writer, Editor, Translator, Commercial Artist, Designer, Photographer, Painter, Sculptor, Actor, Dancer, Musician, Radio and T.V. Announcer, Professional Athlete, Entertainer, and Graphic Art Work.

Agriculture, e.g., occupations in Farming, Ranching, Fishing, Forestry, and Hunting.

Mechanical Work, e.g., occupations in Machine Trades, Bench Work, Structural Work, Processing, Fabricating, Repairing, and Equipment Operating.

Service Work, e.g., occupations in Domestic Service, Food Preparation and Serving, Personal Service, Amusement and Recreation, Building Service, and Protective Service.

Now, let us suppose that as a result of the first step, the adolescent boy feels that he wants to do something in Business. He has decided that he may want to acquire some specialized training before beginning his career. Also, on the basis of his investigation so far and his knowledge of himself, he feels that he does not want to work with people or deal with them on a face-to-face basis. He is more interested in the technical and administrative aspects of business.

His next task is to investigate further the field of Business and to narrow his choice down into terms of the level of training (college, technical or vocational), and the type of work (duties and responsibilities) he would like to do and in which he feels that he could be successful.

He then looks at some of the major areas in the field of Business (excluding clerical work, which he considers to be feminine), viz: Accounting, Purchasing, Sales and Distribution, Banking and Finance, Advertising, Public Relations, Personnel Management, Direct Selling, Market Research, Systems Analysis and Computer Programming and Data Processing. Once he has tentatively chosen one or more of these subgroups, he can then investigate individual occupations and make one or more as specific (but tentative) choices.

He will soon discover many jobs in the business world that cut across occupational groupings. This is important, because in his case the business aspect of the job may be secondary to the type of work. He would like to be in Business, but actually the type of work (duties, job) comes first. For many people, the opposite is true. They are not so concerned with *what* they do, but where they want to work. Some examples of jobs from other fields that occur in Business are Industrial Engineering, Sales

Engineering, Commercial Artist, Applied Statistician, Economist, Corporation Lawyer, Industrial Physician, Industrial Psychologist, Advertising Copy Writer, and Training Director. Each of these jobs has a distinct type of preparation which is common to its field, but the application of the field of knowledge is in Business or Industry.

The point about urging the student to investigate these jobs, as well as the others, is not to add to his confusion and make his ultimate choice more difficult, but rather to expand his view of the world of work. He needs to know that specialized training can open many doors to him. That is, his role identity may be in business, but his job duties have much in common with other people who do not work in the commercial world. Both he and they can, and often will, move out of one and into the other.

This approach emphasizes versatility in training, rather than specificity. One first finds his own vocational identity and then makes a choice in terms of a fairly definite occupation with a fairly specific preparation. However, it will be found that the duties of the job can be performed in many different locations and in many different situations. Furthermore, with experience the individual has a great advantage (over the new job entrant) because he can readily learn closely related tasks and adjust to the new phases and innovations in industry as they occur. It is important to keep this in mind because of the changing aspects of our economy and of our uncertainty about what the occupational structure (types of jobs and their relative frequency) will be like when the adolescent enters the labor market.

Some alarmists would have us believe that the occupational world of tomorrow will be changed so drastically because of technology, e.g., automation, that vocational choice and vocational guidance with adolescents is impossible if not unethical and somewhat immoral. Possibly so, but we suggest that these changes will occur fairly gradually—in any case, enough so that we can educate young people to expect, prepare, and adjust for the changes when they occur. This task is of paramount importance for the future of our adolescents. Part of the primary responsibility for carrying out the task rests on educational and vocational counseling.

If today's adolescents shut their eyes to the necessity for training, and the need for vocational goals that are both broad and specific, they will be at the mercy of the economic forces, which require and will find manpower. Again, we should like to point out that adolescents and adults do not have to make vocational choices (realistic or otherwise), but we submit that if they do not, somebody else will make them for them without worrying about self-actualization, job satisfaction, or need reduction. Our task as vocational counselors is to help adolescents, at various points along the way, make decisions which are in their best interests, as well as in the best interests of society.

Let us return to our adolescent boy who is investigating occupations in Business for the purpose of making a vocational choice. After studying the major areas, he finds that he is most interested in the following specific occupations: Advertising Man, Advertising Copy Writer, and Editor of Trade or Technical Publications. These are, of course, in the general Literary field (Special Talent) as well as in Business, and he should also investigate other related Literary occupations. He has now arrived at a tentative field of choice and some possible jobs in Business. He should keep an open mind regarding the environment in which he wants to work, and he should definitely consider whether he has the special talent for any job which requires writing. He now needs information of a different type, i.e., information about himself and in particular, about the aptitudes for work in the literary field.

So far, in this particular discussion, you might feel that we have been proposing an old-fashioned "cafeteria" system of vocational counseling. A good occupational library, as a program of steps for the student to follow, and his ability to read well would appear to be all that is necessary for him to make a realistic and satisfying vocational choice. Is this, you ask, all there is to vocational counseling? What about aptitude tests? What does the counselor do? Do we even need him? Why can we not handle all of this electronically and solve the whole problem instantaneously by giving our client a computer print-out when he needs it?

Of course, we have been talking about only one, but a very important, phase of vocational counseling. Before discussing briefly some of the other aspects of vocational counseling, we should like to make it very clear that the proper use of occupational information is probably the most important and practical technique of vocational counseling. There are difficulties and drawbacks, but, nevertheless, real vocational decision making simply cannot occur in a vacuum. The adolescent has to have occupational information if he is to choose wisely. The only alternative is for someone else (perhaps on the basis of testing, interviewing, observation, or just sheer guesswork) to tell him what to do. Unfortunately, this latter approach to vocational counseling is still with us, but professional counselors certainly do not subscribe to it and they do not operate that way.

The problem with available occupational information is that it does not go far enough. It describes many things about jobs in terms of economic factors (salary), but it fails to cover adequately the psychological and sociological aspects of jobs. The student would like to know what it is like to be a worker at "x" type of work; what needs can be satisfied on the job; and what personal satisfactions (beyond economic rewards) can be obtained. Information on these things is woefully lacking in our occupational literature. People do work for wages, and they need certain characteristics and potential skills for successful work performance. Much information on these matters can be obtained from published information and from contact with workers. The rest, unfortunately, has to be learned on the job. Our task as vocational counselors is to help adolescents eventually find work in which they can be reasonably successful and happy.

Using the classic model of vocational choice theory (that of matching workers and jobs), we have so far looked at only one side of the coin. Turning to the other side, it is necessary to determine the personal characteristics that bear on the problem of vocational choice. The theory was that knowing what the job requires in the way of aptitudes, personality traits, etc., and knowing what the person has, he or the counselor can then compare the two sets of data and pick out the occupation which is most suitable for the person. Since any rational person naturally will select the best "fit" of himself and the job (so the theory goes), the problem is solved and success and happiness is assured. Actually, there is some merit in this idea if it is not viewed and implemented mechanistically (theoretically it could be computerized very nicely). Unfortunately, it does not work very well in real life. There are other ways of attacking this problem, but, regardless of what theory of vocational choice one uses (Hackman, 1965), the personal characteristics of the adolescent are really the basic starting point. It is he who must choose on the basis of his own expectancies and his own value system.

Before going on, let us add a brief word picture of the hypothetical boy who was investigating occupational information earlier. He is in the eleventh grade in a comprehensive high school and is a C to B student in the general academic curriculum. His best subjects are Social Studies and English, and his poorest are Science and Mathematics. He is reasonably well adjusted, but somewhat quiet. His only extracurricular activity is writing for the school paper; otherwise he has evidenced no special talents or interests in school. He reads a great deal, but with little concentration in any one area. He has never been in trouble, and he seems only mildly interested in school. He states he is not interested in four years of college, although he is open to alternative suggestions. His teachers like him, but they do not really know him. His parents are interested in him and his future. There are no major financial obstacles to further education. This boy is a rather typical, undistinguished, middle-class adolescent who just does not know what he wants to do and is only mildly concerned about it.

If you were his counselor or advisor, would this information assist you in helping him make a vocational choice? Of course it would, but is it enough? Oh, you want to know his IQ? What about aptitude tests? What about College Board scores? What about his measured interests? How does he stack up on a personality inventory? How did he do on the comprehensive National Achievement Testing Program?

Why do we want to know these things? We grant at the outset that they would probably be useful (Cronbach, 1960; Goldman, 1961; Buros, 1965). The first and most important answer is that we want objective measures that will tell us concretely where our student now stands on the traits we have measured. The second answer is that we wish to predict how well he will do later on, all other things being equal. Whichever way you look at it, the purpose of objective information is to assist us in helping our client, and its utility lies in whether or not it does so. The types of tests that are most useful in vocational counseling (looked at from a sequential point of view) will now be discussed.

Tests of General Intelligence and Scholastic Aptitude

These tests tell us something about the adolescent's scholastic promise, his level of trainability, and the degree of job complexity that he will be able to handle. This is a good starting point in vocational testing, if it is approached with caution and due regard for the pitfalls in intelligence testing. At best, intelligence tests measure the present level of the individual's functioning; at the worst, they can be misleading and damaging. Intelligence is not a single unitary trait. It can be broken up into sub-traits such as concrete versus abstract, verbal versus performance, or verbal versus quantitative thinking. Even so-called aptitudes may be considered to be special aspects of intelligence (or vice versa). As predictors of college success, scholastic aptitude tests leave much to be desired, since scores obtained from them do not correlate as highly with grades as many people seem to think. As a matter of fact, high school grades are still the best indicators of success in college.

In spite of the difficulties involved, the measurement of intellectual capacity and functioning is the first step in vocational testing. The level of the student's ability determines to a great extent the next steps in testing and counseling.

Achievement Tests

A student's pattern of achievement in various subjects (taking into account his reading ability) can tell us a great deal about his knowledge, ability, interests, and drive, providing the tests are not just poorly disguised reading or intelligence tests. The individual's performance can be compared to both local and national norms. This shows, if you will, his competitive position in the educational market. Even more important, however, is that the profile (pattern of scores) shows his strengths and weaknesses in achievement. Whatever the reasons may be for his achieving in some areas and not in others (e.g., lack of interest or poor previous background), these differences are of great importance in planning further training. This, in turn, will help to indicate what occupational areas are the most suitable. Grades in school subjects should be considered as well, since they reflect actual performance over a period of time.

Discrepancies often exist between ability (i.e., intelligence), tested achievement, and school performance. In many cases underachievement stands out in bold relief, since the individual does not appear to be working up to his potential. As a result he is labeled, and his parents are told in no uncertain terms that he is an *underachiever*. This shakes up everybody because they really do not know what to do about it. Worse yet, by this time the student may not even care. An underachiever is, quite simply, a student who is behind his age-class group of peers, or one whose test scores fall much lower on the norms than would be expected for his intelligence. A common example is a student who is "bright," and therefore would be expected to do well, but who is failing in school or just getting by.

Many people assume a very high positive correlation between the IQ and performance in school. Thus, for them, high IQ = high grades; average IQ = average grades; and low IQ = low grades (to use an oversimplified example). An individual student who does not fit this pattern (e.g., above-average IQ–below-average grades) is really exhibiting a negative correlation between IQ and grades, and this will never do! Parents, teachers, and counselors must remember that the correlation between intelligence and grades is far from perfect. It should come as no surprise that many boys and girls do not fit into this statistical schema of things at all and that they are not abnormal because they do not. There are other factors involved in achievement besides intelligence. It follows, therefore, that we should expect to find many underachievers in school and that we should not try to make all adolescents come up to the "national average" or another mythical norm which is a generalization or statistical artifact. We should be more disturbed when adolescents do not come up to *their own level of aspiration,* whatever it may be. This is real underachievement, and it may reflect other and more serious problems than so-called underachievement. We seem to spend a great deal of time in attempting to raise the level of aspiration of students without really knowing or trying to understand these levels in the first place. We try to solve this problem by substituting higher goals, which may well be inappropriate for the individual student. In addition, because of our own middle-class value systems, we attempt to change the direction of the aspirations (e.g., toward academic achievement and away from automobile mechanics) without regard for the desires of students. No wonder they rebel and retreat or perhaps sidestep our efforts so adroitly. The stigma attached to being labeled an underachiever is real and often devastating. In fact, it frequently immobilizes all who are concerned with the person so labeled.

Underachievement is a baffling problem, since the reasons for it are so varied and often so difficult to determine in an individual case. Generally speaking, adolescents do not suddenly become underachievers due to a sudden traumatic change in their lives. Failure has a way of feeding on itself. As time goes on, it becomes a way of life and finally results in a complete breakdown from an educational point of view.

Vocational counselors are concerned with underachievement and with academic failure when other indications point to success within the range of abilities of the student. Lack of success in school has a direct bearing on subsequent job training and occupational success. Failure to complete high school, or even grade school, permanently restricts the employability and placeability of an individual in today's job world. At best, it results in occupational as well as educational failure. There are a large number of young job seekers today who have dropped out of school and who cannot find any kind of permanent work. Without help, their chances of ever being employed in good competitive jobs in industry are close to zero. This is a great challenge for vocational counseling and education.

When achievement testing reveals discrepancies such as those we have discussed, one should stop in the process of sequential testing and tackle these problems before going on to further testing or other counseling procedures. As for the particular problem of lack of achievement, one must look at the antecedents, the present situation, and the probable consequences. Problems of lack of achievement, underachievement, and dropping out of school involve educational diagnosis and remediation before vocational guidance and counseling can proceed with any hope of success.

Aptitude Testing

Aptitude refers to potential ability to learn and perform certain kinds of tasks. It does not depend on training to a marked degree. One tends either to have it or not to have it. Aptitude tests are a kind of "quickie" substitute for actual vocational tryouts, which are too slow and too narrow in their application. Thus a high score on a "mechanical" aptitude test purports to predict success in mechanical work of some kind. Early researchers hoped to analyze jobs in terms of the aptitudes needed, and then to construct tests which were predictive by accurately measuring these aptitudes. Thus, with a profile of the individual's scores on the corresponding aptitude tests, one could proceed to match the worker to the job. Many years of research on this problem have failed to fulfill this expectation. As a matter of fact, the correlations of aptitude tests with the criteria of job success are actually very low. In fact, the correlations are so low that very little confidence can be placed on the power of a single aptitude test to predict success on the job. With the exception of the General Aptitude Test Battery of the United States Employment Service, even multiple aptitude test batteries are not much better. We do not deny that aptitude tests are useful at times, but we want to emphasize that we do not have a large number of aptitude tests which actually predict job success. The public still thinks that aptitude testing is a kind of magic that the vocational counselor uses to advise his client. The commonest inquiry we receive at our Vocational and Educational Guidance Clinic is, "Do you give aptitude tests?" not, "Do you do vocational counseling?" If used cautiously by trained counselors, aptitude tests are useful, but they have a limited value in counseling. There is no simple, objective technique for determining an individual's overall vocational potential or vocational satisfaction. A one-shot battery of tests simply does not give enough information about the development of the person, his present situation, or his probable future status.

Personality, Needs, Values, and Interests

This is the most difficult area in which to apply the measurement approach. Personality inventories are commonly used in vocational counseling for three basic purposes. The first is to assess the temperament pattern of the individual as it relates to jobs. While there is no one-to-one relationship between temperament and job performance, nevertheless, the tasks and the climate of jobs do differ. For example, some people are best suited, temperamentally, to dealing with people; others to working alone. Personality inventories give some information that is useful here. The second purpose is to assess the overall personality adjustment, stability, lack of pathology, etc., of the person. Inventories should be followed up with more clinical approaches (such as interviewing and projective techniques) before steps are taken for referral or treatment by professional personnel. The employability of a person is closely related to his personality characteristics and his way of coping with his environment. This is particularly true when he is in a work situation where good interpersonal relationships are basic to his success. Personality maladjustment is a basic cause and heavy contributor to vocational maladjustment. If we can detect incipient trouble in this area for adolescents and get aid for them, we can help to prevent maladjustment and failure on the job later. Lastly, the personality inventory is used to assess the need and value systems of the individual. Since much of this area of an adolescent's life is unconscious, or at least nonverbalized, we sometimes use specialized inventories to obtain information that is pertinent to the problem of vocational choice. While we cannot change the economic world, it is very helpful for the counselor and his client to work through this problem in terms of reality. Adolescents must learn that needs can be satisfied only within limits. This is particularly true in the work setting, where many of an individual's needs (such as self-actualization) simply cannot or may not be satisfied.

Personality measures are useful in the hands of trained counselors. They are really clinical instruments and, as such, are of value in dealing with an individual adolescent only if the counselor knows a great deal about the boy or girl with whom he is working. They are sometimes criticized because they can be faked. This deception on the part of the person taking the inventory is minimal if rapport has been established with him (e.g., conditions for counseling described earlier), if he understands the purpose of the testing, and if he is undergoing it voluntarily. The most serious criticism of using personality "tests" is that they invade the privacy of the individual, often without his consent (Amrine, 1965, 1966). We agree entirely that this can be true in mass testing or testing for employment or selection. For this and other reasons we do not recommend the wholesale use of personality inventories in school. Their use should be restricted to trained counselors and school psychologists who administer them on a one-to-one basis in a clinical setting. Used properly, personality assessment devices are of great value, but in the wrong hands and with the wrong people they can be useless and even dangerous.

Another type of test (actually an inventory) is the Interest Inventory. These are used to help the individual think about and react to a wide variety of job titles and job descriptions. They do not and are not intended to predict success on the job. They help to predict what type of work will be of interest to the student. If used in conjunction with occupational information, they can be among the most valuable tools in the vocational counselors' kit.

Let us return to our hypothetical adolescent. He has narrowed down his vocational choices, through the study of occupational information, to work which requires writing, possibly in the field of Business. In addition to what we already know about him as a person, let us add some further items of testing information.

The reader can put himself in place of the counselor and arrive at a recommendation if he chooses. Although this is a hypothetical, but fairly typical case, we would only suggest that the evidence seems to be quite consistent. The tests are useful in that they seem to corroborate the other information we have at hand. It suggests that this boy might consider going to a specialized school or a community college for more work in

	Percentile	
Intelligence	70	(Above Average)
Achievement		
Mathematics	45	(About Average)
Social Studies	70	(Above Average)
English	90	(High)
Reading	85	(High)
Science	35	(Below Average)
Aptitude		
Mechanical	5	(Very Low)
Clerical	30	(Below Average)
Mathematical	20	(Low)
Art	80	(High)
Interest		
Business Contact	Above Average	(Mild Interest)
Business Clerical	Very Low	(Strong Dislike)
Outdoor	Low	(Dislike)
Social Welfare	Below Average	(Mild Dislike)
Scientific Technical	Very Low	(Strong Dislike)
Mechanical	Very Low	(Strong Dislike)
Service	Very Low	(Strong Dislike)
Aesthetic		
(Special Talent)	High	(Strong Interest)
Personality	Average	(Well-adjusted)

writing. It may turn out that he will decide to continue his education in a four-year college. In any case, he can aim at occupations which involve doing some kind of writing in a business (publishing) or semitechnical field. He is not likely to set the world on fire (few of us do), but he should be a competent and solid citizen on the job.

Summary

We must first make sure that adolescents are exposed to a wide spectrum of reliable and valid information about the world of work. We need to help them look at occupational information realistically and not just to ignore it or to incorporate some part of the information into a private world of fantasy and wishful thinking.

We must assist individual adolescents to evaluate their own characteristics (such as aptitudes, interests, and temperament traits) and relate them to the economic needs and realities of society—both present and future, insofar as this can be done.

We need to help young people learn how to make decisions that are, on the one hand, appropriate for them, and on the other hand, realistic and flexible. This means that they need to know what alternative courses of action are open to them; what the consequences and risks of choosing each of them are; and how these factors relate to their own system of values. They need to become aware that the ultimate responsibility for making choices rests with them, but that we stand ready to help them in the decision-making process.

We need to (and indeed we must) "motivate" adolescents to make the choices, educationally and vocationally, that are feasible for them at their stage of development.

It seems that the most significant role we as teachers, counselors, and parents can play is to do everything we can to make our young people (see chapter by Johnston and Bachman) educationally oriented. We should encourage them to get everything they can from their school experiences. Above all, we should constantly reinforce the importance of high school (or vocational school) graduation. We should stress the importance of good ability in reading, writing, speaking, and arithmetic; for these are the qualifications that employers look for at the entry level of jobs, rather than the specific vocational skills, which are usually learned at work. Boys and girls who are deficient in these basic skills are seriously handicapped, both educationally and vocationally. Special re-medial programs should be set up to handle this problem. However, we need new approaches and new techniques that are not rejected by the student because he sees only more of the same "old stuff." After all, who needs more failures?

We must help disadvantaged young people of all types (not just the so-called economically disadvantaged) to realize the importance of ac-quiring the basic educational skills needed in a modern society. We, in turn, need to realize that these young people have potentialities that are of value. New approaches to education are needed to develop these potentialities. Our schools are struggling with this problem, but until our curricula and instructional techniques change markedly, these boys and girls are not going to be helped very much and their economic future is very grim. Furthermore, vocational counseling is not likely to do much, either.

All of us who are interested in young people must work together on the problem of vocational development. No single group of people in the helping professions, in education, in industry, in the community, or in the family can solve this problem alone. Vocational counseling can be of great help, but let us remember that it is only one approach. It is not a magic formula, nor is it a panacea which will solve the "adolescence problem" by itself.

REFERENCES

Amrine, M. (ed.). Testing and public policy. *American Psychologist,* 1965, *20,* 857–993.

————— (ed.). Camelot and psychological tests. *American Psychologist,* 1966, *21,* 401–470.

Baer, N. F., and Roeber, E. S. *Occupational information: The dynamics of its nature and use.* Chicago: Science Research Associates, 1964.

Berenson, B., and Carkhuff, R. *Sources of gain in counseling and psychotherapy.* New York: Holt, Rinehart and Winston, 1967.

Buros. O. K. (ed.). *The sixth mental measurements yearbook.* Highland Park, New Jersey: Gryphon Press, 1965.

Carkhuff, R., and Berenson, B. *Beyond counseling and therapy.* New York: Holt, Rinehart and Winston, 1967.

Cronbach, L. J. *Essentials of psychological testing.* New York: Harper and Brothers, 1960.

Ginzberg, E. Toward a theory of occupational choice. *Personnel and Guidance Journal,* 1952, *30,* 491–494.

Goldman, L. *Using tests in counseling.* New York: Appleton-Century-Crofts, 1961.

Hackman, R. B. The problem of vocational choice in vocational guidance: An essay. In J. F. Adams (ed.), *Counseling and guidance: A summary view.* New York: Macmillan Co., 1965.

Hopke, W. E. (ed.). *The encyclopedia of careers and vocational guidance.* Chicago: J. G. Ferguson Publishing Co., 1967.

Hoppock, R. *Occupational information.* New York: McGraw-Hill, 1963.

Johnstone, J. W. C., and Rosenberg, L. Sociological observations on the privileged adolescent. In J. F. Adams (ed.), *Understanding adolescence.* Boston: Allyn and Bacon, 1968.

Krumboltz, J. Promoting adaptive behavior: New answers to familiar questions. In J. Krumboltz (ed.), *Revolution in counseling.* Boston: Houghton Mifflin Company, 1966.

—————, and Schroeder, W. Promoting career exploration through reinforcement. *Personnel and Guidance Journal,* 1965, *44,* 19–26.

—————, and Thoresen, C. The effect of behavioral counseling in group and individual settings on information-seeking behavior. *Journal of Counseling Psychology,* 1964, *11,* 324–333.

McDaniel, H. B. *Guidance in the modern school.* New York: Dryden Press, 1956.

Nicholas, O. Vocational development. In A. A. Jersild, *The psychology of adolescence.* New York: Macmillan Co., 1963.

Parsons, T. Youth in the context of American society. In H. Borow (ed.), *Man in a world at work.* Boston: Houghton Mifflin, 1964.

Perluss, S. H. The product: how does it measure up? *Journal of Secondary Education,* 1963, *38,* 10–15.

Rogers, C. R. The necessary and sufficient conditions of therapeutic personality change. *Journal of Consulting Psychology,* 1957, *21,* 95–103.

Rothney, J. W. M. *Guidance practices and results.* New York: Harper and Brothers, 1958.

Super, D. E. *The psychology of careers.* New York: Harper and Brothers, 1957.

Thoresen, C., Krumboltz, J., and Varenhorst, B. Sex of counselors and models: Effect on client career exploration. *Journal of Counseling Psychology,* 1967, *14,* 503-508.

Truax, C., and Carkhuff, R. *Toward effective counseling and psychotherapy.* Chicago: Aldine, 1967.

Tyler, E. *The work of the counselor.* New York: Appleton-Century-Crofts, 1969.

———. Work and individual differences. In H. Borow (ed.), *Man in a world at work.* Boston: Houghton Mifflin, 1964.

———. *The psychology of human differences.* New York: Appleton-Century-Crofts, 1965.

Wrenn, C. G. *The counselor in a changing world.* Washington, D.C.: American Personnel and Guidance Association, 1962.

———. A second look. In *Counseling: A growing profession.* Washington, D.C.: American Personnel and Guidance Association, 1965.

Name Index

Subject Index